D0020928

Brittany & Normandy

Jeanne Oliver, Miles Roddis

Contents

Highlights	4	Loire-Atlantique	181
Getting Started	9	Normandy	199
Itineraries	12	Seine-Maritime	200
The Authors	15	Eure	236
Snapshot	16	Calvados	254
History	17	Manche	291
The Culture	30	Orne	307
Environment	42	Directory	316
Brittany & Normandy Outdoors	46	Transport	333
		Health	344
Food & Drink	50	Language	346
Brittany	65	Glossary	353
Ille-et-Vilaine	66	Behind the Scenes	356
Côtes d'Armor	94	Index	359
Finistère	118	Legend	368
Morbihan	157		

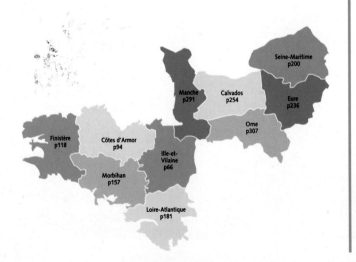

Finistère p118
Côtes d'Armor p94
Morbihan p157
Ille-et-Vilaine p66
Manche p291
Calvados p254
Orne p307
Seine-Maritime p200
Eure p236
Loire-Atlantique p181

Lonely Planet books provide independent advice. Lonely Planet does not accept advertising in guidebooks, nor do we accept payment in exchange for listing or endorsing any place or business. Lonely Planet writers do not accept discounts or payments in exchange for positive coverage of any sort.

Lonely Planet réalise ses guides en toute indépendance et les ouvrages ne contiennent aucune publicité. Les établissements et prestataires mentionnés dans ce guide ne le sont que sur la foi du jugement et des recherches des auteurs, qui n'acceptent aucune rétribution ou réduction de prix en échange de leurs commentaires.

Destination: Brittany & Normandy

Brittany and Normandy wrap up the very best of France and present it with their own distinct-ive flourishes. All of the most delightful elements of French life are present, from scrupulously preserved medieval towns cradling Gothic churches and Romanesque abbeys to a stagger-ingly diverse landscape that includes an endless coastline, rolling pastures, misty marshes, rivers, valleys and forests. Straddling the two regions is Mont St-Michel, France's most visited monument. To the north lie Normandy's timeless and evocative D-Day beaches while Brittany's sandy southern shores around La Baule are devoted to serious sun worshippers.

Of the two regions, Brittany has remained more firmly committed to its unique and col-ourful traditions, most stemming from the Celts who planted their culture here 1500 years ago. Bretons honour their local saints in frequent and festive *pardons* (religious celebrations), dressing up in a swirl of lace headdresses and dancing to *binious* and *bombardes* piping out Celtic tunes. Brittany's mysterious prehistoric megaliths at Carnac set the tone for a region still steeped in magic and legend, where dank and shadowy forests gave rise to tales of the Holy Grail, King Arthur and the Round Table.

Normandy offers no less bewitching pleasures. A string of glittering coastal resorts and alluring fishing ports – Dieppe, Honfleur, Deauville-Trouville, Étretat – have inspired gener-ations of artists, most famously Claude Monet who also immortalised the Rouen cathedral and his splendid gardens at Giverny. Visual treats are abundant, from fine-arts museums displaying Normandy's painters to the historic Bayeux Tapestry. Taste treats? Local markets teem with fresh fish and seafood hauled in daily to Channel ports and the most delectable cheeses from Normandy's cows.

And when you need a break from sightseeing, you can soothe your soul with a stroll along Normandy's desolate Cotentin Peninsula, a bike ride through the Seine Valley or a boat trip through Brittany's canals.

From historic monuments to rugged off-shore islands, Brittany offers a multitude of attractions. Speculate about the **megaliths** (p164) at Carnac or visit Douarnenez's **Musée du Bateau** (p142). Surround yourself with the ecclesiastical tradition of the **enclos paroissiaux** (p136) of the Élorn Valley and marvel at the spectacle of **Mont St-Michel** (p70) abbey rising from the bay.

Relax in outdoor cafés in the cobbled streets of the old city of Dinan (p97)

ROCCO FASANO

MARTIN MOOS

Celebrate Breton music and culture at the Festival de Cornouaille (p148) in Quimper

Promenade along the beach at La Baule (p196), enjoying the passing parade of colourful catamarans

ROCCO FASANO

DAVID TOMLINSON

Explore narrow streets of the walled city of St-Malo (p77) and witness some of the world's greatest tidal variations from the port

MARTIN MOOS

Roam Quimper's old town and visit the Cathédrale St-Corentin with its soaring twin spires (p146)

Watch the sun go down over the waters washing Pointe du Raz (p145)

OLIVIER CIRENDINI

Sandy beaches, fishing ports and superb fine-arts museums entice the visitor to Normandy. Smell the flowers Monet planted and painted at **Giverny** (p244), relive the Battle of Hastings on the **Bayeux Tapestry** (p266) or ponder the *Last Judgment* window at **Coutances cathedral** (p302). Enjoy a cruise on the Seine to riverside **Les Andelys** (p246).

DIANA MAYFIELD

Absorb the ambience of the harbour at Honfleur (p274), lined with slate-faced houses

Marvel at the intricate façade of Rouen's Cathédrale Notre Dame (p204)

FRANCES LINZEE GORDON

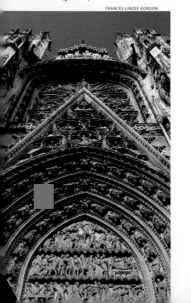

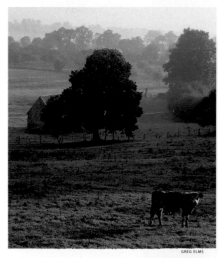

GREG ELMS

Discover the countryside that produces Normandy's delicious cheese and cream (p52)

MARTIN MOOS

Remember those who paid the ultimate price at the American Military
Cemetery, Omaha Beach (p273)

MARTIN MOOS

While away hours tracked by the Gros
Horloge clock in medieval Rouen (p206)

See the fascinating cliff formation of Falaise d'Amont (p234), which hugs the fringes of the
town of Étretat

BÉTHUNE CARMICHAEL

The fertile lands and abundant coastal fisheries of Brittany and Normandy provide a tasty experience. Food is featured in the region's celebrations, as well as everyday life. Festivals based around seafood, apples, cider and much more abound. Cheese and cream are Normandy specialities, while Brittany is renowned for its fresh spring vegetables *(primeur)*.

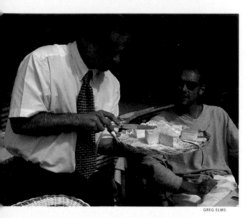

GREG ELMS

Sample some of the cheeses served in the cafés and restaurants of Honfleur (p278)

Savour buckwheat Crêpes Sarrasin and cider at St-Malo (p79)

GREG ELMS

Salivate as the day's catch is unloaded at harbours near the Aber Ildut (p128)

JEAN-BERNARD CARILLET

Getting Started

Normandy and Brittany offer a rich variety of experiences whether your pleasure involves meandering through historic towns or enjoying exhilarating landscapes. No matter what the weather, there's always something to see or do. The busiest months in both places are July and August and, even then, only the seaside resorts are crowded to the point where advance bookings are required. Train transport is generally hassle-free but weekend travel in July and August should also be reserved ahead.

WHEN TO GO

Normandy and Brittany are at their very best in late spring, when the sea pinks and other wildflowers along Brittany's sea cliffs are in bloom and Normandy is bright with apple blossoms. Early autumn is pleasant too, though the days are fairly short and it gets a bit cool for sunbathing; the woods come alive with autumn colours in October and November. Winters are mild but rainy, and obviously less crowded. Most beach resorts shut down at this time, but the coastline is often at its most dramatic as winter storms pound the rocks and reefs.

See Climate Charts (p320) in the Directory chapter for more information

In July and August, the weather is warm and rainy days are at a minimum, making it a good time to plan outdoor pursuits. Museums, chateaux and abbeys are open longer in July and August and often host cultural programmes; most of Brittany's religious *pardons* (p31) are held in summer too. However, this is also the busiest time of year, when the roads are jammed with traffic and the beach resorts are packed to the gills. The region also enjoys small bursts of activity in the week following Easter and during the Toussaint (All Saints' Day) holiday in early November, but nothing like the summer vacation period.

COSTS

Brittany and Normandy are moderately priced compared to the rest of France. You'll pay most for a hotel room in the larger cities all year and in seaside resorts during summer. Train fares can add up, especially for long journeys. Two or more people travelling together may find it cheaper to rent a car, even with the price of petrol and tolls. Staying in three-star hotels and eating two restaurant meals a day will add up to about €80 per person per day. Budget travellers who stay in two-star hotels and rely on do-it-yourself meals can get by on half that amount.

Your euros will go further if you keep in mind a few ways of economising. Travel with someone else – double rooms usually cost only marginally more than singles.

It's cheaper to have coffee or a drink standing at the bar rather than sitting at a table, which usually incurs surcharges. Make lunch the main

---

DON'T LEAVE HOME WITHOUT...

- A copy of your travel insurance policy details
- Photocopies of your important documents
- Good manners. *La politesse* goes a long way in France (p346)
- A four-digit PIN for your credit or debit card (p328)
- A pocket knife to cut Normandy's fine cheeses (p52)

meal of the day – the set-price *menus* (p61) are astoundingly good value, and often cheaper than buying your own food.

You'll get the best exchange rate and low commissions at post offices and by using a credit card (see p328). Use a phonecard instead of pricey International Direct Dial (IDD) services when calling overseas.

Avail yourself of the region's many free sights: bustling marketplaces, tree-lined avenues, cathedrals, churches and nature reserves. Take advantage of discounts for people under 26, students and seniors – especially in museums and on transport (see p322). Look for the words *demi-tarif* or *tarif réduit* (half-price tariff or reduced rate) on admission rates and ask if you qualify.

Avoid taking trains that incur supplements or reservation fees (p343). Buy discount bus/metro passes or carnets of reduced-price tickets rather than single tickets if you'll be in a city any length of time. Arrange car rental before you leave home. If you are staying at least a month, hire a purchase-repurchase car (see p340). Fill up in towns, not on the autoroutes where fuel is more expensive.

TRAVEL LITERATURE

Unique as their cultures are, Normandy and Brittany have incorporated much French-ness into their outlook, making an overview of the French mind-set a good starting point for your readings. Begin with John Ardagh's *France in the New Century: Portrait of a Changing Society*, which has a marvellous chapter on Brittany's independence movement amid an exploration of modern French society. This survey ends in 1990 but provides a good background in understanding more recent developments. *The French*, by Theodore Zeldin, takes a more light-hearted, but still serious, look at French peculiarities. At least, his avowed English prejudices are not as annoying as they could be.

For an in-depth look at Brittany, you will not do better than *The Bretons* by Patrick Galliou & Michael Jones, which treats Brittany's fascinating history with the comprehensiveness it deserves. It's heavy going though and not for the faint-hearted. If your interest is megaliths, pick up a copy of *Statements in Stone* by Mark Patton, which has an extensive section on Brittany with wonderful photos.

Books on Normandy centre on the D-Day experience. *Six Armies in Normandy*, by John Keegan, is the seminal book on the conquest of Normandy, giving appropriate space to all the Allied armies that took part in the invasion. If you want to know what it actually felt like to be a civilian or soldier at the time, peruse the interviews in *The Good War* by Studs Terkel. The man is a gifted listener, coaxing vivid and sometimes astonishing recollections out of his subjects.

INTERNET RESOURCES

Brittany Tourism (www.brittanytourism.com) Practical and cultural information about Brittany and links to regional, departmental and local tourist offices.

Diplomatic & Visa Information (www.france.diplomatie.fr) Includes lists of consulates and embassies with visa information.

Gay & Lesbian (www.france.qrd.org - French only) 'Queer resources directory' for gay and lesbian travellers.

Lonely Planet (www.lonelyplanet.com) Summaries on travel to most places on earth, postcards from other travellers and a bulletin board for questions or advice.

Maison de la France (www.maison-de-la-france.fr) The main tourist office site.

Normandy Tourism (www.normandy-tourism.org)

Weather (www.meteo.fr) Two-day weather forecasts and current conditions.

LONELY PLANET INDEX

Litre of gas/petrol
€1.05

Litre of bottled water
€1.50

Souvenir T-shirt
€15

Street snack (crepe)
€2.50

Bottle of 1664 (beer)
€2

HOW MUCH?

Cinema ticket
€8

Baguette sandwich
€4

Espresso coffee
€2

Mid-range hotel double
€40

Tolls
€5/100km

TOP TENS
MUST-SEE MOVIES

Psych yourself up for Normandy and Brittany with the following shot-on-location flicks:

- *Monsieur Hulot's Holiday* (1953)
  Director: Jacques Tati
- *Les Parapluies de Cherbourg* (The Umbrellas of Cherbourg; 1964)
  Director: Jacques Demy
- *The Longest Day* (1962)
  Directors: Ken Annakin, Andrew Marton, Gerd Oswald
- *Chouans!* (1988)
  Director: Philippe de Broca
- *Tess* (1979)
  Director: Roman Polanski
- *Un Homme et une Femme* (A Man and a Woman; 1966)
  Director: Claude Lelouche
- *Autour de Minuit* (Around Midnight; 1986)
  Director: Bernard Tavernier
- *Dentellière* (The Lacemaker; 1977)
  Director: Claude Goretta
- *The Vikings* (1958)
  Director: Richard Fleischer
- *The Birds* (1963)
  Director: Alfred Hitchcock

OUR FAVOURITE FESTIVALS & EVENTS

Whether toasting their own culture or celebrating foreign films, Normans and Bretons know how to live it up with cider, crepes and Calvados.

- Fête des Marins – Blessing of the Sea
  Honfleur, Whit Sunday & Monday (p277)
- Fête Mediévale – Medieval festival
  Guérande, May (p195)
- Festival Folklorique – Folklore festival
  Trouville, June (p281)
- Festival de Cornouaille – Celebration of Breton music and culture
  Quimper, July (p148)
- The Regattas – Century-old celebration of ships
  Barfleur, August (p298)
- Grand Pardon – Blessing of the Sea
  Granville, July (p305)
- Fête de la Mer – Blessing of the Sea and religious processions
  Fécamp, August (p232)
- Festival Interceltique – Celebration of Celtic music and culture from all Celtic countries and regions
  Lorient, August (p161)
- Festival of American Film – The latest from Hollywood
  Deauville, September (p281)
- Festival du Film Britannique – Festival of British film
  Dinard, October (p81)

TOP READS

There's nothing like a good book to provoke an imaginative journey into a new culture. From Brittany, there's:

- *Les Chouans*
  Honoré de Balzac
- *The Three Musketeers*
  Alexandre Dumas
- *Satori in Paris*
  Jack Kerouac

Normandy has also inspired many acclaimed novelists:

- *Flaubert's Parrot*
  Julian Barnes
- *The Last English King*
  Julian Rathbone
- *The Longest Day*
  Cornelius Ryan
- *Madame Bovary*
  Gustav Flaubert
- *Nausea*
  Jean-Paul Sartre
- *Odo's Hanging*
  Peter Benson
- *Pierre & Jean*
  Guy de Maupassant

Itineraries
CLASSIC ROUTES

THE COASTAL ROUTE
Two to three weeks / 400km

From the crowded resort of **Le Tréport** (p230) to the wind-swept **Cotentin Peninsula** (p293), the Norman coast includes the evocatively named Alabaster Coast, Flowered Coast and Mother of Pearl Coast. The route charts Normandy's maritime and wartime histories, but there's no shortage of wide, sandy beaches, craggy cliffs and ports.

The Coastal Route encompasses startling variations in scenery. It could be done in a very rushed two weeks or a relaxed three weeks.

The port of Le Tréport is small-time compared to the bustle of fishing boats bringing their catch to **Dieppe** (p224). After feasting on the fresh fish of Dieppe, head down the Côte d'Albâtre (Alabaster Coast) to **Fécamp** (p231). Stop in sweet little **Yport** (p233) on the way to **Étretat** (p234) and its looming cliffs. Next stop is **Le Havre** (p220) and the sweeping **Pont de Normandie** (p278) bridging the way to **Honfleur** (p274) and its romantic old harbour. Snooty **Deauville** (p279) and down-to-earth **Trouville** (p279) are the jewels of the Côte Fleurie (Flowered Coast), great for shopping and lazing on the beach, but **Houlgate** (p283) and **Cabourg** (p283) provide a touch of class. Stop off in **Caen** (p256) for its museums and **Bayeux** (p256) for its famous tapestry before heading to the Côte de Nacre (Mother of Pearl Coast) and the **D-Day beaches** (p272). Head inland for a stop at **Ste-Mère-Église** (p299) and the granite town of **Valognes** (p298) before exploring the untamed Cotentin Peninsula and the unique villages of **Barfleur** (p298), **Auderville** (p300) and **Goury** (p301). Big-city shops, restaurants and café life await you in **Cherbourg** (p294).

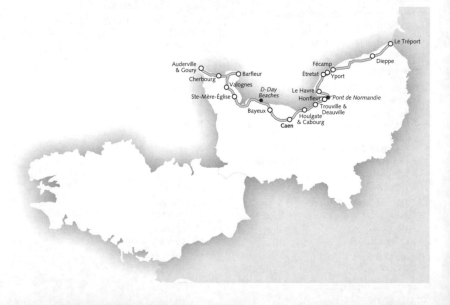

MEDIEVAL MAGIC

Three weeks / 415km

Massive fortifications, towering spires and half-timbered houses crowding narrow streets conjure up the splendour and fragility of medieval France, when God and good walls were considered the only protection from unfriendly neighbours.

From the awesome cathedral at **Coutances** (p301), head south to **Granville** (p303) whose walled upper town offers heady sea views. Go on to the World Heritage Site of **Mont St-Michel** (p68), where walls and swift tides protect the Gothic abbey from everything except a ceaseless onslaught of visitors. It's a short drive to the fairy-tale castle at **Fougères** (p91), surrounded by walls, a moat and an appealing cluster of old streets. Don't miss the extraordinarily well-preserved medieval centre of nearby **Vitré** (p92) before turning towards Brittany's capital at **Rennes** (p85) with its tiny old town. Too modern? Head south to **Vannes** (p172), fetchingly Middle Ages but not middle-aged, thanks to a teeming student population. On your way back up north, stop at scenic **Josselin** (p179), a relaxed spot in the countryside with 16th-century streets and a noble castle. Keep going to **Dinan** (p96) and its enchanting arrangement of cobbled streets, gabled houses, gardens, ramparts and a castle before taking a break at the *belle époque* playfulness of **Dinard** (p81). After a soak at the seaside, hop over to historic **St-Malo** (p75). It was hit hard during WWII, but you can still take a stroll through the old town and around the ramparts.

Between medieval towns, you'll be treated to the best of Normandy and Brittany's countryside. The Medieval Magic route could be done comfortably in three weeks.

TAILORED TRIPS

THE PAINTER'S NORMANDY
Two weeks / 275km

Generations of artists have sought to capture the swirls of light and colour that make up Normandy's landscape. Even if you're not packing an easel, following in their footsteps takes you to some of Normandy's most paintable spots.

Begin in the famous gardens of **Giverny** (p244), which Claude Monet lovingly painted and repainted. Stop in **Gisors** (p248) to admire the marketplace often painted by Pisarro. The French classical painter, Nicolas

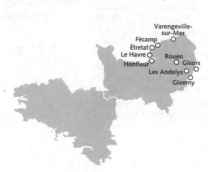

Poussin, is represented in his birthplace, **Les Andelys** (p246), to the southwest. Go on to **Rouen** (p202) whose cathedral was another favourite subject of Monet. The Beaux-Arts Museum here is a good place to catch up with the works of other Normandy painters. **Honfleur** (p274) was a major centre for the Impressionists and is especially linked to Eugène Boudin, whose works hang in an eponymous museum. The Beaux-Arts Museum in **Le Havre** (p220) also has works by Boudin and native son Raoul Dufy. Continue up the coast, stopping at **Étretat** (p234) and **Fécamp** (p231), painted by Monet, to **Varengeville-sur-Mer** (p230), which contains the tomb of Georges Braque.

CELTIC CONNECTIONS
Two weeks / 200km

Nowhere are Brittany's Celtic and maritime characters more apparent than in Finistère with its long and rugged coastline. The Celtic-based native language is still widely spoken, colourful processions mark local religious holidays and many towns boast Brittany's distinctive **enclos paroissiaux** (parish enclosures; p136).

Begin your circuit in **Quimper** (p146), often described as the 'soul of Brittany', where you just might see local costumes on market day. Take the coastal road to **Pointe du Raz** (p145), where fishermen still cast their

lines into a roiling, wind-whipped sea. Their catch may end up for sale in the bustling fish markets of **Douarnenez** (p142). After a stop in captivating little **Locronan** (p143), the most important pilgrimage site in Brittany, head north to **Camaret-sur-Mer** (p140) and experience life on a fishing boat. Next stop is the important naval port of **Brest** (p132); from there take a boat to the wild and beautiful **Île d'Ouessant** (p129). After returning to Brest, take a ride to **Le Folgoët** (p127), which is another important pilgrimage site, and then go on to **Morlaix** (p120), a good base for exploring the *enclos paroissiaux* of the region.

The Authors

JEANNE OLIVER
Coordinating Author & Normandy

Jeanne is a freelance writer who first started visiting Normandy 12 years ago and has been a regular visitor ever since. Her first visits were as a guide to tourists visiting the region but later she returned for the sheer pleasure of it. Jeanne wrote *Normandy* 1 and has updated the Normandy chapter of *France* 5 in addition to working on a dozen other books for Lonely Planet. She makes her home in the south of France.

Jeanne's Brittany & Normandy
I have a strange fondness for salty sea air and white tipped waves, which brings me to the Norman and Breton coast. The sweeping D-Day beaches (p272) exhilarate and awe me, although I much prefer to swim at La Baule (p196). My favourite city is Rouen (p202) not least for the fabulous four-course lunches followed by a healthy walk through the medieval town. In the smaller villages, there's almost always a little river running through the centre. Sometimes there's a walkway along the river or sometimes just benches, perfect for a picnic lunch. I'd visited Mont St-Michel (p68) many, many times and it was always packed with people. Once, in early evening after the tour buses left and during an exceptionally high tide, I finally understood what all the fuss was about. Timing is everything.

MILES RODDIS
Brittany

The first words of French that Miles ever exchanged outside classroom walls were with a Breton onion Johnny (see the boxed text, p123), an exotic figure with beret and bike who came knocking at the door.

A few years later with rather more French vocabulary and onions under his belt, he and a couple of teenage mates cycled all around the coast of Brittany. For him, this guidebook, so immensely satisfying to research, has also been an agreeable journey of nostalgia.

Miles has contributed to over 20 Lonely Planet titles, including *France* and *Walking in France*.

Snapshot

Prosperous and productive, Brittany and Normandy have a per capita income slightly higher and an unemployment rate slightly lower than the national average. Tourism is a big earner in the two regions, although Brittany's tourism industry has recently been hurt by various ecological problems (see p44). Brittany is France's leading agricultural producer, with food processing the biggest employer. Despite a sharp decline in the fishing fleet at the end of the 20th century, the region is a key centre for fishing and marine activity, including seaweed harvest (see the boxed text, p109). Service and hi-tech industries are also expanding. Normandy is second only to Brittany in meat and dairy production with grain crops and vegetables also important. Industry (paper pulp, cars and plastics) is concentrated in Upper Normandy. The ports of Le Havre and Rouen are major employers. Refineries along the Seine produce one-third of France's refined fuel and the nuclear power centre of Paluel produces 12% of its electricity. Politically, both regions are moderate with voting trends that tend to mirror those of the rest of France except that the far-right National Front has been less successful here than elsewhere.

The hottest topic throughout France right now, is the government's decision to ban the display of religious symbols in public schools. Although accepted by the Jewish, Protestant and Catholic faiths, this policy has caused an uproar in France's five-million-strong Muslim community, who argues that its religion requires the veiling of girls and women. The decision nevertheless enjoys broad popular support, since the separation of church and state is one of the bedrock principles of the French republic.

President Jacques Chirac enjoys a solid base of support in Brittany and Normandy. In France, the president is charged with managing the country's foreign affairs and President Chirac's decision to oppose the US invasion of Iraq was highly popular. Although US imports from France have declined as a result, the US market is a less significant factor in Normandy and Brittany's economy, making the overall impact small.

Prime Minister Raffarin is in a more precarious position as many of his domestic reforms have cut into France's generous social safety net. Reducing unemployment benefits for France's *intermittants de spectacle* (part-time performing artists and technicians), reforming the pension system for public employees and reducing the government role in the healthcare system have all provoked widespread and disruptive strikes and demonstrations. Other measures, such as greater enforcement of speed limits and raising tobacco taxes have been grudgingly accepted. The crushing defeat suffered by President Chirac's party in the March 2004 regional elections in Brittany and Normandy, as elsewhere, was widely interpreted as a vote against Raffarin's reforms.

One of Raffarin's greatest strengths is his roots as a local politician from the Poitou-Charentes *région*. The French have a longstanding sense that they are being ruled by an arrogant Parisian elite, a sentiment that is particularly strong in Brittany. Although only a radical few in Brittany seek separation from France, most Bretons and Normans would like greater autonomy in managing their own affairs. It was partly to appease Brittany's noisy clamour for recognition of its distinctive culture that the French government has moved towards regionalisation in recent decades with such policies as allowing Breton in schools. Regionalisation has not, however, had any significant impact on day-to-day life in the region.

FAST FACTS

Population:
6,100,000

Land area:
64,000 sq km

Pop growth:
+0.3%

Unemployment rate:
8.9%

Average hourly wage:
€9.70

Number of cows in Normandy: 6 million

History

PREHISTORY

Brittany's earliest known inhabitants were the Neolithic tribes who raised the cairns, menhirs and dolmens that are still scattered throughout the region, most famously at Carnac (p163). The purpose of these monuments has been a constant subject of debate among archaeologists and historians since the 19th century. All we can say with any degree of certainty is that they were built between 6000 BC and 2000 BC, probably by settled farming communities, and may have had an astronomical and/or religious aspect.

Remnants of Stone Age settlements have been found in Upper Normandy and around Caen, but nothing as impressive as Brittany's monuments. By the time of the Bronze Age (2500 BC) it appears that the ancient Normans and Bretons had begun to trade with the British Isles, mostly in tin and copper. Metals were imported from Britain, forged into swords, hatchets, spears and helmets and sent to inland Europe via the Seine and Loire Rivers.

Statements in Stone by Mark Patton is a large, expensive coffee-table book that examines the megalithic traditions of Western Europe. It has an extensive section on Brittany.

GAULS, ROMANS, CELTS & CHRISTIANS

The defining event in the history of Brittany and Normandy was the arrival of the Celts. From their original heartland in what is now southern Germany, Celtic tribes spread across Western Europe before reaching Brittany and Normandy in the 6th century BC. The Celts, who settled between the Rivers Seine and Loire, named their new homeland Armor, meaning 'the land by the sea'. Their descendants became known as 'Gauls'.

The new settlers formed tribes throughout the region. In Brittany, there were five Gaulish tribes: the Namneti in the south; the Veneti around the Gulf of Morbihan; the Rhedones in the east; the Osismi in the west; and the Coriosolites in the northeast. In Normandy, the Veliocasses made their capital Rouen, whereas the Calètes from the Pays de Caux organised around Lillebonne. Other tribes formed around Lisieux, Évreux, Carentan and Bayeux. They appear to have advanced gradually into the region, living peacefully with – and eventually assimilating – the aboriginal inhabitants. The Celts were a refined and technologically advanced people, who were skilled in the working of wood, iron and pottery. Archaeologists have uncovered many stunning examples of Celtic art, typically decorated with elegantly curved and interlaced designs.

DID YOU KNOW?

The megaliths of Brittany weigh up to 350 tonnes each.

Julius Caesar and the Roman legions marched into the region around 125 BC and defeated the powerful Veneti tribe in 56 BC. The conquest of Gaul was completed with the defeat of Vercingétorix in 52 BC and the region settled into four centuries of Roman rule. The Romans called their newly conquered province Armorica, introducing formal systems of administration and legislation, and building roads, towns and military camps. But the Romanisation of the region was only superficial and the local Gauls managed to retain much of their native culture and traditions, which survived when the Roman Empire began to crumble at the start of the 4th century AD.

TIMELINE	56 BC	AD 460
	Caesar conquers the Veneti tribe	Arrival of Celts from Britain

It was at this point that Brittany received its second great wave of Celtic immigrants. During the 5th and 6th centuries, large numbers of Bretons – the Celtic peoples of what we now call the British Isles – crossed the sea from their homelands in Wales, Cornwall and Ireland and settled in Brittany. The reasons for this migration remain obscure; perhaps they were fleeing attacks from Anglo-Saxons in the east of Britain and marauding Scots in the north, or perhaps their movements were part of a Roman policy to populate the empty lands of Armorica.

Whatever drove them across the English Channel, these new immigrants were responsible for giving the region its modern name and for introducing Christianity. Among the new arrivals were many Welsh and Irish monks and missionaries who set out to evangelise the native Gauls. Their names are remembered in countless churches, towns and villages throughout modern Brittany. The most revered were the 'seven saints', the founders of the seven dioceses of Brittany: Brieuc (St-Brieuc), Tugdual (Tréguier), Pol Aurelian (St-Pol de Léon), Corentin (Quimper), Paterne (Vannes), Samson (Dol de Bretagne) and Maclow (St-Malo).

Meanwhile in Normandy, Christianity was taking root. Rouen, Bayeux, Avranches, Évreux, Sées, Lisieux and Coutances developed into archbishoprics and many ecclesiastical buildings were constructed. By the 6th century, Normandy began to assume recognisable contours. Counties such as Cotentin and Pays de Caux emerged and great abbeys arose at St-Wandrille, Fécamp, Jumièges and Mont St-Michel.

STORMIN' NORMANS

Both Normandy and Brittany fell under Frankish control towards the end of the 8th century when Charlemagne subjugated the region. Yet in 845 Nominoë led the Bretons to victory against the armies of the French king Charles le Chauve (the Bald) at Ballon, near Redon. The resulting treaty guaranteed a peace between the Frankish kingdom and a strong, independent Brittany, reinforced by a further victory won against the Franks by Érispoë, son of Nominoë (who died in 851).

Descendants of Charlemagne proved weak and divided, leaving the region open to Viking raids. Called the 'Norse-men' (hence the word 'Norman'), the Vikings ripped through Rouen, Évreux, Bayeux, Lisieux and Sées in the 9th century, causing immense destruction. They hailed from Scandinavia, mostly Denmark, and sailed unusually rapid ships called *drakkars*. With eyes on the prizes in Normandy's rich abbeys and cathedrals, the Vikings sailed up the Seine, attacking cities along the way, and then dragged their boats overland with horses to set sail on other rivers, unleashing more havoc. In 841, the Vikings attacked Rouen mercilessly before burning and pillaging the abbeys of Jumièges and St-Wandrille. 'A furore Normannorum libera nos, domine' (God, spare us from the Norman fury), prayed the monks, but to no avail.

When bribes and ransom failed to dam the flood of Viking invaders, King Charles (the Simple) tried to negotiate. In 911 at St-Clair-sur-Epte, he ceded Rouen and the territory between the Rivers Bresle, Epte, Avre and Risle (roughly half of modern-day Normandy) to the Viking leader Rollo.

Rollo was a man of large appetites (supposedly so gigantic that no horse could carry him) who continued to devour Normandy. By 924 he had

820	911
The Norse-men (Vikings) ravage the Seine Valley	Treaty of St-Clair-sur-Epte

forced his way into Bayeux, Sées and most of Lower Normandy. After his death in 933 his son, Guillaume Long-Epée, completed his work by seizing Cotentin and the lower Manche, thus setting the boundaries for most of modern Normandy.

Brittany had a different experience. The Normans that began to raid and pillage the eastern marshes were stopped at Dol de Bretagne in 936 and driven out of Brittany by Alain Barbe-Torte, who became duke of Brittany the following year. By creating a duchy of Brittany, the French king allowed the dukes a measure of sovereignty over their own lands without overshadowing the supremacy of the French crown. However, it was a delicate balancing act of diplomacy and force.

The Norman Achievement by David C Douglas is a lively, vivid account of the Norman Conquest of England. *The Norman Conquest* by DJA Matthew is a scholarly book examining the political and cultural effect of the Norman Conquest on England.

THE AGE OF THE WARRIOR-KINGS

Normandy was flourishing economically and culturally but ridden with internal warfare when Guillaume le Batard (William the Bastard, who was later known as 'the Conqueror') assumed the throne in 1035 at the age of seven. As the illegitimate son of Robert I, duke of Normandy, and Arlette, a tanner's daughter, William's origins were hardly auspicious but his future was bright. After a long regency, the adult duke managed to unite his fractious barons and establish a strong central authority. He then began to think about expanding Norman influence and seized the crown of England after the Battle of Hastings in 1066 (see the boxed text, p261).

Brittany was not faring as well. Following the death of Alain Barbe-Torte in 952, the region descended into anarchy once more as the Breton feudal lords (who owed allegiance to the duke) defied the authority of the duke's successors. The Bretons sided with William of Normandy in his invasion of England in 1066 but William's death in 1087 ushered in a new climate of insecurity in the region. His successors battled for control of Normandy and then sought to impose their suzerainty on Brittany. Seeking English aid in the struggle against his rebellious Breton lords, Conan IV, duke of Brittany, married off his daughter in 1171 to Geoffrey, son of the English king Henry II, who already controlled Normandy.

Eleanor of Aquitaine and the Four Kings by Amy Kelly has plenty of fascinating detail about Henry, Richard the Lion-Heart, Eleanor and their activities in Normandy.

Normandy and Brittany were briefly both under Plantagenet control as Henry II assumed the title Duke of Normandy, but their paths diverged in the 13th century. Henry's youngest son, John Lackland, inherited Normandy after the death of his brother Richard the Lion-Heart, then lost it to King Philippe-Auguste in 1204, thereby cementing Normandy into France.

CIVIL WAR IN BRITTANY

Brittany remained an independent duchy but the death of the childless Jean III in 1341 brought about a civil war in Brittany between the supporters of the two claimants to the duke's throne. Jean's half-brother Jean IV de Montfort was backed by the English, while the other claimant, Charles de Blois, had the support of the French king.

The two sides fought it out for a quarter-century in the War of Succession. Several famous episodes of Breton history took place during this conflict, notably the exploits of the Breton hero Bertrand du Guesclin (see the boxed text, p20) and the Combat des Trente (Battle of the Thirty) in 1351, when 30 knights from each side were pitted against each other in a fight to the death.

927
1066

| King Alain Barbe-Torte defeats the last Normans | William the Conqueror defeats Harold at the Battle of Hastings |

BERTRAND DU GUESCLIN

Bertrand du Guesclin (c 1320–80), a Breton knight, was the greatest French soldier of his era. During the War of Succession he fought on the side of Charles de Blois, successfully defending Rennes against an English siege in 1356–57 and defeating the English knight Sir Thomas Canterbury in a duel.

He entered the service of the French king Charles V and won a brilliant victory against the forces of Charles II of Navarre at the Battle of Cocherel in 1364. Later that year he was taken prisoner by the English at Auray, after the death (in battle) of Charles de Blois. He was ransomed for 40,000 gold francs by Charles V, who put him in charge of the *compagnies*, bands of mercenaries who marauded through Spain in an ultimately successful campaign to capture the throne of Castile.

From 1370 until his death, du Guesclin served as Constable of France and notched up several famous victories against the English, reclaiming much of the French territory that they had captured earlier that century. He died as he had lived, besieging an enemy fortress in Languedoc in 1380.

The Age of the Cathedrals by Georges Duby is an authoritative study of the relations between art and society in medieval France.

The War of Succession drew to a close in 1364, when Charles de Blois was killed. The following year the Treaty of Guérande saw Jean V de Montfort, declared duke of Brittany, a title he held until his death in 1399. The Montfort reign saw Brittany achieve the zenith of its power and independence, with the dukes paying little more than lip service to their theoretically feudal relationship with the French crown. The house of Montfort sent its representatives to the Vatican, installed ambassadors in foreign courts and surrounded itself with an all but royal court. From their chateau at Nantes, the Montforts ruled Brittany as an independent country, trying to maintain neutrality between France and England while Normandy was torn apart by the Hundred Years' War.

THE HUNDRED YEARS' WAR

When Edward III of England invaded France through St-Vaast-la-Hougue and triggered the Hundred Years' War, it had a devastating effect on Normandy even as Brittany emerged relatively unscathed. Part of Normandy sided with the English against the Count d'Évreux who had designs on the French throne, and part sided with the French king. As usual, the peasants suffered as rival gangs tore through the Norman countryside pillaging and looting. A semblance of peace was restored when the French king Charles V turned to Betrand du Guesclin. His troops massed in Cocherel on the right bank of the Eure and cleverly lured the forces of Count d'Évreux down from the hill to a devastating defeat, thus ending him as a threat.

A Distant Mirror by Barbara Tuchman is a highly readable account of the vicissitudes of the 14th century with a special focus on the start of the Hundred Years' War.

A form of stability returned when the English consolidated their hold on France and Normandy. Henry VI founded a university at Caen, and law courts functioned in Rouen. Commerce also flourished as suppliers rushed to fill the needs of the occupying army. In 1422 John Plantagenet, the duke of Bedford, was installed as regent of France for England's King Henry VI, then an infant. Henry was crowned as king of France at Notre Dame less a decade later, and the English might have remained in power if Joan of Arc (see the boxed text, p208) hadn't intervened. As it was, the English were finally driven from France in 1453.

The postwar period was a period of rebuilding in Normandy. Louis XI (The Spider King, so called because of his ruthless cunning) granted

1204	1337
Normandy absorbed into France	Start of the Hundred Years' War

Normandy a substantial degree of autonomy both financially and politically. International trade revived, bringing prosperity to Rouen, Dieppe, Fécamp, Honfleur and Cherbourg who exported metal, salt, textiles, spices and fish. Explorers set forth from Normandy's shores starting late in the 15th century. The Canary Islands, Senegal and Newfoundland were important acquisitions of the period. In 1523, Verrazano left from Dieppe on a voyage that founded Manhattan. In 1550, Le Havre native Guillaume Le Testu sailed the coast of Brazil and in 1555 another Le Testu expedition left from Le Havre to colonise the bay of Rio de Janeiro. Ivory, spices and slaves flowed into Normandy's ports from French colonies on the west coast of Africa, allowing commercial shippers to amass fortunes. With all the money flowing into the region, opulent chateaux sprouted throughout the countryside.

Joan of Arc by Mary Gordon is perhaps the most vividly imagined portrait of the Maid; Gordon conveys the immense mystery of her accomplishments. *Joan of Arc* is a fascinating piece by confirmed atheist Mark Twain.

THE END OF INDEPENDENT BRITTANY

Even as its grip on Normandy loosened, the central French authorities sought to tighten their hold on Brittany. Charles VIII (r 1483–98) sent his troops into Brittany in 1487, sparking a series of bloody conflicts that resulted in the surrender of many Breton towns and the death of Duke François II of Brittany in the Battle of St-Aubin du Cormier. His daughter Anne, an only child, became duchess of Brittany at the tender age of 12.

Charles VIII kept up his military pressure with renewed attacks on the peninsula. In 1490 the young Anne made a marriage by proxy to Maximilian I, archduke of Austria, in the hope of gaining the protection of the powerful German empire. In reply, Charles VIII ditched his own fiancée and invoked the terms of a treaty signed after the death of Anne's father, François II, which stipulated that she could not wed without the agreement of the French king. In 1491 he forced her to dissolve her marriage to Maximilian and marry him instead. Although Anne remained sovereign of Brittany – and became queen of France to boot – the French crown had once more got its foot in the door of Breton independence.

It was Anne's fate to become queen of France not once, but twice. On the death of Charles in 1498, she married his successor Louis XII (while still aged only 23), having negotiated a marriage contract which guaranteed her continuing sovereignty over Brittany – a final attempt to keep her native land out of French clutches. But it was in vain. After Anne's death in 1514, her daughter Claude inherited both the duchy of Brittany and the French crown, and married François d'Angoulême, who became King François I. Just 18 years after Anne's death, Brittany and France were joined by a Treaty of Union (see the boxed text, p171), which guaranteed various local freedoms in exchange for recognition of French sovereignty.

Compiled by a true believer, the website www.jeanne-darc.com has tons of information plus links to other sites.

RELIGIOUS WARS

The final years of the 16th century were troubled by the wars of religion that spread through Europe in the wake of the Protestant Reformation. International trade made the Normans broadminded and the region fertile terrain for the spread of Protestantism. The Catholic nobility attempted to preserve a power base, the English helped the Protestants and, as usual, the common people bore the brunt of the massacres and spasms of violence. In 1562, the Huguenots, with the support of the English, attacked and

1341
Start of the War of Succession

1346
Edward of England lands in Normandy

pillaged churches and monasteries. Charles IX, with the connivance of his mother and regent Catherine de Médicis, retaliated by attacking Rouen and pillaging the city for eight days. The St Bartholomew's Day massacre of 1572 left 500 Huguenots dead in Rouen and spawned sporadic killing in Caen and Dieppe.

Even with its minimal Protestant presence, Brittany entered into the fray. In 1588 Philippe de Lorraine, governor of Brittany, joined the Ligue (League), a movement that opposed the accession to the French throne of a Protestant king, the future Henri IV (r 1589–1610). Philippe also plotted to revive the duchy of Brittany for himself and his heirs. Supported by the Breton peasantry, the Ligue entered into open conflict with the French crown. Peace only returned after Henri IV issued the Edict of Nantes in 1598, granting freedom of worship.

Cross Channel by Julian Barnes is a witty collection of key moments in shared Anglo-French history – from Joan of Arc to Eurostar.

FRANCE CRACKS DOWN

The expansion of royal authority under Henri's successor, Louis XIII, and his gifted advisor, Cardinal Richelieu, boded poorly for the autonomy of both Normandy and Brittany. Perhaps because of its proximity to Paris, Normandy was hit first. Rouen's independent-minded Parliament was reduced to a simple law court and its limited autonomy revoked. As a final blow, the young king assaulted the chateau of Caen in 1620 for its fidelity to Marie de Médicis and forced the city into submission.

Brittany's turn came in 1675. The reign of Louis XIV (1638–1715) stirred up trouble in the region, especially over the question of taxes, of which the Sun King was particularly fond. Two peasant revolts were viciously suppressed – the first was against the *papier timbré* ('stamped paper'; an indirect tax on certain official deeds and papers) and the second was an uprising against the feudal system known as the 'Bonnets Rouges' (Red Bonnets) revolts.

The Bretons by Patrick Galliou & Michael Jones is part of a series on the 'Peoples of Europe'. This is an accessible and comprehensive history of the region.

Then in 1718, as a protest against ever-increasing taxes, the Breton nobles (under the banner of 'Les Frères Bretons', the Breton Brothers) signed a pact demanding the French crown adhere to the treaty of union (1532), which stated that Bretons would be liable to pay only taxes that were levied locally. Four of their number were captured and decapitated at Nantes. Just as elsewhere in France, the scenes were set for the discontent that would eventually lead to revolution.

Normandy, on the other hand, fared well under the Sun King. Louis XIV's Finance Minister, Jean-Baptiste Colbert, set up a number of profitable industries in Normandy. Ceramics in Rouen, textiles in Elbeuf and Alençon lace were some of his brainchildren that produced high returns for the region throughout the 17th century. The coastline also remained a launching pad for global expeditions. Colbert set up the West Indies Company in 1664 and put its headquarters in Le Havre. Robert Cavelier de La Salle was born in Rouen and went on to discover Ohio, the Mississippi and then claimed Louisiana for his king. Rich merchants commissioned the most fashionable Parisian architects and designers to create extravagant mansions. Mansard and Le Notre, fresh from their triumph at Versailles, rode out to lend their skills to Normandy's chateaux.

The revocation of the Edict of Nantes in 1685, which had allowed religious freedom, was a disaster for Normandy however. Protestantism had gained a strong foothold and numerous churches were destroyed in Caen, St-Lô and Argentan. Many citizens simply walked out rather than face persecution. Rouen alone lost 20,000 inhabitants, mostly skilled artisans who took their money and know-how to England, France and Germany. The region slid back into poverty.

THE FRENCH REVOLUTION

The revolution of 1789 provoked different reactions in Normandy and Brittany. For Bretons, it was first and foremost a final loss of what independence they retained. Not only was the États de Bretagne (the 'States of Brittany', the region's ruling council whose rights were guaranteed by the treaty of 1532) abolished along with feudalism, but the Breton parliament, a symbol of the region's continuing independence, was dissolved. The power of the clergy, who had an important role in Breton life, was cut at a stroke. The majority of Breton priests, supported by their congregations, refused to accept their new status.

Although the revolutionary government's hostility to the clergy was unpopular in abbey-strewn Normandy, the region stayed loyal to Paris until the purge of the moderate Girondin party and the ascendancy of the radical Jacobins in 1793. Caen became the centre of the Fédéralist party, opposed to the bloody Reign of Terror emanating from Paris. The Terror claimed few victims in Normandy but many churches and abbeys were pillaged, especially in Rouen and Caen. In July 1793 Charlotte Corday – a young woman disgusted by the excesses of the Revolution – left Caen for Paris where she found Jacobin leader Marat in his bath. She stabbed him to death and was then executed herself.

The revolutionary government's forced recruitment of young men provoked anti-recruitment riots in Calvados, but nothing like the Chouan Rebellion in Brittany that claimed tens of thousands of lives between 1793 and 1799 (see the boxed text, p90). Certain parts of Normandy – near Brittany, the Orne and Calvados *départements* and southern Manche – also supported the Chouannerie. The economy suffered as the recruitment drive robbed the region of workers and a blockade affected trade with England, Africa and the Antilles.

One result of this uprising, widely regarded as 'counter-revolutionary', was to create a lasting rift between Brittany and revolutionary (and later republican) France. This attitude was evident in the 'Camp de Conlie' incident during the Franco-German war of 1870–71. Fearing that they had an *armée de chouans* on their hands, France's political and military leaders herded 60,000 Breton soldiers into a muddy and overcrowded camp near Le Mans rather than send them into battle. Many of them died there.

THE 19TH CENTURY

The divergent approaches to the French Revolution stretched into the 19th century as Normandy and Brittany followed different political and economic paths. Once the debris of the Revolution had been cleared, Normandy set about doing what it had always done best – make money. The revolutions of 1830 and 1848 and the 1870–71 war hardly touched Normandy. Politics took place in Paris, close in distance but far from the economic concerns that preoccupied Normans. The opening of the naval

For an overview of Normandy history visit www.normandienet .tm.fr/nn/histoire.htm. There's little on D-Day though.

1598	1675
Edict of Nantes puts an end to religious strife	The 'Stamped Paper' peasant uprising in Brittany

port at Cherbourg, the development of tourism along the coast and the spread of pastures and dairy cows helped transform the landscape and the economy. Coastal Normandy attracted artists and writers, upper Normandy industrialised and lower Normandy remained largely rural.

For Brittany, the 19th century was marked by economic crisis. At sea, maritime trade collapsed following the closure of the French East India Company, the end of the slave trade, and competition from the railways. Many former trading ports, especially in Finistère and Morbihan, turned to the sardine fishery for salvation, while others specialised in crustaceans and shellfish. The boats of Île de Groix and Concarneau set out to hunt tuna, while the schooners of St-Malo and Paimpol scoured the waters of Newfoundland and Iceland in search of *la morue* (cod).

The difficulties experienced by Breton industries towards the end of the 19th century served as a catalyst for radicalisation, manifested in the general strikes of 1893. Brittany went on to experience a series of long and sometimes violent industrial conflicts in the decades before WWI, fought out in the dockyards of Nantes, the canneries of Finistère, the shoe factories of Fougères and the farms of the interior.

If you can read French, there's an overview of Brittany's history at www.bretagne-breizh .com/histoire_bretagne.

WORLD WARS

Both Normandy and Brittany suffered massive losses during WWI, with Brittany taking the heavier blow. The postwar period brought economic hardship to the region as elsewhere and a resurgence of the Breton independence movement. In 1919, 800 Bretons signed a petition demanding the renewal of the treaty of union. In 1923, the Breton flag – the *gwenn ha du* – symbol of Armorican identity, was created by Morvan Marchal. In 1932 the 400th anniversary celebration of the treaty of union was marked by riots and an attack on a train carrying President Herriot from Paris to Nantes.

Normandy's relative calm was shattered on 9 June 1940 when German troops entered Rouen and began their advance across the region to the Channel Islands, where they remained until 1945. A wave of bombardments accompanied their advance, driving the civilian population from their homes. For four years Normandy suffered all the indignities and cruelties of occupation: deportations, forced labour, arrests and executions.

WWII served to expose deep divisions in Breton society. During the war, the ease of crossing the English Channel from Brittany saw many Bretons leaving to join the Free French forces in Britain. Famously, when Charles de Gaulle made his call to arms from London in June 1940, 130 men from the tiny Île de Sein – almost the entire male population – immediately embarked for England. De Gaulle later inspected his first parade of 600 Free French soldiers, asking each one where he had come from. When yet another responded 'Sein', the general exclaimed: 'Mais alors, Sein, c'est le quart de France!' (But then, Sein is one-quarter of France!). The whole island was later awarded the Croix de la Libération (France's highest decoration).

An encyclopaedic discussion of D-Day – replete with pictures and videos – is what you'll find at http://search.eb.com /normandy.

On the other hand, some Breton separatists were attracted to Hitler's regime. Members of the Parti National Breton (PNB) were openly supportive of the Nazis, wheras the Bezenn Perrot (a Breton militia group) even fought in German uniform.

1771	1789
Suppression of the Parliament of Rouen	French Revolution

Invasion

The need for an invasion of continental Europe became apparent to the Allied commanders as early as 1942. Their first target was an astoundingly ill-conceived raid on Dieppe, a strongly fortified port. An Anglo-Canadian force attempting to storm the German defences were met by a wall of machine-gun fire that left 65% of the troops killed or wounded. The debacle demoralised the population and caused the Allies to look towards a more lightly fortified site for their next assault.

The Cotentin beaches were a promising spot for the Allies, largely because the Germans had deemed it unlikely that a place lying so far from Britain and known for its stormy seas would be targeted. The beaches were among the more vulnerable portions of the Atlantic wall, a 3200km defensive system along the Belgian and French coast. The string of pillboxes, blockhouses and gun emplacements were strongest around the narrowest part of the Channel, in the Pas de Calais, far northern France. When German Field Marshal Rommel was placed in charge of the Atlantic defence in 1944 he further strengthened the fortifications by planting antitank obstacles on the beach and underwater obstructions offshore. He also laid nearly six million mines, mostly in Normandy. Remnants of the Atlantic wall are still visible in Pointe du Hoc (p273) and Granville (p303).

For nearly three months prior to D-Day, bombs had rained down on Normandy and northern France, cutting train lines, bridges and arms depots. Resistance fighters on the ground supplemented the air campaign primarily by sabotaging train lines, preventing German reinforcements from reaching the coast. They were deployed inland since the Germans had effectively quarantined the Normandy coast to a depth of at least 50km, making sure that only proven loyalists were allowed near the coastal zone. Allied commanders and resistance fighters communicated via coded messages broadcast by the BBC.

For more about the D-Day landings see the boxed text, p26.

The Battle of Normandy

Four days after D-Day, the Allies held a coastal strip about 100km long and 10km deep, but the Germans were firmly entrenched around Caen. Villers-Bocage was the hub of a crucial road network for the region, but the British armoured thrust there on 13 June was defeated, as was an infantry offensive west of Caen from 25 to 29 June. The situation threatened to degenerate into a stalemate.

The grim Battle of the Hedgerows was fought mainly by the Americans up and down the Cotentin Peninsula. The bocage in northern France (wooded countryside divided into countless fields bordered by walled roads and hedgerows) made ideal territory for defending and the Germans made brilliant use of it. Since the nature of the terrain was not indicated on available maps, Allied commanders failed to foresee the difficulties of fighting in such countryside; the cost in men and morale was high.

On 18 July, American troops captured the vital communications centre of St-Lô after a bombing campaign that so destroyed the city it became known as the 'capital of ruins'. In order to break out of the murderous bocage, General Omar Bradley began a thunderous bombing campaign

Saving Private Ryan (1999) by Stephen Spielberg, a chillingly realistic, Oscar-winning account of the American landing at Omaha Beach, was filmed in Ireland, except for the scenes at the American cemetery.

The star studded *The Longest Day* (1962) was filmed in various locations around Normandy. Daryl Zanuck's epic lacks Spielberg's blood-and-guts battle scenes but it includes actual participants in the battle among the walk-ons.

1793	1843
Beginning of the Chouannerie Rebellion in Brittany	Opening of the Paris–Rouen railroad

D-DAY LANDINGS

The largest amphibious operation in human history kicked off on 6 June 1944 in rough weather and heavy seas. The invasion was carefully timed to take advantage of a full moon for the three airborne divisions and low tides for the landings. Conditions would be optimal only from 5 to 7 June. The invasion was set for 5 June, but the weather turned nasty on 4 June after the invasion force had already embarked, putting Eisenhower in an excruciating position. A delay could fatally imperil the vital secrecy of the operation and force the Allies to resupply the invading army in a period of even worse weather. Meteorologists predicted a window of opportunity on 6 June and Eisenhower gave the go-ahead.

The final plan entailed an assault by three paratroop divisions and five seaborne divisions, along with an armada of 13,000 aeroplanes and 6000 vessels. The initial invasion force was 45,000, and 15 divisions were to follow once successful beachheads had been established. The landing area was to stretch over 80km of the coast from Caen to Ste-Mère-Église. The five sectors involved were code-named Sword, Juno, Gold, Omaha and Utah Beaches.

D-Day – 6 June 1944

Shortly after midnight on the night of 5–6 June, three Allied airborne divisions filled the skies over Normandy with gliders and parachutes. A preliminary bombing began at 3am, followed by artillery fire from the offshore fleet. Even then the scale of the invasion was not apparent to Normandy's German defenders. The high command persisted in the belief that the naval bombardment was a diversionary tactic for an attack elsewhere. Around 6.30am men began pouring out of their landing crafts.

Sword, Juno & Gold Beaches

These beaches, stretching for about 30km from Ouistreham to Arromanches, were attacked by the British 2nd Army, which included sizable detachments of Canadians and smaller groups of Commonwealth, Free French and Polish forces.

At Sword Beach (Colleville Beach), the British 3rd Infantry Division disembarked at 7.25am. The resistance was quickly overcome and the beach secured after about two hours. The infantry was within 5km of Caen by 4pm, but a heavy German armoured counterattack by the crack 21st Panzer division forced the Allies to dig in. Thus, Caen, one of the prime D-Day objectives, was not taken on the first day as planned. The British suffered 630 casualties.

At Juno Beach (Courseulles, Bernières and St-Aubin Beaches), nine Canadian battalions attacked one German battalion but, despite the numerical advantage, underwater obstacles and steady artillery fire took a heavy toll. Two hours later a quarter of the force was still tied down in the landing area, but by noon they were south and east of Creully. At the end of the day, the Canadians had 1000 casualties, including 335 dead.

of the German positions along the St-Lô–Périers road, which ran parallel to the advance route to Avranches. By 28 July, three infantry divisions, followed by four armoured divisions, finally succeeded in punching a hole in the German lines.

Bradley was quick to exploit the advantage, turning to fiery General George S Patton, who was ordered to take his army out of Normandy and into Brittany. After taking the 4th Armoured Division 40km in 36 hours, Patton captured Avranches on 31 July, the exit door from Normandy, leaving the way clear to Brittany.

At Gold Beach, which included the town of Arromanches, the attack by the British forces was at first chaotic; unexpectedly high waters obscured the German underwater obstacles, leading to the loss of numerous armoured vehicles. Fortunately the offshore bombardment had silenced most of the German big guns. By 9am, Allied armoured divisions were on the beach and several brigades pushed inland. By afternoon, they had joined up with the Juno forces and were only 3km from Bayeux – the first town in France to be freed. The British had suffered 400 casualties in securing the beachhead.

Omaha & Utah Beaches

The struggle on Omaha Beach (Vierville, St-Laurent and Colleville Beaches) was by far the bloodiest of the day. Omaha Beach stretched 10km from Port-en-Bessin to the mouth of the River Vire and was backed by 30m high cliffs. The beach was staunchly defended by three battalions of heavily armed, highly trained Germans supported by an extensive trench system, mines and underwater obstacles. The Allied commanders failed to realise that the veteran German 352nd Infantry Division had only recently been moved into position here for training exercises.

The 1st US Infantry Division, known as the 'Big Red One', launched the attack on Omaha Beach and ran into immediate difficulty. The seas were choppy; winds and strong currents buffeted the landing crafts from one end of the beach to the other. Men disembarked under heavy German fire; the naval bombardment had done little damage to German positions at the top of the cliffs. Those who weren't picked off by German gunners as they stepped off the boats, drowned under the weight of their heavy packs. Of the 29 Sherman tanks expected to support the troops, only two made it to shore.

Under relentless German enfilade fire, the men tried to collect themselves in small exhausted groups to seek some shelter under the sea wall or behind the beach obstacles. Man by man and metre by metre, the GIs managed to gain a precarious toehold on the beach and scaled the cliffs. Eventually a naval destroyer opened fire, forcing the Germans to fall back a short distance, and the men were finally able to get off the deadly beach. Nevertheless, 1000 soldiers were killed at Omaha on D-Day, out of a total of 2500 American casualties.

Matters were no better northwest at Pointe du Hoc where Colonel Earl Rudder's Texas Ranger Battalion was struggling up 30m cliffs. His mission was to seize German howitzers, whose fire could imperil the landing at Omaha Beach. A navigational error caused the men to come under direct German fire and casualties were heavy. The Germans had moved the howitzers but the Rangers engaged in two days of bloody fighting before they were finally relieved.

At Utah Beach the 4th US Infantry Division faced little resistance. By noon, the beach had been cleared with the loss of only 12 men. Pockets of troops held large tracts of territory to the west of the landing site, and the town of Ste-Mère-Église was captured. By the end of D-Day, it was clear that the essential conditions for a successful invasion had been met: surprise was total; the Allies had achieved complete mastery of the air and the Germans were unable to reinforce their units. The bad news was that none of the military objectives had been met, and the Allies had lost 10,000 men, two warships, 127 aeroplanes and 300 landing craft.

The Germans decided to counterattack on 7 August. Hitler put together a force of Panzer divisions and moved towards Mortain, intending to cut off the American forces south of Avranches and in Brittany. Allied interceptions of German radio communications allowed them to mount a sturdy air and land defence that inflicted heavy losses on the Germans and stopped the advance cold.

After finally liberating Caen on 19 July, the Canadians moved towards Falaise. Meanwhile, Patton's army was ordered to swing east and then north from Le Mans with the intention of meeting the Canadians at Falaise and

1942	1944
Raid on Dieppe	Battle of Normandy

trapping the German army in what became known as the Falaise pocket. In one of the more controversial decisions of the war, General Bradley ordered Patton to remain at Argentan, apparently fearing a 'friendly battle' between American and Canadian forces.

German commanders sensed the trap and began moving their divisions east just as Polish and American forces raced to close the Falaise-Argentan gap. The Germans fought with the fury of the damned and some quarter of a million men managed to escape to the Seine before the gap was closed on 19 August. Ultimately, their struggle was hopeless. The Germans lost some 10,000 men in the Falaise pocket, with another 50,000 taken prisoner. Allied forces pressed on to the Seine and beyond. The Battle of Normandy was over.

Figures give an accurate picture of the price of victory: the Germans lost 200,000 men and as many were taken prisoner. Some 53,000 Allied soldiers were killed, more than 150,000 were wounded and nearly 20,000 were listed as missing in action. In the five *départmentes* of Normandy, between 15,000 and 35,000 civilians lost their lives.

DID YOU KNOW?

According to a recent poll, 40% of Bretons felt themselves to be Breton first, and French second.

SEPARATISM IN BRITTANY

The aftermath of WWII, which reduced the cities of Lorient, Brest, St-Nazaire and St-Malo to piles of rubble, brought about a change of feeling in the region. Brittany not only seemed ready to accept its role as an integral part of the French state but also showed the desire to direct its own fate. This will was manifested in the improvement of roads and railways and in the modernisation of industry and agriculture. Nevertheless, these changes could not hide the genuine economic difficulties faced by the peninsula, which had to compete with other French regions for national government resources.

BRETON NATIONALISM

Breton nationalism hit international headlines in April 2000, when a bomb attack on a McDonald's restaurant in Quévert, near Dinan, left one person dead. The bombing was attributed to the Armée Révolutionnaire Bretonne (ARB; Breton Revolutionary Army), a terrorist group founded in 1971.

Despite this isolated tragic event, the overwhelming body of nationalist sentiment in Brittany is entirely peaceful. There is a broad spectrum of opinion, from a handful of fanatics who desire nothing less than complete independence, through those who crave greater regional autonomy, to the largely apolitical majority who want only respect and support for Breton culture and language.

The political groupings include the separatist Parti pour l'Organisation d'une Bretagne Libre (POBL; Party for the Organisation of a Free Brittany), the left-wing and federalist Union Démocratique Bretonne (UDB; Breton Democratic Union) and the revolutionary nationalist group Emgann (meaning 'Combat'). Among the demands made by the various nationalist parties are the reunification of Brittany with its former territory in the Loire-Atlantique *départmente*, the protection and promotion of the Breton language, and the establishment of a Breton executive.

In local elections, the separatist parties have never polled more than a few percent of the vote but some of their ideas nevertheless strike a chord with a large proportion of the electorate. Opinion polls published in the regional newspaper *Le Télégramme* in 2000 revealed that 23% of Bretons were sympathetic to some of the causes espoused by separatist parties and 49% were in favour of the compulsory teaching of the Breton language in schools.

1965	1978
Front de la Libération de Bretagne launches its first attacks	*Amoco Cadiz* oil spill on Brittany beaches

But separatist sentiment did not go away. The radical Front de Libér-ation de la Bretagne launched its first attacks in 1965. Anger against the state peaked in the 1970s, provoked by disastrous oil slicks from the wreck of the *Amoco Cadiz* (see the boxed text, p128) and government plans to build a nuclear power station at Plogoff near the scenic Pointe du Raz. These events provided a focus for discontent and stirred up a renewed pride in Breton culture and history. This was expressed in the creation in 1977 of private Breton-language schools , the establishment of annual festivals of Breton music and the development of heritage centres and new museums. The majority of Bretons retain a strong bond with their native culture without feeling the need to belong to any separatist movement.

Brittany today is a distinctive, modern region, now thoroughly inte-grated with the French state yet retaining a strong sense of its own unique history and identity. It enters the 21st century *sans avoir perdu son âme* (without having lost its soul).

REBUILDING NORMANDY

The positive side of a destroyed economy and infrastructure is the oppor-tunity to start from scratch. A network of new roads and train lines connected Normandy's cities with Paris. This opened Normandy's coast and countryside to Parisians looking for seaside vacations and second residences. At the same time, France began moving towards a policy of building economic centres throughout the country rather than maintaining Paris as the seat of all economic opportunity. This policy change benefited Normandy enormously.

DID YOU KNOW?
For centuries Norman French was the official court language of England.

Postwar rebuilding was swift and, with a flood of Allied funds, largely completed by 1951. Speed was essential since housing stock needed to be replenished, but each city approached the task of reconstruction with a different aesthetic. The idea was to conserve reminders of the past, while adapting to the demands of modernity. Rouen erected bland, functional buildings along its devastated river banks but replicated the medieval style of half-timber buildings in the old town. Caen constructed modern buildings out of its traditional white stone and placed its famed university outside the city centre in the style of American campuses. The region has attracted much industry, as well as relying on its traditional agricultural base.

Normandy's natural beauty has led many Parisians to buy second homes in the countryside. Tourists love the coastline in the summer and many come to pay homage to the fallen heroes of WWII.

Although Normandy has never had an independence movement à la Brittany, a number of prominent politicians are endorsing a movement to unify Upper and Lower Normandy. The two regions share a nearly identi-cal culture and history that, supporters of the movement argue, could better be promoted as a tourist destination if the regions were united. Equalising economic opportunity throughout the region both through the promotion of business incentives and governmental initiatives is another goal.

1995	2004
Inauguration of the Pont de Normandie	60th anniversary of the D-Day landings

The Culture

REGIONAL IDENTITY

The sense of regional identity in Brittany is the strongest in continental France. Bretons are extremely proud of their distinctive history, language and culture. Despite a climate that is far from ideal, Bretons need very good reasons to leave their home region and tend to pine for it when they do. Proud, stubborn, hard-drinking (with the highest alcoholism rate in France) and down-to-earth, the Bretons are considered a breed apart by the rest of France. The school system in Brittany is characterised by the existence of bilingual (French and Breton) schools called *Les Écoles Diwan* (Diwan Schools; *diwan* is Breton for 'seed'), where pupils are taught entirely in the Breton language until they are aged seven or eight. From then on the aim is to develop fluent bilingualism in Breton and French. Trade links with Britain and an influx of Brits living out their retirement in Brittany has made the region extremely Anglo-friendly.

Normans tend to identify themselves as Upper or Lower Normans with an intense rivalry that is often manifested on the football field. Lower Normans feel that they have the more beautiful territory whereas Upper Normans tend to consider themselves as more industrious. Despite regional differences, Normans are united in an even more intense rivalry with Brittany. A sense that their regional development is lagging behind their neighbour's, has sparked a drive to unify the two regions (see p29).

LIFESTYLE

One of the major pleasures of visiting Brittany is experiencing its local traditions. Particularly at the *pardons* (colourful religious celebrations; see the boxed text opposite), but also at the *festoù-noz* (night-time dance and music festivals; see the boxed text, p33, for more details), you might spot Bretons wearing their traditional costumes: black dresses covered with lacy white aprons and tall lace headdresses on the women; beribboned black felt hats on the men. Traditional costume and everyday use of the Breton language are most evident in lower Brittany, Finistère and particularly in Cornouaille, the southwestern tip. Other regions have retained little of the traditional Breton way of life.

All in English, www.brittany -bretagne.com has a wealth of information about Brittany's culture.

POPULATION

Brittany

The population of Brittany is relatively stable. Although the birth rate is slightly under the national average, major cities of Rennes, Vannes, Quimper, St-Malo and Lannion have seen their populations increase, largely due to the migration of over-30s professionals, mostly from the Île de France. The centre-west and the northern coast have seen a decline in population. The most densely populated region is Ille-et-Vilaine, whereas the Cote d'Armor is the most sparsely populated. Overall, 47.6% of the population lives in an urban area and 1% of the population is of foreign origin.

It's in French of course but www.normandie.asso.fr agitates for a united Normandy.

Normandy

About 1.4% of the population of Upper Normandy is of foreign origin and 0.6% of Lower Normandy. Upper Normandy has a higher population density than Lower Normandy. The Seine-Maritime is one of the most densely populated *départements* in France, most of which are clustered around Rouen and Le Havre. Eure has the lowest density in Upper Normandy.

POPULAR PARDONS

The *pardons* of Brittany are celebrations of the patron saint of the local parish. Processions, traditional music, dances, games and general merry-making are features of the occasion.

Date	Place	Pardon
3rd Sun in May	Tréguier	St-Yves
last Sun in June	Plouguerneau	St-Pierre et St-Paul
1st Sun in July	Quimper	Ty Mamm Doué
1st Sun in July	Guingamp	Notre Dame de Bon Secours
2nd Sun in July	Locronan	Petite Troménie
mid-July	Pontrieux	Notre Dame des Fontaines
1st Sun after 14 July	Roscoff	Ste-Barbe
26 July	Ste-Anne d'Auray	Ste-Anne d'Auray
15 Aug	Perros-Guirec	Notre Dame de la Clarté
15 Aug	Penmarc'h	Notre Dame de la Joie
15 Aug	Bécherel	Troménie de Haute-Bretagne
3rd Sun in Aug	Rochefort-en-Terre	Notre Dame de la Tronchaye
1st Sun in Sept	Le Folgoët	Notre Dame du Folgoët
8 Sept	Josselin	Notre Dame du Roncier
late Sept	Pontivy	Notre Dame de Joie
1st weekend in Oct	Fougères	Notre Dame des Marais

The interior Manche, central Orne and western Calvados *départements* of Lower Normandy are the least crowded of the region.

Upper Normandy has seen a higher increase in its rural population, especially in the areas close to Paris, as more Parisians choose to live in the country and commute to work. The great urban centres of Rouen and Le Havre have seen an exodus, while in Lower Normandy the economic opportunities in the Calvados region are proving attractive to young workers, especially around the Caen region. The rural population of Lower Normandy has also been swelled by those seeking a rural quality of life unmatched in the cities.

SPORT

Le foot (football, or soccer) is the number-one spectator sport in Brittany and Normandy. Guingamp, Lorient, Nantes and Rennes all have teams in the French 1st division and FC Nantes has played in several European championships. Sailing, however, is Brittany's 'national sport' and the fortunes of local yachtsmen such as Olivier de Kersauson and Bruno Peyron (current holder of the Jules Verne trophy for the round-the-world time record) are followed eagerly on TV. Local yacht and dinghy races are also avidly attended.

The most uniquely Norman spectator sport is horse racing. The most elegant spot to watch the races is in Deauville (p279) which has races almost daily in July and August. Caen also has a racetrack, which is in highest gear in September and October. Cabourg has races in January, July, August, October and in December, while Lisieux has race meetings several times a month from March to November.

The world's most prestigious bicycle race, the Tour de France, often passes through Normandy and one of the Tour's greatest riders, Jacques Anquetil, was a Norman. The race takes place for three weeks in July and, despite some doping scandals, is still a major event across France.

DID YOU KNOW?

Up until WWII, Breton children were punished for speaking their native language in school.

DID YOU KNOW?

Caen has welcomed the Tour de France bicycle race 32 times since the first Tour de France in 1903.

MEDIA
Newspapers & Magazines

Ouest-France is Normandy and Brittany's most respected daily newspaper, with separate editions for each *département*. In Normandy, *Paris Normandie* is simple to read if your French is basic. In Brittany, *La Télégramme* is another daily crammed with the minutiae of local life. The bimonthly *Normandie Magazine* is in French and English and covers cultural, business, political and economic news.

In larger towns, newsagents and newsstands at railway stations usually carry English-language dailies including the *International Herald Tribune*, the *Guardian*, the *Financial Times*, the *New York Times* and the colourful *USA Today*. Also readily available are *Newsweek*, *Time* and the *Economist*.

Radio

You can pick up a mixture of the BBC World Service and BBC for Europe on 648kHz AM. The Voice of America (VOA) is on 1197kHz AM but reception is often poor. By law, at least 40% of musical variety broadcasts must consist of songs in French (stations are fined if they don't comply). This helps explain why so many English-language hits are re-recorded in French (which can be a real hoot).

TV

Some good French programmes include *Le Vrai Journal* on Canal+ on Sunday. It's a popular, hard-hitting programme of investigative journalism hosted by one Karl Zéro (surely not his real name). Another great show is the satirical *Les Guignols*, with Spitting Image-type latex puppets.

Weekend-to-weekend TV listings (such as *Tél'7 Jours* or *Télérama*) are sold at newsstands. Foreign movies that haven't been dubbed and are shown with subtitles are marked 'VO' *(version originale)*.

Since 2000 there has been a local cable channel, TV Breizh, which broadcasts material of local interest, often in the Breton language.

Upmarket hotels often offer Canal+ and access to CNN, BBC World, Sky and other English-language networks.

ARTS
Music

No-one in Normandy is humming ancient Viking tunes, but in recent years there has been a resurgence of interest in the traditional music of Brittany. Although preserving basic forms and melodies, Breton music has also borrowed from the musical styles and instruments of other cultures, primarily Irish and Scottish. There is a great affinity between Breton musicians and those from other Celtic regions (see the boxed text, p161), and they have each sought to explore musical adventure on each other's shores.

Many of the instruments used in Breton music hail from the medieval and Renaissance periods. The *biniou kozh*, a simple double-reed bagpipe specific to Brittany, has a bag made of goat skin. The *biniou* is most commonly paired with a *bombarde*, the Breton version of the shawm, a precursor of the oboe. It is very loud and strident (once you've heard one at close quarters you'll never forget it) – its name is a rather descriptive allusion to its tonal quality. Later, the clarinet made its way into Breton music and is still used today. Over the centuries, Breton dances and weddings often had several hundred participants so it became necessary to design instruments that could be heard above the noise of the dancing. Since the *biniou*, the smallest of all bagpipes, could not be made any louder – they made it very shrill so that its sound would carry.

France Today by John Ardagh is a good introduction to modern-day France, its politics, its people and their idiosyncrasies.

Feminism in France by Claire Duchen is a work that charts the progress of feminism in France from 1968 to the mid-1980s.

FEST-NOZ FESTS

The communal celebration called a *fest-noz* (night festival; plural *festoù-noz*) developed in rural Brittany as an opportunity for socialising, dancing and singing. Born out of this localised gathering and kindled by a new interest on the part of Brittany's younger people, the idea of *fest-noz* has grown into a hugely popular phenomenon. Some hold that the *fest-noz* is an avenue for the preservation of pure Breton music and dance traditions and feel the larger, more commercial events are diluting their tradition. The younger, hybrid bands feature prominently in *festoù-noz*, which have become a wonderful way for travellers and visiting musicians to come into direct contact with Breton culture and music and to witness first hand where it is going.

At a typical *fest-noz*, the evening will start with music played on *bombarde* and *biniou kozh*, followed by unaccompanied singers, then expanding as the evening progresses to include bands as large as 10 pieces with some combination of violin, diatonic accordion, *bombarde*, flute, clarinet, bagpipes, guitar, bouzouki, *veuze* (one-drone bagpipe), *uilleann* (elbow) pipes, tin whistle, Celtic harp, *bodhrán* (goatskin drum), saxophones, percussion, fretless bass and other modern instruments. This music is incredibly vibrant and constantly evolving, and so has attracted attention from around the world, especially among progressive traditional musicians. The *fest-deiz* is a similar event, only held in the daytime.

Several instruments and stylistic elements have been integrated into Breton music from Ireland and Scotland. The diatonic accordion and fiddle have woven themselves strongly into the music of Brittany. The fiddle made its entrance not only through Irish music but also as a result of the jazz music played by American servicemen and the great French jazz players such as Stéphane Grappelli. Although the bouzouki was originally Greek, Bretons quickly adapted its unique sound to their music.

Each town in Brittany has its own marching pipe band. The Breton pipe bands use Scottish highland pipes and look to the Scots for inspiration. They took the basic musical structure of the Scottish marching tunes and added the *bombarde* and Breton melodies to their repertoire.

The music in the western part of Brittany is quite different from that of the eastern part, which has had more influence from the rest of France and Europe. It is in eastern Brittany that you are more likely to hear the hurdy-gurdy (*chalumeau*), associated more with central France, and more modern instruments such as clarinets and oboes. The *biniou* and *bombarde* hail from western Brittany.

Many current artists and bands have contributed to the unique and vital music of Brittany: Alan Stivell, Gwerze, Kornog, Korventenn, Dan Ar Braz, Skolvan, Storvan, Tri Yann, Glaz, Bleizi Ruz, Bagad St-Nazaire, Bagad Kemper, Jacky and Patrick Molard, Christian Lemaître, Jean-Michel Veillon, Soig Siberil, Alain Genty, Den, Barzaz and Pennoù Skoulm.

Literature

BRITTANY

The modern study of Breton literature, culture and folk tradition dates from the publication in 1838 of the *Barzhaz Breizh* (Breton Anthology) by the aristocratic Théodore Hersart de Villemarqué. It is a collection of Breton poems, songs and fairy tales that Villemarqué gathered on his travels around Brittany, by speaking to local people and assiduously writing down epic tales and verses that had been, until then, an oral tradition.

François-Auguste-René de Chateaubriand (1768–1848) is without doubt the most famous literary figure to emerge from Brittany. The first French Romantic novelist, his early works evoke his idyllic childhood at the Château de Combourg north of Rennes.

DID YOU KNOW?

The brilliant philosopher-lover Peter Abelard (of Abelard and Helöise) was born in Brittany, near Nantes.

The work of philosopher Ernest Renan (1823–92), born in Tréguier, was deeply concerned with religion and especially its relationship with science. His principal work, *La Vie de Jésus* (The Life of Jesus), made an impact right across Europe. A lesser-known writer of the 19th century was Auguste Brizeux (1803–58) from Lorient, who penned a rustic epic called *Bretons*.

The prolific Jules Verne (1828–1905), born in Nantes, produced no less than 63 novels in his lifetime, many of which have been translated into English and numerous other languages. Several have become classics, notably *Le Tour du Monde en Quatre- Vingts Jours* (Around the World in Eighty Days; 1873) in which the pedantic Englishman Phileas Fogg and his newly hired, scatter-brained manservant Passpartout circumnavigate the globe in order to win a bet. Other well-known works include *De la Terre à la Lune* (From the Earth to the Moon; 1865) and *Vingt Milles Lieues Sous les Mers* (Twenty Thousand Leagues Under the Sea; 1869).

Notable 20th-century Breton writers include Louis Guilloux (1899–1980) from St-Brieuc, author of *Sang Noir* (Black Blood), who wrote enchantingly about his home town. The best-selling author from Quimper, Per Jakez Hélias (1914–95), touched hundreds of thousands of readers with *Le Cheval d'Orgueil* (The Horse of Pride; 1974), an epic novel based on the author's youth and recounting the daily life of poor, Breton-speaking rural families in Bigouden in southwestern Finistère in the early 20th century.

Several Breton poets are also worthy of mention. Anatole Le Braz (1859–1926) was a teacher and lecturer in Rennes, who published various essays on Celtic drama and folklore, and several collections of poems. His chief work was *La Légende de la Mort chez les Bretons Armoricains* (Celtic Legends of the Beyond: A Celtic Book of the Dead). Théodore Botrel (1868–1925) from Dinan was a songwriter as well as a poet and is most famous for penning the words to the popular song *La Paimpolaise* (1895), about local folklore of Paimpol.

The surrealist poet and painter Max Jacob (1876–1944) was born in Quimper but lived mostly in Paris and later in St-Benoît-sur-Loire. Tragically, both he and his family were denounced as Jews during WWII and were murdered in the French concentration camp at Drancy in 1944.

The poetry of Xavier Grall (1930–81), who is commemorated by a riverside garden in Pont-Aven, captures in words the rhythms of tide and wind, and records in vivid imagery the lives and feelings of the fishermen and sailors of Brittany. One of his most beautiful works is *Les Vents M'ont Dit* (The Winds Have Told Me).

NORMANDY

The most celebrated early work attributed to a Norman poet was the 11th-century epic poem *Chanson de Roland* (Song of Roland). It was the earliest work of French literature and recounts the heroic death of Charlemagne's nephew Roland, ambushed on the way back from a campaign against the Muslims in Spain in 778.

In the 15th century, poets turned their attention to matters of the heart. Alain Chartier of Bayeux (c1390–c1430) began his career with a patriotic work recounting the French defeat at Agincourt and then launched the trend of romanticism by writing *La Belle Dame Sans Merci* (The Beautiful Woman Without Pity), which inspired the John Keats poem of the same title. Chartier's allegorical love poems became enormously popular.

The 17th century is known as *le grand siècle* because it was the century of great French classical writers. Pierre Corneille (1606–84) of Rouen was a leading figure of the classical period and one of France's greatest playwrights. He began his career with comedy and tragicomedy, then turned

DID YOU KNOW?

William the Conqueror and his troops went into the Battle of Hastings singing the *Chanson de Roland*.

out the celebrated *Le Cid* (El Cid) based upon the Spanish hero. Matters of conscience preoccupied his tragedies, especially the conflict between reason and romantic yearnings. He wrote three other fine tragedies – *Horace*, *Cinna* and *Polyeucte* set in ancient Rome – before inventing the comedy of manners in the 1643 *Le Menteur* (The Liar) .

The 19th century brought Gustave Flaubert (1821–80), a Rouen native and author of *Madame Bovary*, a landmark in French literature. The shallow, corrupt Emma Bovary is portrayed with unflinching realism, marking a turn away from romantic, classical themes. Based upon a real-life story in Ry (see p217), the book sparked a government prosecution to have it banned for immorality which of course assured its popular success.

Guy de Maupassant was another influential Norman writer. Born in Fécamp, and a failed law student like his friend Flaubert, de Maupassant had a pessimistic view of human nature. His short-story collection *Contes de la Bécasse* (Tales of the Woodcock), written in Étretat, evoked the oppressive class hierarchy found in bourgeois Norman life, and his grim psychological study of two brothers, *Pierre et Jean*, was set in Le Havre.

The Norman coastal village of Cabourg is the background for Proust's *À l'Ombre des Jeunes Filles en Fleur* (In the Shadow of Young Girls in Flower) part of *À la Récherche du Temps Perdu* (Remembrance of Things Past). Marcel Proust (1871–1922) spent time in the village as a child and returned each year until WWI. His largely autobiographical novel explores in evocative detail the true meaning of past experience recovered from the unconscious by 'involuntary memory'.

The 20th century opened with the works of the philosopher-essayist Émile Chartier (1868–1951), known as Alain and born in Mortagne au Perche. His aphoristic essays, *Propos sur le Bonheur* (About Happiness) and *Propos sur l'Éducation* (On Education) expressed a humanistic philosophy opposed to war and political tyranny. Perhaps the best-known philosopher of the 20th century was Jean-Paul Sartre (1905–80) whose existential philosophy was forcefully prefigured by his novel *Nausée* (Nausea), written while he was teaching at Le Havre. His companion, philosopher and feminist Simone de Beauvoir, taught at the school in Rouen for four years.

The Bayeux Tapestry by David M Wilson is an excellent overview of the making of the Bayeux Tapestry. It has beautiful photographs.

Architecture
PREHISTORIC

Brittany's earliest monuments are the hundreds of menhirs (standing stones), dolmens (stone burial chambers) and cairns (burial mounds made of small stones) that are found throughout the region, but especially in Morbihan. Dating from perhaps 6000 BC to 2000 BC, the original purpose of these megalithic structures remains a mystery, although many of them appear to be orientated towards the rising and setting points of the sun and moon.

Menhirs often occur in isolation, as with the Grand Menhir Brisé near Locmariaquer (see p165 for details), which once stood 20m high but is now lying broken on its side. More commonly they are arranged in cromlechs (stone circles or rectangles), of which there are only a few in Brittany, or in parallel lines called *alignements* (alignments). The most spectacular examples are to be seen at Carnac (p163), where the alignments of Ménec and Kermario contain more than 1000 menhirs each.

A dolmen (from the Breton for 'stone table') consists of a horizontal stone slab placed on top of two or more upright slabs to form a burial chamber. A long, rectangular chamber composed of many slabs is called an *allée-couverte* (covered corridor, or gallery tomb); La Roche aux Fées (p93) in Eastern Brittany is a good example.

Most dolmens and gallery tombs were originally covered by a mound of earth (tumulus) or small stones (cairn) but in many examples the stones have long since been removed for use as building materials. The 80m-long Tumulus de Barnenez (p123), near Morlaix in northern Finistère, is Brittany's finest surviving example of a burial cairn.

GALLO-ROMAN

The Romans constructed a large number of public works all over the country from the 1st century BC: aqueducts, fortifications, marketplaces, temples, amphitheatres, triumphal arches and bathhouses. They also established regular street grids at many settlements. Little remains of the Roman presence except remnants of an amphitheatre at Lillebonne, foundations of Roman buildings in Lisieux (p283) and the Gallo-Roman wall (p238) at Évreux.

ROMANESQUE (10TH TO 12TH CENTURIES)

Following the 11th-century conquest of England, Normandy was rich in resources, and engaged in a flurry of new construction. The new style was termed Romanesque because the architects adopted many architectural elements (such as round arches and barrel vaulting) from the Gallo-Roman buildings still standing at that time. Romanesque buildings typically have heavy walls, plain columns, small doors and windows topped by round arches, and a lack of ornamentation bordering on the austere.

The effect is remarkably graceful, despite the architectural limitations of barrel vaulting which precluded the construction of large windows. Norman builders often constructed Oriental-style cupolas or installed square lantern towers to create light. The naves usually had three storeys with wide, high bays; galleries broke the monotony of thick walls; and the façade was often flanked by tall towers in an H shape.

Mont St-Michel and Chartres by Henry Adams, the turn-of-the-century writer and historian, brings a fine sensibility to Normandy's most famous monument.

The Benedictine monks were the primary instigators of Normandy's 11th-century abbeys. They're in ruins now, but the abbeys of Jumièges (p216) and St-Wandrille (p217) still convey a sense of the majesty of the Norman Romanesque style. The abbey of Mont St-Michel (p70), though expanded in later centuries, contains remains of the 11th-century structure. The abbeys in Caen – Abbaye aux Hommes and Abbaye aux Dames (p260) – are the best surviving examples of Romanesque architecture in Normandy.

The finest Romanesque church in Brittany is the 11th-century Église Ste-Croix (p156) in Quimperlé, based on the circular plan of the Church of the Holy Sepulchre in Jerusalem.

GOTHIC (12TH TO 15TH CENTURIES)

The Romanesque style remained popular until the mid-12th century, when it was supplanted by the Gothic style, originating in the Île de France. Gothic structures are characterised by ribbed vaults carved with great precision, pointed arches, slender verticals, chapels (often built by rich people or guilds) along the nave and chancel, refined decoration and large stained-glass windows. The use of flying buttresses to support the walls allowed windows to be larger, creating a light, spacious interior. The cathedral of Rouen (p204) was the first cathedral in Normandy to incorporate the Gothic style in the St-Romain tower but it is in the cathedral (p302) at Coutances, built between 1218 and 1275, that early Gothic style can be seen in its purest form. One of the other features of Gothic cathedrals are the huge, colourful rose windows as seen in Rouen cathedral.

PARTS OF A CATHEDRAL

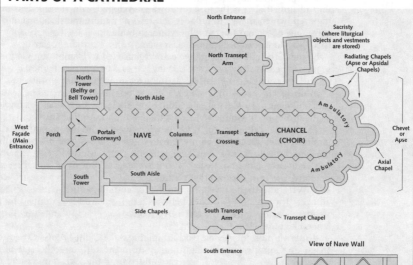

View of Nave Wall

Labels on the diagram: North Entrance; Sacristy (where liturgical objects and vestments are stored); North Transept Arm; Radiating Chapels (Apse or Apsidal Chapels); North Tower (Belfry or Bell Tower); North Aisle; Ambulatory; West Façade (Main Entrance); Porch; Portals (Doorways); NAVE; Columns; Transept Crossing; Sanctuary; CHANCEL (CHOIR); Chevet or Apse; Axial Chapel; South Tower; South Aisle; Ambulatory; Side Chapels; South Transept Arm; Transept Chapel; South Entrance.

View of Nave Wall labels: Clerestory Windows; Triforium; Aisle (behind the columns).

NOTE: Very few churches incorporate all of the elements shown here some of which are found only in Gothic cathedrals from certain periods. Romanesque churches have a much simpler layout.
Many cathedrals in Brittany are oriented roughly east to west so that the chancel faces more or less east towards Jerusalem. As a result, the main entrance is usually at the base of the west façade and the transept arms extend north and south from the transept crossing as shown here.

USEFUL TERMS:

Ambulatory
The ambulatory, a continuation of the aisles of the nave around the chancel, forms a processional path that allows pilgrims relatively easy access to radiating chapels, saints' relics and altars around the chancel and behind the altar.

Clerestory Windows
The clerestory windows, a row of tall windows above the triforium (see below), are often difficult to see because they're so high above the floor.

Cloister
The cloister (cloître), a four-sided enclosure surrounded by covered, colonnaded arcades, is often attached to a monastery church or a cathedral. In monasteries, the cloister served as the focal point of the monks' educational and recreational activities.

Crypt
The crypt (crypte) is a chamber under the church floor, usually at the eastern end, in which saints, martyrs, early church figures and worthy personages are buried. In many Gothic churches, the crypt is often one of the few extant parts of earlier, pre-Gothic structures on the site. A visit to the crypt, usually reached via stairs on one or both sides of the chancel, may involve a small fee.

Narthex
The narthex is an enclosed entrance vestibule just inside the west entrance. It was once reserved for penitents and the unbaptised.

Rood Screen
A rood screen, also known as a jube (jubé), is an often elaborate structure separating the chancel from the nave. Because rood screens made it difficult for worshippers to see religious ceremonies taking place in the chancel, most were removed in the 17th and 18th centuries.

Rose Window
The circular stained-glass windows commonly found in Gothic cathedrals over the west entrance and at the northern and southern ends of the transept arms are known as rose or wheel windows. The stained-glass panels are usually separated from each other by elaborate stone bar tracery, which people inside the church see in silhouette.

Treasury
A treasury (trésor) is a secure room for storing and displaying precious liturgical objects. It may be open shorter hours than the church itself. Visiting often involves a small entry fee.

Triforium
The triforium is an arcaded or colonnaded gallery above the aisle, choir or transept. Most triforia are directly above the columns that separate the aisles from the nave or the ambulatory from the chancel. From the late 13th century, larger clerestory windows often replaced the triforium.

In the 14th century, the Rayonnant (Radiant) Gothic style – named after the radiating tracery of the rose windows – developed, with interiors becoming even lighter, thanks to broader windows and more translucent stained glass. One of the most beautiful Rayonnant buildings is the Église St-Ouen (p207) in Rouen, whose stained glass forms a sheer curtain of glazing.

By the 15th century, decorative extravagance led to Flamboyant Gothic, so named because its wavy stone carving was said to resemble flames. Beautifully lacy examples of Flamboyant architecture include Rouen cathedral's Tour de Beurre (p205) and the Église St-Maclou (p208) in Rouen. The beautiful buildings of La Merveille on Mont St-Michel provide a superb example of the evolution of Gothic style from the 13th to the 16th century.

The Gothic cathedrals of Brittany were inspired by their counterparts in Normandy, but cannot compete with them in size or ostentation. Only the superb bell tower of the Chapelle Notre Dame du Kreisker (p125) in St-Pol de Léon (south of Roscoff) comes close. Its 78m spire, the tallest in Brittany, was modelled on that of the Église St-Pierre in Caen (destroyed in WWII), and itself served as a model for countless other church spires all over Brittany. The Kreisker belfry is a tall, square tower topped by a slender, soaring spire, perforated by Gothic tracery and flanked by four lance-like pinnacles.

Brittany's most impressive Gothic building is the Cathédrale St-Corentin (p146) in Quimper, which dates mostly from the 13th to 15th centuries, although its twin 76m spires were not added until the 19th century and it was extensively restored in the 20th.

Although less imposing, the smaller Gothic village churches and the chapels of Brittany have a unique charm, ranging from the plain but elegant Chapelle Notre Dame de Rocamadour (p140) in Camaret-sur-Mer to the quaint tilted spire of the Chapelle St-Gonéry in Plougrescant (p112).

RENAISSANCE (16TH CENTURY)

The Renaissance had its first impact on France at the end of the 15th century, when Charles VIII began a series of invasions of Italy. His chief minister, Georges d'Amboise, introduced the style to Normandy by importing Italian artists and artisans to build his chateau in Gaillon. In the beginning of the 16th century, the architect Rouland Le Roux applied elements of the new style to the Bureau des Finances (p206), which is now the tourist office in Rouen, and the tombs of the Amboise cardinals in Rouen's cathedral. In this early period, Renaissance decorative motifs (columns, tunnel vaults, round arches, domes) were blended with the rich decoration of Flamboyant Gothic. In the Bureau des Finances, Renaissance pilasters and bas-reliefs combine well with Gothic canopies. Also in Rouen, the early Renaissance style is apparent in Aître St-Maclou (p208) and the Gros Horloge (p206). The cathedral and St-Maclou church show Renaissance influences in several stained glass windows and sculptures. In Caen (p256), the apse of the St-Pierre church is a wonderful example of the early Renaissance style.

Many private mansions in Normandy's cities were built in a Renaissance style and some smaller towns have 16th-century Renaissance churches. The exquisite carved porch of the Ry church (p217) is especially notable. The style became more mannered later on in the 16th century and fell out of favour in Normandy although there are scattered restored mansions from the period in Rouen, Honfleur, Bernay and Lyons-la-Forêt. Because French Renaissance architecture was very much the province of the aristocracy and designed by imported artists, the middle classes – resentful French artisans among them – remained loyal to the indigenous Gothic style, and Gothic churches continued to be built throughout the 16th century.

'Renaissance architecture was the province of the aristocracy; the middle classes remained loyal to the indigenous Gothic style'

In Brittany, the elegant Renaissance style appeared in the palaces of the Breton aristocracy – the interior façade of the Rohan family's Château de Josselin (p179) in central Brittany is a superb example. The style was also adopted by church architects; in the case of the Basilique Notre Dame de Bon Secours (p111) in Guingamp, it was adopted halfway through construction. One of its twin bell towers is Gothic, the other Renaissance.

Painting
BRITTANY
Brittany has not produced any internationally famous artists but its romantic history, picturesque harbours, wild coastline and luminous light have inspired many well-known painters including Paul Gauguin (1848–1903; see p155) and Claude Monet (1840–1926; see p169).

NORMANDY
The Rouen painters Jean Jouvenet (1644–1717) and Jean Restout (1692–1768) achieved some note in Normandy with their religious paintings, but it was Nicolas Poussin (1594–1665) who became the most influential painter of the age. Voltaire wrote that French painting began with Poussin, who was born near Les Andelys. Influenced by Titian and Raphael at first, Poussin later developed a style based on mathematically controlled composition, restrained colour and themes from antiquity. His classical style became the official 'Academic' style of French painting and the standard by which all succeeding painters were judged up to the 20th century. Several Poussin canvases are in the Musée des Beaux-Arts in Rouen (p209).

By the 18th century, other landscape painters were becoming interested in Normandy. The most influential was Joseph Turner (1775–1851) who made a point of coming to France each year. He produced several paintings of the Normandy ports of Dieppe and Rouen that strongly influenced the later Impressionists. Monet's seminal *Impression, Soleil Levant* (Impression, Sunrise) strongly resembles a Turner watercolour of Rouen.

The 19th century was Normandy's golden age of painting. The century began with Rouen-native Théodore Géricault (1791–1824), whose forceful, dramatic works realistically depicting human suffering launched the romantic movement in France. An entire room of Géricault paintings is part of Rouen's Musée des Beaux-Arts.

Gréville-born Jean-François Millet (1814–75) took a different approach. After studying art in Cherbourg and Paris, he joined the Barbizon school, a group of French painters who devoted themselves to paintings of outdoors scenes. They based themselves in the town of Barbizon on the Île de France. Millet painted peasants with extraordinary naturalism, rejecting the idealised historical scenes that the French Academy admired. The Barbizon school's emphasis on painting outdoors and its choice of everyday scenes foreshadowed Impressionism. Rouen's Musée des Beaux-Arts displays several Millet paintings.

During a time when many painters left Normandy to work and study, Honfleur-born Eugène Boudin (1824–98) spent most of his life living and working on the Normandy coast. Enchanted with the opportunities afforded by working in the open air, Boudin took advantage of Normandy's new popularity to paint the elegantly dressed women frequenting the coastal resorts. Boudin's paintings are displayed in the museums of Le Havre (p222), Honfleur (p276), Trouville (p280), Caen (p260) and Rouen (p209), but he is mainly remembered as Claude Monet's first teacher.

The Dutch painter Johan Barthold Jongkind (1819–91) also influenced young Monet, educating his eye to observe varying intensities of light and

The French by Theodore Zeldin is a highly acclaimed and very insightful survey of French passions, peculiarities and perspectives. It's intelligent, informative and humorous.

subtleties of colour. Norman by choice if not by birth, Jongkind lived all along the coast where he painted Honfleur, Tréport and Le Havre. In the 1860s, Boudin, Jongkind and Monet were a frequent threesome around Honfleur, painting and socialising together.

Of all the painters fascinated by the Norman landscape, Monet (1840–1926) was the most influential and most rooted in the region. In his long life he spanned every phase of Impressionism, beginning with landscape painting in Le Havre and ending with the first steps towards abstraction in Giverny. Although he painted in London, the south of France and around Paris, the everchanging skies of Normandy afforded him limitless opportunities to explore light in all its daily and seasonal variations. He returned again and again, finally settling in Giverny where he spent 43 years (see p244). Some of Monet's paintings are displayed in the museums of Honfleur (p276), Le Havre (p222), Rouen (p209) and Vernon (p244).

Throughout the 19th century, painters made regular sojourns to the Normandy coast. Honfleur became the first painter's hub with a friendly inn La Ferme St-Siméon, outside town, welcoming Boudin, Bazille, Pissarro and Sisley among others. Étretat's cliffs and pebbly beach attracted Delacroix, Corot and Courbet in the 1860s and '70s. Courbet found Trouville particularly appealing, inviting his American friend Whistler to stay with him at the Hôtel des Roches Noires in 1866. Renoir set up his easel in Pourville where he painted *Madame Charpentier et ses Enfants* (Madam Charpentier with her Children), while Manet headed for Cherbourg. Camille Pissarro (1830–1903) chose Rouen where he took a room overlooking the Seine in 1883, executing a series of river scenes. Degas 'discovered' Dieppe in the 1880s, attracting his admirers, including Whistler, to the port. Fécamp, Varengeville, Ste-Adresse and Le Havre also welcomed a succession of artists.

By end of the century, a school of painters (pupils of Zacharie at the École des Beaux-Arts) arose in Rouen. The École de Rouen was dominated by Albert Lebourg (1849–1928), who came to Rouen as a young artist and sold his first canvas to an Algerian. After painting in Algeria, Auvergne, Brittany and Holland, he returned to Rouen relatively successful, with pieces hanging in several Paris museums. In his later years, he executed a number of paintings of the Seine in an Impressionistic style. His works are on view in the fine-arts museums of Caen (p260) and Rouen (p209).

The 20th century opened with another revolution in painting. The Fauvists (wild beasts) rejected the Impressionist's use of soft colours and turned to a harsh, almost violent, palette of ochre, green and vermilion. The short-lived movement was begun in 1898 by Matisse and was promulgated by a group of three painters from Le Havre: Othon Friesz (1879–1949), Raoul Dufy (1877–1953) and Georges Braque (1882–1963). The three artists met in Paris in 1900 and turned out a number of works in the style, but by 1908 they had taken separate stylistic paths and the movement died out. After returning from service in WWI, Braque turned to still life and birds in paintings and lithographs. At the end of his life he set up a studio in Varengeville (p230) where he created stained glass windows for the local church and painted Norman landscapes. The museum in Dieppe (p225) has several of his lithographs.

When Raoul Dufy abandoned Fauvism, he turned to colours that were vigorous without being strident and applied them to watercolours dominated by a rigorous use of line. His subjects were outdoor scenes at Normandy's resorts and ports, especially sailing and horse racing, rendered in a light, happy style. The museum in Le Havre (p222) has a selection of Dufy's paintings.

Linnea in Monet's Garden by Cristina Bjork is a beautifully illustrated lesson in art appreciation for kids over seven. It is set in Giverny.

Cinema

Whether because of its proximity to Paris, the cinephile paradise or its photogenic landscapes, Normandy has been a major centre for the production of film since practically the beginning of talkies. Directors as diverse as Claude Lelouche, François Truffaut and Joseph Losey have found the right settings for their films in Normandy's countryside or on the beach. The environment is somewhat less hospitable for foreign film-makers. Stephen Spielberg wanted to make *Saving Private Ryan*, his D-Day movie, in Normandy but found the labour costs prohibitive.

Fortunately, there's no shortage of fine French flicks set in Normandy. *Les Parapluies de Cherbourg* (The Umbrellas of Cherbourg; 1964), Jacques Demy's delightful musical, was filmed on location with Catherine Deneuve. Roman Polanski's *Tess* (1979) was filmed in the countryside south of Cherbourg as a substitute for the English countryside. *Un Homme et une Femme* (A Man & a Woman), Claude Lelouche's poignant romance, was filmed in Deauville in 1966, as was the recent sequel with the same stars, Trintignant and Anouk Aimée. Also filmed in Deauville was *Dentellière* (The Lacemaker; 1977) with Isabelle Huppert and scenes from Bernard Tavernier's 1986 great jazz movie, *Autour de Minuit* (Around Midnight). Bernard Blier filmed *Préparez vos Mouchoirs* (Get Out Your Handkerchiefs) in Tréport in 1976 and Dieppe was the location for the final scene of *Journal d'Une Femme de Chambre* (Diary of a Chambermaid), Luis Buñuel's 1963 classic.

Claude Chabrol filmed his 1990 adaptation of *Madame Bovary* in Lyons-la-Forêt and Luc Besson's recent *Jeanne d'Arc* was partly filmed in Sées. Louis Malle's *Le Voleur* (The Thief; 1967) was filmed in Évreux. François Truffaut shot *Deux Anglaises et le Continent* (Two English Girls; 1971) in Auderville; scenes from *400 Coups* (400 Blows; 1958) were around Criqueboeuf, and scenes from *Jules et Jim* (1961) were shot outside Vernon. Most recently, Laurent Cantet's *Ressources Humaines* (Human Resources; 2000) took a look at factory life in Gaillon, employing many locals as actors.

Appreciation of film, as well as film-making, is strong in Normandy. In addition to its September Festival of American Film, since 1998 Deauville (p281) has been hosting a yearly Festival of Asian Cinema at the beginning of March. Rouen began a Festival of Nordic Cinema (p210) in 1987 that introduced Gabriel Axel's *Babette's Feast* to the world. It has continued to seek out little-known Scandinavian directors. Cherbourg (p294) hosts a British Film Festival in the second week of October that introduces popular British films to France.

Brittany's dramatic coastline and beautifully preserved historic towns and castles have also caught the eye of many a location manager. *The Vikings* (1958), starring Kirk Douglas and Tony Curtis in swashbuckling mode, was filmed at several locations on the northern coast, most recognisably at Fort La Latte.

Roman Polanski, unable to find anywhere sufficiently unspoilt in England, chose the Finistère village of Locronan for *Tess* (1979), his adaptation of Thomas Hardy's novel *Tess of the d'Urbervilles*, but some scenes were filmed in Normandy. *Chouans!* (1988), directed by Philippe de Broca, and starring a young Sophie Marceaux well before her first clinch with James Bond, is a French-language historical adventure set in eastern Brittany.

However, two of the most famous films to be shot in Brittany made the most of the region's seaside resorts. The superb *Monsieur Hulot's Holiday* (1953), starring and directed by that master of slapstick Jacques Tati, was filmed in the tiny resort of St-Marc-sur-Mer, a few kilometres southwest of St-Nazaire. And if you've ever wondered where the seaside scenes in Alfred Hitchcock's *The Birds* (1963) were filmed, it was Dinard.

Les Parapluies de Cherbourg (The Umbrellas of Cherbourg, 1964), Jacques Demy's classic, is one of the most broadly appealing movies to come out of France's New Wave. Every word of dialogue is sung and Catherine Deneuve has never been more luminous.

Roman Polanski's *Tess* (1979), based on the Thomas Hardy novel *Tess of the D'Urbervilles*, is a moody and disturbing look at an unfortunate young woman, brilliantly played by Nastassja Kinski.

Environment

THE LAND

Brittany

Brittany is contained within a blunt, westward-thrusting peninsula about 250km long and on average about 100km wide. It is surrounded on three sides by the open sea – the English Channel to the north and the Atlantic Ocean to the west and south. If you include the 'lost' *département* of Loire-Atlantique (see p182), as this book does, then Brittany covers an area of around 34,000 sq km – slightly larger than Belgium.

The interior is a largely featureless, rocky landscape. There are few real hills, save for the rolling, gorse- and heather-clad *landes* (moors) of the Montagnes Noires and the Monts d'Arrée (p138) in the west. The abundance of granite is a characteristic feature of Brittany, whether in spectacularly weathered coastal outcrops or in the dressed masonry of churches and domestic buildings.

The coastline is incredibly tortuous, with a diversity of scenery that is one of Brittany's most appealing features – from soaring sea cliffs to vast, sandy beaches, and from grass-covered dunes to sinuous, rocky creeks. Brittany is characterised by an abundance of *rias* (known as *abers* in Breton). These are deep river valleys that were eroded on dry land by active rivers, but which were flooded by the sea when ocean levels rose at the end the last Ice Age around 12,000 years ago. The most notable include the Golfe du Morbihan (p175), the Ria d'Étel (between Lorient and Auray) and Aber-Wrac'h and Aber-Benoit (p127) in northern Finistère.

This flooding of the landscape is also responsible for the picturesque scatter of islands – ranging from the maze of rocks, reefs and islets fringing the northern coast, to the 20km-long Belle-Île-en-Mer (p168) in the south – that is such a feature of Breton seascapes.

Normandy

Normandy covers an area of around 30,000 sq km, including a 550km coastline that stretches from Le Tréport in the northeast to Mont St-Michel in the southwest. North of the Seine estuary at Honfleur the coastline is composed of the high chalky cliffs that gave the coastline its name, the Côte d'Albâtre (p220). South of the estuary the Côte Fleurie (Flowered Coast; p274) offers long stretches of sand interspersed by low cliffs, sand dunes and salt marshes that continue to the Côte de Nacre (Mother of Pearl Coast; p266) west of Caen. The coastline of the Cotentin Peninsula (p293) is marked by rocky inlets with occasional stretches of sandy beach.

The interior is gentle, rarely surpassing 200m in height. Inland from the Côte d'Albâtre, the Pays de Caux is a vast chalky plateau sliced by the Rivers Bresle and Béthune. The central axis that runs from Caen to Falaise is a treeless plain, which becomes chalky as you continue south to Alençon. The Seine bisects the region into Upper and Lower Normandy each of which is crisscrossed by the meandering rivers that create such a bucolic landscape. South of the Seine, the River Iton cuts through the wheat fields of the St-André plain. In the east, Normandy's other major river, the Eure, flows into the Seine. Further west, the Rivers Touques and Dives and their many tributaries water the Pays d'Auge, a plateau that marks the beginning of bocage country. These parcels of land divided by hedgerows run southwest to the Armorican massif, which forms the backbone of Brittany and Normandy.

DID YOU KNOW?

Between 1970 and 1980, over 100 sq km (25,000 acres) of forestland in Normandy was lost, largely to the timber industry.

WILDLIFE
Brittany

Brittany is a paradise for those interested in natural history. Its diversity of habitats, especially along the coast, has favoured the establishment of a wide range of plant and animal species.

Brittany is one of only half a dozen regions in France where the otter still thrives, albeit in small numbers. Look in the ponds and canals of the Parc Naturel Régional de Brière (p194), in the rivers of the Monts d'Arrée (p138), and in the coastal waters of the Presqu'île de Crozon (p139) and the islands of Molène (p132) and Ouessant (p129). In the Monts d'Arrée the otter cohabits with a small population of European beaver *(le castor)*, reintroduced to the area in 1968.

The wide range of coastal habitats supports many species of bird, both resident and migratory (see the boxed text, p175). The tidal mudflats and sheltered inlets attract spoonbill, little egret, avocet, brent geese *(bernache cravant)* and a whole range of waders and waterfowl, while chough *(craves à bec rouge)* – members of the crow family, with glossy black plumage and bright red bills and feet – can be seen soaring on the updraughts above the sea cliffs of the Île d'Ouessant. About 20 pairs of Montagu's harrier *(busard cendré)*, a rare bird of prey, nest on the moors of the Monts d'Arrée.

The islets of the Molène archipelago provide nesting sites for the rarely seen storm petrel (Europe's smallest sea bird, which spends most of its life away from land), and in spring and summer the sea cliffs and islets of northern Brittany are crowded with nesting sea birds of many species: cormorant, guillemot, razorbill, puffin, tern, and the ever-present herring gull and black-headed gull.

The sea around the Breton coast – and in particular the Mer d'Iroise (around the islands of Ouessant and Molène in North Finistère) – is incredibly rich in marine life, including significant populations of dolphin and grey seal. The bay of Mont St-Michel hosts a large population of native ducks feeding on the watery grasses and is an international thoroughfare for migrating birds such as grey geese and black scoters. Seals arrive each year to nurse their young and large dolphins travel in schools seeking cuttlefish. The Atlantic salmon, a connoisseur of clean water, returns each year to spawn in the headwaters of around 20 Breton rivers, notably the Aulne and the Élorn.

Animal life along the country's littoral – including Normandy and Brittany – features on www.conservatoire-du-littoral.fr, a French-language site.

Normandy

Fauna is scarce in Normandy's forests but the wetlands are rich in wildlife. On the southeast of the Cotentin Peninsula, the Baie des Veys is one of the best spots in Normandy for bird life. Covering some 130 sq km (32,000 acres), this vast swamp at the confluence of salt and fresh water harbours a nesting population of sheldrakes and ducks, while thousands of rails arrive in winter. Shrikes, sandpipers and grey curlews also make an appearance. The bay is under the protection of the World Wide Fund for Nature.

The Marais Vernier is a vast 5060-hectare marsh in the Seine Valley with exceptional bird life. Grey herons and white swans were recently reintroduced and there are black-tailed godwits, white spoon-bills and avocets. White Camargue horses and Scottish cows have also been introduced into the marsh; they are not indigenous. For more on horse- and cow-breeding traditions in Normandy, see the boxed texts (p313 and p52).

The cliffs of Étretat (p234) are host to arctic auks that come to the temperate coastal climes for three months each year to reproduce. They lurk in the cracks of the cliffs and lay one sole egg. Unfortunately, these trusting birds make an easy target for hunters who decimate the population each spring.

REGIONAL PARKS
Brittany

Brittany has two *parcs naturels régionaux* (regional natural parks) – the Parc Naturel Régional d'Armorique (p138) in the west and the Parc Naturel Régional de Brière (p194) in the southeast.

The Armorique regional park in Finistère was founded in 1969 and covers 1720 sq km, stretching from the Monts d'Arrée to the Presqu'île de Crozon and includes Île d'Ouessant and the Molène archipelago. It encompasses a wide range of landscapes, from the windswept moors of the Monts d'Arrée to the striking sea cliffs of the Pointe de Dinan.

The 400-sq-km Parc Naturel Régional de Brière, dating from 1970, protects the unique ecology of the Brière fenland, a vast area of reed beds, marshes, ponds and canals to the north of St-Nazaire. The park is a haven for otters, waterfowl, amphibians and aquatic plants, and continues to manage the reed beds as a resource for the region's numerous thatched cottages.

For links to Normandy and Brittany's parks see www.parcs-naturels-regionaux.tm.fr.

Normandy

Normandy has four *parcs naturels régionaux*, which are large, locally managed spaces that include small towns and villages and often have special visitors programmes, ecomuseums and cultural tours.

The Parc Naturel Régional de Normandie-Maine is the southernmost park and includes part of the Orne *département* and the Maine *département* in the Loire Valley. The countryside is a luscious combination of wooded cliffs, forests, bocage and open countryside. Of all the park's forests, the loveliest is the Forêt d'Écouves (p312), within easy reach of Alençon.

The Parc Naturel Régional des Marais du Cotentin et du Bessin covers the bird sanctuary of Baie des Veys as well as 300 sq km of wetlands, home to many species of migrating birds. The marshes also harbour small mammals and many insects.

The Parc Naturel Régional du Perche lies at the far southern tip of Lower Normandy and contains a number of oak and beech forests, most notably the Forêt de Bellême, with many kilometres of shady trails. This regional park is particularly rich in plant life with some 1200 different species, 140 of which are protected.

In Upper Normandy, the Parc Naturel Régional de Brotonne includes the vast Forêt de Brotonne, with its towering beech and oak trees, as well as the Marais Vernier wetlands. The park spans the northern and southern banks of the Seine, linked by the soaring Pont de Brotonne near Caudebec-en-Caux which makes a good base for exploring the park.

ENVIRONMENTAL ISSUES
Brittany

Although Brittany has suffered repeated oil slicks from offshore wrecks, the most consistent environmental threat comes from intensive agriculture (notably pig farming). In addition to polluting the groundwater and many waterways, run-off from fertilisers and animal waste enters the sea (via the rivers), where the nitrates contained in the run-off contribute to the phenomenon of *les marées vertes* ('green tides'). Abnormal 'blooms', their rapid growth caused by a combination of warm weather and high levels of nitrates, of a species of seaweed known as sea lettuce drift at the mercy of tide and wind, eventually washing up in thick strands on the beaches (mostly in northern Brittany). Exposed to the sun, the seaweed quickly begins to decay, producing an overpowering and unpleasant stench. As well as causing a setback for the tourist industry, these blooms

DID YOU KNOW?

The oil tanker *Erika* dumped 10,000 tonnes of oil along the Brittany coast in 1999, killing at least 35,000 sea birds.

also threaten coastal fisheries, notably the scallops of the Baie de St-Brieuc. The EU has implemented regulations intended to limit agricultural waste from polluting the water, but France, under pressure from the powerful agricultural lobby, has refused to enforce them. Local people are hoping that the prospect of legal action and steep fines from the EU will force changes, but no-one is holding their breath.

However, the problem should not be overstated – the quality of the sea water on Brittany's beaches, scoured and rinsed daily by powerful tidal currents, is generally among the best in Europe.

Normandy

If Normandy was colour-coded to reflect ecological problems, the tip of the Cotentin Peninsula would be bright red, largely because of radioactive discharge from the COGEMA nuclear waste treatment plant at La Hague (p300). With 230 million litres of waste pumped into the Channel each year, Greenpeace has labelled COGEMA 'the single largest source of radioactive contamination in the EU' and has waged a long-running battle against the plant.

Intensive agriculture has also degraded the environment, especially around the intensively farmed Caen-Falaise plain, leaving unacceptably high levels of nitrates and pesticides in the groundwater. The natural flushing action of the sea keeps the northwestern Manche far less polluted, but the Calvados coast between Courseulles and Honfleur is subject to occasional outbreaks of green tides, just as in Brittany. Sea water in Upper Normandy is generally cleaner than that in Lower Normandy. The primary threat to the Upper Normandy coastline is erosion, which has eaten away at the chalky cliffs of the Côte d'Albâtre.

All the environmental hotspots in France are covered by www .greenpeace.fr.

Brittany & Normandy Outdoors

Opportunities for water activities, vigorous or gentle, are almost limitless, whether you make diving, windsurfing, sailing or surfing the core of your holiday or just a tempting add-on. If you're experienced, you can simply hire equipment and enjoy the independence. For beginners and those wanting to improve their skills, even quite small resorts offer instruction, ranging from a couple of one-on-one hours to full week programmes. Courses in English, however, are very much the exception.

The popularity of the outdoors throughout Brittany and Normandy puts great pressure on the natural environment. Enjoy the outdoors in a responsible way, follow park regulations and play a small part in helping to preserve the ecology of the countryside and coastlines of the region. As they say: leave only your footprints.

For information about regulations for individual national parks, see www.parcsnationaux-fr.com.

WALKING

Plunging cliffs, windswept promontories and stirring seascapes – that same coast which gives so much scope for aquatic fun will also tempt walkers, whether you're out for an impromptu after-dinner family amble or a challenging – but never overly demanding – outing of several days. Most tourist offices have a leaflet describing easy walks in their vicinities.

It's not all spume and spindrift. Head inland to enjoy shady forest walking around **Huelgoat** (p138) or deep within the **Forêt de Paimpont** (p180), where Merlin the magician once cast his spells. To be assured of gradient-free strolling, walk the banks of one of the canals that crisscross Brittany.

In both Normandy and Brittany you can hike year round; if you wrap up well, winter walking borders on the inspirational when the crowds have long since left and the waves lash the shores.

The GR34

This trail ranks as one France's longest *Sentiers de Grande Randonnée* (GRs; long-distance trails). Hugging the Brittany coast, it runs for over 2000km all the way from Mont St-Michel to Port-Navalo on the Golfe du Morbihan. We're not suggesting for a nanosecond that you push for an entry in the *Guinness Book of Records* and complete every kilometre. Wherever you come across the characteristic red-and-white striped GR trail markers, you can be sure you're on a safe walk that follows the best of the coastline. Many stretches, especially near coastal towns, are also called the *Sentier des Douaniers* (customs officers' trail), a reminder of the distant days when the paths were patrolled by armed officers on the lookout for smugglers.

Discover how regional nature parks integrate heritage preservation in local development at www.parcs-naturels-regionaux.tm.fr.

Among the most attractive stretches:

Cancale to St-Malo via Pointe du Grouin (25km; p74)
Plage de Trestraou to Ploumanac'h (5km; p83)
Plage du Prieuré to Plage de St-Enogat via Pointe du Moulinet (4km; p113)
Presqu'île de Crozon peninsula walk from Camaret-sur-Mer to Crozon (40km, two days; p139)
Vannes to Port-Navalo (50km, two to three days; p176)

Alan Castle's admirable *Brittany Coastal Path* describes in detail a 580km stretch from Mont St-Michel to Morlaix at the eastern limit of Finistère and also gives suggestions for a further 98 day walks. The **Fédération Française de**

la Randonnée Pédestre (www.ffrp.asso.fr - French only) covers nearly the whole route in a series of excellent *topoguides* (French only).

Other tempting trails:

Belle-Île-en-Mer (p169) Pick a section of the island's coastal footpath or undertake the full circuit (95km, four days).

Canal Towpaths Among many attractive stretches of the Ille-et-Rance Canal, the towpath running east and west of the charming little village of **Hédé** (p90) stands out. Similarly, long stretches of the **Nantes–Brest Canal** (see, for example, p179) are absolutely flat and ideal for walks with young children.

Île d'Ouessant (p129) A coastal footpath (45km, two to three days) hugs this island's wild, rocky coastline. If you're over for the day, a couple of tempting shorter walks (8km & 12km) lead from Lampaul, the island's only village.

Lonely Planet's *Walking in France* devotes a chapter to some longer and more challenging walks in Brittany and Normandy.

SAILING & CANAL CRUISING

Brittany's long, indented coastline with its stunning scenery calls to sailors from the smallest cabin boy to gnarled salts. Traditionally the land of seafarers, and latterly the birthplace of such famous international yachtsmen as Éric Taberly and Alain Colas, Brittany in particular is one of Europe's most popular cruising grounds. Each year, hundreds of British yachts cross the Channel to spend their summer holidays on the northwestern coast of France, adding to the thousands of French boats that crowd the region's many marinas and harbours. The Brittany regional tourist board publishes a brochure, *Sailing in Brittany*, and there are several yachtsmen's pilot books and cruising guides to Brittany and Normandy available in English.

Companies such as English-owned **Brittany Sailing** (☎ 02 98 17 01 31; www .brittanysail.co.uk; L'Ancrage, Kergalet, 29160 Lanveoc) offer an easy introduction to sailing, combining one week's cruise on a skippered yacht with a week onshore in a cottage B&B (from €750 per person). They also offer training courses leading to Royal Yachting Association qualifications (€565 to €610 for five days).

If you merely want to test the Breton waters or include sailing within a more general holiday, there are plenty of centres besides Point Passion Plage (see below) where you can hire dinghies and catamarans by the hour and either sail independently or follow a course of instruction.

POINT PASSION PLAGE

It's a brilliantly simple idea: 36 aquatic centres throughout Brittany have banded together under the beach umbrella **Point Passion Plage** (☎ 02 98 02 49 67). Look for their flags at seaside resorts large and small. Each centre keeps its individuality yet undertakes to observe common minimum standards and – of special benefit to visitors passing through or just wanting to sample an activity – common tariffs.

You buy a **Pass'sensations**, a carnet of tickets (€80/140 for 25/50), which you can use anywhere within the network and which gives a discount of up to 30% on normal hire and instruction rates. So, for example, you could start learning to windsurf in St-Malo, pick up the dagger board again further west at Erquy, ride the waves at Perros-Guirec, then simply hire a board to round off the experience at one of Finistère's fine beaches.

Standard undiscounted hourly rates throughout the network:

- windsurfing €14
- dinghy for two €30
- catamaran €30-40
- sea kayak €10-14

Possibilities for boat hire and sailing instruction in Normandy include **Albâtre Plaisance** (www.albatre-plaisance.com - French only), with centres in **Le Havre** (☎ 02 35 43 53 79; 56 rue des Sauveteurs) and **Fécamp** (☎ 06 13 17 16 44; 2 rue du Commandant Riondel); and **École de Voile de Cherbourg** (☎ 02 33 94 99 00; www.ev-cherbourg.info - French only; Centre Albert Livory, Plage Napoléon).

In principle, the whole of the coastline is suitable for sailing – though bear in mind that conditions can change rapidly. Particularly safe areas include wide sheltered bays and estuaries such as the Golfe du Morbihan, Baie de Morlaix, the Abers of northwest Brittany and the protected Rade de Brest.

For a relaxing inland holiday, nothing can rival hiring a **canal cruiser** and putt-putting along a section or two of Brittany's several hundred kilometres of navigable inland waterways. These were mostly scoured out on the order of Napoleon in the early 19th century.

The **Ille-et-Rance Canal** (85km, 47 locks; p89) links Dinan with Rennes, from where the **River Vilaine** (137km, 12 locks) leads to the sea at Arzal. The **Nantes–Brest Canal** (p178) threads its way through the heart of central Brittany from the Rade de Brest to the River Loire at Nantes. Navigable sections nowadays are the River Aulne from Le Faou to Carhaix (85km, 46 locks) in the west and from Pontivy to Nantes via Josselin (208km, 104 locks; p179) in the east. The latter section links to the Vilaine at Redon. The **River Blavet** from Pontivy downstream to Hennebont is also navigable (60km, 28 locks).

Several companies rent canal boats that can sleep from three to 10 people. No previous experience is needed – a quick lesson in boat-handling and how to operate the locks is all you need, then it's anchors away. Typical high-season (July and August) rates are around €1350 per week for a boat that sleeps three to five people.

Companies offering canal boat hire:

Bretagne Croisières (☎ 02 99 71 08 05; www.bretagnecroisieres.com - French only; 75 rue de Vannes, 35600 Redon) With a recently opened centre in Dinan (same contact details).

Bretagne Plaisance (☎ 02 99 72 15 80; www.bretagne-plaisance.fr; 12 quai Jean-Bart, 35600 Redon)

CYCLING

If you're a head-down, conquer the cols and notch up the kilometres cyclist, leave your bike at home. Normandy and Brittany call much more to touring bikers who like their cycling gentle and to savour a good meal at day's end. Working westwards, Normandy's chalky cliffs, pastures and apple orchards give way to the more rugged coastline of Brittany's Côtes d'Armor, then the wilder, dramatic seascapes of Finistère. Inland, it can be hillier. But most times you can wheel effortlessly through forest and along quiet country lanes that follow a gently undulating countryside or pedal on the level beside canals and languid rivers.

'Wheel effortlessly through forest and along quiet country lanes or pedal on the level beside canals'

Maps & Books

Lonely Planet's *Cycling France* has a chapter devoted to day and multiday rides in Normandy and Brittany. The **Fédération Française de Cyclotourisme** (FFCT; www.ffct.org - French only) issues two useful guides in French: *La France à Vélo: Bretagne* and *La France à Vélo: Normandie*, both published by Éditions Franck Mercier.

The **Institut Géographique National** (IGN; www.ign.fr - French only) publishes two maps specifically for cyclists in Normandy, each highlighting more than 50 circuits: *La Calvados à Bicyclette* at a scale of 1:100,000 and *Itinéraires*

Cyclotouristiques en Haute-Normandie at 1:200,000. Both feature in its *Plein Air* (Open Air) series.

Touring Companies

Belle France (☎ 0870 405 40 56; www.bellefrance.co.uk; Spelmonden, Old Oast, Goudhurst, Kent CN17 1HE, UK) A British-based company that arranges cycle tours in Normandy, among several other French destinations.

Breton Bikes (☎ 02 96 24 86 72; www.bretonbikes.com; 14 Grande Rue, 22570 Plelauff) Friendly, knowledgeable, British-owned and based in a small village in central Brittany. Offers a wide choice of independent or guided cycling holidays with accommodation in hotels or camping.

Cycling for Softies (☎ 0161 248 82 82; www.cycling-for-softies.co.uk) Indeed fulfils the promise of its enticing name. You're unaccompanied, though well supported with documentation, and stay in small, family hotels, selected – among other criteria – for the quality of their cuisine.

Euro-bike & Walking Tours (☎ 1-800-321-6060; www.eurobike.com; PO Box 990, DeKalb, Illinois 60115, USA) Offers tours that embrace both Normandy and Brittany, with an option that nudges into the Loire Valley too.

Randonnée (☎ 1-800-465-6488; www.randonneetours.com; 100-162 Albert St, Winnipeg, Manitoba R3B 1E9, Canada) Arranges self-guided cycling itineraries in Brittany.

DIVING

The waters off Normandy are the last resting place of some spectacular wrecks from the D-Day landings. Experienced divers can explore, for example, the *Carbonelle*, lying off Omaha Beach, still bearing its cargo of Sherman tanks, or the *Léopoldville*, an 11,500-tonne liner converted into a troopship that rests 8km off the Cherbourg coast.

For more information about these and other dives and for details of local courses, contact the **Association Sport Cultures Loisirs Paul Éluard** (ASCL; ☎ 02 35 53 95 72; www.pauleluard-plongee.com - French only; Hangar 17, quai Johannès Couvert, 76000 Le Havre) or **Club d'Exploration Sous-Marine de la Manche** (CESMM; ☎ 02 35 48 15 21; 14 rue Frédéric Bellanger, 76600 Le Havre).

Wrecks abound off Brittany too, particularly beneath the turbulent waters of the entrance to the Channel. It can be chilly down there; winter temperatures are near 10°C, climbing to 17° to 18°C in July and August.

Major holiday resorts have diving centres that offer courses at all levels, especially for beginners, leading to a PADI certificate or an equivalent qualification. Most function between March and October, and offer daily diving between June and September, but are often only active at weekends outside the summer season. To test the waters if you're a beginner, sign on for a *baptême*, a one-to-one trial dive accompanied by an instructor.

There are more than 20 diving centres around the Brittany coast. Some leading ones:

Saint Malo Plongée Émeraude – Centre Bleu Émeraude (☎ 02 99 19 90 36; www.saint maloplongee.com - French only; Terre-plein du Naye)

Aber-Benoit Plongée (☎ 02 98 89 75 66; www.aberbenoitplongee.com - French only; quai du Stellac'h, Aber Benoit) Offers a dive down to the wreck of the *Amoco Cadiz*.

Centre d'Activités Plongée Trébeurden (CAP; 02 96 23 66 71; www.plongeecap.com - French only; Corniche de Goas Trez, Trébeurden)

Club Léo-Lagrange Camaret (☎ 02 98 27 90 49; www.club-leo-camaret.net; 2 rue du Stade, Camaret-sur-Mer)

TYPICAL DIVE PRICES:

try dive
€30-40

one-week beginner's course
€300-380

one-week intermediate or advanced course
€325-400

single dive with/without instructor
€35/30 (20-25% less if you use your own equipment)

Food & Drink

The pleasures of the table are equally important in Normandy and Brittany, but the table is likely to contain different items. Norman cuisine tends to be more elaborate, making full use of butter and cream sauces while Breton cuisine tends to be more down-to-earth. Seafood is the one constant: each region takes full advantage of a long coastline that brings in heaps of fresh fish and shellfish.

There's a wealth of recipes and food information from all over France on the French site www.cuisine.tv.

STAPLES & SPECIALITIES
Brittany

Brittany is famous for its fresh produce and simple country cuisine rather than for any fancy gourmet dishes. Very little cheese is produced here and the region's only wine – a Muscadet – slipped outside Brittany's administrative borders when the Loire- Atlantique *département* around Nantes was moved into the Pays de la Loire region. (Because of its closes ties to Brittany, we included Loire-Atlantique in this guide.) However, Brittany produces some of France's finest seafood and its best *primeurs* (early spring vegetables), especially cauliflower, carrots, artichokes, peas and pink onions. The inland pastures support herds of small, black-and-white dairy cattle, and sheep graze on the salty turf of the *marais salants* (salt marshes), while the pigs of Brittany produce some of the country's finest smoked sausages. Sea salt from Guérande (see the boxed text, p196) is a prized ingredient.

FISH & SEAFOOD

The waters around Brittany provide a rich harvest of *poissons* (fish) and *fruits de mer* (seafood), making the region a paradise for seafood lovers: enjoy oysters from Cancale and the Morbihan Gulf coast; scallops and sea urchins from St-Brieuc; crabs from St-Malo; and lobsters from Camaret, Concarneau and Quiberon.

Countless seafood restaurants all around the region dish up this bounty, from humble cafés serving the traditional Breton snack of *moules-frites* (mussels and chips), to gourmet dining rooms offering the king of Breton fish dishes, *bar de ligne au sel de Guérande* (line-caught sea bass baked in a salt crust; see the boxed text, p145).

Most fish and seafood dishes are cooked simply and accompanied by a *beurre blanc* (butter sauce). Traditional Breton seafood dishes include *cotriade* (known as *godaille* in the Loire-Atlantique *département*), a hearty soup of fish and shellfish – sometimes called the 'bouillabaisse of the north'.

The most famous seafood dish from Brittany, however, is *homard à l'armoricaine* – lobster flambéed in brandy and simmered in white wine. Its origins are hotly debated – some experts insist that the name is a corruption of 'homard à l'américaine' and that the dish was invented in Paris in the 19th century by a Languedocien chef who had previously worked in Chicago.

MEAT & CHARCUTERIE

Although Breton farmers raise beef cattle, pigs, sheep and poultry, their produce is rather overshadowed by the fame of the region's seafood. The *agneau de pré-salé* (salt-meadow lamb), raised on the shores of the Baie du Mont St-Michel, is particularly good; the sheep graze on the salty meadows near the high-water mark, adding flavour to their meat.

Brittany's *charcuterie* (which is an all-encompassing term for pork butchery) includes the famous *andouille* (smoked pork-tripe sausage, usually eaten cold), *andouillette* (pork-tripe sausage that is usually grilled or stewed in cider) and *boudin* (black pudding, usually fried and served with stewed apples).

CREPES & GALETTES

Crepes and *galettes* are probably Brittany's best-known and most widespread culinary speciality. Both are large thin pancakes made by spreading batter on a hot griddle (known as a *bilig* in Breton). The difference is that *galettes* are made using buckwheat flour *(sarrasin* or *blé noir)* and crepes using ordinary wheat flour *(froment)*. Crepes usually have a sweet filling, while *galettes* are usually savoury. The classic *galette* filling is ham, egg and cheese, but you can choose anything from just a smear of butter to scallops in a wine and cream sauce.

CAKES & PASTRIES

The rich and filling Breton cake called *kouign amann* (butter cake) originates in Douarnenez, but is now made all over Brittany. It is prepared using a leavened bread dough, rolled out thinly and spread with butter and sugar, then folded and refolded and rolled out, in a way similar to that used in making flaky pastry.

Far (also called *far breton* or *farz forn*) is a heavy, golden flan flavoured with vanilla and often containing prunes. Other sweet toothed specialities of the region include *galettes de Pont-Aven* (not pancakes, but shortbread-like biscuits), *niniches de Quiberon* (cane-sugar lollipops) and *salidou* (caramel).

Bouquet De Bretagne: Seasonal Recipes from Le Bretagne, Questembert by Georges Paineau. This Brittany chef takes a literary look at Brittany's cuisine to supplement his recipes.

Normandy

Normandy is famous for the incredible richness and superior quality of its local produce. Dairy products are the 'white gold' of the region. Each Norman cow produces an average of five tonnes of milk annually, which is why the region supplies something like half of France's milk, butter, cream and cheese. Norman cuisine is based on butter and cream sauces, which are slathered over eggs, chicken, fish, veal, seafood, vegetables and desserts. If a dish is *à la normande*, it's bound to contain butter, cream or both.

The best Normandy butter comes from Isigny-sur-Mer on the border between the Calvados and Manche *départements*. It's an exceptionally flavourful butter, sought after by chefs around France, although the butter from Ste-Mère-Église is also very highly regarded.

DID YOU KNOW?

Normandy is France's largest producer of mussels, turning out some 25,000 tonnes a year.

Fish and seafood are also of superior quality in Normandy. Oysters from the Cotentin Peninsula and turbot are major delicacies throughout France. Look for *lisettes* (little mackerel) and *coquilles St-Jacques* (scallops) from Dieppe, shrimp from Honfleur, cod from Fécamp and crabs, clams and mussels all along the coast.

Meat and poultry are menu staples in the interior. The savoury lamb *pré-salé* from Mont St-Michel needs no sauce, but Normandy's fine beef, chicken and veal are often served in cider or Calvados-based sauces. Some think it's heresy, but don't be surprised to see a meat dish topped with a sauce based on one of Normandy's fine cheeses.

Charcuteries (delicatessens) abound in Normandy, their windows displaying various terrines, pâtés and tripe. Also common is *galantine*, a cold dish of boned, stuffed, pressed meat (especially pork) that is presented in its own jelly, often with truffles and pistachio nuts.

CHEESE

Normandy is renowned for its cheese, much of it produced in the Pays d'Auge region of Lower Normandy. It's the birthplace of France's most popular cheese, Camembert, a luscious, creamy cheese with a complex flavour. The area around Camembert village had long been renowned for its cheese, but it wasn't until 1791 that farmer Marie Harel developed the Camembert formula based on certain tips from a renegade priest she was sheltering. It was a big success at the market of nearby Vimoutiers and eventually in the court of Napoleon III. Unfortunately, much commercially produced Camembert is bland and flavourless since it's made from pasteurised milk. Look for Camembert made from *lait cru* (raw milk) and then let it get soft and runny before eating it. Don't put it into the refrigerator. The best brands are Monsieur Mellon and the Lepetit family.

Pont l'Évêque is another popular cheese from Auge country and is Normandy's oldest cheese. The town lies between Deauville and Lisieux and it's said that the grass feeding the region's cows is particularly oily, which gives the cheese its unique flavour. The process differs from that of Camembert cheese, requiring a longer ageing process and more frequent turning. The best label is Briouze.

Livarot became the most sought after Norman cheese in the 19th century and is the most complicated to make. Called the 'colonel' because of the five imprinted stripes on its rind, Livarot sits in a cellar for a month and is periodically washed with fresh or lightly salted water. Look out for Livarot from the Graindorge cheese maker.

The *petits suisses* cheese from the Bray region has pleased generations of French children. Merging *crème fraîche* with white cheese, this creamy cheese emerged in the 19th century as a dessert. Other popular Normandy cheeses include the heart-shaped Neufchâtel made near Neufchâtel-en-Bray, the *pavé d'Auge* and *brillat-savarin* made near Forges-les-Eaux and *la Bouille* from the town of the same name. Most Norman cheeses are best in spring and autumn.

Links to information about Normandy's luscious cheeses can be found at www.fromages.org, a French-language site.

SOLE NORMANDE

It may not have been invented in Normandy, but the shellfish-rich coastal waters of Normandy provided the raw materials to dress up dull sole fillets. Based on a white butter-and-cream sauce, the dish varies from town to town. In Dieppe they add mussels, mushrooms and sometimes crab. In Fécamp the sauce is enhanced with shrimp butter and in Le Havre and Trouville shrimp replaces the mussels and mushrooms. Some restaurants only add scallops to the sauce.

NORMANDY COWS

There are cows and there are cows and then there are Normandy cows. Easily recognisable by the distinctive spectacle markings around their eyes, Normandy cows are a breed unto themselves. They're relatively new, dating only from the 19th century when the need to feed a growing population forced farmers to look for ways to increase the quality and output of their cows. For the best milk and meat, breeders mixed three regional cows: the large, heavy Cotentine; the Augeronne, which was smaller but produced good meat; and the Cauchoise of Flemish stock. The breed was officially recognised in 1883.

La race normande is a cow with qualities. It's hardy, not fussy about its climate or cuisine. It produces more milk than other breeds and the milk is of a higher quality, with more curds, making it more expensive. The meat is highly prized by chefs around France for its tenderness and flavour and the breed has now gained a following around the world.

CANETON ROUENNAIS

Rouen is famous for its duck dishes but the most extreme is *Caneton Rouennais*. The duckling is strangled in order to retain its blood, then roasted for only 20 minutes. A red-wine sauce is prepared using the duck's heart and liver. At the table, the duck is put through a duck press (which every kitchen has) to release the blood, which is then combined with the sauce. The dish is so special that there's an association devoted to its preparation. L'Ordre des Canardiers (the Order of Canardiers) licenses chefs qualified to prepare the duckling, publishes a magazine and even has a website (www.canardiers.asso.fr) where you can find the recipe for the dish and a list of master *canardiers* around the world.

TRIPES À LA MODE DE CAEN

Cow intestines may not be to everyone's taste but when France was poor and rural, every part of the animal had to be eaten. Caen is the place to taste your tripe dish, made by stewing the intestines with carrots, onions, leeks, herbs, spices, cider and Calvados. Naturally, there's an association, the Tripière d'Or, that awards yearly prizes for the best *tripes à la mode de Caen*.

DID YOU KNOW?

Tripe à la mode de Caen was invented by a monk from the Abbaye aux Hommes in the 16th century.

ANDOUILLE DE VIRE

More guts, this time from a pig. It's rolled into a sausage that is then seasoned and smoked for two months before being served cold and cut into small rounds. The technique has been perfected in Vire but the sausage is served throughout Normandy.

BOUDIN

Blood sausage has its fans and the place to eat your *boudin* is Mortagne-au-Perche. It's made with one-third pig's blood, one-third onion and one-third pig fat, and often served with baked or fried apple. The Knights of the Boudin Tasters (Chevaliers du Goûte Boudin), based in Mortagne-au-Perche, is an order of *boudin* lovers so devoted to their product, they must swear to eat it at least once a week.

OMELETTE À LA MÈRE POULARD

At the foot of the Mont St-Michel abbey, Grandma Poulard (long since deceased) created an extraordinarily fluffy omelette that is still made in the Mère Poulard restaurant (p71) – and other restaurants in town. There's no real secret to the omelette; it's cooked over a wood fire in a long-handled pan and taken away from the heat from time to time during the process.

DRINKS
Nonalcoholic Drinks
WATER

All tap water (*eau du robinet*) in France is filtered and purified but the high level of pollutants in Brittany's rivers has made most Bretons distrustful of tap water. Most will order bottled *eau de source* (mineral water) in a restaurant, which comes *plate* (flat or noncarbonated) or *gazeuse* (fizzy or carbonated). Normans are more comfortable ordering *une carafe d'eau* (a jug of water), which comes from the tap.

SOFT DRINKS

A *citron pressé* is a glass of iced water (either flat or carbonated) with freshly squeezed lemon juice and sugar. The French are not particularly fond of drinking very cold things, so if you'd like your drink with ice cubes, ask for *des glaçons*.

COFFEE

The most ubiquitous form is espresso, made by forcing steam through ground coffee beans. A small, black espresso is called *un café noir, un express* or simply *un café*. You can also ask for *un grand* (large) *café*.

Un café crème is espresso with steamed milk or cream. *Un café au lait* is lots of hot milk with a little coffee served in a large cup or, sometimes, a bowl. A small *café crème* is *un petit crème*. *Une noisette* (literally 'hazelnut') is an espresso with just a dash of milk. Decaffeinated coffee is *un café décaféiné* or *un déca*.

TEA & HOT CHOCOLATE

Thé (tea) is also widely available and will be served with milk if you ask for *un peu de lait frais* (a little cold milk). Herbal tea, popular as a treatment for minor ailments, is called *tisane* or *infusion*. French *chocolat chaud* (hot chocolate) can be either excellent or completely undrinkable.

Alcoholic Drinks

CIDER

Cidre is equally popular with Normans and Bretons which makes sense considering that the border between Normandy and Brittany is one of France's main apple-growing regions. The apples are harvested between September and December, then crushed and pressed in January. Winter cold slows down the fermentation process, which can last up to three months. Large manufacturers filter, pasteurise and sometimes add carbon dioxide before putting the cider in bottles.

The length of the fermentation process determines the sweetness of the cider. *Cidre doux* (sweet) has an alcohol content of 2.5% to 3%; brut (dry) has an alcohol content of about 4.5%. Most cider is bubbly and, like champagne, comes in corked bottles. Look for *sec* (at least a year old), *pur jus* (no added water), *mousseux* (naturally carbonated) or *bouché* (cider fermented in the bottle).

WINE

Normandy is the only French region that has never had a wine business and, since the Loire-Atlantique *département* was transferred to the Pays de la Loire region, Brittany proper no longer has any vineyards. However, the light and dry white wines produced in the Muscadet de Sèvre-et-Maine vineyards around Nantes are widely available throughout Brittany and Normandy and make an excellent accompaniment to a seafood dinner.

BEER

True to its Celtic roots, Brittany produces a number of excellent local beers, such as Coreff, Dremmwell, Cervoise Lancelot and Telenn Du. See the boxed text (p121) for more details.

MEAD

You may occasionally see locally made *chouchen* (Breton for mead) available in bars and cafés. It's a rich and sweet drink halfway between beer and wine, with an alcohol content around the 18% mark. Made by fermenting diluted honey, its origins date back to the time of the Celts and Druids.

APERITIFS

Pommeau is a refreshing Norman aperitif made from apple juice and Calvados (see Digestifs, opposite). It's made by stopping the fermentation

THE AOC LABEL

The label *Appellation d'Origine Contrôlée* (AOC) is the highest honour that can be bestowed on a French product. It signals that the product comes from a specific region and is made according to specific standards. Although the label is most regularly applied to wine, in Normandy certain cheeses and ciders have also received the label. The 'made-in Normandy' *(fabriqué en Normandie)* label means little since the original milk or apples could have come from outside Normandy.

Camembert received its AOC label in 1983, which means that the cheese must have been made either in the Pays d'Auge, the Orne bocage or the Cotentin Peninsula. Pont l'Évêque can be made anywhere in Normandy plus the Mayenne *departement* of the Loire Valley. Livarot cheese must be produced in a narrow area confined to the southeast of Calvados and northeast of the Orne; Neufchâtel is limited to a 30km-radius of the town in Pays de Bray.

Cider and Calvados from the Pays d'Auge also benefit from the AOC quality-control label. No other cider has an AOC label but Calvados from 10 other areas in Normandy – Avranches, Cotentin, the Pays de Bray and the Orne Valley, among others – has achieved the lesser distinction of being *réglementée* (regulated). Calvados from the Pays d'Auge is made only from apples around the Deauville region and it is subject to a double distillation.

of freshly pressed apples and adding Calvados, which preserves the apple flavour, the natural sugars of the fruit and an agreeable acidity. It is then aged in an oak barrel for 18 months. Drink *pommeau* cool but without ice. The alcohol content is a moderate 16% to 18% and it's particularly good with oysters, *foie gras* or apple-based desserts.

Poiré is good if you can find it, but unfortunately it is becoming increasingly rare. Essentially a dry cider made from pears, *poiré* is a light drink that you may find in the Orne Valley.

DIGESTIFS

Need stronger stuff? Calvados is the pride of Normandy and, with an alcohol content of 50% to 55%, this apple brandy takes the sting out of a rainy Norman winter. Calvados is cider that has been allowed to age for at least a year, but the process is more complicated. Some 40 different kinds of apples can go into the making of a good Calvados, many of them cultivated specifically for the brandy. After a one- or two-step distillation process the brandy is aged for at least one year, first in a new oak barrel and then in a series of progressively older oak barrels that lend it a particular woody taste.

Its quality derives from the length of time it passes in the oak barrels. Three-star Calvados has been aged two years, *vieux* Calvados has aged three years, *Vieille Réserve* or VSOP (Very Special Old Pale) has aged five years, and Hors d'Age Extra or Napoleon has aged at least six years.

Calvados can be drunk at the end of a meal with coffee or in the middle of a meal – the *trou normand* (Norman hole; see p59).

Bénédictine is a heady plant-based liqueur made in Fécamp, although it is not widely imbibed in Normandy. For details see p232.

CELEBRATIONS

With such a wealth of fresh produce and a bountiful harvest from the sea, it's no surprise that Normans and Bretons are inclined to celebrate their good fortune. Food festivals abound. The starring product is usually surrounded by a supporting cast of regional products adding up to a blockbuster food-fest. Some of the best known:

March
Foire au Boudin (☎ 02 33 85 11 18) If blood sausage is your passion, come to Mortagne-au-Perche the third weekend in March.

May
Fête de Fromage (☎ 02 31 64 12 77) Pont L'Evêque hosts this cheesy fair on the second weekend in May to display its prize product.
Foire aux Cerises (☎ 02 31 51 39 60) On Pentecost weekend, Vernon celebrates its juicy cherries.

April
Fête de la Coquille St-Jacques (☎ 02 96 72 30 12) Scallops are the treat at this fest, held alternately in Erquy, St-Quay-Portrieux and Loguivy.

June
Fête de la Morue (☎ 02 96 73 60 12) This cod festival in Binic is a throwback to the port's days as a fishing centre.

July
Fête de la Mer et du Maquereau (☎ 02 31 14 60 70) Tasty and nutritious mackerel are available on the last weekend of July in Trouville.

August
Foire aux Picots (☎ 02 31 48 81 10) On 1 August, Lisieux celebrates poultry, *fois gras* and other meaty matters.
Fête des Filets Bleus (☎ 02 98 97 01 44) The 'Blue Nets' festival, is a celebration of the local fishing industry in Concarneau; held on the third weekend in August.

Normandy Gastronomique by Jane Sigal. Recipes, restaurants and a look at Normandy's culinary products make this book worthwhile for the gastronome.

September
Fête de la Crevette (☎ 02 31 89 23 30) Honfleur is proud of its grey shrimp and honours them on the third weekend in September.
Fête du Fromage (☎ 02 35 93 22 96) Neufchâtel-en-Bray is awash in its luscious cheese for this festival in mid-month.

October
Foire de la Pomme et de la Citrouille (☎ 02 31 69 29 86) The last weekend in October Pont d'Ouilly stages a fest to show off apples and pumpkins.
Fête de la Cagouille et de la Citrouille (☎ 02 31 14 60 70) Here's the chance to sample snails in all their glory in Trouville on the last weekend of October.
Fête du Ventre et de la Gastronomie (☎ 02 32 08 32 40) The glories of gastronomy are celebrated in and around the place du Vieux-Marché in Rouen in mid-month.

November
Foire aux Harengs (☎ 02 32 14 40 60) Dieppe doesn't bring in the herring as it did, but this fair in mid-month is a reminder of the good old days.

December
Foire aux Dindes (☎ 02 33 28 74 79) In mid-month Sées sells turkey and *foie gras*, along with related products in stalls throughout town.

WHERE TO EAT & DRINK
Types of Eateries
RESTAURANTS & BRASSERIES
Some of the best French restaurants in the country are attached to hotels and those on the ground floor of budget hotels often have some of the best deals in town. Almost all are open to everyone.

Restaurants usually specialise in a particular variety of food (for example, regional, traditional, North African or Vietnamese), whereas brasseries – which look very much like cafés – serve more standard fare. Unlike restaurants, which usually open only for lunch and dinner, brasseries keep going from morning until night and serve meals (or at least something solid) at all times of the day.

Don't count on eating in a smoke-free environment anywhere in the country. French eateries are required to set aside a section for nonsmokers, but the law is widely ignored, especially in small family-run establishments. In our reviews of restaurants in this guide, we have used a nonsmoking icon to indicate that an establishment has designated nonsmoking areas that are adhered to.

ETHNIC RESTAURANTS
Ethnic restaurants are not particularly cheap or plentiful in Normandy and Brittany. There's invariably a Chinese restaurant, usually with a strong Vietnamese influence, in most towns, and often a North African restaurant serving couscous with stewed vegetables and meat. The larger cities have Indian restaurants too. Rennes has a particularly extensive selection of exotic restaurants.

SALONS DE THÉ
Salons de thé (tearooms) are trendy and somewhat pricey establishments that usually offer quiches, salads, cakes, tarts, pies and pastries in addition to tea and coffee.

CREPERIES
Traditional creperies are found all over Brittany and Normandy specialising in crepes and *galettes* (see p51). You can order as few or as many as you like; a typical lunch would consist of one or two savoury *galettes* followed by a sweet crepe.

Self-Catering
Most French people buy a good part of their food from small neighbourhood shops, each with its own speciality. At first, having to go to four shops and stand in four queues to fill the fridge (or assemble a picnic) may seem rather a waste of time, but the whole ritual is an important part of the way many French people live their daily lives. It's perfectly acceptable to purchase only meal-size amounts: a few *tranches* (slices) of meat to make a sandwich, perhaps, or a *petit bout* (small chunk) of sausage.

BOULANGERIES
Fresh bread is baked and sold at *boulangeries* (bakeries), which supply 75% of the country's bread. All *boulangeries* have 250g, long and thin baguettes, and fatter 400g loaves of *pain* (bread), both of which should be eaten within four hours of baking. If you're not very hungry, ask for a *demi baguette* or *demi pain*. A *ficelle* is a thinner, crustier version of the baguette – like very thick breadsticks. Bread is baked at various times of the day so fresh bread is readily available as early as 6am and also in the afternoon. Most *boulangeries* close one day a week but the days are staggered so that you'll always find one open somewhere (except perhaps on Sunday afternoon).

PATISSERIES
Mouth-watering pastries are available at patisseries (cake and pastry shops), which are often attached to bakeries. Some of the most common

DID YOU KNOW?

You can tell if a croissant has been made with margarine or butter by the shape: margarine croissants have their tips almost touching, while those made with butter have them pointing away from each other.

pastries include *tarte aux fruits* (fruit tarts), *pain au chocolat* (similar to a croissant but filled with chocolate), *pain aux raisins* (a flat, spiral pastry filled with custard and sultanas) and *religieuses* (éclairs with one cream puff perched on top of another to resemble a nun's headdress).

FROMAGERIES

If you buy your cheese in a supermarket, you'll end up with unripe and relatively tasteless products unless you know your stuff. Here's where a *fromagerie*, also known as a *crémerie*, comes in. The owners will advise you and usually let you taste before you decide what to buy. Just ask: 'Est-ce que je peux le goûter, s'il vous plaît?'

FRUIT & VEGETABLES

Fruits and *légumes* are sold by a *marchand de fruits et légumes* (green-grocer) and at food markets and supermarkets. Most small groceries have only a limited selection. You can buy whatever quantity of produce suits you, even if it's just three carrots and a peach. *Biologique* means that it has been grown organically (without chemicals).

'Buy whatever quantity suits you, even if it's just three carrots and a peach'

MEAT & FISH

A general butchery is a *boucherie* but for specialised poultry you have to go to a *marchand de volaille*, where *poulet fermier* (free-range chicken) will cost much more than a regular chicken. A *boucherie chevaline*, which is easily identifiable by the gilded horse's head above the entrance, sells horse meat.

Fresh fish and seafood are available from a *poissonnerie*. All around the coast of Brittany you can buy fresh shellfish direct from the growers; look for signs saying *ostréiculture* (oyster-farming) and *mytiliculture* (mussel-farming).

ÉPICERIES & ALIMENTATIONS

A small grocery store with a little bit of everything is known as an *épicerie* (literally 'spice shop') or an *alimentation générale*. Most *épiceries* are more expensive than supermarkets, though some – such as those of the Casino chain – are more like minimarkets. Some *épiceries* open on days when other food shops are closed and many family-run operations stay open until late at night.

SUPERMARKETS

City centres usually have at least one department store with a large *super-marché* (supermarket) section. Chains include Monoprix, Prisunic and Nouvelles Galeries. Most larger supermarkets have a delicatessen and a cheese counter; many also have inhouse bakeries.

The cheapest place to buy food is a *hypermarché* (hypermarket), such as those of the Carrefour, Intermarché and Marché Plus chains, where you'll pay up to 40% less for staples than at an *épicerie*. Unfortunately, they are normally on the outskirts of town.

FOOD MARKETS

In most towns and cities, many food products are available one or more days a week at *marchés en plein air* (open-air markets), also known as *marchés découverts*, and up to six days a week at *marchés couverts* (covered marketplaces), often known as *les halles*. Markets are cheaper than food shops and supermarkets and the merchandise, especially fruit and vegetables, is generally fresher and of better quality.

VEGETARIANS & VEGANS

Vegetarians form only a small minority in France and are not very well catered for; specialised vegetarian restaurants are few and far between. Only the cities are likely to have vegetarian establishments, and these may look more like laid-back cafés than restaurants. Other options include *saladeries*, casual restaurants that serve a long list of *salades composées* (mixed salads). Indian restaurants usually have a variety of vegetarian options and it's possible to order the North African dish, couscous without the meat. Most towns of any size will have a store specialising in organic (bio) products and many large supermarkets now have an organic section where you can buy soy yogurt, milk and other health-food products.

WHINING & DINING

It can a be challenge in unfamiliar territory to find food to suit all tastes, without the need for the kids to 'behave' like adults in a fancy restaurant. Picnic lunches can be fun and as a side benefit can keep costs down. Prepare your own sandwiches from fine cheese, local pâté and a touch of fresh produce. Finish with some fruit and a scrumptious pastry and *voilà!* Every town has a supermarket or open-air markets to stock up on supplies and the local cafeteria is good for a hot lunch or dinner. Many Casion supermarkets have cafeterias; otherwise look for the Flunch chain.

Even in the better restaurants lunch is usually much more casual than dinner, so it might be wise to sit down for a family meal at lunch and grab a *croque-monsieur* at a café for dinner. Many restaurants are child friendly and have high-chairs and half portions available; generally the more expensive and exclusive they are the more intolerant they get. If in any doubt ask when you make a booking. Sunday lunch is a family affair in France and generally the best time to drag the kids to a restaurant. Weekend nights would be the worst time.

For more information on travelling with your children, see p320.

HABITS & CUSTOMS
Traditional Meals

As the pace of French life becomes more hectic, the three-hour midday meal is becoming increasingly rare, at least on weekdays. Dinners, however, are still turned into elaborate affairs whenever time and finances permit. For visitors, the occasional splurge can be the perfect end to a day of sightseeing.

A fully fledged, traditional French meal is an awesome event, often comprising six distinct courses and sometimes more. The meal is always served with wine (red, white or rosé, depending on what you're eating). The fare served at a traditional *déjeuner* (lunch), usually eaten around 1pm, is largely indistinguishable from that served at *dîner* (dinner), usually begun around 8.30pm.

The Norman Table: The Traditional Cooking of Normandy by Claude Guermont. The Norman-born author presents 200 classic Norman recipes.

THE NORMAN HOLE

With even everyday meals stretching to four courses, it's not surprising that Normans need to take a break in the middle of the meal. After the starter and main course, Normans typically down a little glass of Calvados – known as the *trou normand* (Norman hole) – to help their digestion.

According to nutritionists, Calvados actually dilates the stomach lining, eliminating the impression of satiety and encouraging the diner to eat more.

At the more elegant restaurants, the traditional shot has been replaced by a serving of sorbet topped with Calvados.

DOS & DON'TS

■ In France it is not customary to rest one hand on your lap while eating. Both hands should be visible.

■ 'Doggie bags' are also not customary but are tolerated in larger establishments with a large tourist clientele.

■ Many French people seem to feel that 'going Dutch' (ie splitting the bill) at restaurants is an uncivilised custom. In general, the person who did the inviting pays for dinner, though close friends and colleagues will sometimes share the cost.

And a few don'ts:

■ When buying fruit, vegetables or flowers anywhere except at supermarkets, do not touch the produce or blossoms unless invited to do so. Show the shopkeeper what you want and they will choose for you.

■ In a restaurant, do not summon the waiter by shouting 'garçon', which means 'boy'. Saying 's'il vous plaît' (please) is the way it's done nowadays.

■ When you're being served cheese (eg as the final course for dinner), remember two cardinal rules: never cut off the tip of the pie-shaped soft cheeses (such as Brie or Camembert); and cut cheese whose middle is the best part (eg blue cheese) in such a way as to take your fair share of the crust.

BREAKFAST

In the continental tradition, the French start the day with a *petit déjeuner* (breakfast) usually consisting of a croissant and a light bread roll with butter and jam, accompanied by a *café au lait* (coffee with lots of hot milk), a small black coffee or hot chocolate. Buying rolls or pastries from a patisserie (cake and pastry shop) is an alternative to eating at your hotel or a café.

LUNCH & DINNER

For many Breton people, especially in rural areas, lunch is still the main meal of the day. Restaurants will generally serve lunch between noon and 2pm or 2.30pm, and dinner from 7pm or 7.30pm to sometime between 9.30pm and 10.30pm. Very few restaurants (except for brasseries, cafés and fast-food places) are open between lunch and dinner, and most are closed on Sunday.

Cuisine Grandmere: From Brittany, Normandy, Picardy and Flanders by Jenny Baker. Recipes and practical tips from the north of France.

Desserts

The best-known Norman dessert is the scrumptious *tarte normande*, a kind of apple pie with no top crust. The apples are sometimes cooked in cider and the tart may be served with warm cream. In Yport, a similar dish called *tarte au sucre* is served. By all means try to sample *tergoule*, sometimes called *terrinée*, a delicious concoction made from rice, sugar, milk and cinnamon, subjected to a long bake in the oven. Sailors' wives invented the dish in Honfleur when their husbands brought back cinnamon from their travels to exotic destinations. The dessert is often enjoyed with *falue*, which is an egg-based bread. You also might find *bourdelots* or *douillons*, apples or pears encased in pastry, on the dessert menus of the region. Other dessert delicacies include the *sablés* (a round, crumbly pastry) and *fouaces* (hearth cake) of Caen and the *sucre de pomme* (apple sweet) of Rouen.

Sweet treats from Brittany include crepes, Breton cake *kouign amann* and *far Breton* (also see p51).

Menus

Most restaurants offer at least one fixed-price, multicourse meal known in French as a *menu*, *menu à prix fixe* or *menu du jour* (menu of the day). A *menu* (not to be confused with a *carte*, the French equivalent of the English word 'menu') almost always costs much less than ordering a la carte. In some places, you may also be able to order a *formule*, which usually has fewer choices but allows you to pick two out of three courses. In many restaurants, the lunch *menus* are a much better deals than the equivalent those available at dinner.

When you order a three-course *menu*, you usually get to choose a starter, such as salad, pâté or soup; a main dish – several meat, poultry or fish dishes, including the *plat du jour* (dish of the day) are generally on offer; and one or more final courses (usually cheese or dessert).

Boissons (drinks), including wine, cost extra unless the menu says *boisson comprise* (drink included), in which case you may get a beer or a glass of mineral water. If the *menu* says *vin compris* (wine included), you'll probably be served a small *pichet* (jug) of wine. The waiter will always ask if you would like coffee to end the meal but this will almost always cost extra.

COOKING COURSES

You can learn how to prepare fine Norman (and French) dishes at the following places:

On Rue Tatin (www.susanloomis.com) English-language cooking lessons held in Louviers.
La Manoir de L'Aufragère (www.laufragere.com) Also in English, this course is offered in a Norman farmhouse.

On Rue Tatin: Living and Cooking in a French Town by Susan Herrmann Loomis. This journalist-cook recounts her life and cuisine in Louviers (see Cooking Courses)

EAT YOUR WORDS

For pronunciation guidelines, see the Language chapter, p346.

Useful Phrases

A table for two, please. — *Une table pour deux, s'il vous plaît.*
  ewn ta·bler poor der seel voo play
Do you have a menu in English? — *Est-ce que vous avez la carte en anglais?*
  es·ker voo za·vay la kart on ong·lay
What's the speciality here? — *Quelle est la spécialité ici?*
  kel ay ler spay·sya·lee·tay ees·ee
I'd like the dish of the day. — *Je voudrais avoir le plat du jour.*
  zher voo·dray a·vwar ler pla doo zhoor
I'd like the set menu. — *Je prends le menu.*
  zher pron ler mer·new
I'm a vegetarian. — *Je suis végétarien/végétarienne.(m/f)*
  zher swee vay·zhay·ta·ryun/vay·zhay·ta·ryen
I'd like to order the... — *Je voudrais commander ...*
  zher voo·dray ko·mon·day
The bill, please. — *La note, s'il vous plaît.*
  la not seel voo play

Menu Decoder

agneau de pré-salé – salt-meadow lamb
bar de ligne au sel de Guérand – line-caught sea bass baked in a salt crust
blanquette de veau/d'agneau – veal/lamb stew with white sauce
bonhomme normande – duck in a cider and cream sauce
Calvados – apple brandy
canard flambé au Calvados – duck with Calvados

confit de canard/d'oie – duck/goose preserved and cooked in its own fat
croque-monsieur – grilled ham and cheese sandwich
entrées chaudes – warm starter
entrées froides – cold starter
galantines – cold dishes of boned, stuffed, pressed meat (especially pork) presented in its own jelly, often with truffles and pistachio nuts
huîtres plates – flat or native oysters
marmite Dieppoise – fish soup from Dieppe
pommeau – aperitif made from partially fermented apple juice to which Calvados is added
poulet vallée d'Auge – chicken in cream and cider
quenelles – dumplings made of a finely sieved mixture of cooked fish or (rarely) meat
salade Fécampoise – salad of potatoes, smoked herring and eggs
sandwich garni – filled sandwich
sole à la normande – sole with mussels, shrimps and mushrooms
tripes à la mode de Caen – a heavily spiced tripe stew

Lonely Planet's *World Food France* shares the secret ingredients behind regional dishes.

English–French Glossary

BASICS

breakfast	le petit déjeuner	**poultry**	volaille
lunch	le déjeuner	**game**	gibier
dinner	le dîner	**dessert**	dessert
vegetable	légume	**grocery store**	l'épicerie
fish	poisson	**chip shop**	friture
meat	viande		

MEAT

beef	bœuf	**large sausage**	saucisson
black pudding	boudin noir	**liver**	foie
boar	marcassin	**mutton**	mouton
brains	cervelle	**pheasant**	faisan
cooked/prepared meats	charcuterie	**pork**	porc
		pork belly	poitrine de porc
chicken	poulet	**rabbit**	lapin
duck	canard	**rib steak**	entrecôte
guinea fowl	pintade	**snail**	escargot
ham on the bone	jambonneau	**tongue**	langue
ham	jambon	**turkey**	dinde
horse	cheval	**veal**	veau
kebab	brochette	**venison**	cerf
lamb	agneau		

FISH & SEAFOOD

anchovy	anchois	**oyster**	huître
bream	brème	**prawn**	scampi
clam	palourde	**ray**	raie
cod (fresh)	cabillaud	**red mullet**	rouget
cod (salted)	morue	**salmon**	saumon
crab	crabe	**scallop**	coquille St-Jacques
crayfish	langouste	**sea bream**	daurade
eel	anguille	**shrimp**	crevette
herring	hareng	**sole**	sole
lobster	homard	**squid**	calmar
mackerel	maquereau	**trout**	truite
monkfish	lotte	**tuna**	thon
mussel	moule		

VEGETABLES

artichoke	artichaut	**leek**	poireau
asparagus	asperge	**mushroom**	champignon
avocado	avocat	**olive**	olive
bean	haricot	**onion**	oignon
Brussels sprouts	choux de Bruxelles	**parsley**	persil
cabbage	chou	**peas**	petit pois
capsicum (red/	poivron rouge/vert	**potato**	pomme de terre
green pepper)		**pumpkin**	citrouille
carrot	carotte	**shallot**	échalote
celery	céleri	**spinach**	épinards
chicory	chicon	**sweet corn**	maïs
cucumber	concombre	**truffle**	truffe
eggplant	aubergine	**zucchini**	courgette
garlic	ail		

STAPLES

bread	pain	**pepper**	poivre
butter	beurre	**rice**	riz
cheese	fromage	**salt**	sel
egg	œuf	**sugar**	sucre
goat's cheese	fromage de chèvre	**vinegar**	vinaigre
jam	confiture	**wholemeal or**	galette
milk	lait	**buckwheat**	
olive oil	huile d'olive	**pancake**	

DESSERTS

apple cooked in pastry	bourdelot
apple tart	tarte normande
cake	gâteau
flan with prunes	far
ice cream	glace
jelly	gelée
pancake	crêpe (sweet); galette (savoury)
pear cooked in pastry	douillon
sweet apple dessert	sucre de pomme
sweet, cinnamon-flavoured rice pudding	teurgoule
tart (pie)	tarte
waffle	gaufre

COOKING METHODS

baked	au four
browned on top with cheese	gratiné
coated in breadcrumbs	pané
cooked over a wood stove	au feu de bois
grilled	grillé
in pastry	en croûte
roasted	rôti
sautéed	sauté
smoked	fumé
spit-roasted	à la broche
steamed	à la vapeur
stuffed	farci
with a cream or butter sauce	à la normande

DRINKS

beer	bière
caffeinated coffee	un décaféiné or déca
cider	cidre
espresso with just a dash of milk	noisette
espresso with milk or cream	café crème
espresso	un café/espresso
fizzy, carbonated	gazeuse
herbal tea	tisane/infusion
hot chocolate	chocolat chaud
hot milk with a little coffee	café au lait
iced water with lemon and sugar	citron pressé
milk	lait
squash, fruit syrup	sirop
water	eau
wine	vin

Brittany

RICHARD MILLS

Ille-et-Vilaine

CONTENTS

Mont St-Michel	**68**
Around Mont St-Michel	**71**
Avranches	71
Pontorson	72
Dol de Bretagne	73
Côte d'Émeraude	**74**
Cancale	74
Pointe du Grouin	75
St-Malo	75
Dinard	81
St-Lunaire	85
St-Briac-sur-Mer	85
Eastern Brittany	**85**
Rennes	85
Around Rennes	89
Fougères	91
Vitré	92
Around Vitré	93

Ille-et-Vilaine marks the interface between Brittany and France proper. Indeed, Mont St-Michel, this chapter's main must-see feature, lies just over the border, in neighbouring Normandy. But you'll find such manmade divisions irrelevant as you explore the Côte d'Émeraude (Emerald Coast), which nudges westwards into the neighbouring *département* of Côtes d'Armor. Here, peninsulas and promontories offer spectacular sea views while at their feet, rocky reefs and islets are fringed with golden sands, emerald-green shallows and aquamarine depths.

If, like summertime thousands, you arrive by ferry from the UK at St-Malo, pause to explore the narrow streets of Intra-Muros, the old quarter, its massive granite buildings almost entirely reconstructed after the devastation of WWII. The short drive eastwards to Cancale, famous for its oyster beds, is a must for all seafood scoffers.

Westwards, across the Rance estuary (do take the scenic passenger ferry across its mouth if you're travelling light) lies the chic seaside resort of Dinard with its casino, select beaches and distinctive striped bathing tents. Prefer somewhere quieter for the kids? Then the smaller resorts of St-Briac or St-Lunaire could be for you.

It would be something of a shame if, like many travellers, you stuck only to the coast. The interior, a region of fertile farmland and gently rolling countryside and the one-time frontier between Brittany and France, has a couple of imposing defensive castles at Fougères and Vitré, while Rennes, the *département* capital, is a bustling university city with an attractive old quarter.

HIGHLIGHTS

- Catch **Mont St-Michel** (p68) surrounded by water at high tide

- Shuck and slurp down a dozen oysters from Cancale's **marché aux huîtres** (p74)

- Circle the 17th-century ramparts of St-Malo's **walled old city** (p77)

- Cruise up the **River Rance** (p82) to the medieval city of Dinan

- Relax on Dinard's swanky **Grand Plage** (p82)

- Walk the towpath on the **Ille-et-Rance Canal** (p89) near Hédé, north of Rennes

- Browse the second-hand bookshops of **Bécherel** (p90)

- Patrol the walls of Fougères' magnificent **fortress** (p91)

POPULATION: 867,500	AREA: 6775 SQ KM

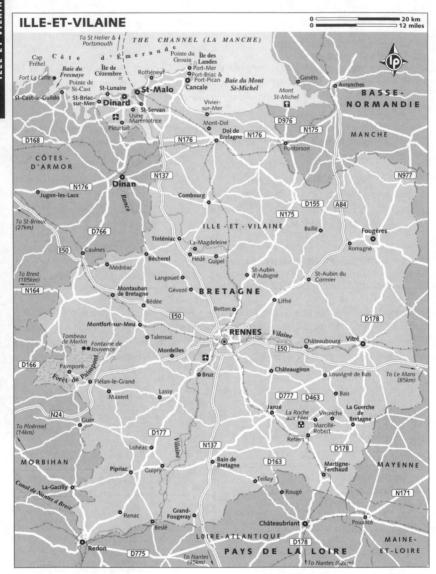

MONT ST-MICHEL

pop 55

Administratively speaking, Mont St-Michel falls in Normandy, not Brittany. We include it here because its history is as much Breton as Norman – and because it's an easily ac-

cessible and popular day trip from St-Malo, Rennes, or, if you have wheels, towns and coastal resorts even further west.

There are few sights in France as inspiring as its pinnacled Gothic pyramid, piercing the mists of an autumn morning or reflected in the rippling waters of the advancing tide. The downside is that, just like the pilgrim sites of old, Mont St-Michel is also one of France's biggest tourist traps. Its single street is lined with shoddy souvenir shops whose vendors maintain a longstanding tradition from the time when medieval merchants would sell fake relics to the faithful. The Mont's genuine spiritual and architectural attractions are best appreciated in the early morning or low season, when the crowds – the Mont receives over three million visitors each year, the majority in high summer – have thinned and a semblance of peace has returned.

History

In 708 the Archangel Michael appeared in a vision to the Bishop of Avranches. Within decades, the oratory that he ordered to be built on the island of Mont St-Michel had become a place of pilgrimage. Richard I, duke of Normandy, installed Benedictine monks there in AD 966; their simple Romanesque church was replaced with a magnificent, fortified Gothic abbey, constructed from the 13th to 16th centuries. After the monks were evicted during the anticlerical excesses of the French Revolution – when it was renamed Mont Libre (Free Mountain) – the Mont served as a prison until 1863. Listed as a historic monument, its restoration began under Napoleon III and in 1966 the abbey was symbolically returned to the Benedictine order; a small monastic community now lives there. In 1979 Mont St-Michel became one of the earliest entries on Unesco's list of World Heritage Sites.

Shifting Sands

Mont St-Michel is a tidal island, surrounded by the vast sandbanks that fill the Baie du Mont St-Michel. At low tide, the sea can be up to 12km away. The Mont is only surrounded by water for a couple of hours, around the time of high water during the highest tides (specifically, when the height of the tide, as given in tide tables available from the tourist office, rises above 12m).

Since the building of the causeway and the canalisation of the River Couësnon in the 19th century, the area around Mont St-Michel has been silting up; one million cubic metres of sediment are deposited each year. The shoreline is advancing and, if nothing is done, Mont St-Michel will soon become part of the mainland, like Mont-Dol (see Dol de Bretagne, p73).

In 1995, action was initiated to combat the build up of sand. The first step was a research programme into the tidal currents and deposition patterns of the Baie du Mont St-Michel. Now, a massive €107 million project is under way, with the ambitious aim of emulating King Canute on the grand scale, by altering the tidal flow around the island so that the deposition of sand is reduced and, it's hoped, even reversed. The causeway, and the car parks outside the Mont that detract from the grandeur of the setting, will be replaced by a low bridge, beneath which the tidal currents can flow and eddy. There'll be a massive new car park about 2.5km south of the Mont and a shuttle will carry visitors to the island. The bridge will also have a boardwalk so that you can stroll out if you wish. The planned admission charge of about €5 per person will include use of the car park and travel on the shuttle. Work is due to be completed in 2009; in the meantime, the Mont remains accessible. The project website (www.projetmontsaintmichel.fr) details progress and plans.

Orientation

Mont St-Michel is a tiny, tidal island, barely 300m in diameter and a kilometre in circumference, linked to the mainland by a 2km causeway (soon to be a bridge; see above). A single gateway, the Porte de l'Avancée, gives access to the Mont's single street, Grande Rue, lined with souvenir shops and places to eat. The nearest town is Pontorson, on the mainland 9km to the south.

Information

The **tourist office** (☎ 02 33 60 14 30; www.ot-mont saintmichel.com; ☼ 9am-7pm Jul & Aug, 9am-noon & 2-5.30pm Sep-Jun) is just to the left as you enter the Porte de l'Avancée.

Sights
GRANDE RUE

The tiny island has only one small street, **Grande Rue**, leading up to the abbey. Flanked by gabled and half-timbered houses – now the home to a racket of souvenir emporia – it heaves with humanity from June to September. To your right as you enter the Porte de l'Avancée are a pair of huge **cannons**, abandoned by the invading English in 1434 after they unsuccessfully tried to capture Mont St-Michel during the Hundred Years' War.

Of the several **'museums'** (adult/child per museum €4/2) you pass, two might merit a visit. Children may find the **Archéoscope,** a smart 20-minute multimedia history of the Mont with lights, video and even smoke, as exciting as the actual bricks and mortar. The **Musée de la Mer et de l'Écologie** is informative about Mont St-Michel's complex tidal patterns and warrants a visit if model ships excite you.

ABBAYE DU MONT ST-MICHEL

The Mont's main attraction is its famous **abbey** (☎ 02 33 89 80 00; adult/18-25/under 18 €7/4.50/free, incl 1hr guided tour; ✆ 9am-7pm May-Sep, 9.30am-6pm Oct-Apr). Once inside, you are able to wander around the public parts of the abbey at will (ask for the English version of the guide pamphlet), but it's well worth taking the guided tour (tours in English are held three to eight times daily, depending on the season). Another way of visiting at your own pace is to hire an **audioguide** (€4). For a more scholarly insight into the abbey and monastic life, sign on for the two-hour **visite conférence** (lecture tour, French only; adult/12-25/under 12 €4/3/free; ✆ 10.30am, 11.30am, 2pm & 3pm Jul & Aug, 10.30am & 2pm Sat, Sun Sep-Jun), which also visits parts of the building not covered in the ordinary tour.

To see the abbey under a very different light and in relative tranquillity, plan your day – or rather, night – to take in **Les Songes** (adult/12-25/under 12 €10/7/free; ✆ 9pm-12.30am Mon-Sat Jul & Aug), when you can wander around the illuminated abbey to soft music.

The **Église Abbatiale** (Abbey Church) was built on the island's rocky summit. The crossing (the intersection of the nave and the transepts) rests on solid rock while the nave, choir and transepts are supported by massive vaults. The church is a fairly harmonious mix of architectural styles: the nave and south transept (11th and 12th centuries) are Romanesque whereas the choir (late 15th century) is Flamboyant Gothic.

The buildings on the north side of the Mont are known collectively as **La Merveille** (The Marvel). The intimate **cloister** is surrounded by a double row of delicately sculpted arches resting on granite columns. The **refectory**, barrel vaulted with wooden panels, like the church, is illuminated by a series of recessed windows. The Gothic **guest hall**, dating from 1203, retains two huge fireplaces. The **Chapelle de Notre Dame Sous Terre** (Chapel of Our Lady Underground), one of the oldest parts of the abbey, was only rediscovered in 1903. What looks like a treadmill for giant gerbils is, in fact, a hoist – turned by prisoners in the days when the abbey was a jail – to haul up provisions.

TURNING TIDES

Although there's a high and low tide in the bay each day, the water must reach a level of at least 12m to be perceptible in Mont St-Michel, which only occurs 15 or 16 days a month. The gravitational pull of the sun and moon cause the tides. When the sun, moon and earth are aligned, the tides are at their highest; when they are at right angles, tides are lowest. The tides reach their peak twice a month during the full-moon and new-moon periods, but the most impressive 15m tides only occur twice a year: around the full-moon period of the vernal equinox (around 21 March) and the new-moon period of the autumnal equinox (around 23 September).

For the first six months of the year the highest tides are around the full-moon period. They increase with each full moon until they reach a peak during the full-moon period around the vernal equinox. Thereafter the full-moon tides decrease and the new-moon tides increase until the summer solstice (21 June), when the highest tide is at the new-moon period. For the last six months of the year high tides increase around the new moon until they peak near the autumnal equinox. Then the new-moon tides decrease and the full-moon tides increase until the winter solstice (21 December), when you have the highest tides at the full moon.

For a traveller who wants to experience the high tides of the Baie, the best plan is to come during the full-moon period of the vernal equinox or the new-moon period of the autumnal equinox. The next best plan is to come during the full-moon period during the first six months of the year or the new-moon period the rest of the year. Otherwise, come during the full- or new-moon period any time of the year. To be precise, the days you're targeting are 36 to 48 hours after the full or new moons.

Other Sights & Activities

If you want to feel the sand between your toes and approach the Mont at pilgrim pace, sign on for a 4½- to five-hour walk across the sand flats; it is led by a qualified guide. Organised by two local companies on most days between late April and October, **walks** (adult/child €5.50/4) set out from Genêts, 5km west of Avranches, departure time depending upon the day's tides. Dress code: shorts and bare feet. Also pack a snack and maybe an anorak for the wind chill. For details and reservations, contact **Chemins de la Baie** (☎ 02 33 89 80 88; www.cheminsdelabaie.fr - French only; 14 place des Halles, Genêts) or **La Maison du Guide** (☎ 02 33 70 83 49; www.decouvertebaie.com - French only; 1 rue Montoise, Genêts).

The **Maison de la Baie** (see p74) at Vivier-sur-Mer, west of Mont St-Michel, also has a varied programme of walks, including a tramp across the sands to the Mont.

You won't be able to canter right up to the Mont on your steed like a latter-day knight, but you *can* have a lovely trot across the salt meadows with some wonderful views of the island in a posse organised by the **Centre Équestre La Tanière** (☎ 02 33 58 13 53; randobaie@aol.com; route de Mont St-Michel, Moidrey; 2hr/half day €35/46).

Sleeping & Eating

There are eight hotels within the walls of Mont St-Michel and several more at the end of the causeway. All tend to be fully booked in summer, often by large coach parties. We recommend that you beat a retreat to somewhere – such as Pontorson or St-Malo – that's less seething.

The tourist restaurants around the base of the Mont have lovely views, but they aren't bargains; *menus* start at around €13. Cosy **Crêperie La Siréne** (☎ 02 33 60 08 60; galettes €6.40-8.20) offers reasonable value.

La Mère Poulard (☎ 02 33 89 68 68; Grande Rue; lunch menus €29-39, dinner menus €45-55; ☺ 11am-10pm) Established in 1888, this tourist institution turns out its famous *omelettes à la Mère Poulard* (soufflé omelettes cooked in a wood-fired oven) at astronomical prices. Visiting film stars, politicians and business tycoons have left behind autographed photos that adorn the walls. The choices also include seafood, free-range chicken and *agneau pré-salé* (lamb from animals that have grazed the surrounding salt meadows).

Getting There & Away

Parking per vehicle costs €4.

The nearest train station is at Pontorson (see p73), 9km south of Mont St-Michel.

Courriers Bretons (☎ 02 99 19 70 70) operates between Mont St-Michel and Pontorson (€1.70, 15 minutes, seven to 10 daily) and also to/from St-Malo (€9.20, 1½ hours, up to four daily).

AROUND MONT ST-MICHEL

Avranches and Pontorson, both nominally in Normandy, feature here in our guide since their history and current prosperity are closely related to Mont St-Michel's.

AVRANCHES
pop 9250

The history of Avranches, perched on a high granite spur that is overlooking Baie du Mont St-Michel, is closely intertwined with that of the mount itself, 19km southwest across the bay. It was Bishop Aubert of Avranches who ordered the first oratory to be built on Mont St-Michel early in the 8th century. Today, Avranches holds the abbey's rich repository of manuscripts and documents.

In 1172, the English king Henry II submitted himself to public flagellation outside the cathedral as penance for having ordered the murder of Thomas à Becket, archbishop of Canterbury. The cathedral has long since crumbled but a plaque marks the spot.

The town, which was the last barrier to the Allied advance into Brittany and southern Normandy, also witnessed General George S Patton's 'Avranches breakthrough' of 31 July 1944 (see p26).

Orientation & Information

Avranches' compact town centre is located at the northern end of rue de la Constitution, its main street. The **tourist office** (☎ 02 33 58 00 22; www.ville-avranches.fr; 2 rue Général de Gaulle; ☺ 9.30am-12.30pm & 2-7pm daily Jun-Sep, 9.30am-12.30pm & 2-6pm Mon-Fri, 10am-12.30pm & 2.30-5pm Sat Oct-May) is just off place Littré in the town centre.

The train station is 1km northwest of the town centre.

Sights

Basilique St-Gervais (place St-Gervais) houses the rich **Trésor St-Gervais** (adult/12-25/under 25 €1.55/0.80/free; 9.30am-12.30pm & 2-6pm Jun-Sep). This is a precious collection of liturgical objects and robes. More immediately attention-grabbing is the skull of Bishop Aubert, poked through (so it's said) by the penetrating finger of St Michael, who grew weary of trying to persuade the procrastinating bishop to build an oratory in his name ('for heaven's sake, *listen* to me, Aubert!').

The **Bibliothèque du Fond Anciens** (02 33 89 29 49; place Littré; admission €3.05; 10am-6pm Jul & Aug, 10am-noon & 2-6pm Jun & Sep), the town hall library – also a stone's throw from the tourist office – has a priceless collection of illuminated manuscripts from Mont St-Michel's abbey. Exquisitely illustrated, they date from the 8th to the 15th centuries and treat both religious and temporal themes. Because of their fragility, only 30 of the more than 200 manuscripts are displayed at a time. In 2006, the collection is scheduled to move to premises that better reflect its worth – the **Centre du Livre Manuscrit** (place d'Estouteville).

The most interesting feature of the **Musée Municipal d'Avranches** (02 33 58 25 15; place Jean de St-Avit; adult/12-25/under 25 €2.30/1.25/free; 10am-12.30pm & 2-6pm Jun-Sep), near the tourist office, is its reconstruction of a monastic studio that explains how the illuminated manuscripts of Mont St-Michel were created. It also displays furniture, clothes and *objets d'art* from the 19th century, plus vestiges of the former cathedral.

You can buy a **combined ticket** (adult/12-25/under 25 €4.60/2.30/free), which is valid for all three sites.

The site of the old cathedral where Henry II did penance is marked by a **platform** surrounded by a chain. Heading out to the west on rue d'Office, it is one block north of the tourist office.

General Patton's vital 'Avranches breakthrough' is commemorated by a monument and WWII tank on **place Patton**. It's a small slice of American territory; the earth was brought over from the USA.

For a wonderful view of Baie du Mont St-Michel head to **Le Jardin des Plantes**, only 200m southwest of the tourist office, and at the same time savour the rich variety of rare plants and trees.

Sleeping & Eating

Hôtel La Renaissance (02 33 58 03 71; 17 rue des Fossés; d/tr/q €28/33/38) is the town's cheapest option. The restaurant downstairs offers sandwiches, crepes and basic dishes.

Hôtel Le Jardin des Plantes (02 33 58 03 68; www.le-jardin-des-plantes.fr; 10 place Carnot; s/d with shower €26/28, d with bathroom €52-79) A Logis de France, this hotel occupies a large country house near the Jardin des Plantes. Rooms, varying in size, are cheerfully decorated in bright fabrics. Its elegant **restaurant** (menus €13.50-25.50; closed Sat-Sun Sep-Easter) is a favourite with locals.

Restaurant Le Littré (02 33 58 01 66; 8 rue Docteur Gilbert; menus €15-23; Tue-Sat) Beside place Littré, *menus* are short and simple and the dishes equally uncomplicated. But, whether you dine in the cosy bar or the more plush surroundings of its dining room, you'll eat very well indeed at this much-garlanded restaurant.

Getting There & Away

The bus station is beside the tourist office. **STN** (02 33 58 03 07) connects Avranches with Granville (one hour, four to six daily) and, in summer only, Mont St-Michel (35 minutes, one daily). **Courriers Bretons** (02 33 60 11 43) runs to/from Pontorson (€4.40, 30 minutes, one to four daily), where there are connections to Rennes and St-Malo.

Avranches is on the Caen–Rennes line. Northbound, infrequent trains run to Caen (€18.40, 1¾ hours) via Coutances (40 minutes) and Bayeux (1½ hours). Southbound, they serve Rennes (€13.20, 50 minutes) via Pontorson (15 minutes).

PONTORSON

pop 4200

Pontorson, with its wider variety of accommodation options, makes an attractive base for travellers visiting Mont St-Michel, 9km north.

Orientation & Information

Route D976 from Mont St-Michel runs right into Pontorson's main thoroughfare, rue du Couësnon.

The **tourist office** (02 33 60 20 65; www.mont-saint-michel-baie.com - French only; place de l'Église; 9am-noon & 2-6pm Mon-Fri, 10am-noon & 3-6pm Sat Sep-Jun, longer hours plus 10am-noon Sun Jul & Aug), beside the town hall, has **Internet** (per hr €8).

Sights & Activities

The 12th-century **Église Notre Dame de Pontor-son**, although no match for its flamboyant sister to the north, is a good example of Norman Romanesque ecclesiastical architecture. To the left of the main altar is a 15th-century **relief** depicting the life of Christ in 22 panels. Mutilated during the Wars of Religion (1562–98) and again during the Revolution, every one of its figures has been decapitated. To illuminate it, press the switch beside the sacristy door, just to the left.

Sleeping & Eating

Camping Haliotis – no, it's not the Breton for bad breath – (☎ 02 33 68 11 59; www.camping -haliotis-mont-saint-michel.com - French only; adult/pitch €4.20/3.50; ⊗ Apr-Oct; ⊛) Just off blvd Général Patton, this complex has a heated pool.

Centre Duguesclin (☎ 02 33 60 18 65; aj@ville -pontorson.fr; blvd Général Patton; dm €8.40; ⊗ year-round) About 1km northwest of the train station, this modern, renovated HI-affiliated youth hostel has self-catering facilities.

Hôtel l'Arrivée (☎ 02 33 60 01 57; 14 rue Docteur Tizon; r from €15.40, with shower from €21, with bathroom from €35; ⊗ closed Mon Sep-Jun) Across place de la Gare from the train station, the Arrivée is an economical option with a bar/restaurant below. Hall showers are extra.

Hôtel La Tour Brette (☎ 02 33 60 10 69; latourbrette@ wanadoo.fr; 8 rue du Couësnon; d €30 Sep-Jun, €35 Jul & Aug; P) A Logis de France that's an excellent deal. Rooms, all with bathroom, are as cheerful as the staff and there's free parking. It also runs a splendid **restaurant** (menus €10-25).

Hôtel La Cave (☎ 02 33 60 11 35; www.hotel-la -cave.com; 37 rue Libération; basic rooms €28, with shower €32, with bathroom €39-44; P) A small and welcoming family hotel, bedecked with flowers. The **restaurant** (menus €11-22) too has a range of tempting dishes.

Hôtel de Bretagne (☎ 02 33 60 10 55; www.le bretagnepontorson.com; 59 rue du Couësnon; s €35-48, d €39-64) Another attractive, mid-range Logis de France option. Rooms are brighter than its rather dreary reception area might have you believe. Its restaurant, more formal than those of its competitors, offers excellent service and food, ranging from its *formule deux plats* (two courses; €11) to a gourmet *menu* at €38.

Hôtel Montgomery (☎ 02 33 60 00 09; www.hotel -montgomery.com; 13 rue du Couësnon; s €46-52, d €75-83; P ☐) The Montgomery is in a gorgeous

16th-century townhouse that retains many of its original features, including several Renaissance frescoes. Each room is individually and tastefully decorated and the **restaurant**, open exclusively to hotel guests, will tempt the most serious dieter.

You'll find a few cheap, but unexceptional eateries along main rue du Couësnon but if you're looking for anything in any way special, choose a hotel restaurant.

Getting There & Around

Courriers Bretons (☎ 02 33 60 11 43) buses run between Pontorson and Mont St-Michel (€1.70, 15 minutes, seven to 10 daily) and also to/from St-Malo (€7.80, one hour).

Train services to/from Pontorson include Caen (2¼ hours, two daily) via Folligny, Rennes (one hour, two daily) via Dol, Coutances (55 minutes, three daily) and Cherbourg (2½ hours, two daily). For Paris via the TGV, change in Rennes.

You can rent **bicycles** – a great way to approach Mont St-Michel – from **Couësnon Motoculture** (☎ 02 33 60 11 40; 1 bis rue du Couësnon), **Camping Haliotis** (☎ 02 33 68 11 59; off blvd Général Patton) and **VMPS** (☎ 02 33 60 28 76, 06 86 90 95 01). VMPS delivers to your hotel or camp site. For a **taxi**, call ☎ 02 33 60 33 23.

DOL DE BRETAGNE

pop 4550

Dol de Bretagne, seat of a former bishopric founded in the 6th century by St Samson, became the religious capital of the region in 848, under Nominöe, the first king of Brittany. It's now a charming, somewhat sleepy town, dominated by its massive cathedral.

Orientation & Information

Grande Rue des Stuarts, which is the main street in the old town, lies a block south of the cathedral and has some fine half-timbered houses.

Dol's **tourist office** (☎ 02 99 48 15 37; 3 Grande Rue des Stuarts; ⊗ 10am-7pm Jul & Aug, 2.30-6.30pm Mon, 10am-12.30pm & 2.30-6.30pm Tue-Sat Sep-Jun) has an Internet point.

Sights

The town's main attraction is its magnificent granite **Cathédrale St-Samson** (place de la Cathédrale; ⊗ 9am-noon & 2-6pm). Almost 100m long and 20m high, the cathedral dates largely from the 13th century, when it was rebuilt after having been torched by the army of King John of England in 1203. There's a magnificently wrought flamboyant porch on the south side, its impact marred by some incongruous 19th-century bas-reliefs. This adornment apart, it seems from the outside as much fortress as church; inside, the soaring Gothic vaults stand witness to the skill of its builders. The stained-glass windows in the choir, Brittany's oldest, date from the late 13th century.

Immediately south of the cathedral in the former bishop's palace is the **Cathédraloscope** (☎ 02 99 48 35 30; place de la Cathédrale; adult/child €6.60/ 4.30; ☺ 10am-12.30pm & 1.30-7pm Apr-Oct), which depicts the history, technology, craftsmanship and symbolism of cathedral building in Europe. Ask for an English translation at reception.

It's well worth driving or hiking the 2km north to **Mont-Dol**, a 65m high, flat-topped hill. Like Mont St-Michel, it was once an island; unlike crowded Mont St-Michel, you'll be almost alone to enjoy the superb view over the surrounding countryside.

The **Maison de la Baie** (☎ 02 99 48 84 38; www .maison-baie.com - French only; Port le Vivier; ☺ year-round), at Vivier-sur-Mer, 7km north of Dol has a permanent **exhibition** (adult/child €2.5/free) about the complex ecology of the Baie du Mont St-Michel. There's a varied programme of **guided coastal walks** (€9 to €13, 8 to 15km, four to six hours).

Getting There & Away
Dol is served by both train and bus from St-Malo and Rennes (see p80 and p89 for details).

CÔTE D'ÉMERAUDE

The beautiful Côte d'Émeraude (Emerald Coast) stretches west from the oyster beds of Cancale to the broad beaches of Pléneuf-Val-André. Its tempting coastline of rocky reefs and islets fringed with golden sand, emerald-green shallows and aquamarine depths.

CANCALE
pop 5200
Cancale, a relaxed little fishing port 14km east of St-Malo, is famed for its *parcs à huîtres* (oyster beds). The town even has a

small museum dedicated to oyster farming and shellfish.

Orientation & Information
From the upper town, clustered around the church on Place de l'Église, rue du Port leads steeply downhill to the harbour at Port de la Houle. Quai Gambetta is to the right, quai Thomas to the left.

The **tourist office** (☎ 02 99 89 63 72; www.ville -cancale.fr; ☺ 9.30am-noon & 2-5pm Mon-Sat) is at the top of rue du Port. Startlingly uninformed – even about its own opening hours – it does, however, rent bicycles (per half-day/day from €8/11).

There's a tourist office **annexe** (☺ school holidays) on quai Gambetta in the wooden house where the fish auction takes place

Activities
The falling tide reveals banks of oyster beds off Port de la Houle. Each year, these beds produce around 4000 tonnes. That's one whole lot of oyster, yet it pales beside the 10,000 tonnes that were dredged from the sea annually in the early 20th century. Most sought-after – and more expensive – are the *huîtres plates* (flat oysters), native to the bay and cultivated in deeper water. More plentiful are the *huîtres creuses* (hollow oysters), originally imported from Brittany's western coast and recognisable by the crinkly shells.

You can take a guided tour of the oyster industry and visit the small museum at the **Ferme Marine** (Marine Farm; ☎ 02 99 89 69 99; Corniche de l'Aurore; adult/child €6.10/3.10; tours in English 2pm mid-Jun–mid-Sep, in French 11am, 3pm & 5pm mid-Jun– mid-Sep, 3pm Mon-Fri mid-Feb–mid-Jun & mid-Sep–Oct), southwest of the port.

The **marché aux huîtres** (oyster market) is a cluster of little stalls in the shadow of the Pointe des Crolles lighthouse. Oysters, numbered according to size and quality, cost from €2.50 per dozen for the smallest *huîtres creuses* (No 5) to as much as €20 for saucer-sized *plates de Cancale*.

An excellent **coastal walk** begins above rue des Parcs, just north of the lighthouse at Port de la Houle, and leads 7km north to Pointe du Grouin (opposite).

Sleeping
Camping Municipal Le Grouin (☎ 02 99 89 63 79; fax 02 99 89 96 31; Pointe du Grouin; 2 adults, tent & car

€11.20; ☯ Mar-Oct) This site is 6km north of Cancale near Pointe du Grouin, and has a view of the sea and overlooks a fine beach. There are several other camping grounds in the area.

Auberge de Jeunesse (☎ 02 99 89 62 62; cancale@fuaj.org; Port-Pican; dm €8.85; ☯ Nov-Sep). Cancale's HI-affiliated youth hostel is a large, chalet-style building overlooking the beach at Port-Pican, 3km north of the town. The bus from St-Malo to Cancale continues to Port-Pican. The hostel is a five-minute walk downhill from the bus stop.

Hôtel La Mère Champlain (☎ 02 99 89 60 04; 1 quai Thomas; d €30-45, with sea view €50-65) Rooms at this recently renovated hotel, on the corner at the foot of rue du Port, have great sea views. There's a nice restaurant deck, complete with crisp linen, heavy cutlery and waiters with black bow ties.

Eating

Cancale boasts over 50 restaurants, most of which specialise in – you've guessed it – oysters, starting at around €6.50 per dozen.

Le Surcouf (☎ 02 99 89 61 75; 7 quai Gambetta; menus €18-50, mains €19-24; ☯ closed Wed-Thu except Jul & Aug) Le Surcouf is among the best of the many quality seafood restaurants that line the waterfront.

Au Pied d'Cheval (☎ 02 99 89 76 95; 10 quai Gambetta; ☯ 9am-9pm) This typically rustic little Breton place sells oysters direct from the farm. The prices are excellent – the *assiette du capitaine* (captain's plate) offers half a dozen oysters and a glass of Muscadet for €5.60, while the *super plateau* (mixed seafood platter) feeds two people for a bargain €30.50.

Getting There & Away

Buses stop behind the church on place Lucidas and at Port de la Houle, next to the pungent fish market. **Courriers Bretons** (☎ 02 99 19 70 70) and **TIV** (☎ 02 99 82 26 26) have year-round services to/from St-Malo (€3.80, 30 minutes). At least three Courriers Bretons buses daily continue to Port-Pican and Port-Mer, near Pointe du Grouin.

POINTE DU GROUIN

This nature reserve lies on a headland near Port-Mer at the tip of the wild, beautiful coast between Cancale and St-Malo. Cancale tourist office's free map covers the coastline

well. **Île des Landes**, just offshore, is home to a colony of giant black cormorants, whose wingspan can reach 170cm.

Via the GR34 coastal hiking trail, Pointe du Grouin is 7km from Cancale and 18km from St-Malo. By the D201 road, it's 4km from Cancale and 18km from St-Malo.

ST-MALO

pop 52,700

The port of St-Malo is one of Brittany's most popular tourist destinations. Squatting at the mouth of the River Rance, it is famed for its walled city, nearby beaches – and one of the world's highest tidal ranges.

History

The old walled city was originally an island, which became linked to the mainland by the sandy isthmus of Le Sillon in the 13th century. The 6th-century Welsh monk MacLow converted the locals to Christianity and later became their bishop. He was buried on the island, bequeathing his name to the town that grew up there.

Isolated and easily defended, the town of St-Malo grew to be fiercely independent. During the Wars of Religion in the late 16th century, the city even briefly declared itself an independent republic. This spirit was encapsulated in the adopted motto: 'Ni français, ni breton, malouin suis' ('Neither Frenchman, nor Breton, but of St-Malo am I').

St-Malo was a key port during the 17th and 18th centuries, serving as a base for both merchant ships and government-sanctioned pirates, known euphemistically as privateers. Although fortification began in the 12th century, the most imposing military architecture dates from the 17th and 18th centuries, when the English, the favourite targets of Malouin privateers, posed a constant threat. St-Malo was also the home port of La Grande Pêche à la Morue, the great cod fishery of the Grand Banks of Newfoundland (see the boxed text, p107).

During August 1944, the battle to drive the German forces out of St-Malo destroyed approximately 80% of the old city. The main historical monuments were faithfully reconstructed while the rest of the area was rebuilt in the style of the 17th and 18th centuries.

ILLE-ET-VILAINE

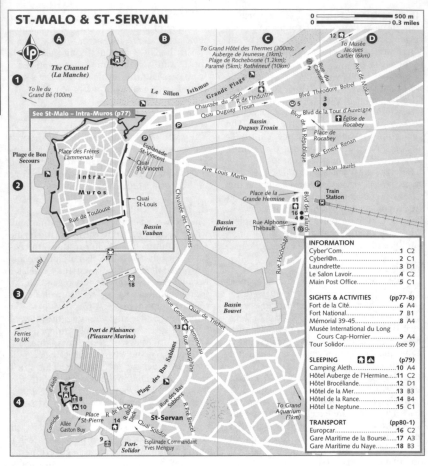

ST-MALO & ST-SERVAN

INFORMATION	
Cyber'Com	1 C2
Cyberl@n	2 C1
Laundrette	3 D1
Le Salon Lavoir	4 C2
Main Post Office	5 C1

SIGHTS & ACTIVITIES	(pp77-8)
Fort de la Cité	6 A4
Fort National	7 B1
Mémorial 39-45	8 A4
Musée International du Long Cours Cap-Hornier	9 A4
Tour Solidor	(see 9)

SLEEPING	(p79)
Camping Aleth	10 A4
Hôtel Auberge de l'Hermine	11 C2
Hôtel Brocéliande	12 D1
Hôtel de la Mer	13 B3
Hôtel de la Rance	14 B4
Hôtel Le Neptune	15 C1

TRANSPORT	(pp80-1)
Europcar	16 C2
Gare Maritime de la Bourse	17 A3
Gare Maritime du Naye	18 B3

Orientation

The St-Malo conurbation consists of the harbour towns of St-Malo and St-Servan plus the modern suburbs of Paramé and Rothéneuf to the east. The old walled city of St-Malo is known as Intra-Muros ('within the walls') or Ville Close. From the train station, it's a 15-minute walk west along ave Louis Martin.

Information

INTERNET ACCESS

Cyber'Com (Map p76; ☎ 02 99 56 05 83; 26 bis blvd des Talards; per hr €3.60; ☉ 9am-noon Tue, Wed, Fri & Sat, 2-6pm Mon-Sat)

Cyberl@n (Map p76; ☎ 02 99 56 07 78; 68 chaussée de Sillon; per hr €4; ☉ noon-1am Mon-Sat, 3pm-1am Sun)

LAUNDRY

Laundrette (Map p76; 25 blvd de la Tour d'Auvergne; ☉ 7.30am-9pm)

Le Salon Lavoir (Map p76; 20 blvd des Talards; ☉ 7am-9pm)

POST

Main Post Office (Map p76; 1 blvd de la Tour d'Auvergne)

Post Office **Annexe** (Map p77; old city)

TOURIST INFORMATION

Tourist Office (Map p77; ☎ 02 99 56 64 48; www.saint-malo-tourisme.com; esplanade St-Vincent; ☉ 9am-7.30pm Mon-Sat, 10am-6pm Sun Jul & Aug, 9am-12.30pm & 1.30-6.30pm Mon-Sat, 10am-12.30pm & 2.30-6pm Sun Easter-Jun & Sep, 9am-12.30pm & 1.30-6pm Mon-Sat Oct-Mar)

Sights & Activities
THE RAMPARTS
The narrow streets of St-Malo's old walled city can become claustrophobically over-crowded in summer. Escape to the **ramparts** (Map p76), constructed at the end of the 17th century to the designs of the great military architect Vauban, and which mostly survived the bombing of the town in 1944. You can make a complete circuit, a distance of around 2km; there's free access at several places, including all the main city gates.

From the northern stretch of the ram-parts, you can look across to the remains of **Fort National** (Map p76; ☎ 02 99 85 34 33; admission free; ☺ Jun-Sep). Accessible only at low tide, this fort was also designed by Vauban and long used as a prison.

INTRA-MUROS (WALLED CITY)   Map p77
The town's centrepiece is **Cathédrale St-Vincent** (place J de Châtillon; ☺ 9.30am-6pm). Constructed between the 12th and 18th centuries and severely damaged by the 1944 bombing; its rebuilding was completed in 1971 with the erection of a new spire. A mosaic **plaque** on

> ### COMBINED TICKET
>
> A **combined ticket** (adult/child €11.40/5.70) gives access to St-Malo's three major monu-ments: the Musée du Château de St-Malo, Musée International du Long Cours Cap-Hornier and Mémorial 39–45.

the floor of the nave marks the spot where Jacques Cartier knelt to receive the blessing of the bishop of St-Malo before his voyage of discovery to Canada in 1535 (see the boxed text, p78). Cartier's tomb – all that remains post-1944 is his head – is in a chapel on the north side of the choir. The striking modern bronze altar features the symbols of the four Apostles: a book (Matthew), lion (Mark), bull (Luke) and eagle (John). Beyond, the harlequin colours of the modern stained glass in the traceried windows of the east wall positively glow.

Within the **Château de St-Malo**, built by the dukes of Brittany in the 15th and 16th cen-turies, is the **Musée du Château** (☎ 02 99 40 71 57; adult/child €4.60/2.30; ☺ 10am-12.30pm & 2-6pm Apr-Sep,

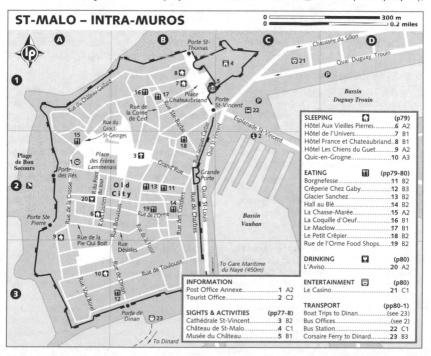

ST-MALO – INTRA-MUROS

0 — 300 m
0 — 0.2 miles

Bassin Duguay Trouin

Bassin Vauban

Chaussée du Sillon

Quai Duguay Trouin

Esplanade St-Vincent

Place Chateaubriand

Place des Frères Lammenais

Place du Grout-St-Georges

Plage de Bon Secours

Old City

Porte St-Thomas

Porte St-Vincent

Grande Porte

Porte Ste Pierre

Porte des Bés

Porte de Dinan

To Gare Maritime du Naye (450m)

To Dinan

SLEEPING	🛏	(p79)
Hôtel Aux Vieilles Pierres	6	A2
Hôtel de l'Univers	7	B1
Hôtel France et Chateaubriand	8	B1
Hôtel Les Chiens du Guet	9	A2
Quic-en-Grogne	10	A3

EATING	🍴	(pp79-80)
Borgnefesse	11	B2
Crêperie Chez Gaby	12	B3
Glacier Sanchez	13	B2
Hall au Blé	14	B2
La Chasse-Marée	15	A2
La Coquille d'Oeuf	16	B1
Le Maclow	17	B1
Le Petit Crêpier	18	B2
Rue de l'Orme Food Shops	19	B2

DRINKING	🍷	(p80)
L'Aviso	20	A2

INFORMATION		
Post Office Annexe	1	A2
Tourist Office	2	C2

SIGHTS & ACTIVITIES		(pp77-8)
Cathédrale St-Vincent	3	B2
Château de St-Malo	4	C1
Musée du Château	5	B1

ENTERTAINMENT	🎭	(p80)
Le Casino	21	C1

TRANSPORT		(pp80-1)
Boat Trips to Dinan	(see 23)	
Bus Offices	(see 2)	
Bus Station	22	C1
Corsaire Ferry to Dinard	23	B3

Tue-Sun Oct-Mar). The museum covers the history of the city and the St-Malo region. Its most interesting exhibits are in the Tour Générale – the history of cod fishing of the Grand Banks on the ground floor and the photos of St-Malo after WWII.

ÎLE DU GRAND BÉ

At low tide you can walk out to the rocky islet of **Île du Grand Bé**, to the west of the old city, and visit the tomb of the great French writer François-René de Chateaubriand. Access to the beach is via the Porte des Bés (Map p77), but be warned: when the tide comes in – much faster than you'd expect – the causeway remains impassable for about six hours. Check tide times with the tourist office.

ST-SERVAN   **Map p76**

The rocky peninsula of **St-Servan**, 1.5km south of Intra-Muros, was once the site of the Cité d'Aleth, the Gallo-Roman settlement Christianised by MacLow in the 6th century. Today the coastal suburb extends east around the harbour of **Port-Solidor** and along **Plage des Bas Sablons**. The peninsula is crowned by **Fort de la Cité**, built in the mid-18th century and used as a German base for several years during WWII. The bunkers flanking its walls were heavily scarred by the

---

CARTIER & CANADA

Jacques Cartier (1491–1557), one of St-Malo's most famous sons, was commissioned by King Francis I to make a voyage of discovery to North America in the hope of discovering gold, spices and a sea passage to Asia. He set sail in 1535 but found none of these things. However, during this and a second voyage in 1541, Cartier explored the St Lawrence River as far as Ottawa and laid the foundations for France's colonisation of Quebec and eastern Canada.

Jacques Cartier's manor house on his former estate in Rothéneuf, an eastern suburb of St-Malo, houses the **Musée Jacques Cartier** (☎ 02 99 40 97 73; rue David-MacDonald-Stewart, Limoelou, Rothéneuf; adult/child €4/3; ⏰ 10-11.30am & 2.30-6pm daily Jul & Aug, Mon-Sat Jun & Sep, guided visits 10am & 3pm Oct-May). The exhibits recall Cartier's great voyages of exploration, and the restored rooms evoke everyday life in the 16th century.

Allied shells in August 1944. One now hosts **Mémorial 39–45** (☎ 02 99 82 41 74; adult/child €4.60/2.30; guided visits 2pm, 3.15pm & 4.30pm Tue-Sun Apr-Jun & Sep-Mar, 6 times daily Jul & Aug). Through photos, documents, weapons and a 45-minute film in French, it depicts St-Malo's violent WWII history and liberation.

To the south, the 14th-century **Tour Solidor** dominates the bay. Within is the **Musée International du Long Cours Cap-Hornier** (Museum of the Cape Horn Route; ☎ 02 99 40 71 58; adult/child €4.60/2.30; ⏰ 10am-12.30pm & 2-6pm daily Apr-Sep, Tue-Sun Oct-Mar). This museum, a must for anyone who's felt even the most distant call of the sea, displays nautical instruments, ship models, and exhibits about the ships and sailors who followed the Cape Horn route from the 17th to early 20th centuries. The view from the top of the tower is superb.

The **Grand Aquarium** (☎ 02 99 21 19 00; ave Général Patton; adult/child €12.50/9; ⏰ at least 10am-6pm Feb-Dec) is about 4km south of the city centre, close to the main road to Dinard. This vast, modern complex, one of Europe's top aquariums, is an excellent wet-weather alternative for keeping kids amused. They will particularly enjoy the minisubmarine descent and *bassin tactile* (touch pool), where you can fondle rays, turbot – even a baby shark (don't fear for their fingers; it's small and not noticeably carnivorous!). Bus No 5, direction Grassinais, passes by every half hour.

BEACHES   **Map p76**

Just west of the old city walls is **Plage de Bon Secours**, which has a protected tidal pool for bathing. St-Servan's **Plage des Bas Sablons** has a cement wall that keeps the sea from receding completely at low tide. The **Grande Plage**, much larger, stretches northeast along the isthmus of Le Sillon; **Plage de Rochebonne** is another kilometre or so to the northeast. The walk from Grande Plage to Plage des Bas Sablons via the ramparts of the old city is particularly enjoyable at sunset.

BOAT TRIPS

Corsaire (☎ 02 23 18 15 15) runs ferries from just outside the Porte de Dinan (Map p77) to Îles Chausey (adult/child €25/15 return, 1½ hours, July and August), the Île Cézembre (€10.50/6, 20 minutes each way, April to September) and Dinan (one way/return €17.30/23, 2½ hours, May to September). For ferries to Dinard, see p81.

Sleeping

Camping Aleth (Map p76; ☎ 02 99 81 60 91; camping@ville-saint-malo.fr; allée Gaston Buy, St-Servan; 2 people, tent & car €10.80; ⌣ Apr-Sep) Camping Aleth (also spelt Alet), at the western tip of St-Servan is nearest to the old town. Next to Fort de la Cité, it enjoys an exceptional view in all directions. Take bus No 1 in July and August or No 6 year-round.

Auberge de Jeunesse (☎ 02 99 40 29 80; info@centrevarangot.com; 37 ave du Père Umbricht; dm €12.60-14.10, s €19-21.30, d €26-30.60, all incl breakfast) Choose the more expensive option for a considerably more luxurious stay than the usual hostel fare. St-Malo's HI-affiliated youth hostel is about 2km northeast of the train station and near the beach. Take bus No 5 from the train station or No 1 (July and August only) from the bus station and tourist office.

BEYOND THE WALLS   Map p76
There are plenty of hotels to suit all budgets near the train station and around the beaches of Sillon and Grande Plage.

Hôtel Auberge de l'Hermine (☎ 02 99 56 31 32; fax 02 99 40 44 61; 4 place de l'Hermine; s €23, with shower €27, d with bathroom €29-46) This attractive little two-star place is tucked away in a hidden square a block west of the train station.

Hôtel Le Neptune (☎ 02 99 56 82 15; 21 rue de l'Industrie; d €20-27.50, with bathroom €27-38) Close to Grande Plage, this is a comfortable family-run place above a small, cheerful bar.

Hôtel Brocéliande (☎ 02 99 20 62 62; 43 chaussée du Sillon; d €84-125) Also a family hotel but in a very different league, the Brocéliande is a delightful, cosy place. Most rooms – including the breakfast room with its picture-window – directly overlook the Grande Plage. Each of the nine bedrooms ('Merlin', 'Arthur') is named after a hero of Arthurian legend, and is individually and tastefully decorated.

Grand Hôtel des Thermes (☎ 02 99 40 75 75; www.thalassotherapie.com, 100 blvd Hébert; s €60-147, d €87-314) Exuding old-world elegance, this hotel – 'grand' in every sense – caters mainly to *curistes* indulging in its various types of thalassotherapy, as well as offering beauty treatments and fitness courses. Prices vary with the season, size of room and view.

HOTELS – INTRA-MUROS   Map p77
Hôtel Aux Vieilles Pierres (☎ 02 99 56 46 80; 4 rue des Lauriers; d €27.50, with shower €29, with bathroom €45) This friendly, intimate, family-run hotel, the cheapest in the old city, has only six rooms so it's wise to reserve in advance. For dinner, step no further than its equally cosy, downstairs restaurant.

Hôtel les Chiens du Guet (☎ 02 99 40 87 29; chiens duguet@hotmail.com; 4 place du Guet; d €31, with shower €39, with bathroom €45) Near Porte St-Pierre and a pace or two from Plage de Bon Secours, this is another good-value, welcoming hotel with a more than decent restaurant. Its 12 rooms are both quiet and clean, and prices fall by about 30% between October and March.

Hôtel France et Chateaubriand (☎ 02 99 56 66 52; www.hotel-fr-chateaubriand.com; place Chateaubriand; s €62.50-71.50, d €73-94) This is a smart, two-star place directly opposite the entrance to the chateau. Its 80 rooms – the more expensive ones overlook the sea – are plush, evoking the Baroque, and several have wheelchair access.

Hôtel de l'Univers (☎ 02 99 40 89 52; www.hotel-univers-saintmalo.com; place Chateaubriand; s €43-69, d €56-78) On the same square, this is another attractive mid-range option. More modestly priced, the Univers lacks the France et Chateaubriand's sea views. But oh, what a bar (see Drinking, p80)!

Quic-en-Grogne (☎ 02 99 20 22 20; 8 rue d'Estrées; s €48, d €53-62; Ⓟ) Here's another tranquil, mid-range choice. Occupying two floors (there's no lift so be prepared to flex your muscles and drag your bags), it's in a quiet street off main rue de Dinan.

HOTELS – ST-SERVAN   Map p76
Hôtel de la Rance (☎ 02 99 81 78 63; hotel-de-la-rance@wanadoo.fr; 15 quai Sébastopol; d €55-81) This small, welcoming, 11-room hotel overlooking Port-Solidor has spacious and stylish rooms – try to get one at the front with a balcony and sea view.

Hôtel de la Mer (☎ 02 99 81 61 05; 3 rue Dauphine; d €22-29) This hotel, overlooking Plage des Bas Sablons and with a couple of public car parks nearby, is particularly convenient if you are looking for somewhere to stay after arriving on an evening ferry from the UK. All 11 rooms have a bathroom and it represents an excellent deal. It's best to book ahead.

Eating   Map p77
Rue Jacques Cartier in the walled city, to the left as you enter Porte St-Vincent, is lined with tourist restaurants and there are lots of creperies and pizzerias in the area

bounded by Porte St-Vincent, the cathedral and the Grande Porte. Both **Hôtel aux Vieilles Pierres** and its near neighbour **Hôtel les Chiens du Guet** (see p79) run great little restaurants that merit a visit in their own right.

Le Petit Crêpier (☎ 02 99 40 93 19; 6 rue Ste-Barbe; dishes €5.50-8; ☽ closed Tue & Wed except Jul & Aug) This famous creperie is known for its gourmet specialities such as a *galette* with plaice in a seaweed and Muscadet sauce or a crepe with a mousse of dates and spices.

La Chasse-Marée (☎ 02 99 40 85 10; 4 rue du Grout-St-Georges; mains €11.50-23, menus €14-23) Here you can enjoy excellent seafood, beef and lamb in a dining room with exposed timber beams. The dinner *menu* includes half a dozen oysters, a main course and cheese.

La Coquille d'Oeuf (☎ 02 99 40 92 62; 20 rue de la Corne de Cerf; menus €12-23.50) Neat, trim and with a nautical theme, this small restaurant with its tables for two makes for intimate dining. Given the quality of the cuisine, dishes are very reasonably priced.

Borgnefesse (☎ 02 99 40 05 05; 10 rue du Puits-aux-Braies; mains €11.50, full meal €21; ☽ closed Sun & lunch Mon & Sat year-round, plus 2 weeks late-Jun–early Jul). You're assured of a hearty welcome at Borgnefesse, where fish and seafood are the main elements on the short but impressive menu. If your French is up to it, ask the owner, an exuberant Captain Haddock figure, to explain just why his restaurant is called Borgnefesse (But One Buttock)…

QUICK EATS

Le Maclow (☎ 02 99 56 50 41; 22 rue Ste-Barbe; sandwiches €2.50-4) Although it looks like a burger chain clone, this little sandwich bar is fine for cheap, no-nonsense takeaway grub.

Other places worth trying for a snack include the tiny, hole-in-the-wall **Crêperie Chez Gaby** (2 rue de Dinan), which has excellent *galettes* and crepes costing from €1.50 to €5.50, and **Glacier Sanchez** (☎ 02 99 56 67 17; 9 rue de la Vieille Boucherie), serving up great ice cream (€3.80 for three scoops).

SELF-CATERING

Among the food shops along rue de l'Orme is a truly excellent **cheese shop** (☽ Tue-Sat) at No 9, a **fruit and vegetable shop** at No 8 and two **boulangeries**. Just down the street and well worth the browse is the **Hall au Blé**, once the town's grain store and now sheltering its **covered market**.

Drinking   Map p77

Hôtel de l'Univers (☎ 02 99 40 89 52; place Chateaubriand) has a magnificent, snug **bar** that's all wood, from the gleaming, polished bar itself to the heavy overhead beams. The wallpaper is scarcely visible for maritime photos and prints. If you find the ambience there a bit too heavy, head for **l'Aviso** (☎ 02 99 40 99 08; 12 rue du Point du Jour; ☽ 5pm-2am), with 300 beers on offer, over 10 of them on draught. Indulge in a little local cultural research by sampling one or two Breton speciality ales (including several of those we list in the boxed text, p121) at this cheerful place for serious hopheads. Not least of its charms are the welcoming young bar staff and background jazz and blues (on occasion, live).

Entertainment

In summer, classical music concerts are held in Cathédrale St-Vincent and elsewhere in the city.

Getting There & Away

AIR

See Dinard Getting There & Away (p84) for flight details. A daytime/evening taxi from St-Malo to Dinard airport costs around €18/25. **TIV** (☎ 02 99 40 82 67) runs a bus to Dinard airport, leaving St-Malo's train station two hours before the daily Ryanair departure time.

BOAT

Brittany Ferries (reservations in France ☎ 0825 82 88 28, in the UK ☎ 0870 556 1600; www.brittany-ferries.com) sail between St-Malo and Portsmouth daily, April to mid-November, and at least five times weekly, mid-November to March. The journey time is nine hours.

Condor Ferries (in France ☎ 08 25 16 03 00, in the UK ☎ 0845 345 2000; www.condorferries.co.uk) does daily high speed runs between St-Malo and both Poole (mid-May to mid-December) and Weymouth (February to December) via Jersey or Guernsey. Between mid-May and mid-September, it has daily sailings between St-Malo and both Jersey and Guernsey (Îles Anglo-Normandes).

Hydrofoils and catamarans depart from the Gare Maritime de la Bourse, while car ferries leave from the Gare Maritime du Naye (Map p76).

From April to September, **Corsaire** (☎ 02 23 18 15 15) operates the **Bus de Mer** (Sea Bus;

adult/child return €5.70/3.50, 10 minutes, hourly) shuttle service between St-Malo and Dinard. Boats depart from the quay (Map p77) outside the Porte de Dinan at the southern end of the walled city. You can also travel by boat from St-Malo along the River Rance to Dinan (see p98).

BUS

The bus station is beside the tourist office on esplanade St-Vincent. All intercity buses also call by the train station. The bus office is in the same building as the tourist office.

Courriers Bretons (☎ 02 99 19 70 80) has services to Cancale (€3.80, 30 minutes), Fougères (€13.90, 1¾ hours, one to three daily), Pontorson (€7.80, one hour) and Mont St-Michel (€9.20, 1½ hours, three to four daily). It also offers all-day tours to **Mont St-Michel** (adult/child return €19.50/17.50, twice weekly April to June and September, four times weekly July and August).

TIV (☎ 02 99 40 82 67) has buses to Dinard (€3.40, 30 minutes, hourly) and to Rennes (€9.90, one to 1½ hours, three to six daily).

CAT (☎ 02 96 68 31 20) bus No 10 goes to Dinan (€5.70, 50 minutes, three to eight daily) via the Barrage de la Rance.

CAR & MOTORCYCLE

Avis (☎ 02 99 40 18 54) has a desk at both the train station and Gare Maritime du Naye (Map p76). **ADA** (☎ 02 99 56 06 15) also has a desk in the train station, while **Europcar** (☎ 02 99 56 75 17; 16 blvd des Talards) is across the street.

TRAIN

Trains or SNCF buses run between St-Malo and Rennes (€11, one hour, frequent), Dinan (€7.60, one hour, five daily), Dol de Bretagne (€3.90, 20 minutes, eight daily) and Lannion (€21.60, four hours, seven daily). Change trains at Rennes for Paris' Gare Montparnasse (€53, 4¼ hours, eight to 10 daily).

Getting Around

St-Malo city buses (single journey €1.10, 10-trip carnet €7.80, 24-hour pass €3.20) operate until about 8pm with some lines extending until around midnight in summer. Between esplanade St-Vincent and the train station, take bus No 1 (July and August only), 2, 3 or 4.

You order a **taxi** on ☎ 02 99 81 30 30.

DINARD
pop 11,000

Dinard is one of France's oldest *stations balnéaires* (seaside resorts). During the late 19th and early 20th centuries, it attracted a well-heeled clientele that included many members of the British aristocracy. Today it retains something of the feel of a late-19th-century resort, with its striped bathing tents, seaside carnival rides and pinnacled *belle époque* mansions perched above the water.

The town's long-standing links with Britain are honoured with an excellent annual festival of British cinema, held in early October. For information about shows and dates go to www.festivaldufilm-dinard.com (French only) .

Orientation

Dinard's focal point is the fashionable Plage de l'Écluse (also called Grande Plage), flanked by Pointe du Moulinet and Pointe de la Malouine. To get to this beach from the Embarcadère (where the boats coming from St-Malo dock), climb the stairs from the waterfront and walk 200m northwest along rue Georges Clemenceau.

Information

Cyberk@w@ (☎ 02 99 46 79 01; 32 rue de la Gare; per hr €4; 11-1am Tue-Sat, 2-11pm Sun & Mon) For Internet access.
Lavomatic de la Poste (10 rue des Saules; 8am-7pm daily Jun-Sep, Mon-Sat Oct-May)
Main Post Office (place Rochaid)
Tourist Office (☎ 02 99 46 94 12; www.ville-dinard.fr; 2 blvd Féart; 9.30am-7.30pm Jul & Aug, 9am-12.15pm & 2-6pm Mon-Sat Sep-Jun) Staff will book accommodation for free.

Sights

As befits a classic seaside resort, Dinard's main attractions are its beaches, cafés and waterfront walks.

The **promenade du Clair de Lune** (Moonlight promenade), with its free sound-and-light spectacle in summer, runs from just north of place du Général de Gaulle to the Embarcadère. From this viewpoint you can see St-Malo's old city across the mouth of the River Rance.

If you are even just slightly mechanically minded, pay a visit to the visitors centre of the **Barrage de la Rance** megatidal station (see the boxed text, p83).

DINARD

0 — 300 m
0 — 0.2 miles

INFORMATION
Cyberk@w@.....................................1 A3
Lavomatic de la Poste.....................2 B2
Main Post Office.............................3 B3
Police Station.................................4 B3
Tourist Office.................................5 C2

SIGHTS & ACTIVITIES   (pp82-3)
Alfred Hitchcock Statue.................6 C2
Piscine Olympique........................7 C2
Wishbone Club (Windsurfing, Kayaks
    & Catamarans).........................8 D1

SLEEPING   (pp83-4)
Hôtel de la Gare.............................9 A3
Hôtel de la Plage..........................10 C2
Hôtel de la Valleé.........................11 D2
Hôtel du Parc...............................12 A2
Hôtel Printania............................13 D2
Hôtel-Restaurant du Prieuré....14 B4

To Pointe de
la Malouine (150m)

Pointe du
Moulinet

Les Roches
Bonnes

The Channel
(La Manche)

Seawater
Pool

Plage de l'Écluse
(Grande Plage)

Promenade des Alliés

Anse
du Bec

Baie du
Prieuré

To Plage de St-Énogat (400m);
Camping Municipal du
Port Blanc (800m);
St-Lumaire (4km);
St-Briac-sur-Mer (14km)

Place
Maréchal
Joffre

Blvd Wilson

Place de la
République

Rue Levavasseur

Place
Rochaid

Ave Édouard VII

Place de
Newquay

Place du
Général
de Gaulle

Plage du
Prieuré

To Barrage de la Rance
(3.5km); Airport (4.5km);
St-Malo (12km)

Trail to Barrage de
la Rance

To
St-Malo

EATING   (p84)
Bar La Croisette...........................15 B2
Covered & Outdoor Market.........16 B3
Crêperie Côté Mer.......................17 C2
La Médicis...................................18 B3
L'Escale à Corto..........................19 D2
Lindfield & Company...................20 B2
Newport Café..............................21 B2
Restaurant Didier Méril...............22 B2

TRANSPORT   (pp84-5)
Breiz Cycles.................................23 B2
Bus Station.................................24 A3
Embarcadère (Ferry to
    St-Malo)..................................25 D3
Le Gallic Bus Stop..................(see 5)
SNCF Office (Train
    Information)............................26 C3

Activities

TOURS

Guided walks (2.30pm & 4.30pm Mon & Wed-Sat) covering the town's history, art and architecture, depart from the tourist office.

From May to September, you can take a **boat** along the River Rance (one way/return €17.30/23, 2½ hours). There's usually one sailing a day, the morning departure time linked to the tide. The return trip (by boat) runs the following day. You can also return by bus (see p84).

SWIMMING

Broad, sandy **Plage de l'Écluse** (or Grande Plage) is fringed with Dinard's trademark blue-and-white striped bathing tents and overlooked by fashionable hotels, a casino and a string of pointy-roofed, neo-Gothic villas. Picasso used the beach as the setting for several canvases in the 1920s and you may see reproductions of them planted in the sand. A statue of film director Alfred Hitchcock, with a seagull perched on each shoulder, balances on a giant egg near the entrance to Plage de l'Écluse in honour of the annual festival of British film.

The **Piscine Olympique** (☎ 02 99 46 22 77; promenade des Alliés; adult/student €4/2.55; ⏰ 10am-12.30pm & 3-7.30pm Mon-Sat, 10am-6.30pm Sun), an indoor Olympic-sized swimming pool right beside the beach, is filled with heated sea water.

Plage du Prieuré, 1km to the south, might not be as smart as Plage de l'Écluse but it's less crowded. **Plage de St-Énogat** is 1km west of Plage de l'Écluse, on the far side of Pointe de la Malouine.

WALKING & CYCLING
Beautiful seaside trails extend along the coast in both directions. A complete traverse of the splendid shoreline from Plage du Prieuré to Plage de St-Énogat via Pointe du Moulinet is a must. You can continue along the GR34 in either direction, though not always so close to the waterline. For this and other hiking opportunities in the *département*, pack the Institut National Géographique (IGN) 1:50,000 map *Ille-et-Vilaine: Randonnées en Haute Bretagne*, which highlights walking trails.

WINDSURFING & KAYAKING
During high season, there's scope for some intense aquatic activity on all three of Dinard's beaches.

At Plage de l'Écluse, **Wishbone Club** (☎ 02 99 88 15 20; ☒ 9am-9pm Jun-Sep, 10am-noon & 2-6pm Oct-May), next to the open-air swimming pool, offers windsurfing lessons (€30 per hour) and also hires out boards (€14 to €19 per hour, €30 to €40 per half-day) and catamarans/kayaks (€30/10 per hour).

In July and August, **Espace Mer et Loisirs** (☎ 06 81 45 55 35) at Plage du Prieuré and **Windschool** (☎ 02 99 46 83 99) at Plage de St-Énogat both offer kayak and windsurfing.

Sleeping
Camping Municipal du Port Blanc (☎ 02 99 46 10 74; fax 02 99 16 90 91; rue Sergeant Boulanger; 2 adults, tent & car €15.50; ☒ Apr-Sep) Close to the beach and about 2km west of Plage de l'Écluse.

Dinard can be an expensive place to stay; you might want to base yourself in St-Malo and hop over on the ferry. Prices drop by a good 15% in the low season.

Hôtel de la Gare (☎ 02 99 46 10 84; 28 rue de la Corbinais; d €20-26) Station Hotel, still so called even though trains no longer pass and the station is long demolished, is a fair hike from the beach, but the rooms are undeniably good value – as is **L'É'picurien** (menu €9; ☒ lunch only Mon-Fri), its Routard restaurant.

Hôtel du Parc (☎ 02 99 46 11 39; hotel.du.parc@ infonie.fr; 20 ave Édouard VII; basic d €28, with bathroom €52; ☒ Easter-Sep & school holidays) This medium-sized hotel, 500m from Plage de l'Écluse, is a favourite with English school groups. Corridors are dingy but the rooms, though smallish, are more than adequate and bathed in light.

Hôtel-Restaurant du Prieuré (☎ 02 99 46 13 74; fax 02 99 46 81 90; 1 place du Général de Gaulle; d from €38.50; ☒ Feb-Dec, closed Sun evening & Mon except Jul & Aug) This is a lovely, old-fashioned little place overlooking the beach. Of its seven rooms, five have views across the water to St-Malo and it runs a fine restaurant (see p84).

Hôtel Printania (☎ 02 99 46 13 07; www.printania hotel.com; 5 ave George V; s/d €50/55, d with sea view €75-

---

TAPPING THE TIDE

A major miracle of French engineering links the towns of St-Malo and Dinard. To take in its enormity, stop in the parking area at the western, Dinard, side of the busy bridge that carries the four-lane D168 highway.

The bridge, stretching for 750m across the Rance estuary, lops a good 30km from the journey between the two towns. But, though impressive in its own right, it's a minor feature compared to the **Usine Marémotrice de la Rance** (☎ 02 99 16 37 00) that juts beside it, fed from the 24 turbines that quietly whir beneath the highway.

Built between 1961 and 1966, this tidal power station generates over 3% of Brittany's electricity needs – enough to keep the fair-sized city of Rennes alight and cooking year-round. Churning out over 600 million kwh annually, those 24 turbines exploit the lower estuary's extraordinarily high tidal range. Here, where the estuary is still almost 1km wide, there's an incredible difference of 13.5m between high and low tide. Driven by this ever-reliable rise and fall – the height of a four-storey building, twice a day, every day without fail – the turbines are almost constantly turning.

On the downside, silt piles up in worrying quantities and the environmental impact upon the estuary (especially its fish and bird life) has been heavy. This said, on balance the power station comes out clean – if not quite as clean as its non-polluting way of producing power.

Espace Découverte (admission free; ☒ 1-7pm Tue-Sun), at the western end of the bridge, illustrates the power station's construction and its environmental impact on the Rance estuary.

82; ☿ mid-Mar–mid-Nov) This charming Breton-style hotel, complete with mature wood and leather furniture, has a superb location overlooking the Baie du Prieuré. The breakfast room has grand views across the water to St-Servan.

Hôtel de la Vallée (☎ 02 99 46 94 00; www.hotel delavallee.com; 6 ave George V; r €61-80 with breakfast; ☿ mid-Dec–mid-Nov) Facing the Printania on the other side of the little harbour of Anse du Bec, the Vallée looks in the wrong direction for expansive views. That said, it's a pleasant blend of traditional and modern with bright, cheerful rooms.

Hôtel de la Plage (☎ 02 99 46 14 87; hotel-de-la-plage@wanadoo.fr; 3 blvd Féart; d €60.50-88; ☿ mid-Dec–mid-Nov) The merest stroll from the Plage de l'Écluse, the 'Beach Hotel', a fine, stone-built structure indeed merits its name. Its 18 rooms are well appointed and the dearer ones have a balcony with sea views.

Eating

There's no shortage of good cafés and restaurants. Rue Yves Verney, which stretches from Plage de l'Écluse to place de la République, is lined with trendy eateries.

Bar La Croisette (☎ 02 99 46 43 32; 4 rue Yves Verney; menus €11 & 17; ☿ mid-Dec– mid-Nov, closed Tue Oct-Mar) La Croisette, easily recognised by the blonde, bikini-clad mannequin on the roof, is a cheerful eatery and bar where portions are ample. It carries a good selection of wines by the glass.

Newport Café (☎ 02 99 46 50 18; 8 rue Yves Verney; ☿ Jan-Nov) This trendy café has cane chairs and glass tables on a wooden boardwalk-style deck that's a sun trap at lunchtime. Primarily a pancake place, it serves great *moules-frites* (mussels with chips/french fries; €10).

Restaurant Didier Méril (☎ 02 99 46 95 74; 6 rue Yves Verney; menus €23-99; ☿ Feb-Dec, closed Wed except school holidays) Sandwiched between these two cheery bar-cafés, this is an altogether more sophisticated place that takes its food *very* seriously. With a young, talented, creative chef, it has rapidly gained a reputation that extends way beyond Brittany.

Crêperie Côte Mer (☎ 02 99 16 80 30; 29 blvd Wilson; galettes €2.60-7.20, other dishes €4.60-7.80) A crisp little creperie with pine tables, the Côte Mer serves grills, salads and *moules-frites* as well as crepes, *galettes* and ice cream.

Lindfield & Company (☎ 02 99 16 96 77; www .lindfield.biz - French only; 48 rue Levavasseur; snacks €2-4;

☿ daily Jul & Aug, Tue-Sat Sep-Jun) Dinard's long-standing British connection lives on in this very English tearoom, where *les anglophiles* can be found at *le tea time*, partaking of Earl Grey and muffins.

L'Escale à Corto (☎ 02 99 46 78 57; 12 ave George V; mains €12.80-22; ☿ dinner only Tue-Sun) This fashionable, intimate restaurant specialises in fish and seafood. Meals are all à la carte, varying with the seasons and featuring creative dishes such as sea bream with ginger and lime, and saffron-scented scallops.

Some of Dinard's best restaurants are in hotels. **Hôtel-Restaurant du Prieuré, Hôtel Printania** and **Hôtel de la Vallée** are all top-notch places for fish and seafood (see p83).

SELF-CATERING

Dinard has a large **covered market** (place Rochaid; ☿ 7am-1.30pm). Outdoor market days are Tuesday, Thursday and Saturday.

La Médicis (☎ 02 99 46 92 11; 33 blvd Féart), strictly for the sweet toothed, is a delightful specialist chocolate shop.

Getting There & Away

AIR

Ryanair (☎ 02 99 160066; www.ryanair.com) has daily flights to/from London (Stansted). Dinard airport is 5km south of the town on the D168. A daytime/evening taxi from Dinard to the airport costs around €10/15.

BOAT

From April to September, **Corsaire** (☎ 02 23 18 15 15) operates the **Bus de Mer** (Sea Bus; adult/child €5.70/3.50 return, 10 minutes, hourly) shuttle service between Dinard and St-Malo.

BUS

TIV (☎ 02 99 40 82 67) buses connect Dinard with the train station in St-Malo via the Barrage de la Rance (€3.40, 30 minutes, hourly). Dinard bus station is southwest of the town centre at place de Newquay; Le Gallic bus stop, outside the tourist office, is more convenient.

TAE (☎ 02 99 26 16 00) runs five buses daily between Dinard and Rennes (€11.80, two hours) via Dinan (€3.80, 25 minutes).

TRAIN

Although trains no longer run to Dinard, there's an **SNCF ticket office** (31 bis blvd Féart).

Getting Around
You can hire bikes (€5.50/8 per half/full day) and motor scooters (€11/38 per hour/day) at **Breiz Cycles** (☎ 02 99 46 27 25; 8 Rue St-Énogat).

For a **taxi**, call ☎ 02 99 46 88 80 or 02 99 88 15 15.

ST-LUNAIRE
pop 2300

St-Lunaire is a mere 5km west of Dinard. With turn-of-the-century villas overlooking the golden sands of **La Grande Plage,** it's like a miniature version of its larger, more famous neighbour. Take a stroll out to **Pointe du Décollé**, the rocky point to the west of the beach, for the great coastal views in both directions: east to St-Malo and Île de Cézembre, and west towards Cap Fréhel.

The peninsula of Pointe du Décollé is bordered by La Grande Plage to the east and, to the west, the vast Plage de Longchamps – which is more exposed and favoured by windsurfers.

The **tourist office** (☎ 02 99 46 31 09; blvd Général de Gaulle; ☒ 9am-7pm Jul & Aug, 2.30-5pm Mon & Thu-Fri Sep-Jun) is towards the eastern end of La Grande Plage.

Restaurant du Décollé (☎ 02 99 46 01 70; 1 Pointe du Décollé; menus €19-36, mains €15-27; ☒ Wed-Sun) Whether dining on the terrace or sitting beside the picture window, you'll enjoy great cuisine and grand views towards Dinard and the Rance estuary.

Frequent buses between Dinard and St-Briac call at St-Lunaire. You can hire bikes from **Alain Rozé** (☎ 02 99 88 92 68).

ST-BRIAC-SUR-MER
pop 2100

St-Briac is another pretty village, clustered around a pine-fringed bay where pleasure boats bob. The Presqu'île du Nessey, to the west of the village, is capped with a late-19th-century chateau. There's also a string of beaches to the west and north. The tiny **tourist office** (☎ 02 99 88 32 47; www.saint-briac.com; ☒ 9am-7pm Jul & Aug, 2-5pm Mon-Tue & Thu-Sat Apr-Jun & 1-15 Sep, 2-5pm, Tue & Sat 16 Sep-Mar) is beside the traffic lights on the main coast road.

Camping Émeraude (☎ 02 99 88 34 55; www.camping-emeraude.com; 7 chemin de la Souris; person €5, pitch €7-11; ☒ Apr-Sep) This pleasant, wooded site, particularly popular with families, is about 700m north of the village centre.

Hôtel de la Houle (☎ 02 99 88 32 17; hoteldelahoule@wanadoo.fr; 14 blvd de la Houle; d €50-65, with sea view €75) Antique hunters will love this hotel – the owners are dedicated *brocanteurs* (buyers of bric-a-brac) and their charming 12-room hotel doubles as an antiques shop. You can even make a bid for the furniture!

TIV (☎ 02 99 44 83 33) runs frequent buses between St-Briac and Dinard (€1.80, 15 minutes) via St-Lunaire.

EASTERN BRITTANY

RENNES
pop 212,500

Although Rennes, capital of Ille-et-Vilaine and also Brittany, may hardly feel Breton at all, it's an attractive place in its own right with a charming old quarter and all the animation and zest that goes with a large university town. The city has occupied an important crossroads since Roman times. Capital of Brittany since its incorporation into France in the 16th century, Rennes developed at the junction of the highways linking the northern and western ports of St-Malo and Brest with the former capital, Nantes (see p183), and the inland city of Le Mans.

Orientation
The city centre is divided by La Vilaine, a river channelled into a cement-lined canal which disappears underground just before the central square, place de la République. The northern area includes the pretty, pedestrianised old city whereas much of the south is garishly modern.

Information
BOOKSHOP
Comédie des Langues (☎ 02 99 36 72 95; 25 rue St-Malo) A good selection of fiction in English.

INTERNET ACCESS
France Telecom (place de la République; per 20min €1; ☒ noon-7pm Mon-Sat) Beside the post office.
Next Génération (☎ 02 99 27 09 72; 36 rue d'Antrain; per 15min €1; ☒ 11am-7pm Mon-Sat)
Point Internet (in city information kiosk, place de la République)

LAUNDRY
Laundrette (3 place de Bretagne, ☒ 7am-10pm)
Laundrette (23 rue de Penhoët, ☒ 7am- 8pm)

ILLE-ET-VILAINE

RENNES

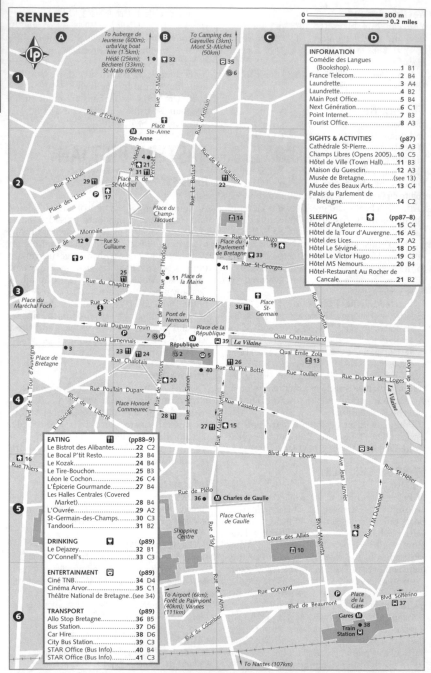

To Auberge de Jeunesse (600m); urbaVag boat hire (1.5km); Hédé (25km); Bécherel (33km); St-Malo (60km)

To Camping des Gayeulles (3km); Mont-St-Michel (50km)

INFORMATION		
Comédie des Langues		
(Bookshop)......................	1	B1
France Telecom...................	2	B4
Laundrette.........................	3	A4
Laundrette.........................	4	B2
Main Post Office..................	5	B4
Next Génération..................	6	C1
Point Internet.....................	7	B3
Tourist Office.....................	8	A3

SIGHTS & ACTIVITIES	(p87)	
Cathédrale St-Pierre.............	9	A3
Champs Libres (Opens 2005)...	10	C5
Hôtel de Ville (Town Hall).....	11	B3
Maison du Guesclin..............	12	A3
Musée de Bretagne...............	(see 13)	
Musée des Beaux Arts............	13	C4
Palais du Parlement de		
Bretagne........................	14	C2

SLEEPING	(pp87–8)	
Hôtel d'Angleterre................	15	C4
Hôtel de la Tour d'Auvergne...	16	A5
Hôtel des Lices...................	17	A2
Hôtel Le Sévigné.................	18	D5
Hôtel Le Victor Hugo............	19	C3
Hôtel MS Nemours...............	20	B4
Hôtel-Restaurant Au Rocher de		
Cancale.........................	21	B2

EATING	(pp88–9)	
Le Bistrot des Alibantes........	22	C2
Le Bocal P'tit Resto..............	23	B4
Le Kozak...........................	24	B4
Le Tire-Bouchon.................	25	B3
Léon le Cochon...................	26	C4
L'Épicerie Gourmande..........	27	B4
Les Halles Centrales (Covered		
Market).........................	28	B4
L'Ouvrée...........................	29	A2
St-Germain-des-Champs........	30	C3
Tandoori...........................	31	B2

DRINKING	(p89)	
Le Dejazey........................	32	B1
O'Connell's........................	33	C3

ENTERTAINMENT	(p89)	
Ciné TNB...........................	34	D4
Cinéma Arvor.....................	35	C1
Théâtre National de Bretagne..	(see 34)	

TRANSPORT	(p89)	
Allo Stop Bretagne...............	36	B5
Bus Station........................	37	D6
Car Hire............................	38	D6
City Bus Station..................	39	C3
STAR Office (Bus Info)..........	40	B4
STAR Office (Bus Info)..........	41	C3

POST
Main Post Office (place de la République)

TOURIST INFORMATION
Tourist Office (☎ 02 99 67 11 11; www.ville-rennes.fr;
11 rue St-Yves; ☺ 9am-6/7pm Mon-Sat, 11am-6pm Sun)
Staff will book local accommodation for a fee of €1.

Sights
OLD CITY
Much of medieval Rennes was gutted by
the great fire of 1720, started by a drunken
carpenter who accidentally set a pile of shav-
ings alight. The half-timbered houses that
survived now make up the old city, Rennes'
most picturesque quarter.

Among the prettiest streets to wander
are **rue St-Michel** and **rue St-Georges**. The latter
runs into the enormous place de la Mairie
and place du Palais, site of the 17th-century
Palais du Parlement de Bretagne, the former
seat of the rebellious Breton parliament
and more recently, the Palais de Justice. In
1994 this building too was destroyed by fire,
started by angry fishermen during a protest
over income tax rates. Now restored, it
houses the Court of Appeal.

One of the most stylish half-timbered
houses, **Maison du Guesclin** (3 rue St-Guillaume),
named after a 14th-century Breton warrior
and these days a teahouse, has a pair of
quaint wooden carved figures on either side
of its twin doors. Nearby is the outwardly
reserved 17th-century **Cathédrale St-Pierre**
(☺ 9.30am-noon & 3-6pm), whose neoclassical
interior with its clean lines comes as a
welcome surprise.

MUSEUMS
The city's former university building on the
southern bank of the Vilaine now houses
the **Musée des Beaux-Arts** (☎ 02 99 28 55 85; 20 quai
Émile Zola; adult/child €4/2; ☺ 10am-noon & 2-6pm Wed-
Mon). The museum is unexceptional save for
the rooms devoted to the art of the Pont-
Aven school (which included Paul Gauguin) and watercolours and decorative art
of local artist Ernest Guérin (1887–1953).

Temporarily sharing premises are the
most important elements of the **Musée de
Bretagne** (☎ 02 99 28 55 84), with displays on
Breton history and culture. It's scheduled
to move to a new cultural complex – the
futuristic **Champs Libres** (cours des Alliés), due to
open in 2005. This huge centre will also

house the **Espace des Sciences**, an interactive
science museum including a planetarium
and displays on the geology of Brittany.

Activities
To see Rennes from a special perspective,
hire an electric boat from **urbaVag** (☎ 02 99
33 16 88; rue Canal St Martin; per hr €14-25) and cruise
its waterways. Boats take up to seven passengers and the price drops significantly for
each extra hour of rental.

Festivals & Events
Rennes is at its most lively during the
Tombées de la Nuit festival in the first week of
July, when the old city is filled with music,
theatre and people dressed up in medieval
costume.

Yaouank (☎ 02 99 30 06 87) is a huge *fest-noz*
(night festival), held on the third Saturday
in November (see the boxed text, p33, for
more on *festoù-noz*).

Sleeping
Camping des Gayeulles (☎ 02 99 36 91 22; fax 02 23
20 06 34; rue Professeur Audin; 2 adults, tent & car €11.45;
☺ Apr-Oct) Rennes' only camping ground is
the municipal one in Parc des Bois, about
4.5km northeast of the train station. Take
bus No 3 from place de la Mairie to the
Gayeulles stop.

Auberge de Jeunesse (☎ 02 99 33 22 33; rennes@
fuaj.org; 10-12 Canal St-Martin; dm €12.70 incl breakfast;
☺ year-round) The city's bustling youth hos-
tel is 2.5km northwest of the train station.
Just five minutes' walk from the old town,
it's in a lovely setting on the banks of the
canal. Take bus No 18 (last run about 8pm)
from place de la Mairie to the Auberge de
Jeunesse stop.

Hôtel de la Tour d'Auvergne (☎ 02 99 30 84 16;
fax 02 23 42 10 01; 20 blvd de la Tour d'Auvergne; d €23,
with bathroom €36) The spick-and-span rooms at
this warm, inviting place, only a 10-minute
walk from the old town, are a real bargain.

Hôtel d'Angleterre (☎ 02 99 79 38 61; fax 02 99 79
43 85; 19 rue Maréchal Joffre; basic s €23, d with shower €32,
with bathroom €36-45) The Angleterre is another
good, fairly economical choice. It's set in
a grand old town house with monumental
staircases, echoing corridors and spacious,
if somewhat tired, rooms.

Hôtel Le Sévigné (☎ 02 99 67 27 55; www.hotelle
sevigne.fr - French only; 47 bis ave Jean Janvier; s €48-65, d €67-
70) The 44-room Sévigné is a trim, two-star

ILLE-ET-VILAINE

option near the train station. All rooms have satellite TV and modem points.

Hôtel MS Nemours (☎ 02 99 78 26 26; www.hotel nemours.com - French only; 5 rue de Nemours; s €43-53, d €53-61) A glance around reception in the MS Nemours will reveal that the owner is a fan of traditional sailing vessels. The rooms, with bathroom and TV, are correspondingly neat and shipshape.

There are only a handful of hotels in the old-town area.

Hôtel-Restaurant Au Rocher de Cancale (☎ 02 99 79 20 83; 10 rue St-Michel; d €37-48) One of the few options in the old town is this fine restaurant (right), set in a half-timbered house in a lively street full of bars, which has four pretty, renovated rooms upstairs.

Hôtel Le Victor Hugo (☎ 02 99 38 85 33; fax 02 99 36 54 95; 14 rue Victor Hugo; s €29.50, d with bathroom €40-45) East of the old town, the Victor Hugo has decent accommodation. Although it's rather faded, this is more than compensated for by the warmth of the welcome.

Hôtel des Lices (☎ 02 99 79 14 81; www.hotel-des -lices.com - French only; 7 place des Lices; s €51-54, d €54.50-60) Overlooking the busy Saturday market square, the bright and breezy Hôtel des Lices has access for handicapped travellers. It offers comfortable, attractive, soundproofed rooms in a superb location; the ones on the upper floors have good views over the old town.

Eating
RESTAURANTS
Lovely rue St-Georges is *the* street for indulging in crepes, pizza and ethnic food from India to Brazil. Rue St-Malo these days comes a close rival for exotic eating. Rue St-Michel and rue de Penhoët are good for snacks and café fare.

L'Ouvrée(☎ 02 99 30 16 38; 18 place des Lices; menus €14.50-31.60; ☺ lunch Sat & Sun, dinner Tue-Fri) Highly reputed L'Ouvrée is a place that cares passionately about food, from the crusty brown bread to the subtle blends of the main dishes, served on piping hot plates and so attractively presented that it's almost a shame to tuck into them. The muted, mellow background jazz adds to the enjoyment.

Le Tire-Bouchon (☎ 02 99 79 43 43; 2 rue du Chapitre; ☺ Mon-Fri) Decked out like a traditional bistro, Le Tire-Bouchon more than merits a visit for the quality of its cooking – especially the home-made desserts – and its carefully selected wine list.

St-Germain-des-Champs (☎ 02 99 79 25 52; 12 rue Vau St-Germain; mains €9, menu €15; ☺ lunch Tue-Fri, dinner Fri & Sat) Even ardent carnivores will enjoy eating at this organic-food-only vegetarian restaurant with its tranquil rear terrace. Best to look and pick; the smudgy chalkboard is all but illegible. It also does sandwiches and dishes to take away (€4.50 to €6).

Léon le Cochon (☎ 02 99 79 37 54; 1 rue Maréchal Joffre; mains €10.50-12.50; ☺ closed Sun Jul & Aug only) Justifiably basking in the plaudits of about every French gastronomic guidebook, 'Leo the Pig' – where pork features prominently on the menu – is great value. Leave your tip in the piggy bank on the bar...

Le Bocal P'tit Resto (☎ 02 99 78 34 10; 6 rue d'Argentré; mains €11; ☺ Mon-Fri & dinner Sat) This imaginative little gourmet place – little it is; you'd be well advised to reserve – serves up delightful, unexpected concoctions. The décor is as original and as quirkily pleasing as the cuisine.

Le Bistrot des Alibantes (☎ 02 99 84 02 02; 36 rue de la Visitation; lunch menu €10, dinner menu €17; ☺ closed Sun, dinner Mon & Tue) This attractive bistro, with antique furniture and wooden floors, has a range of classic French and Breton dishes. The lunch *menu* is particularly good value.

Hôtel-Restaurant Au Rocher de Cancale (☎ 02 99 79 20 83; 10 rue St-Michel; mains €9-13, menus €14-25; ☺ Mon-Fri) This delightful restaurant serves mainly fish. Settle into its *plateau du rocher* (€20), a seafood combination with oysters, winkles, whelks and *amandes de mer*, a kind of giant clam.

Tandoori (☎ 02 99 78 21 29; 13 rue de Penhoët; mains €7.30-10.10; ☺ closed lunch Mon) Tiny Tandoori is a friendly, family-run restaurant specialising in Indian and Sri Lankan dishes. It also does takeaway.

Le Kozak (☎ 02 99 79 18 66; 3 rue d'Argentré; plat du jour €7, menus €15-25; ☺ Tue-Fri & lunch Sat) Kitted out with Slav knick-knacks and folk costumes, Le Kozak, away from Rennes' cluster of ethnic eateries, does Russian dishes from starter to finish.

SELF-CATERING
Les Halles Centrales (place Honoré Commeurec; ☺ 7am-6.30pm Mon-Sat) is the larger of the two covered markets in Rennes. Every Saturday morning, there's also a huge fresh produce market on place des Lices.

L'Épicerie Gourmande (☎ 02 99 79 55 86; 16 rue Maréchal Joffre) For delicious sandwich fillings, call by this delicatessen with its wonderful range of spicy, scented sausages and pâtés, both tinned and fresh.

Drinking
Place and rue St-Michel, plus rue St-Malo, have lots of music bars and cafés, including **Le Dejazey** (☎ 02 99 38 70 72; 54 rue St-Malo), which regularly has live jazz.

O'Connell's (☎ 02 99 79 38 76; place du Parlement de Bretagne) is a convivial Irish bar with live folk music sessions every Wednesday evening.

Entertainment
Nondubbed films ('VO' for 'version originale') are screened at **Cinéma Arvor** (☎ 02 99 38 72 40; 29 rue d'Antrain) and **Ciné TNB** (☎ 02 99 31 55 33; 1 rue St-Hélier) at the Théâtre National de Bretagne.

Getting There & Away
AIR
Rennes' **airport** (☎ 02 99 29 60 00; www.rennes .aeroport.fr - French only), about 6km southwest of town, has direct flights to a number of French provincial destinations. Its sole international flight is the Saturday run to/from Shannon, in Ireland.

BUS
The **bus station** (☎ 02 99 30 87 80) is immediately east of the train station on place de la Gare. **Cariane Atlantique** (☎ 02 40 18 42 00) offers services to Nantes (€14.50, two hours). **CTM** (☎ 02 97 01 22 01) runs an express bus service to/from Pontivy (€13.90, two hours, eight daily). **TAE** (☎ 02 99 16 93 06) runs five times daily to Dinard (€11.80, two hours) via Dinan (€8, 1½ hours); and **TIV** (☎ 02 99 26 11 26) serves St-Malo (€9.90, one to 1½ hours, three to six daily), Fougères (€7.60, one hour) and Paimpont (€2.50, one hour).

CAR & MOTORCYCLE
ADA (☎ 02 99 67 43 79), **Europcar** (☎ 02 23 44 02 72), **National Citer** (☎ 02 23 44 02 78) and **Hertz** (☎ 02 23 42 17 01) all have offices at the train station.

HITCHING
Allo Stop Bretagne (☎ 02 99 67 34 67; www.allostop rennes.com - French only; 20 rue d'Isly; ⏰ 9.30am-12.30pm & 2-6pm Mon-Sat), in the Trois Soleils shopping centre, matches up hitchers with drivers for a fee of €6.10.

TRAIN
Destinations with frequent services include St-Malo (€11, one hour), Dinan (€11.60, one hour), Vitré (€6.10, 35 minutes), Vannes (€16.10, 1½ hours), Nantes (€18.50, 1¼ hours), Brest (€28.70, two hours), Quimper (€27, 2½ hours) and Paris' Gare Montparnasse by TGV (€57.50, 2¼ hours).

Getting Around
St-Jacques airport is connected to the city – well, almost; you're left with a five-minute walk at the airport end – by bus No 57, which stops at place de la République.

Rennes has an efficient local bus network and a *very* smart, 22nd-century, single-line metro, both run by **STAR** (☎ 08 20 03 20 02; www.star.fr - French only). Bus and metro tickets (single journey €1, 10-trip carnet €9.20, 24-hour pass €3) are interchangeable.

To get to the town centre from the train or bus station, take bus No 17 to place de la République.

The **metro** line links the northwest of the city to the southeast via place de la République and the train station. Main stations of interest to visitors are Gares (train and bus stations), République (place de la République) and Ste-Anne (old town).

Ring ☎ 02 99 30 79 79 for a **taxi**.

AROUND RENNES
The environs of Rennes were once the border between Brittany and the rest of France and are characterised by a series of imposing defensive castles, such as those of Fougères and Vitré. It is a region of fertile farmland and gently rolling countryside, bisected from

---

DETOUR: ILLE-ET-RANCE CANAL

If you're heading south from Dinan or the coast, following the busy N137, and fancy stretching your legs a little, pull off at **Hédé**, 25km before Rennes. Take a minor road on the left at the end of the village. This leads to a pretty cluster of canal-side houses called **La Magdeleine**. From its bridge, you can stroll up or downstream along the towpath of the **Ille-et-Rance Canal**. Long abandoned as a commercial waterway, it's increasingly popular with walkers, small boat traffic – and families of aquatic birds who pass by or call it home.

ILLE-ET-VILAINE

north to south by the bucolic waterway of the Ille-et-Rance Canal.

Hédé
pop 1930

This former mill town, 25km north of Rennes on the road to St-Malo, lies close to the Ille-et-Rance Canal, which offers good gentle walks along the towpath in either direction. The little bridge of **La Magdeleine**, in the middle of an impressive flight of 11 locks – the **Onze Écluses**, is on a minor road just 1km north of Hédé. Heading east, you can follow the canal for 8km through rural scenery, then return to Hédé along a minor road via the village of Guipel, south of the canal.

The **Maison du Canal** (☎ 02 99 45 48 90; adult/child €2.50/1.70; ☼ 10.30am-12.30pm & 1.30-7pm Jul & Aug, 2-6pm Wed-Mon Apr-Jun, Sep & Oct, 2-6pm Sun Nov-Mar), an interpretation centre that explains the history and workings of the canal, is beside the bridge in a former lock-keeper's house.

Hostellerie du Vieux Moulin (☎ 02 99 45 45 70; fax 02 99 45 44 86; Vallée des Moulins; d €40-45), on the western edge of Hédé, is a flower-bedecked hotel and restaurant in a lovely old water mill. For dinner, stray no further than its **restaurant**, which offers superb fish and beef dishes (€12 to €17).

Bécherel
pop 670

This *petite cité de caractère* – as it styles itself – sitting on a hilltop 33km northwest of Rennes, is built of weathered stone the colour of Harris tweed. Its narrow streets of tidy 17th- and 18th-century houses are dressed in muted shades of slate, rust and olive, with lintels, sills and cornerstones picked out in silver-grey granite.

Bécherel, tiny though it is, has France's biggest concentration of second-hand bookshops. The maze of little streets around the church is lined with bookshops, galleries and studios guaranteed to provide many hours' browsing. On the first Sunday of every month there's a second-hand book fair in the market square.

The town's **tourist office** (☎ 02 99 66 75 23; www .becherel.com - French only; 9 place Jehanin; ☼ 10am-12.30pm & 2-5.30pm Tue-Sun) is opposite the village church.

Drop in for a coffee and some nostalgia at the **Librairie Salon-de-Thé** (☎ 02 99 66 74 48; 1 rue Porte St-Michel), below the church. Within this wondrous combination café-bookshop-junk shop, customers compete for space with old cane fishing rods, Art Deco table lamps, 1960s toasters, assorted ironmongery and a piano.

THE CHOUAN REBELLION: NOT JUST A HOOT

It was a bit like Astérix and Obelix, France's legendary cartoon characters from 'the little village in Gaul' who held out against the Roman invaders despite all odds. Only this time, a much later time, this Breton last stand against the French revolutionaries in distant Paris was very much for real...

Chouan – the Breton word for 'owl' – was the nickname of Jean Cottereau, leader of a Breton revolt in 1793 against the Revolutionary Convention, the caucus that took control of France in the wake of the French Revolution. It's an odd name for a group of passionate rebels, and folk wisdom has it that the term came from the rebels' use of owl-like hooting calls to communicate in darkness. Whatever, the name Chouan soon stuck as a term for the entire Breton rebellion.

The Chouans often get a bad press as provincial counter-revolutionaries. In fact they were more concerned with defending the cause of Brittany rather than those of the overthrown French crown, even though their motives were spiced with more than a pinch of self-interest. Several issues bugged them. The new republican government had enforced conscription for wars outside Breton territory, something strictly against the terms of the 1532 treaty of union, when Brittany agreed to become a part of France. The Breton clergy, in a region that was still deeply religious, had lost status and power and was subject to the extreme, often violent anticlericalism, of the Revolution. Then again, the abolition of an ancient tax on salt ruined their lucrative smuggling trade...

The Chouans paid for their opposition with heavy-handed repression; Cottereau and other Chouan leaders were executed in 1794. It's a saga deeply embedded in the Breton – even French – consciousness; the country's greatest 19th-century novelist, Honoré de Balzac, dramatically recounts the story of the rebellion in his novel *Les Chouans* and it's also the central theme of the French film classic *Chouans!*

FOUGÈRES

pop 22,800

Fougères occupies a picturesque loop in the River Nançon, overlooking a massive medieval fortress that once formed part of the line of defences along the eastern marches of Brittany.

Orientation & Information

The centre of the *haute ville* (upper town), which stretches from place Aristide-Briand southwest to place de l'Hôtel de Ville, sits high up on the eastern bank of the Nançon. From here, rue de la Pinterie drops steeply westwards to the castle.

The **tourist office** (☎ 02 99 94 12 20; www.ot -fougeres.fr; 2 rue Nationale; 🕑 9am-7pm Mon-Sat, 10am-noon & 2-6pm Sun Jul & Aug, 9.30am-12.30pm & 2-6pm Mon-Sat, 1.30-5.30pm Sun Easter-Jun, Sep & Oct, 2-6pm Mon, 10am-12.30pm & 2-6pm Tue-Sat Nov-Easter) is on place du Théâtre.

Sights & Activities

WALKING TOUR

From the tourist office, head west to rue Nationale, turn left and continue southwest. On the right, set back in a small square, is the **Beffroi (1)**, a granite bell tower, dating from 1397 and Brittany's oldest. The **Musée de l'Horlogerie Ancienne (2;** ☎ 02 99 99 40 98; adult/child €4.20/3.50; 🕑 9am-noon & 2-7pm Tue-Sat, 2-6.30pm Sun & Mon mid-Jun–Aug, 9am-noon & 2-7pm Tue-Sat Sep–mid-Jun) is on the left at No 37. This fascinating little clock museum was established over 25 years ago at the rear of his shop by Alain le Floch, one of Brittany's last practising watchmakers.

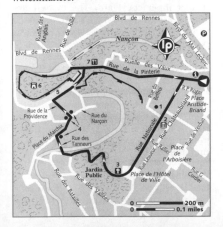

At the end of the street, go into the public garden behind **Église St-Léonard (3)**, from where there's a superb view over the castle and lower town. Descend steeply through the gardens and cross the bridge into the lower town. Go along rue des Tanneurs and turn right into place du Marchix, passing several fine medieval **half-timbered houses (4)**. Take rue de la Providence, the second street on the left and, at the end, turn right alongside the **castle moat (5)**. Pass through the gate in the old city walls beside a splashing mill stream. At the top of the hill, turn left to visit the **castle (6)**, or right to climb back up rue de la Pinterie to the tourist office – or maybe pause for a pancake at **Crêperie des Remparts (7;** see below).

CHÂTEAU

The pride of Fougères is its magnificent medieval **castle** (☎ 02 99 99 79 59; place Pierre-Symon; adult/child €4.50/2; guided visit €3.50/2.80; 🕑 9am-7pm mid-Jun–mid-Sep, 9.30am-noon & 2-6pm Apr–mid-Jun, 10am-noon & 2-5pm mid-Sep–Dec, Feb & Mar, closed Jan) It's possible to make an almost complete circuit of the ramparts, spiked with five massive towers dating from the 12th to the 14th centuries. Ask for the free guide leaflet in English.

Sleeping & Eating

Hôtel Les Voyageurs (☎ 02 99 99 08 20; hotel-voyageurs -fougeres@wanadoo.fr; 10 place Gambetta; s €30-52, d €37-69; P ⊠) The 37-room Voyageurs is an attractive, well-kept hotel with a small private garage (€6 supplement). It has an excellent **restaurant** (☎ 02 99 99 28 89; menus €16-37).

Hôtel Balzac (☎ 02 99 99 42 46; fax 02 99 99 65 43; 15 rue Nationale; d €31-40) The recently renovated Balzac, in an 18th-century town house on a partly pedestrianised street, is quieter than the Voyageurs. A friendly place, its owner speaks fluent English.

Le St-Léonard (☎ 02 99 94 36 23; 20 rue Nationale; menus €12, €16 & €25; 🕑 closed lunch Sat, dinner Sun & Mon) Both meat and fish dishes are grilled before your eyes over a wood fire at this cosy restaurant with its creative *menus*. The €12 menu is only available at lunchtime on weekdays.

Le Bretagne (☎ 02 99 99 04 70; 10 place Carnot; menus €12.50-15.50; 🕑 Tue-Sun) With an attractive terrace, this place offers traditional French cuisine in healthy portions.

Crêperie des Remparts (☎ 02 99 94 53 53; 102 rue de la Pinterie; galettes €2.80-7.50) Close to the castle

ILLE-ET-VILAINE

but away from the crush of place Pierre-Symon, this atmospheric creperie has tables that spill across the street into a garden terrace on the city walls.

Getting There & Away

The **bus station** (☎ 02 99 99 08 77; place de la République) is 1km south of the tourist office. **TIV** (☎ 02 99 99 02 37) runs frequent buses between Fougères and Rennes (€7.60, one hour). **Courriers Bretons** (☎ 02 99 19 70 70) has a service to/from St-Malo (€13.90, 1¾ hours, one to three daily).

The nearest train station is in Vitré, 31km to the south; an **SNCF** (☎ 08 92 35 35 35) bus runs three times daily between Fougères and Vitré (€5.80, 35 minutes).

VITRÉ

pop 15,900

Vitré is another border town, its defensive nature emphasised by the dramatic castle with its witches hat turrets. The old town is a beautifully preserved medieval relic with narrow streets of half-timbered houses just as picturesque as those of its more famous counterparts, Dinan and Quimper.

Orientation & Information

Vitré's compact old town lies immediately north of the train station, between the castle and place de la République.

The **tourist office** (☎ 02 99 75 04 46; www.ot-vitre.fr; place Général de Gaulle; ⏰ 10am-12.30pm & 2-7pm Jul & Aug, 2.30-6pm Mon, 9.30am-12.30pm & 2.30-6pm Tue-Sat Sep-Jun) is right outside the train station.

Sights & Activities

WALKING TOUR

From the tourist office, head downhill (west) to place St-Yves and turn right along narrow, picturesque rue d'Embas and its continuation, rue Poterie. The colourful **half-timbered houses (1)** in the old town date mostly from the 16th and 17th centuries, when Vitré was at its peak of prosperity, its fortune built on the manufacture of sailcloth and other textiles exported through St-Malo.

At the far end of rue Poterie turn left along rue Duguesclin, then first left into rue Notre Dame. **Hôtel Ringues (2)**, on the left at No 27, was built for a rich merchant in the 16th century and is now a community centre – surely one of the most opulent in the country. The Gothic **Église Notre Dame (3;**

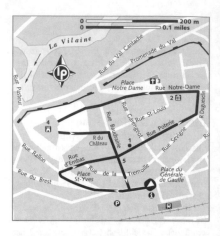

1537), opposite the Ringues, has some fine Renaissance stained glass and a 19th-century painted timber ceiling. Note too the unusual external pulpit on the south side. Continue west along rue Notre Dame to the **chateau (4)**. To return to the tourist office, take rue du Château and turn right down **rue de la Baudrairie (5)** – the 'street of the leatherworkers' – Vitré's best-preserved medieval street.

THE CASTLE

Vitré's most imposing feature is its **medieval castle** (☎ 02 99 75 04 54; place du Château; adult/child €4/2.50; ⏰ 10am-6pm Jul-Sep, 10am-noon & 2-5.30pm Apr-Jun, 10am-noon & 2-5.30pm Wed-Fri, 2-5.30pm Sat-Mon Oct-Mar), perched on a rocky outcrop overlooking the River Vilaine. An impressive, twin-turreted gateway leads from the cobbled square of place du Château into the triangular inner courtyard. The castle dates originally from 1060 – there's a Romanesque porch to the north of the gateway – but was expanded in the 14th and 15th centuries.

Tour St-Laurent, at the southern corner, of the castle contains the **Musée du Château** (admission included in castle ticket). A beautifully restored room in the neighbouring Tour de l'Argenterie houses a 19th-century *cabinet de curiosités*, whose bizarre exhibits include a foetal skeleton, an albino crow and a glass case full of stuffed frogs in humorous poses.

Sleeping and Eating

Hôtel Le Petit Billot (☎ 02 99 75 02 10; www.petit-billot.com; 5 bis place Général Leclerc; s/d €38.50/51; **P**) Five minutes' walk east of the train station, the 21-room Petit Billot has modern rooms with cable TV and modem points.

Hôtel du Château (☎ 02 99 74 58 59; fax 02 99 75 35 47; 5 rue Rallon; s/d €34.50/41.50; ☎ closed last week Aug) About 300m west of the train station, this hotel is on a quiet road at the base of the chateau's ramparts. Pick a room on the 2nd or 3rd floor, from where there's a view of the castle, attractively illuminated on summer evenings.

Le Potager (☎ 02 99 74 68 88; 5 bis place Général Leclerc; menus €14.80 & €22) This recently established restaurant, run by a youthful team, is next door to Hôtel Le Petit Billot. It offers a pair of particularly creative *menus*, each excellent value.

Le Chêne Vert (☎ 02 23 55 14 62; 2 place Général de Gaulle; mains €5.50-7) The 'Green Oak', directly opposite the train station, has a sunny terrace where you can enjoy snacks, sandwiches and salads.

Getting There & Away

SNCF (☎ 08 92 35 35 35) runs three buses daily between Vitré and Fougères (€5.80, 35 minutes). There are about a dozen trains each day between Vitré and Rennes (€6.10, 35 minutes).

AROUND VITRÉ
La Roche aux Fées

The 'Fairies' Rock', hidden on a back road to the west of La Guerche de Bretagne, is about 30km southwest of Vitré. It is one of Brittany's most evocative prehistoric sites, set among trees on the crest of a hill. Dating from around 2500 BC, this roofed corridor, 11m long and 2m wide, is made of huge slabs of schist weighing up to 40 tonnes. It was originally covered by a cairn but the stones have long gone.

GETTING THERE & AWAY

You'll need wheels. Take the D178 from Vitré to La Guerche de Bretagne, then follow the D463 towards Rennes. Turn left after 5km in Visseiche (signposted Marcillé and Jazné). At the far end of the village of Marcillé-Robert, descend the hill, cross the end of the lake and turn left (signposted Retiers). One kilometre later take the first road on the right (signposted Thiel de Bretagne), then continue for 3km to the second crossroads, where a signpost for La Roche aux Fées directs you to the right. The car park and monument lie 500m further on, beyond the houses.

Côtes d'Armor

CONTENTS

West of the River Rance	**96**
Dinan	96
St-Cast-le-Guildo	100
Côte de Penthièvre	**101**
Pays de Fréhel	101
Erquy	101
Pléneuf-Val-André	103
St-Brieuc	104
Côte du Goëlo	**106**
Binic	106
St-Quay-Portrieux	106
Kermaria	106
Paimpol	107
Around Paimpol	108
Île de Bréhat	109
Côte de Granit Rose	**111**
Guingamp	111
Tréguier	111
Around Tréguier	112
Perros-Guirec	113
Sept-Îles	115
Trégastel	115
Trébeurden	116
Lannion	117

Unlike neighbouring Ille-et-Vilaine and Finistère, the *département* of Côtes d'Armor (in Breton, 'Armor' means of or beside the sea) looks almost exclusively outwards, over the sea from which it makes its living. The working harbour of Paimpol was once the home port of France's Icelandic fishing fleet, Erquy remains the country's prime port for dredging *coquilles St-Jacques* (scallops), and small bands of seaweed harvesters still work its more remote shores at low tide.

The sea, as it recedes inexorably twice a day, also reveals some of Brittany's finest beaches – long, broad, safe strands of golden sand backed by small, well-resourced resorts, each ideal for a family holiday. The largest of these is exclusive Perros-Guirec, separated by a fine clifftop walk from its charming little sister, Ploumanac'h. To the west at tiny Trégastel, there's a great aquarium, should you ever tire of exploring the golden beaches and pink granite rocks.

But life needn't be all beach lolling; there's plenty of scope for water-sports enthusiasts too, with Erquy in particular and its neighbour Pléneuf-Val-André offering a variety of aquatic activities. Set aside a full day to venture inland and visit the walled, medieval city of Dinan, left behind a bit by the tide of coastal development but still hugely – excessively in high summer – popular with day visitors.

CÔTES D'ARMOR

HIGHLIGHTS

- Meander the cobbled streets of Dinan's **old town** (p97)
- Hike the colourful **coastal path** (p101) from Fort La Latte to Cap Fréhel
- Hire a bike on the **Île de Bréhat** and explore its scenic delights (p109)
- Fly a kite on the **Sillon de Talbert** (p109)
- Take a tranquil break in the cloister of Tréguier's **Cathédrale St-Tugdual** (p111)
- Watch winter storms batter the rocky coast near **Plougrescant** (p112)
- Walk the **coastal trail** (p113) between Perros-Guirec and Ploumanac'h

- POPULATION: 542,400
- AREA: 6878 SQ KM

CÔTES D'ARMOR

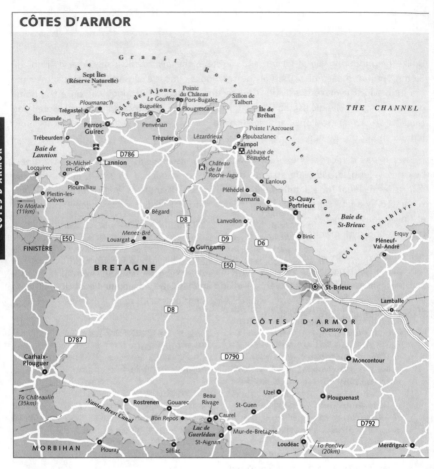

WEST OF THE RIVER RANCE

DINAN
pop 11,000

'Dinan is a lovely old town, fashioned and formed against a cliff like a swallow's nest.' So said Victor Hugo, mightily impressed, when he visited the town in 1836.

Perched above the River Rance about 25km south of Dinard and St-Malo, this walled, medieval city is one of Brittany's most beautiful towns and a hugely popular tourist attraction. Visit, if you can, in spring or autumn, when the sun is usually present and high-season hordes satisfyingly absent.

Dinan was founded around a thousand years ago. It was famously defended against an English siege in 1357 by Bertrand du Guesclin, a knight noted for his hatred of the English (there's an equestrian statue of the old warrior, brandishing his sword, on place du Champ). Subsequently, it became the property of the dukes of Brittany. It grew into a prosperous commercial town, famous in the 19th century for producing leather and sailcloth. Although the town was badly knocked about during the French Revolution, a good portion of its medieval ramparts and some beautiful 15th-century half-timbered houses still stand today.

Orientation

Nearly everything of interest to travellers – except the picturesque port area on the River Rance – is contained within the tight confines of the old city, with its heart at place des Cordeliers and adjacent place des Merciers.

Information

@rospace (☎ 02 96 87 04 87; 9 rue de la Chaux; per 15min €1.50; ☷ 10am-12.30pm & 1.30-7pm Tue-Sat) Internet access.
Main Post Office (7 place Duclos)
Tourist Office (☎ 02 96 87 69 76; www.dinan -tourisme.com; 9 rue du Château; ☷ 9am-7pm Mon-Sat, 10am-12.30pm & 2.30-6pm Sun mid-Jun–mid-Sep, 9am-12.30pm & 2-6pm Mon-Sat mid-Sep–mid-Jun)

Sights

THE OLD TOWN

The cobbled streets of the **old town** are Dinan's main draw, with attractive half-timbered houses overhanging central place des Cordeliers and place des Merciers. A few paces south, the **Tour de l'Horloge** (adult/under 18 €2.50/1.60; ☷ 10am-6pm Apr-Sep), a 15th-century clock tower whose tinny chimes ping every quarter-hour, rises from rue de l'Horloge. It's well worth the climb up to its tiny balcony.

Basilique St-Sauveur (place St-Sauveur; ☷ 9am-6pm) encompasses a range of architectural styles. Entering through a triple-arched Romanesque doorway, you are immediately struck by the asymmetry of the nave with its austere wooden box-pews: a plain Roman-esque wall to the right and ribbed Gothic vaults to the left. Then the eye is drawn towards the soaring Gothic chancel, its clean lines interrupted by a florid baroque altarpiece that would be more at home in some Latin land. In the north transept is a 19th-century monument enclosing a 14th-century grave slab, which is reputed to contain the heart of Bertrand du Guesclin (see opposite).

Just east of the church is the **Jardin Anglais** (English Garden), a former cemetery and nowadays a pleasant little park. Continue to the ramparts and the 13th-century **Tour Ste-Cathérine**, from where there's a great view down over the viaduct and port.

CHÂTEAU & MUSÉE DE DINAN

Dinan's **museum** (☎ 02 96 39 45 20; rue du Château; adult/child €3.90/1.50; ☷ 10am-6.30pm Jun-Sep, 1.30-5.30pm Oct-Dec & Feb-May) is in the keep of the ruined 14th-century castle, next to the tour-ist office. It focuses on the town's history,

CÔTES D'ARMOR

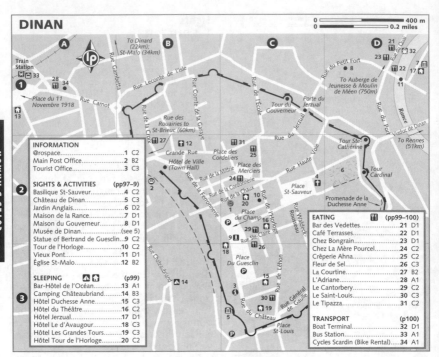

DINAN

0 —————— 400 m
0 —————— 0.2 miles

To Dinard (22km);
St-Malo (34km)

Train Station

To Auberge de Jeunesse & Moulin de Méen (750m)

Place du 11 Novembre 1918

Rue Comte de la Garaye

Rue des Rouairies to St-Brieuc (60km)

Porte du Jerzual

Tour du Gouverneur

To Rennes (51km)

Viaduc de Dinan

Tour Ste-Cathérine

Tour Cardinal

Promenade de la Duchesse Anne

Grande Rue

Hôtel de Ville (Town Hall)

Place des Cordeliers

Place des Merciers

Place St-Sauveur

Place du Champ

Place Du Guesclin

Place St-Louis

INFORMATION	
@rospace	1 C2
Main Post Office	2 B2
Tourist Office	3 C3

SIGHTS & ACTIVITIES	(pp97–9)
Basilique St-Sauveur	4 C2
Château de Dinan	5 C3
Jardin Anglais	6 D2
Maison de la Rance	7 D1
Maison du Gouverneur	8 D1
Musée de Dinan	(see 5)
Statue of Bertrand de Guesclin	9 C2
Tour de l'Horloge	10 C2
Vieux Pont	11 D1
Église St-Malo	12 B2

SLEEPING	(p99)
Bar-Hôtel de l'Océan	13 A1
Camping Châteaubriand	14 B3
Hôtel Duchesse Anne	15 C3
Hôtel du Théâtre	16 C2
Hôtel Jerzual	17 D1
Hôtel Le d'Avaugour	18 C3
Hôtel Les Grandes Tours	19 C3
Hôtel Tour de l'Horloge	20 C2

EATING	(pp99–100)
Bar des Vedettes	21 D1
Café Terrasses	22 D1
Chez Bongrain	23 D1
Chez La Mère Pourcel	24 C2
Crêperie Ahna	25 C2
Fleur de Sel	26 C2
La Courtine	27 B2
L'Adriane	28 A1
Le Cantorbery	29 C2
Le Saint-Louis	30 C3
Le Tipazza	31 C2

TRANSPORT	(p100)
Boat Terminal	32 D1
Bus Station	33 A1
Cycles Scardin (Bike Rental)	34 A1

dwelling on its textile industry, and includes a collection of polychrome wooden statues from the 16th century, as well as a fine collection of *coiffes* (women's lace headdresses) of the region.

OLD PORT

Rue du Jerzual and its continuation, steep **rue du Petit Fort**, are both lined with art galleries, antiques shops, creperies and restaurants. The **Maison du Gouverneur** (Governor's House; 24 rue du Petit Fort; adult/child €1.60/0.80) is a particularly fine half-timbered house. The port extends northwards from the **Vieux Pont** (Old Bridge), while the 19th-century **Viaduc de Dinan** soars high above to the south. There are boats for hire, several restaurants and some good walks along the river in both directions.

Cross the bridge and turn left for **Maison de la Rance** (☎ 02 96 87 40 00; quai Talard; adult/child €4.60/3; 🕑 10am-7pm daily Jul & Aug, 11am-12.30pm & 2-6pm Tue-Sun Apr-Jun, Sep & Oct), an interactive interpretation centre that presents the natural history and industrial heritage of the River Rance.

Activities
WALKING

Ask at the tourist office for its leaflet *Discovery Tours*, in English, which plots three walking itineraries: a tour of **old Dinan**, a walk around the town's premier **religious sites**, and a 3.5km circuit of the medieval **ramparts**, although not always following the top of the walls. The finest stretch is from Tour Ste-Cathérine south to Porte St-Louis, with superb views over the Rance Valley.

BOAT TRIPS

You can hire self-navigating motorboats from **Danfleurenn Nautic** (☎ 06 07 45 89 97; per hr/3hr €28/69; 🕑 Easter–mid-Nov). If you prefer someone else at the helm, the **Jaman IV** (☎ 02 96 39 28 41; adult/child €9/7; sailings Apr-Oct) offers one-hour cruises with commentary.

From May to September, **Corsaire** (☎ 02 96 39 18 04) runs boats along the River Rance to Dinard and St-Malo (one way/return €17.30/23, 2½ hours). There's usually one sailing a day, the morning departure time linked to the tide and the return trip (by boat) occurring the following day. To return to Dinan by bus, see p100.

All three operators have booths at the port.

Festivals & Events

The **Fête des Remparts** (☎ 02 96 87 94 94; admission per day adult/under 12 €15/free) is held every second year over a weekend in the second half of July (most recently 24–25 July 2004). Dinannais dressed in medieval garb are joined by some 40,000 visitors for a rollicking, two-day festival in the old city. Events include military re-enactments, jousting contests, street theatre, parades, fireworks and a medieval market. There are events all over the old town and a bracelet around your wrist serves as proof that you've paid up.

In the first half of July, there's an annual **Celtic harp festival** that also recalls the town's sailors who used to trawl the Newfoundland fishing grounds.

Sleeping

Camping Châteaubriand (☎ 02 96 39 11 96; fax 02 96 85 06 97; 103 rue Chateaubriand; tent, car & 2 adults €7; ☺ Jun-Sep) The nearest camping ground is this small, unexceptional, two-star place at the foot of the ramparts. There is a nearby pool.

Auberge de Jeunesse Moulin de Méen (☎ 02 96 39 10 83; dinan@fuaj.org; Vallée de la Fontaine des Eaux; dm €8.85; ☺ year-round) Dinan's HI-affiliated youth hostel is in a lovely old water mill in a green valley beside the River Rance about 750m north of the port. It has limited camping space and five much-coveted double rooms. Staff, if they are free, will collect you from the train station if you phone in advance. To get there on foot – a pleasant stroll in its own right – follow rue du Quai north from the port, then turn left along a signposted lane.

Bar-Hôtel de l'Océan (☎ 02 96 39 21 51; fax 02 96 87 05 27; 9 place du 11 Novembre; d from €18, with bathroom from €30) This hotel, one of several inexpensive options near the train station, is a reasonable budget choice. For a good night's slumber, ask for a room away from the bar.

The following hotels are all in the old town.

Hôtel du Théâtre (☎ 02 96 39 06 91; 2 rue Ste-Claire; s/d €14.50/22, d with bathroom €27) Rooms here have all the comforts of a monastic cell, but they're cheap and the location is ideal. If no-one's around, call by Crêperie du Beffroi, just around the corner.

Hôtel Duchesse Anne (☎ 02 96 39 09 43; fax 02 96 87 57 26; 10 place de Duguesclin; d €28, with bathroom €34-38) This is another inexpensive, central place with cramped yet acceptable accommodation. It runs a reasonable restaurant and there's public parking opposite.

Hôtel Les Grandes Tours (☎ 02 96 85 16 20; carregi@wanadoo.fr; 6 rue du Château; d €31, with bathroom €45-48; ☺ Feb–mid-Dec; **P**) Venerable, altogether larger and once upon a time called Hôtel des Messageries, it was here that Victor Hugo slept with his very good friend Juliette Drouet in 1836. Handy for visiting the chateau, it has smallish but nicely renovated rooms.

Hôtel Tour de l'Horloge (☎ 02 96 39 96 92; hiliohotel@wanadoo.fr; 5 rue de la Chaux; d €44-66) The 12-room Horloge occupies a charming 18th-century house on a cobbled, pedestrianised lane. Top-floor rooms have exposed wooden beams and a splendid view of the clock tower.

Hôtel Le d'Avaugour (☎ 02 96 39 07 49; www.avaugourhotel.com; 1 place du Champ; d €118-170 incl breakfast; ☺ mid-Feb–mid-Nov) Housed in an elegant 18th-century town house just inside the city walls, the Avaugour is a peaceful luxury hotel with tastefully decorated rooms and a pretty rear garden. There is ample public parking opposite the hotel.

Hôtel Jerzual (☎ 02 96 87 02 02; www.bestwestern.com/fr/jerzual; 26 quai Talard; s €68-99, d €78-138; **P** ⚒) Outside the city walls, the Jerzual overlooks the port. Modern yet sensitively constructed in stone and slate, its 52 rooms have every last comfort and the restaurant merits a visit for its own sake. For the active, there's a pool, gym and sauna, and the hotel rents bikes – ideal for a towpath spin.

Eating

RESTAURANTS – OLD TOWN

Dinan's old town heaves with restaurants, many of them tourist traps. The following are not.

Le Cantorbery (☎ 02 96 39 02 52; 6 rue Ste-Claire; menus €22-32; ☺ closed Wed year-round & dinner Sun Oct-Apr) Occupying a most magnificent 17th-century house, this elegant, intimate restaurant changes its choices regularly, according to the rhythm of the seasons, and does an excellent-value lunch *menu* (€13.50).

Chez La Mère Pourcel (☎ 02 96 39 03 80; 3 place des Merciers; mains €18-33, menus €28-62.50; ☺ Tue-Sat

& lunch Sun) La Mère Pourcel is a Dinan institution: a wonderful beamed dining room, mostly from the 15th-century, that serves specialities of the region, including lobster, duckling, pigeon and salt-marsh lamb.

Le Saint-Louis (☎ 02 96 39 89 50; 9-11 rue de Léhon; lunch menu Mon-Fri €11.50, dinner menus €16.50 & €20; ☾ closed Wed & lunch Mon) This popular place is famous for its good-value, all-you-can-eat buffets of various hors d'oeuvres, cheeses and desserts. In fine weather, walk through to the charming floral patio at the rear.

Fleur de Sel (☎ 02 96 85 15 14; 7 rue Ste-Claire; mains €10-15.50, menus €25-34; ☾ closed Tue & Wed except Jul & Aug) Seafood dominates at this crisp, minimalist restaurant – a medieval-free zone! The food is almost as spare as the décor but what's there is consistently of quality. More unusual offerings in season include prawns flambéed with whisky.

Crêperie Ahna (☎ 02 96 39 09 13; 7 rue de la Poissonnerie; galettes €6-7.85; ☾ Mon-Sat) This excellent place, in the family for three generations, tosses up gourmet, inventive crepes and *galettes* (savoury buckwheat pancakes); the speciality of the house is a *galette* filled with duck breast and cooked with garlic-and-herb butter.

Le Tipazza (☎ 02 96 39 09 08; 14 rue de la Lainerie; mains €11.50-14.50) The décor could be the set for a pantomime of Aladdin, but this North African place serves delicious couscous dishes and, on Thursday and Friday, *tajine* (slow-cooked casserole of lamb with dried fruits and spices).

La Courtine (☎ 02 96 39 74 41; 6 rue de la Croix; menus €16-35; ☾ closed dinner Sun & Wed except Jul & Aug) Booking is recommended for this cosy, romantic restaurant that also does takeaways.

RESTAURANTS – PORT

The quay north of the old bridge has several good places to eat.

Chez Bongrain (☎ 02 96 87 57 51; 9 rue du Quai; menus €15-24) In a medieval half-timbered house, this rustic little restaurant serves fresh, local produce and specialises in fondues and *pierrades* (strips of meat that you cook to taste on a hot stone).

Bar des Vedettes (☎ 02 96 39 04 14; 11 rue du Quai; galettes €2.70-5.40) This is a good spot for a riverside snack; excellent *moules-frites* (mussels and chips/french fries; €10.50) come with a choice of cream, curry or *marinière* sauces.

Café Terrasses (☎ 02 96 39 09 60; 2-4 rue du Quai; mains €11.30-22) Café Terrasses enjoys a prime location overlooking the river. Under the direction of its dynamic young owner, it has a pleasant bistro atmosphere with a decidedly Breton overlay, and relies on the best of local produce. Crepes, whipped up with fresh farm eggs and milk, are the only dessert – but what a dessert!

SELF-CATERING

L'Adriane (☎ 02 96 39 11 38; 34 rue Carnot) is the place for hearty Breton specialities, cooked up for the neighbourhood, not the passing trade. In addition to the usual bready fare, this small bakery conjures up dishes such as *kouign amann*, a rich cake, and *far breton*, a rich, thick flan.

Getting There & Away

Buses leave from place Duclos and the bus station. **CAT** (☎ 02 96 39 21 05) bus No 10 goes to St-Malo (€5.70, 50 minutes, three to eight daily), and No 13 serves St-Cast-le-Guildo (€6.85, 50 minutes, one to five daily, weekdays only). **TAE** (☎ 02 99 26 16 00) runs five daily services to Dinard (€3.80, 25 minutes) and Rennes (€8, 1½ hours).

Trains run to St-Malo (€7.60, one hour, five daily) via Dol de Bretagne (€4.70, 25 minutes, 10 daily).

Getting Around

Cycles Scardin (☎ 02 96 39 21 94; 30 rue Carnot) rents bikes for €12/72 per day/week. There are also available **taxis** by calling ☎ 02 96 39 06 00 or ☎ 06 08 00 80 90).

ST-CAST-LE-GUILDO

pop 3300

St-Cast is famed for its vast, fine-white-sand beaches: **Plage de la Grande-Grève**, along which the town extends, and **Plage de Pen-Guen** to the south. There are several smaller beaches west of **Pointe de St-Cast**, a headland with a grand panorama eastwards to Île d'Hébihens, St-Jacut, St-Briac-sur-Mer and St-Malo.

The town's **tourist office** (☎ 02 96 41 81 52; www .ot-st-cast-le-guildo.fr - French only; place Charles de Gaulle; ☾ 9am-7.30pm Mon-Sat, 10am-12.30pm & 3-6.30pm Sun Jul & Aug, 9.30am-noon & 2-6pm Mon-Fri Sep-Jun) is one block inland towards the northern end of Plage de la Grande-Grève.

Camping Le Châtelet (☎ 02 96 41 96 33; www.le chatelet.com; rue des Nouettes; per person €3.30-5.50, per pitch €11-18; 🕙 May–mid-Sep) This four-star site is poised above the lovely little Fresnaye beach, west of Pointe de St-Cast.

Hôtel Port Jacquet (☎ 02 96 41 97 18; www.port-jacquet.com - French only; 32 rue du Port; d €46-54) This comfortable hotel has a wonderful location overlooking the harbour and beach. Its **L'Étoile des Mers restaurant** (menus €12.20-23.65) is particularly good for seafood. Try for starters the *moules de bouchot au cidre*, a jagged hillock of mussels simmered in cider, cream and spices.

CAT (☎ 02 96 39 21 05) bus No 13 goes to Dinan (€6.85, 50 minutes, one to five daily, weekdays only), while No 14 goes to St-Malo (€5.50, one hour, two or three daily). In July and August, Bus No 2 runs three to six times a day to St-Brieuc (€8.40, two hours) via Erquy and Pléneuf.

CÔTE DE PENTHIÈVRE

Côte de Penthièvre (Coast of Penthièvre, an ancient county of Brittany), stretching from Cap Fréhel southwest to St-Brieuc, is characterised by sea cliffs of coarse pink sandstone and huge sandy beaches, like damp deserts at low tide.

CAT (☎ 02 96 68 31 20) bus No 2 operates on the coastal route two to seven times daily between St-Brieuc and Erquy (€6.70, 1¼ hours) via Pléneuf-Val-André.

PAYS DE FRÉHEL

The cliff-bound peninsula to the west of Baie du Fresnaye is a vast expanse of wild heath, carpeted with heather, gorse and lichen and frequented by moorland birds. This protected area is awash with colour during spring and summer, when the wildflowers compete with the yellow gorse and purple heather. There are several good **beaches** southwest of Cap Fréhel, served by the small beach resorts of Pléhérel-Plage and Sables-d'Or-Les-Pins.

The easternmost of the Pays de Fréhel's two headlands is crowned by the spectacular **Fort La Latte** (☎ 02 96 41 30 31; adult/child €3.90/2; 🕙 10am-7pm daily Jul & Aug, 2-6.30pm daily Apr-Jun & Sep, 2.30-5.30pm Sat & Sun Oct-Mar), as much a castle as a fort. The original 14th-century chateau was expanded during the reign of Louis XIV to help defend the port of St-Malo against the English.

Clearly visible from Fort La Latte, and linked to it by a 5km coastal footpath, are the 70m-high cliffs of **Cap Fréhel**, from which pokes a 30m-tall, square-towered **lighthouse**. It overlooks a smaller round tower, the **Phare Vauban** (Vauban Lighthouse; 1685), one of the oldest in France (see the boxed text below). The surrounding sea cliffs of deep pink, stratified sandstone are alive with sea birds in spring and summer.

ERQUY
pop 3800

Erquy stretches languidly around a big, west-facing bay that empties at low tide. Fringed by the long, white-sand **Plage du Centre**, it's Europe's number-one scallop-fishing port (see the boxed text, p102). During the season (October to April), the

---

SENTINELS OF THE SEA

The hazardous waters around the shores of Brittany, strewn with reefs and islands and washed by strong tidal currents, have long been a graveyard for unwary mariners. Today the coast is waymarked by a complex network of *phares* (lighthouses), each with its own distinctive appearance in daylight and an equally distinctive pattern of flashes by night.

The **Phare Vauban** on Cap Fréhel, now overshadowed by a more modern lighthouse, dates from 1685 and is one of the oldest light towers in France, while the original **Phare du Stiff** on the Île d'Ouessant was built in 1699. However, it was in the second half of the 19th century and the early 20th century that most of Brittany's lighthouses were erected.

Famous lights around the Breton coast include the **Phare d'Île Vièrge** (1902) off Aber-Wrac'h, at 82.5m the tallest in Europe; the **Phare du Créac'h** (1863) on the Île d'Ouessant, the most powerful in the world, visible up to 53km away; and the **Phare St-Mathieu** (1835) south of Le Conquet, a slender white-and-red pillar rising amid the ruins of a 16th-century abbey.

The history of Brittany's lighthouses is recorded in the Musée des Phares et des Balises on the Île d'Ouessant (p129).

town's restaurants dish up all imaginable variations of *coquilles St-Jacques*, and the town celebrates its status with a Fête de la Coquille St-Jacques every three years.

The **tourist office** (☎ 02 96 72 30 12; www.erquy -tourisme.com; blvd de la Mer; ☺ 9.30am-7pm Mon-Sat, 10am-12.30pm & 3.30-6.30pm Sun Jul & Aug, 9.30am-12.30pm & 2.30-6pm Mon-Sat Sep-Jun) is beside the bay, about 1km south of the port.

A coastal path leads northwest from the harbour for 2km to **Cap d'Erquy**, a nature reserve bounded by cliffs of pink sandstone and giving good views west across the Baie de St-Brieuc. There are also several smaller beaches to the east of Cap d'Erquy, plus the magnificent 2km stretch of **Plage de Caroual**, southwest of town.

In the **Maison de la Mer**, which is a large, white, rectangular building at the port, three organisations provide all kinds of watery activity. The **École de Voile d'Erquy** (Erquy Sailing School; ☎ 02 96 72 32 62; www.everquy.org - French only) offers lessons and equipment hire for activities, including dinghies (€22 to €30), catamarans (€30 to €40), windsurf boards (€14 to €19) and kayaks (€10 to €14). These hire prices are per hour in July and August; for the rest of the year, the same rates get you two hours' rental.

Histoire d'Eau (☎ 02 96 72 49 67) runs a one-day *baptême en mer* (initiation dive), courses in scuba diving and a package of five dives for €90.

The **Sainte Jeanne** (☎ 06 08 18 30 94; adult/child €25/12.50) is a painstakingly restored commercial sailing sloop that used to ply the Brittany and UK coasts. She does a half-day sail every day in July and August. Maximum capacity is 18 so advance reservation is essential.

Sleeping & Eating

Camping de la Plage de St-Pabu (☎ 02 96 72 24 65; per person/site €4/7.80; ☺ Apr–mid-Oct) This family-oriented camping area is close to the beach at St-Pabu, about 5km southwest of Erquy.

Camping Le Vieux Moulin (☎ 02 96 72 34 23; www .campingvieuxmoulin.com; 14 rue des Moulins; per person/ tent/car €4.90/11/4.20, ☺ May-early Sep; ☒) About 1km northeast of town and a similar distance from the northern beaches, this four-star camping ground is a kids' paradise of playgrounds and activities.

Hôtel-Crêperie Le Reflet de la Mer (☎ 02 96 72 00 95; 18 rue du Port; s/d/tr €17/27/33; ☺ Apr-Sep) This delightful little seafront hotel, spick and span with whitewashed walls and blue shutters, has seven rooms with shared shower and toilet. Choose one of the three with a sea view and you can also watch the *boules*, played with passion on the pitches below your window. The hotel has an excellent and inexpensive creperie.

Hôtel-Restaurant Le Relais (☎ 02 96 72 32 60; fax 02 96 72 19 57; 60 rue du Port; d €46-57; ☺ closed Thu Oct-Mar) Overlooking the harbour, Le Relais has 12 rooms with bathroom and toilet, all

---

WHAT A LOAD OF SCALLOPS!

Small Erquy, at once active fishing port and seaside resort, well merits the title 'Capitale de la Coquille St-Jacques' (Capital of Scallops). Each year, around 50% of France's scallop harvest is pulled from the Baie de St-Brieuc that sweeps before it. Around 60 *coquilliers* (scallop-fishing boats), that between them land about 1500 tonnes of scallops each year, call its harbour home.

Scallops burrow deep into the offshore sandy sea beds and the fishermen catch them by towing along the bottom rake-like dredges backed by nets. As you can imagine, this causes major disturbance to the sea-floor habitat so, in order to limit the turmoil and also to avoid overfishing, scallop harvesting is severely regulated. The privileged boats that are accorded licences can dredge only between October and April, no more than two or three times a week – and then for a maximum of 45 minutes each day. As they scurry and delve, a patrol launch circles among them while a spotter plane snoops overhead, each ensuring that no boat breaks the rules. And woe betide the transgressor; as if the stiff fine wasn't enough, the opprobrium of your peers ensures that the lesson is well learnt.

Every third year in April, Erquy hosts a two-day **Fête de la Coquille St-Jacques** (Scallop Festival), with cooking demonstrations and tastings, special restaurant menus, processions, art exhibitions, folk music and fireworks. Erquy's next festival will be in April 2005 (neighbouring Loguivy-sur-Mer plays host in 2004 and St-Quay-Portrieux's turn comes around in 2006). Contact each town's tourist office for details.

facing the bay. Its **restaurant** (🕲 Easter-Sep) is a decent dining option.

L'Escurial (☎ 02 96 72 31 56; blvd de la Mer; menus €18.30-38.20, fish dishes €20-23; 🕲 closed Mon & dinner Sun except Jul & Aug) This classy restaurant, beside the tourist office, is the place to sample the delights of Erquy's *coquilles St-Jacques* and other seafood.

PLÉNEUF-VAL-ANDRÉ
pop 3800

Founded in 1880, Pléneuf-Val-André is a classic seaside resort with a vast beach and a lovely promenade, lined with early-20th-century villas and an Art Deco casino.

Orientation & Information
'Pléneuf' refers to the town centre, clustered around the church and 2km inland. 'Val-André' is the beach resort, spread along the 1.8km-long Plage Val-André. The equally impressive beaches of Plage des Vallées and its continuation, Plage de la Ville Berneuf, sweep away northwards beyond a small headland.

The **tourist office** (☎ 02 96 72 20 55; www.val-andre.org; rue Winston Churchill; 🕲 9am-1pm & 2-7pm Mon-Sat, 10am-12.30pm & 3-5pm Sun Jul & Aug, 9am-12.30pm & 2.30-6pm Mon-Sat Sep-Jun) is in the large waterfront La Rotonde building.

For a choice of splendid, but none-too-demanding, two- to 3½-hour coastal walks, pick up the tourist office's *Randonnées Pédestres Autour de Pléneuf-Val-André*. The text is in French but the maps are quite sufficient in themselves to guide you.

Sights & Activities
Like Erquy, Val-André's attractions include beaches, water sports and coastal walking. At the northeastern end of the beach is **Anse Piégu**, a sunny little cove. Just offshore is the rocky island and nature reserve of **Le Verdelet**, open to visitors but accessible on foot only at exceptionally low tides. From the southwestern end of the beach, you can follow the coastal path around the headland to the picturesque little harbour of **Dahouët**, from where the fishing boats bound for Newfoundland would set sail.

Point Passion Plage (☎ 02 96 72 91 20; Port Piégu), within the small port at the northern end of Plage Val-André, and **Centre Nautique** (☎ 02 96 72 95 28), on the headland south of Plage Val-André, both hire sailing dinghies, kayaks,

catamarans and sailboards. Prices are the same as Erquy's (see opposite).

Outside high summer, the vast, firm sands of Plage de la Ville Berneuf are crisscrossed by aficionados of *le char à voile* (sand-yachting). Both places mentioned above offer an introductory session (€14) and courses.

If you only swing your clubs once all holiday, do the rounds of **Golf Blue Green** (☎ 02 96 63 01 12; pleneuf.val.andre@bluegreen.com; rue de la plage des Vallées; per round €30-44), venue of the French Open in 2002 and 2003.

Château de Bienassis (☎ 02 96 72 22 03; adult/child €4.40/2.80; 🕲 10.30am-12.30pm & 2-6.30pm Mon-Sat, 2-6.30pm Sun mid-Jun–mid-Sep) is along the Erquy road, 6km east of the town centre. Built between the 15th and 17th centuries, this large, well-preserved castle retains its original moat and machicolated walls.

Sleeping
Camping La Ville Berneuf (☎ /fax 02 96 72 28 20; Plage de la Ville Berneuf; per person/tent/car €3.80/3.20/2.60; 🕲 Mar–mid-Nov) This small, well-sheltered site is about 4km northeast of town and only 100m from the beach.

Hôtel du Commerce (☎ 02 96 72 22 48; 2 place de Lourmel; d €25, with bathroom €35; 🕲 year-round) The cheapest hotel in town is near the church, about 2km inland from the beach.

Hôtel de la Mer (☎ 02 96 72 20 44; hdlm2@wanadoo.fr; 63 rue Amiral Charner; d €35-60; 🕲 year-round) This pretty little flower-bedecked hotel is one block in from the promenade and about 1km south of the tourist office. It has an impressive **restaurant** (menus €14.50-37.50).

Eating
Art et Saveur (☎ 02 96 63 19 17; 28 quai des Terres-Neuvas, Dahouët; mains €7-14; 🕲 Apr-Oct) Dine inside, surrounded by the exhibition of the moment, at this attractive art-gallery-cum-restaurant, or on its terrace, overlooking the port of Dahouët. Go for one of the mixed platters – say, the *Islandaise* (€11), with slivers of salmon, sardines, smoked tuna and seafood pâté – accompanied by a glass of chilled Muscadet (€3.50). If your French is up to it, you'll have fun deciphering the aphorisms and bons mots on the place mats.

Au Biniou (☎ 02 96 72 24 35; 121 rue Clemenceau; menus €15.50-39.50; 🕲 closed Wed & dinner Tue except Jul & Aug) Only 150m from the tourist office, this fine restaurant offers a range of subtle fare, much of it hauled from the sea.

Getting There & Away
CAT (☎ 02 96 68 31 20) bus No 2 for St-Brieuc stops at the church in Pléneuf and at the large building (La Rotonde) near the tourist office and the beach.

ST-BRIEUC
pop 48,900
St-Brieuc, which is the administrative and commercial capital of the Côtes d'Armor *département*, is also a transport hub. Like many other northern Brittany towns, it owes its name to a Welsh monk who arrived on Brittany's shores as a missionary in the 6th century.

Orientation
St-Brieuc sits a few kilometres inland from the southern shore of the Baie de St-Brieuc. The town's centre occupies a triangular patch of raised ground between the Rivers Gouët, to the north, and the Gouédic, to the southeast.

The old town clusters around Cathédrale St-Étienne. The main shopping street, rue St-Guillaume, is a few blocks east.

Information
Médicap (☎ 02 96 68 90 31; 4 rue Jouallan; per hr €3.10; ☼ 10am-7pm Mon-Fri, 2-7pm Sat)
Post Office (place de la Résistance)
Tourist Office (☎ 02 96 33 32 50; www.baiedesain tbrieuc.com; 7 rue St-Gouéno; ☼ 9am-7pm Mon-Sat, 10am-2pm Sun Jul & Aug, 9am-noon & 1.30-6pm Mon-Fri, 9am-12.30pm & 2-6pm Sat Sep-Jun)

Sights
St-Brieuc will never be at the top of anyone's sightseeing list, but it is a pleasant town nonetheless and wandering its streets makes a change from the crowded beaches of the coastal resorts. The highlight of the massive, fortress-like **Cathédrale St-Étienne** (place Général de Gaulle; ☼ 8am-7pm) is its fine 16th-century organ gallery at the western end. Recorded music throbs through the cathedral from the equally impressive organ itself, its 2500 pipes fashioned in the mid-19th century.

The old town's few remaining **medieval houses** can be seen around **place au Lin** and **rue Fardel**. Most venerable is the half-timbered **Maison Ribault** (1480; 32 rue Fardel). Today it's the headquarters of the local bakers' association,

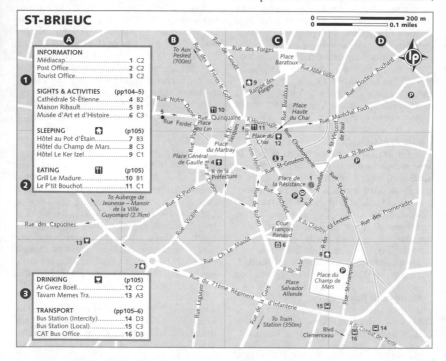

ST-BRIEUC

0 .... 200 m
0 .... 0.1 miles

INFORMATION
Médicap.........................1 C2
Post Office.....................2 C2
Tourist Office.................3 C2

SIGHTS & ACTIVITIES   (pp104–5)
Cathédrale St-Étienne......4 B2
Maison Ribault................5 B1
Musée d'Art et d'Histoire...6 C3

SLEEPING 🏠 (p105)
Hôtel au Pot d'Étain........7 B3
Hôtel du Champ de Mars...8 C3
Hôtel Le Ker Izel............9 C1

EATING 🍴 (p105)
Grill Le Madure...............10 B1
Le P'tit Bouchot.............11 C1

DRINKING 🍸 (p105)
Ar Gwez Boell................12 C2
Tavarn Memes Tra...........13 A3

TRANSPORT   (pp105–6)
Bus Station (Intercity).......14 D3
Bus Station (Local)..........15 C3
CAT Bus Office...............16 D3

To Aux Pesked (700m)
To Auberge de Jeunesse – Manoir de la Ville Guyomard (2.7km)
To Train Station (350m)

recognisable by the swinging iron sign denoting their trade.

The **Musée d'Art et d'Histoire** (☎ 02 96 62 55 20; cour François Renaud; adult/child €2.20/1.20; ☺ 9.30-11.45am & 1.30-5.45pm Tue-Sat, 1.30-5.45pm Sun) has well-laid-out exhibits covering fishing, seafaring, the textile industry, and the social and religious lives of the Côtes d'Armor region.

Sleeping

Auberge de Jeunesse – Manoir de la Ville Guyomard (☎ 02 96 78 70 70; saint-brieuc@fuaj.org; rue de la Ville Guyomard, Les Villages; per person incl breakfast €12.70; ☺ year-round) St-Brieuc's HI-affiliated hostel is a beautifully restored, 15th-century Breton manor house in a large, peaceful park about 3km northwest of town. Rooms have two to four beds. It's a 300m walk from the end of bus line No 3 at Centre Commercial Les Villages.

Hôtel au Pot d'Étain (☎ 02 96 77 43 00; fax 02 96 77 42 99; 3 rue de Brest; s/d €23/26, s with bathroom €31-37, d with bathroom €34-42; P) Run by a cheery, waggish young couple, this is an engaging budget choice, complete with inexpensive restaurant. Spick-and-span rooms are set back from the street around a cluttered rear patio, where parking is free.

Hôtel Le Ker Izel (☎ 02 96 33 46 29; fax 02 96 61 86 12; 20 rue du Gouët; s €35-40, d €51) The Ker Izel is on a quiet street just a few minutes' walk from the cathedral. Accommodation here is bright as a new pin and comfy, if slightly cramped.

Hôtel du Champ de Mars (☎ 02 96 33 60 99; hotel demars@wanadoo.fr; 13 rue Général Leclerc; s €39-45, d €42-48) Rooms here are a little lacking in charm, but the hotel is modern, comfortable, central and run by a friendly and welcoming husband-and-wife team.

Eating

For ethnic food tastes – Lebanese, Moroccan, Caribbean and more – browse the budget restaurants along **rue des Trois Frères le Goff.**

Le P'tit Bouchot (☎ 02 96 61 58 66; 4 rue Houvenagle; mains €9-13; ☺ closed Wed, lunch Sun & dinner Tue) Mussels, mussels and more mussels – *au lardon* (with bacon), *au safran* (with saffron), *au cidre* (with cider), *au curry*. This homely little restaurant prepares mussels whichever way you like them, along with many other seafood dishes.

Grill Le Madure (☎ 02 96 61 21 07; 14 rue Quinquaine; mains €13.50-14.50, lunch menu €11; ☺ closed lunch Sat & Sun Sep-Jul, lunch all of Aug) The Madure specialises

in meat, especially beef steaks, grilled on a wood-fired barbecue. Side dishes include tasty salads and delicious potatoes baked in the embers of the fire.

Aux Pesked (☎ 02 96 33 34 65; 59 rue du Légué; menus €19 & €30-85; ☺ closed Mon, lunch Sat & dinner Sun) This stylish place has an elegant dining room in muted marine colours. Everything – down to the monogrammed plates in the form of a glum fish that looks about to leap up and bite you back – exudes taste. With its picture window and open terrace overlooking the Gouët Valley, the place streams with light. Its gourmet fare leans heavily towards the sea. Service is impeccable – perhaps a little too attentive for comfort – and the weekday lunch *menu* (€19) is magnificent value.

Drinking

St-Brieuc has several lively bars, many concentrated around the cathedral, especially in rue Fardel and place du Chai. One of the town's most popular is **L'Iliade** (☎ 02 96 33 46 99; 5 rue du Légué), also known as Tavarn Noz, a large and convivial Breton pub with many little corners where you can chat over a beer or six. Other typical Breton bars with regular live music are **Tavarn Memes Tra** (☎ 02 96 68 52 36; 4 rue de Quintin) and **Ar Gwez Boell** (☎ 02 96 33 05 63; 2 bis place Haute du Chai).

Getting There & Away
BUS

St-Brieuc lies at the centre of a bus network covering Côtes d'Armor. The **CAT office** (☎ 02 96 68 31 20; 6 rue Combat des Trente) is beside the *gare interurbaine* (intercity bus station).

Bus No 9 travels along the northwestern coast to Paimpol (€7.60, 1½ hours), then Pointe l'Arcouest (for the ferry to Île de Bréhat, summer service only), via Binic and St-Quay-Portrieux. Bus No 6 heads west to Lannion (€8.40, two hours) via Guingamp (€5.70, one hour), while No 2 heads east to Pléneuf-Val-André (€5.70, one hour), Erquy (€6.70, 1¼ hours) and – in July and August only – St-Cast (€8.40, two hours).

An SNCF express bus goes to and from Vannes (€14.80, two hours, four daily) via Pontivy (€10, 1¼ hours).

TRAIN

St-Brieuc lies on the main TGV line between Paris (€52.10 to €62.70, three hours), Rennes (€14.90, 50 minutes) and Brest (€19.80, 1¼ hours). You can also travel by train to Guin-gamp (€5.20, 20 minutes, four to 11 daily) and Lannion (€10.30, one hour).

CÔTE DU GOËLO

The Côte du Goëlo stretches northwest from St-Brieuc to Île de Bréhat, taking in the holiday resorts of Binic and St-Quay-Portrieux and the fishing harbour of Paimpol. The 100m-high sea cliffs at Pointe de Plouha, north of St-Quay-Portrieux, are Brittany's highest.

CAT (☎ 02 96 68 31 20) bus No 9 runs along the coast between St-Brieuc, Binic, St-Quay-Portrieux, Paimpol (€7.60, 1½ hours) and (summer services only) Pointe l'Arcouest, the ferry point for the Île de Bréhat.

BINIC
pop 3200

Binic is an attractive little fishing harbour. In the 19th century it was one of the main ports involved in La Grande Pêche (see the boxed text opposite) but these days its main business is tourism. Each year in late May it hosts a three-day **Fête de la Morue** (Cod Festival), which sees a gathering of around 20 old sailing vessels.

Binic's **tourist office** (☎ 02 96 73 60 12; ave Général de Gaulle; ☼ 9.30am-12.30pm & 2-7pm Mon-Sat, 10am-12.30pm & 2-5pm Sun Jul & Aug, 10am-noon & 2-5pm Mon-Sat Sep-Jun) has information about the town, activities and accommodation.

Hôtel Le Benhuyc (☎ 02 96 73 39 00; www.benhuyc .com; 1 quai Jean Bart; d €45-68) This attractive three-star hotel has several rooms with views of the harbour. Its **restaurant** (mains €10-15) specialises in seafood.

ST-QUAY-PORTRIEUX
pop 3400

St-Quay is another former cod-fishing port turned seaside resort. Its first hotel opened in 1845 and in the early part of the 20th century it became a major centre for thalassotherapy. Today it's a busy summer resort, thronged in August with Parisians enjoying the beaches.

The massive breakwaters of Port d'Armor shelter the only deep-water harbour between Cherbourg and Brest, capable of holding up to 1000 yachts and fishing boats. Controversial at first – it's not a pretty sight and was

slow to attract yachties – it's accepted these days as a boon to the local economy.

St-Quay co-hosts the **Fête de la Coquille St-Jacques** (Scallop Festival) every third April (the next one here is in 2006), taking turns with Loguivy-sur-Mer (2004) and Erquy (2005).

Information
St-Quay's **main tourist office** (☎ 02 96 70 40 64; www.saintquayportrieux.com; 17 bis rue Jeanne d'Arc; ☼ 9am-7pm Mon-Sat, 9am-12.30pm & 3.30-6pm Sun Jul & Aug, 9am-12.30pm & 2-6/6.30pm Mon-Sat Sep-Jun) is at the northern end of town, near Plage du Casino. There's a seasonal **annexe** (☎ 02 96 70 50 60; 20 quai de la République; ☼ 10.30am-12.30pm & 3.30-6.30pm Jul & Aug) at Port d'Armor.

Sleeping & Eating
Camping Bellevue (☎ 02 96 70 41 84; campingbellevue@ free.fr; 68 blvd du Littoral; per person/site €4.20/6.25; ☼ Easter–mid-Sep; ☎) This camping ground is close to the coast (but not the beaches), about 1km north of the tourist office.

Hôtel Le Commerce (☎ 02 96 70 41 53; 4 rue Clemenceau; s €23, d €39-46; P). The Commerce, close to the beach between the old port and Port d'Armor, is the cheapest hotel in town – but none the worse for that, with its basic but comfy rooms.

Hôtel-Restaurant Le Gerbot d'Avoine (☎ 02 96 70 40 09; www.gerbotdavoine.com; 2 blvd du Littoral; d €43-60) Slightly higher up the price and comfort scale is this grand, old-fashioned granite house. A welcoming Logis de France with 20 rooms, it's only a couple of minutes' walk north from Plage du Casino. Its quality **restaurant** (menus €14-36) serves traditional Breton cuisine.

Hôtel Le Ker Moor (☎ 02 96 70 52 22; www .ker-moor.com; 13 rue Président Le Sénécal; d €70-110; ☼ mid-Jan–mid-Dec) Set dramtically beneath a mock-Moorish villa on a cliff overlooking the sea, the Ker Moor has stylish, modern rooms with sea-view balconies. Sadly, its once highly reputed restaurant is nowadays reserved for corporate clients.

KERMARIA
pop 770

This tiny village is unremarkable, except for its 13th-century **Chapelle de Kermaria-an-Iskuit** (Chapel of the House of Mary, Restorer of Health), which hosts a famous *pardon* on the third Sunday in September. A fresco, from the late 15th century, runs the length of the nave; it depicts the *Danse Macabre* (Dance of Death), a common theme of the time. Death, represented by skeletons and corpses, dances with the living to remind us that we are all mortal, and that wealth and status are no protection – the dancing figures include a monk and a ploughman as well as a king and a cardinal. If the church is locked, call M Cojean (☎ 02 96 20 35 78).

From St-Quay-Portrieux, follow the road towards Paimpol and, when you reach the centre of Plouha, turn left (west) onto the D21 towards Pléhédel. Kermaria is 3km along this road.

PAIMPOL
pop 8400
Paimpol is a working fishing harbour, once famous as the home port of the Icelandic fishery. Then, the town's fishermen would set sail for the seas around Iceland for seven months or more at a stretch. Many, victims of storms or disease, never returned and are now recalled in folk tales and *chants de marins* (sea shanties). See the boxed text below.

Orientation & Information
The centre of Paimpol, to the south of the two harbours, is around the market square of place du Martray. The bus and train stations are both 100m south of this square.

Au Lavoir Pampolais (23 rue 18 Juin; ☺ 8am-8pm) Just north of the train station, this place will wash, dry and fold your clothes while you look around town.

Tourist Office (☎ 02 96 20 83 16; www.paimpol -goelo.com; place de la République; ☺ 9.30am-7.30pm Mon-Sat, 10am-6pm Sun Jun-Sep, 9.30am-12.30pm & 1.30-6.30pm Mon-Sat Oct-May)

Sights & Activities
Paimpol has the feel of a working port, with constant nautical comings and goings at the harbour's two crowded docks.

The splendid **Musée de la Mer** (☎ 02 96 22 02 19; rue Labenne; adult/child €4.15/2.05; ☺ 10.30am-12.30pm & 2.30-6pm mid-Jun–Aug, 2.30-6pm mid-April–mid-Jun & early Sep), in a former cod-drying factory, charts the region's maritime heritage, notably the Icelandic cod fishery of the 19th century.

For something of Paimpol's land-bound history, visit the **Musée du Costume Breton** (☎ 02 96 22 02 19; adult/child €2.45/1.30; ☺ 10.30am-12.30pm & 2.30-6pm Jul & Aug). (A combined ticket, giving access to both museums, costs €5.25/ 2.55 adult/child.)

Not only railway buffs will enjoy travelling on a train between Paimpol and Pontrieux, following the scenic Trieux Valley line and pulled by a 1920s 4-6-0 steam locomotive. **La Vapeur du Trieux** (Trieux Steam; ☎ 08 92 39 14 27; www.vapeurdutrieux.com; Gare de Paimpol, ave du Général de Gaulle; adult/child return €20/10; departures twice daily Thu-Sun Jun-Sep, more frequently mid-Jul Aug). The outward trip includes a 40-minute stop at **Traou-Nez manor house** for a snack and Breton music. Reservations are required.

Sleeping
Camping Municipal de Cruckin (☎ 02 96 20 78 47; rue de Cruckin; up to 3 adults, tent & car €11.65; ☺ Easter-Sep) This quiet, two-star camping ground is on the beautiful Baie de Kérity, 2km southeast of town off the road to Plouha.

Auberge de Jeunesse (☎ 02 96 20 83 60; paimpol@ fuaj.org; Château de Kerraoul) Occupying an 18th-century mansion, this HI-affiliated hostel should reopen during 2005 after undergoing extensive renovations.

LA GRANDE PÊCHE
It was the fishermen of Brittany who, way back in the 16th century, pioneered La Grande Pêche à la Morue (the Great Cod Fishery), long-lining for cod on the Grand Banks of Newfoundland. Braving the stormy waters of the north Atlantic, the *morutiers* (cod-fishing boats) would be away from their home ports for up to six months at a time, their crews suffering lives of unimaginable hardship – a tradition that continued until the 1930s.

During the peak of La Grande Pêche in the late 19th and early 20th centuries, boats from St-Malo favoured the Newfoundland (Terre-Neuve) fishing grounds, while the fishermen of Paimpol and Binic frequented the Icelandic fishery. Their *goélettes* (schooners), with a crew of only a dozen or so men, were small and fast but often exposed to dangerous conditions. In the 19th and early 20th centuries, the Paimpol region lost a total of 100 ships and more than 2000 men to the sea in only 80 years.

Hôtel Le Terre-Neuvas (☎ 02 96 55 14 14; fax 02 96 20 47 66; 16 quai Duguay Trouin; d €31-37; ❤ mid-Jan–mid-Dec) With a good location beside the harbour, the Terre-Neuvas is Paimpol's best budget choice. The more expensive rooms have sea views.

Hôtel Le Repaire de Kerroc'h (☎ 02 96 20 50 13; kerroch@chateauxhotels.com; 29 quai Morand; d €60-99) Don't be deterred by the naff suit of armour that greets you on entry to the hotel; the more upmarket, 11-room Kerroc'h is set in a lovely 18th-century privateer's mansion overlooking the marina. Most of the rooms – even the less expensive ones – overlook the harbour.

K" Loys (☎ 02 96 20 40 01; www.k-loys.com; 21 quai Morand; d €65-120) Each of the 15 rooms at cosy 'Chez Louise', in its time a shipowner's mansion, is individually and tastefully decorated. One, accommodating up to four, has facilities for disabled travellers.

Eating

Both Hôtel Le Terre-Neuvas and the elegant Hôtel Le Repaire de Kerroc'h (see above) have good restaurants.

Crêperie-Restaurant Morel (☎ 02 96 20 86 34; 11 place du Martray; galettes €4.20-6.90) On Paimpol's main square, the Morel is much favoured by locals during the low season, especially on market day (Tuesday). Help your *galette* down with a glass of refreshing draught cider.

Bar-Brasserie Le Neptune (☎ 02 96 20 53 03; 23 quai Morand; mains €7.50-12; ❤ Tue-Sun) This cosy little waterfront bar does good, filling light meals and snacks, including a tasty pile of *moules-frites* (€8).

L'Islandais (☎ 02 96 20 93 80; 19 quai Morand; menus €16.50 & €24.50) This attractive, bustling, harbourside restaurant serves, predominantly and appropriately, fish and seafood. For something lighter, try the salads (€7.70) or a *galette* (€3.40 to €6.10).

Every Tuesday morning Paimpol's **market** spreads over place Gambetta and place du Martray. At the weekend, vendors sell freshly shucked **oysters** at quai Duguay Trouin.

Getting There & Around

In summer, buses (€2.10, six to seven daily) run to Pointe l'Arcouest to connect with the Île de Bréhat ferries (see p110).

There are several trains or SNCF buses that operate daily between Paimpol and Guingamp (€5.80, 45 minutes), where you can pick up connections to Brest, St-Brieuc and Rennes.

You can rent bikes from **Cycles du Vieux Clocher** (☎ 02 96 20 83 58; place Verdun; per day €11). It's south of the tourist office near the Vieux Clocher (Old Bell Tower).

AROUND PAIMPOL
Abbaye de Beauport

About 2.5km southeast of Paimpol town centre lie the graceful Gothic ruins of **Abbaye de Beauport** (☎ 02 96 55 18 55; Kérity; adult/child €4.5/2 incl guided tour; ❤ 10am-7pm mid-Jun–mid-Sep, 10am-noon & 2-5pm mid-Sep–mid-Jun). Founded in 1202, the abbey flourished for several centuries as a port and overnight stop for English pilgrims heading for Santiago de Compostela in Spain. The tour takes in the abbey and its sheltered harbour, apple orchards and rose gardens.

Château de la Roche-Jagu

Around 10km southwest of Paimpol, on the banks of the Trieux, stands the scenic 15th-century country-house-cum-castle of **Château de la Roche-Jagu** (☎ 02 96 95 62 35; La Roche-Jagu; adult/child €4/1.50; ❤ 10am-7pm mid-Jun–mid-Sep, 10.30am-12.30pm & 2-6pm mid-Sep–Nov & Feb–mid-Jun). Built

---

DETOUR: SILLON DE TALBERT VIA THE D20

It's tempting to belt along the straight, swift inland D786 that runs between Paimpol and Lannion. But build in a couple of hours to turn right at Lézardrieux and take the quiet D20 that runs due north for 10km, running parallel to the estuary of the River Trieux as far as land's end at the tip of the **Sillon de Talbert**. Two hours for only 20km, there and back? Yes, because you'll probably want to make a brief pause near **Pommelin**, where the road meets a tiny branch of the estuary – and to walk a stretch of the breezy Sillon de Talbert, watch the sea birds and, if your timing's right, see the local **seaweed harvesters** tossing strands of kelp into their carts (see the boxed text, p109).

If you don't want to retrace your wheel marks, continue along the D20 as it snakes around to rejoin the main D786 at Tréguier.

on the site of an older castle, the chateau was both fortress, guarding the approach to the river harbour of Pontrieux, and aristocratic residence. While the side facing the river is stern and forbidding, the landward façade is a delightful example of Flamboyant Gothic domestic architecture. There are good short walks within the attractive **gardens** (admission free; ⊙ dawn-dusk) and along the river.

Sillon de Talbert

Ten kilometres northwest of Paimpol, the point of land between the Rivers Trieux and Jaudy merges with the sea in a vast tidal no-man's-land of shifting sandbanks, mud flats and rocky reefs. Along its centre lies the Sillon de Talbert, a snaking ribbon of sand, gravel and marram grass around 3.5km long but never more than 100m wide. This delicate spit of land, shaped by tidal currents, makes for pleasant, breezy walking and attracts crowds of expert kite-flyers on windy days. At the far end of the spit is a nature reserve where terns and ringed plovers nest in spring and seaweed is harvested from the surrounding tidal flats.

From Paimpol, head west on the Tréguier road. Turn right (north) in the village of Lézardrieux, immediately after crossing the River Trieux, and follow signs to the Sillon de Talbert.

ÎLE DE BRÉHAT

pop 425

Not so much an island as an archipelago, Île de Bréhat – just 3.5km long and 1.5km wide – is surrounded by a tide-washed maze of pink granite reefs and islets. An exceptionally mild microclimate nurtures luxuriant and exotic flora such as palms, fig trees, eucalyptus, mimosa, honeysuckle, camellias, geraniums – and hydrangeas that can sprout up to 200 football-sized flower heads per bush.

Cars aren't allowed on the island, but Bréhat is overrun with visitors in summer (more than 4000 invading daily via the Pointe l'Arcouest ferry on peak days). The best times to visit are spring and autumn, when the crowds are less oppressive.

Orientation & Information

The island has two roughly equal parts – Île Sud (South Island) and Île Nord (North Island) – umbilically joined by the small,

> **THE SEAWEED HARVESTERS**
>
> All along the north coast of Brittany, from Île de Bréhat to Pointe de Corsen in northern Finistère, the receding tide exposes vast areas of sea bed covered in a thick growth of seaweed (goémon). For centuries, a small band of seaweed harvesters (goémoniers) has collected the weed washed up along the shore or set out in boats to dredge it fresh from its rocky bed. Long used as an agricultural fertiliser, the seaweed is today dried and used for various purposes in the food and cosmetics industries.
>
> The **Centre d'Étude et de Valorisation des Algues** (☎ 02 96 22 93 50; Armor-Pleubian; adult/child €4/2.50; ⊙ 3-4.30pm Thu-Sun) is a research laboratory 2km southeast of the Sillon de Talbert with exhibits (in French only) on the harvesting and use of Brittany's seaweed crop.

(see Sleeping & Eating, p110)

scarcely noticeable Pont ar Prat. The ferry lands at Port-Clos in the south of the island. Le Bourg is the only place approaching the status of a village.

The island's **tourist office** (☎ 02 96 20 04 15; syndicatinitiative.brehat@wanadoo.fr; ⊙ 10am-6pm Tue-Fri, 10am-1pm & 2-5.30pm Mon & Sat Jul & Aug, 10am-12.30pm & 2-4.30pm Mon-Sat Apr-Jun & Sep, 10am-12.30pm & 2-4.30pm Mon & Fri Oct-Mar) is just east of the main square in Le Bourg.

Activities

If you're here for only a few hours, the best way to spend your time is to hike from Port-Clos to the **Phare du Paon** (Peacock Lighthouse – we can't claim to have spotted any though a couple of pheasants scuttled away through the undergrowth) on the wild, northern point of the island, a distance of around 4km (allow 1½ hours each way). The road takes you through Le Bourg, with its pretty little square and a 12th-century church. On the way to the lighthouse, be sure to build in a rest stop at **Ferme et Fromagerie de Bréhat** (see Sleeping & Eating, p110).

If time permits, make a detour up to the tiny, whitewashed **Chapelle St-Michel**, built in 1852 on the highest point of the island (30m), from where the view is superb. In the bay below is the **Moulin à Marée du Birlot** (1638), a tidal grain mill powered by the retreating sea.

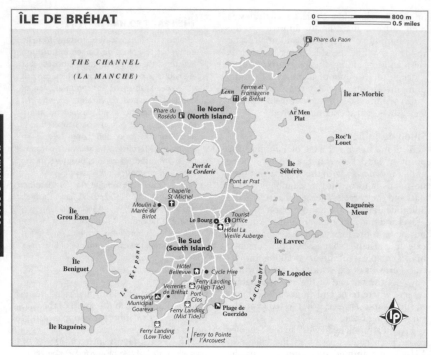

ÎLE DE BRÉHAT

THE CHANNEL
(LA MANCHE)

Phare du Paon

Ferme et
Fromagerie
de Bréhat

Lenn

Île ar-Morbic

Phare du
Rosédo

Île Nord
(North Island)

Ar Men
Plat

Roc'h
Louet

Port de
la Corderie

Île
Séhérès

Pont ar Prat

Chapelle
St-Michel

Moulin à
Marée du
Birlot

Île
Grou Ézen

Le Bourg

Tourist
Office

Raguénès
Meur

Hôtel La
Vieille Auberge

Île Sud
(South Island)

Île Lavrec

Île
Beniguet

Hôtel
Bellevue

Cycle Hire

Île Logodec

Verreries
de Bréhat

Ferry Landing
(High Tide)

Camping
Municipal
Goareva

Port-
Clos

Plage de
Guerzido

Ferry Landing
(Mid Tide)

Île Raguénès

Ferry Landing
(Low Tide)

Ferry to Pointe
l'Arcouest

A renovated 17th-century fortress on the hilltop to the west of Port-Clos now houses the **Verreries de Bréhat** (Bréhat Glassworks; ☎ 02 96 20 09 09; La Citadelle; admission €2 mid-Jun–mid-Sep, free mid-Sep–mid-Jun; ☽ 10am-6pm daily mid-Jun–mid-Sep, 10am-1pm & 2-6pm Mon-Fri mid-Sep–mid-Jun). On weekdays, you can watch the glass-blowers at work and buy the finished products. Only the shop is open on Saturday and Sunday.

The island's best beach is **Plage du Guerzido**, about 500m southeast of Port-Clos. There are other good bathing spots on the southern side of Île Nord, along the shore west of Pont ar Prat.

Sleeping & Eating
Camping Municipal Goareva (☎ 02 96 20 02 46; Port-Clos; up to 3 adults & tent €8; ☽ May-Sep) The island's only camping facility, west of Port-Clos, enjoys a lovely setting among the pine trees around the citadel.

Hôtel Bellevue (☎ 02 96 20 00 05; www.hotel-belle vue-brehat.com - French only; Port-Clos; d €83-97; ☽ Mar-Dec) The best of Bréhat's three hotels commands a superb view over the harbour at Port-Clos; of its 17 rooms, 11 have sea views.

You can dine outdoors on garden terraces shaded by huge pine trees.

Hôtel La Vieille Auberge (☎ 02 96 20 00 24; vieille -auberge.brehat.com@wanadoo.fr; Le Bourg; d €83.50-100; ☽ Easter-Nov) This 15-room hotel is set in an atmospheric old *bréhatin* house (1711) of pink granite. It has a peaceful, flower-filled garden at the back and a good seafood restaurant out front.

Ferme et Fromagerie de Bréhat (☎ 02 96 20 04 06; Kervilon, Île Nord; ☽ Easter-Sep) Stop by for a glass of milk or chilled cider and pick up a baby cheese (€2) or open sandwich at this roadside stall, where the farmer sells fresh dairy produce from his Jersey herd.

Getting There & Away
Vedettes de Bréhat (☎ 02 96 55 79 50; www.vedettes debrehat.com) operates the ferries (adult/child return €7.50/6.50, 15 minutes, hourly sailings from 8.30am to 7pm April to September, at least eight daily October to March) to Île de Bréhat from Pointe l'Arcouest, 6km north of Paimpol.

Between April and September, the same company also offers 45-minute boat trips around the island (adult/child €12/9) from Port-Clos.

During the summer there are also boats to Île de Bréhat from St-Quay-Portrieux, Binic, Perros-Guirec, Pléneuf-Val-André and Erquy. Ask for details at the respective tourist offices.

Getting Around

Cars are not allowed on the island. Several places, including a couple just beyond the high-tide arrival jetty, rent bikes (around €10/13 per half/full day).

The little tourist train that negotiates the narrow lanes had broken down when we last visited and its future was uncertain.

CÔTE DE GRANIT ROSE

With its huge, rounded outcrops of deep-pink granite contrast with golden sand and emerald-green water, the Côte de Granit Rose (Pink Granite Coast) is one of Brittany's most beautiful stretches of coastline.

GUINGAMP

pop 8800

You may well pass through Guingamp en route to the Côte de Granit Rose to the north. It's a busy industrial and university town that sits at a cultural crossroads – between the 'true' Brittany to the west and 'Gallic' Brittany to the east; and between Armor (coastal Brittany) to the north and Argoat (inland Brittany) to the south. Once an important textile centre, its name is the likely source of the English word 'gingham' (checked cloth).

Guingamp's very attractive, tree-lined, triangular town square has a few medieval houses at the downhill end and **Basilique Notre Dame de Bon Secours** at the top. Built from a patchwork of dark-green schist and rusty granite, the church's twin bell towers are of different ages and styles – Gothic to the left, Renaissance to the right as you look above its finely carved but severely weathered main door.

The **tourist office** (☎ 02 96 43 73 89; place Champ au Roy; ⏰ 10am–noon & 2–6pm Mon-Sat Jul & Aug, Tue-Sat Jun & Sep, Tue, Fri & Sat Oct-May) is in the modern Centre Culturel, one block northeast of the church. It also has Internet access (€1 per 15 minutes).

Sleeping

Demeure Ville Blanche (☎ 02 96 44 28 53; www.demeure-vb.com; 5 rue Général de Gaulle; s €49-66, d €56-78) Should you find yourself overnighting in Guingamp, you may as well splash out on its best hotel. The Ville Blanche is a grand 17th-century town house, fully renovated and furnished in period style, but with all modern comforts, including a video recorder and stereo in each room.

Getting There & Away

There are frequent buses from Guingamp to St-Brieuc (€5.70, one hour) and Lannion (€6.65, one hour). Trains run to/from St-Brieuc (€5.20, 20 minutes, four to 11 daily), Lannion (€7, 40 minutes, three to 11 daily) and Paimpol (€5.80, 45 minutes, one to five daily).

TRÉGUIER

pop 2950

With its narrow streets of weathered granite and half-timbered houses huddled around a magnificent cathedral, Tréguier commands a hilltop overlooking the confluence of the Rivers Jaudy and Guindy. It was founded in the 6th century by yet another of those itinerant Welsh monks, St Tugdual, and soon became a bishopric. Before the French Revolution, Tréguier – today merely a local market town – was one of the most important urban centres in Brittany, thanks to the flax trade. It still retains vestiges of its past glory and makes a good base for exploring the surrounding region.

Orientation & Information

The most interesting part of Tréguier clusters around the market square of place du Martray, on the southern side of the hilltop cathedral. To reach the marina on the Jaudy, to the east of the town centre, go down rue St-André or rue Ernest Renan.

The **tourist office** (☎ 02 96 92 22 33; www.paysdetreguier.com - French only; 67 rue Ernest Renan; ⏰ 9am-7pm Tue-Sat, 10am-1pm & 2-7pm Sun & Mon Jul & Aug, 9.30am-12.30pm & 1.30-5.30pm Mon-Fri Sep-Jun) is at the lower end of rue Ernest Renan, beside the Jaudy.

Sights

Tréguier's glory is its magnificent Gothic **Cathédrale St-Tugdual** (place du Martray; free guided visits 10am-noon & 2-6pm Jul & Aug). Most of the building

CÔTES D'ARMOR

dates from the 14th and 15th centuries, but as you enter the south porch from place du Martray, ahead of you are two Romanesque arches at the base of the **Tour Hastings** – all that remains of an earlier 10th-century church.

To appreciate the grandeur of the cathedral, stand between the massive fluted columns of the crossing, craning your neck to see the soaring ribbed vaulting of the nave and choir. Just west of the crossing is the exuberantly Gothic, canopied **tomb of St-Yves**, surrounded by votive candles and offerings. It is an 1890 copy of the 15th-century original, which was destroyed after the Revolution.

A door to the right of the Tour Hastings leads out into the **cloister**, a peaceful flower garden lined with graceful 15th-century Gothic tracery and a few ancient Templar grave slabs.

Flanking place du Martray and the narrow streets around it – notably rue Ernest Renan, rue St-Yves and rue Colvestre – are some interesting 16th-century **half-timbered houses**.

Festivals & Events

Mercredis en Fête (Festival Wednesdays) are six Wednesdays of fun and activity in July and August, animating place des Halles and place du Martray. There's a bustling market in the morning and concerts of traditional music, variety shows and general enjoyment in the afternoon and evening.

The **Pardon de St-Yves**, held on the third Sunday of May, is Tréguier's major event of the year. Around 15,000 pilgrims take part in a religious procession in honour of St Yves, patron saint of – now here's a paradox – both lawyers and the poor.

Sleeping

For the nearest camping grounds, see Plougrescant (right).

Hôtel Le Saint-Yves (☎ 02 96 92 33 49; 4 rue Colvestre; s/d €18/26, d with shower €30, with bathroom €38) This little seven-room hotel, above a bar and just 100m west of the cathedral, is great value, especially considering its central location.

Hôtel L'Estuaire (☎ 02 96 92 30 25; fax 02 96 92 94 80; 5 place Général de Gaulle; d with shower €29, with bathroom €44-50) This hotel, recently acquired and renovated by a British couple, overlooks the river near the foot of rue Ernest Renan. Its bar is bright and convivial and the restaurant merits a visit in its own right.

Hôtel Aigue Marine (☎ 02 96 92 97 00; www.aigue marine.fr; Marina; d €66-88; ☉ Mar-Dec; **P** **☒**) The three-star Aigue Marine is a modern luxury hotel overlooking the marina, about 150m upstream from Hôtel L'Estuaire. Many of the rooms have balconies, there's an outdoor heated pool at the rear and it has a more than decent restaurant.

Eating

Crêperie des Halles (☎ 02 96 92 39 15; 16 rue Ernest Renan; galettes €4.30-10; ☉ Tue-Sun) This rustic little creperie is a favourite with locals for its good food and reasonable prices. Last orders are 30 minutes before closing (1.30pm at lunchtime, 9pm at night), when they lock the door. Turn up early – and on market days don't hold out much hope of getting a table! The place is 100% nonsmoking – a rarity in France.

Le Hangar (☎ 02 96 92 47 46; Marina; ☉ dinner only Tue-Sun Apr-Sep) In an old boathouse, with an outdoor dining deck overlooking the marina, this good-value seafood restaurant attracts a young and lively yachtie crowd. It does mussels in seven different ways (€8 to €10.30) and an overflowing seafood platter (€28).

Getting There & Away

CAT (☎ 02 96 68 31 20) bus No 7 links Tréguier with Paimpol (€4.50, 30 minutes) and Lannion (€4.50, 35 minutes). The nearest train stations are at Paimpol and Lannion.

AROUND TRÉGUIER
Plougrescant

The small village of Plougrescant (population 1400), 7km north of Tréguier, has a delightfully eccentric little church, **Chapelle St-Gonéry**. Its 10th-century tower is topped by a distinctly skew-whiff steeple, grafted on in the 17th century, that leans alarmingly to one side.

Camping Le Varlen (☎ 02 96 92 52 15; fax 02 96 92 50 34; 4 route de Pors Hir; 2 adults, tent & car €14.60; ☉ year-round) At Pors Hir, Le Varlen is about 2km north of Plougrescant.

Manoir de Kergrec'h (☎ 02 96 92 56 06; kergrec.h@ wanadoo.fr; Kergrec'h; d with breakfast €100; **P**) As far as could be from a humble tent, this 17th-century chateau is set in beautiful gardens approximately 600m east of Chapelle St-Gonéry. With its spacious medieval rooms and antique furniture, plus a breakfast fit for a duke and duchess, it's a wonderful romantic hideaway.

Côte des Ajoncs

The coast between Tréguier and Perros-Guirec is known as the Côte des Ajoncs (Gorse Coast) because of its wild conjunction of yellow-flowered gorse bushes, grassy heath land and weather-worn granite coated with hairy green lichen. The most northerly point is **Pointe du Château**, with views of the Sept-Îles offshore. About 1km to the west at Castel Meur is **Le Gouffre**, a spectacular cleft in the sea cliffs, and **La Maison Entre Les Deux Rochers**, an picturesque little house built between two huge granite outcrops – the subject of innumerable Breton postcards.

Further west again lie the picturesque villages of **Buguélès** and **Port Blanc**, both with good sandy beaches.

CAT (☎ 02 96 68 31 20) bus D runs between Tréguier and Penvénan via Plougrescant, Pors Hir and Buguélès for a flat fare of €1.90. Buses run twice a day in July and August and once daily the rest of the year. The same service also runs several times a day between Penvénan and Lannion via Port Blanc.

PERROS-GUIREC

pop 7900

The chic resort of Perros-Guirec perches on a rocky peninsula at the eastern end of the Côte de Granit Rose. It's an exclusive town, flanked by a sheltered new marina to the southeast and the old fishing port of Ploumanac'h about 3km to the northwest; in between lies a coastline of pink and orange granite cliffs and coves where sea otters still feel at home.

Orientation

Perros has two distinct parts: the upper town and commercial centre on the crest of the peninsula, and the marina area to the south. They're about 1km apart if you make your way up through the maze of backstreets, or double that distance if instead you follow the main coastal road (blvd de la Mer and blvd Clemenceau) around Pointe du Château, at the eastern end of town.

Information

Laverie du Port (7 rue Anatole le Braz; ⊗ 9.15am-7.15pm) Get your clothes washed at this laundry.
Tourist Office (☎ 02 96 23 21 15; www.perros-guirec.com; 21 place de l'Hôtel de Ville; ⊗ 9am-7.30pm Mon-Sat, 10am-12.30pm & 4-7pm Sun Jul & Aug, 9am-12.30pm & 2-6.30pm Mon-Sat Jun-Sep)

Sights & Activities

With the possible exception of tiny **Église St-Jacques**, a little, lopsided gem, half Romanesque and half Gothic, there are no real sights in Perros-Guirec. The coastal scenery is the main attraction; here nature has taken the raw seaside materials of rock, sand and sea and assembled them in a particularly appealing fashion. Baking on the beach, chilling in a café or mastering the art of windsurfing are among the activities on offer, but by far the best is exploring the coastline on foot.

Of a number of **beaches** close to Perros, the main one is **Plage de Trestraou**. Near Pointe du Château, **Plage de Trestrignel**, is a smaller and prettier spot – and therefore much more crowded.

The former fishing village of **Ploumanac'h**, 3km northwest of Perros but now virtually a suburb, has a pretty harbour with an old tide-powered water mill and a good, safe family beach at **Plage de St-Guirec**.

WALKING

The **Sentier des Douaniers** (custom officer's trail) follows the spectacular 5km coastline from Plage de Trestraou to Ploumanac'h through a wilderness of massive, pink granite boulders and outcrops.

The **Vallées des Traouïero** are two narrow, wooded ravines (Grand and Petit Traouïero) that lead inland. Footpaths along the valley floors snake through a jumble of huge, moss-coated boulders, ivy-clad tree trunks and fern-fringed streams. The path along the Grand Traouïero starts on the shore just west of the tidal mill. About 1.5km inland you can head east for 500m and then return to Ploumanac'h along the Petit Traouïero (a total of 4km). Ask the tourist office for its *Sentiers de Petites Randonnées*, a wallet of 15 sheets describing these and other walks in the area, each with a fairly explicit map.

WATER SPORTS

The **Centre Nautique** (☎ 02 96 49 81 21; Plage de Trestraou; ⊗ year-round) rents out equipment and offers courses for catamaran, dinghy, windsurfer and kayak.

Sleeping

Many accommodation places close for much or all of October as staff take their own well-earned annual break.

CÔTES D'ARMOR

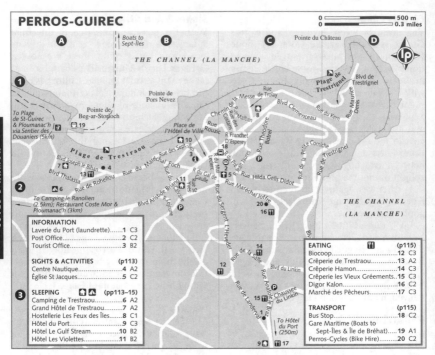

PERROS-GUIREC

Boats to Sept-Îles

THE CHANNEL (LA MANCHE)

Pointe du Château

0 — 500 m
0 — 0.3 miles

Plage de Trestrignel

Blvd de Trestrignel

Pointe de Pors Nevez

Pointe de Beg-ar-Storloch

To Plage de St-Guirec & Ploumanac'h via Sentier des Douaniers (5km)

Place de l'Hôtel de Ville

Plage de Trestraou

Blvd Clemenceau

Rue Maurice Denis

Rue du Kern

Rue de la Petite Corniche

Rue de Trestrignel

Blvd Joseph le Bihan

Rue du Maréchal Foch

Rue de Rohellou

Blvd Thalassa

To Camping le Ranolien (2.5km); Restaurant Coste Mor & Ploumanac'h (3km)

Blvd Aristide Briand

Rue Ernest Renan

Rue du Gal de Gaulle

Rue Hilda Gelis Didot

Rue Maréchal Joffre

THE CHANNEL (LA MANCHE)

Rue du Sergent l'Héveder

Rue de la Salle

Blvd du Linkin

Chaussée du Linkin

Rue Anatole le Braz

Rue de Landerval

To Hôtel du Port (250m)

To Hôtel du Port

INFORMATION
Laverie du Port (laundrette)........1 C3
Post Office......................................2 C2
Tourist Office................................3 B2

SIGHTS & ACTIVITIES (p113)
Centre Nautique...........................4 A2
Église St Jacques..........................5 C2

SLEEPING (pp113–15)
Camping de Trestraou.................6 A2
Grand Hôtel de Trestraou...........7 A2
Hostellerie Les Feux des Îles......8 C1
Hôtel du Port................................9 C3
Hôtel Le Gulf Stream.................10 B2
Hôtel Les Violettes....................11 B2

EATING (p115)
Biocoop.......................................12 C3
Crêperie de Trestraou...............13 A2
Crêperie Hamon.........................14 C3
Crêperie les Vieux Gréements...15 C3
Digor Kalon.................................16 C2
Marché des Pêcheurs................17 C3

TRANSPORT (p115)
Bus Stop......................................18 C2
Gare Maritime (Boats to
Sept-Îles & Île de Bréhat)........19 A1
Perros-Cycles (Bike Hire).........20 C2

Camping de Trestraou (☎ 02 96 23 08 11; fax 02 96 23 26 06; 89 ave du Casino; 2 adults, tent & car €20; ☺ May–mid-Sep) Ideally positioned, this camping ground is close to the centre of Perros-Guirec and only a few minutes' walk from Plage de Trestraou.

Camping le Ranolien (☎ 02 96 91 43 58; chemin de Ranolien, Ploumanac'h; 2 adults, tent & car €37; ☺ Apr–mid-Sep; ☎) This luxury, four-star site has the best location of all – it is close to the sea and on the rocky coast between Perros and Ploumanac'h.

HOTELS – PERROS-GUIREC
Hôtel Les Violettes (☎ 02 96 23 21 33; fax 02 96 23 10 08; 19 rue du Calvaire; s/d €30/34, d with shower €38, with bathroom €45) This Victorian-style hotel with restaurant and small bar has smallish rooms and is guaranteed to give you a warm welcome.

Hôtel du Port (☎ 02 96 23 21 79; www.cafeduport.fr; 85 rue Ernest Renan; d €38-47) Hôtel du Port has a dozen modern, double-glazed rooms, with bathroom, TV and telephone. The more expensive ones have balconies overlooking the marina.

Hôtel Le Gulf Stream (☎ 02 96 23 21 86; www.gulf-stream-hotel-bretagne.com; 26 rue des Sept-Îles; d €30-40, with bathroom €50-60) The Gulf Stream is a lovely, ivy-cloaked, mansard-roofed villa perched above the eastern end of Plage de Trestraou. Its 12 modest – and very pleasant – rooms (eight with a sea view) contrast with its decidedly upmarket restaurant, which also overlooks the beach.

Hostellerie Les Feux des Îles (☎ 02 96 23 22 94; www.feux-des-iles.com; 53 blvd Clemenceau; s €61-90, d €72-110) Surrounded by a large, flower-filled, clifftop garden looking out towards the Sept-Îles, 'Island Lights' is a magnificent stone villa with a modern wing attached. Its restaurant specialises in gourmet seafood.

Grand Hôtel de Trestraou (☎ 02 96 49 84 84; www.grand-hotel-trestraou.com; 45 blvd Joseph le Bihan; d €65-95; ☺ Mar–mid-Nov) For the ultimate in pampering, the Grand offers elegant rooms with a sumptuous *belle époque* décor, and there's also the option of thalassotherapy treatment.

HOTELS – PLOUMANAC'H
Hôtel de l'Europe (☎ 02 96 91 40 76; www.hotelde leurope-perros.com; 158 rue de St-Guirec; d €42-62 Jul & Aug,

€38-49 Sep-Jun; (P)) This friendly hotel is only 30m from the beach at Plage de St-Guirec. Cyclists will feel particularly at home; the local club meets in the bar and the owner's son was pursuit champion of Brittany. Rooms are soundproofed and higher prices are for sea views.

Hôtel Le Phare (☎ 02 96 91 41 19; www.hotel -le-phare.com; 39 rue St-Guirec; d €42-59; (P)) The 24-room *phare* (lighthouse), a Logis de France, further away from the beach (500m) at the entrance to town, represents good value. Breakfast (€6) is a compulsory extra charge in high season.

Eating

Crêperie du Trestraou (☎ 02 96 23 04 34; blvd Thalassa; galettes €2.80-9.20; ⊗ closed Mon & Thu except Jul & Aug) Although this creperie looks more like a standard pizza joint from the outside, it has an excellent selection of crepes and *galettes*, as well as salads, seafood and grills.

Crêperie Hamon (☎ 02 96 23 28 82; 36 rue de la Salle; galettes €3-6.50; ⊗ 7-9pm Tue Sat) This eccentric little place has only a handful of tables in what seems like a domestic living room. But the food and atmosphere are great – the chef's party trick is to toss crepes over his shoulder for the waitress to catch. Reservations are essential.

Crêperie les Vieux Gréements (☎ 02 96 91 14 99; 19 rue Anatole le Braz; galettes €5.50-9; ⊗ Tue-Sun, closed 2 weeks in Oct & 1-15 Dec) In an old shipowner's house overlooking the marina, it also has a pleasant outdoor terrace. On the 1st floor is a *moulerie*, serving mussels, mussels and more mussels.

Digor Kalon (☎ 02 96 49 03 63; 89 rue du Maréchal Joffre; menus €12-17.50; ⊗ evenings only, closed Mon-Tue except Jul & Aug) This Celtic-themed pub-cum-restaurant is an Aladdin's cave of bric-a-brac. The food – snacky stuff such as mixed tapas (€6.50), mussels (€8.50 to €9.50) and Breton cakes – is good and it does a great line in local beers.

Restaurant Coste Mor (☎ 02 96 91 65 55; 162 rue St-Guirec, Ploumanac'h; ⊗ Easter-Oct) This great, mainly seafood restaurant has an unbeatable spot near Plage de St-Guirec at Ploumanac'h. With *menus* from €12 to €82, there's something for every palate and pocket.

SELF-CATERING

At the **Marché des Pêcheurs** (Marina; ⊗ 8.30am-12.30pm Jul & Aug, 2-3 times weekly Sep-Jun), fisherfolk

sell their catch directly. Nearby, **Biocoop** (67 rue Anatole le Braz) is a neat little cooperative that sells only organic produce.

Getting There & Around

CAT (☎ 02 96 68 31 20) bus No 15 links Perros-Guirec with Lannion (€3, 30 minutes, five to eight daily) via Ploumanac'h, Trégastel and Trébeurden. **Perros-Cycles** (☎ 02 96 23 13 08; 129 rue Maréchal Joffre) rents city/mountain bikes for €12/23 per day.

SEPT-ÎLES

The ornithological reserve of the Sept-Îles (Seven Islands) and countless smaller rocks and islets lie 5km offshore to the north of Ploumanac'h. In spring and summer this chain of rocky islands draws around 20,000 pairs of nesting sea birds, including colonies of gannets, puffins, guillemots, razorbills, shags and fulmars.

Only **Île aux Moines** (Monks' Island) can be visited. The others are part of a nature reserve managed by the Ligue pour la Protection des Oiseaux (LPO), the French equivalent of the UK's Royal Society for the Protection of Birds. There's not much to see there except a lighthouse (closed to the public), the ruins of a 15th-century monastery and an 18th-century fort, but views of the surrounding islands and distant coast are superb.

There are boat trips (several daily April to September, two to three times weekly February, March, October and November) to the Sept-Îles from Perros-Guirec's **Gare Maritime** (☎ 02 96 91 10 00) and also from Ploumanac'h and Trégastel (July and August). Trips last between 1¼ and 3½ hours; a 2¾-hour trip (including 45 minutes on Île aux Moines) costs €16/10 per adult/child.

TRÉGASTEL

pop 2300

Trégastel, one of Brittany's most popular beach resorts, attracts huge crowds in summer to its strands of fine white sand and surrounding *chaos de granit rose* (jumble of pink granite). Unlike Perros-Guirec, which manages to retain its charm even in the depths of winter, Trégastel is a bit grey and dreary once the summer crowds head home.

You'll recognise the **tourist office** (☎ 02 96 15 38 38; www.ville-tregastel.fr - French only; place Ste-Anne; ⊗ 9.30am-1pm & 2-7pm Mon-Sat, 10am-12.30pm Sun Jul

CÔTES D'ARMOR

& Aug, 9.30am-noon & 2-5.30/6pm Mon-Sat Sep-Jun) by the menhir in the window.

Apart from the attractions of sun, sand and sea, there's good easy hiking on the **Sentier des Douaniers** coastal path. For a pleasant shorter walk, do the circuit of **Presqu'île Renote**, a near-island to the north of town, joined to the mainland by a causeway-cum-car park and fringed by the popular beach of **Plage de Toul Drez**.

For rainy days, there's the **Aquarium Marin** (☎ 02 96 23 48 58; blvd Coz Pors; adult/child €4.70/2.70; 10am-7pm Jul & Aug, 10am-noon & 2-6pm Apr-Jun & Sep). Ingeniously built amid huge, rounded granite outcrops, it has 28 aquariums sunk into the rock. It also explains the ecology of the Brittany coast, complete with a working tidal model of the shores from Trégastel to Ploumanac'h.

Sleeping & Eating

Hôtel-Restaurant Beauséjour (☎ 02 96 23 88 02; www.beausejour.fr.fm; 5 Plage du Coz Pors; d €55-60, €67-85 Jul & Aug; mid-Feb–mid-Nov; P) The address says it all – this welcoming hotel, decorated in a nautical style, is right beside the beach at Coz Pors. It has a good seafood **restaurant** (Apr-Sep).

Hôtel de la Corniche (☎ 02 96 23 88 15; www.hotel delacorniche.fr.fm - French only; 38 rue Charles le Goffic; d €48-65; closed Sun & Mon except Jul & Aug) The Corniche is a lovely early-20th-century villa about 10 minutes' walk from the sea. The restaurant serves seafood and traditional Breton cuisine.

TRÉBEURDEN

pop 3500

Trébeurden, 10km southwest of Trégastel, is the last of the beach resorts along the Côte de Granit Rose. It offers much the same attractions as both Perros-Guirec and Trégastel – good beaches and spectacular coastal scenery – but on a smaller and more intimate scale.

The **tourist office** (☎ 02 96 23 51 64; www.ville -trebeurden.fr.st - French only; 9am-7pm Mon-Sat & 10am-1pm Sun Jul & Aug, 9am-12.30pm & 2-6pm Mon-Sat Sep-Jun) is on place de Crec'h Héry.

Cosmopolis

With three very different, equally engaging attractions, this place is 3km east of the town, just north of the village of Pleumeur-Bodou.

Under the giant dome of **Le Radôme** (☎ 02 96 46 63 80; adult/child €7/5.50; 11am-7pm daily Jul & Aug, 11am-6pm daily May-Jun, 11am-6pm Mon-Fri, 2pm-6pm Sat & Sun Apr & Sep) is a museum of telecommunications. Occupying a former ground station for the Telstar satellite and covering 200 years of telecommunications history, including the latest Internet technology, it's geek heaven.

The **Planétarium de Bretagne** (☎ 02 96 15 80 32; adult/child €6.25/5; Feb-Dec) has some shows in English in July and August. Even more visual is the **Village Gaulois** (☎ 02 96 91 83 95; adult/child €4/3.50; 10.30am-7pm daily Jul & Aug, 2-6pm Sun-Fri Apr-Jun & Sep), a mock-up of a village in Gaul at the time of the Romans. It's realistic and ideal for the kids; they'll search in vain for Astérix and Obélix, Gaul's most famous fictional warriors.

Île Grande

Île Grande (Big Island), a few kilometres north of Trébeurden, is connected to the mainland by a little bridge. It has four sandy beaches and an attractive coastal path (allow two hours for a complete circuit). On it is a **Station Ornithologique** (bird-watching centre; ☎ 02 96 91 91 40; adult/child €2.50/1.50; 10am-1pm & 2-6pm daily Jul & Aug, 2-6pm Sat & Sun Sep-Jun), where TV screens show live pictures of nesting birds from remote-controlled cameras installed by the LPO on the Sept-Îles nature reserve (see p115).

Sleeping

Camping Kerdual (☎ /fax 02 96 23 54 86; chemin du Can, Pors Mabo; per person/tent/car €4.20/4.20/2.40; May–mid-Sep) There are half a dozen good camping grounds in and around Trébeurden; this one is right on the beach at Pors Mabo, 1km south of the town centre.

Auberge de Jeunesse Le Toëno (☎ 02 96 23 52 22; trebeurden@fuaj.org; route de la Corniche; dm €8.40; Mar-Dec) This HI-affiliated youth hostel is bang on the coast, 2km north of Trébeurden on the road towards Île Grande. CAT bus No 15 passes within 200m.

Hôtel Ker an Nod (☎ 02 96 23 50 21; www.ker annod.com - French only; 2 rue Pors Termen; d €40-60; Apr-Dec) This 21-room Logis de France, perched above the beach of Pors Termen, has large windows on the seaward side. It's run by an engaging young couple, who keep a shipshape little restaurant, strong on seafood and creative fish dishes (try the hot oysters bathed in a butter and Muscadet sauce).

Hôtel-Restaurant Ti Al Lannec (☎ 02 96 15 01 01; www.tiallannec.com; 14 allée de Mézo-Guen; s €78-97, d €144-231; ☺ mid-Mar–mid-Nov; P) One of the most delightful hotels on Brittany's north coast, the Ti Al Lannec is a grand, early-20th-century villa perched among pines and flowerbeds and overlooking the sweeping bay of Plage de Tresmeur. It has a couple of rooms for disabled travellers, and extras include massage and beauty treatments, a fitness centre and a spa. You can dine in style at its much-acclaimed **restaurant** (menus €32-64).

LANNION
pop 19,400

Formerly a port on the River Léguer, Lannion today is a bustling business town whose fortunes have been revived since it became a centre for the electronics and communications industries. It has a pleasant riverside setting and retains a few reminders of its medieval past in the half-timbered houses around place du Général Leclerc and the Templar church of Brélévenez.

Orientation & Information

The old town centre lies on the east bank of the Léguer. Train and bus stations are on the west bank on ave Général de Gaulle, about 500m south of the tourist office.

The **tourist office** (☎ 02 96 46 41 00; www.ot-lannion.fr; quai d'Aiguillon; ☺ 9am-7pm Mon-Sat, 10am-1pm Sun Jul & Aug, 9.30am-12.30pm & 2-6pm Mon-Sat Sep-Jun) is beside the river on the east bank.

Sights & Activities

Place Général Leclerc, Lannion's pleasant old town square, is lined with picturesque 16th- and 17th-century **half-timbered houses**.

From the square, rue St-Malo and rue des Augustins lead to the River Léguer at Pont Ste-Anne. Upstream from here extends the town's **stade d'eau** vive, an artificial whitewater course where national canoeing and kayaking competitions are held.

Perched on a hilltop to the north of the town centre, and reached via a picturesque staircase at the end of rue de la Trinité, is the ancient **Église de Brélévenez** (rue des Templiers).

Supposedly founded by the Knights Templar, it has a 13th-century semicircular, granite apse with Romanesque pillars and capitals. Even if churches aren't your prime turn-on, it's worth climbing the 140 steps to reach it for the view over the town and river.

Sleeping & Eating

Head for the coast at bedtime unless you're hostelling or happy with the bland comforts of a chain hotel.

Auberge de Jeunesse Les Korrigans (☎ 02 96 37 91 28; lannion@fuaj.org; 6 rue du 73ème Territorial; dm B&B €12.70; ☺ year-round) Lannion's HI-affiliated youth hostel is 400m west of the train and bus stations. It's a luxury place for a hostel with accommodation in four-bed rooms, each with bathroom.

Crêperie l'Akène (☎ 02 96 37 06 59; 8 rue Duguesclin; galettes €2.50-7.30; ☺ closed Sun except Jul & Aug) L'Akène is a traditional Breton creperie, one block downhill from place Général Leclerc, with home-made cider served by the boulot (bowl). If you really can't take yet another galette, crunch on one of the refreshing salads (€5.65 to €7).

Le Lannionais (☎ 02 96 46 74 79; 31 place du Général Leclerc; tartines €6-12; ☺ closed Tue Oct-Mar & mid-Nov–mid-Dec) Set in a splendid half-timbered house on the old-town square, this café-bar serves delicious tartines (toast with various toppings), quiches, cakes and other snacks, as well as locally brewed beers.

Getting There & Around

CAT (☎ 02 96 68 31 20) buses link Lannion with Guingamp (€6.65, one hour), Perros-Guirec (€3, 30 minutes), Tréguier (€4.50, 35 minutes), St-Brieuc (€8.40, two hours) and Morlaix (€8.40, 1¼ hours).

Lannion is a rail terminus, with a line that runs south to join the main Paris–Rennes–Brest route at Plouaret-Trégor (15 minutes away), where you may have to change trains. There are frequent trains from Lannion to Guingamp (€7, 40 minutes), St-Malo (€21.60, four hours), St-Brieuc (€10.30, one hour), Morlaix (€7.30, 50 minutes) and Brest (€13.90, 1¾ hours).

Around town, you can call ☎ 06 07 06 84 27 for a **taxi**.

CÔTES D'ARMOR

Finistère

CONTENTS

North Coast	**120**
Morlaix	120
Tumulus de Barnenez	123
Roscoff	123
St-Pol de Léon	125
Île de Batz	126
Côte des Légendes	126
Le Folgoët	127
Pays des Abers	127
Pays d'Iroise	**128**
Portsall to Le Conquet	128
Le Conquet	129
Île d'Ouessant	129
Île Molène	132
Brest	132
Inland	**136**
Les Enclos Paroissiaux	136
Parc Naturel Régional d'Armorique	138
Presqu'île de Crozon	**139**
Ménez-Hom & Around	139
Crozon & Morgat	139
Camaret-sur-Mer	140
Around Camaret	141
Cornouaille	**142**
Douarnenez	142
Locronan	143
Audierne & Around	144
Pointe du Raz	145
Île de Sein	145
Quimper	146
Le Pays Bigouden	149
Bénodet	150
Concarneau	151
Îles de Glénan	154
Pont-Aven	154
Quimperlé	156

To really delve into Breton culture and tradition, push west to Finistère, its heartland. On the northern knuckle of this fist thrust into the Atlantic you stand the greatest chance of hearing Breton spoken. Here too is the greatest concentration of *enclos paroissiaux* (parish closes), intricately sculpted groups of monuments decorating village churchyards and peculiar to Brittany.

The islands off the coast of France and Brittany's most westerly *département* – Ouessant, Molène, Beniguet and Batz – are buffeted by wild seas and strong tidal currents, while some 350 lighthouses, beacons, buoys and radar installations stand watch over the busy, treacherous sea lanes leading into the Channel.

Cornouaille (meaning Cornwall) differs in mood from the wilder, more sparsely populated north. Holiday resorts are livelier, fishing ports are bigger and more bustling, and the coastline is more dramatic. Here too, the typical whitewashed fisherfolk's houses, with their bright-blue shutters, contrast with the more dour grey granite cottages of the north.

Seething with visitors in summer but unmissable all the same is Pointe du Raz, Finistère's longest finger, poking deep into the ocean and the Breton equivalent of Cornish Land's End. The tang of salt remains strong in the still-active fishing ports and seaside resorts of Douarnenez (give yourself a good half-day to explore its huge maritime museum) and Concarneau, where you can visit the bustling fish market's daily auction.

FINISTÈRE

HIGHLIGHTS

- Walk the rugged coastline at **Île d'Ouessant** (p129)
- Savour the underwater worlds of Brest's **Océanopolis** (p134)
- Read stories in stone on the intricate calvaries of the **enclos paroissiaux** (parish encloses; p136) of the Élorn Valley
- Play the sailor on the traditional wooden boats in Douarnenez' vast **Musée du Bateau** (p142)
- Catch the sunset at stunning **Pointe du Raz** (p145)
- Explore the Gothic cathedral and old town of **Quimper** (p146)
- Watch the return of the fishing fleet at **Le Guilvinec** (p150)
- Wander the river banks at pretty **Pont-Aven** in low season (p154)

Île d'Ouessant
Brest
Élorn Valley
Pointe du Raz
Douarnenez
Quimper
Pont-Aven
Le Guilvinec

- POPULATION: 852,400
- AREA: 6733 SQ KM

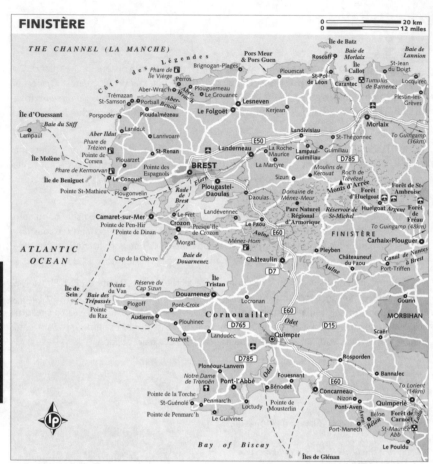

FINISTÈRE

NORTH COAST

MORLAIX
pop 17,000

Morlaix, which is unusually set at the bottom of a deep valley, is the principal city of northeastern Finistère. Although there aren't too many worthwhile sights as such, its web of steep, narrow *venelles* (alleys) reveals some hidden corners and unexpected views. It makes an excellent base for exploring both the coast to the northwest and the *enclos paroissiaux*, the richly sculpted closes surrounding so many of the parish churches along the Élorn Valley to the southwest.

Orientation

At the heart of Morlaix (see map p122) is the wide-open space of place des Otages, overlooked – and rather overwhelmed – by a high railway viaduct at the northern end and the town hall to the south. The old town is south of the town hall. From the train station, take rue de Léon south, then turn left and descend the stairs of rue Courte.

Information

Cyber@rena (☎ 02 98 88 15 83; 16 rue Basse; per hr €3; ☻ 11am-midnight Mon-Fri, 11am-1am Sat, 2pm-1am Sun) Internet access.

Post Office (15 rue de Brest)

Tourist Office (☎ 02 98 62 14 94; officetourisme.morl aix@wanadoo.fr; place des Otages; ☻ 10am-12.30pm &

1.30-7.30pm Mon-Sat, 10.30am-12.30pm Sun Jul & Aug,
10am-noon & 2-6pm Tue-Sat Sep-Jun)

Walking Tour

Start at the **tourist office (1)**, which cowers beneath the 14 soaring, 58m-high arches of the viaduct, built in 1863 to carry the Paris–Brest train line. Go up the steps leading to the late-15th-century Flamboyant Gothic **Église St-Melaine (2**; ☺ 9am-noon & 2-6pm), with its star-studded barrel-vault roof and some fine polychrome wooden statues, including St Peter and the eponymous St Melaine looking down protectively over the altar.

Turn right to take rue Ange de Guernisac and its continuation, rue au Fil, passing several fine half-timbered houses and – if you can resist – several creperies, to debouch into place des Jacobins.

The **Musée des Jacobins (3**; ☎ 02 98 88 68 88; place des Jacobins; adult/child €4/2; ☺ 10am-12.30pm & 2-6.30pm daily Jul & Aug, 10am-noon & 2-6pm Mon & Wed-Fri, 2-6pm Sat Easter-Jun & Sep-Oct, 10am-noon & 2 5pm Mon & Wed-Fri, 2-5pm Sat Nov-Easter) occupies a 15th-century former convent. Exhibits cover the history, archaeology and art of the Haut-Léon and Trégor regions of northeastern Finistère, and the museum incorporates the beautiful early-Gothic convent church (1230).

From the museum, head southeast to cross place du Dossen, then bear right along narrow venelle aux Archers, which leads uphill to Morlaix's medieval old town.

Turn right on the pedestrianised rue du Mur and emerge onto a terrace overlooking place Allende, which is bordered by several picturesque timber houses, notably the

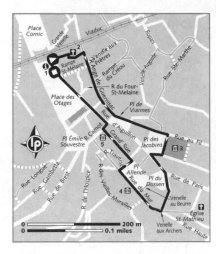

early-16th-century **Maison de la Reine Anne (4**; Queen Anne's House; ☎ 02 98 88 23 26; 33 rue du Mur; adult/child €1.50/free; ☺ 10am-6.30pm Mon-Sat Jul & Aug, to 6pm May-Jun, to 5pm Sep). Return to place des Otages along characterful Grand' Rue, overhung with more old timber houses. Best preserved is **La Maison à Pondalez (5**; ☎ 02 98 62 14 94; 9 Grand' Rue; admission €2; ☺ 10.30am-12.30pm & 3-6pm Tue-Sat Jul & Aug, 10.30am-12.30pm & 2-6pm Wed-Sat Sep-Jun, term time), carefully restored by the local authorities. Ask for the English version of the guide sheet.

Sleeping

Hôtel-Restaurant des Halles (☎ 02 98 88 03 86; fax 02 98 63 47 96; 23 rue du Mur; s/d €25/28, with shower €28/31) This homely hotel, right on place Allende, is Morlaix's best budget choice. It's primarily

FINISTÈRE

BRETON BEERS

In 1624 John Facan, an Irish Catholic fleeing English persecution in his homeland, founded Brittany's first commercial brewery at Quimper. By the 19th century there were around 100 breweries in the region, but the industry declined in the 20th century and, by the beginning of 1985, there was only one working brewery left in Brittany (in Rennes) – and that belonged to the international brewing giant Kanterbrau.

However, that same year saw the opening of a microbrewery in Morlaix, an event that marked a rekindling of interest in real Breton beers. The Deux Rivières began producing the delightful real ale known as Coreff, and was followed in 1990 by the brewery of Bernard Lancelot at Le Roc St-André in Morbihan, whose beers include the dark Telenn Du (brewed from fermented *sarrasin*, or buckwheat flour), the rich Cervoise Lancelot (flavoured with honey) and the pale Blanche Hermine (wheat and malted barley).

Today there are around 15 microbreweries in Brittany, including Trégor and Diaouligs in Côtes d'Armor, Britt near Concarneau, Tri Martelod in Bénodet and An Alarc'h in the Monts d'Arrée.

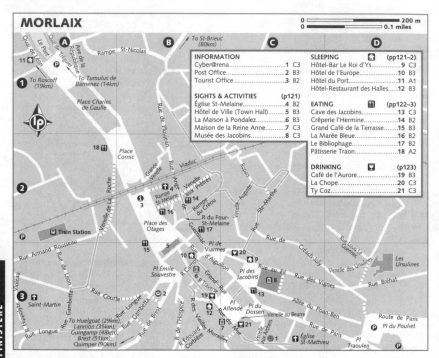

MORLAIX

INFORMATION	
Cyber@rena.....................1 C3	
Post Office........................2 B3	
Tourist Office....................3 B2	

SIGHTS & ACTIVITIES	(p121)
Église St-Melaine................4 B2	
Hôtel de Ville (Town Hall).....5 B3	
La Maison à Pondalez...........6 B3	
Maison de la Reine Anne.......7 C3	
Musée des Jacobins..............8 C3	

SLEEPING	(pp121–2)
Hôtel-Bar Le Roi d'Ys..............9 C3	
Hôtel de l'Europe...................10 B3	
Hôtel du Port........................11 A1	
Hôtel-Restaurant des Halles.....12 B3	

EATING	(pp122–3)
Cave des Jacobins.................13 C3	
Crêperie l'Hermine.................14 B2	
Grand Café de la Terrasse......15 B3	
La Marée Bleue....................16 B2	
Le Bibliophage.....................17 B2	
Pâtisserie Traon....................18 A2	

DRINKING	(p123)
Café de l'Aurore...................19 B3	
La Chope.............................20 C3	
Ty Coz................................21 C3	

an unpretentious **restaurant** (menus €11-15), serving good, wholesome food at reasonable prices.

Hôtel-Bar Le Roi d'Ys (☎ 02 98 63 30 55; 8 place des Jacobins; s/d €23/31) This 11-room place has a pleasant location near the museum and the added attraction of bikes available for use by guests. The more-expensive rooms, with private bathroom, are well worth opting for.

Hôtel de l'Europe (☎ 02 98 62 11 99; www.hotel -europe-com.fr; 1 rue d'Aiguillon; d €55-85) The Hôtel de l'Europe, occupying an elegant 19th-century building and with well over 100 years in business, is a wonderful choice. The public areas have attractive moulded ceilings, carved panelling and sculpted woodwork (bought up and reinstalled by an earlier, prescient owner), while bedrooms are bright and cosy.

Hôtel du Port (☎ 02 98 88 07 54; www.lhotel duport.com; 3 quai de Léon; s €40, d €46-58) After its recent fundamental face-lift, Hôtel du Port makes another seductive mid-range option. Rooms are bright, airy and clean as a new pin, and the owner speaks good English.

Eating

Crêperie l'Hermine (☎ 02 98 88 10 91; 35 rue Ange de Guernisac; meals €8-16) Among rue Ange de Guernisac's several tourist-oriented restaurants, l'Hermine stands out for good value, with seafood *galettes* (buckwheat pancakes) and flambéed crepes for as little as €6.

Le Bibliophage (☎ 02 98 62 65 45; 15 rue Ange de Guernisac; mains €5-6; ☺ 11am-6.30pm Tue-Sat) The 'Book Gobbler', at once both bookshop and café, serves appetising soups, salads and sandwiches.

Grand Café de la Terrasse (☎ 02 98 88 20 25; 31 place des Otages; mains €10-15.50) This much-restored, classical French brasserie (the ceiling and magnificent central spiral staircase are original) comes complete with waiters in waistcoats and black bow ties, serving salads, seafood and meat dishes.

La Marée Bleue (☎ 02 98 63 24 21; rampe St-Melaine; menus €13.50-36; ☺ Tue-Sat & lunch Sun) One of Morlaix's best eating places, the Marée Bleue concentrates on seafood, prepared in a variety of original ways, but also serves meat dishes.

Pâtisserie Traon (☎ 02 98 88 08 51; 24 place Cornic) This place has a mouthwatering window display of traditional Breton cakes and pastries, including *kouign amann* (butter cake), prepared using a 40-year-old recipe.

For some subtle little wine to wash down a picnic lunch, head to the **Cave des Jacobins** (☎ 02 98 88 05 54; 15 place des Jacobins; ☝ Tue-Sat), which has a wide range of excellent wines.

Drinking

Although Morlaix isn't Brittany's liveliest nightspot, there are a few decent bars in the old town.

Café de l'Aurore (☎ 02 98 88 03 05; 17 rue Traverse; ☝ Mon-Sat) This is a convivial spot to enjoy a Breton beer and, occasionally, live music. Buy a beer and you can log on for free at the one Internet station.

Ty Coz (☎ 02 98 88 07 65; 10 venelle au Beurre; ☝ Fri-Wed) Opposite l'Aurore on place Allende, this old-style Breton tavern is in a medieval half-timbered house.

La Chope (☎ 02 98 88 28 77; 2 rue des Fontaines; ☝ Tue-Sun) A short walk away, tiny and intimate La Chope serves cider on draft, plus two varieties of Coreff, Morlaix's very own real ale.

Getting There & Away

CAT (☎ 02 96 68 31 20) bus No 16 runs between Morlaix and Lannion (€8.40, 1¼ hours, two to six daily).

Morlaix lies on the main train line from Paris to Brest. There are frequent trains from Morlaix to St-Brieuc (€11.50, 45 minutes), Brest (€8.60, 45 minutes), Roscoff (€8.60, 45 minutes) and Quimper (€15.90, 2½ hours, change at Landerneau).

TUMULUS DE BARNENEZ

At least 6000 years old, **Tumulus de Barnenez** (Plouezoc'h; adult/child €3.80/free; ☝ 10am-6.30pm daily May-Aug, 10am-12.30pm & 2-5.30pm Tue-Sun Sep-Apr) is one of Brittany's biggest and most important prehistoric structures. Around 80m long and 10m high, the burial cairn (tumulus) dominates a scenic peninsula overlooking the Baie de Morlaix. The heaped stones conceal no fewer than 11 granite burial chambers. Two of these have been exposed by quarrying work at the northern end – in 1955 the site narrowly escaped being used as a source of road stone before being classified as a historic monument. The adjacent museum explains how the cairn was constructed.

ROSCOFF

pop 3600

Sheltered from the savage seas of the English Channel by the little island of Batz, Roscoff (Rosko in Breton), with its 16th-century granite houses clustered around a small bay, is the southernmost, smallest and arguably most attractive French channel-ferry port.

Orientation & Information

Roscoff ranges around a north-facing bay, with its fishing port and pleasure harbour on the western side. The car-ferry terminal is at Port de Bloscon, 2km east of the town centre.

The **ferry terminal** has a 24-hour banknote exchange and ATM.

Ferry Laverie (23 rue Jules Ferry; ☝ 9am to 8pm) Laundrette.

Post Office (19 rue Gambetta)

Tourist Office (☎ 02 98 61 12 13; www.roscoff -tourisme.com; 46 rue Gambetta; ☝ 9am-12.30pm & 1.30-7pm Mon-Sat, 10am-12.30pm Sun Jul & Aug, 9am-noon & 2-6pm Mon-Sat Sep-Jun)

Sights

The oldest part of Roscoff is squeezed between rue Amiral Réveillère and the waterfront. An open square, which is guarded on its seaward side by a little lookout tower, occupies the former site of the medieval **Chapelle St-Ninian**, where a six-year-old Mary Queen of Scots, on her way to marry the French dauphin, gave thanks after disembarking at Roscoff in 1548. Only the Gothic doorway survives.

LES JOHNNIES

Roscoff's hinterland is known for its early fruit and vegetables that flourish in Finistère's mild climate: cauliflower, tomatoes, new potatoes, artichokes and onions – especially onions. Before the days of large vehicular ferries, Roscoff farmers would load up small fishing boats with locally grown pink onions, sail to Britain and go from house to house with them strung from their bicycles. They were known affectionately as 'Onion Johnnies' and were the origin of the stereotypical Frenchman in English popular culture – with striped Breton jersey, beret, moustache and a string of onions round his neck.

FINISTÈRE

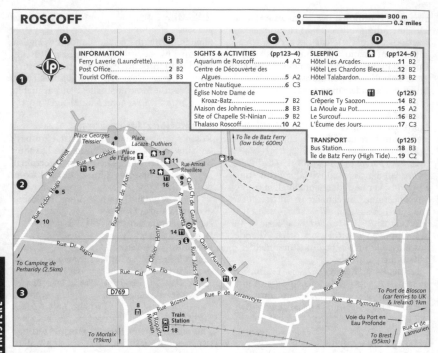

ROSCOFF

0 _____ 300 m
0 _____ 0.2 miles

A	**B**	**C**	**D**

INFORMATION
Ferry Laverie (Laundrette).........1 B3
Post Office...........................2 B2
Tourist Office.......................3 B3

SIGHTS & ACTIVITIES (pp123–4)
Aquarium de Roscoff.................4 A2
Centre de Découverte des
  Algues............................5 A2
Centre Nautique.....................6 C3
Église Notre Dame de
  Kroaz-Batz........................7 B2
Maison des Johnnies.................8 B3
Site of Chapelle St-Ninian 9 B2
Thalasso Roscoff...................10 A2

SLEEPING (pp124–5)
Hôtel Les Arcades..................11 B2
Hôtel Les Chardons Bleus...........12 B2
Hôtel Talabardon...................13 B2

EATING (p125)
Crêperie Ty Saozon.................14 B2
La Moule au Pot....................15 A2
Le Surcouf.........................16 B2
L'Écume des Jours..................17 C3

TRANSPORT (p125)
Bus Station........................18 B3
Île de Batz Ferry (High Tide)....19 C2

Nearby, the 16th-century Flamboyant Gothic **Église Notre Dame de Kroaz-Batz**, with its Renaissance belfry, is one of Brittany's most spectacular churches. Both it and the old shipowners' houses in the streets of the surrounding area are decorated with carvings of ships, anchors and other nautical motifs.

The **Aquarium de Roscoff** (☎ 02 98 29 23 25; place Georges Teissier; adult/child €4/2; ☻ 10am-noon & 1.30-6.30pm mid-Jul–mid-Aug, 1.30-5.30pm Apr–mid-Jul & mid-Aug–Sep) is located just to the northwest of the church.

The **Maison des Johnnies** (☎ 02 98 61 25 48; 48 rue Brizeux; admission €4; ☻ afternoons daily mid-Feb–mid-Mar & Jun–mid-Sep, Sat & Sun mid-Mar–May & late Sep) is a museum devoted to the itinerant onion sellers of times past, who are accorded near-hero status locally.

The **Centre de Découverte des Algues** (☎ 02 98 69 77 05; 5 rue Victor Hugo; admission free; ☻ 9am-noon & 2-7pm Mon-Sat) has a small permanent exhibition about the history, harvesting and multiple uses of seaweed. It also organises a rich programme of lectures in French and guided walks.

Activities

Roscoff's **Centre Nautique** (☎ 02 98 69 72 79; quai d'Auxerre) rents out windsurfing boards and catamarans.

In the 1890s, Roscoff was the first resort in France to promote thalassotherapy. Today, **Thalasso Roscoff** (☎ 08 25 00 20 99; www.thalasso -roscoff.com - French only; rue Victor Hugo) offers a huge range of health-inducing activities, including a heated seawater pool, *hammam* (Turkish bath) and spa bath (each €9 or all three for €16), and an introductory half-day session (€79 or €99). The higher price includes a massage and both (you're paying for this, remember!) have you coated in a thick seaweed paste.

Sleeping

Camping de Perharidy (☎ 02 98 69 70 86; www.aqua camp.fr; Le Ruguel; per person/tent/car €2.70/2.45/1.15; ☻ Easter-Sep) This camping ground, close to a sandy beach, is in the grounds of a lovely 19th-century mansion about 3km southwest of Roscoff.

Hôtel Les Arcades (☎ 02 98 69 70 45; 15 rue Amiral Réveillère; d with toilet €31, with bathroom €47-57;

FINISTÈRE

Mar–mid-Nov) This two-star hotel, run by the same family for nearly a century, overlooks the bay. It has simple but spruce modern rooms and – who knows? – you may find yourself in the same bed that Jane Fonda and Roger Vadim once shared…

Hôtel Les Chardons Bleus (☎ 02 98 69 72 03; fax 02 98 61 27 86; 4 rue Amiral Réveillère; d €48-58; Mar-Jan) The 'Thistles', a Logis de France establishment, is good value, with quiet rooms and a pleasant restaurant.

Hôtel Talabardon (☎ 0298612495; www.bestwestern-talabardon.com; place de l'Église; s €69-87, d €78-96; Mar-Oct) Roscoff's oldest hotel, established in 1890, offers spacious, comfy rooms, many with balconies looking over the sea. You may find the welcome rather frostier than the weather.

Eating

In Roscoff, France's premier crabbing port, seafood reigns supreme.

La Moule au Pot (☎ 02 98 19 33 60; 13 rue Édouard Corbière; May-Oct, closed Wed except Jul & Aug) With fresh flowers, wooden beams, a huge fireplace and a leafy rear terrace, the 'Mussel in the Pot' is a wonderful place for a substantial snack. Go for one of the giant salads (€8) or *moules frites* (mussels and chips/french fries; €11), lubricated with a small pot of Muscadet (€3).

Crêperie Ty Saozon (☎ 02 98 69 70 89; 30 rue Gambetta; crepes €2-7.50; dinner only Tue-Sat) With its stone walls, old timber beams, antique furniture and classical music, this place feels more like a Cotswolds tearoom than a French creperie. The food, however, is Breton through and through and this lovely place is – so rare in France – nonsmoking throughout.

L'Écume des Jours (☎ 0298612283; quai d'Auxerre; menus €18-43; closed Wed Jul & Aug, Tue-Wed Sep-Jun) In a beautiful 16th-century house overlooking the harbour, this is one of Roscoff's top seafood restaurants, with a warm, friendly atmosphere. Highly recommended.

Le Surcouf (☎ 02 98 69 71 89; 14 rue Amiral Réveillère; Feb-Dec, closed Wed Jul & Aug, Tue & Wed other months) This pleasant, brasserie-style restaurant specialises in seafood, drawing strongly on local produce and culinary tradition.

Hôtel Les Arcades has a quality restaurant that's strong on seafood, does a particularly good-value lunch *menu* and has superb views of the harbour. The gourmet restaurant (*menus* €19 to €44) of **Hôtel Talabardon** also has stunning views over the bay (see Sleeping, left).

Getting There & Away

The combined bus and train station is on rue Ropartz Morvan.

BOAT

Brittany Ferries (reservations ☎ 08 25 82 88 28; www.brittany-ferries.com) links Roscoff to Plymouth in England (five to nine hours, one to three daily, year-round) and Cork in Ireland (14 hours, one weekly, June to September). Boats leave from Port de Bloscon, about 2km east of the town centre.

For boats to Île de Batz, see p126.

BUS & TRAIN

Cars Bihan (☎ 02 98 83 45 80) operates buses from Roscoff to Brest (€9.40, 1½ to two hours, up to four daily), departing from the ferry terminal (Port de Bloscon) and passing by the town centre.

There are regular trains and SNCF buses to Morlaix (€8.60, 45 minutes), where you can make connections to Brest, Quimper and St-Brieuc.

ST-POL DE LÉON

pop 7400

Five kilometres south of Roscoff, St-Pol de Léon (Kastell Paol in Breton) is a busy market town serving the surrounding vegetable farms and is also a minor beach resort. Historically, it was the seat of western Brittany's first bishop, Pol Aurelian.

The broad main square, place de l'Évêché, is dominated by the twin 55m-tall Gothic towers of **Cathédrale St-Pol de Léon** (9am-noon & 2-6.30pm), built between the 13th and 16th centuries. From the balcony above the main west door, the bishop would bless the crowds gathered in the square below. The little door at the foot of the south tower opens into a tiny chapel, once reserved for the use of lepers.

From the square, rue Général Leclerc leads south for 200m to St-Pol de Léon's most famous building, the **Chapelle Notre Dame du Kreisker** (10am-noon & 2-6pm Jul & Aug, 10am-6pm Oct & Feb-Jun). Built in the 14th century on the site of an even older church that had been sacked by English invaders, the chapel's original bell tower was toppled

FINISTÈRE

by lightning in 1628. Its soaring successor, constructed in the late 17th century, is Brittany's tallest at 78m. It is topped by a graceful, slender spire and pierced by lace-like tracery. Its elegance was so admired that you'll see its replica on a smaller scale atop many a Breton church. In July and August, you can climb 169 steps to the balcony at the base of the spire (40m up).

The **tourist office** (☎ 02 98 69 05 69; place de l'Évêché; ☉ 9am-noon & 1.30-7pm Mon-Sat, 10am-noon Sun Jul & Aug, 9am-noon & 2-5.30pm Mon-Sat Sep-Jun) is just off the square in front of the cathedral. In July and August it runs free guided tours in French of the cathedral.

ÎLE DE BATZ
pop 600

A 20-minute ferry trip north of Roscoff, Île de Batz (pronounced ba; Enez Vaz in Breton) is a charming little island with some good beaches. Just 3.5km by 1.5km, it's one big, fertile vegetable garden, its soil fertilised with seaweed.

The main attraction of the island is simply wandering around and exploring the coastal scenery; you can make a complete circuit of the island in about two hours. At the eastern tip is a botanic garden, the **Jardins Georges Delaselle** (☎ 02 98 61 75 65; adult/child €3.50/1.75; ☉ 1-6pm daily Jul & Aug, 2-6pm Wed-Mon Apr-Jun & Sep, 2-6pm Sat & Sun Oct). Founded in the 19th century, the garden contains a luxuriant display of more than 1500 plants from five continents.

You can climb the 198 steps to the top of the island's **lighthouse** (☎ 02 98 61 75 85; adult/child €1.70/1; ☉ 1-5.30pm daily Jul & Aug, 2-5pm Thu-Tue Jun & 1-14 Sep) for a magnificent wrap-around panorama.

Sleeping

Accommodation is limited. There's a basic, unofficial **camping ground** (per person/tent €1/1; ☉ mid-Jun–mid-Sep) beside the beach on the western side of the island, 10 minutes' walk from the ferry.

Auberge de Jeunesse (☎ 02 98 61 77 69; fax 02 98 61 78 85; dm €8.50; ☉ Apr-Oct) This is the cheapest option if you want a roof over your head.

Grand Hôtel Morvan (☎/fax 02 98 61 78 06; d incl breakfast €52; ☉ Mar-Nov) The larger of the island's two hotels, the Morvan is a welcoming, 1950s-style, family hotel. It is decorated with traditional Breton furniture and old photographs.

Getting There & Around

The island ferry (adult/child/bike €6/3.50/5 return, 20 minutes) to/from Roscoff runs every 30 minutes between 8am and 8pm from late June to mid-September; there are about eight sailings daily during the other months.

Vélos et Nature (☎ 02 98 61 75 75), **Le Saout** (☎ 02 98 61 77 65) and **Prigent** (☎ 02 98 61 77 65) all rent bicycles.

CÔTE DES LÉGENDES

The coastline between Plouescat and Plouguerneau is known as the Côte des Légendes (Coast of Legends), famous for its tales of shipwrecks.

Information

The **tourist office** (☎ 02 98 04 70 93; ☉ 9.30am-12.30pm & 2-7pm Mon-Sat, 10.30am-12.30pm Sun Jul & Aug, 9.30am-noon Mon-Sat, 2-5pm Thu-Sat Sep-Jun), together with the office at Lannilis, covers this and the Pays des Abers area.

DETOUR: PLOUESCAT & THE ABER-WRAC'H ESTUARY

From the busy N12-E50 motorway linking Morlaix and Brest, turn north onto the D30 at Landivisiau and head for **Plouescat**. Alternatively, if you're coming from Roscoff, take the D10 westwards, 6km south of the port. West of Plouescat (worth a pause to explore its splendid 16th-century timber-roofed **covered market** in the main square) and beside the D10 are Brittany's finest sand dunes – lonely, wild, over 5km long and ideal for a breezy walk. After savouring their solitude, drop into the **Maison des Dunes et de la Randonnée**, a small interpretive centre that organises guided nature walks in summer.

Continue along the D10 as far as Plouguerneau, from where the D71 leads 5km northwest to the pretty little resort of **Lilia**, snug in its small bay at the mouth of the Aber-Wrac'h estuary. Before pushing on, take a short, dead-end road to the **Phare d'Île Vièrge**, Europe's tallest lighthouse at 82.5m, against whose slender finger the waves pound.

FINISTÈRE

Sights & Activities

West of Roscoff is the town of Plouescat (see the boxed text opposite). Nearby are the beautiful white-sand beaches of **Pors Meur** and **Pors Guen**.

West of Plouescat, the coast is indented by the Grève de Goulven, a shallow tidal bay fringed to the east by the sand dunes of **Keremma**. Wander through the impressive dunes, over 5km long, then call by the **Maison des Dunes et de la Randonnée** (☎ 02 98 61 69 69; admission free; ☒ 10.30am-6pm daily Jul & Aug, 2.30-5.30pm Mon-Fri Sep-Jun), beside the D10, which has a display and interpretive trail and organises guided nature walks (Sunday to Friday July to August, Sunday only September to June).

To the west of the Grève de Goulven is the popular seaside resort of **Brignogan-Plages**, ranged around a pretty little cove and surrounded by tortuous outcrops of pale grey granite. Just west of town is the **Menhir Marz**, 8m high and 'Christianised' by having a small stone cross added to its summit.

Twenty kilometres of wild but unexceptional coast continue west to the rugged peninsula near the town of **Plouguerneau** and the pretty seaside village of **Lilia**, with views across reef-strewn seas to the slender sentinel of the **Phare d'Île Vierge**. In July and August, **Vedettes des Abers** (☎ 02 98 04 74 94; adult/child €2.50/2; 12.30-7.30pm incl lighthouse visit) does the short hop from the headland north of the village to the lighthouse.

Sleeping & Eat

Hôtel-Restaurant Le Castel-Ac'h (☎ 02 98 37 16 16; Lilia; d €45-60; ☒ closed 1-21 Jan) This modern Logis de France has a fine waterfront location, where nearly all rooms overlook the cove. Recently taken over by a dynamic young couple who've given it a fundamental face-lift, it has two restaurants: a **terrace** (menus €15-30) with picture windows, offering meals that are strong on fish and seafood, and the adjacent, stylishly furnished, more intimate gourmet **restaurant** (menus €35-55).

Hôtel-Restaurant Castel Régis (☎ 02 98 83 40 22; www.castelregis.com; Plage du Garo, Brignogan-Plages; d €50-100; ☒ May-Sep) This charming 22-room hotel has a great location, practically overhanging the sea at the eastern end of the cove. Rooms have a nautical décor and the more expensive ones overlook the sea.

LE FOLGOËT

pop 3100

Le Folgoët, 11km south of Brignogan-Plages, is Brittany's second-most-important place of pilgrimage after Locronan. Legend tells how, in the early 14th century, a local simpleton called Salaün lived in the hollow trunk of an oak tree in the woods near Lesneven (Folgoët is Breton for Fool's Wood). He knew only the words 'Itron Gwerc'hez Vari' (Breton for Our Lady the Virgin Mary) and repeated them constantly, every day of his life until he died. When he was buried, a lily grew upon his grave, with a golden pistil shaped into the words 'Ave Maria'. When the villagers dug up the grave, they found that the lily sprouted from Salaün's mouth.

In honour of this miracle, a chapel was constructed on the site of the spring where Salaün used to drink. Completed in 1423, the **Basilique de Notre Dame du Folgoët** is one of Brittany's finest examples of Gothic architecture. The splendid south porch is lined with statues of major saints – St Peter stands between the double doors – while the interior contains a 15th-century stone rood screen, the fringes of its three arches filled with delicate Gothic tracery. At the eastern end are four intricately carved granite altars and a statue of Our Lady of Folgoët. On the exterior of the eastern wall is the **Fontaine de Salaün**, fed by the spring beneath the altar.

The Grand Pardon de Notre Dame du Folgoët takes place on the Sunday closest to 8 September. A more bizarre event is the Pardon de St-Christophe, on the fourth Sunday in July, when thousands of motorists gather to have their cars blessed.

PAYS DES ABERS

Between Plouguerneau and Portsall, the coastline is indented by two long inlets of the sea: Aber-Wrac'h and Aber-Benoit (the Breton – and also the Welsh – word 'aber' means river mouth). Both inlets are former river valleys, flooded by a rise in sea level after the last Ice Age.

Information

The Aber area's **tourist office** (☎ 02 98 04 05 43; www.abers-tourisme.com - French only; 1 place de l'Église; ☒ 9.30am-12.30pm & 2-7pm Mon-Sat, 10.30am-12.30pm Sun Jul & Aug, 9.30am-noon Mon-Sat, 2-5pm Mon-Wed Sep-Jun) is in the village of Lannilis.

FINISTÈRE

FINISTÈRE

Sights & Activities

Aber-Wrac'h, the more northerly of the two inlets, is also the longer (32km) and definitely the more scenic. The little port of Aber-Wrac'h, which is on the southern shore is a popular yachting harbour. Further west, the dunes of the **Presqu'île Ste-Marguerite,** at the mouth of the inlet, make for bracing coastal walks.

Vedettes des Abers (☎ 02 98 04 74 94) runs boat trips (adult/child €10/5.50, from June to September) along Aber-Wrac'h from the port of Perros, on the northern side, 4km west of Plouguerneau.

Aber-Benoit has good sandy beaches on the southern side, where it meets the sea at Corn Ar Gazel. The tiny harbour at St-Pabu is home to the diving school **Aber-Benoit Plongée** (☎ 02 98 89 75 66; www.aberbenoit plongee.com - French only; quai du Stellac'h), which offers beginners dives for €36, as well as courses. The most popular dive site – for experienced divers only – is the wreck of the *Amoco Cadiz*.

Sleeping & Eating

Camping des Abers (☎ 02 98 04 93 35; per person/ tent/car €3.10/4.70/1.40; ☺ May-Sep) Among the dunes at Landéda, west of Aber-Wrac'h, this is one among several good camping grounds in the area.

Hotel La Baie des Anges (☎ 02 98 04 90 04; www .baie-des-anges.com - French only; 350 route des Anges, Landéda; d €80-114) This luxury hideaway is perched above the sea on the Bay of Angels, on the southern shore of Aber-Wrac'h. Expect a warm welcome, huge rooms, hot baths and a breakfast that verges on a work of art.

PAYS D'IROISE

The sea where the waters of the Atlantic Ocean and English Channel mingle around the island of Ouessant is known as the Mer d'Iroise. The land that faces it, from Portsall round to Brest – the Pays d'Iroise – is one of the least-developed parts of the Brittany coast, a ragged ribbon of pale-grey granite riddled with narrow creeks and tiny white-sand beaches.

PORTSALL TO LE CONQUET

The neat little harbour town of **Portsall**, 8km west of Aber-Benoit, made the news in 1978 when the supertanker *Amoco Cadiz* was wrecked a short distance offshore, causing one of the world's worst environmental disasters (see the boxed text below).

The minor road that hugs the coast from Portsall to Landunvez (signposted 'Route Touristique') offers a panorama of reefs, lighthouses and beacons, the sea dotted with fishing boats trailing white curtains of seagulls, and the distant forms of ships entering and leaving the Channel. Halfway along is the roadside stone cross and tiny chapel of **St Samson**, with a spring further down towards the sea, where it is said the saint drank after arriving from Wales in 548.

Pointe de Corsen, 7km south of Aber Ildut, is the most westerly point of the Brittany mainland. However, this headland is rarely visited – the crowds tend to overlook its geographical credentials in favour of the more dramatic headland of Pointe du Raz (p145). The view extends to the low outline

---

LES MARÉES NOIRES

Each day, at least 150 ships pass through the shipping channels west of Île d'Ouessant in Finistère, carrying a total of around 700,000 tonnes of oil and 90,000 tonnes of toxic substances. And in these waters the wind speed reaches more than 60km/h – a near gale – on more than 100 days every year.

So it's no surprise that Brittany has suffered more than any other part of Europe from the environmental nightmare of *les marées noires* (oil slicks; literally 'black tides'). The list of ships that have come to grief in Breton waters in the last few decades is a lengthy one.

The worst and most infamous environmental disaster happened when the oil tanker *Amoco Cadiz* foundered on the rocks off Portsall in northern Finistère in March 1978 after her steering gear failed. As the ship broke up, more than 226,500 tonnes of crude oil escaped from her tanks to pollute the shores of northwestern France. (By comparison, the *Exxon Valdez* disaster in Alaska in 1989 involved only 35,500 tonnes of oil.)

of Île d'Ouessant on the horizon, while the nearer Île Molène seems a town floating unsupported on the sea.

Hostellerie du Castel (☎ 02 98 48 63 35; fax 02 98 48 75 12; d €54-60; ☯ Easter-Sep). This pretty 15-room hotel, its granite walls clad with ivy, is in the little hamlet of Kersaint, 1km south of Portsall.

LE CONQUET
pop 2150

Perched on the westernmost tip of Brittany, the pretty fishing village of Le Conquet (called, engagingly, Konk Leon in Breton) is close to some pristine beaches and lovely coastal paths. It's largely ignored by tourists, who generally do no more than leave their cars here before piling onto the ferries headed for Île d'Ouessant.

Information

The **tourist office** (☎ 02 98 89 11 31; www.leconquet.fr; ☯ 9am-12.30pm & 2.30-6.30pm Mon-Sat, 9am-noon Sun Jul & Aug, 9am-noon Tue-Sat Sep-Jun) is in the town hall in the Parc de Beauséjour.

Sights & Activities

The tourist office's free town plan details a couple of good **walks** in and around Le Conquet. One leads via a long footbridge across the river mouth and along the clifftops to **Phare de Kermorvan** (admission €1.50; ☯ 3.30-6pm Jul & Aug), a 37m lighthouse on the rocky northern point guarding the harbour entrance. To its north lies the lovely, wide sandy beach of **Plage des Blancs Sablons**.

A 5km hike along the coastal path south of Le Conquet leads to **Pointe St-Mathieu**. At the foot of its conspicuous lighthouse are the spectacular ruins of the 16th-century Benedictine **Abbaye St-Mathieu**.

Sleeping & Eating

Camping le Théven (☎ 02 98 89 06 90; Les Blancs Sablons, Kermorvan; per person/site €2.95/2.95; ☯ Apr-Sep) This site lies 400m east of Plage des Blancs Sablons. Prices may have altered substantially since it was about to change owners when we last visited.

Le Relais du Vieux Port (☎ 02 98 89 15 91; 1 quai du Drella'ch; d €37-55; ☯ year-round) Le Relais, with seven comfortable rooms (three of them with four-poster beds), enjoys an appealing setting beside the waterfront at the old (inner) harbour and is excellent value. Staff

are friendly and there's also a cosy **restaurant** (menu €24) on the ground floor that serves everything from crepes and salads to full-blown meals.

Hostellerie de la Pointe St-Mathieu (☎ 02 98 89 00 19; www.pointe-saint-mathieu.com; Pointe St-Mathieu; s/d from €58/63; dinner menus €25-64) Across the road from the lighthouse and abbey (5km south of Le Conquet), this hotel is a lovely option with a swimming pool, a stylish bar and a gourmet restaurant with a Gothic fireplace and stone vaulting.

Getting There & Away

Buses operated by **Les Cars St-Mathieu** (☎ 02 98 89 12 02) link Brest with Le Conquet (€4.25, 45 minutes, six daily).

Ferries to the islands of Ouessant (below) and Molène (see p132) depart from the *embarcadère* (ferry terminal) in the outer harbour.

ÎLE D'OUESSANT
pop 950

Île d'Ouessant (Enez Eusa, meaning 'Island of Terror', in Breton; Ushant in English) is a wild, rugged, hauntingly beautiful island, 20km from the mainland. About 7km long and 4km wide, it serves as a beacon for more than 50,000 ships entering the Channel each year.

Traditionally, the sea provided the islanders with both a livelihood and resources. The menfolk, traditionally sailors, would be away for as much as two years at time and it was the women who tilled the fields and pulled in the seaweed. The interior of the houses, partitioned by little more than wooden panels, could almost be the inside of a boat, with furniture often made from driftwood, washed up from wrecks. To mask its imperfections, it was usually painted in bright colours – blue and white symbolising the Virgin Mary or green for hope.

Although the island is no longer isolated (day visitors by the thousand pour from the ferries in high summer), a few local traditions persist. Old women still make delicate lace crosses in memory of husbands who never returned from the sea, little black sheep are free to roam where they please and the delicious local dish *ragoût de mouton* (lamb roasted in an extempore peat oven) retains its popularity.

FINISTÈRE

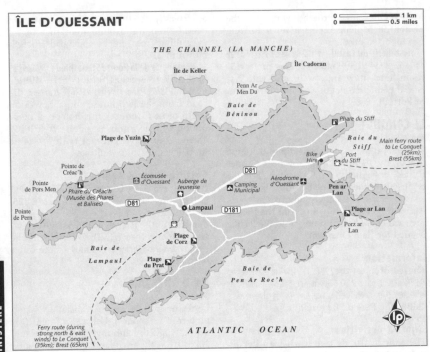

ÎLE D'OUESSANT

Orientation & Information

The ferry landing is at Port du Stiff on the east coast. The island's only village is Lampaul, on the west coast, 4km from the ferry landing. It has a handful of hotels, restaurants and shops.

The tiny **tourist office** (☎ 02 98 48 85 83; www.ot -ouessant.fr - French only; ⊙ 10am-noon & 1.30-5pm Mon-Sat, 10am-noon Sun) is on place de l'Église in Lampaul.

Sights & Activities
MUSEUMS

The black-and-white striped **Phare du Créac'h** is the world's most powerful lighthouse, its light (two white flashes every 10 seconds) visible for over 50km. Beneath the light is the island's main museum, the **Musée des Phares et Balises** (Lighthouse and Beacon Museum; ☎ 02 98 48 80 70; adult/child €4/2.50; ⊙ 10.30am-6.30pm Jun-Sep, 1.30-5/5.30pm Oct-Jun). In the old lighthouse generator rooms, it tells the story of these vital navigation aids. Unless you're of a technical bent, you'll probably find the section on shipwrecks and underwater archaeology more interesting.

The small **Écomusée d'Ouessant** (☎ 02 98 48 86 37; Maison du Niou; admission €2.30; ⊙ as for Musée des Phares et Balises) occupies two typical local houses, one re-creating a traditional homestead and the other exploring the island's history and customs.

BEACHES

Plage de Corz, 600m south of Lampaul, is the best beach. Other good spots are **Plage du Prat**, **Plage de Yuzin** and **Plage Ar Lan**. All are easily accessible by bike from Lampaul or Port du Stiff.

WALKING

A footpath (45km) hugs the island's rocky coastline, passing through wild scenery. A good walk (8km; about two hours) is from Lampaul west along the coastal path to Pointe de Pern, then along the northern coast to the Phare du Créac'h and back to Lampaul by the road. For a longer walk (12km; about three hours), follow the path along the northern coast from Port du Stiff to the pretty beach of Plage de Yuzin via Penn Ar Menn Du, then head south to Lampaul.

The tourist office sells an English-language version of its brochure *Circuits de Randonnée Pédestre* (€2.30), with stylised maps and descriptions of four coastal walks varying between 10km and 16km.

CARRIAGE RIDE

Calèches du Ponant (☎ 02 98 48 89 29), just south of Lampaul beside the road to Plage de Corz, offers trips in a traditional horse-drawn carriage (per hour per carriage of up to eight people €45).

Sleeping & Eating

Camping Municipal (☎ 02 98 48 84 65; fax 02 98 48 83 99; Stang Ar Glan, Lampaul; per person/site €2.65/2.65; ✆ May-Sep) The island's only camping ground is 750m northeast of Lampaul in a lumpy field beside the main road.

Auberge de Jeunesse (☎ 02 98 48 84 53; fax 02 98 48 87 42; La Croix-Rouge, Lampaul; dm incl breakfast €13.35; ✆ closed last 3 weeks Jan) This hostel, in an old granite house on the hill above Lampaul, has two- to six-person bedrooms. Since it's frequently occupied by walking and school groups, reservations are essential.

Hôtel La Duchesse Anne (☎ /fax 02 98 48 80 25; Lampaul; d €38-41; ✆ Apr–mid-Feb) This tiny hotel, in an imposing pink house overlooking Lampaul's tiny harbour, is excellent value. Renovated rooms have bathrooms and the top price – just €3 extra – gets a sea view.

Hôtel Roc'h Ar Mor (☎ 02 98 48 80 19; www.rocharmor.com - French only; Lampaul; d €48-75; ✆ mid-Feb–Dec) This modern 15-room hotel has bright, cheerful rooms and enjoys a superb location next to the Baie de Lampaul. There's one wheelchair-accessible room.

Both hotels have good restaurants with terraces overlooking the sea.

Crêperie Ti A Dreuz (☎ 02 98 48 83 01; Lampaul; galettes €3-9; ✆ Easter–mid-Sep) This pretty little blue-and-white creperie (named 'the slanting house' because of its somewhat wonky walls) serves delicious *galettes*. Try the *ouessantine*, with its creamy potato, cheese and sausage topping.

Ty Karn (☎ 02 98 48 87 33; Lampaul; lunch menu €12-15, dinner €20-28) The ground floor of this hyperfriendly place is a bar, offering tasty midday snacks in summer, while upstairs is an agreeable restaurant. Whichever you choose, you won't be disappointed.

If you forgot the sandwich filling, you'll find three minimarkets in Lampaul.

Getting There & Away

AIR

Finist'air (☎ 02 98 84 64 87; www.finistair.fr) flies from the Aéroport International de Brest-Guipavas, about 9km northeast of Brest, to Ouessant in a mere 15 minutes. There are two flights daily (adult/child €61/35).

BOAT

Two companies operate ferries to Ouessant year-round. The fares we quote here are all return.

Penn Ar Bed (☎ 02 98 80 80 80; www.pennarbed.fr) sails from the Port de Commerce in Brest (adult/child €29.50/17.70, 2½ hours) and from Le Conquet (€25.50/15.30, 1½ hours). Most boats call at Île Molène en route. Boats run between each port and the island two to five times daily from May to September and once daily between October and April.

In season, Penn Ar Bed also operates from Camaret (adult/child €26.40/15.80, two hours, once daily mid-April to mid-September).

Finist'mer (☎ 02 98 89 16 61; www.finist-mer.fr) runs faster boats to the island up to six times daily from Le Conquet (adult/child €24/14, 40 minutes, mid-April to September) and from Camaret (€25/15, one hour, mid-May to mid-September).

Buy ferry tickets at the ports or at the Brest or Le Conquet tourist offices. In high summer, it's prudent to reserve at least one day in advance and check in 30 minutes before departure.

Getting Around

BICYCLE

Several bike-hire operators have kiosks at the Port du Stiff ferry terminal and compounds just up the hill. There are also outlets in Lampaul. The going rate for town/mountain bikes is €10/14.

Cycling on the coastal footpath is forbidden – the fragile turf is strictly for walkers.

MINIBUS

Several of the islanders – including **Dominique Etienne** (☎ 06 07 90 07 43), **Lucien Malgorn** (☎ 06 84 42 12 70), **Robert Quantin** (☎ 06 07 90 07 36) and **Christiane Lucas** (☎ 06 07 90 07 62) – run minibus services. They meet the ferry at Port du Stiff and will shuttle you to Lampaul or your accommodation for a flat fare of €1.50 (in July and August book ahead to guarantee a seat).

FINISTÈRE

For the return journey, the pick-up point is the car park beside Lampaul's church.

The minibus owners also offer two-hour **guided tours** (€12 per person) of the island.

ÎLE MOLÈNE

pop 270

Île Molène (Mol Enez, meaning 'Bald Island', in Breton) is barely 1km across. It's the only inhabited island among the dozens of tide-washed rocks, reefs and sandbanks that lie scattered between Le Conquet and Île d'Ouessant. The entire Molène archipelago was designated a Biosphere Reserve by Unesco in 1988 and is a haven for a variety of marine life, including seals, dolphins and, in season, whales, plus thousands upon thousands of sea birds.

The islanders have long been famous as expert seafarers, though nowadays those remaining are mostly engaged in lobster and crab fishing, or gathering seaweed from the vast expanse of sea bed revealed at low tide.

There's a **tourist information point** (☎ 02 98 07 37 35; mid-Jun–mid-Sep) by the ferry jetty.

One hour is long enough to make a full circuit of Île Molène on foot. The single village of **Le Bourg**, with its maze of narrow streets lined with houses of grey or white-washed granite, huddles around the harbour in the east of the island. The **Musée du Drummond Castle** (☎ 02 98 07 38 41; Le Bourg; adult/child €1.85/0.75; 2-6pm Jul & Aug, 3-5pm May, Jun, Sep & Oct) tells the tragic tale of the *Drummond Castle*, a British passenger liner that foundered on the rocks of the Pierres Vertes, west of Molène, in 1896. Only three people survived and 251 died. Britain's Queen Victoria, in a gesture of thanks to the Molénois who had risked their lives rescuing survivors, presented a bell tower to the island's church.

The island has a handful of rooms to rent and one hotel – the charming 10-room **Hôtel Kastell An Daol** (☎ 02 98 07 39 11; kastell.an .daol@libertysufr.fr; d €54-64; 10 Feb-10 Jan, closed Mon Oct-Apr).

Getting There & Away

Most Penn ar Bed ferries that serve the Île d'Ouessant (see p131) also call at Île Molène. From Le Conquet, the crossing to Molène (adult/child €22.40/13.40) takes one hour. A return ticket costs €21.65/13.10.

BREST

pop 149,600

With its magnificent natural harbour, Brest is one of France's most important naval and commercial ports. Flattened by air attacks during WWII, it was hastily rebuilt as a modern – and not particularly attractive – city. The medieval port area and its narrow streets are long gone. However, you will still see the crisp, white uniforms of French sailors everywhere, whether enjoying lunch in a café or lurching from bar to bar on shore leave.

History

Brest grew around its castle, built to defend the harbour on the River Penfeld. The original 11th-century fortress was seized by English invaders in 1342 before returning to the possession of the dukes of Brittany by the end of the 14th century. Following the 1532 union of Brittany and France, the castle and its harbour became a royal fortress.

FINISTÈRE

ASLEEP AT THE HELM

On the morning of 12 November 2001, the inhabitants of Île Molène awoke to find the massive, 9650-tonne container ship *Melbridge Bilbao* aground on the rocks just a few hundred metres off the western shore of their island. But this was no ordinary shipwreck. The weather was fine, the sea was as flat as a millpond and visibility was excellent. The French coastguard had spotted the ship on radar 50 minutes before it crashed onto the rocks and had repeatedly tried to contact it by radio, but to no avail.

What had gone wrong? Incredibly, it seemed that the autopilot had been programmed incorrectly – the ship, en route from Cuba to Rotterdam, should have been around 40 miles north of Ouessant – and the entire crew, officers included, had been asleep! The 150m-long vessel had sailed, blind but unharmed, at its cruising speed of 17 knots through some of the most dangerous and rock-infested waters in Brittany before thumping into Île Molène.

Fortunately, there were no injuries, no loss of life, no leakage of fuel oil, and no serious damage to the ship's hull. Indeed, the crew's streak of luck extended to running aground on a rising tide – the ship was able to float off the rocks less than five hours after hitting them.

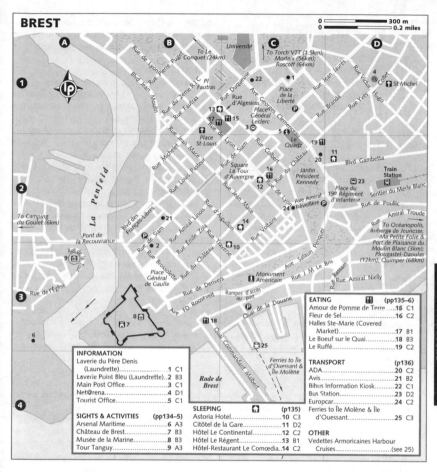

BREST

INFORMATION
Laverie du Père Denis
  (Laundrette)....................................1 C1
Laverie Point Bleu (Laundrette)..2 B3
Main Post Office...............................3 C1
Net@rena..4 D1
Tourist Office..................................5 C1

SIGHTS & ACTIVITIES (pp134–5)
Arsenal Maritime.............................6 A3
Château de Brest.............................7 B3
Musée de la Marine.........................8 B3
Tour Tanguy....................................9 A3

EATING (pp135–6)
Amour de Pomme de Terre 15 C1
Fleur de Sel..16 C2
Halles Ste-Marie (Covered
  Market)..17 B1
Le Bœuf sur le Quai.........................18 B3
Le Ruffé..19 C2

SLEEPING (p135)
Astoria Hotel....................................10 C3
Citôtel de la Gare............................11 D2
Hôtel Le Continental......................12 C2
Hôtel Le Régent...............................13 B1
Hôtel-Restaurant Le Comœdia...14 C2

TRANSPORT (p136)
ADA...20 C2
Avis..21 B2
Bibus Information Kiosk.........22 C1
Bus Station.......................................23 D2
Europcar..24 C2
Ferries to Île Molène & Île
  d'Ouessant.....................................25 C3

OTHER
Vedettes Armoricaines Harbour
  Cruises...(see 25)

FINISTÈRE

During Louis XIV's reign, Brest and its naval dockyards became one of France's four main military ports. Its strategic importance was paramount during WWII. Occupied by German forces, Brest suffered intense bombardment and virtually the entire city was razed. Today, it's still a major port and naval base although its shipbuilding and heavy industries have waned. It's in the process of reinventing itself as a centre for high-tech, tourism and service industries.

Orientation

Brest sprawls along the north shore of the deep natural harbour known as the Rade de Brest. The castle (Château de Brest), naval base (Arsenal Maritime) and Port de Commerce are on the waterfront beside the mouth of the Penfeld. From the castle, rue de Siam runs northeast to place de la Liberté, the city's main square, where it intersects with ave Georges Clemenceau, the main northwest to southeast traffic artery.

Information

INTERNET ACCESS

Net@rena (☎ 02 98 33 61 11; 30 rue Yves Collet; per hr €3.50; ☯ 11am-1am Mon-Thu, 11am-4am Fri-Sat, 1-11pm Sun)

LAUNDRY

Laverie du Père Denis (8 place de la Liberté; ☯ 7am-8.30pm)

Laverie Point Bleu (7 rue de Siam; ☯ 7am-9.30pm)

POST
Main Post Office (place Général Leclerc)

TOURIST INFORMATION
Tourist Office (☎ 02 98 44 24 96; office.de.tourisme
.brest@wanadoo.fr; place de la Liberté; ☒ 9.30am-7pm
Mon-Sat, 10am-noon Sun mid-Jun–mid-Sep, 10am-
12.30pm & 2-6pm Mon-Sat mid-Sep–mid-Jun)

Sights & Activities

CHÂTEAU DE BREST

Commanding the old harbour at the mouth of
the River Penfeld, Brest's **castle** miraculously
escaped destruction by WWII bombing.
On the site of a 3rd-century Roman fort –
notice fragments of the Roman walls in its
ramparts – it dates mostly from the 16th
century. There are striking views of the harbour and naval base from the ramparts.

Today the castle houses the **Musée de la
Marine** (Naval Museum; ☎ 02 98 22 12 39; adult/child
€4.60/free; ☒ 10am-6.30pm daily Apr–mid-Sep, 10am-noon

& 2-6pm Wed-Mon mid-Sep–Mar), recording the city's
naval tradition and with ship models and
objects mainly of interest to enthusiasts.

TOUR TANGUY

Across the Penfeld from the castle is the
14th-century round tower known as **Tour Tan-
guy** (☎ 02 98 00 88 60; place Pierre Péron; admission free;
☒ 10am-noon & 2-7pm daily Jun-Sep, 2-5pm Wed-Thu,
2-6pm Sat & Sun Oct-May). Its paintings, photos
and dioramas trace the history of Brest, with
emphasis on how the city looked on the eve
of WWII. Don't miss the documented visit
of three Siamese ambassadors in 1686 who
presented the court of Louis XIV with gifts
of gold, silver and lacquer; rue de Siam was
named in memory of the occasion.

OCÉANOPOLIS

Brest's biggest tourist attraction is the ultra-
modern aquarium complex **Océanopolis** (☎ 02
98 34 40 40; www.oceanopolis.com - French only; port de

BREST'S BOAT BONANZA

As we moved along the coast of Brittany researching this guide, so many owners of traditional
craft told us their latest timetables and prices – then added 'but not, of course, in early July'.
Why such a collective shutdown, we wondered at first, just when the major holiday season is
getting under way?

They and some 2000 more traditional vessels were bound for Brest and the world's largest
gathering of sailing vessels. For six hectic, action-packed July days every four years, this seaward-
looking city hosts a quite extraordinary maritime festival that pulls in some 17,000 sailors and
yachties from all over the world, plus more than a million visitors.

Moored alongside over 7km of quayside are examples of typical Breton sailing boats – swift,
tri-masted *bisquines* that once plied the Newfoundland fishing grounds; *dundées* with their bluff
bows, once the mainstay of coastal fishing; the heavier, straight-keeled *chasse-marée* (tide-chaser),
a tough coastal trader that could moor almost in a puddle; and the shallow-drafted *sinagot* with
its black hull and tan sails.

In 2004, replicas of famous vessels included the *Endeavour*, Captain Cook's ship when he visited New Zealand and claimed Australia for the British crown; *Matthew*, in which Jacques Cartier
explored the St Lawrence River (see the boxed text, p78); and, from Russia, the 18th-century
Schtandart, designed and commissioned by Tsar Peter the Great.

You can visit the larger ships tied up at the quay. Everywhere, look for the *toiles de mer*, a
wooden plank brought by each new crew and painted or carved to represent its boat or home
port. If the rich, arcane vocabulary of the seas (gaff-rigged yawls, top-sail schooners, luggers,
galleasses, ketches and caravels, they're all there) baffles or bores you, there are plenty of other
diversions. Restaurants work overtime, the city's overflowing bars are filled with the sound of
sea shanties and Breton music, and there's a nightly firework spectacle.

Each festival has its special invitees. Among the stars of the 2004 moot were the *jangadas*,
traditional sailing boats from northwestern Brazil, and *la banda*, musicians from the Pirata Bar
de Fortaleza – a watering hole known to every mariner who's covered that coast. Highlighted
too were papyrus pirogues from Lake Tana in Ethiopia with their accompanying team of dancers and musicians.

Brest's next such invasion from the sea will be in July 2008.

FINISTÈRE

Plaisance; adult/child €14.50/10; ☼ 9am-6pm daily Apr-Aug, 10am-5pm Tue-Sun Sep-Mar). You can happily spend all day exploring this huge complex, about 3km east of the city centre. In its three aquarium pavilions (temperate, polar and tropical) are kelp forests, seals, penguins, sharks and so much more. Take bus No 7 from place de la Liberté.

BOAT TRIPS

From April to September, **La Société Maritime Azenor** (☎ 02 98 41 46 23) has cruises (adult/child €13.50/9, 1½ hours, two or three times daily) around the harbour and naval base, departing from both the Port de Commerce (near the castle) and the Port de Plaisance du Moulin Blanc (opposite Océanopolis). **Vedettes Armoricaines** (☎ 02 98 44 44 04) operates similar cruises, sailing from the Port de Commerce. The tourist office sells tickets for both.

For a more intimate maritime experience, **Escalenrade** (☎ 06 82 19 52 44) provides full-day and half-day cruises in a skippered yacht for about €50 per person for a full day.

Festivals & Events

The big summer attraction is **Les Jeudis du Port** (Harbour Thursdays; admission free; ☼ 7.30pm-midnight Thu mid-Jul–late Aug), with live bands, concerts, street theatre and children's events.

Brest 2008 is the title of the next moot of around 2000 traditional sailing craft from around the world that the city hosts in an intensive week of July every four years (for details of this extraordinary gathering, see the boxed text opposite).

Sleeping

Camping du Goulet (☎ 02 98 45 86 84; campingdugoulet@wanadoo.fr; Ste-Anne du Portzic; per person/tent/car €3.40/3.90/1.30; ☼ year-round) This huge, hilly, three-star camping ground is near the sea on the outskirts of Brest, 6km southwest of the city centre. Take bus No 14 from the train station to Le Cosquer stop.

Auberge de Jeunesse (☎ 02 98 41 90 41; brest.aj.cis@wanadoo.fr; rue de Kerbriant; dm incl breakfast €12.10; ☼ year-round) Brest's modern youth hostel, just a stone's throw from the beach at Moulin Blanc, is also close to Océanopolis and the marina. Take bus No 7 from the train station to the terminus (Port de Plaisance).

Brest's hotels are mainly chain places, short on character. Exceptions include:

Hôtel-Restaurant Le Comœdia (☎ 02 98 46 54 82; 23 rue d'Aiguillon; s/d €23/27) The 15-room Comœdia ranks among the town's best budget deals, with clean, simple rooms and a good **restaurant** below.

Hôtel Le Régent (☎ 02 98 44 29 77; www.brestle-regent.fr.st – French only; 22 rue d'Algésiras; s/d €30/33) With its lovely Art Nouveau café-bar, this place speaks attitude and offers excellent value. All 18 rooms have private bathroom and at weekends rates fall as low as €24.

Citôtel de la Gare (☎ 02 98 44 47 01; info@hotelgare.com; 4 blvd Gambetta; s/d with shower €35/40, s with bathroom €43-58, d with bathroom €48-58; P) Handy for both train and bus stations, this is a welcoming place, recently renovated, where most rooms have a view of the harbour.

Hôtel Le Continental (☎ 02 98 80 50 40; fax 02 98 43 17 47; 41 rue Émile Zola; s €98-129, d €105-136) The Continental is the smartest place in Brest's city centre. The exterior of the building is just plain dull but the Art Deco interior sucks your breath away. Having recently slipped away from an international chain and now reasserting its identity, the Continental is all the better for it.

Astoria Hotel (☎ 02 98 80 19 10; fax 02 98 80 52 41; 9 rue Traverse; d €25, with bathroom €40-50; P) Don't be fooled by the unimpressive exterior of this friendly family hotel; rooms, some with a balcony overlooking the quiet street, are bright, airy and good value.

Eating

Amour de Pomme de Terre (☎ 02 98 43 48 51; 23 rue Halles St-Louis; menus €9-26) 'Potato Love' serves up all manner of dishes – just as long as they have potatoes...baked, mashed, au gratin, any old way. You get a delightful minisalad of the freshest fruit and veg from the covered market opposite – and a dip into a basket of rich dried sausages, from which you hack off a hunk.

Fleur de Sel (☎ 02 98 44 38 65; 15 bis rue de Lyon; mains €16-23.50; ☼ closed Sun & lunch Sat) This stylish Art Deco restaurant, with minimalist décor and a warm atmosphere, serves creative French cuisine, including dishes such as veal kidneys sizzled in truffle vinegar.

Ma Petite Folie (☎ 02 98 42 44 42; Port de Plaisance; menus €18-25; ☼ Mon-Sat) This superb seafood restaurant is in an old lobster-fishing boat, forever beached at Moulin Blanc. Take bus No 7 from the train station to the last stop (Port de Plaisance).

FINISTÈRE

Hôtel-Restaurant Le Comœdia (☎ 02 98 46 54 82; 23 rue d'Aiguillon) boasts an attractive wood-panelled restaurant with an excellent-value lunch *menu* (€7.25).

Le Ruffé (☎ 02 98 46 07 70; 1 bis rue Yves Collet; mains €13.50-18, menus €25-30; ☯ lunch only) With its unostentatious maritime décor, the airy, friendly and highly regarded Le Ruffé is among the best places in town for seafood and quality, creative fish dishes.

Le Boeuf sur le Quai (☎ 02 98 43 91 34; 2 quai Commandant Malbert; menus €12-22) If you just can't face another fish dish, seek haven at 'The Ox on the Quayside'. Down by the docks and defiant, it serves strictly red meat and poultry.

Halles Ste-Marie, Brest's covered market, is a rich resource for self-caterers.

Getting There & Away
AIR
Ryanair operates twice daily flights to/from London (Stansted).

BOAT
Ferries to Île Molène and Île d'Ouessant (for details, see p131) leave from the Port de Commerce.

BUS
Brest's **bus station** (☎ 02 98 44 46 73) is beside the train station. There are buses to Le Conquet (€4.25, 45 minutes, six daily) and Roscoff (€9.40, 1½ to two hours, four daily).

CAR & MOTORCYCLE
There are several hire companies:
ADA (☎ 02 98 44 44 88; 9 ave Georges Clémenceau)
Avis (☎ 02 98 44 63 02; 20 bis rue de Siam)
Europcar (☎ 02 98 44 66 88; rue Voltaire).

TRAIN
There are frequent trains or SNCF buses to Quimper (€13.30, 1¼ hours), Lannion (€13.90, 1¾ hours), St-Brieuc (€19.80, 1¼ hours) and Morlaix (€8.60, 45 minutes), which has connections to Roscoff (€11.70, 1½ hours). There are also around 15 TGV trains daily to Rennes (€28.70, two hours) and Paris (Gare Montparnasse; €63.80, 4½ hours).

Getting Around
Torch'VTT (☎ 02 98 46 06 07; 93 blvd Montaigne) rents bicycles.

The local bus network **Bibus** (☎ 02 98 80 30 30) has an information kiosk on place de la Liberté. A single ticket costs €1, a carnet of 10 €8.30 and a day pass €3.

To order a **taxi** call ☎ 02 98 80 43 43 or ☎ 02 98 42 11 11.

INLAND

LES ENCLOS PAROISSIAUX
The region around the Élorn Valley, between Morlaix and Brest, has a concentration of traditional Breton **parish enclosures**, featuring elaborate *calvaires* (calvaries) and *ossuaires* (ossuary chapels for the storage of disinterred bones), dating mostly from the 15th to 17th centuries. Don't overlook their **churches** (☯ mostly 9am to 6pm), which were often constructed well after the close complex and resonate with haunting recorded liturgical music. Within, the colourful – some might say gaudy – polychrome, wooden rood screens and altarpieces, plus finely carved wooden pulpits, baptistries and organ lofts, contrast with the squat stone sculptures of the closes, which seem to have more in common with a more distant, naive, medieval ecclesiastical tradition.

You can make a circular route by car or bike, taking in most of those we describe – and, time and energy allowing, grafting on Sizun too. It makes for a great day outing from either Morlaix or Brest.

St-Thégonnec
St-Thégonnec has a **calvary**, among the last to be built, that's one of Brittany's most imposing. Enter the close through its sturdy triumphal arch, constructed in 1587 with clear Renaissance influences. The calvary shows scenes from the Passion; as you face it, the death of Christ is to the left and the risen Christ to the right. Around the other three sides are scenes of Christ's torment. Examine the faces of those abusing him, some grinning and snarling grotesquely.

The **church** suffered a serious fire in 1998 and, although open to the public, is still undergoing restoration work. Happily, the magnificent carved pulpit (1683) survived the blaze unscathed.

Guimiliau
The elaborate **calvary** at Guimiliau, dating from the 1580s, seethes with skilfully carved figures – more than 200 of them – showing

scenes from the life of Christ. The four Evangelists stand guard at the four corner buttresses. Look for the one nonbiblical scene, illustrating the local legend of Katell Golet, a woman who took the Devil as her lover. Like something that crept in from a horror comic, the sculpture shows her at the mouth of hell, a rope around her neck and her breasts bared as a demon flays her flesh with a pitchfork. Beside this cameo is a portrayal of the Last Supper, the disciples peering over Jesus' shoulder, seemingly more concerned about what's on the menu (whole roast lamb, you'll see) than looming tragedy.

The **church** has a beautiful Renaissance porch, lined with statues of the 12 Apostles, as in many such churches. Its archway is decorated with three bands of intricate carving. Inside, the finely wrought pulpit, organ loft and baptistry were all carved between 1675 and 1677.

Lampaul-Guimiliau

The **close** at Lampaul-Guimiliau, 4km west of Guimiliau, is relatively plain, except for the ossuary chapel's quaint wooden door, decorated with grape vines. The interior of the **church** (1553), by contrast, has a lavish, naively carved, painted timber rood beam, decorated with scenes from the Passion and surmounted by a large wooden Crucifixion. By even greater contrast, the rest of the church (especially the Entombment in the southeast corner) is pure, extravagant baroque. Back outside, take a look at the church's curious truncated spire, which was struck by lightning in 1809.

La Roche-Maurice

The village of La Roche-Maurice and its ruined 12th-century castle have a delightful setting on a hillside overlooking the River Élorn. The most interesting part of the **close** is the ossuary chapel, built of honey-coloured granite and dark-grey schist. Here, a low frieze of sculpted panels represents earthly society – a bishop with his staff, a baker bearing his shovel, a lawyer and his money bag. At the left-hand end, above a holy water stoup, perches the figure of Ankou (Death) with the chilling words 'je vous tue tous' – 'I kill you all' – chiselled into the stone.

The **church** has a magnificent painted wooden rood screen where capitals representing grotesque monsters support the 12 apostles. Note too the fine original 17th-century stained glass at the eastern end.

La Martyre

About 5km southeast of La Roche-Maurice is the village of La Martyre, which has the oldest **close** in the region, dating from around 1460. A triumphal arch topped by a lichen-mottled calvary leads into the close, with its macabre ossuary chapel adorned with a male figure holding a skull and a thighbone.

Above the stoup just inside the lopsided porch to the church, a broken figure of Ankou clutching a severed head delivers a stern warning.

Plougastel-Daoulas

More conveniently visited as an excursion from Brest, the modern commercial town of Plougastel-Daoulas, is famous for its early 17th-century **calvary**. It was shattered, like the entire town, during the WWII bombing of Brest – and its postwar reconstruction was funded by the very American airmen who dropped the bombs. The calvary has around 180 figures, the whole topped by a tall cross bearing the crucified Christ, a Piéta (scene of the Virgin Mary holding the body of Christ) and a pair of knights and archangels. The two smaller crosses represent the two thieves who were crucified along with Jesus Christ. The good thief has an angel perched on his cross; the bad one, a demon. The warty lumps on the shaft of the cross represent the pustules that appeared on the skin of plague victims and signify that this is a *croix de peste* (plague cross), erected to celebrate the end of the epidemic.

Bus No 25 (€1, 40 minutes, every half-hour) travels between Brest's place de la Liberté and place du Calvaire in Plougastel-Daoulas.

Sizun
pop 1900

The peaceful village of Sizun, 40km southwest of Morlaix, has one of the prettiest parish closes in Brittany. Beyond a commanding Renaissance triple arch, topped with a miniature calvary, is an elaborately carved 16th-century ossuary chapel and a church with a finger-slim spire, grafted on in the 18th century.

Down in the valley of the Élorn – here little more than a stream – and 2km west of the village is the **Maison de la Rivière** (☎ 02 98 68 86 33; Moulin de Vergraon; adult/child €4/2.50; ◯ 10am-6.30pm daily Jul & Aug, 10am-noon & 2-5pm Mon-Sat, 2-5pm Sun Sep-Jun). In and around an old water mill, exhibits describe the ecology and hydrology of Brittany's river systems, including features on otters and beavers, plus the cleaning up of the previously polluted Élorn.

The **tourist office** (☎ 02 98 68 88 40; 3 rue de l'Argoat; ◯ 9am-12.30pm & 2-7pm Mon-Sat, 10am-12.30pm Sun Jul & Aug, 9.30am-noon & 2-5.30pm Mon-Sat Sep-Jun) is across the road from the church.

PARC NATUREL RÉGIONAL D'ARMORIQUE

Established in 1969, the 1100-sq-km **Armorica Regional Park** (☎ 02 98 81 90 08; http://pnr-armorique .fr - French only) takes in the Monts d'Arrée and the unspoiled forests around Huelgoat. It also stretches westwards for approximately 70km along the Presqu'île de Crozon (Crozon Peninsula).

Huelgoat
pop 1750

Huelgoat, 30km south of Morlaix, lies at the eastern extremity of a small Y-shaped lake that empties into the Argent, a mere trickle of a river. It's an excellent base for exploring what's left of the forested Argoat. The village borders the unspoiled Forêt d'Huelgoat – where King Arthur's treasure is said to be buried – with its unusual rock formations, caves, menhirs and abandoned silver and lead mines. To the east and northeast are the Forêt de Fréau and the Forêt de St-Ambroise. All have a good network of walking trails.

Between June and September, the **tourist office** (☎ 02 98 99 72 32; fax 02 98 99 75 72; ◯ 10am-12.30pm & 2-5.30pm Mon-Sat Jul & Aug, 10am-noon and 2-4.30pm Mon-Fri Sep-Jun) is in the **Moulin du Chaos**, an old mill beside the bridge at the eastern end of the lake. During the rest of the year it operates within the **town hall** (place Alphonse Penven).

Huelgoat gets very busy in summer and the forest trails are best appreciated in the relative peace of spring and autumn. An undemanding **walking trail** (round trip 45 minutes, comfortably, including a stop at signed features) heads downstream from the bridge, initially on the opposite bank

to the tourist office. Here, the river disappears into a picturesque, wooded valley where giant granite boulders lie pell-mell, each upholstered with a luxuriant growth of shaggy green moss. La Grotte du Diable (the Devil's Grotto), a chamber with a waterfall reached via a narrow steel ladder and steps hacked into the rock, is counterbalanced, spiritually speaking, by the Ménage de La Vièrge (Virgin Mary's Kitchen), a clutter of large boulders. La Roche Tremblante is a massive boulder, weighing around 100 tonnes, that rocks slightly if you push in *just* the right place.

Longer hiking trails (1½ to two hours) lead along the Promenade du Canal to some old silver mines and to the unremarkable Grotte d'Artus (Arthur's Cave).

SLEEPING & EATING

Camping Municipal du Lac (☎ 02 98 99 78 80; rue Général de Gaulle; per person/site €2.80/3.30; ◯ mid-Jun–mid-Sep) This camping area is on the lakeside around 500m west of the town centre.

Hôtel-Restaurant du Lac (☎ 02 98 99 71 14; fax 02 98 99 70 91; 9 rue Général de Gaulle; d €45-58; ◯ mid-Feb–mid-Dec) Huelgoat's only hotel, a Logis de France that's a mere 200m from the tourist office, is fine – if not as charming as its name and lakeside location might suggest. Its popular **restaurant** serves steaks, pizzas and salads.

Crêperie des Myrtilles (☎ 02 98 99 72 66; 26 place Aristide-Briand; crepes €2-6, menus from €8; ◯ Jan-Oct, closed Mon except Jul & Aug) This pretty little creperie on the town's main square has a pleasant summer terrace. Try the juicy, signature *crêpe aux myrtilles* (crepes with bilberries, picked locally).

GETTING THERE & AWAY

EFFIA (☎ 02 98 93 06 98) runs at least two bus services daily to Morlaix (€8.70, one hour) to the north and Carhaix to the southeast. Buses stop in front of the Chapelle de Notre Dame in place Aristide-Briand.

Les Monts d'Arrée

Les Monts d'Arrée form a long, narrow ridge that rises like a breaking wave to the east of Sizun and west of Huelgoat. This band of granite bedrock, more resistant to erosion than the surrounding schist, runs in a straight line, southwest to northeast, for over 20km. Its highest point is the **Roc'h** de Trévézel (383m), a tortured outcrop of granite bursting through the shaggy coat of heather and gorse. The view on a clear day is panoramic, from the Rade de Brest to the Baie de Morlaix.

Ten kilometres west of the Roc'h de Trévézel, on the road to Sizun, are the **Moulins de Kerouat** (☎ 02 98 68 87 76; Commana; adult/child €4.50/2.10; ☺ 11am-7pm daily Jul & Aug, 10am-6pm Mon-Fri, 2-6pm Sat & Sun Jun, 2-6pm Sun mid-Mar–May, Sep & Oct). This group of more than a dozen buildings, dating from the 17th to early 20th centuries, includes water mills, bakeries, workshops and a furnished house. The regional park has restored the hamlet as a living example of a rural Breton community of old. Ask for the English version of the guidance leaflet.

PRESQU'ÎLE DE CROZON

The Crozon Peninsula, which is part of the Parc Naturel Régional d'Armorique, has wild and spectacular sea cliffs at Pointe de Dinan and Pointe de Pen-Hir and, in Morgat and Camaret-sur-Mer, a pair of sheltered resort towns with beaches.

MÉNEZ-HOM & AROUND
Ménez-Hom
The 330m-high, grass- and heather-clad rounded hump of Ménez-Hom guards the eastern end of the peninsula. The summit – a surfaced road leads right to the top – offers a superb panorama over the Baie de Douarnenez and is a very popular hanggliding and paragliding site. The **Club Celtic de Vol Libre** (☎ 02 98 81 50 27; www.vol-libre-menez -hom.com - French only) organises half-day hanggliding and parapente sessions for €70.

Landévennec
To the north of Ménez-Hom, the Aulne empties into the Rade de Brest close to the pretty little village of Landévennec, which is famous for the ruins of the Benedictine **Abbaye St-Guénolé**. The abbey **museum** (☎ 02 98 27 35 90; admission €4; ☺ 10am-7pm daily Jul–mid-Sep, 2-6pm Sun-Fri May, Jun & late Sep) records the history of the site, which has been occupied since at least Roman times. Although the ruins are medieval, the abbey was establisehd by St Guénolé in AD 485, making Landévennec the oldest Christian site in Brittany. Not far away, a new abbey is home to a contemporary community of monks, who run a little shop selling, in addition to the usual tourist paraphernalia, some delicious homemade fruit jellies.

CROZON & MORGAT
pop 7800
Crozon, the largest town on the peninsula and itself unremarkable, provides shops and services for the more alluring resort of Morgat, 2km south, which makes a good base for exploring this outstandingly beautiful peninsula.

Information
Along the main road to Camaret, the **Crozon tourist office** (☎ 02 98 27 07 92; crozon.maison.du .tourisme@wanadoo.fr; blvd Pralognan; ☺ 9.15am-7.30pm Mon-Sat, 10am-1pm Sun Jul & Aug, 9.15am-noon & 2-5/6pm Mon-Sat Sep-Jun) is approximately 500m west of the church.

The seasonal **Morgat tourist office** (☎ 02 98 27 29 49; ☺ 9.15am-7.30pm Mon-Sat, 3-7pm Sun Jul & Aug) is beside the promenade at the corner of blvd de la Plage and the road to Cap de la Chèvre.

Sights & Activities
Morgat is ranged along a promenade overlooking a fine sandy **beach**. Beyond the marina at the southern end, the coastal path offers an excellent 8km hike along the sea cliffs to **Cap de la Chèvre**.

A couple of Morgat-based companies, **Vedettes Rosmeur** (☎ 02 98 27 10 71) and **Vedettes Sirènes** (☎ 02 98 26 20 10), operate 45-minute boat excursions to the colourful **sea caves** along the coast. The tours cost around €9/6 per adult/child and boats depart from Morgat harbour several times daily from April to September.

The **Centre Nautique** (☎ 02 98 16 00 00; ☺ year-round), beside the marina, hires yachts, windsurf boards and kayaks.

POINTE DE DINAN
Six kilometres westwards from Crozon-Morgat, **Pointe de Dinan** is bounded by 40m cliffs of pale-grey quartzite that are topped by a thick rug of heather, moss and ground-hugging gorse. It commands great views over the **Château de Dinan**, a heap of stratified rock attached to the mainland by a natural archway.

FINISTÈRE

Sleeping

Camping Les Pieds Dans l'Eau (☎ 02 98 27 62 43; St-Fiacre; tent, car & 2 adults €12.35; ⊙ mid-Jun–mid-Sep) 'Camping feet in the water' (almost literally so at high tide since the beach is only a well-cast pebble away) is one of nine camping grounds along the peninsula.

Hôtel de la Baie (☎ 02 98 27 07 51; hotel.delabaie@presquile-crozon.com; 46 blvd de la Plage, Morgat; d with shower €32, with bathroom €35-47; ⊙ year-round; **P**) This jolly, family-run hotel on Morgat's promenade is one of the best deals in town – and one of the very few to remain open year-round.

Eating

La Grange de Toul-Boss (☎ 02 98 27 17 95; 1 place d'Ys, Morgat; galettes €3-7.50, mains €10-18.50, menus €13) Just a few paces from the Morgat tourist office, this combined restaurant, creperie and tearoom is housed in an old barn decorated in traditional Breton style. The *menu* is exceptionally good value. Starters include half a crab or six oysters, mains are principally large portions of fish and the range of sticky desserts includes *far Breton* (vanilla flan).

Crêperie du Kreisker (☎ 02 98 26 15 49; 2 rue Kreisker, Morgat; galettes €2-5.75; ⊙ May-Sep) This little creperie, next door to Hôtel de la Baie, serves traditional Breton crepes at very reasonable prices. Try the *galette Avar Doual*, filled with meltingly delicious cheese, potatoes, bacon and onion.

Les Échoppes (☎ 02 98 26 12 63; 24 quai du Kador, Morgat; menus €15-30; ⊙ lunch & dinner Jul & Aug, dinner only May, Jun & Sep) This tiny, unassuming stone cottage at the southern end of the waterfront is Morgat's best restaurant. It specialises in seafood – the catch of the day is advertised on a sign outside – and is so small we advise reserving a table, whatever the day.

Getting There & Around

SCETA (☎ 02 98 93 06 98) and **Transports Salaün** (☎ 02 98 27 02 02) between them run up to five buses daily from Quimper to Crozon (€9.30, 1¼ hours) and on to Camaret. **EFFIA** (☎ 02 98 93 06 98) has a service from Camaret and Crozon to Brest (€9, 1¼ hours, up to four daily). Buses also run between Morgat, Crozon and Camaret several times daily (€1.60, 10 minutes).

To rent a bike, contact **Presqu'île Loisirs** (☎ 02 98 27 00 09; 13 rue de la Gare, Crozon), opposite Crozon's tourist office, **Point Bleu** (☎ 02 98 27 09 04; quai Kador, Morgat) or, in summer, the **open-air stall** in front of Morgat's tourist office. The going rate is about €10 per day.

CAMARET-SUR-MER

pop 2700

Camaret is an attractive and lively town in summer, though decidedly drowsy out of season. It makes a good alternative to Morgat as a base for exploring the region. Originally a centre of the sardine-fishing industry, in the late 19th and early 20th centuries Camaret became France's premier port for *la pêche à la langouste* (crayfish fishing). Fleets of specially designed sailing boats called *dundées* set out to scour the banks of Biscay, the Irish Sea and even the Indian Ocean in search of this elusive, expensive crustacean.

Today, the decaying hulks of abandoned fishing boats line the breakwater in Camaret harbour, sad testimony to the decline of the industry. The town is now a popular yachting harbour and depends on the annual flood of summer visitors for a living.

Information

The **tourist office** (☎ 02 98 27 93 60; www.camaret-sur-mer.com - French only; 15 quai Kléber; ⊙ 9am-7pm Mon-Sat, 10am-1pm Sun Jul & Aug, 10am-noon & 2-5pm Mon-Sat Sep-Jun) is on the waterfront.

Sights & Activities

The elegant little **Tour Vauban** (☎ 02 98 27 82 60; adult/child €3/2; ⊙ 2-5pm mid-Mar–mid-Sep) guards the breakwater that shelters the harbour's northern flank. Constructed in 1689, it houses a small exhibition on the various fortifications in the Camaret region.

The 17th-century **Chapelle Notre Dame de Rocamadour** is a short distance away. Long and relatively plain, its timber roof like an inverted ship's hull, this simple chapel is dedicated to the sailors and fishermen of Camaret, who have adorned it with votive offerings of oars, life buoys and model ships. Outside, glance up at the bell tower; part of it – unrepaired to this day – was carried away by a cannonball fired during the English navy's assault on Brest in 1694.

BOAT TRIPS

The old slipway opposite the chapel is now home to Charpentiers Marine Camarétois, a modern boat yard that continues the traditions of wooden boat building. One of its finest products is the **Belle Étoile** (☎ 02 98 27 86 91; half/full-day cruise €28/42; daily sailings Apr-Oct), a faithful reproduction of a 19th-century *dundée*, built in 1992 and moored opposite the yard on the town quay.

In summer, **Pesketour** (☎ 02 98 27 98 44), run by a local ex-fisherman who also organises sea-fishing expeditions, offers boat trips (adult/child €13.50/9, 1½ hours, twice daily) to the Tas de Pois sea stacks off Pointe de Pen-Hir, a run also undertaken by **Vedettes Azénor** (☎ 02 98 41 46 23).

Sleeping & Eating

Camping Municipal du Lannic (☎ 02 98 27 91 31; rue du Grouannoc'h; 2 adults, tent & car €7.30; ☼ Easter-Oct) This basic site is less than 400m from the waterfront. Opposite the marina near Hôtel du Styvel, take the road towards Pointe de Pen-Hir and turn left at rue de Penzance.

Hôtel Vauban (☎ 02 98 27 91 36; fax 02 98 27 96 34; 4 quai du Styvel; d with toilet €28, with bathroom €31-34; ☼ Feb-Nov; **P**) The 16-room Vauban is a convivial place, its bar much favoured by the old salts of Camaret. With harbour views to the front and an extensive garden at the back, plus quiet, comfortable rooms, it ranks as one of Brittany's best bargains.

Hôtel de France (☎ 02 98 27 93 06; fax 02 98 27 88 14; 19 quai Gustave Toudouze; d with shower €35, with bathroom €45-71; ☼ Easter-Oct; **P**) The charming Hôtel de France has cosy, wood-panelled rooms, many with sea views, and a good **restaurant** (menus €17-28), also overlooking the bay.

Hôtel Thalassa (☎ 02 98 27 86 44; www.hotel-thalassa.com - French only; quai du Styvel; d €48-125; ☼ Apr-Sep; **P** 🛋) The modern Thalassa is Camaret's top hotel, offering guests a heated sea-water pool, fitness centre and steam room. Paying top whack gets you a spacious room with a large balcony overlooking the marina.

For *galettes* and crepes, try either **Crêperie Rocamadour** (☎ 02 98 27 93 17; quai Kléber), close to the tourist office, or **Les Embruns** (☎ 02 98 27 90 39; quai Gustave-Toudouze), which is near Hôtel de France.

Le Langoustier (☎ 02 98 27 99 00; Plage du Correjou; ☼ mid-Mar–Oct), is a snug, intimate little place, imaginatively decorated with a strong nautical theme (much more than the all-too-common couple of nets slung up a wall), at the landward end of the harbour bar. It's an everything place, where you can munch on a pizza (€6 to €12), nibble at a hearty salad (€4 to €8), go for a *menu* (€13.50 to €37) or tuck into one of the variety of fresh fish dishes (€10 to €20).

Getting There & Away

BOAT

Vedettes Azénor (☎ 02 98 41 46 23; www.azenor.com - French only) runs a seasonal ferry (adult/child €8/5 one way, 25 minutes, four daily July to August, three daily Tuesday to Sunday April to June & September) between Brest's Port de Commerce and the Presqu'île de Crozon. Some ferries dock at Camaret, but most of the arrivals and departures are from the little port of Le Fret, 7km east of Camaret; a minibus links it with Camaret (€1.50, 10 minutes) at ferry arrival time.

Vedettes Armoricaines (☎ 02 98 44 44 04) also operates between Brest and Le Fret (adult/child €5/3, 30 minutes, at least one daily Monday to Friday).

Penn Ar Bed and Finist'mer provide a summer-only ferry service between Camaret and Île d'Ouessant (see p131).

BUS

Camaret is served by the same bus lines as Crozon-Morgat (see opposite).

AROUND CAMARET

On the western fringes of Camaret, beside the road which leads to Pointe de Pen-Hir, are the **Alignements de Lagatjar**, a field of around 40 prehistoric standing stones, arranged in lines.

Pointe de Pen-Hir, 3km south of Camaret, is a spectacular headland bounded by steep sea cliffs – it's a popular rock-climbing site, so don't lob stones down the crags! There are two WWII memorials on the headland: one commemorates the Bretons who died; the other, a bunker, is to the soldiers and sailors who perished during the Battle of the Atlantic. The line of sea stacks off the point is known as the **Tas de Pois** – rather more euphonic in French than its translation, the 'Pile of Peas'.

The peninsula to the north of Camaret ends at the **Pointe des Espagnols**, a steep bluff overlooking Le Goulet (the Bottleneck), the narrow entrance to the Rade de Brest. As befits such a strategic position, the headland is riddled with old fortifications and gun emplacements.

CORNOUAILLE

Cornouaille, Finistère's most southerly part, has a name that commemorates the early Celts who sailed from Cornwall and other parts of Britain to settle here. This is where Breton customs are strongest and where you're most likely to hear people speaking Breton. The area's major city, Quimper, stages an annual summer festival celebrating Celtic culture.

DOUARNENEZ
pop 17,000

Until well into the 20th century, Douarnenez was the centre of France's sardine-fishing industry, home port to more than 1000 sardine boats whose catch was processed by 34 canneries. So strongly was the town identified with the small, silvery fish that its inhabitants picked up the Breton nickname 'penn sardin' (sardine-head). Today Douarnenez is still an important fishing port, but it has also reinvented itself as a guardian of Brittany's – and France's – maritime traditions.

Douarnenez has two other claims to fame: in the 19th century it invented *kouign amann*, the famous Breton butter cake; and in 1924 it elected France's first Communist mayor.

Orientation

The action part of Douarnenez sits on a stubby peninsula. The main drag – which changes its name from rue Jean Jaurès to rue Jean Bart to rue Ernest Renan as it progresses northwards – follows the crest of the peninsula, passing just east of the umbilically joined main squares, place Édouard Vaillant and place de la Résistance. From this main thoroughfare, streets fall steeply west to the narrow, river-mouth harbour of Port Rhu. To the east, the narrow alleys of the old town lead more gently down to the old port of Rosmeur. The northern end of the peninsula is dominated by the warehouses of the busy fishing port.

Information

Café des Halles (3 place des Halles) One Internet point, free for clients.
Le Lavoir (2 rue du Centre; 🕑 7am-7pm) Wash clothes at this laundrette.

Post Office (rue Berthelot)
Tourist Office (🕾 02 98 92 13 35; www.douarnenez -tourisme.com - French only; 2 rue Docteur Mével; 🕑 10am-noon & 2-7pm Mon-Sat, 10am-1pm Sun Jul & Aug, 10am-noon & 2-5/6pm Mon-Sat Sep-Jun) Beside place Édouard Vaillant.

Sights & Activities

The town's liveliest area is the waterfront on Port Rhu, where Douarnenez's maritime traditions are celebrated in the quayside **Port-Musée** and **Musée du Bateau** (🕾 02 98 92 65 20; quai du Port Rhu; combined ticket adult/child €6.20/3.85; 🕑 10am-7pm daily mid-Jun–mid-Sep, 10am-12.30pm & 2-6pm Tue-Sun Apr–mid-Jun & mid-Sep–Oct). The Port-Musée includes around 20 traditional vessels afloat at the quayside, ranging from *Notre Dame de Rocamadour*, a Breton *langoustier* (cray-fishing boat), to the Norwegian three-masted sailing ship *Anna Rosa*. Workshops along the quay preserve the old skills of wooden boat building, sail making and net repairing.

Nearby, the Musée du Bateau occupies a former sardine cannery. Its vast interior contains around 40 smaller traditional boats from various parts of the world, including an Inuit kayak, a Welsh coracle and a West African outrigger canoe, as well as local designs.

On the other side of town is the old port area of **Rosmeur**, an attractive waterfront lined with fishermen's bars and touristy restaurants.

BEACHES

At the northern end of town, the tiny beaches of **Plage des Dames** and **Plage de Pors Cad** face the little **Île Tristan**, accessible at most low tides and once the island hideaway of the infamous 16th-century pirate known as La Fontenelle. There are bigger and better beaches 2km east of town at the immense **Plage du Ris** and 1km west at **Plage des Sables Blancs** in the suburb of Tréboul.

Festivals & Events

Every two years in late July (most recently 16–20 July 2004), Douarnenez plays host to the **Rendez-Vous des Marins** (🕾 02 98 92 29 29), a spectacular gathering of several hundred traditional sailing vessels, from the smallest dinghy to the tallest tall ship. The gathering is also called the Fête des Vieux Gréements, or Festival of Old Sailing Rigs.

FINISTÈRE

Les Arts Dînent à l'Huile (sardines in oil – try saying this toe-curling pun out loud!) is an annual event, held in late July or early August, where musicians, performers, artists and sailors from a sardine-fishing port elsewhere in the world are invited to Douarnenez for a few days of music and revelry. In 2002 the Portuguese came to town, while in 2004 it was Senegal's turn. For information call ☎ 02 98 92 27 13 or see www.lesartsdinent.com (French only).

Sleeping & Eating

Camping Croas Men (☎ 02 98 74 00 18; www.croas -men.com; 27 bis rue de Croas Men; 2 adults, tent & car €10.30; ☼ Apr–Oct) This small, pleasant site is a few blocks west of the marina at Tréboul, itself about 1km west of the town centre.

Hôtel-Restaurant Le Kériolet (☎ 02 98 92 16 89; fax 02 98 92 62 94; 29 rue Croas Talud; d €42-47; menus €12-33) The Kériolet, on the main road a little over 500m south of the town centre, has eight pleasant rooms, the dearer ones with a view of the bay. The seafood restaurant is excellent value, whichever of the varied *menus* you settle for.

Hôtel Le Bretagne (☎ 02 98 92 30 44; 23 rue Duguay Trouin; d €30, with bathroom €42-47) The Bretagne is just a block south of the main square. It's well worth paying the €5 difference for one of the recently renovated and altogether more congenial rooms.

Hostellerie Le Clos de Vallombreuse (☎ 02 98 92 63 64; www.closvallombreuse.com – French only; 7 rue Estienne d'Orves; d €70-76; ☒) Tucked away just north of the town centre, behind the church, this grand early-20th-century villa offers 25 elegant rooms, a stylish, wood-panelled **dining room** (menus €16-38) and a huge garden with swimming pool. Out of season, when singles/doubles drop as low as €43/49, it represents exceptional value.

Crêperie au Goûter Breton (☎ 02 98 92 02 74; 36 rue Jean Jaurès; crepes €2.30-5; ☼ closed lunch Sun Jul & Aug, all day Sun & Mon Sep-Jun) In business for over 50 years, this welcoming, agreeably and eccentrically furnished creperie is Douarnenez' oldest and best. You can also select from a range of 10 different ciders (€1.60 a bowl) to accompany one of the tasty traditional Breton crepes and walk away with a jar of tasty home-made jam or jelly, honey or pure fruit juice.

Restaurant Le Vivier (☎ 02 98 92 73 72; place de l'Enfer; menus €12 & €18.50-35; ☼ closed Mon & dinner Sun) This choice place, opposite the Musée du Bateau and named after the *vivier* (lobster tank) in the middle of the dining room, has a great-value lunch *menu* at only €12.

Getting There & Away

The bus station is on place de la Résistance, opposite the tourist office. **CAT** (☎ 02 98 90 68 40) runs buses to/from Quimper (€6, 35 minutes, six to 10 daily). Three or four daily continue to Pointe du Raz (€7) via Audierne (€4.75). **Voyages d'Ys** (☎ 02 98 92 05 42) also runs between Douarnenez and Pointe du Raz.

LOCRONAN

Devoid of modern buildings, and unspoilt even by telephone wires or electricity cables (they are all underground), Locronan possesses an outward appearance that has changed little since the 18th century. For this, it has been much in demand as a film location – most famously in 1979 for Roman Polanski's *Tess*.

It may have evaded the passage of time, but Locronan certainly doesn't escape the passage of thousands of tourists every year. Finding a parking place in July and August is well nigh impossible. To savour the atmosphere of *les temps perdus*, it's best to visit very early in the morning – at dawn, say – or outside the summer season.

From the 14th to the 19th centuries, Locronan was famed for its sailcloth, the mainstay of the town's economy. Today, tourism brings wealth and the village enjoys fame as the site of **La Grande Troménie** (see the boxed text, p144).

As you enter the 15th-century **parish church** through a side chapel, you are confronted by the tomb of St Renan, patron saint of Locronan village, his supine effigy poking a crosier into the mouth of a benign-looking monster.

The **tourist office** (☎ 02 98 91 70 14; www.locronan .org – French only; place de la Mairie; ☼ 10am-1pm & 2-7pm Mon-Sat Jun–mid-Sep, plus Sun morning Jul–mid-Sep, 10am-noon & 2-6pm Mon-Fri Apr-Jun & mid-Sep–end Sep) is on the main square.

There's only one hotel in the village itself – a splendid Logis de France offering great value. **Hôtel du Prieuré** (☎ 02 98 91 70 89; www.hotel -le-prieure.com – French only; 11 rue du Prieuré; s/d €51.50/59; ☼ mid-Mar–Oct; ℗) occupies an old granite house with 14 comfortable rooms and runs

LA GRANDE TROMÉNIE

La Grande Troménie – the biggest and most important religious event in Brittany – attracts thousands of pilgrims to Locronan. Dressed in traditional Breton costume, and singing traditional songs, the pilgrims follow a sacred trail through the surrounding countryside. The 12km route has 12 'stations', each marked by a tiny chapel housing an effigy of a saint. But why 12? The Stations of the Cross? The months of the calendar? No one knows for sure.

People think that the Troménie may have its origins in the Druidic practice of touring the sacred groves in the Forêt de Névet, west of the village. St Ronan, the 5th-century Irish hermit who brought Christianity to these parts, took this pagan ritual and dressed it in Christian clothing.

La Grande Troménie takes place every six years, from the second to the third Sundays in July; the next occurrence is in 2007.

The Petite Troménie is just that – a smaller but still spectacular version of the extravaganza held every six years. Following a 6km route, it takes place annually on the second Sunday in July.

a more than creditable restaurant. Reservations are essential between June and September and you'll appreciate the free hotel parking if you arrive on a day during the busy summer season.

Between two and seven buses travel daily between Locronan and both Quimper and Camaret.

AUDIERNE & AROUND

pop 2500

Audierne, at the head of a scenic *aber* (as in Welsh, the word *aber* means 'mouth of a river'), is both active fishing harbour and family seaside resort. In summer, boats ferry day-visitors from the harbour to offshore Île de Sein.

Orientation & Information

The town straggles along the western bank of the Goyen estuary, with the marina to the north, the fishing harbour in the middle, and the harbour entrance to the south.
Laverie du Port (2 place de la République; 9am-10pm) Laundrette.
Tourist Office (☎ 02 98 70 12 20; www.audierne -tourisme.com - French only; 8 rue Victor Hugo; ☺ 9.30am-12.30pm & 2-7pm Mon-Sat Jul & Aug, 9am-noon & 2-6pm Mon-Sat Sep-Jun) Beside the market square – and main parking area – in the centre of town.

Sights & Activities

Audierne's **Aquarium** (☎ 02 98 70 03 03; www .aquarium.fr - French only; rue du Goyen; adult/child €10.50/7.50; ☺ 10am-7pm daily Apr-Sep, 2-5pm Sun-Thu Oct-Dec & mid-Feb–Mar) overlooks the Goyen at the northern end of town. Its tanks and display areas re-create the various marine and freshwater habitats of Brittany and there's a

pleasant outdoor café-terrace built out over the river.

At the southern end of the harbour, on the way to the beach, you can visit **Les Grands Viviers** (☎ 02 98 70 10 04; route de la Plage), the largest covered holding tanks in Europe. A sort of death row for crustaceans, it's where thousands of freshly caught lobsters, crabs and crayfish await that final journey to the restaurant kitchens. The Viviers were closed when we last visited, pending a move to new premises – though the lobsters are unlikely to appreciate the upgrade.

From the breakwater at the southern end of town, a beautiful sandy **beach** stretches west for over 1km.

CAP SIZUN

The scenic and rocky headland of **Cap Sizun**, 8km northwest of Audierne, is thronged with nesting sea birds in spring and early summer. Since 1958 the cliffs have been protected as the **Réserve du Cap Sizun** (☎ 02 98 70 13 53; adult/child €2/free; ☺ 10am-6pm daily Jul & Aug, 10am-noon & 2-6pm Apr-Jun). You can rent binoculars (€1.50) and take a **guided tour** (€4; daily July to August, Saturday only April to June) with an ornithologist.

Sleeping

Hôtel du Roi Gradlon (☎ 02 98 70 04 51; www.auroi gradlon.com - French only; 3 ave Manu Brusq; d €46-61) Externally, this isn't Brittany's prettiest hotel, but the views from the restaurant, and the spacious, comfortable rooms – most of which overhang Audierne's beautiful beach – more than compensate. Some rooms in the annexe, just a short walk away, also have sea views.

FINISTÈRE

Hôtel-Restaurant Le Cabestan (☎ 02 98 70 08 82; www.hotel-cabestan.com - French only; 2 rue Laënnec, Esquibien; d €30-48) This homely place – it has a lounge with leather armchairs and a grandfather clock – is on the village square, 2km west of the harbour at Esquibien.

Getting There & Away
BOAT
In summer there are ferries between Audierne and the Île de Sein (right). The ferry terminal is 2km southwest of Audierne harbour; take the road to the beach and keep going.

BUS
CAT (☎ 02 98 90 68 40) buses run regularly from Quimper to Audierne (€6.10, one hour), some via Douarnenez and some continuing to Pointe du Raz.

POINTE DU RAZ
Although it is not quite the most westerly point on the French mainland – that honour goes to Pointe de Corsen (see p146) – the dramatic scenery of Pointe du Raz has seen it become the French equivalent of England's Land's End (its Breton name, Penn Ar Bed, means just that: 'land's end'). Each year almost one million people visit this cliff-girt headland, with its statue of **Notre Dame des Naufragés** (Our Lady of the Shipwrecked) gazing out across the perilous tidal races of the Raz de Sein to the distant reefs of the Île de Sein.

A new car park and commercial centre, cleverly landscaped so as to be invisible from a distance, were built well short of the actual point; you can take a shuttle bus for the last 800m or, even better, walk along the coastal path.

In high summer, Pointe du Raz is a heaving mass of humanity. Its true majesty is best appreciated out of season, in winter, when only the hardy few venture out to see the winds whip the waves into a foam-streaked fury. If you're feeling adventurous, you can scramble out along the final rocky ridge, aided by fixed ropes and steel cables, to the very extremity of the headland.

To the north of the point stretches the broad, sandy beach of the **Baie des Trépassés** (Bay of the Dead), so named because it was from here that boats once ferried dead druids to the Île de Sein for burial.

Getting There & Away
CAT (☎ 02 98 90 68 40) runs four buses daily (six in July and August) from Quimper to Pointe du Raz (€7, 1½ hours) via Douarnenez and Audierne.

ÎLE DE SEIN
pop 250
Tiny Île de Sein – just 3km long and only a few hundred metres across – seems not so much a fragment of the mainland as a sinuous ribbon of sea bed that has broken temporarily through the waves. Its highest point is barely 6m above the high-water mark and on a number of occasions – most recently in 1839, 1866 and 1919 – a conjunction of storms and exceptionally high tides has flooded the island, forcing the inhabitants to seek refuge on the roofs of their houses and in the church bell tower. The government

FINISTÈRE

LES LIGNEURS DU RAZ

Twice a day the ebb tide pours southwards through the gap between Pointe du Raz and the Phare de la Vieille, and twice a day the flood surges north again. Every six hours or so, at speeds of up to seven knots, these powerful tidal streams turn the sea around the headland into a spectacular torrent of standing waves, foaming breakers and swirling eddies.

The *ligneurs* (line fishermen) of Pointe du Raz make their living from this maelstrom where few sailors dare venture. From April to October their small boats (generally 7m or 8m long), each helmed by a single fisherman, dart nimbly between the rocks and the breakers to fish for the big *bars* (sea bass) which come to hunt mackerel and sprat in the turbulent waters. The fish are caught using lures and live bait trailed on a line behind the boat.

Their catch – mostly big fish weighing up to 6kg each – is much sought after by restaurateurs, and is sold under the name *bar de ligne* (line-caught sea bass). Look out on restaurant menus for the classic dish *bar au sel de Guérande* – a whole sea bass, delicately flavoured with fennel seeds and baked in a crust of sea salt.

has repeatedly tried to persuade the Seinois to abandon their island, but the attempts have been to no avail.

Lobster fishing, once the main source of income, has declined and tourism is now the main industry: hordes of day-visitors descend on Sein – a mere 8km beyond Pointe du Raz – in July and August. Still, it's a place with character, especially out of season, with its little village of white houses huddled together for protection and the tang of salt spray and seaweed on the breeze. A bracing walk along the length of the island and a visit to its two tiny museums (one on the island's history, the other dedicated to the local lifeboat service) make for a great day trip.

Sleeping & Eating

The island has two hotels, both open year-round, and a handful of rooms to let by the week; contact the tourist office in Audierne (p144) for details. Most are booked solid in July and August.

Hôtel-Restaurant d'Ar-Men (☎ 02 98 70 90 77; www.hotel-armen.com - French only; route du Phare; d €47-62) Have no worries about getting a sea view here – the water is only 20m away on one side of the hotel, and 30m on the other! Its 10 rooms are cheerfully decorated in blue, white and yellow, and there's a homely seafood restaurant.

Hôtel-Restaurant Les Trois Dauphins (☎ /fax 02 98 70 92 09; quai des Paimpolais; d €38-54) A charming little place with a good creperie, the 'Three Dolphins' has seven wood-panelled rooms with large windows, some of which enjoy a small balcony and stunning views towards Pointe du Raz.

Getting There & Away

Penn Ar Bed (☎ 02 98 70 70 70) runs ferries (adult/child return €21.80/13.10, one hour) year-round from Audierne to the Île de Sein, with three sailings daily in July and August. The rest of the year there's one boat a day, departing from Audierne at 9.30am and leaving Sein at 4pm.

Vedettes Biniou (☎ 02 98 70 21 15) also has a summer service (adult/child return €21.50/13, three times daily July to August) from Audierne.

Both of the above companies have ticket offices in Audierne town centre and at the ferry terminal.

QUIMPER

pop 59,400

Quimper (kam-*pair*), lying where the small Rivers Odet and Steïr meet, takes its name from the Breton word *kemper*, meaning 'confluence'. Very Breton in character, Quimper, capital of the *département* of Finistère, is very much its cultural and artistic capital too; it's even sometimes referred to as the 'soul of Brittany'.

Orientation

The old city, much of it pedestrianised, clusters around the cathedral on the north bank of the Odet, overlooked by Mont Frugy on the south bank.

Information

INTERNET ACCESS

Eixxos (☎ 02 98 64 40 56; 12 blvd Dupleix; per hr €3.50; ☺ 11am-10pm Mon-Thu, 11am-1am Fri-Sat, 2-10pm Sun)

Stargames Café (☎ 02 98 95 71 97; 17 rue des Gentilhommes; per hr €4; ☺ 1pm-1am Mon-Sat, 5-11pm Sun)

LAUNDRY

Lav' Seul Laundrette (9 rue de Locronan; ☺ 7am-9pm)

Laverie de la Gare (4 ave de la Gare; ☺ 8am-8pm)

POST

Main Post Office (blvd Amiral de Kerguélen)

TOURIST INFORMATION

Tourist Office (☎ 02 98 53 04 05; www.quimper-tourisme.com - French only; place de la Résistance; ☺ 9am-7pm Mon-Sat, 10am-1pm & 3-5.45pm Sun Jul & Aug, 9am-12.30pm & 1.30-6/6.30pm Mon-Sat Sep-Jun, 10am-12.45pm Sun Jun & 1-15 Sep) The office can reserve accommodation and arranges a weekly guided city tour in English from July to August.

Sights & Activities

CATHÉDRALE ST-CORENTIN

The twin spires and soaring vertical lines of Quimper's **cathedral** dominate the city centre. Begun in 1239, it wasn't completed until the 1850s, when the spires that meld so harmoniously into the original structure were added. The inside, scrubbed, renovated and repainted, gives an extraordinary feeling of light and space. The choir is at a distinct angle to the nave. Was this a limitation imposed by the nature of the terrain, or, as in similar off-centre churches, a symbolic representation of Christ's drooping head

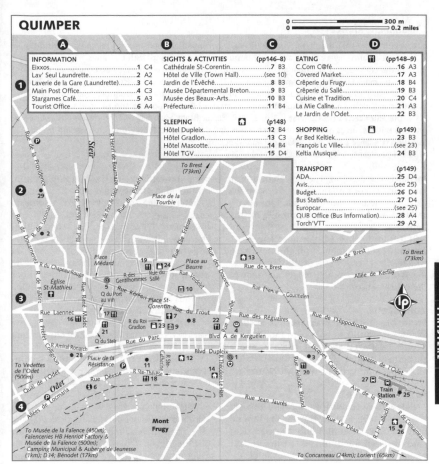

QUIMPER

INFORMATION	
Eixxos..................................1 C4	
Lav' Seul Laundrette...............2 A2	
Laverie de la Gare (Laundrette)...3 C4	
Main Post Office.....................4 C3	
Stargames Café......................5 A3	
Tourist Office........................6 A4	

SIGHTS & ACTIVITIES	(pp146–8)
Cathédrale St-Corentin.................7 B3	
Hôtel de Ville (Town Hall)........(see 10)	
Jardin de l'Évêché......................8 B4	
Musée Départemental Breton......9 B3	
Musée des Beaux-Arts...............10 B3	
Préfecture...............................11 B4	

SLEEPING	(p148)
Hôtel Dupleix..........................12 B4	
Hôtel Gradlon.........................13 C3	
Hôtel Mascotte.......................14 B4	
Hôtel TGV..............................15 D4	

EATING	(pp148–9)
C.Com C@fé.............................16 A3	
Covered Market........................17 A3	
Crêperie du Frugy.....................18 B4	
Crêperie du Sallé......................19 B3	
Cuisine et Tradition...................20 C4	
La Mie Câline...........................21 A3	
Le Jardin de l'Odet....................22 B3	

SHOPPING	(p149)
Ar Bed Keltiek.........................23 B3	
François Le Villec..................(see 23)	
Keltia Musique.........................24 B3	

TRANSPORT	(p149)
ADA......................................25 D4	
Avis...................................(see 25)	
Budget..................................26 D4	
Bus Station.............................27 D4	
Europcar..............................(see 25)	
QUB Office (Bus Information)......28 A4	
Torch'VTT..............................29 A2	

FINISTÈRE

on the cross? No-one knows for sure. High up on the west façade, between the spires, is an equestrian statue of King Gradlon, the city's mythical 5th-century founder.

MUSEUMS

The former bishop's palace beside the cathedral houses the **Musée Départemental Breton** (☎ 02 98 95 21 60; 1 rue du Roi Gradlon; adult/child €3.80/ 2.50; ☉ 9am-6pm daily Jun-Sep, 9am-noon & 2-5pm Tue-Sat, 2-5pm Sun Oct-May), with superb exhibits on the history, furniture, costumes, crafts and archaeology of the area. Adjoining the museum is the **Jardin de l'Évêché** (Bishop's Palace Garden; admission free; ☉ 9am-5/6pm).

The **Musée de la Faïence** (☎ 02 98 90 12 72; 14 rue Jean-Baptiste Bousquet; adult/child €4/2.30; ☉ 10am-6pm

Mon-Sat mid-Apr–mid-Oct), behind the Faïenceries HB Henriot factory (see the boxed text, p148), occupies a one-time ceramics factory and displays more than 2000 pieces of choice china.

The **Musée des Beaux-Arts** (☎ 02 98 95 45 20; 40 place St-Corentin; adult/child €4/2.50; ☉ 10am-7pm daily Jul & Aug, 10am-noon & 2-6pm Wed-Mon Apr-Jun & Sep-Oct, 10am-noon & 2-6pm Wed-Sat & Mon, 2-6pm Sun Nov-Mar), in the town hall, displays European paintings from the 16th to early 20th centuries.

WALKING

A pleasant way to get a feel of Quimper is simply to stroll – along the banks of River Odet, where flowers cascade from its numerous foot bridges, or around place

---

QUIMPER FAÏENCE

It was in 1690 that the first *faïencerie* (faïence works) was established in Quimper, creating the tin-glazed earthenware that was hugely popular in the 17th and 18th centuries.

In the 18th century Quimper grew into an important faïence centre as skilled craftsmen arrived from the main French faïence-making cities of Nevers, Rouen and Moustiers, bringing with them the latest glazes, patterns and techniques. In the 19th century the Quimper *faïenceries* began producing highly popular Breton designs, illustrating Breton legends and pastoral scenes.

The **Faïenceries HB Henriot** (☎ 02 98 90 09 36; rue Haute; adult/child €3/1.50), close to the Musée de la Faïence, gives guided tours seven times daily, Monday to Friday. The shop behind the factory has a large selection of Quimperware crockery.

Médard, rue Kéréon, rue des Gentilhommes and its continuation, rue du Sallé, to place au Beurre. Most of old Quimper's **half-timbered houses** are concentrated in this tight triangle.

If you're feeling a little more energetic, start off by climbing 72m-high **Mont Frugy**, which offers great views of the city. Follow the switchback path that starts just east of the tourist office.

BOAT TRIPS

From May to September **Vedettes de l'Odet** (☎ 02 98 52 98 41) run boat trips (adult/child €20.50/12.50, 1½ hours) from Quimper along the wonderfully scenic Odet estuary to Bénodet, departing from quai Neuf.

Festivals & Events

The **Festival de Cornouaille** (www.festival-cornouaille .com - French only), a showcase for traditional Celtic music, costumes and culture, takes place between the third and fourth Sundays of July. After the traditional festival, classical-music concerts are held at different venues around town. Ask the tourist office for times and venues of local *festoù-noz* (night festivals).

Sleeping

Oh how we ransacked Quimper for something more than the standard hotel-chain provision!

Camping Municipal (☎ /fax 02 98 55 61 09; ave des Oiseaux; per person/tent/car €3/0.75/1.50; ⊗ year-round) This site is 1km west of the old city. From quai de l'Odet follow rue Pont l'Abbé northwest and continue straight ahead where it veers left. Alternatively, take bus No 1 from the train station to the Chaptal stop.

Auberge de Jeunesse (☎ 02 98 64 97 97; quimper@ fuaj.org; 6 ave des Oiseaux; dm €8.40) Quimper's youth hostel is beside the camping ground, on the edge of a wooded park.

Hôtel Gradlon (☎ 02 98 95 04 39; www.hotel-grad lon.com – French only; 30 rue de Brest; d €72-90; ⊗ closed 20 Dec-20 Jan) This comfortable place is full of character. Public areas have been recently and tastefully renovated. Rooms are set around a pretty courtyard with a rose garden at its heart, and there's a convivial bar with an open fire for winter evenings. One room is equipped for disabled travellers. All in all, a home away from home…

Hôtel TGV (☎ 02 98 90 54 00; www.hoteltgv.com – French only; 4 rue de Concarneau; d €32-46) One among several hotels around the train station, the TGV has small but well-appointed rooms. A reader reports that noise from the bar beneath can be intrusive so aim high, for one of the top-floor rooms.

Hôtel Dupleix (☎ 02 98 90 53 35; www.hotel -dupleix.com – French only; 34 blvd Dupleix; d €82-105; Ⓟ) The Dupleix, reliable if bland, is part of a business complex overlooking the River Odet opposite the town hall. All rooms are modern and well equipped and some have a balcony and view of the cathedral.

Hôtel Mascotte (☎ 02 98 53 37 37; www.hotel -sofibra.com; 6 rue Théodore Le Hars; s €55-66, d €63-74) The Mascotte is spruce and reliable, if short on character. Rooms are double glazed and sizable, and there's adjacent public parking. Just don't expect anything out of the ordinary…

Eating

Crêperie du Frugy (☎ 02 98 90 32 49; 9 rue Ste-Thérèse; galettes €3.70-6.55; ⊗ closed lunch Sun & Mon) This tiny place, in the shadow of Mont Frugy, dishes up excellent, inexpensive crepes and *galettes*.

Crêperie du Sallé (☎ 02 98 95 95 80; 6 rue du Sallé; galettes €3-9; ⊗ Tue-Sat) Locals crowd into this bright and breezy creperie at lunchtime, so

FINISTÈRE

arrive early to guarantee a table. Sample some real Breton specialities tucked away inside your *galette,* such as *saucisse fumée* (smoked sausage; €6.60) and *coquilles St-Jacques* (scallops; €8.60).

Le Jardin de l'Odet (☎ 02 98 95 76 76; 39 blvd Amiral de Kerguélen; menus €19-35; ☺ Mon-Sat) This stylish Art Deco restaurant overlooks part of the Jardin de l'Évêché. Specialising in Breton and French cuisine, it selects familiar dishes, then twists and modifies them creatively.

CAFÉS
Stoke up a hookah at **Stargames Café** (☎ 02 98 95 71 97; 17 rue des Gentilhommes; ☺ 1pm-1am Mon-Sat, 5-11pm Sun). Primarily an Internet café, Stargames also has a lovely little oriental café, all cushions and low seating, on the ground floor.

SELF-CATERING
La Mie Câline (14 quai du Steir) is a hugely popular bakery where you can get a whopping filled baguette, pastry and soft drink for only €5.20. If the midday line is too long – or if you want something a bit more subtle – just cross the stream to **C.Com C@fé** (9 quai du Port au Vin). Here they do great sandwiches and garnished salads – so the midday queues are likely to be just as long.

Cuisine et Tradition (45 ave de la Gare) is a delicatessen with a huge choice of cured meats, tarts, pies and prepared dishes.

For the freshest fruit, veg and sandwich fillings, visit the **covered market** (quai du Steir).

Entertainment
From late June to the first week in September, there's traditional Breton music and dance (admission €4) every Thursday evening at 9pm in the Jardin de l'Évêché.

Shopping
Ar Bed Keltiek (Celtic World; ☎ 02 98 95 42 82; 2 rue du Roi Gradlon) has a wide selection of Celtic books, music, pottery and jewellery.

Keltia Musique (☎ 02 98 95 45 82; 1 place au Beurre) carries an excellent range of CDs, cassettes and books on Breton and Celtic music and art.

François Le Villec (☎ 02 98 95 31 54; 4 rue du Roi Gradlon) is an excellent place to shop for faïence and creative textiles based on traditional Breton designs.

Getting There & Away
BUS
The **bus station** (☎ 02 98 90 88 89) is beside the train station.

CAT (☎ 02 98 90 68 40) bus destinations include Brest (€13.25, 1¼ hours), Audierne (€6.10, one hour), Douarnenez (€6, 35 minutes, six to 10 daily), Pointe du Raz (€7, 1½ hours) and Bénodet (€5.70, 40 minutes, up to six daily).

Caoudal (☎ 02 98 56 96 72) runs buses to Concarneau (€4.60, 45 minutes, seven to 10 daily); three daily continue to Quimperlé (€8.80, 1½ hours).

CAR
ADA (☎ 02 98 52 25 25), **Europcar** (☎ 02 98 65 10 05) and **Avis** (☎ 02 98 90 31 34) have offices right outside the train station. **Budget** (☎ 02 98 52 04 87; 8 rue de Concarneau) is nearby.

TRAIN
There are frequent trains to Brest (€13.30, 1¼ hours, up to ten daily), Lorient (€9.50, 40 minutes, six to eight daily), Vannes (€15.40, 1½ hours, seven daily), Rennes (€26.90, 2½ hours, five daily) and Paris (Gare Montparnasse; €64, five hours, eight daily).

Getting Around
BICYCLE
Torch'VTT (☎ 02 98 53 84 41; 58 rue de la Providence; ☺ Tue-Sat) rents mountain bikes for €15 per day. The friendly owner is a fount of information about local cycle routes.

CAR & MOTORCYCLE
Leave your car in the vast **Parking de la Providence** (rue de la Providence), which can accommodate more than 1000 vehicles.

TAXI
For a **taxi**, call ☎ 02 98 90 21 21.

LE PAYS BIGOUDEN
The southwestern corner of Cornouaille, from Penmarc'h to Bénodet, clings proudly to its culture and traditions, notably the *coiffe bigoudène,* the up to 30cm tall lace headdress that village women still occasionally wear on Sunday.

Pont-l'Abbé
Pont-l'Abbé, 'capital' of the Pays Bigouden, is a former port with a 14th-century chateau

FINISTÈRE

and a Carmelite monastery. The castle's keep houses the **Musée Bigouden** (☎ 02 98 66 09 03; adult/child €3.50/1.80; ☺ 10am-12.30pm & 2-6pm daily Jun-Sep, 10am-noon & 2-5pm Mon-Sat Easter-May), which includes an exhibition of local costumes and lace *coiffes*.

The **Maison de Tourisme** (☎ 02 98 82 30 30; www .ouest-cornouaille.com; Rond Point de Kermaria; ☺ 10am-7pm Mon-Sat Jul & Aug, 9am-noon & 2-6pm Mon-Fri Sep-Jun), at the entrance to town and readily recognisable by the long-beached trawler beside it, covers the whole of western Cornouaille and is very clued up.

Pont-l'Abbé's own **tourist office** (☎ 02 98 82 37 99; www.ot-pontlabbe29.fr - French only; 10 place de la République; ☺ 10am-12.30pm & 2-5pm Mon-Sat, 10am-12.30pm Sun Jul & Aug, 9am-noon & 2-5.30pm Mon-Sat Sep-Jun) is scheduled to move to 11 place Gambetta in early 2005.

Hôtel de Bretagne (☎ 02 98 87 17 22; fax 02 98 82 39 31; 24 place de la République; s €41-50, d €46-62), an attractive Logis de France, is on the main square and has Pont-l'Abbé's best **restaurant** (menus €26 & 31; ☺ closed dinner Sun).

Pointe de Penmarc'h

The reefs around Pointe de Penmarc'h mark Brittany's exposed southwestern extremity. Here the little fishing villages of **St-Guénolé** and **Kérity** huddle beneath the watchful eye of **Phare d'Eckmühl** (admission free; ☺ 10.30am-noon & 2.30-5.30pm), one of the few lighthouses regularly open to the public.

To the north of Penmarc'h, the west-facing sand and shingle beaches around **Pointe de la Torche** are battered by Atlantic swells savoured by surfers and windsurfers. There are several surf shops behind the beach where you can hire gear or book lessons.

Notre Dame de Tronoën

Five kilometres north of Penmarc'h and 8km west of Pont-l'Abbé is the little chapel of Notre Dame de Tronoën. Its lichenous, weather-worn **calvary** (1540) displays around 100 carved figures.

Le Guilvinec

Although Le Guilvinec, around 6km east of Penmarc'h, seems small, it's one of France's major ports for landing fresh fish. Today, its hard-pressed fishing industry has had a makeover as a tourist attraction too. **Haliotika** (☎ 02 98 58 28 38; adult/child €5.80/3.30; ☺ 2.30-7pm Mon-Fri, 3-6.30pm Sat & Sun mid-Mar–mid-Oct) is, despite the name, nothing to do with Breton bad breath. Huge fun, it's an exciting, interactive venture with a museum-exhibition centre and a terrace overlooking the quay. From it, you can watch the trawlers unload and enjoy the noise and spectacle of *la criée*, the daily **fish auction** (☺ 4.45-6pm Mon-Fri).

BÉNODET
pop 2800

Once a favourite retreat of both Marcel Proust and Winston Churchill, Bénodet is a charming, upmarket holiday resort and yachting harbour at the mouth of the River Odet.

Orientation & Information

Avenue de la Mer, the town's main north–south axis, leads from the Quimper road to the main beach of Plage du Trez. The attractive waterfront, on the eastern bank of the Odet, lies 700m west.

The **tourist office** (☎ 02 98 57 00 14; www.benodet .fr; ☺ 9am-7pm Mon-Sat, 10am-6pm Sun Jun-Sep, 9.30am-noon & 2-5/6pm Mon-Sat Oct-May) is near the roundabout at the northern end of ave de la Mer. It also has an **Internet point**, accessible with a France Telecom card.

Sights & Activities

Plage du Trez, south of the town centre, is Bénodet's main beach. Almost as appealing is **Plage du Coq**, a narrow strand 500m to the north, beneath the lighthouse of Phare de la Pyramide. At **Le Letty**, 2km southwest of Bénodet, dunes of coarse white sand stretch unbroken for 4km to Pointe de Mousterlin.

The small **Musée du Bord de Mer** (Seaside Museum; ☎ 02 98 57 00 14; adult/child €4/2; ☺ 10am-9pm Jun-Sep), co-located with the tourist office, evokes the world of bathing tents, briny and early seaside holidays.

Between April and September, **Vedettes de l'Odet** (☎ 02 98 57 00 58) operates **boat trips** (adult/child €20.50/12.50, 2¼ hours) along the scenic estuary of the Odet and also upstream to Quimper, where you can disembark and take a later boat back. Between May and September, it also runs a ferry service to the Îles de Glénan (see p154). In July and August, it offers daily **fishing trips** (adult/child from €28/18). Its ticket office is on the waterfront.

Odet Locations (☎ 02 98 54 63 22; Cale du Bac), just beside the passenger ferry terminal, rents

FINISTÈRE

out kayaks/canoes (€6.50/8 per hour) and a range of other craft, motorised or sailing.

Sleeping & Eating

Camping du Poulquer (☎ 02 98 57 04 19; www.camping dupoulquer.com; 23 rue Poulquer; tent, car & 2 adults €19.30; ☯ mid-May–Sep; ☒) This convenient, shaded, three-star site is just a few minutes' walk east of Plage du Trez.

Hôtel Abbatiale (☎ 02 98 66 21 66; www.hotel abbatiale.com; 4 ave de l'Odet; s €59, d €80-95; P ☒) A 50-room hotel overlooking the waterfront, the Abbatiale has smart, modern rooms and a thalassotherapy centre.

La Croisette (☎ 02 98 57 06 39; 3 ave de l'Odet; menus €17.50-29; ☯ closed Tue Nov–Mar) Justifiably popular, this seafood restaurant has a lob-ster tank as its centrepiece, and great views over the river.

Le Safran (☎ 02 98 57 24 63; 10 ave de l'Odet; menus from €23; ☯ dinner only Thu-Tue plus lunch Sun) Cosy, intimate Le Safran is another excel-lent seafood restaurant, the ideal spot for a romantic dinner.

Getting There & Away

CAT (☎ 02 98 90 68 40) operates buses between Quimper and Bénodet (€5.70, 40 minutes, up to six daily).

CONCARNEAU

pop 18,600

Concarneau (Konk-Kerne in Breton), 24km southeast of Quimper, has the refreshingly unpretentious air of a working fishing port. It is an attractive, walled old town perched on a rocky islet, with several good beaches nearby.

It also is home to France's third-largest fish market, deferring only to Boulogne and Lorient. Concarneau's fortune was originally founded on the Atlantic sardine fishery, which collapsed at the turn of the 20th century. Today Concarneau is home port to around 30 seine-netters, which hunt tuna as far afield as the coast of Africa and even the Indian Ocean, and another 150 boats that fish home waters; look out for handbills announcing the size of the incom-ing fleet's catch.

Orientation

Concarneau hugs the western side of the har-bour at the mouth of the River Moros. Ville Close, the walled town, sits on an island in the middle of the harbour, separating the Port de Plaisance to the south from the busy fishing-boat quays of the Port de Pêche to the north. Quai d'Aiguillon and quai Peneroff run from north to south beside the harbour.

Information
INTERNET ACCESS

Cyberesp@ce As Sap (☎ 02 98 50 68 46; 3 place Duguesclin; per hr €6; ☯ 10am-3pm & 5-8pm daily May-Sep, 10.30am-12.30pm Mon, 10.30am-12.30pm & 2-7pm Tue-Sat Oct-Apr)

LAUNDRY

Laundrette (place de l'Hôtel de Ville; ☯ 7am-8pm)
Laundrette (21 ave Alain Le Lay; ☯ 7am-8pm)

POST

Post Office (14 quai Carnot)

TOURIST INFORMATION

Tourist Office (☎ 02 98 97 01 44; www.villeconcarneau .fr - French only; quai d'Aiguillon; ☯ 9am-7pm daily Jul & Aug, 9am-12.30pm & 1.45-6.30pm Mon-Sat, 9.30am-12.30pm Sun Apr-Jun & 1-15 Sep, 9am-noon & 2-6pm Mon-Sat mid-Sep–March.

Sights
VILLE CLOSE

The **walled town**, fortified between the 14th and 17th centuries, is on a small island linked to place Jean Jaurès by a bridge and a barbican; a ferry (see p154) runs from the eastern end of the island to the eastern side of the harbour. Wander along rue Vauban and place St-Guénolé, their old stone houses packed with shops, restaurants and galleries, and return via the **ramparts** on the southern side of the island for views over the town, port and bay.

Just beyond the gate of Ville Close is the excellent **Musée de la Pêche** (Fisheries Museum; ☎ 02 98 97 10 20; 3 rue Vauban; adult/child €6/4; ☯ 9.30am-8pm Jul & Aug, 10am-noon & 2-6pm Sep-Jun; closed 3 weeks in Jan). It has real fishing boats, model ships and exhibits on everything you could possibly want to know about the fishing industry, including the chance to explore a retired trawler, the *Hemerica*.

Should you indeed want to know more, especially about fishing today, sign on for **Vidéo Mer** (☎ 06 80 26 34 25; quai de la Criée; adult/child €5/3), a 1½-hour **guided visit** of the Port de Pêche run by ex-journalist Yvon Lachèvre. His engaging patter's in French but it's a way

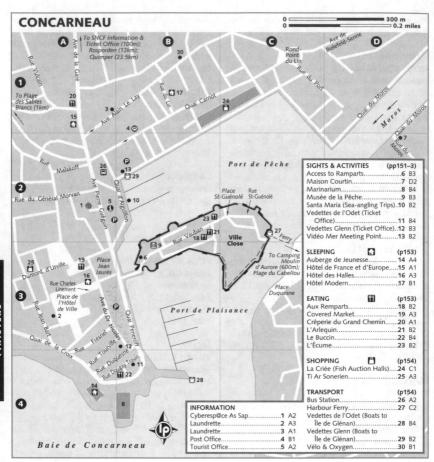

CONCARNEAU

0 ———————— 300 m
0 ———————— 0.2 miles

To SNCF Information &
Ticket Office (100m);
Rosporden (12km);
Quimper (23.5km)

To Plage
des Sables
Blancs (1km)

Rue Vulcain

Ave de la Gare

Rue du Lin

Quai Carnot

30

17

24

Rond-
Point
du Lin

Ave de
Bielefeld-Senne

Rue du Port

Quai du Moros

Moros

Quai du Moros

Rue du Port

Rue
Malakoff

Ave Alain Le Lay

3

4

Ave Pierre Guéguin

Quai d'Aiguillon

26

13
29

P

1

5

10

P

Port de Pêche

Place
St-Guénolé

Rue
St-Guénolé

23

18 21

Rue Vauban

Ville
Close

9

6

27

Ferry

To Camping
Moulin
d'Aurore (600m);
Plage du Cabellou

Place
Duquesne

Rue du Général Morvan

Dumont d'Urville

25

19

16

Place
Jean
Jaurès

Rue Charles
Linement

Place de
l'Hôtel
de Ville

2

Ave du Dr Nicolas

Quai de la Croix

Rue Jean Bart

Quai Penéroff

Rue Fresnel

Rue Tourville

Rue Duquesne

Rue Douary Troun

12

11

22

Port de Plaisance

14

8

28

Baie de Concarneau

SIGHTS & ACTIVITIES	(pp151–3)
Access to Ramparts	..6 B3
Maison Courtin	..7 D2
Marinarium	..8 B4
Musée de la Pêche	..9 B3
Santa Maria (Sea-angling Trips)	.10 B2
Vedettes de l'Odet (Ticket Office)	.11 B4
Vedettes Glenn (Ticket Office)	.12 B3
Vidéo Mer Meeting Point	.13 B2

SLEEPING	(p153)
Auberge de Jeunesse	.14 A4
Hôtel de France et d'Europe	.15 A1
Hôtel des Halles	.16 A3
Hôtel Modern	.17 B1

EATING	(p153)
Aux Remparts	.18 B2
Covered Market	.19 A3
Crêperie du Grand Chemin	.20 A1
L'Arlequin	.21 B2
Le Buccin	.22 B4
L'Écume	.23 B2

SHOPPING	(p154)
La Criée (Fish Auction Halls)	.24 C1
Ti Ar Sonerien	.25 A3

TRANSPORT	(p154)
Bus Station	.26 A2
Harbour Ferry	.27 C2
Vedettes de l'Odet (Boats to Île de Glénan)	.28 B4
Vedettes Glenn (Boats to Île de Glénan)	.29 B2
Vélo & Oxygen	.30 B1

INFORMATION	
Cyberesp@ce As Sap	.1 A2
Laundrette	.2 A3
Laundrette	.3 A1
Post Office	.4 B1
Tourist Office	.5 A2

to visit *la criée*, the fish auction (otherwise closed to the public), and there's a 30-minute film about deep-sea fishing off Ireland.

Simon Allain, an ex-fisherman, heads **À l'Assaut des Remparts** (☎ 02 98 50 56 55; adult/child €5/3). He too runs guided visits to the auction halls and to a cannery, plus other fishy venues. Ask at the tourist office – not, it must be said, in France's first division for accurate information, graciously given – which should be able to tell you the current schedule.

OTHER SIGHTS

The **Marinarium** (☎ 02 98 50 81 64; place de la Croix; adult/child €5/3; ⏰ 10am-7pm Jul & Aug, 10am-noon & 2-6pm Apr-Jun & Sep, 2-6pm Oct-Dec & Feb) is at the harbour's southernmost point. The world's

oldest institute of marine biology, founded in 1859, it has 10 large aquariums (the largest containing 120,000L of sea water) as well as exhibits on oceanography and marine flora and fauna.

Maison Courtin (☎ 02 98 97 01 80; 3 quai du Moros; adult/child €2/free; ⏰ tours 9.30am, 10.30am, 11.30am, & 2.30pm daily Jun-Sep, 10.30am & 11.30am Mon-Fri Oct-May) is one of Concarneau's last functioning canning factories, nowadays specialising in gourmet products such as *crème de sardines au whisky*. Cannery tours include a film of the cannery in peak production and free sampling of its products.

Plage des Sables Blancs is on Baie de la Forêt, 1.5km northwest of the town centre; take bus No 2, northbound, from the tourist office.

FINISTÈRE

For **Plage du Cabellou**, 5km south of town, take bus No 2, southbound.

Activities
BOAT TRIPS
Vedettes de l'Odet (☎ 02 98 50 72 12) and **Vedettes Glenn** (☎ 02 98 97 10 31) run day trips to the Îles de Glénan archipelago (see p154). Both have offices near the Port de Plaisance.

In July and August, Vedettes Glenn also operates four-hour **river trips** (adult/child €23/12, sailings at 2.15pm Tuesday to Friday and Sunday) from Concarneau along the gorgeously scenic estuary of the River Odet.

In July and August you can also take a **day cruise** (adult/child €38/26, 10am to 6pm) to the Îles de Glénan on the **Belle Angèle** (☎ 02 98 65 10 00), a beautiful, three-masted sailing ship built in 1992 to a 19th-century design. It leaves from quai d'Aiguillon.

WALKING
The tourist office sells a walking guide, *Balades au Pays des Portes de Cornouaille* (€4; in French), that describes half a dozen walks around Concarneau. One good walk, the Boucle de Moros (5km), is a loop trail following the banks of the Moros upstream.

SEA ANGLING
If you fancy catching your own fish, the **Santa Maria** (☎ 02 98 50 69 01; adult/child €31/16 incl equipment hire; 🕑 8am Mon, 8am & 1.30/2pm Tue-Fri) operates four-hour sea-angling trips daily in July and August. It's moored alongside quai d'Aiguillon near the tourist office.

Sleeping
Camping Moulin d'Aurore (☎ 02 98 50 53 08; www .moulinaurore.com - French only; 49 rue de Trégunc; 2 adults, tent & car €12.75; 🕑 Apr-Sep) This site is only 600m southeast of the harbour and a mere 50m from the sea. Take bus No 1 or 2 to Le Rouz stop from the tourist office, or the ferry from Ville Close, then walk southeast along rue Mauduit Duplessis.

Auberge de Jeunesse (☎ 02 98 97 03 47; concarneau .aj.cis@wanadoo.fr; quai de la Croix; dm €9.40; 🕑 yearround) A friendly hostel right on the waterfront, next to the Marinarium.

Hôtel des Halles (☎ 02 98 97 11 41; www.hoteldes halles.com; place de l'Hôtel de Ville; s €42, d €45.50-54) Only a few minutes' stroll from Ville Close, the Halles is a quiet, older-style hotel with comfortable, renovated rooms.

Hôtel de France et d'Europe (☎ 02 98 97 00 64; hotel.france-europe@wanadoo.fr; 9 ave de la Gare; d €48-59; P) The 26 rooms at this conveniently central place, a member of the Citôtel group, are all bright and modern. One (€61) has facilities for disabled travellers, and there's a small fitness room.

Hôtel Modern (☎ 02 98 97 03 36; fax 02 98 97 89 06; 5 rue du Lin; d €40, with bathroom €55-60; P) With its friendly landlady, this is a cosy, 1950s, put-your-feet-up kind of place in a quiet backstreet.

Eating
Crêperie du Grand Chemin (☎ 02 98 97 36 57; 17 ave de la Gare; crepes €1.30-3.80; 🕑 closed Mon except Jul & Aug) For excellent Breton crepes, try this unpretentious little place. Your basic *crêpe au beurre* (buttered crepe) costs only €1.30 or you can make a meal of it with crepes from starter to finish (three-course *menus* €8 to €12.30).

Le Buccin (☎ 02 98 50 54 22; 1 rue Dougay Trouin; menus €16-34; 🕑 closed Thu, lunch Sat & dinner Sun except Jul & Aug) Elegant Le Buccin (the Whelk) is where Concarneau's gourmets gather to enjoy whatever harvest of the sea has been landed at the Port de Pêche that morning.

You can eat well in Ville Close – and prices aren't necessarily top-tourist.

Aux Remparts (☎ 02 98 50 65 66; 31 rue Théophile Louarn; 🕑 Easter-Oct) Indulge in the very Breton lunchtime *menu* (€11) of fish soup, *moules frites* and *far breton*. Or, for something a bit lighter, choose from the inventive range of *galettes* (€6 to €8.45).

L'Écume (☎ 02 98 97 15 98; 3 place St-Guénolé; menus €10-13; 🕑 Thu-Tue mid-Mar–mid-Sep) This is another good place for a meal or substantial snack. As you tuck in, glance around at the collection of old postcards that plaster the walls of this cosy retreat with wooden tables and a maritime theme.

L'Arlequin (☎ 02 98 50 50 98; 4 place St-Guénolé; pizzas €5-8.50, salads €7-9, menus €13-20) L'Arlequin, with a pretty little terrace and a small, pleasant interior, is just off the main square and all the quieter for that. While the menu has something for everyone, we suggest that you go for one of the fresh fish dishes.

SELF-CATERING
There's a **covered market** on place Jean Jaurès and a busy open-air **farmers market** in the same square on Monday and Friday.

FINISTÈRE

FINISTÈRE

Shopping

Ti Ar Sonerien (☎ 02 98 50 82 82; 12 rue Dumont d'Urville) specialises in all things Celtic: CDs, music, books, *bodhráns* (Celtic drums), bagpipes and even tin whistles.

Getting There & Away

BUS

Caoudal (☎ 02 98 56 96 72) runs buses from Quimper to Concarneau (€4.60, 45 minutes, seven to 10 daily), three of which continue to Quimperlé.

TRAIN & BUS

The nearest train station is at Rosporden, 12km northeast on the Quimper–Lorient line and linked to Concarneau by SNCF bus. There's an **SNCF information and ticket office** (ave de la Gare) 750m north of the tourist office.

Getting Around

BOAT

A stubby little **passenger ferry** (€0.60; ⏱ 8am-11pm Jul & Aug, 8am-6.30/8.30pm Mon-Sat, 9am-12.30pm & 2-6.30pm Sun Sep-Jun) links Ville Close with place Duquesne on the eastern side of the harbour.

CYCLE

Vélo & Oxygen (☎ 02 98 97 09 77; 65 ave Alain Le Lay) rents bikes for €10 per day.

TAXI

Call ☎ 02 98 97 10 93 or ☎ 02 98 50 70 50.

ÎLES DE GLÉNAN

The Îles de Glénan is a group of nine little islands – barely more than a few scraps of rock and sand – about 20km south of Concarneau, famous for their unspoilt beaches and transparent turquoise waters. The only island accessible to visitors, **Île de St-Nicolas**, is a mere 900m by 300m. Four of the other islands are home to a world-famous sailing school, the Centre Nautique des Glénans, while the rest are kept as nature reserves for flocks of nesting sea birds. There is no accommodation on the islands and camping is forbidden.

The most frequent services are from Bénodet. **Vedettes de l'Odet** (☎ 02 98 57 00 58) offers a straightforward day trip (adult/child €24/12.50, one to four sailings daily May to September, Wednesday and Thursday April

and October) with time to explore Île St-Nicholas. It also operates a guided cruise (adult/child €37/19.50) around the islands in a glass-bottomed boat, with English commentary, and can provide one- to four-seater kayaks once you arrive at the islands for €15 to €35 extra.

Vedettes de l'Odet also sails from Concarneau (twice daily mid-July to August, Thursday June to mid-July), departing from the Port de Plaisance, and Quimper (limited dates, July to August), returning by bus from Bénodet.

Vedettes Glenn (☎ 02 98 97 10 31) sails to the islands from Concarneau (adult/child €23/12, 10am and 2.15pm July to August), departing from the Port de Pêche.

In July and August there are also cruises to the islands on a traditional coastal vessel (see p153).

PONT-AVEN

pop 3000

Originally a mill town and coastal port – there were once 14 water mills on the river here – picturesque Pont-Aven's current fame dates from the late 19th century, when it was frequented by a group of penniless artists that included one Paul Gauguin.

Orientation & Information

The main feature of Pont-Aven is the bridge over the Aven from which the town takes its name. Beside it is quite the cutest little stone toilet you're ever likely to perform in. The harbour is downstream on the west bank, and the woods of Bois d'Amour upstream.

The **tourist office** (☎ 02 98 06 04 70; www.pont aven.com; 5 place de l'Hôtel de Ville; ⏱ 9.30am-7.30pm Mon-Sat, 10am-1pm & 3-6.30pm Sun Jul & Aug, 10am-12.30pm & 2-6/7pm Mon-Sat Sep-Jun, 10am-1pm Sun Apr-Jun & Sep) is set back on the main square, 75m east of the bridge.

Sights & Activities

The **Musée de Pont-Aven** (☎ 02 98 06 14 43; place de l'Hôtel de Ville; adult/child €4/2.50; ⏱ 10am-7pm Jul & Aug, 10am-12.30pm & 2-6/6.30pm Sep-Dec & Feb-Jun) is off the main square. Exhibits include photos of the town during the late 19th century, and a collection of paintings, drawings and etchings by Émile Bernard, Paul Sérusier and other contemporaries of Gauguin, but only one canvas by the master himself, *Le Sabotier* (The Clog Maker).

Upstream from the bridge is the **Promenade Xavier Grall**, an attractive garden walkway forged amid the boulders and willows of the river bed. You can continue walking upstream along the river's west bank to the woods of **Bois d'Amour**, scene of a famous meeting between Gauguin and Sérusier. Downstream from the bridge, beyond a scenic jumble of mossy boulders and millraces, is the **harbour** area. The road ends here but you can keep walking along the west bank of the Aven for 9km to the little seaside resort of **Port-Manech**.

Boat Trips

From mid-April to mid-September **Vedettes Aven-Bélon** (☎ 02 98 71 14 59) runs **boat trips** (€9 to €12) from the harbour and along the Aven estuary to Port-Manech, taking in the adjacent Bélon estuary. Departure times depend on the tides – there's barely 20cm of water in the harbour at low tide.

Sleeping & Eating

Pont-Aven accommodation doesn't come cheap, but it's a very appealing place to stay once the hordes have gone home. Sadly, the Pension Gloanec, where Gauguin and his artist pals once stayed, now houses the local newsagent.

Hôtel des Ajoncs d'Or (☎ 02 98 06 02 06; fax 02 98 06 18 91; 1 place de l'Hôtel de Ville; s/d €49/76; Feb-Dec) This big, white hotel with blue shutters overlooks the main square. Double glazing attenuates the noise that would otherwise penetrate the rooms at the front.

Hostellerie Moulin de Rosmadec (☎ 02 98 06 00 22; fax 02 98 06 18 00; venelle de Rosmadec; d €79) In a 15th-century water mill beside the Aven, just downstream from the bridge, the Rosmadec has the best **restaurant** (menus €25-69; closed dinner Sun except Jul & Aug) and most charming accommodation in town. It has only four rooms so reservations are essential.

Hôtel Roz Aven (☎ 02 98 06 13 06; rozaven@ wanadoo.fr; 11 quai Théodore Botrel; d €49-92) Try to get one of the four lovely wood-panelled rooms in the 16th-century thatched cottage that forms part of this riverside hotel.

Hôtel des Mimosas (☎ 02 98 06 00 30; fax 02 98 06 18 40; 22 square Théodore Botrel; d €49-60; mid-Nov–mid-Oct) Tucked away at the far end of the harbour, the Mimosas, run by a friendly young couple, has quiet, good-value rooms and a convivial bar and bistro.

Le Rive Gauche (☎ 02 98 09 14 94; promenade Xavier Grall; mains €9.25-14, menus €15-28; Wed-Sun) This bright, flower-bedecked restaurant and tearoom overhanging the river is reached from the wooden walkways upstream from the bridge.

Shopping

In high summer, Pont-Aven has more than 70 **art galleries**, selling work that ranges from tourist tat to seriously good. There are also a few good, if expensive, antiques shops. Besides art, the town is famous for its **galettes**. Nothing to do with the usual pancakelike *galette*, the Pont-Aven version is a kind of biscuit made with flour, eggs and butter. Buy straight from the manufacturer at traditional **Biscuiterie Traou Mad** (10 place Gauguin), just east of the bridge.

Getting There & Away

Caoudal (☎ 02 98 56 96 72) bus No 14a runs four times daily (twice on Sunday) from Quimper to Pont-Aven (€5.90, 1¼ hours) via Concarneau, and continues on to Quimperlé.

FINISTÈRE

FINISTÈRE

QUIMPERLÉ
pop 11,500

Quimperlé sits 12km inland at the head of the Laïta estuary, where the Rivers Isole and Ellé meet to form the River Laïta (like Quimper, the town takes its name from the Breton *kemper*, meaning 'confluence').

Orientation & Information

The old town, clustered around Église Ste-Croix, nestles in the fork between the two rivers; Quartier St-Michel lies uphill on the Laïta's west bank.

The **tourist office** (☎ 02 98 96 04 32; www.ville-quimperle.fr - French only; 45 place St-Michel; 🕑 9.30am-6.30pm Mon-Sat, 10am-noon Sun Jul & Aug, 9am-12.30pm & 2-5/6pm Mon-Sat Sep-Jun) is on the main square in the *haute ville* (upper town), a short, steepish walk from river level.

Sights

Quimperlé's **old town** retains a handful of 16th-century **half-timbered houses**, notably along the narrow, winding alley of rue Dom-Morice northwest of the church.

Up the hill on the far side of the Isole – with its little weir and salmon ladder – lies the **Quartier St-Michel**, with the Gothic church of **Notre Dame de l'Assomption** and more old houses ranged around the market square of place St-Michel (market day is Friday).

ÉGLISE STE-CROIX

The glory of Quimperlé is the 11th-century church of **Ste-Croix** (🕑 9am-6pm). Circular, like the Church of the Holy Sepulchre in Jerusalem, it's Brittany's finest example of Romanesque architecture. In the original Romanesque crypt is the 15th-century **tomb of St Gurloës**, said to have the power to cure migraines; a hole allowed sufferers to place their heads inside the tomb.

One of the splendours of the church is the intricately carved Renaissance statuary that frames the main doorway on the inside; it's behind you as you enter, so you tend not to notice it until you're leaving. Above the doorway is Christ in glory with the four Apostles below – Matthew, Mark, Luke and John from left to right, indicated by their traditional symbols (book, lion, bull and eagle).

Sleeping & Eating

La Maison d'Hippolyte (☎ 02 98 39 09 11; 2 quai Surcouf; d incl breakfast €45) This characterful little B&B near the river behind the tourist office has four rooms and a flower-filled garden where you can take breakfast on sunny mornings. You may find that the owner is holding an art exhibition in his front room.

Hôtel Le Vintage (☎ 02 98 35 09 10; bistrodelatour@wanadoo.fr; 20 rue Brémond d'Ars; s €55, d €77-107) This 18th-century town house – which is recognisable from a distance by the bunch of metal grapes dangling outside – is in the heart of old Quimperlé. It offers 10 charming, individually – some would say idiosyncratically – decorated rooms.

Restaurant-Crêperie La Grignotière (☎ 02 98 39 31 87; 5 rue du Bourgneuf; crepes €4-6.50, grills €10.50-13; 🕑 lunch Mon-Sat, dinner Thu-Sat) This old granite house with stone fireplace and timber beams serves a range of tasty crepes, *galettes*, salads, grills and omelettes.

Restaurant Dom-Morice (☎ 02 98 39 23 59; 4 rue Dom-Morice; salads €7, pizzas €7.50-10) Set in a snug, half-timbered house, this popular spot serves delicious pizzas cooked in a wood-fired oven – get there early at weekday lunch times.

Bistro de la Tour (☎ 02 98 39 29 58; 2 rue Dom-Morice; menus €19-39; 🕑 closed lunch Sat & dinner Sun) This elegantly cluttered place – the owners also go in for antiques dealing – not only serves the finest cuisine but is justly renowned for its cellars, stacked with some 700 varieties of wine and 300 whiskies (we did say they went in for collecting…).

Getting There & Away

Caoudal (☎ 02 98 56 96 72) bus No 14a runs four times daily between Quimper and Quimperlé (€4.60, 45 minutes, seven to 10 daily).

The train station is 700m west of the old town on blvd de la Gare. There are frequent trains from Quimperlé to Quimper (€7.10, 30 minutes), Brest (€17.30, two hours) and Lorient (€3.60, 15 minutes).

Morbihan

CONTENTS

The Coast   **159**
Lorient   159
Around Lorient   162
Carnac   163
Quiberon   166
Belle-Île-en-Mer   168
Île d'Houat & Île d'Hoëdic   170
Auray   171
Vannes   172
Golfe du Morbihan   175
Inland   **176**
Lac de Guerlédan   176
Pontivy   177
Vallée du Blavet   178
Josselin & Around   179
Ploërmel   180
Around Ploërmel   180
Forêt de Paimpont   180

Morbihan, land of mystery and legend. Around Carnac is the world's greatest concentration of megalithic sites, while Celtic legend maintains that King Arthur and his court held sway in the deep forests that once cloaked the interior.

Morbihan is the one Breton *département* whose interior charms can rival its coastal beauty. Beat but a short retreat from the seaside crowds to enjoy delightful walking along the rural waterways of the Canal de Nantes à Brest (Nantes–Brest Canal) or within the Forêt de Paimpont, where Merlin the magician once cast his spells. You can pick from a host of picturesque villages and ramble around the medieval castles of Pontivy and Josselin.

Not that the coast lacks charm. The Golfe du Morbihan, with the *département* capital of Vannes nestling at its heart, is a shallow gulf (Morbihan means 'Little Sea' in Breton), dotted with over 40 islands. The wild western coast of the slender Quiberon Peninsula, in places no more than 100m wide, contrasts with the sandy beaches on its eastern flank, while the town at its tip is the jumping-off point for day visits to the island of Belle-Île-en-Mer.

If you're around in early August, head to Lorient's Festival Interceltique, 10 days of pan-Celtic artistic celebration – everything from traditional dance to folk fused with jazz and rock – and France's biggest cultural festival.

HIGHLIGHTS

- Dance till you drop at Lorient's **Festival Interceltique** (p161)
- Ponder the meaning of the megaliths at **Carnac** (p164)
- Take a boat trip to **Belle-Île-en-Mer** (p168)
- Explore the old town in **Vannes** (p172)
- Canoe down the **River Blavet** (p178)
- Learn about 19th-century farm life at the 'living museum' of **Poul Fétan** (p178)
- Walk the wooded banks of the **Canal de Nantes à Brest** (p179)
- Cycle forest trails in the **Forêt de Paimpont** (p180)

Pontivy ★

Poul Fétan ★ Josselin ★ Forêt de Paimpont ★

Lorient ★

★ Vannes

Carnac ★

★ Belle-Île-en-Mer

POPULATION: 643, 900	AREA: 6843 SQ KM

MORBIHAN

THE COAST

LORIENT

pop 62,000

In the 17th century the Compagnie des Indes (the French East India Company) founded the Port de l'Orient, a name later abbreviated to Lorient. During WWII the town sheltered U-boat pens. Although the city was almost entirely destroyed during fierce fighting in 1945, it remains an important port.

Lorient (meaning 'An Oriant' in Breton) is not a pretty city – like Brest, it was almost completely rebuilt following WWII – and has few specific attractions. All the same,

its tidy streets, upbeat atmosphere and large student community make it well worth a visit. Fans of Celtic music and culture will certainly enjoy the Festival Interceltique, which takes the city by storm every summer in August.

Orientation

Lorient extends on the western side of a large natural harbour, the Rade de Lorient, at the mouth of Le Scorff. The centre of town is near the canal-like Port de Plaisance, about 1km south of the train and bus stations. You can reach it by walking down cours de Chazelles and its continuation, rue Maréchal Foch, or by taking bus No D, direction Carnel.

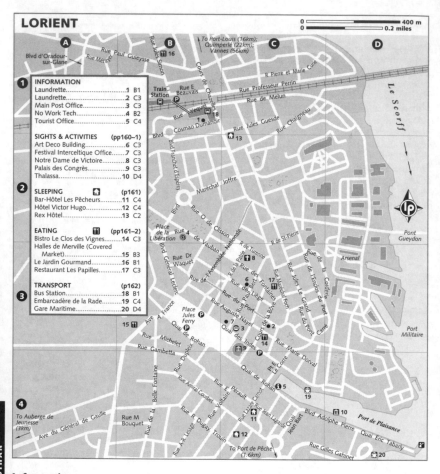

LORIENT

INFORMATION	
Laundrette.....................1	B1
Laundrette.....................2	C3
Main Post Office............3	C3
No Work Tech................4	B2
Tourist Office................5	C4

SIGHTS & ACTIVITIES	(pp160–1)
Art Deco Building...........6	C3
Festival Interceltique Office.......7	C3
Notre Dame de Victoire...8	C3
Palais des Congrès.........9	C3
Thalassa......................10	D4

SLEEPING	(p161)
Bar-Hôtel Les Pêcheurs...11	C4
Hôtel Victor Hugo..........12	C4
Rex Hôtel.....................13	C2

EATING	(pp161–2)
Bistro Le Clos des Vignes...14	C3
Halles de Merville (Covered	
Market)....................15	B3
Le Jardin Gourmand......16	B1
Restaurant Les Papilles...17	C3

TRANSPORT	(p162)
Bus Station..................18	B1
Embarcadère de la Rade...19	C4
Gare Maritime..............20	D4

Information

INTERNET ACCESS

No Work Tech (☎ 02 97 84 72 09; 5 place de la Libér ation; per hr €4; ⏲ 2pm-1am Mon, 10am-1am Tue-Sat, 3-11pm Sun)

LAUNDRY

Laundrettes (blvd Cosmao Dumanoir) Two together beside the bus station.
Laundrette (15 cours de la Bôve)

POST

Post Office (9 quai des Indes)

TOURIST INFORMATION

Tourist Office (☎ 02 97 21 07 84; www.lorient -tourisme.com; quai de Rohan; ⏲ 9am-7pm Mon-Sat,

10am-1pm Sun Jul & Aug; 9am-12.30pm & 1.30-6pm Mon-Fri, 9am-noon & 2-6pm Sat Apr-Jun & Sep; 10am-12.30pm & 1.30-5pm Mon-Fri, 10am-12.30pm Sat Oct-Mar)

Sights & Activities

Lorient doesn't have much in the way of inspiring architecture – the concrete church of **Notre Dame de Victoire** resembles a nuclear reactor and the grimy Palais des Congrès is a good imitation of a warehouse – but there are a few nice 1930s **Art Deco buildings** spared by the bombers, notably the house at the corner of rue de Liège and rue Paul Bert.

The oceanographic research vessel **Thalassa** (☎ 02 97 35 13 00; quai de Rohan; adult/child €5.90/4.50; ⏲ 9am-7pm daily Jul & Aug; 9am-12.30pm & 2-6pm Tue-Fri, 2-6pm Sat-Mon Sep-Jun), now on a permanent

MORBIHAN

mooring at the Port de Plaisance, enjoys a new life as an oceanography museum and hands-on exhibition.

In July and August **Nautibus** (☎ 02 97 21 28 29) runs four boat trips (adult/child €10/5) daily around the estuary, including a peek into the vast WWII submarine base. The tourist office sells tickets.

Compagnie des Îles (☎ 02 97 46 18 19) also does cruises (adult/child €11.50/8; Jun-Sep) around the estuary and up the River Blavet.

The cruises and boat trips leave from Embarcadère de la Rade at the end of quai des Indes.

Festivals & Events

For 10 days in early August, Lorient throbs to the **Festival Interceltique**, a celebration of Celtic culture, especially music, literature and dance (see the boxed text below). People from the Celtic countries and regions join the Bretons in celebrating their common heritage.

Sleeping

Auberge de Jeunesse (☎ 02 97 37 11 65; lorient@ fuaj.org; 41 rue Victor Schoelcher; dm €8.85) Lorient's HI-affiliated hostel is 3km out of town in a beautiful waterside setting on the banks of the River Ter. Take bus No B2 from the bus stop outside the bus station on cours de Chazelles.

Bar-Hôtel Les Pêcheurs (☎ 02 97 21 19 24; fax 02 97 21 13 19; 7 rue Jean Lagarde; d €18-21, with shower or toilet €23-29, with bathroom €34; ⏲ Mon-Sat; P) The

cheery 'Fishermen', with its rooms above a cosy neighbourhood bar, is excellent value. There's no reception; ask at the bar for a room. You might find the bar a bit noisy in the evenings, though it usually closes well before bedtime.

Hôtel Victor Hugo (☎ 02 97 21 16 24; hotelvictor hugo.lorient@wanadoo.fr; 36 rue Lazare Carnot; d €27, with bathroom €42-48; P) The 30-room Victor Hugo is warm and welcoming. Even though it's on a quiet road, rooms overlooking the street are sound-proofed. The hotel's public areas are bright and rooms tasteful and spotless.

Rex Hôtel (☎ 02 97 64 25 60; www.rex-hotel-lorient .com; 28 cours de Chazelles; s €43, d €46-54; P) The Rex, handy for the train station, has recently had a major facelift. The rooms positively gleam and all are double glazed. Owned by a pair of brothers, it's a tautly run ship – almost literally so; the reception desk is shaped like a boat's prow, there's woodwork everywhere and a tape of the lapping ocean and seagulls mewing plays in the small lounge.

Eating

Bistro Le Clos des Vignes (☎ 02 97 64 15 72; 7 cours de la Bôve; menus €11 & €15.75) All polished wood, brass rails and crisp white tablecloths, this lively bistro dishes up seafood and Lyonnais specialities. A snack of *moules au curry* (mussels in curry sauce) is only €6.40. Finish off with a selection from the splendid cheeseboard. The €11 *menu* is available only for lunch on weekdays.

FESTIVAL INTERCELTIQUE

The Festival Interceltique, held each August in Lorient, is the biggest cultural festival in France, attracting around 500,000 visitors. For 10 days, the city rocks to the beat of *bodhráns* (Celtic drums) and marching bands, while the bars and cafés are packed to bursting with the drinkers happily tapping their feet to the reedy strains of the *bombarde* and *biniou kozh* (Breton bagpipes).

The festival celebrates all music and dance of Celtic origin, from 1000-year-old traditional songs to modern folk, rock and jazz with a Celtic influence. Performers – ranging from local musicians to international pipe bands – arrive from all the Celtic nations and regions of Europe (Brittany, Cornwall, Galicia, the Isle of Man, Ireland, Wales and Scotland), and indeed from all over the world.

Major concerts and events are spread among a dozen or so large venues, from a marquee on place Jules Ferry to the Moustoir stadium just beyond, while smaller bands perform in bars and on the streets throughout the city centre. A 'grand parade of Celtic nations' makes its way through the city on the opening weekend. Admission to most events is by ticket only, but much of the music on the street and in the bars is free, as are the *festoù-noz* in the evenings.

A programme of events (printed or on the Web) is usually available from the end of March. For more information, contact the Lorient tourist office or the **Festival Interceltique office** (☎ 02 97 21 24 29; www.festival-interceltique.com; 7 quai des Indes, 56100 Lorient).

Restaurant Les Papilles (☎ 02 97 21 08 44; 63 rue Maréchal Foch; mains €9.50-11, menus €20-25; 🕐 closed Sat & Mon, dinner Sun) Les Papilles has classic French cuisine at reasonable prices; the lunch *menu* (€11.50) is particularly good value.

Le Jardin Gourmand (☎ 02 97 64 17 24; 46 rue Jules Simon; meals €18-48; 🕐 Tue-Sat) The décor is decidedly minimalist at this highly regarded restaurant, a couple of blocks north of the train station. The food – both mainstream French and Breton – by contrast, is rich and subtle. The *menu*, based upon what's best in the market that morning, changes regularly. There is usually only one *menu*, from which you select as many courses as you wish.

Self-caterers should stock up at the **Halles de Merville** (ave A France), one of Lorient's two covered markets. Outside, there's a busy farmers' market on Wednesday and, with many more stalls, Saturday.

Getting There & Away
BOAT
Car ferries to the Île de Groix (right) and passenger ferries to Belle-Île (p168) depart from Gare Maritime (ferry terminal).

Boats to Port-Louis leave from the Port de Pêche (1.6km south of the city centre) from Monday to Saturday, and the Embarcadère de la Rade, on quai des Indes opposite the tourist office, on Sunday. Bus No H links the train and bus stations to Port de Pêche, passing through place Jules Ferry.

BUS
The **Gare d'Échanges** (☎ 02 97 21 28 29), Lorient's bus station, is linked to the train station by a covered footbridge. TIM bus Nos 14 and 17 goes to Pontivy (€9, one to 1¾ hours, four to five daily).

TRAIN
There are several trains a day from Lorient to Quimper (€9.50, 40 minutes), Quimperlé (€3.60, 15 minutes), Auray (€5.60, 25 minutes), Vannes (€7.90, 40 minutes) and Rennes (€22.70, 1½ hours). Lorient is also served by TGVs from Paris' Gare Montparnasse (€59.10 to €69.70, four hours).

Getting Around
City **buses** (☎ 02 97 21 28 29) run until around 8pm (single ticket €1.15, 10-trip carnet €9.70, 24-hour pass €3.50).

For a **taxi**, call ☎ 02 97 21 29 29.

AROUND LORIENT
Port-Louis
Port-Louis is a lovely little town at the mouth of the Scorff estuary, 5km south of Lorient. Its tidy cobbled streets, lined with elegant, 18th-century shipowners' houses, overlook a magnificent **citadel** (adult/student €4.60/3; 🕐 10am-6.30pm Apr–mid-Sep, 2-6pm Wed-Mon mid-Sep–mid-Dec, Feb & Mar) built at the end of the 16th century to defend the entrance to Lorient's harbour.

Inside the citadel are two worthwhile museums. The **Musée de la Compagnie des Indes** (☎ 02 97 82 19 13) traces the history of the French East India Company and its lucrative trade with India, China, Africa and the New World from 1660 to the end of the 18th century. It is a fascinating display of documents, maps, artefacts and pictures.

The **Musée National de la Marine** (☎ 02 97 82 56 72) illustrates the themes of safety at sea and underwater archaeology, with a rich treasure trove from the world's oceans.

The **Batobus** (☎ 02 97 21 28 29) runs between Lorient and Port-Louis, leaving every half-hour between 6.45am and 8pm (one way €1.15). It departs from Lorient's Port de Pêche from Monday to Saturday and from the Embarcadère de la Rade on Sunday.

Île de Groix
Île de Groix, 8km long by 3km wide, lies about 14km offshore from Lorient. Until 1940 it was a major tuna-fishing port but today relies on tourism, agriculture and small businesses. The island has some excellent beaches and a 25km coastal footpath. The **Trou de l'Enfer** on the southern coast is an impressive blow-hole in the cliffs – a spectacular sight in stormy weather.

On the quayside at Port-Tudy, where the ferry arrives, is the **Écomusée – La Mémoire de l'Île** (☎ 02 97 86 84 60; adult/student €4.10/3.10; 🕐 9.30am-12.30pm & 3-7pm daily Jul & Aug, 10am-12.30pm & 2-5pm May-Jun & Sep Tue-Sun Apr, Oct-Nov, Wed & Sun Dec-Mar) An unmissable introduction to Groix, the museum, in a former canning factory, records the island's history and culture in artefacts, photos and films, as well as describing its geology and natural history.

The island's **tourist office** (☎ 02 97 86 53 08; www.groix.fr - French only; 🕐 9am-1pm & 2-7pm daily Jul & Aug, 9am-12.30pm daily except Thu, 2-5.30pm Mon-Fri May, Jun & Sep, 9am-noon & 2-5pm Mon-Fri except Thu morning Oct-Apr) is located on the quay opposite the ferry landing.

GETTING THERE & AROUND

The **Société Morbihannaise de Navigation** (SMN; ☎ 08 20 05 60 00; www.smn-navigation.fr) operates car ferries (adult/child €22.55/13.60, 45 minutes, seven to eight daily), departing from Lorient's Gare Maritime for Port-Tudy on Île de Groix. Bicycles travel free.

You can rent bicycles, cars and motor scooters on the island from **Loca Loisirs** (☎ 02 97 86 80 03) and **Coconut's Location** (☎ 02 97 86 81 57), both on quai de Port-Tudy.

CARNAC

pop 4600

Carnac (Garnag in Breton) has the world's greatest concentration of megalithic sites, erected between 5000 BC and 3500 BC. About 32km west of Vannes, it consists of an attractive old village, Carnac-Ville, and a more modern seaside resort, Carnac-Plage, with its 2km-long sandy beach on the sheltered Baie de Quiberon.

Orientation & Information

Carnac-Ville is 1.5km north of Carnac-Plage. The main megalithic sites of Le Ménec and Kermario are 1km north of Carnac-Ville.

INTERNET ACCESS

Le Bao-Bab (3 allée du Parc, Carnac-Plage; per hr €4) A friendly bar with four terminals.

POST

Main Post Office (ave de la Poste, Carnac-Ville)

TOURIST INFORMATION

Main Tourist Office (☎ 02 97 52 13 52; www.carnac.fr; 74 ave des Druides, Carnac-Plage; ☉ 9am-7pm Mon-Sat, 3-7pm Sun Jul & Aug, 9am-noon & 2-6pm Mon-Sat Sep-Jun)
Annexe (☎ 02 97 52 13 52; place de l'Église, Carnac-Ville; ☉ Jun-Sep & school holidays)

Sights

MUSÉE DE PRÉHISTOIRE

Before visiting the megaliths, pass by the **Museum of Prehistory** (☎ 02 97 52 22 04; 10 place de la Chapelle, Carnac-Ville; adult/under 25/child €5/2.50/free; ☉ 10am-6pm Mon-Fri, 10am-noon & 2-6pm Sat & Sun Jun-Sep, 10am-noon & 2-5pm Wed-Mon Oct-May). Founded by Scotsman James Miln in 1882, the museum chronicles life in and around Carnac from the Palaeolithic and Neolithic eras to the Middle Ages, and elucidates the various theories that attempt to explain the motivations of the megalith builders. There's

---

MORBIHAN'S MIGHTY MEGALITHS

Remember roly-poly, menhir-wielding Obélix, the classic French cartoon star, and his little Gallic chum Astérix, heroes of so many epic encounters with the invading Romans? Even he would have been challenged by the density of megaliths (the word means 'big stone' in Greek) on the Morbihan peninsula. In fact, the whole Morbihan region is a showcase of Neolithic landmarks – menhirs, dolmens, cromlechs, tumuli and cairns, the very vocabulary is mostly Breton in origin. The most famous of these are the *alignements* (parallel rows of standing stones) around Carnac, the greatest concentration of megaliths in the world. These stones were erected between 5000 BC and 3500 BC, at a time when hunter gatherers were abandoning their seminomadic life in favour of a more settled existence, sustained by agriculture and animal rearing.

Carnac's megalithic sites stretch 13km north from Carnac-Ville and east as far as the village of Locmariaquer. Don't expect Britain's Stonehenge though; most menhirs are no more than 1m high and scarcely reach your thigh – yet they predate Stonehenge by at least 1000 years. What *will* impress you is the sheer weight of their numbers – over 3000 of them. And their cumulative weight too; nowadays it seems as though every last camping ground and hotel garden has a menhir or two on display, freshly carved by mechanical stone cutters and hauled into place by the bulldozer. But just how *did* the original constructors hew, then haul these blocks (the heaviest weighs 300 tonnes), millennia before the wheel and the mechanical engine reached Brittany?

And why? The question continues to bewilder historians. Theories and hypotheses, from the inspired to the barking mad, are multiple. A fertility cult (those thousands of erect, phallic menhirs are a stiff argument in favour of such an interpretation)? Manifestations of sun-worship? The stylised representation of some divinity, long-forgotten by the corporate consciousness? For the moment, the cumulative best offer of all this pondering is the vague yet commonly agreed notion that they served some kind of sacred, religious purpose – the same spiritual impulsion that has led to so many of the world's greatest monuments built by humankind.

MORBIHAN

a free English-language booklet to guide you through the two floors of exhibits.

MAISON DES MÉGALITHES

Opposite the Alignements du Ménec is the **Maison des Mégalithes** (☎ 02 97 52 89 89; route des Alignements; admission free; ☼ 9am-8pm Jul & Aug, 9am-5.15pm Sep-Apr, 9am-7pm May-Jun). Recently opened, 'Megalith House' is an information centre with rolling video, topographic models and a good selection of books about the sites (including the official English-language *The Carnac Alignments*; €6). Here is where you sign on for guided visits to the alignments (see the next section).

A terrace on top of the building gives a good view of the menhirs.

THE MEGALITHS

For more about Carnac's **megalithic sites**, see the boxed text (p163).

To get a feel for the sites and set them in time, start off with visits to the Musée de Préhistoire and Maison des Mégalithes. From the latter, there's no better way than to walk or bike between the alignments of Le Ménec and Kerlescan, with menhirs almost constantly in view. Between June and September, seven buses a day link these two sites with both Carnac-Ville and Carnac-Plage villages.

Visiting the alignments varies with the season and the pressure of numbers. Because of severe erosion, they are fenced off to allow vegetation to regenerate. However,

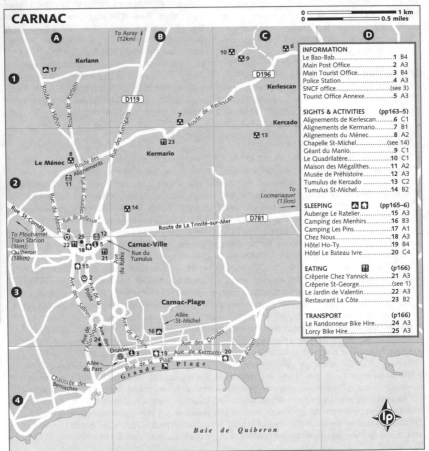

CARNAC

INFORMATION	
Le Bao-Bab.................................1 B4	
Main Post Office.........................2 A3	
Main Tourist Office.....................3 B4	
Police Station..............................4 A3	
SNCF office............................(see 3)	
Tourist Office Annexe.................5 A3	

SIGHTS & ACTIVITIES	(pp163–5)
Alignements de Kerlescan..........6 C1	
Alignements de Kermario..........7 B1	
Alignements du Ménec...............8 A2	
Chapelle St-Michel..................(see 14)	
Géant du Manio.........................9 C1	
Le Quadrilatère........................10 C1	
Maison des Mégalithes............11 A2	
Musée de Préhistoire...............12 A3	
Tumulus de Kercado................13 C2	
Tumulus St-Michel...................14 B2	

SLEEPING	(pp165–6)
Auberge Le Ratelier.................15 A3	
Camping des Menhirs..............16 B3	
Camping Les Pins....................17 A1	
Chez Nous................................18 A3	
Hôtel Ho-Ty.............................19 B4	
Hôtel Le Bateau Ivre................20 C4	

EATING	(p166)
Crêperie Chez Yannick..............21 A3	
Crêperie St-George................(see 1)	
Le Jardin de Valentin...............22 A3	
Restaurant La Côte..................23 B2	

TRANSPORT	(p166)
Le Randonneur Bike Hire..........24 A3	
Lorcy Bike Hire........................25 A3	

MORBIHAN

Baie de Quiberon

MEGALITHIC GLOSSARY

The word megalith comes from ancient Greek for 'giant stone'. These terms appear frequently when discussing megalithic sites.

- **Alignment** – *alignement* in French; a series of standing stones arranged in straight lines
- **Cairn** – a heap of dry stones, usually covering a burial chamber
- **Cromlech** – a circle of standing stones
- **Dolmen** – from the Breton 'dol men' (stone table); a horizontal stone slab supported by two or more vertical slabs set on edge to create a chamber
- **Menhir** – from the Breton 'men hir' (standing stone); a single upright stone
- **Tumulus** – a mound of stone and/or earth covering a burial chamber

between 10am and 5pm from October to May, you can wander through parts of all three alignments. Exactly where changes so check the frequent site billboards or ask at the Maison des Mégalithes. For the rest of the year, there are **guided visits** (€4; in English at least once daily Jul & Aug, Sat & Sun Apr-Jun & Sep).

Just outside Carnac-Ville, **Tumulus St-Michel**, 400m northeast of place de l'Église at the end of rue du Tumulus, dates back to at least 5000 BC. Long closed to the public, it fails to impress – until, that is, you realize that the entire hillock is artificial and required the shifting of over 25,000 cu metres of stone and soil. From the top, capped by a battered orientation table and much weathered 16th-century cross, there's a fine view of the estuary and wooded inland plain.

The largest field of menhirs – with no fewer than 1099 stones – is the **Alignements du Ménec**, 1km north of Carnac-Ville. Its rows of stones are easily seen from the road. From here, the D196 heads northeast for about 1.5km to the equally impressive **Alignements de Kermario** (1029 menhirs in 10 lines). Climb the stone observation tower midway along the site to see the alignment from above – 1200m long, over 100m wide and threading like rows of pulled teeth. Another 500m further on are the **Alignements de Kerlescan**, a smaller grouping.

Between Kermario and Kerlescan and 500m to the south of the D196 is the small **Tumulus de Kercado** (admission €1). Dating from 3800 BC and one of the world's best preserved tumuli, it was the burial site of a Neolithic chieftain. During the French Revolution it was used as a hiding place for Breton royalists.

From the small parking area 300m further along the D196, a pleasant 15-minute, round-trip wooded walk brings you to the **Géant du Manio**, an outsize menhir, highest in the whole complex. Just to its north is **Le Quadrilatère**, a group of mini-menhirs, close set in a rectangle.

Near Locmariaquer, 13km southeast of Carnac-Ville, the major monuments are the **Table des Marchands**, a 30m-long dolmen, and the **Grand Menhir Brisé** (adult/student/child €4.60/3/ free; ☯ 9am-8pm Jul & Aug, 9am-7pm May & Jun, 9.30am-12.30pm & 2-5.15pm Sep-Apr). The latter is the region's largest menhir, which once stood 20m high but now lies broken on its side.

Just south of Locmariaquer by the sea is the **Dolmen des Pierres Plates**, a 24m-long chamber whose rocky walls are decorated with impressive engravings.

Sleeping

There are over 15 camping grounds around Carnac.

Camping Les Pins (☎ 02 97 52 18 90; route du Hahon, Kerlann; person/pitch €3.50/6.85; ☯ Apr-Sep) The pleasant three-star Les Pins is 2km north of Carnac-Ville; follow rue de Courdiec and fork left 200m beyond the megaliths.

Camping des Menhirs (☎ 02 97 52 94 67; www.les menhirs.com; 7 allée St-Michel, Carnac-Plage; person/pitch €7/26; ☯ May-late Sep) This luxury site – complete with pool, sauna, massage and cocktail bar – is just 300m north of the beach.

Chez Nous (☎ 0297520728; chez.nous56@wanadoo.fr; 5 place de la Chapelle, Carnac-Ville; d with bathroom €33-40; ☯ Easter-Oct) Mme Chabert (the proprietor) refuses to bow to the *normes Européennes*, devised by a distant Brussels bureaucrat, that threaten to push so many small French hoteliers out of business. She's simply closed up her hotel and continues with her equally charming five-room annexe with its antique-furnished guest salon. So, while there won't be an electric razor point in the bathroom, for example, you will relax in a home from home. A true bargain that merits your patronage.

MORBIHAN

Auberge Le Ratelier (☎ 02 97 52 05 04; www.le-ratelier.com; 4 chemin du Douet, Carnac-Ville; d €35, with shower €38, with bathroom €48; ❤ year-round) This delightfully rustic eight-room hotel, occupying a former farmhouse with low ceilings and traditional timber furnishings, is in a quiet street one block southwest of place de l'Église.

Hôtel Ho-Ty (☎ 02 97 52 11 12; fax 02 97 52 89 52; 15 ave de Kermario, Carnac-Plage d €47-59; ❤ Easter-Oct) Only a minute's walk from the beach, the Ho-Ty is a traditional family seaside hotel in a lovely blue-and-white 1930s building. Given its location, the eight recently renovated rooms represent great value.

Hôtel Le Bateau Ivre (☎ 02 97 52 19 55; fax 02 97 52 84 94; 71 blvd de la Plage, Carnac-Plage; d €78/112 with breakfast; ❤ year-round) Set in landscaped gardens with a small heated swimming pool and overlooking the beach, the Bateau Ivre is one of Carnac's more luxurious hotels. We quote the mid-season tariff; in August it's significantly overpriced.

Eating

Crêperie St-George (☎ 02 97 52 18 34; 8 allée du Parc, Carnac-Plage; galettes €3.20-6.70, menu €9; ❤ Apr-Sep & school holidays) Set in the Galeries St-George shopping centre, this chic, modern creperie is one of the best-value eating places in town.

Crêperie Chez Yannick (☎ 02 97 52 08 67; 8 rue du Tumulus, Carnac-Ville; galettes €2.80-7.20; ❤ closed Mon & dinner Sun except Jul & Aug) Just southeast of place de l'Église, Carnac's oldest creperie – whose general fare leans heavily towards seafood – has a lush garden terrace draped with trailing vines.

Auberge Le Ratelier (☎ 02 97 52 05 04; 4 chemin du Douet, Carnac-Ville; menus €17-40; ❤ daily May-Sep, Thu-Mon Oct-Apr) This hotel restaurant serves gourmet *menus* in a pleasant low-beamed dining room with whitewashed walls. Not least of its many pleasures is the deliciously nutty home-made bread. The English version of the *menu*, with its 'banana greediness to rhum' and other verbal titbits, is also to be savoured.

Le Jardin de Valentin (02 97 52 19 12; 2 rue St-Cornély, Carnac-Ville; salads €9, menus €8.50-12; ❤ Jan–mid-Nov) This delightful little place is tucked away down a short alley. The food stresses the fishy – though the goldfish in its bowl on the ship-shaped bar is strictly not for consumption. You can eat in the stylishly decorated

restaurant or outside in the courtyard. Save room for one of the creative desserts.

Restaurant La Côte (☎ 02 97 52 02 80; Kermario; menus €21-65; ❤ Feb-Dec, closed Mon, lunch Sat & dinner Sun except Jul & Aug) Close to the Kermario megaliths, La Côte serves top-quality dishes cooked with an adventurous twist.

On Wednesday and Sunday there's a **produce market** just off place de l'Église in Carnac-Ville.

Getting There & Away

The main bus stops are in Carnac-Ville outside the police station on rue St-Cornély and in Carnac-Plage beside the tourist office. Buses go to Auray (€3.80), Vannes (€6.70) and Quiberon (€3.70).

The nearest train station is in Auray, 12km to the northeast (see p172). SNCF has an office above the main tourist office in Carnac-Plage.

Getting Around

You can hire bikes from **Lorcy** (☎ 02 97 52 09 73; 6 rue de Courdiec, Carnac-Ville) and **Le Randonneur** (☎ 02 97 52 02 55; 20 ave des Druides, Carnac-Plage).

For a **taxi**, call ☎ 02 97 52 75 75.

QUIBERON
pop 5200

Quiberon is a popular seaside town at the far tip of a slim, 14km-long peninsula that narrows at one point to a spit barely 100m across, guarded by the 19th-century Fort de Penthièvre.

Orientation & Information

One main road, the D768, leads along the peninsula and into Quiberon, ending at the train station. From here rue de Verdun winds down to the sheltered bay of Port-Maria, fringed by the town's main beach, La Grande Plage, to the east and the ferry harbour to the west.

The **tourist office** (☎ 02 97 50 07 84; 14 rue de Verdun; ❤ 9am-7.30pm Mon-Sat, 10am-1pm & 2-7pm Sun Jul & Aug; 9am-12.30pm & 2-6pm Mon-Sat Sep-Jun) is between the train station and Grande Plage.

Sights & Activities

In the 1950s, Quiberon still had more than a dozen **sardine-canning factories**; now only two remain. **Conserverie La Belle-Iloise** (☎ 02 97 50 08 77; rue de Kerné; ❤ 9-11.30am & 2-6pm daily Jul & Aug, 10-11am & 3-5pm Mon-Fri Sep-Jun), north of the train station, does guided visits around its former cannery.

Grande Plage attracts families, although the bathing spots further out towards the peninsula's tip are larger and less crowded. The peninsula's rocky western flank is known as the **Côte Sauvage** (Wild Coast). It's great for a windy walk but too rough for swimming. The spooky, Gothic-style mansion perched on the rocks of Beg Er Lan, south of the harbour, is the privately owned **Château de Turpault**.

Plage de Penthièvre, 9km north of Quiberon, is a major centre for **windsurfing**, **sand-yachting** and the relatively new sport of **kite-surfing** (*flysurf*). **Flysurf** (☎ 02 97 52 39 90; 1 ave de St-Malo, Penthièvre) offers instruction and equipment hire for sand-yachting and kite-surfing.

If you fancy a shot at **sea-kayaking**, contact **Sillages** (☎ 02 97 30 95 29; eric.marion2@wanadoo.fr; Plage de St-Joseph) in Portivy, 6km north of Quiberon, whose instructors speak English.

Sleeping

The peninsula's 15 camping grounds are all close to the sea, mostly on the more sheltered eastern side.

Camping Municipal du Rohu (☎ 02 97 50 27 85; fax 02 97 30 87 20; Le Petit Rohu; 2 adults, tent & car €8.50; ☒ Apr-Sep) Right beside the beach, it's on the east coast, about 3km north of town.

Camping du Conguel (☎ 0297501911; www.camping duconguel.com; blvd de la Teignouse; 2 adults, tent & car €14-30; ☒ Apr-Oct) This luxury four-star site, with pool and aquapark, is 2km east of town centre, beside Plage du Conguel. Rates rocket in July and August but are otherwise reasonable.

Auberge de Jeunesse – Les Filets Bleus (☎ 02 97 50 15 54; 45 rue du Roc'h Priol; dm €7.35; ☒ Apr-Sep) Quiberon's HI-affiliated hostel is in a quiet part of town, 800m east of the train station. There's limited camping in the grounds.

Hôtel Le Roc'h Priol (☎ 02 97 50 04 86; www.hotel rochpriol.fr; 1-5 rue des Sirènes; d €69-78; ☒ mid-Feb–mid-Nov; P) The bright, modern Roc'h Priol is in a quiet corner of town, 800m east of the centre.

Hôtel L'Océan (☎ 02 97 50 07 58; fax 02 97 50 27 81; 7 quai de l'Océan; d €30-55; ☒ Easter-Sep). You can't miss this pleasant family hotel, overlooking the harbour. Look for the big white house with multicoloured shutters and a couple of jolly *trompe l'oeil* windows painted on the side wall. The top rate gets you a private bathroom and harbour view.

Hôtel Albatros (☎ 02 97 50 15 05; fax 02 97 50 27 61; 24 quai de Belle-Île; d €61-78; ☒ year-round) The modern, 35-room Albatros is bang in the middle of things, on the waterfront between the harbour and Grande Plage. Paying top whack will secure a comfy room with a big balcony and a view of Belle-Île.

Eating

Creperies, pizzerias and snack bars line quai de Belle-Île, promenade de la Plage and rue de Port Maria.

La Closerie de St-Clément (☎ 02 97 50 40 00; 36 rue de St-Clément; galettes €4-8.20; ☒ closed Wed & dinner Sun except Jul & Aug) This rustic creperie, with gnarled timber beams and chunky wooden furniture, has a garden terrace for summer and a cosy fireplace for winter. The menu has salads as well as crepes and *galettes*.

Restaurant-Crêperie du Vieux Port (☎ 02 97 50 01 56; 42-44 rue Surcouf; menu €11, galettes €4-7, mains around €12; ☒ mid-Feb–Oct) Overlooking Port-Haliguen, 1km northeast of Grande Plage, this pleasant eatery occupies an old stone house with a beautiful, flower-filled garden.

On the seafront and an easy walk from the ferry terminal, **La Criée** (☎ 02 97 30 53 09; 11 quai de l'Océan; mains €15-18; ☒ Tue-Sun Feb-Dec) This splendid restaurant outlet of Maison Michel Lucas, the fish shop and smoke house just up the road offers quite the finest seafood (laid out enticingly on a table for you to take your pick) and freshest fish in town.

Getting There & Away
BOAT
For ferries from Quiberon to Belle-Île, and to the smaller islands of Houat and Hoëdic, see p170.

BUS
Buses connect Quiberon with Carnac, Auray and Vannes year-round. They stop at the train station and at place Hoche between the tourist office and the beach.

CAR & MOTORCYCLE
Drive your car into Quiberon town centre during July and August and you'll spend the day stuck in a traffic jam. During high summer, we strongly recommend leaving your vehicle at the 1200-place **Sémaphore car park** (up to four hours €3.40, 24 hours €9), 1.5km north of the beach, then walking or taking the free shuttle bus into town. Better

still, leave the car at Auray station and hop on the Tire-Bouchon train.

TRAIN

A shuttle train, the 'Tire-Bouchon' (corkscrew), runs several times a day between Auray and Quiberon in July and August only (€2.50, 40 minutes). From September to June a SNCF bus service links Quiberon and Auray train stations (€6, 50 minutes) four times a day.

Getting Around

Cycles Loisirs (☎ 02 97 50 31 73; 3 rue Victor Golvan), 200m north of the tourist office, charges €8/13 a day to rent a touring/mountain bike. **Cyclomar** (☎ 02 97 50 26 00; 47 place Hoche) rents both bikes and scooters. The shop is around 200m south of the tourist office and it runs an operation from the train station during July and August. To order a **taxi** ring ☎ 02 97 50 11 11.

BELLE-ÎLE-EN-MER
pop 5200

Belle-Île-en-Mer, around 15km south from Quiberon, is just what its name suggests: a beautiful island in the sea. About 20km by 9km, Belle-Île is the biggest of Brittany's islands, exposed to the full force of Atlantic storms on its ragged southwestern coast, but with relatively sheltered waters to the east. Although the population swells to over 35,000 in summer, the place rarely feels crowded.

History

Geoffrey I, duke of Brittany, bestowed the island upon the monks of Redon Abbey in 1005, then in the 17th century it became a possession of the French Crown. Louis XIV commanded the military engineer Vauban to reinforce the island's simple citadel to defend the port of Le Palais against assaults by the English and Dutch navies. The British navy succeeded in capturing Belle-Île in 1761, but two years later exchanged it for the Mediterranean island of Menorca; later in the 18th century the Acadian families, expelled by the British from eastern Canada, resettled here.

Information

Turn left as you leave the ferry in Le Palais for the main **tourist office** (☎ 02 97 31 81 93; www.belle-ile.com; quai Bonnelle; 8.45am-7pm Mon-Sat, 10am-12.30pm & 5-6.30pm Sun Jul & Aug, 9am-12.30pm & 2-6pm Mon-Sat Sep-Jun).

There's a summer-only **information kiosk** (☎ 02 97 31 69 49; Easter-Sep) on the quay in Sauzon.

Sights & Activities

Le Palais, the main village, is a cosy port dominated by its citadel, expanded and strengthened by Vauban in 1682. The citadel now houses the **Musée Historique** (☎ 02 97 31 84 17; adult/child €6.10/3.05; 9.30am-7pm Jul & Aug, 9.30am-6pm Sep & Oct & Apr-Jun, 9.30am-noon & 2-5pm Nov-Mar), which records the island's often-turbulent history.

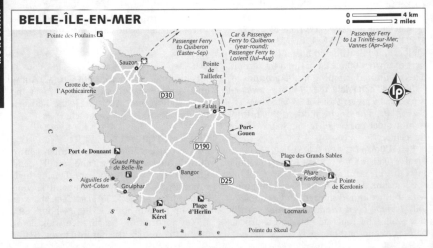

BELLE-ÎLE-EN-MER

0 — 4 km
0 — 2 miles

Pointe des Poulains
Passenger Ferry to Quiberon (Easter–Sep)
Car & Passenger Ferry to Quiberon (year-round); Passenger Ferry to Lorient (Jul–Aug)
Passenger Ferry to La Trinité-sur-Mer; Vannes (Apr–Sep)
Sauzon
Pointe de Taillefer
Grotte de l'Apothicairerie
D30
Le Palais
Port-Gouen
Port de Donnant
D190
Plage des Grands Sables
Grand Phare de Belle-Île
Bangor
D25
Phare de Kerdonis
Pointe de Kerdonis
Aiguilles de Port-Coton
Goulphar
Port-Kérel
Plage d'Herlin
Locmaria
Pointe du Skeul

ARTISTS & BELLE-ÎLE

The beauty of Belle-Île has been an inspiration to many famous artists. During the summer of 1886, while Paul Gauguin was making his first brief visit to Pont-Aven on the mainland, Claude Monet (1840–1926) spent 10 weeks on Belle-Île and turned out no fewer than 39 canvases, the best known being his four takes of the Aiguilles de Port-Coton.

In 1896 Vincent Van Gogh (1853–90) sketched several portraits of the islanders, notably at Sauzon, and in 1897 Henri Matisse (1869–1954) painted a number of images Le Palais harbour.

In the late 1940s, Hungarian-born Victor Vasarely (1908–97), a leading figure in the Op Art movement, spent several holidays on Belle-Île. The ovoid abstractions, irregular shapes and contrasting shades typical of his work during this period are said to have emerged from his study of the rounded pebbles on the beach at Sauzon.

Other 20th-century artists inspired by visits to Belle-Île include André Masson (1896–1987), Jean Hélion (1904–87) and the American Ellsworth Kelly (b 1923).

The little port of **Sauzon** with its pastel-painted houses is an even prettier entry point to the area. A 5km hike northwest along the coastal trail (or a 3.5km bike ride along the road) leads to scenic **Pointe des Poulains**, the island's northern extremity.

Belle-Île's wild and deeply eroded south-western coast, known with reason as the **Côte Sauvage**, has spectacular rock formations – notably the sea stacks of the **Aiguilles de Port-Coton** – a few small, natural harbours and a number of caves. The most famous cave, **Grotte de l'Apothicairerie** (Cave of the Apothecary's Shop), is an awesome cavern where the waves roll in from two sides.

BEACHES

Port de Donnant has a beautiful beach, popular with surfers, though swimming here is dangerous. The best beaches for children are **Port-Kérel** and **Plage d'Herlin**, which is a little harder to get to. **Plage des Grands Sables**, 2km long, is the island's biggest and busiest strand.

WALKING & CYCLING

The large-scale, explicit maps in *Guide des Randonnées Pédestres et Cyclistes* (Walking and Cycling Trail Guide; €8), on sale at the tourist offices, are excellent for navigation, even if your French isn't too hot. Bikes are banned on the coastal footpath.

The ultimate hike is a circuit of the **coastal footpath**, a total distance of 95km, which a fit walker can cover in four full days. You can either camp or stay the night in a *chambre d'hôte* (B&B) or *gîte d'étape* (walkers' accommodation); the tourist office has a full list of each.

Day 1: Le Palais to Pointe des Poulains, and back to Sauzon for the night (23.5km)
Day 2: Sauzon to Port Kérel; stay the night at Bangor (30.5km)
Day 3: Bangor to Locmaria (23km)
Day 4: Locmaria to Le Palais (17.5km)

Sleeping

There are 10 camping grounds dotted around Belle-Île; most are two-star places, open from April or May to September or October.

Les Glacis (☎ 02 97 31 41 76; Le Palais; adult/child €3/2, tent site €2; ☼ Apr-Sep) This municipal camping area, at the base of the citadel, couldn't be handier for Le Palais.

Auberge de Jeunesse Haute Boulogne (☎ 02 97 31 81 33; belle-ile@fuaj.org; Le Palais; dm €8.85; ☼ closed Oct) This modern HI-affiliated hostel is to the north of the citadel in Le Palais.

For walkers, there's a **gîte d'étape** (☎ 02 97 31 55 88; per person €11.50) at Port-Gouen, about 2km south of Le Palais and a **gîte communal** (☎ 02 97 31 73 75; dm €5.50) in Locmaria.

Hôtel La Frégate (☎ 02 97 31 54 16; fax 02 97 31 33 13; quai de l'Acadie, Le Palais; d €29, with bathroom €39; ☼ Apr–mid-Nov) Among the hotels facing the ferry dock, the Frégate is a good economical choice, although the interior décor doesn't live up to the appeal of the colourful exterior. There's a lively bar beneath and a spacious guest living room overlooking the harbour.

Hôtel Vauban (☎ 02 97 31 45 42; 1 rue des Ramparts, Le Palais; s €39, d €61-70; ☼ mid-Feb–Oct) The Vauban has 16 comfortable, spacious rooms and a grand location, perched high above the ferry landing and right beside the coastal path. By car, it's signed from place de la République. On foot, turn second left up a steep, narrow alley that becomes rue des Remparts.

MORBIHAN

Hôtel Castel Clara (☎ 02 97 31 84 21; www.castel
-clara.com; Goulphar; d €134-569; 🕙 mid-Feb–mid-Nov;
🐟) The four-star Castel Clara sits above
the little harbour of Goulphar on the
southwestern coast. The island's top hotel,
it was once a favourite retreat of the late
President Mitterrand. Among its many
luxuries are a heated seawater pool and a
thalassotherapy centre.

The local **chambres d'hôtes** (B&Bs) are
often better value than hotel rooms – ask
the tourist office for its comprehensive list.
Prices average about €40 for a double room
with breakfast.

Eating

Le Goéland (☎ 02 97 31 81 26; 3 quai Vauban, Le Palais;
mains €10-16; 🕙 Thu-Mon Mar–mid-Nov) The Goéland (seagull) is by far the best eating place
in Le Palais, whether you choose the lively
bar-brasserie on the ground floor or the
more formal restaurant upstairs. The menu
concentrates on seafood, augmented by local
lamb, fattened on the island, and salads.

Traou-Mad (☎ 02 97 31 84 84; 9 rue Willaumez,
Le Palais; galettes €4-8; 🕙 Easter-Nov) The small,
friendly Traou-Mad (Breton for 'good
things') is a pleasant, all-timber place where
you could almost be dining amidships. Serving up excellent *galettes*, crepes and salads,
it's on a narrow alley to the left off rue
Carnot, which heads uphill from place de
la République.

Getting There & Away
FROM QUIBERON
The shortest crossing to Belle-Île is from
Quiberon. **SMN** (☎ 08 20 05 60 00; www.smn
-navigation.fr) runs both car ferries (45 minutes,
year-round) and high-speed passenger ferries (20 minutes, July to August) to Le Palais, and passenger ferries to Sauzon (April
to mid-September). The adult/child return
fare is €21.90/13.20 for normal boats and
€25/15.10 for the fast ferry. The return fare
for a bicycle is €12.60; for a car it's €101 to
€193 depending on length. There are at least
five crossings a day, more than double that
in July and August.

FROM LA TRINITÉ-SUR-MER
In July and August **Navix** (☎ 02 97 46 60 00,
www.navix.fr - French only) runs two boats a day
from La Trinité to Le Palais (adult/child
return €28.50/18, one hour).

FROM VANNES
Navix also operates a ferry at least daily between May and mid-September from Vannes
to Belle-Île, most calling by La Trinité or
Port-Navalo.

FROM LORIENT
From mid-July to the end of August, SMN
runs a fast passenger-only ferry (adult/child
€25/15.10, one hour, once daily) from the
Gare Maritime in Lorient to Sauzon.

Getting Around
There are lots of places in Le Palais where
you can hire bicycles/motor scooters for
around €12/35 a day.

ÎLE D'HOUAT & ÎLE D'HOËDIC
pop 340
Houat and Hoëdic (Breton for 'duck' and
'duckling') are two small islands to the east
of Belle-Île, both capped by ancient forts. **Île
d'Houat**, 5km long and barely 1km wide, is a
low-lying slab of turf-topped granite, nib-
bled around the edge by little bays of golden
sand. It has a single fishing village of blue-
shuttered houses overlooking the harbour of
Port St-Gildas, and a superb beach, **Tréac'h Er
Gourèd** (or Grande Plage), at its eastern end.
A hike around the coastal footpath (15km)
takes around three hours.

Île d'Hoëdic, with a handful of small, sandy
beaches, is even smaller – you can comfortably make a circuit of the island in 1½ hours.

Sleeping
Houat's **town hall** (☎ 02 97 30 68 04) tolerates
semi-wild **camping** (2 adults & tent €5) among
the dunes of En Tal, at the northern end of
Grande Plage with access to beach showers
and toilets. On Hoëdic there's one official
camping ground, **camping municipal** (☎ 02 97
52 48 88; 2 adults & tent €5; 🕙 Jun–mid-Sep).

Houat has two hotels – **Hôtel-Restaurant
des Îles** (☎ 02 97 30 68 02; fax 02 97 30 66 61; d €56;
🕙 Easter-Nov) and **Hôtel l'Ezenn** (☎ 02 97 30 69 73; d
€42; 🕙 year-round), a lovely place with four of its
rooms overlooking the sea at no extra cost.

Hôtel Les Cardinaux (☎ 02 97 52 37 27; fax 02 97
52 41 26; d €45-75; 🕙 closed 3 weeks Oct) is Hoëdic's
only hotel.

Houat's town hall will provide a list of
private rooms to rent, with rates around €35
for a double. Book well in advance for July
and August.

TREATY OF UNION

When Anne de Bretagne died in 1514 with no male heir, her title to the duchy of Brittany was inherited by her daughter Claude. Claude became Queen of France through her marriage to King Francis I (r 1515–47), who persuaded his wife to bequeath her inheritance to their son, the future Henry II.

The union of Brittany and France was formalised in a treaty proclaimed at Vannes in August 1532. Although Brittany would thenceforth be ruled by a governor representing the French Crown, the treaty allowed Bretons certain rights, including those of paying only Breton taxes and being tried by Breton courts, plus the stipulation that only Bretons would be allowed to occupy important religious offices. Like many such unions, however, it was observed more often in the breach than in the keeping.

Getting There & Away

SMN runs ferries from Quiberon to Houat (adult/child €21.90/13.20, 30 to 55 minutes, two to six daily) and Hoëdic (same fares and frequency, one hour). There are also services between the two islands (adult/child one way €5.20/3.60, one to three daily).

In July and August, **Compagnie Vendéenne** (☎ 02 40 23 34 10) runs two weekly boats (adult/child €10.50/6.75, 40 to 50 minutes, variable days) between Le Palais on Belle-Île and Houat and Hoëdic.

AURAY

pop 11,300

The busy commercial town of Auray lies at the tidal limit of the River Auray, which flows into the western end of the Golfe du Morbihan. Its main attraction is the old port area of St-Goustan.

Orientation & Information

The upper town, on the western side of the river, is centred on place Notre Dame, where there's plenty of parking. From here, rue du Lait leads east past the tourist office to place de la République. From this square, rue du Château curves steeply down to the river and St-Goustan. The train station is 2km northwest of the town centre.

The **tourist office** (☎ 02 97 24 09 75; www.auray -tourisme.com - French only; 20 rue du Lait; ❂ 9am-7pm Mon-Sat & 9am-noon Sun Jul & Aug, 9am-noon & 2-6pm Mon-Sat Sep-Jun, closed Sat afternoon Sep-Apr) is in a lovely deconsecrated chapel.

Sights & Activities

Walking east from the tourist office, cross place de la République and drop down rue du Château, lined with little galleries and antique shops. As you round a bend, the picturesque old port of **St-Goustan** reveals itself. Colourful 16th- and 17th-century half-timbered houses cluster around cobbled place St-Sauveur on the quayside. For more quaint wattle-and-daub and stone houses, walk along **quai Franklin** – so named because Benjamin Franklin landed here from the recently formed United States, seeking to win over France in an alliance against England – then return to place St-Sauveur along the parallel rue du Petit Port. The **Promenade du Loc'h**, a short loop trail on the western bank, offers good views over St-Goustan.

Sleeping & Eating

Hôtel Le Cadoudal (☎ 02 97 24 14 65; fax 02 97 50 78 51; 9 place Notre-Dame; d €27, with bathroom €25-40) The 14-room Cadoudal is in a fine old stone house overlooking Auray's main square. The bar beneath is lively but unintrusive.

Hôtel Le Celtic (☎ 02 97 24 05 37; fax 02 97 50 89 79; 38 rue Clemenceau; d €27, with shower €41, with bathroom €54; P) The 19-room Celtic is another homely spot. Family-run and friendly, it has simple, comfy rooms and a breakfast area with a big granite fireplace.

Hôtel Le Marin (☎ 02 97 24 14 58; fax 02 97 24 39 59; 1 place du Roland; d €52-72) This little hotel, the only one in the port area, is within a stone's throw of the river. It has 12 cosy rooms, each named after an offshore Breton island.

The cobbled square of place St-Sauveur in St-Goustan is a sun trap at lunch time and a half-dozen cafés and seafood restaurants take advantage of the setting; take your pick.

L'Églantine (☎ 02 97 56 46 55; 17 place St-Sauveur; mains €12-19, menus €14-33), a stylish place where deep-freeze is a dirty word, is the top table for the freshest of fish and seafood.

MORBIHAN

Getting There & Away

Auray lies on the main TGV route between Quimper and Paris (from €55.70 to €66.30, six daily). There are frequent trains to Vannes (€3.30, 12 minutes), Lorient (€5.60, 25 minutes) and Quimper (€13.20, one hour) and a bus service to Carnac (€3.80).

For travel to Quiberon, see p166.

VANNES

pop 55,000

Gateway to the islands of the Golfe du Morbihan, Vannes (Gwened in Breton) is a lovely town – small enough to feel intimate, close enough to the sea to taste the salt air and old enough to have an interesting history. Its medieval heart, lively with students from the Vannes campus of the Université de Rennes, must be as vital as it was centuries ago.

History

In pre-Roman times Vannes was the capital of the Veneti, a Gaulish tribe of intrepid sailors who fortified their town with a sturdy wall (a long section of which remains) and built a formidable fleet of sailing ships. The Veneti were conquered by Julius Caesar after a Roman fleet defeated them off Brittany's south-eastern coast in the 1st century BC. Under the 9th-century Breton hero Nominoë, the town became the centre of Breton unity. In 1532 the union of the duchy of Brittany with France was proclaimed in Vannes.

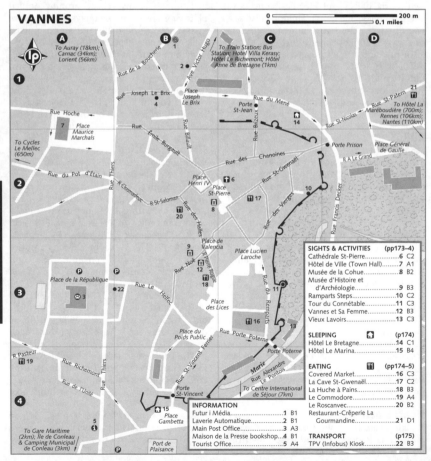

VANNES

SIGHTS & ACTIVITIES	(pp173–4)
Cathédrale St-Pierre	6 C2
Hôtel de Ville (Town Hall)	7 A1
Musée de la Cohue	8 B2
Musée d'Histoire et d'Archéologie	9 B3
Ramparts Steps	10 C3
Tour du Connétable	11 C3
Vannes et Sa Femme	12 B3
Vieux Lavoirs	13 C3

SLEEPING	(p174)
Hôtel Le Bretagne	14 C1
Hôtel Le Marina	15 B4

EATING	(pp174–5)
Covered Market	16 C3
La Cave St-Gwenaël	17 C2
La Huche à Pains	18 B3
Le Commodore	19 A4
Le Roscanvec	20 B2
Restaurant-Crêperie La Gourmandine	21 D1

TRANSPORT	(p175)
TPV (Infobus) Kiosk	22 B3

INFORMATION	
Futur i Média	1 B1
Laverie Automatique	2 B1
Main Post Office	3 A3
Maison de la Presse bookshop	4 B1
Tourist Office	5 A4

MORBIHAN

Orientation

Vannes' small Port de Plaisance, bristling with yacht masts, sits at the end of a canal-like waterway, 1.5km from the Golfe du Morbihan. The Île de Conleau, about 3.5km south of town, is linked to the mainland by a causeway. It's sometimes called Presqu'île de Conleau (Conleau Peninsula).

Information

Futur i Média (☎ 02 97 01 84 09; 14 rue de la Boucherie; per hr €4; ☺ noon–1am Mon-Fri, 2pm–1am Sat & Sun) For Internet connections.

Laverie Automatique (5 ave Victor Hugo; ☺ 7am-9pm)

Main Post Office (2 place de la République)

Maison de la Presse (☎ 02 97 47 18 79; 6 rue Joseph Le Brix) A good map selection and a few English novels.

Tourist Office (☎ 02 97 47 24 34; www.pays-de-vannes.com; 1 rue Thiers; ☺ 9am-7pm daily Jul & Aug, 9.30am-12.30pm & 2-6pm Mon-Sat Sep-Jun). Occupies a lovely 17th-century half-timbered house.

Sights & Activities
WALKING TOUR

Vannes' **old town** is a maze of narrow alleys ranged around the massive cathedral. From the crowded café terraces of place Gambetta, enter the old town through the baroque **Porte St-Vincent** (1; 1747) and take rue St-Vincent Ferrier to place des Lices, perhaps pausing there to pick up the wherewithal for a picnic lunch from the smart new **covered market** (2). Bear left up rue Pierre Rogue and at the corner of rue Noë look out on the left for **Vannes et sa Femme** (3), a 16th-century carving of a smiling man and wife.

Continue up rue des Halles and turn right into picturesque **place Henri IV** (4), lined with half-timbered houses. Bear right again into place St-Pierre, beneath the Gothic splendour of **Cathédrale St-Pierre** (5), built in the 13th century and remodelled several times over the centuries. Opposite the cathedral is the entrance to the 13th-century halls of **La Cohue** (6; right).

Turn left past the cathedral, then right and go left again onto rue des Vierges, just inside the city walls. A section of the **ramparts** (7), which afford views over the manicured formal gardens to the east, is accessible via stairs tucked away off this street. Continuing, head north along rue des Vierges and turn right to pass through the 13th- to 15th-century **Porte Prison** (8), the oldest surviving city gate. Look back now;

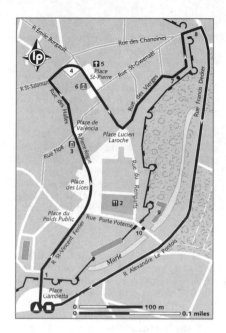

the gate and its tower are much more impressive seen from beyond the walls.

Turn right and return to place Gambetta along rue Francis Decker and its continuation, rue Alexandre Le Pontois, passing the **Vieux Lavoirs** (9; old laundry houses) beside the **Porte Poterne (10)**; despite their picturesque medieval appearance, they date from the early 19th century.

MUSEUMS

The **Musée de la Cohue** (☎ 02 97 47 35 86; 9-15 place St-Pierre; adult/child €4/2.50; ☺ 10am-6pm Jul-Sep, 1.30-6pm Oct-Jun) is named after the venerable 14th-century building that houses it. Over the centuries La Cohue has been a produce market, a law court and the seat of the Breton parliament. Today it's a museum of fine arts, displaying mostly 19th-century paintings, sculptures, engravings and temporary exhibits.

The **Musée d'Histoire et d'Archéologie** (☎ 02 97 47 35 86; 2 rue Noë; adult/child €3/1.50; ☺ 10am-6pm mid-Jun–mid-Sep), in the 15th-century Château Gaillard, exhibits primarily artefacts from the megalithic sites at Carnac and Locmariaquer plus Roman and Greek finds. Outside the summer season, it's closed for extensive renovation works.

BOAT TRIPS

From April to September **Navix** (☎ 02 97 46 60 00) has a range of cruises on the Golfe du Morbihan, departing from Gare Maritime, 2km south of the tourist office. The 'Grand Tour du Golfe' (adult/child €21/13.50; 3¼ hours) includes optional visits to Île aux Moines and Île d'Arz (extra €5/3.50).

Festivals & Events

The **Fêtes d'Arvor** in mid-August is a vibrant three-day celebration of Breton culture with parades, concerts and numerous *festoù-noz*. Vannes also hosts a four-day **Jazz Festival** in late July or early August. **Les Nuits Musicales du Golfe,** a series of classical music concerts, take place in August.

Sleeping

Camping Municipal de Conleau (☎ 02 97 63 13 88; fax 02 97 40 38 82; ave du Maréchal Juin; person/tent site €4/8; ⊗ Apr-Sep) This three-star camping ground, about 3km south of the tourist office, has views over the calm waters of the gulf. Take bus No 2 from place de la République.

Centre International de Séjour (☎ 02 97 66 94 25; cis.sene@wanadoo.fr; route de Moustérian; dm €10.40; ⊗ year-round) An out-of-town option for hostellers is this 100-bed centre just beyond Séné, 7km southeast of Vannes. Take bus No 4 from place de la République to Le Stade stop.

Hôtel Le Richemont (☎ 02 97 47 17 24; www.hotel -richemont-vannes.com; 26 place de la Gare; d with toilet €33, with bathroom €47-52; **P**) Don't be misled by the naff mock-medieval breakfast room; the 28 bedrooms are comfortable, sound-proofed and strictly contemporary.

Hôtel Anne de Bretagne (☎ 02 97 54 22 19; 42 rue Olivier de Clisson; d €32, s/d with bathroom 41/55; **P**). This is another friendly port of call with well-kept rooms that represent good value for money.

Hôtel Le Bretagne (☎ 02 97 47 20 21; hotel.le .bretagne@wanadoo.fr; 34-36 rue du Mené; d €31-37) Just outside the old city walls yet conveniently central, Le Bretagne is another good economical choice. Others realise this too so you'd do well to reserve in advance.

Hôtel Le Marina (☎ 02 97 47 22 81; lemarinahotel@ aol.com; 4 place Gambetta; s/d €32/35, with shower €43/46, with bathroom €51/55) This comfortable, welcoming hotel, with views over the marina and the crowded cafés below, has relaxing, modern rooms.

Hôtel Villa Kerasy (☎ 02 97 68 36 83; www.villa kerasy.com; 20 ave Favrel-et-Lincy; s/d from €90/122; ⊗ closed mid-Nov–mid-Dec & early Jan; **P**) Villa Kerasy is the brainchild of one man, Jean-Jacques Violo, who has created this bijou hotel where every one of its 12 luxurious rooms is themed on historic ports of the East India trading route, from Port-Louis to Pondicherry and Canton. The tranquil garden was designed by a Japanese landscape artist, there's a cosy tearoom with a log fire in winter and the artefacts and accoutrements have been chosen with flair.

Hôtel La Marébaudière (☎ 02 97 47 34 29; www .marebaudiere.com; 4 rue Aristide-Briand; d €56-95; **P**) The Marébaudière is a large Breton villa with 41 modern, refurbished rooms set in its own grounds just 10 minutes' walk east of the old town.

Eating

RESTAURANTS

Restaurant-Crêperie La Gourmandine (☎ 02 97 01 00 20; 18 rue St-Patern; mains €9-15, menus €8-15) The name reflects the twin strengths of this cosy, affable, warmly recommended eatery, on the ground floor of a half-timbered house. For a full meal, go for a *menu* or pick from the short but creative à la carte selection. For something lighter, snack on one of the special *galettes*. Or – come on, be creative! – go for the basic, bedrock *galette* and choose your own toppings (€0.90 to €1.90).

La Cave St-Gwenaël (☎ 02 97 47 47 94; 23 rue St-Gwenaël; galettes €3-6.50; menu €9; ⊗ Tue-Sat) In the basement of a medieval building opposite the cathedral, the St-Gwenaël is another excellent creperie offering good food and a warm atmosphere.

Le Roscanvec (☎ 02 97 47 15 96; 17 rue des Halles; menus €17-74; ⊗ Mon-Sat Jul & Aug, Tue-Sat Sep-Jun) The Roscanvec is one of a number of tempting eateries that are found along rue des Halles and are a cut above the lot. It combines a great setting – in a fine old house on a narrow medieval street – with a superb selection of seafood and game. The cheapest *menu* is available for weekday lunches only, while the most expensive offers lobster in just about every way it can be served.

Le Commodore (☎ 02 97 46 42 62; 3 rue Pasteur; menus €18.50-26.50; ⊗ closed Sun, lunch Mon & Sat) With a décor of model ships, flags, ropes and nets, it's no surprise to learn that the fare here is predominantly seafood.

MORBIHAN

SELF-CATERING

On Wednesday and Saturday morning, a **produce market** takes over place du Poids Public and the surrounding area. To buy fresh meat and fish and a multitude of sandwich fillings, you just need to slip around the corner to the **covered market**. The cheerful vendor who sells from the first stall on the right was a finalist in the all-Brittany 2003 *kouign amann* (butter cake) championships; a slice really does just about melt in your mouth.

La Huche à Pains (23 place des Lices) is a popular patisserie that sells *kouign amann* and other enticing Breton pastries.

Getting There & Away

BOAT

Between May and mid-September, Navix operates boats between Vannes and Belle-Île (see p170).

BUS

TIM (☎ 02 97 01 22 10) bus No 3 serves Pontivy (€8.85, 50 minutes, three to six daily). Bus Nos 23 and 24 travel via Auray to Carnac (€6.70, 1¼ hours) and then on to Quiberon (€7.90, 1¾ hours). Bus No 7 runs from Vannes to Port-Navalo (€6, 45 minutes) via Sarzeau. An SNCF express bus goes to/from St-Brieuc (€14.80, two hours, four daily) via Pontivy (€8.85, 55 minutes).

The small bus station is opposite the train station.

CAR & MOTORCYCLE

Europcar (☎ 02 97 42 43 43) and **ADA** (☎ 02 97 42 59 10) have offices in the train station. **Budget** (☎ 02 97 54 25 22) is just opposite, in the bus station.

TRAIN

There are frequent trains west from Vannes to Auray (€3.30, 12 minutes), Lorient (€7.90, 40 minutes) and Quimper (€15.40, 1½ hours). Heading east, trains go to Rennes (€16.10, 1½ hours) and Nantes (€16.90, 1½ hours). For Quiberon (€9.30 to €11), take the train to Auray and continue by SNCF bus or, in July and August, by train.

Getting Around

TPV (☎ 02 97 01 22 23) runs eight city bus lines until 8.15pm (single ticket €1.10, 10-trip carnet €8.20). For information, call at the **Infobus kiosk** (place de la République). Bus Nos 3 and 4 link the train station with place de la République.

You can hire bikes from **Cycles Le Mellec** (☎ 02 97 63 00 24; 51 ter rue Jean Gougaud), west of the centre, for €12 a day.

To order a **taxi**, ring ☎ 02 97 54 34 34.

GOLFE DU MORBIHAN

The Golfe du Morbihan ('mor bihan' is Breton for 'little sea') is a shallow, island-choked gulf some 20km by 15km, connected to the open sea by a narrow channel barely 1km across.

The Islands

There are about 40 inhabited islands in the Golfe du Morbihan, most privately owned by artists, actors and the like. There are several small villages on the two largest islands, **Île d'Arz** and **Île aux Moines**. Although there's little on them to see apart from palm groves, beaches and good coastal walks, they're popular day-trip destinations from Vannes.

Tiny **Île de Gavrinis**, at the western end of the gulf, has one of Morbihan's most important

MORBIHAN

BIRD-WATCHING IN MORBIHAN

The Golfe du Morbihan's unique ecosystem is complex and influenced by several factors: a mild, sunny climate, strong tidal currents, the mixing of fresh and salt water, large expanses of salt marsh and tidal mud flats, numerous small, sheltered islands and diverse flora. This ecological unit provides a haven for many species of birds, both resident species and migratory waterfowl and waders fleeing the rigours of the northern European winter. You've a great chance of spotting, among many others, spoonbill, white egret, grey heron, shelduck, curlew, sandpiper and various species of waders, ducks and grebes.

One excellent place to go bird-watching is the **Réserve Naturelle de Séné** at Brouel-Kerbihan, 6km southeast of Vannes. The reserve, open at all times, has four observation hides. There is also a **visitor centre** (☎ 02 97 66 92 76; adult/child €3.80/2.30; ☺ open daily 10am-1pm & 2-7pm Jul–mid-Sep, Sun & hols only Feb-Jun).

prehistoric monuments, the **Cairn de Gavrinis** (☎ 02 97 42 63 44; 30-minute guided tour €8.50, incl ferry; ❧ 9.30am-6.30pm Jul & Aug, 9.30am-12.30pm & 1.30-6.30pm Apr-Jun & Sep). The chambered burial cairn – a 14m-long dolmen corridor covered by a huge heap of stones – is 8m high and dates from 3500 BC. The dolmen slabs are richly decorated with strange symbols, some possibly images of stone axes. The island is reached by boat from Larmor-Baden, 14km southwest of Vannes.

GETTING THERE & AWAY

Le Passeur de l'Île d'Arz (☎ 02 97 50 83 83) runs ferries from Île de Conleau, 4km south of Vannes, to Île d'Arz (adult/child return €14/8, 15 minutes, hourly year round).

Izenah (☎ 02 97 26 31 45) boats make the short crossing from Port-Blanc, 13km southwest of Vannes, to Île aux Moines (adult/child return €3.50/2, five minutes, half-hourly all year).

From Vannes' Gare Maritime **Navix** (☎ 02 97 46 60 00) offers a range of cruises on the Golfe du Morbihan between the months of April and September. Its 'Grand Tour du Golfe' (adult/child €21/13.50; 3¼ hours) includes optional visits to Île aux Moines and Île d'Arz (supplement €5/3.50).

Presqu'île de Rhuys

The Presqu'île de Rhuys is the peninsula that bounds the southern edge of the Golfe du Morbihan. It's a little off the beaten track with no major sights but there are several pretty villages – notably **Arzon**, with the picturesque tidal mill of Pen Castel, and the harbour of **Port-Navalo**.

The impressive moated and turreted 13th-century **Château de Suscinio** (☎ 02 97 41 91 91; adult/child €5/2; ❧ 10am-7pm daily Jun-Sep, 10am-noon & 2-7pm daily Apr & May, 10am-noon & 2-5/6pm Thu-Wed Oct-Mar) is 4km southeast of Sarzeau. Once a seat of the dukes of Brittany, it now houses a historical museum, its prize exhibit a medieval tiled floor that once graced the castle's chapel. Minor roads running east beyond the castle lead to the vast 5km sweep of sandy beach at **Landrézac**.

In summer you can hike the GR34 coastal path from Vannes to Port-Navalo (50km; allow two or three days), then take the boat to return to Vannes.

TIM bus No 7 runs several times daily between Vannes and Port-Navalo (€6, 45 minutes) via Sarzeau.

INLAND

For inland Morbihan, we've exercised a little geographic licence, redrawing *département* boundaries by a kilometre or two. Technically, most of Lac de Guerlédan falls within Côtes d'Armor where the Forêt de Paimpont straddles the border with Ille-et-Vilaine. Practically, visitors more often approach each from coastal resorts to the south.

LAC DE GUERLÉDAN

When a hydroelectric dam was built across the River Blavet, west of Mur-de-Bretagne, in 1928, it ended through-navigation on the Canal de Nantes à Brest (Nantes–Brest Canal) but created a beautiful, sinuous, tree-fringed lake, popular with bathers, hikers and water-sports enthusiasts.

Orientation

The lake stretches for around 12km between the dam (Barrage de Guerlédan) in the east and the hamlet of Bon Repos in the west. The nearest towns are Mur-de-Bretagne (2km east of the dam) and Gouarec (5km west of Bon Repos). The lake shore can be reached by road at Beau Rivage (near Caurel) on the northern side, and at Anse de Sordan on the south. Elsewhere, you'll have to walk or take a boat. The 40km GR341 hiking trail makes a complete circuit of the lake.

Information

There's a **tourist office** (☎ 02 96 28 51 41; otsi.guer ledan@wanadoo.fr; place de l'Église; ❧ 10am-12.30pm & 2-6.30pm Mon-Sat, 10.30am-12.30pm Sun Jul & Aug, 10am-12.30pm & 2-5pm Mon-Sat May-Jun, 10am-noon & 2-5pm Mon-Fri Sep-Apr) in Mur-de-Bretagne.

Sights & Activities

There are bathing beaches and plenty of summer water-sports facilities at **Beau Rivage**, on the northern shore of the lake near the village of Caurel, and at the little bay of **Anse de Sordan** on the southern shore. North of the village of St-Aignan, a road leads to a viewpoint and picnic area overlooking the **Barrage de Guerlédan**.

One kilometre west of the lake is a picturesque old bridge, weir and lock on the Nantes–Brest Canal, close to the ruined **Abbaye de Bon Repos**. The abbey was founded by Cistercian monks in 1184 but most of the grand ruins, which are gradually being restored, date from the 18th century. There's a huge **sound and light spectacle** (reservations ☎ 02 96 24 85 28; adult/child €15/7) here that illuminates the night sky on five evenings around the second weekend of August.

A few kilometres south of Bon Repos is **Les Forges des Salles** (☎ 02 96 24 95 67; adult/child €5/3; ✆ 2-6.30pm daily Jul & Aug, 2-6.30pm Sat & Sun Easter-Jun, Sep & Oct). This is a beautifully preserved iron-working village of the 18th and early 19th centuries, complete with smelting furnace, workshops, school and chapel.

Sleeping & Eating

There are several camping grounds close to the lake.

Camping Nautic (☎ 02 96 28 57 94; fax 02 96 26 02 00; Beau Rivage, Caurel; 2 adults, tent & car €18; ✆ mid-May–Sep) This large four-star lakeside site has many facilities, including pool and water-sports equipment hire.

Camping Tost Aven (☎ 02 96 24 85 42; Le Bout du Pont, Gouarec; 2 adults, tent & car €8.85; ✆ mid-Jun–Sep). A quieter, cheaper alternative is the Tost Aven site, which offers pleasant tent sites beside wooded canal banks.

The nearest **Auberge de Jeunesse** (☎ 02 96 28 54 34; 10 rue du Sénéchal, St-Guen; dm €7.35; ✆ mid-Jun– mid-Sep) is located in the village of St-Guen. HI-affiliated, it's about 4km northeast of Mur-de-Bretagne.

There are hotels in Mur-de-Bretagne, Caurel and Gouarec.

Hôtel du Blavet (☎ 02 96 24 90 03; louis.le-loir@ wanadoo.fr; Gouarec; d €36-60; ✆ Mar-Jan) A fine old stone villa overlooking the canal in Gouarec, the Blavet offers 15 traditionally furnished rooms, all with private bathroom and TV. For the top rate of €60 you and your loved one can cavort in a gorgeous four-poster bed; ask for room No 6.

Hôtel Le Beau Rivage (☎ 02 96 28 52 15; fax 02 96 26 01 16; Beau Rivage, Caurel; s €39-46, d €43-45; ✆ Nov-Sep) The Beau Rivage is a modern hotel with a great lakeside location, although the room décor is a bit 1970s-motel. It has a **restaurant** (menus €17-38; ✆ closed Sun & Mon evening & Tue except Jul & Aug) that has panoramic views of the lake and serves excellent seafood and classic French cuisine.

Crêperie du Vieux Moulin (☎ 02 96 28 54 72; galettes €2.90-7.50; ✆ Wed-Mon year-round), next door, also has a wonderful picture window that overlooks the lake and offers a warm welcome year round – *a fortiori* in winter, when a log fire glows in the open hearth.

Good places at the other end of the lake include **Crêperie de Bon Repos** (☎ 02 96 24 86 56; St-Gelven) next to the abbey, and **Café de l'Abbaye**, beside the old bridge over the canal.

Getting There & Away

Three or four buses daily, operated by **EFFIA** (☎ 02 98 93 06 98), run from Loudéac, calling by St-Guen, Mur de Bretagne (25 minutes), Caurel, Bon Repos and Gouarec (45 minutes). Loudéac – the nearest train station – is served by trains and SNCF buses from St-Brieuc (€7.40, 45 minutes), Pontivy (€4.10, 30 minutes) and Vannes (€11.25, one hour 20 minutes).

PONTIVY

pop 15,000

The impressive chateau of Pontivy recalls the town's former status as the capital of the Pays de Rohan, the lands of central Brittany once owned by the powerful Rohan family. Following the Revolution, Pontivy became an important military and strategic centre when Napoleon ordered the canalisation of the Blavet and the construction of barracks,

MORBIHAN

DETOUR: LAC DE GUERLÉDAN CIRCUIT

The 25km circuit of **Lac de Guerlédan** makes for a lovely half day out. Even though you're rarely in sight of water, the central Brittany countryside is consistently pretty. From Mur-de-Bretagne, head west along the lightly travelled N164 as far as the lakeside hamlet of Bon Repos and push 1km to its west to take in the romantic ruins of the **Abbaye de Bon Repos** (opposite).

Returning to Bon Repos, take the D15 southwards to pass near **Les Forges des Salles** (above), an intact early 19th-century iron-working village. After around 8km, an optional diversion to the left drops you down to the lake at **Anse de Sordan**, a great spot for a picnic or swim.

Continuing, and when you're only a couple of kilometres short of Mur-de-Bretagne, there's a stunning view down over the lake and the dam at its eastern end.

a new town hall and a courthouse. It was in his honour that the 'new town' was christened Napoléonville.

Orientation & Information

The Pontivy town centre lies on the eastern bank of the Blavet, where the main street (rue Nationale, becoming rue Général de Gaulle) runs north–south.

The **tourist office** (☎ 02 97 25 04 10; www.pays -pontivy.com - French only; 61 rue Général de Gaulle, ⏲ 10am-noon & 2-6pm year-round) is immediately north of the castle.

Sights & Activities

The chunky, late-15th-century **Château des Rohan** (☎ 02 97 25 12 93; adult/child €4/1.75 Jul-Sep, €1.25/0.80 Oct, Nov & Feb-Jun; ⏲ 10.30am-6.30pm daily Jul-Sep, 10am-noon & 2-6pm Wed-Sun Apr-Jun, 2-6pm Wed-Sun Feb, Mar, Oct & Nov) squats menacingly behind a massive ditch and earthwork at the northern end of town.

South of the castle is Pontivy's **old town**, enlivened by several half-timbered houses around place du Martray and along pedestrianised rue du Fil and rue du Pont. South again is **Napoléonville** with its orderly grid of streets, lined with elegant 18th- and 19th-century buildings.

At the north end of Pontivy the **Nantes–Brest Canal** parts company with the River Blavet, the canal ascending eastwards towards Josselin, while the river (itself canalised) flows southwest to meet the sea at Lorient. Pontivy is one of Brittany's main centres for canal-cruising.

Sleeping

Auberge de Jeunesse (☎ 02 97 25 58 27; fax 02 97 25 76 48; dm €8.85; ⏲ daily Jul & Aug, Mon-Fri Sep-Jun) Based in a former flour mill on the Île de Récollets, this hostel is about 1.5km north of the bus station.

Hôtel du Porhoët (☎ 02 97 25 34 88; fax 02 97 25 57 17; 41 rue Général de Gaulle; s/d €26/33, with bathroom s €37-39, d €37-45) The Porhoët, 80m north of the tourist office, is a good mid-range choice with comfy rooms, a friendly welcome and a cosy bar.

Hôtel Le Rohan (☎ 02 97 25 02 01; fax 02 97 25 02 85; 90 rue Nationale; s/d €50/64; [P]) In an elegant 19th-century town house close to the bus station, this is the fanciest place in town. Each of its 16 rooms is individually decorated. In summer enjoy breakfast on the sheltered terrace.

Eating

Restaurant La Pommeraie (☎ 02 97 25 60 09; 17 quai du Couvent; mains €15, 3-course menu €29, 4-course menu €39; ⏲ Tue-Sat) The Pommeraie is a small, smartly dressed restaurant overlooking the Blavet. It serves classic French cuisine and does a good-value lunch *menu* at €18. For a total gastronomic blow-out, attempt the seven-course special (€52).

Getting There & Away

Pontivy, which long ago lost its train service, lies on the main north-south SNCF bus route between Vannes (€8.85, 55 minutes, three daily) and St-Brieuc (€10, 1¼ hours, four daily). There is also a **CTM** (☎ 02 97 01 22 01) regional express bus service between Pontivy and Rennes (€13.90, two hours, eight daily) via Josselin (€6, 30 minutes) and Ploërmel (€7.70, 45 minutes). TIM bus Nos 14 and 17 run between Pontivy and Lorient (€9, one to 1¾ hours, four to five daily) while No 3 goes to/from Vannes (€8.85, 50 minutes, three to six daily).

Buses leave from the former train station, off rue Nationale.

VALLÉE DU BLAVET

The scenic, winding valley of the Blavet extends from Lac de Guerlédan, 17km north of Pontivy, to meet the sea at Lorient. You can follow its route by bicycle or canoe or on foot.

St-Nicolas des Eaux

The little riverside hamlet of St-Nicolas des Eaux, 15km south of Pontivy, sits beneath a narrow neck of land pinched between two meanders of the Blavet. Atop this ridge is the **Site de Castennec**, the site of a Neolithic and, later, Roman fort. Although little remains today, the spot is marked by a small stone look-out tower that affords a stunning view along the valley. Immediately south of Castennec, the tiny chapel of **Ermitage de Gueltas** is built below an overhanging rock outcrop on the western bank of the river.

Poul Fétan

Two kilometres south of the little hamlet of Quistinic, and overlooking the northern bank of the Blavet, is the 'living museum' of **Poul Fétan** (☎ 02 97 39 51 74; adult/child €6/3; ⏲ 10am-7pm Jul-Sep). This pretty village of thatched cottages, complete with a working pottery, preserves the traditional crafts and farming practices of 19th-century central Brittany. There's even an *auberge* (inn) where you'll be able to sample food and drink of the era.

Quistinic, which is not served by public transport, is 25km south of Pontivy.

JOSSELIN & AROUND
The picturesque village of Josselin (population 2600), 30km southeast of Pontivy, was the seat of the counts of Rohan for several centuries. Overlooking the River Oust, they built an imposing castle that hosted many of the dukes of Brittany during their progressions through the duchy.

Orientation & Information
Josselin lies on the Oust, which is part of the Nantes–Brest Canal. Its centre, place Notre Dame, is a beautiful square of 16th-century half-timbered houses. Rue Olivier de Clisson runs north from the square; the castle and tourist office are just to its south, below rue des Trente, the main through street.

The **tourist office** (☎ 02 97 22 36 43; www.pays dejosselin.com - French only; place de la Congrégation; 🕑 10am-6pm daily Jul & Aug, 10am-noon & 2-6pm Mon-Fri, 10am-noon Sat Sep-Jun) is beside the castle entrance.

Sights & Activities
The three huge round towers of the 14th-century **Château de Josselin** (☎ 02 97 22 36 45; adult/child €6.30/4.30, incl guided tour; 🕑 10am-6pm daily mid-Jul–Aug, 2-6pm daily Jun–mid-Jul & Sep, 2-6pm Sat & Sun Apr, May & Oct) dominate the riverbanks. Behind them, the elegant Gothic-Renaissance palace dates from the late 15th and early 16th centuries. The castle can only be visited by **guided tour** (in French; in English 11am & 2.30pm Jul & Aug, 2.30pm Sep). Within the castle complex is the **Musée des Poupées** (Doll Museum; adult/child €5.50/3.90), with a collection of over 600 dolls from around the world. A combined ticket, allowing entry to both, costs €11/7.70.

Parts of the **Basilique Notre Dame du Roncier** (place Notre Dame) date from the 12th century. Note the superb 15th- and 16th-century stained glass in the south aisle. In the chapel northeast of the choir is the finely carved marble tomb of Olivier de Clisson and his wife. De Clisson fortified the chateau during the Hundred Years' War. In July and August, go up the **bell tower**

(admission free) for a splendid view of the castle and river.

Walking
A pleasant 15-minute stroll west along the towpath beside the Oust leads to the **Île de Beaufort**, an island stretching between the river with its weir and the lock that allows canal boats to pass. It's a beautiful picnic spot, with grassy banks shaded by willow, poplar and oak.

For even more agreeable strolling – which could take you as far as Nantes or Brest, time and energy permitting – take time to enjoy a stretch of the canal that here scythes through delightful shady woodland.

Guéhenno
About 10km southwest of Josselin is the village of Guéhenno, which has one of central Brittany's most beautiful **calvaries** (representation of the Crucifixion).

Sleeping & Eating
Camping du Bas de la Lande (☎ 02 97 22 22 20; campingbasdelalande@wanadoo.fr; Guégon; 2 adults, tent & car €12; 🕑 May-Sep) This camping ground is about 2km west of Josselin, on the southern bank of the Oust.

There's no youth hostel but the village runs a **gîte d'étape** (☎ 02 97 75 67 18; dm €7.80, €8.80 in winter; 🕑 year-round). It's southeast of the chateau beside the Oust.

Hôtel Restaurant du Château (☎ 02 97 22 20 11; www.hotel-chateau.com - French only; 1 rue Général de Gaulle; d €30, with shower €41, with bathroom €53.50-58 incl breakfast; 🅿) For just €3.50 extra – and even that paltry addition only applies between June and September – you can reserve a room with the most magnificent view of the chateau, looming above this delightfully cosy hotel, a Logis de France. Its **restaurant** (menus €14-40) also has a gorgeous picture window.

There are several popular creperies on and around place Notre Dame. Down the hill, **Crêperie-Grill Sarrazine** (☎ 02 97 22 37 80; 51 rue Glatinier; galettes & salads from €6, menus from €9) packs in the locals.

Getting There & Away
Josselin lies on the main **CTM** (☎ 02 97 01 22 01) bus route between Pontivy (€6, 30 minutes) and Rennes (€10.70, 1½ hours). The Rennes-bound bus also stops at Ploërmel (€2.70, 15 minutes).

MORBIHAN

PLOËRMEL

pop 5000

Ploërmel is a market town and transport hub, at the junction of the main east–west route between Rennes and Lorient, and the north–south route from St-Malo to Vannes. It was named after the English monk and missionary St Arthmael (plou arthmael is Breton for 'the parish of Arthmael'), remembered in the town's heavy **Église de St-Armel**. The arches of the north porch (on the opposite side of the church from the main road) are intricately carved with comic figures, as well as scenes from the life of Christ.

On the lane leading east from the tourist office is the remarkable **Maison des Marmousets** (1586; 7 rue Beuamanoir), the carved figures on its timber façade include jesters, caryatids and a bishop. Were they were carved as caricatures of the figures on the church porch? To satirise the royal court? Or simply by a carpenter with a droll sense of humour? No-one knows.

Ploërmel's **tourist office** (☎ 02 97 74 02 70; 5 rue du Val; ⏲ 9.30am-7pm Mon-Sat, 9.30am-12.30pm Sun Jul & Aug, 10am-12.30pm & 2-6.30pm Mon-Sat Sep-Jun) is 150m northwest of the church.

Hôtel Le Cobh (☎ 02 97 74 00 49; fax 02 97 74 07 36; 10 rue des Forges; d €46-100) Named after Ploërmel's twin town in Ireland, the Cobh is a friendly, old-fashioned hotel – it dates from 1916 – with a cosy bar and tempting restaurant.

Ploërmel is on the express bus route between Rennes and Pontivy (see p178).

AROUND PLOËRMEL

Malestroit, 18km south of Ploërmel, is a picturesque little village on the Nantes–Brest Canal. It's the starting point for pleasant strolls along the towpath. In summer you can hire a motor boat from **Canal Loc 56** (☎ 02 97 73 79 03; quai Plisson), beside the canal lock in Malestroit. Boats taking up to five people cost €25/65 per hour/three hours.

Not far west of Malestroit is the **Musée de la Résistance Bretonne** (☎ 02 97 75 16 90; St-Marcel; admission €6; ⏲ 10am-7pm daily mid-Jun–mid-Sep, 10am-noon & 2-6pm daily Apr–mid-Jun, 10am-noon & 2-6pm Wed-Mon mid-Sep–Mar), an open-air museum that tells the story of Brittany's part in WWII.

FORÊT DE PAIMPONT

The Paimpont Forest, straddling the *départements* of Morbihan and Ille-et-Vilaine, is 40km southwest of Rennes, and 20km northeast of Ploërmel. Deep in this forest, the young King Arthur traditionally received the sword Excalibur from Viviane, the mysterious Lady of the Lake. Visitors still come in search of the spring of eternal youth, where the magician Merlin first met Viviane, who became his lover.

The best base for exploring Forêt de Paimpont is the lakeside village of **Paimpont**. Its **tourist office** (☎ 02 99 07 84 23; ⏲ 10am-noon & 2-6pm Wed-Mon Feb-Sep) is beside the 12th-century **Église Abbatiale** (Abbey Church). It has a free walking/cycling map of the forest (62km of trails) – or buy the more complete *Tour de Brocéliande*, detailing over 150km of trails. In July and August there are guided tours of the lower (€2.50) and upper (€4) forests.

On the eastern fringes of the forest are two sites associated with Arthurian legend; both deeply disappointing. The **Tombeau de Merlin** (Merlin's Tomb) is an uninspiring lump of broken stone with a sapling sprouting from the middle, although that has not stopped starry-eyed romantics covering it in votive ribbons, grassy wreaths and hand-written notes and prayers. And the **Fontaine de Jouvence** (Fountain of Youth), further down the path and little more than a muddy puddle, is itself badly in need of rejuvenation.

Sleeping & Eating

Camping Municipal de Paimpont (☎ 02 99 07 89 16; rue du Chevalier Lancelot du Lac; 2 adults, tent & car €8; ⏲ May-Sep) This small camping area is near the lake.

Auberge de Jeunesse (☎ 02 97 22 76 75; dm €7.35; ⏲ Jun-Sep) This hostel occupies a lovely stone farmhouse at Choucan en Brocéliande, in the countryside and 5km north of Paimpont.

Hôtel Le Relais de Brocéliande (☎ 02 99 07 81 07; relais-de-broceliande@wanadoo.fr; 7 rue du Forges, Paimpont; d €32-48, menus €14.50-68.60). This 24-room hotel has pleasantly rustic rooms with all mod cons, as well as an excellent restaurant.

For a cheaper bite, try the **Crêperie au Temps des Moines** (☎ 02 99 07 89 63; 16 ave Chevalier Ponthus) in a pleasing granite house overlooking the lake.

Getting There & Around

TIV (☎ 02 99 30 87 80) runs buses from Rennes (€2.50, one hour). You can rent mountain bikes (per half/full day €9/14) from **Bar Le Brécilien** (☎ 02 99 07 81 13; rue Général de Gaulle), beside Paimpont's tourist office.

Loire-Atlantique

CONTENTS

Nantes	183
St-Nazaire	191
Parc Naturel Régional de Brière	194
Presqu'île de Guérande	**195**
Guérande	195
La Baule	196
Le Croisic	197
Batz-sur-Mer	198

The *département* of Loire-Atlantique belongs to both maritime Brittany and the freshwater world of the River Loire. To escape the crowds, punt the reedy fens of the Parc Naturel Régional de Brière or drop by the saltpans and small folk museums along the Guérande Peninsula. The sweeping, 500m-wide golden beach at the swanky seaside resort of La Baule is one of Brittany's best. Further along the peninsula is Le Croisic, a more intimate little gem that's at once active fishing port, marina and seaside resort.

Upriver lies Nantes, the culturally dynamic departmental capital, with its throbbing night-life and pleasantly pedestrianised old quarter. Betwixt and between, perched at the mouth of the Loire estuary, is the port of St-Nazaire, famous for its shipbuilding yards (from which the *Queen Mary 2*, the biggest cruise liner ever built, was launched in December 2003) and as the principal base for the German submarines that prowled the Atlantic in WWII.

Administratively speaking, Loire-Atlantique – which these days falls within the Pays de la Loire region – is no longer Breton. But we juggle unrepentantly with geography and include this hunk of western France here because of its strong historical and cultural links to Brittany, of which Nantes was once the capital. Indeed we may be prescient: recent opinion polls indicate that as much as 80% of the populace would favour being reassimilated.

HIGHLIGHTS

- Explore the frondy delights of Nantes' **Jardin des Plantes** (botanic gardens; p186)
- Stay out late to savour Nantes' throbbing **nightlife** (p190)
- Devote a day to the attractions of **St-Nazaire**, a city still confidently rising from its WWII devastation (p191)
- Punt through reed beds in the **Parc Naturel Régional de Brière** (p194)
- See salt-panners at work in the *marais salants* of **Guérande** (p196)
- People-watch, sitting beside stylish **La Baule**'s promenade (p196)
- Bike or drive the spectacular circular coast road from **Le Croisic** (p197)

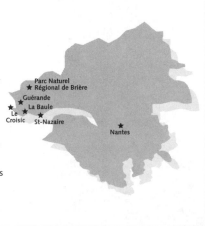

- POPULATION: 1,134,300
- AREA: 6815 SQ KM

LOIRE-ATLANTIQUE

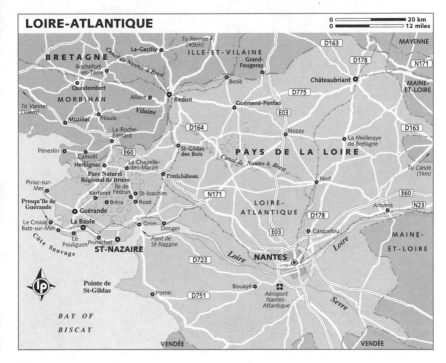

LOIRE-ATLANTIQUE

NANTES
pop 534,200

Nantes, France's seventh-largest city, is the most important commercial and industrial centre in west-central France. Enjoying a mild Atlantic climate, it's a lively place, rich in cafés and restaurants, with fine museums, carefully tended parks and gardens, an ultra-modern tram system, a university of 33,000 students and (of course – it's beside the Loire) an imposing chateau.

In 1598 the Edict of Nantes, a landmark royal charter guaranteeing civil rights and freedom of worship for France's Protestants, was signed here by Henri IV.

During the Reign of Terror (September 1793 to July 1794) the local representative of the sinisterly named Committee of Public Safety deemed the guillotine too slow. Instead, suspected counter-Revolutionaries were stripped, tied together in pairs and loaded onto barges that were then sunk in the middle of the River Loire.

Outside the pleasantly pedestrian old city, Nantes has its fair share of 1960s concrete creations, most notably the 29-storey Tour de Bretagne (Brittany Tower), looming between place de Bretagne and cours des 50 Otages, its name another reminder of the city's Breton roots.

Orientation

Central Nantes sits snugly on the north bank of the Loire, 55km east of the Atlantic coast. The city's two main arteries, both served by tram lines, are the north–south, partly pedestrianised cours des 50 Otages (named in memory of 50 people taken hostage and shot by the Germans on 22 October 1941) and a broad east–west boulevard that connects the train station with quai de la Fosse. They intersect near the Gare Centrale bus/tram hub. The pedestrian ways running beside these two major thoroughfares are called *allées*.

The old city is to the east, between cours des 50 Otages and the Château des Ducs de Bretagne.

Information
BOOKSHOPS

Géothèque (☎ 02 40 47 40 68; 10 place du Pilori) A top-notch place for maps and guidebooks.

NANTES

A   B   C   D

1   2   3   4   5   6

Rue Talensac
Rue Basse Porte
Rue de Bel Air
Rue Paul Bellamy
Rue de Versailles
6   7
48
20
49
60
Église St-Similien
Rue Sarrazin
Rue Jeanne d'Arc
Place Viarme
Place Viarme

Rue Porte Neuve
Rue Jean Jaurès
Rue Le Nôtre
Allée des Tanneurs
Allée de l'Erdre
2
50 Otages
Rue St-Léonard
Rue de Strasbourg

Place Ste-Elisabeth
Rue Clöphine Coiturin
Rue R President Édouard Hérriot
26
Jean Jaurès
Rue d'Elton
Rue Jean Jaurès
10
Rue du Marais
Rue de l'Hôtel de Ville
Town Hall

Palais de Justice
Rue Mercoeur
Place Aristide Briand
Rue Léopold Cassegrain
12
Place de Bretagne
25
Place du Cirque
67
33
44
Rue du Moulin

Rue Deshoulières
Rue Marceau
Rue La Fayette
Rue de Budapest
Rue Cacault
Allée Duguesse Cours des 50 Otages
Rue des Trois Croissants
14
Rue des Halles
1
Rue de la Marne

45
Rue du Calvaire
Rue de Feltre
11
Rue de la Bâronire
Rue de la Bâclere
Rue de la Marne
Rue Beauregard
Église Ste-Croix

Place Delorme
Rue Copernic
Rue Louis Préaubert
Rue du Châpeau Rouge
Rue Contrescarpe
Église St-Nicolas
34
Rue Jean Bart
Allée du Port Maillard
Place du Bouffay
51

Rue Franklin
Rue de la Contrie
Rue Boileau
39
42
Rue Rubens
62
46
47
Place Royale
Rue du Calade
Rue du Orléans

Rue Racine
54
Rue Scribe
Commerce
32
65
Gare Centrale Bus/Tram Hub
55
9
13

56
61
27
Rue Molière
Rue Crébillon
Rue Santeuil
Rue de la Fosse
40
59
Place du Commerce
Commerce
57
Allée Brancas
Allée Jean Bart
Cours Olivier de Cisson

Place de la Monnaie
23
Place Graslin
43
36
Rue Siffait
52
Passage Pommeraye
68
Place de la Bourse
Palais de la Bourse
Franklin Roosevelt
Allée Duguay Trouin
Rue Kervégan
53
Allée Turenne

22
Rue Voltaire
41 3
Rue Piron
Rue Jean-Jacques Rousseau
Île Feydeau
Hôtel Dieu

Cours Cambronne
31
Rue Fourcroy
28
Square JB Daviais
Rue Gaston Veil

Rue M Sibille
Rue Maréchal de Lattre de Tassigny
Médiathèque
P
P

Quai de la Fosse

To Bellevue Tram Terminus;
Maillé Brézé (300m);
Musée Jules Verne (1km)

Loire
(Bras de la Madeleine)

Quai de Tourville
Quai André Morice
Quai Moncousu
4

LOIRE-ATLANTIQUE

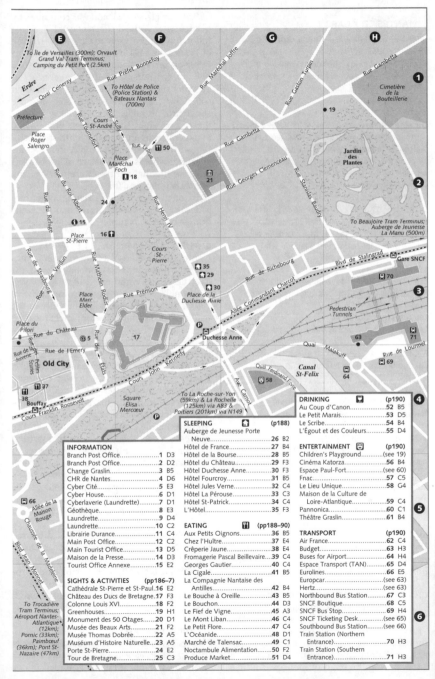

INFORMATION

Branch Post Office.....................1	D3
Branch Post Office.....................2	D2
Change Graslin.........................3	B5
CHR de Nantes.........................4	D6
Cyber Cité..............................5	E3
Cyber House...........................6	D1
Cyberlaverie (Laundrette)............7	D1
Géothèque.............................8	E3
Laundrette.............................9	D4
Laundrette............................10	C2
Librairie Durance.....................11	C4
Main Post Office......................12	C2
Main Tourist Office...................13	D5
Maison de la Presse...................14	D3
Tourist Office Annexe................15	E2

SIGHTS & ACTIVITIES (pp186–7)

Cathédrale St-Pierre et St-Paul.16	E2
Château des Ducs de Bretagne.17	F3
Colonne Louis XVI....................18	F2
Greenhouses..........................19	H1
Monument des 50 Otages...........20	D1
Musée des Beaux Arts................21	F2
Musée Thomas Dobrée...............22	A5
Muséum d'Histoire Naturelle......23	A5
Porte St-Pierre........................24	E2
Tour de Bretagne......................25	C3

SLEEPING (p188)

Auberge de Jeunesse Porte Neuve.....................................26	B2
Hôtel de France.......................27	B4
Hôtel de la Bourse....................28	B5
Hôtel du Château.....................29	F3
Hôtel Duchesse Anne.................30	F3
Hôtel Fourcroy........................31	B5
Hôtel Jules Verne.....................32	C4
Hôtel La Pérouse......................33	C3
Hôtel St-Patrick.......................34	C4
L'Hôtel.................................35	F3

EATING (pp188–90)

Aux Petits Oignons...................36	B5
Chez l'Huître..........................37	E4
Crêperie Jaune........................38	E4
Fromagerie Pascal Beillevaire.....39	C4
Georges Gautier......................40	C4
La Cigale...............................41	B5
La Compagnie Nantaise des Antilles.................................42	B4
Le Bouche à Oreille...................43	B5
Le Bouchon............................44	D3
Le Fief de Vigne.......................45	A3
Le Mont Liban.........................46	C4
Le Petit Flore..........................47	C4
L'Océanide.............................48	D1
Marché de Talensac...................49	C1
Noctambule Alimentation...........50	F2
Produce Market.......................51	D4

DRINKING (p190)

Au Coup d'Canon.....................52	B5
Le Petit Marais........................53	D5
Le Scribe...............................54	B4
L'Égout et des Couleurs..............55	D4

ENTERTAINMENT (p190)

Children's Playground...............(see 19)	
Cinéma Katorza.......................56	B4
Espace Paul-Fort....................(see 58)	
Fnac....................................57	C5
Le Lieu Unique........................58	G4
Maison de la Culture de Loire-Atlantique......................59	C4
Pannonica.............................60	C1
Théâtre Graslin........................61	B4

TRANSPORT (p190)

Air France..............................62	C4
Budget.................................63	H3
Buses for Airport......................64	H4
Espace Transport (TAN)..............65	D4
Eurolines..............................66	E5
Europcar...............................(see 63)	
Hertz..................................(see 63)	
Northbound Bus Station..............67	C3
SNCF Boutique........................68	C5
SNCF Bus Stop........................69	H4
SNCF Ticketing Desk..............(see 65)	
Southbound Bus Station..........(see 66)	
Train Station (Northern Entrance)..............................70	H3
Train Station (Southern Entrance)..............................71	H3

NANTES CITY CARD

The tourist offices sell the **Nantes City Card** (€14/24/30 for 1/2/3 days), a pass allowing free admission to city museums, a guided tour, a river cruise and unlimited free travel on buses and trams.

Librairie Durance (☎ 02 40 48 68 79; 4 allée d'Orléans) Has a fair choice of English-language novels downstairs.
Maison de la Presse (junction cours des 50 Otages & rue des Trois Croissants) Carries some English-language newspapers.

INTERNET ACCESS
Cyber Cité (☎ 02 40 89 57 92; 14 rue de Strasbourg; per hr €3; ✆ 1pm-1am) Has more than 80 terminals.
Cyber House (☎ 02 40 12 11 84; 8 quai de Versailles; per hr €3; ✆ 2pm-2am Mon-Fri, 3pm-2am Sat)

LAUNDRY
Cyberlaverie (10 quai de Versailles; ✆ 8am-10pm) Also has three Internet terminals (using France Telecom phonecards).
Laundrette (8 allée des Tanneurs)
Laundrette (3 allée Duguay Trouin; ✆ 7am-8.30pm)

MONEY
Change Graslin (17 rue Jean-Jacques Rousseau)

POST
Main Post Office (place de Bretagne) Has a small Postal Museum.

TOURIST INFORMATION
Nantes' **tourist offices** (☎ 02 40 20 60 00; www.nantes -tourisme.com) moved house in 2003 and may appear incorrectly on older maps.
Main Tourist Office (3 cours Olivier de Clisson; ✆ 10am-6pm Mon-Sat)
Annexe (2 place St-Pierre; ✆ 10am-1pm & 2-6pm)

Sights
If you're an assiduous museums and monuments visitor, the Nantes City Card (see the box above) is a worthwhile investment.

CHÂTEAU DES DUCS DE BRETAGNE
The **Château des Ducs de Bretagne** (Chateau of the Dukes of Brittany; ☎ 02 40 41 56 56; 4 place Marc Elder; admission free; ✆ 10am-6pm), Nantes' major historical building, rises above its moat in the east of the old city. Construction began in 1466, during the reign of François II, duke

of Brittany (1435–88), and was continued by his daughter Anne de Bretagne (1477–1514) following her marriage to Charles VIII, king of France, in 1491. After the Edict of Nantes (1598) it served as a barracks and a prison.

From the outside, the chateau appears to be your standard medieval castle, all high walls and crenellated towers. Step into the courtyard, though, give a quick glance at the heavyweight **Harnachement**, built in the 18th century as an armoury for the barracks, then turn to savour the wholly Renaissance charm of what is more palace than fortification, its highlight the lacy fretwork of the **Tour de la Couronne d'Or**.

Extensive renovations, lasting more than a decade and costing more than €18 million, should be completed by 2008.

CATHÉDRALE ST-PIERRE ET ST-PAUL
Nantes' **cathedral** (place St-Pierre; ✆ 9am-7pm) has recently had a good scrubbing down, just like the castle. Although it took over four-and-a-half centuries to be completed (in 1891), there's a pleasing Gothic unity to the whole. The interior was completely restored after a fire in 1972.

The **tomb of François II**, the last duke of Brittany to rule independently (1458–88), is a masterpiece of Renaissance sculpture. In the southern transept, it was commissioned by his daughter, Anne de Bretagne, and carved in Italian marble. The reclining figures are François and his second wife, Marguerite de Foix. The statues at the corners represent the four cardinal virtues: Prudence (with mirror and dividers, and an old man's face at the back of her head), Temperance (with reliquary and bridle), Fortitude (strangling a dragon) and Justice (with sword and scales). Above the tomb is the largest **stained-glass window** in France, a modern, glowing creation 25m high.

For another perspective of the cathedral, pass behind into **place Maréchal Foch**, a monumental square from the centre of which rises the **Colonne Louis XVI** (1790), with its disproportionately tiny statue atop a thick pillar. On the southern side lies the old **Porte St-Pierre**, a vestige of the medieval city walls.

JARDIN DES PLANTES
Nantes' **Jardin des Plantes** (blvd de Stalingrad; admission free; ✆ 8am-6pm) is one of France's most exquisite botanic gardens. Founded in the

early 19th century, it has lawns like putting greens, beautiful flowerbeds, duck ponds, fountains and even a few California redwoods (sequoias). At its northern end are greenhouses and a children's playground.

ÎLE FEYDEAU

The channels of the Loire that once surrounded the **Île Feydeau** (the neighbourhood where Jules Verne was born) were filled in after WWII, but the area's 18th-century mansions still stand. Built by rich merchants from the ill-gotten profits of the slave trade, some are adorned with stone carvings of the heads of African slaves.

Passage Pommeraye, which is a delightful 19th-century shopping arcade, is two blocks northwest of Île Feydeau. Its ornate interior shelters exclusive art galleries and designer shoe shops and is fun for window and serious shoppers alike.

MUSEUMS

Two blocks to the east of the cathedral is the renowned **Musée des Beaux Arts** (Fine Arts Museum; ☎ 02 40 41 65 65; 10 rue Georges Clemenceau; adult/child/student €3.10/free/1.60; ☺ 10am-6pm Wed-Tue, 10am-8pm Fri), displaying mainly paintings, including three by Georges de la Tour.

On the western edge of the city centre is the ageing but excellent **Muséum d'Histoire Naturelle** (Natural History Museum; ☎ 02 40 99 26 20; 12 rue Voltaire; adult/child/student €3.10/free/1.60; ☺ 10am-6pm Wed-Mon). Founded in 1799, it features a vivarium with pythons, crocodiles and a green iguana. Entry is from leafy place de la Monnaie.

Immediately west is the **Musée Thomas Dobrée** (☎ 02 40 71 03 50; 18 rue Voltaire; adult/child €3/1.50; ☺ 9.45am-5.30pm Tue-Fri, 2.30-5.30pm Sat & Sun). Partly housed in the Manoir de la Touche, a 15th-century bishops' palace, it has exhibits

of classical antiquities, medieval artefacts, Renaissance furniture and items relating to the French Revolution. One highlight is the **heart of Anne de Bretagne**, encased in ivory and gold following the death of the 37-year-old queen in 1514.

The 133m-long French navy destroyer **Maillé Brézé** (☎ 02 40 69 56 82; 1hr guided tour adult/child €4.60/2.30, 1½hr tour €7/2.40; ☺ 2-6pm daily Jun-Sep, 2-5pm Wed, Sat & Sun Oct-May), in service from 1957 to 1988, is moored on quai de la Fosse, about 1km west of the main tourist office. The excellent (and obligatory) guided tour is available in English in the summer. The longer tour includes a visit to the engine room. Ask for the free guide pamphlet in English.

Activities

BOAT TRIPS & RIVERSIDE WALKS

Promenade de l'Erdre is a network of riverside paths along both banks of the River Erdre from the Monument des 50 Otages. It extends north for about 7km. The **Île de Versailles**, an island on the northern bank 500m northeast of the monument, is home to a Japanese garden, a children's playground and a jetty where you can hire electric-powered boats from **Ruban Vert** (☎ 02 51 81 04 24; up to 4 people €20 per hr; ☺ 2-7pm Mon-Fri, 10am-7pm Sat & Sun Apr-Oct).

Bateaux Nantais (☎ 02 40 14 51 14; quai de la Motte Rouge; tram stop Motte Rouge), 1km northeast of the Monument des 50 Otages, runs river cruises (adult/child €9/5, 1½hours, daily July to August, Saturday and Sunday April to May and September to November).

Festivals & Events

The **Festival des Trois Continents** (☎ 02 40 69 74 14; www.3continents.com) is a prestigious annual festival of Third World cinema, held in the last week of November.

VOYAGES EXTRAORDINAIRES

Jules Verne (1828–1905), whose fabulous tales evoking extraordinary journeys took him and his readers to unexplored realms of the world, is considered the father of science fiction. Born in Nantes of seafaring parents, he ran off to sea to be a cabin boy, only to be dragged home by an authoritarian father, who pushed his son through school and into law studies, which Verne quit.

After moving to Paris in 1848, the Verne family retained a holiday home in Nantes. Today, it's the **Musée Jules Verne** (☎ 02 40 69 72 52; 3 rue de l'Hermitage; adult/child €1.50/0.75; ☺ 10am-noon & 2-6pm Mon & Wed-Sat, 2-6pm Sun). Documents, models, posters and first-edition books evoke the novelist's progressive vision, expounded in such works as De la Terre à la Lune (From the Earth to the Moon) and Le Tour du Monde en 80 Jours (Around the World in 80 Days).

Sleeping

BUDGET

Camping du Petit Port (☎ 02 40 74 47 94; camping -petit-port@nge.fr; 21 blvd du Petit Port; per person/site €2.25/4.60; ☺ year-round) This big, luxury camping ground is in a wooded area close to the Erdre and about 3km north of the train station. Take tram No 2, northbound, to the Morrhonnière stop.

Nantes has two central and HI-affiliated **Auberges de Jeunesse**, both with self-catering facilities.

Porte Neuve (☎ 02 40 20 63 63; fax 02 40 20 63 79; 1 place Ste-Élisabeth; dm incl breakfast €8.85; ☺ year-round) A stone's throw from place de Bretagne, this couldn't be closer to the heart of town. Jean Jaurès tram stop is less than 100m away.

La Manu (☎ 02 40 29 29 20; nanteslamanu@fuaj.org; 2 place de la Manu; dm €8; ☺ year-round) Just 600m east of the train station's northern entrance. Take tram No 1 to the Manufacture stop.

Hôtel du Château (☎ 02 40 74 17 16; fax 02 40 14 01 15; 5 place de la Duchesse Anne; s/d €22/27, d with shower €26-32, with bathroom €39) This little hotel, which also runs a quality restaurant, is sandwiched between a couple of more costly neighbours in a peaceful location near the chateau.

Hôtel Fourcroy (☎ 02 40 44 68 00; fax 02 40 44 68 21; 11 rue Fourcroy; s/d €30/32; P) Hidden in a side street, this excellent-value, 19-room hotel has been run by the same family since 1978. Rooms, all soundproofed and with bathroom, are spacious, pleasant and well kept.

Hôtel St-Patrick (☎ 02 40 48 48 80; hot.saint -patrick@wanadoo.fr; 7 rue St-Nicolas; d €26, with shower €29.50, with bathroom €33.50) This friendly 24-room hotel offers simple, modern rooms and a copious buffet breakfast (€4.95). There are five floors but no lift, so you might want to ask for a room near ground level. Reception is on the 3rd floor.

Hôtel de la Bourse (☎ 02 40 69 51 55; fax 02 40 71 73 89; 19 quai de la Fosse; d €19, with shower €22, with bathroom €24) Close to the Médiathèque tram stop, this tidy one-star hotel offers one of the best deals in town.

MID-RANGE & TOP END

Hôtel Duchesse Anne (☎ 02 51 86 78 78; infos.hda@ wanadoo.fr; 3-4 place de la Duchesse Anne; d €52-63; P) This charming hotel, just east of the chateau, is great value, with elegant, spacious bedrooms and palatial bathrooms.

L'Hôtel (☎ 02 40 29 30 31; www.nanteshotel.com; 6 rue Henri IV; s/d €68/74; ✗) You have to be confident to simply call yourself 'The Hotel', and this friendly, well-maintained, 31-room hotel indeed speaks style. Most bedrooms are non-smoking. All the five attractive ground-floor rooms has a small, leafy patio.

Hôtel de France (☎ 02 40 73 57 91; fax 02 40 69 75 75; 24 rue Crébillon; d €63-102) In the heart of Nantes' main shopping area, this stunning three-star hotel occupies a venerable 18th-century mansion. Rooms with high ceilings are decorated in different period styles.

Hôtel La Pérouse (☎ 02 40 89 75 00; www.hotel -laperouse.fr; 3 allée Duquesne; s €71-92, d €85-110; P ✖) The clean lines, uncluttered furnishings and use of space in this hotel border on the breathtaking. But, although avant-garde in design, it couldn't be more traditional in its attentive service. In bedrooms and public areas, glass and mellow wood – you could almost eat the gorgeous honey-coloured parquet flooring – predominate.

Hôtel Jules Verne (☎ 02 40 35 74 50; 3 rue du Couëdic; d €74-87; P ✗ ✖) This thoroughly modern hotel, a member of the Best Western group, does a particularly fine buffet breakfast. It's well worth investing the extra for one of the top-range 'Prestige' rooms; those on the top (7th) floor have splendid views over the cathedral and city.

Eating

Several brasseries and cafés with sunny pavement terraces offer inexpensive fare on and around place du Commerce. The pedestrian streets in the old city, especially around rue de la Juiverie, rue des Petites Écuries and rue de la Bâclerie, teem with cheap, snacky places. Pizza, tapas, couscous, crepes and Asian cuisines are just some of the offerings.

Crêperie Jaune (☎ 02 40 47 15 71; 1 rue des Échevins; galettes €5.50-7.50; ☺ Mon evening-Sat) This delightful little creperie offers some of the best *galettes* in Nantes, notably the *pavé nantais* (€7.50), a filling combination of ham, cheese, eggs and mushrooms.

Chez L'Huître (☎ 02 51 82 02 02; 5 rue des Petites Écuries; mains €7-12; ☺ Mon-Sat) This tiny hole-in-the-wall restaurant is dedicated to seafood and a variety of smoked or marinated fish dishes. As the name implies, the oyster rules – the *formule apérihuître* (half a dozen oysters and a glass of Muscadet) is excellent value at €8.

Le Petit Flore (☎ 02 40 48 24 88; 1 rue des Vieilles Douves; mains €8.20-11; ☺ noon-10pm Mon-Sat) Off place Royale, this is a must for anyone into

LE PETIT BEURRE

France's best-known butter biscuit – the *petit beurre*, with its just-asking-to-be-nibbled, tooth-combed edge and characteristic rounded corners – comes from Nantes. It's the timeless creation of the LU biscuit factory, born out of an unassuming cake shop run by Monsieur Lefèvre, who married eligible young Mademoiselle Utile (hence the name).

In 1889 three tonnes of biscuits were produced daily at the **Ancienne Usine LU** on allée Baco. Less than a decade later, a workforce of more than 1000 was cooking up 15 tonnes of 200 different biscuits, using ingredients that couldn't be simpler or – if you forget the sugar – healthier: wheat flour, butter, sugar, fresh milk – and 25,000 eggs daily.

Lefèvre's son, Louis, was the real business mind. He bought a dairy to guarantee a flow of fresh milk, snapped up a forest to provide the wood for packing cases, and established the company metalwork shop to stamp out the distinctive biscuit tins. When advertising was in its infancy, he was already a master of marketing. 'To tempt the appetite, first attract the eye,' he would say. LU became famous for its innovative Art Nouveau advertising posters and hoardings (home-owners who agreed to lease a wall of their house were handsomely rewarded – in biscuits). On a more intimate scale, the designs on the tins that graced the shelves of any self-respecting French larder were created by some of the famous artists of the day. And on the firm's 50th anniversary, Louis, reluctant to miss even the smallest promotional trick, gave each of his workers a week's wages, snug inside a *petit beurre*–shaped purse.

One of the factory's fancy octagonal towers (1905–09), a beautiful example of early-20th-century eclecticism with its ornate dome and sculpted angel, still stands on the corner of allée Baco and ave Carnot (its twin was destroyed during WWII). Living on, too, is the original warehouse, topped with two squat, biscuit-box-shaped towers, and with the original, giant-sized *petit beurre* still clinging to its façade.

Nowadays the old LU factory is a lively entertainment complex, retaining the initials 'LU' (see Le Lieu Unique, p190).

healthy living. Salads and delicious sweet and savoury *tartines* (tarts) star on the menu of this charming spot. At lunch time, count on a short wait for a table.

Le Mont Liban (☎ 02 40 89 18 31; 3 rue des Vieilles Douves; mains €5-7) Next door to Le Petit Flore, this popular, authentic Lebanese spot does an astonishingly good-value lunchtime *menu* (€8). Its cuisine is delicate, lightly perfumed and worth the wait.

La Cigale (☎ 02 51 84 94 94; 4 place Graslin; breakfast special €11, lunch menu €11.50, dinner menu €23; ☺ 7.30am-12.30am; ✗) Eat here and you're dining in a classified national historic monument. The quite magnificent La Cigale, a Nantes institution, is famed for its lunches and pre- or post-theatre dinners. Waiters scurry and the interior, decorated with colourful 1890s tile-work, mirrors and painted ceilings, positively shimmers. It has a nonsmoking area.

Aux Petits Oignons (☎ 02 40 71 84 84; 2 rue Suffren; mains €11.50-16, menu €22) This delightful place dishes up hearty regional fodder. You can tuck into *tripoux* (tripe), *cuisses de gren-ouilles* (frogs' legs), *andouillette de troyes* (a big, fat offal sausage) or pan-fried *rognons de veaux* (calf kidneys).

Le Bouche à Oreille (☎ 02 40 73 00 25; 14 rue Jean-Jacques Rousseau; lunch menu €11, mains €8-15; ☺ closed lunch Sat & Sun) Plastic, pottery and even rubber pigs – there must be more than 50 of them – bedeck the bar, indicating the origin of many of the sausages and meat dishes at this traditional Lyonnais *bouchon* (bistro-style restaurant). Dine like Gargantua on the delicious *saucisse de morteau* (a meaty sausage from the Jura region in eastern France) or *quenelles* (poached pike dumplings). Or go for the best black pudding you'll ever taste, served with a veritable hillock of buttered mashed potato.

Le Bouchon (☎ 02 40 20 08 44; 7 rue Bossuet; mains €12-16; ☺ closed Sun & Mon, lunch Sat) In a half-timbered house down a cobbled lane, this restaurant has a low-beamed interior and a gorgeous flower-filled summer garden. The weekday lunchtime *menu* is great value at €13.50.

L'Océanide (☎ 02 40 20 32 28; 2 rue Paul Bellamy; menus €17.80-36) L'Océanide, all decked out in blue and white, is *the* place for seafood. Most diners opt for a seafood platter or select from the lobsters and langoustines crawling their last in the display tanks.

SELF-CATERING

The huge **Marché de Talensac** spills out from the covered market halls and along rue Talensac. On place du Bouffay there's an altogether smaller **produce market**, where Wednesday is organic food day.

Pedestrian rue Contrescarpe has some lovely little food shops. You can buy excellent cheese at **Fromagerie Pascal Beillevaire** (☎ 02 40 12 02 70; 8 rue Contrescarpe) while **La Compagnie Nantaise des Antilles** (☎ 02 40 48 24 07; 8 rue Rubens) is the place to pick up fresh ground coffee.

Chocolates to make your mouth water are exquisitely displayed amid polished wood, brass and mirrors at the old-fashioned *chocolatier* **Georges Gautier** (☎ 02 40 48 23 19; 9 rue de la Fosse). Choice wines are sold at **Le Fief de Vigne** (☎ 02 40 47 58 75; 16 rue Marceau).

Just north of place Maréchal Foch is **Noctambule Alimentation** (☎ 02 40 37 92 87; 89 rue Maréchal Joffre; ☻ 5.30pm-1am), a late-opening shop.

Drinking

There are lively pubs and cafés in the alleys around place du Bouffay in the old city. Hip young Nantais head for the bars around rue Scribe such as **Le Scribe** (☎ 02 40 69 36 13; 14 rue Scribe), while the Île Feydeau district around rue Kervégan is home to many gay bars, including **Le Petit Marais** (☎ 02 40 20 15 25; 15 rue Kervégan) and **L'Égout et les Couleurs** (☎ 02 40 20 58 58; 2 rue Kervégan).

Au Coup d'Canon (☎ 02 40 71 88 04; 12 rue Jean-Jacques Rousseau) This is one of the few remaining traditional wine bars in town. A lively, smoky den where the rough stone walls are lined with *objets trouvés*, it offers a huge selection of wines, plenty by the glass. To soak up the wine, go for their *formule* meal (€11), which changes regularly, or the platter of five different cheeses (€8.40).

Entertainment

The weekly *Nantes Poche* (€0.45) has listings of films, live music and other action, as does the monthly freebie *Pulsomatic* and the more intermittent *L'Olympic* and *Tribal*, all of them much thinner in content and distributed in bars and clubs. The tourist office publishes the free monthly *Le Mois Nantais*, with sports and culture listings.

FNAC (☎ 02 51 72 47 23; Palais de la Bourse, place du Commerce) sells tickets for cultural events. The **Maison de la Culture de Loire-Atlantique** (☎ 02 51 88 25 25; 10 Passage Pommeraye) dispenses theatre tickets and programmes.

CLUBS

Pannonica (☎ 02 51 72 10 10; www.pannonica.com; 9 rue Basse Porte) This popular basement jazz joint hosts everything from trad to electronic jazz and poetry readings. Most shows begin around 9pm; admission is from €5 to over €20, based on the band's pulling power.

Le Lieu Unique (☎ 02 40 12 14 34; 2 rue de la Biscuiterie; www.lelieuunique.com - French only). The name says it all – 'The Unique Place'. In the former LU biscuit factory (see the boxed text, p189), this animated cultural venue is a wonderful example of how to recycle a redundant industrial hulk. It has everything: a lively bar that's open until the wee hours, a club, a restaurant, a cinema, a bookshop, a theatre, a performance space and live music.

OPERA, THEATRE & MUSIC

Nantes' main theatre is the **Théâtre Graslin** (☎ 02 40 69 77 18; 1 rue Molière). The theatre is the home base of **Nantes Opéra** (☎ 02 40 69 77 18).

Espace Paul-Fort (☎ 02 51 72 10 10; 9 rue Basse Porte) is Nantes' main venue for rock concerts.

CINEMA

The art-house **Cinéma Katorza** (☎ 08 92 68 06 66; 3 rue Corneille; admission €6) screens films in their original languages.

Getting There & Away

AIR

Aéroport Nantes-Atlantique (☎ 02 40 84 80 00; www.nantes.aeroport.fr - French only) is about 12km southwest of the town centre. Flights serve several French cities and there are at least two planes a day to/from London (Gatwick).

Air France (☎ 08 20 82 08 20; 6 place Royale) has a sales office in town.

BUS

Regional buses in the Pays de la Loire are run by **Réseau Atlantic** (☎ 08 25 08 71 56), a consortium of operators. Nantes has two bus stations. Generally speaking, the one on allée de la Maison Rouge serves the region south of the Loire, while northbound buses leave from the one at 1 allée Duquesne.

Eurolines (☎ 08 92 89 90 91; www.eurolines.fr) has a particularly scruffy office at the southbound bus station. In summer there are daily direct services to/from London (€80, 14½ hours) and also (via Tours or Paris) to/from Amsterdam (€67) and Brussels (€58).

CAR & MOTORCYCLE
Budget (☎ 02 40 20 25 70), **Europcar** (☎ 02 40 47 19 38), **Hertz** (☎ 02 40 35 78 00) and others have offices outside the train station's southern entrance.

TRAIN
The **train station** (☎ 08 36 35 35 35) has two entrances: Accès Nord (northern entrance; 27 blvd de Stalingrad) and Accès Sud (southern entrance; rue de Lourmel), linked by a foot tunnel. In town, the **SNCF Boutique** (12 place de la Bourse) and the **SNCF ticketing desk** (2 allée Brancas), inside TAN's Espace Transport, both supply tickets and train information.

There are frequent trains to and from St-Nazaire (€9.20, 50 minutes) and direct services to Vannes (€16.90), Rennes (€18.50), Brest (€35.60) and Bordeaux (€37).

Getting Around
TO/FROM THE AIRPORT
The TAN-Air bus (€6, 20 minutes) links the airport with the Gare Centrale bus/tram hub and the southern entrance of the train station. Bus times correspond with flight arrivals/departures.

BICYCLE
Ville à Vélo (The Town by Bike; 1st hr free, 2nd hr €1.50, half-day €4.50, day €7.50) is a splendid cycle-hire scheme run by the municipality. Pick up a bike at one of several rental points in car parks around town, including the Gare Nord train station, Parking Talensac, near the Marché de Talensac covered market, and Parking Bretagne, beneath the Tour de Bretagne.

PUBLIC TRANSPORT
TAN (ticket €1.20, 10-trip carnet €9.60, 24hr pass €3.30) runs Nantes' urban mass transit network. The ultramodern tram system has three lines that intersect at Gare Centrale (Commerce). Most bus lines run until 8pm or 9pm, and TAN runs an hourly night service until 12.30am on all three tram lines and seven bus routes; all pass by Gare Centrale.

TAN maintains an information and ticket office, **Espace Transport** (☎ 08 10 44 44 44; 2 allée Brancas), just across the street from the Gare Centrale hub.

ST-NAZAIRE
pop 68,600
The industrial port of St-Nazaire and its shipbuilding yards are strategically located at the mouth of the Loire estuary, 55km downstream from Nantes. This was the last pocket of Europe to be liberated at the end of WWII – but not before 85% of it had been destroyed by allied blanket bombing. Completely rebuilt in the 1960s, the modern city is a rectilinear grid of dull, concrete buildings interspersed with bleak parking lots.

Originally a small community of fisherfolk and river pilots, St-Nazaire grew into a major port in the mid-19th century in order to accommodate the vastly increased human and freight traffic with the Americas. Its harbour is France's fourth largest, processing an estimated 25 million tonnes of freight annually. St-Nazaire's famous shipyards, the Chantiers de l'Atlantique, have built around 120 warships and 80 ocean liners, including the world-famous SS *Normandie* and SS *France* and – the latest wonder, a huge source of civic pride – the new Cunard liner *Queen Mary 2*, which slid down the slipway in late December 2003. At 345m long and displacing 150,000 tonnes, she's the biggest cruise liner ever built.

The city's aeronautics industry employs more than 4000 people in the manufacture and assembly of major hunks of the Airbus and the new A380, the largest passenger aircraft ever constructed. Total's primary oil refinery in France is 10km east, in Donges, on the estuary's northern bank.

Those who fancy themselves as ship's captains or captains of industry can have fun fantasising at Escal'Atlantic, devoted to the great passenger liners of the past, the WWII submarine base, the contemporary dockyards and the Airbus assembly line.

Orientation
Avenue de la République forms a north–south axis between the train station and rue du Général de Galle. The port, with its giant basins and shipyards, lies to the east of, and parallel to, ave de la République.

Information
Forum Espace Culture (☎ 02 51 76 39 39; 76 ave de la République; per hr €4; ☷ 2-7pm Mon, 10am-7pm Tue-Sat) For Internet access, pay in advance at the cash desk by the entrance to this department store.

LOIRE-ATLANTIQUE

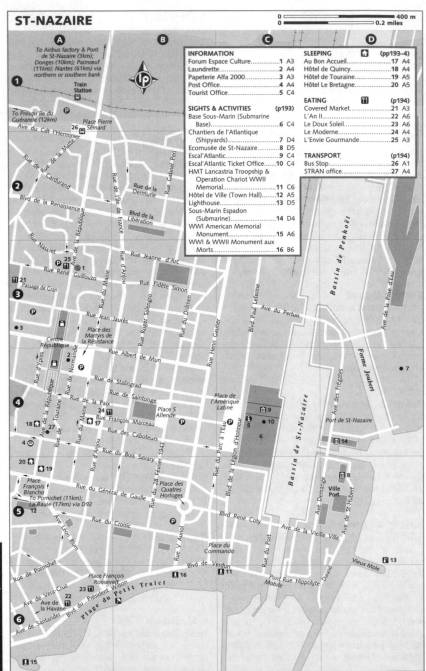

ST-NAZAIRE

0 ——————— 400 m
0 ——————— 0.2 miles

INFORMATION
Forum Espace Culture..............1 A3
Laundrette...............................2 A4
Papeterie Alfa 2000.................3 A3
Post Office...............................4 A4
Tourist Office...........................5 C4

SIGHTS & ACTIVITIES (p193)
Base Sous-Marin (Submarine
    Base)...................................6 C4
Chantiers de l'Atlantique
    (Shipyards)..........................7 D4
Ecomusée de St-Nazaire..........8 D5
Escal'Atlantic.........................9 C4
Escal'Atlantic Ticket Office......10 C4
HMT Lancastria Troopship &
    Operation Chariot WWII
    Memorial............................11 C6
Hôtel de Ville (Town Hall)........12 A5
Lighthouse.............................13 D5
Sous-Marin Espadon
    (Submarine).......................14 D4
WWI American Memorial
    Monument..........................15 A6
WWI & WWII Monument aux
    Morts.................................16 B6

SLEEPING (pp193–4)
Au Bon Accueil.......................17 A4
Hôtel de Quincy......................18 A4
Hôtel de Touraine...................19 A5
Hôtel Le Bretagne...................20 A5

EATING (p194)
Covered Market.......................21 A3
L'An II....................................22 A6
Le Doux Soleil........................23 A6
Le Moderne............................24 A4
L'Envie Gourmande.................25 A3

TRANSPORT (p194)
Bus Stop.................................26 A1
STRAN office...........................27 A4

To Airbus factory & Pont
de St-Nazaire (3km);
Donges (10km); Paimœuf
(11km); Nantes (61km) via
northern or southern bank

Train Station

To Presqu'île du
Guérande (12km)

Place Pierre Sémard
Ave du Cdt l'Herminier

Rue de la Malte

Rue de Cardurand

Blvd de la Renaissance

Rue Nassiet

Ave de la République

Rue de l'Île de France

Rue de la Dermurie

Rue Gabriel Petit

Blvd de la Libération

Rue René Guillouzo

Passage de Gran

Rue d'Anjou

Rue Jeanne d'Arc

Rue Fidète Simon

Rue du Maine

Rue Jean Jaurès

Place des Martyrs de la Résistance

Centre République

Rue d'Ypres

Rue Roger Salengro

Rue du Dolmen

Rue Albert de Mun

Rue de Normandie

Rue de Stalingrad

Rue de Saintonge

Rue de la Paix

Rue François Marceau

Place S Allende

Rue des Caboteurs

Rue du Bois Savary

Rue de Touraine

Ave de la République

Rue du 28 Février 1943

Place des Quatres Horloges

Place François Blancho

To Pornichet (11km);
La Baule (17km) via D92

Rue du Général de Gaulle

Ave Léon Blum

Rue du Croisic

Blvd René Coty

Place du Commando

Rue V Auriol

Blvd de Verdun

Place François Roosevelt

Rue de Pornichet

Ave de Vera Cruz

Ave de la Havane

Blvd du Président Wilson

Ave de Santander

Plage du Petit Traict

Bassin de Penhoët

Ave de la Prise d'Eau

Blvd Paul Leferme

Ave du Pertuis

Rue Henri Gautier

Forme Joubert

Place de l'Amérique Latine

Rue du Parc à l'Eau

Blvd de la Légion d'Honneur

Bassin de St-Nazaire

Ave des Frégates

Port de St-Nazaire

Ave Demange

Ville Port

Ave de St-Hubert

Ave de la Vieille Ville

Pont Rue Hippolyte Mobile

Rue du Pont

Durand

Vieux Mole

Laundrette (place des Martyrs de la Résistance; ☺ 8am-7.30pm Mon-Sat, 9am-1pm Sun)
Main Post Office (11 ave de la République)
Papeterie Alfa 2000 (90 rue Albert de Mun) For regional maps and guidebooks.
Tourist Office (☎ 08 20 01 40 15; www.saint-nazaire -tourisme.com; blvd de la Légion d'Honneur; ☺ 9am-7pm daily Jul-Aug, 9am-12.30pm & 1.30-6pm daily Apr-Jun & Sep-Oct, 9.30am-12.30pm & 2-5.30pm Tue-Sun Feb-Mar & Nov-Dec) Within one of the old WWII submarine pens.

Sights

The **Escal'Atlantic ticket office** (☎ 08 10 88 84 44; blvd de la Légion d'Honneur; ☺ 9.30am-12.30pm & 1.30-5.30pm daily Apr-Oct, 10am-12.30pm & 2-6pm Wed-Sun Nov-Dec & Feb-Mar), beside the tourist office, is the sole point for admission tickets to the Escal'Atlantic exhibition itself, Base Sous-Marin, Chantiers de l'Atlantiques, the Airbus factory and Écomusée de St-Nazaire.

BASE SOUS-MARIN (SUBMARINE BASE)

During the Battle of the Atlantic in 1940–42, when packs of U-boats prowled the North Atlantic hunting down convoys of Allied ships carrying vital supplies from America to Britain, the Germans built their main **submarine base** at St-Nazaire. The massive U-boat pens, with bomb-proof walls and roofs of reinforced concrete several metres thick, lie on the western side of the harbour. You can wander freely around most of the pens and climb onto the **roof** (☺ 10am-sunset) via the stairs or lift near the tourist office for a spectacular view over the harbour and the shipbuilding yards. Up there, too, is a fascinating photographic display of the docks before they were supplanted by the submarine base and of the effects of allied bombing.

Two adjacent pens have been converted into **Escal'Atlantic** (☎ 08 10 88 84 44; www.escal -atlantic.com; adult/child high season €13/10, low season €10.50/8.50; ☺ 9.30am-7.30pm daily Jul & Aug, 9.30am-12.30pm & 1.30-6pm Apr-Jun & Sep-Oct, 10am-12.30pm & 2-6pm Wed-Sun Nov-Dec & Feb-Mar, closed Jan), a multimedia exhibition dedicated to the history of *paquebots* (ocean liners).

VILLE-PORT

On the opposite side of the harbour basin from the submarine base, **Ville-Port** is a redeveloped area. In July and August a free *navette* (shuttle boat) crosses to the main attraction here, the **Écomusée de St-Nazaire** (☎ 02 40 22 35 33; www.ecomusee-saint-nazaire.com; ave de St-Hubert;

admission free; ☺ as for Escal'Atlantic). This museum charts the history of the town's shipbuilding and aerospace industries.

More interesting is the nearby **Sous-Marin Espadon** (www.sousmarin-espadon.com; adult/child high season €7.60/6.10, low season €5.30/3.80; ☺ as for Escal' Atlantic). The 78m-long submarine *Espadon* (Swordfish) was built for the French navy in 1958 and decommissioned in 1986. It's berthed in the fortified lock between the harbour basin and the river – the concrete roof was designed to protect U-boats from Allied bombs while passing through the lock. The visit takes in the torpedo room, the claustrophobic crew accommodation and the instrument-cluttered control room. Admission includes an audioguide in English.

Just east of the submarine is the **Forme Joubert**, 350m long, 50m wide and one of the largest dry docks in the world.

OTHER SIGHTS

Escal'Atlantic arranges visits to the **Airbus factory** (www.visite-airbus.com; adult/child high season €10/7.60, low season €7.60/6), in the suburb of Gron near the Pont de St-Nazaire. Here the Airbus and significant hunks of the A380 are constructed. Two-hour tours leave by bus from the Escal'Atlantic office. **Chantiers de l'Atlantique** (adult/child €15/10) is the shipyards. There are guided visits between February and December, also arranged through Escal'Atlantic. Phone for current opening hours and advance reservations for both – which are essential.

It's pleasant to wander along the sea front to the south and west of Ville-Port, past the **lighthouse** on the Vieux Môle (Old Jetty), the **Pont Mobile** (Swing Bridge) and several **monuments**. Around ave de Santander and ave de la Havane there are a few surviving pre-WWII buildings with wooden façades and wrought-iron balconies. Ever-present on the horizon is the graceful, 3.3km-long **pont de St-Nazaire** (1975), the suspension bridge that carries the coastal road across the Loire.

Sleeping

Hôtel de Touraine (☎ 02 40 22 47 56; hoteltouraine@ free.fr; 4 ave de la République; d €36-38). This friendly, family-run, one-star hotel is a block north of the town hall. In summer, you can breakfast in the attractive garden.

Hôtel Le Bretagne (☎ 02 51 76 30 00; www.hotel-le -bretagne.com - French only; 7 ave de la République; d with shower €32, with bathroom €45) The attractive Le Bretagne, like its near neighbour, Hôtel de Touraine, is right in the heart of the city, convenient for both beach and tourist sights.

Hôtel de Quincy (☎ 02 40 66 70 82; fax 02 40 22 04 30; 15 ave de la République; d with shower €38, with bathroom €43) The two-star Hôtel de Quincy, with its 23 comfortable rooms and decent restaurant beneath, is another good mid-range choice.

Au Bon Accueil (☎ 02 40 22 07 05; au-bon-accueil44@wanadoo.fr; 39 rue Marceau; d €68.60-73.20; P) This three-star Logis de France, one of the few buildings near the docks to have survived the WWII bombardment, is solid and comfortable, its 12 rooms recently renovated. In a quiet street, it's only a 500m walk from the action around the Base Sous-Marin. Head back in time for dinner (see Eating below).

Eating

L'An II (☎ 02 40 00 95 33; 2 rue Villebois Mareuil; menus €20-39) This restaurant is among the best places in town for seafood. Its speciality – which you need to order in advance – is *godaille de St-Nazaire* (€29 for two), a hearty fish soup-cum-stew with potatoes and vegetables, rather like a northern version of bouillabaisse. Rare for France, its wine list does more than acknowledge wines from the rest of the world. Trust the fish of the day, *cuisiné suivant l'humeur du chef* (cooked according to the chef's mood).

Le Moderne (☎ 02 40 22 55 88; 46 rue d'Anjou; menus €15.50-27; 🕙 closed Mon, dinner Sun & Wed) This small, exclusive place, popular with business people, serves traditional regional dishes including *choucroute de mer* (seafood with sauerkraut).

Le Doux Soleil (☎ 02 40 70 30 20; 31 blvd du Président Wilson; menu €8.50, galettes €6.70-7.50; 🕙 closed Tue evening & Wed Sep-May) Near L'An II, this welcoming, airy place serves a good selection of savoury *galettes* and sweet crepes.

The much-garlanded restaurant of **Au Bon Accueil** (☎ 02 40 22 07 05; au-bon-accueil44@wanadoo.fr; 39 rue Marceau; menus €20-38; 🕙 closed Sun evening) serves excellent fare in its period dining room. Catching the flavour of the moment, and more contemporary, is its top-of-the-line(r), gourmet *menu Queen Mary 2*.

L'Envie Gourmande (85 ave de la République) sells fine regional wines, gourmet food and chocolate to make you melt.

The **covered market** (place du Commerce; 🕙 6am-3pm Tue, Fri & Sat) sells fresh and fishy produce.

Getting There & Away
BUS
West of St-Nazaire, the Presqu'île du Guérande is well served by **Réseau Atlantic** (☎ 08 25 08 71 56) buses, which operate from the bus stop in front of the train station. Bus No 81 runs about hourly from St-Nazaire to La Baule (€3, 30 minutes), Batz-sur-Mer (€4, 55 minutes) and Le Croisic (€4, one hour). Bus No 80 runs to Guérande (€3, 35 minutes).

TRAIN
From St-Nazaire, trains head along the coast to Le Croisic (€4.90, 30 minutes, 10 or more daily), mostly stopping en route at Pornichet, La Baule, Le Pouliguen and Batz-sur-Mer. Eastbound, there are frequent trains to/from Nantes (€9.20, 50 minutes).

Getting Around
STRAN (tickets €1, 10-trip carnet €8.60) runs the urban bus services. It has an **information office** (☎ 02 40 00 75 75; 18 ave de la République). For a **taxi**, call ☎ 02 40 66 02 62.

PARC NATUREL RÉGIONAL DE BRIÈRE
The Parc Naturel Régional de Brière embraces an area of 400 sq km north of St-Nazaire. At the core of this wetland is the **Grande Brière**, a 7000-hectare marsh of reed beds, water meadows and ponds by the dozen. Since 1471 it has belonged to the local inhabitants, who, over the centuries, have learned how to farm this harsh environment, through which the GR3 and GR39 hiking trails thread.

The park is crisscrossed by 120km of canals that every so often splay out into abandoned peat-digging sites, now small lakes. Peat was traditionally cut in July, when water levels were at their lowest, then left to dry until winter, when it would be burned as fuel. Reeds, rich in wildlife, cover around 50% of the park. Some are harvested as roofing material for the traditional thatched cottages, of which around 3000 still remain.

Information
The **Maison du Tourisme de Brière** (☎ 02 40 66 85 01; 38 rue de le Brière; 🕙 10am-12.30pm & 2.30-6.30pm daily Jun-Sep, 10am-12.30pm & 2-6pm Mon-Sat Oct-May) is in the village of La Chapelle-des-Marais on the park's northern edge.

IGN's 1:25,000 map *Parc Naturel Régional de Brière* (Sheet 1022ET) is vital for anyone intent on exploring the park in depth.

Sights & Activities

The park has three small **museums** (◔ 10.30am-1pm & 2.30-6.30pm Apr & Jun-Sep, 2-5pm Oct-Mar & May).

In the picturesque village of Île de Fédrun, near the Maison du Parc, is **La Maison de la Mariée** (The Bride's House; ☎ 02 40 66 85 01; 130 Île de Fédrun; adult/child €3/2), a museum that illustrates the Brièron tradition of making bridal headdresses from orange blossom.

A few kilometres south of St-Joachim, in the village of Rozé, is the **Maison de l'Éclusier** (Lock Keeper's House; ☎ 02 40 91 17 80; adult/child €3/2), which explains the ecology and hydrology of the marshes of the park. Next to the museum, a botanical trail leads across reed beds and meadows.

On the western side of the park is the remarkable conservation village of **Kerhinet**. This pedestrian-only hamlet has 18 thatched cottages, one of which houses the **Musée du Chaume** (Museum of Thatching; ☎ 02 40 66 85 01; adult/child €3/1.50). Others contain arts and crafts workshops.

Don't miss the opportunity to take a **promenade en chaland** – an outing through the reed beds in a traditional wooden punt. The main embarkation points are at Île de Fédrun and Bréca, 3km east of Kerhinet. A 1½-hour trip for one to three people costs around €25.

The **Tour de la Brière** is a marked hiking trail that makes a circuit of the marshes; a complete tour takes around three days. The trail crosses the road just north of Rozé.

Sleeping & Eating

The Maison du Tourisme de Brière (p194) has lists of *chambres d'hôtes* (B&Bs) and *gîtes* (holiday cottages) in the park.

Auberge de Kerhinet (☎ 02 40 61 91 46; fax 02 40 61 97 57; Kerhinet; d €50, menus €21-38; ◔ mid-Jan–mid-Dec) Within this incredibly picturesque thatched cottage are a handful of cosy little rooms and a delightfully rustic restaurant.

Auberge de Bréca (☎ 02 40 91 41 42; menus €22-45; ◔ closed Sun evening & Thu Sep-Jun) This is another lovely thatched building on the very edge of the marshes, with a restaurant serving traditional local fare that includes eel, partridge and frogs' legs.

Getting There & Away

STRAN Ty'Bus (☎ 02 40 00 75 75) runs buses from St-Nazaire to La Chapelle-des-Marais via Rozé and St Joachim from Monday to Saturday.

PRESQU'ÎLE DE GUÉRANDE

The Guérande Peninsula, a fist of land that thrusts into the Atlantic northwest of St-Nazaire, presents a contrasting landscape of salt marshes and sandy beaches. In summer a carpet of poppy-red to bright-green *salicornes*, an aquatic plant that is pickled and eaten, covers many of the saltpans, while bathers flock to the beaches at La Baule to dip their toes into its sparkling blue waters.

Cliffs and dunes sweep west towards Le Croisic, an old fishing settlement marooned on Pointe du Croisic, the peninsula's southwesternmost point.

GUÉRANDE

pop 14,300

Guérande, a fortified medieval town walled in by 14th-century ramparts, is where most of the peninsula's *paludiers* (saltpan workers) live. Over a weekend in mid-May Guérande regresses by several hundred years to celebrate its **Fête Mediévale**. The populace dons medieval costumes, stalls are erected within and around the ramparts and, at night, there's a spectacular sound-and-light show.

Information

The **tourist office** (☎ 02 40 24 96 71; www.ot-guerande .fr - French only; place du Marché du Bois; ◔ 9.30am-7pm Mon-Sat Jul-Aug, 9.30am-12.30pm & 1.30-6pm Mon-Sat Sep-Jun, 10am-1pm Sun mid-Jun–mid-Sep) is just north of Porte St-Michel, the main entrance to the walled town. In July and August it runs daily guided tours (in French; adult/child €5.30/2.50) of the old town and ramparts.

Walking Tour

The well-preserved ramparts and towers apart, there's not a lot to see in Guérande, but it's a pleasant place to wander around for a while. Enter the old town through the 15th-century **Porte St-Michel**, which houses the **Musée du Château de Guérande** (☎ 02 40 42 96 52; rue St Michel; adult/child/student €3.50/1.70/2.50; ◔ 10am-12.30pm & 2.30-7pm daily Jun-Sep, 10am-noon & 2-6pm daily except Mon am Apr-May & Oct). The displays concentrate on the salt-making industry and the traditional costume of the region. From the top floor you can walk along the medieval ramparts.

LES MARAIS SALANTS

The shallow bay between Guérande and Le Croisic is a 2000-hectare patchwork of *marais salants* (saltpans), the most northerly still to be worked in Europe. Sea salt, harvested here for around 1000 years, is still collected today by teams of *paludiers* (saltpan workers). *Sel de Guérande* is a much sought-after culinary ingredient that features on many a Breton restaurant menu. *Fleur de sel* (flowers of salt) – the delicate crystals raked by hand from the surface of the saltpans – is considered the highest quality.

Two exhibitions near Guérande explain the history and technology of salt-harvesting **Terre de Sel** (☎ 02 40 62 08 80; Pradel; adult/child €3.15/1.95; 9.30am-12.30pm & 2.30-7pm Jul & Aug, 10.30am-12.30pm & 2.30-6pm Apr-Jun & Sep), 2km west of Guérande, and **La Maison des Paludiers** (☎ 02 40 62 21 96; 18 rue des Prés Garnier, Saillé; adult/child €3.50/2.40; 10am-12.30pm & 2-5pm year-round), 4km south of Guérande.

From the museum, stroll along rue St Michel to the **Collégiale St-Aubin** (9am-noon & 2-6pm), in the heart of the walled town. This 15th-century church has an unusual exterior pulpit and is famous for its summer organ recitals (admission free; 9pm Friday July and August).

A left turn at the church leads down rue de Saillé to the **Musée de la Poupée** (Doll Museum; ☎ 02 40 15 69 13; 23 rue de Saillé; adult/child €3.50/2; 10.30am-12.30pm & 2.30-6.30pm daily May-Nov, 2-6pm Tue-Sun Dec & Feb-Apr), with a collection of around 300 dolls and other toys dating from 1830 to 1930. Exit through the Porte de Saillé at the end of the street and turn left to return to Porte St Michel.

Sleeping & Eating

Camping Le Pré du Château de Careil (☎ 02 40 60 22 99; chateau.careil@free.fr; Château de Careil; 2 adults, tent & car €18-21; May-Sep) Some 4km south of Guérande on the road to La Baule, this four-star camping ground occupies the grounds of a 14th-century castle.

Hôtel-Restaurant des Remparts (☎ 02 40 24 90 69; fax 02 40 62 17 99; 14-15 blvd du Nord; d €46, half-board required Jul-Aug; year-round, closed Sun evening Sep-Jun) No more than 50m from the tourist office – and indeed overlooking the ramparts –

this hotel with eight unexceptional rooms represents good value. Rather more exciting and equally reliable is its excellent **restaurant** (menus €16-26; Tue-Sun Apr-Sep, lunch only Oct-Mar).

Hôtel-Crêperie Roc-Maria (☎ 02 40 24 90 51; fax 02 40 62 13 03; 1 rue des Halles; d €54-57, galettes €3-7, menu €9.80) Just off rue de Saillé, this fine old granite house with timber beams is a family-run hotel and creperie. Try the *galette gourmande*, filled with black pudding and braised apples and doused with flaming Calvados.

Getting There & Away

Réseau Atlantic (☎ 08 25 08 71 56) buses link Guérande with St-Nazaire, La Baule and Le Croisic (change at Le Pouliguen). The main bus stop is on place de l'Europe.

LA BAULE

pop 16,400

La Baule, one of the most glamorous resorts on France's Atlantic coast, dates from 1879 and the height of *la belle époque*. It is best known for its vast golden beach, sheltered to the north by pine forests, planted in 1840 to stabilise the shifting sand dunes. Luxury hotels, a casino, surf shops and lively restaurant terraces line the promenade that hugs the beach.

Orientation & Information

South-facing La Baule sprawls for 3km along the Baie de Pouliguen, merging into the neighbouring resorts of Pornichet to the east and Le Pouliguen to the west. Crowded ave Général de Gaulle (if ever a street cried out to be pedestrianised...) links the promenade to place de la Victoire and the tourist office, 500m north of the sea front.

Cyberbaule (☎ 02 40 60 21 28; 136 ave Général de Gaulle; per hr €4.50; 10am-9pm Mon-Wed, 10am-midnight Thu-Sat, 10am-1pm & 3-6pm Sun) Internet access.

Tourist Office (☎ 02 40 24 34 44; www.labaule.fr; place de la Victoire; 9.30am-7.30pm daily Jul-Aug, 9.15am-12.30pm & 2-6pm Mon-Sat, 10am-1pm & 2.30pm-5pm Sun Sep-Jun) Opposite the bus station.

Sights & Activities

The sweeping, golden **beach** extends over 500m offshore at low tide. There are several places along the sea front where you can hire sailing dinghies, windsurfers, kayaks and catamarans, with or without instruction.

Tired of the beach? Stroll the quiet lanes around the town hall (west of ave Général de Gaulle) and grand old **villas** and holiday homes, many from the 19th and early 20th centuries. Styles range from rustic cottage to country manor to Art Nouveau palace.

Ave Général de Gaulle and the **promenade** are lined with chic shops, cafés and restaurants – prime people-watching territory.

Sleeping & Eating
La Baule is not a cheap place to stay and in the high season (July and August), accommodation can be difficult to find.

Camping Les Ajoncs d'Or (☎ 02 40 60 33 29; www .ajoncs.com; chemin du Rocher; 2 adults, tent & car €13.50-18; ☺ Apr-Sep) None of La Baule's camping grounds is close to the beach. This attractive, pine-shaded site is about 600m northeast of the train station.

Hôtel Le Coralli (☎ 02 40 60 29 82; fax 02 40 60 82 26; 2 ave Pierre 1er de Serbie; d with shower €35, with bathroom €38-44) This small, intimate hotel, right across the street from the train station, has only eight rooms and is excellent value.

Hôtel des Dunes (☎ 02 51 75 07 10; www.hotel -des-dunes.com; 277 ave Lattre de Tassigny; d with shower €40, with bathroom €47-51) Some of the rooms are a bit on the small side, but all are comfortable and homely and the welcome's friendly. The Dunes is a few minutes' walk west from the tourist office and about 10 minutes from the beach.

Hôtel La Palmeraie (☎ 02 40 60 24 41; www.hotel -lapalmeraie-labaule.com - French only; 7 ave des Cormorans; d €73.50-110; ☺ Apr-Sep) La Palmeraie is a delightful, old-style hotel set around a palm-shaded garden, only a short haul from the beach.

Hôtel Hermitage Barrière (☎ 02 40 11 46 46; www .lucienbarriere.com; 5 esplanade Lucien Barrière; d €189-270, with sea view €260-461) This vast, white, Normandy-style villa hulks above the beach just west of the casino and is La Baule's most prestigious pad. Facilities include a pool, thalassotherapy, tennis and a sailing school.

Crêperie la Bôle (☎ 02 40 60 19 73; 36 ave Général de Gaulle; salads €7.50-9, galettes €6.50-8; ☺ closed Tue-Wed except Jul & Aug) This bustling pancake house's *menu* (€10.90), offering a couple of galettes, a crepe dessert and a *bolée* (bowl) of cider, makes a tasty meal.

La Croisette (☎ 02 40 60 73 00; 31 place Maréchal Leclerc; salads from €10, carpaccios from €12) This is a delightful brasserie with wooden decking where your *carpaccio* is garnished with one of 13 marinades, whipped up before your eyes.

Getting There & Around
La Baule is linked to St-Nazaire (17km west) by train (€3.30, 20 minutes) and bus (€3, 30 minutes). The **bus station** (☎ 02 40 11 53 00; place de la Victoire) is opposite the tourist office; the train station (La Baule-Escoublac) is 200m to the northeast, off ave Georges Clemenceau.

In summer a *petit train* shuttles back and forth along the promenade between the casino and Le Pornichet.

Location Chaillou (☎ 02 40 60 07 06; 3 place de la Victoire; ☺ daily Easter-Sep, Tue-Sat Oct-Easter), across the square from the tourist office, rents out bikes (from €7 per day). To be really cool, glide the prom on a pair of rollerblades (€7 per hour). To really, really make heads turn, sashay along with your chosen one on a tandem (€14 per day).

LE CROISIC
pop 4300
Le Croisic, 10km west of La Baule, is an active fishing port, marina and seaside resort, at the end of the narrow peninsula that guards the southern edge of the Guérande saltpans.

Orientation & Information
The harbour and old town are on the northern edge of the peninsula, just inside the narrow entrance to the bay. The train station is just east of the harbour.

The **tourist office** (☎ 02 40 23 00 70; www.ot -lecroisic.com; place du 18 Juin 1940; ☺ 9am-1pm & 2-7pm Mon-Sat, 10am-1pm & 3-5pm Sun May-Sep, 9am-12.30pm & 2-6.30pm Tue-Sat Oct-Apr) is in a little cottage to the right as you exit the train station.

Sights & Activities
Activity centres on the harbour, where a fleet of around 50 fishing boats lands its catches of shrimp, langoustine, crab, scallop, sea bass and many other species. The 19th-century **Ancienne Criée** (Old Auction Room), where freshly landed fish was once sold, dominates the waterfront, while inland the old town's streets are dotted with charming **half-timbered houses**; you can see some lovely examples on place de l'Église, place du Pilori and rue St-Christophe.

The western end of the harbour is overlooked by **Mont Lénigo**, a landscaped hillock created by ships dumping their stone ballast; **Mont Esprit** is its counterpart at the eastern end. Paths lead to both summits, from where you can enjoy good views over the **Grand**

DETOUR: THE CROISIC PENINSULA

Most drivers take the N171 from **La Baule** to **Le Croisic**. But for consistently fine views, build in an extra half-hour (including some stopping time) to loop around the stubby peninsula along the D45. Little travelled, except in high summer, and ideal for cyclists, this minor road hugs the coast all the way to Le Croisic. The seascape from Pointe du Croisic across to the cluster of rocky islets known collectively as **La Calebasse** is stunning – all the more so if you time your tour at sunset.

Traict – the bay to the north, which reveals a vast expanse of sandbanks at low tide – and the 850m-long jetty and lighthouse (1872).

The town's main tourist sight is the **Océarium** (☎ 02 40 23 02 44; ave de St-Goustan; adult/child €10/7; ☺ 10am-7pm Jun-Aug, 10am-noon & 2-6pm Sep-Dec & Feb-May), a marine aquarium with 45 tanks, an underwater tunnel and a strong but never overly didactic educational slant.

In July and August **Le Port Liberté** (☎ 06 68 64 65 42) sets out on boat trips and sea-fishing excursions from quai du Lénigo. The tourist office sells tickets for a 1¼-hour trip along the coast (€10), day trips to the offshore islands (€25 to €32) and half-day fishing trips (€32).

There are a dozen pleasant, sandy **beaches** between rocky cliffs along the southern and western shores of the peninsula, from Port Lin around to St Goustan, all within 20 to 30 minutes' walk from the town centre.

The coast road along the rim of the peninsula west from Le Croisic makes a wonderful circuit by car, even better by bike – and at its very best as the sun sets over the bay.

Sleeping & Eating

Le Croisic gets very busy at weekends and in July and August.

Camping de l'Océan (☎ 02 40 23 07 69; www.camping -ocean.com; route de la Maison Rouge; up to 3 adults & site €13-30 according to season; ☒) Of the four camping grounds on the peninsula, this fancy three-star option, near Plage St Goustan, has shady pitches, a pool and water slides.

Hôtel-Bar Le Paris (☎ 02 40 23 15 19; 66 rue du Traict; d €28-35) All rooms above this small, popular bar opposite the train station have full bathroom and represent excellent budget value.

Hôtel Le Castel Moor (☎ 02 40 23 24 18; www.castel -moor.com; Baie du Castouillet; d €49-71; ☺ Feb-Dec; P))

The Castel Moor is a lovely modern villa set in a trim garden about 1.5km west of the town centre. Most of its 19 rooms overlook the sea, and its restaurant is a great place for seafood. Half board (from €78/107 for one/two) is compulsory in July and August.

Hôtel Fort de L'Océan (☎ 02 40 15 77 77; www.fort -ocean.com - French only; Pointe du Croisic; d €138-244) This four-square granite villa stands in splendid isolation on a rocky promontory at the western extremity of the peninsula, surrounded by 17th-century fortifications. Its eight rooms are elegant and luxurious, there's an outdoor pool, and the **restaurant** (menus €32-58) is just as special as the hotel.

The quays alongside the port are lined with brasseries where you can enjoy oysters, eat bowlfuls of *bouillabaisse bretonne* (a local fish soup-cum-stew), or indulge in the local speciality, *bar au sel de guérande* (sea bass baked in a crust of Guérande salt).

Getting There & Around

Le Croisic is at the end of the train line from St-Nazaire (€4.90, 30 minutes); the last stretch of the line from Batz-sur-Mer cuts straight through saltpans and is especially picturesque. There are some direct trains between Nantes and Le Croisic (€12.30, 1½ hours, five or more daily) and more frequent options if you change in St-Nazaire.

For details of buses, see p194. Hire bicycles at **Garage Moderne** (☎ 02 40 62 92 81; 34 rue du Trait), 100m from the tourist office and station.

BATZ-SUR-MER
pop 3130

Batz-sur-Mer, 4km east of Le Croisic, is an attractive little place, squeezed between saltpans to the north and the ocean to the south. The 57m-high, 14th-century belfry of **Église St-Guénolé** towers over the ruins of the 15th-century **Chapelle du Mûrier**, devastated by a hurricane in 1820. A few hundred metres south of the church is the pleasant sandy beach of **Plage St-Michel**.

On the main road, 200m northeast of the church, is the **Musée des Marais Salants** (Saltpan Museum; ☎ 02 40 23 82 79; 29 bis rue Pasteur; adult/child €4/3; ☺ 10am-12.30pm & 2.30-6.30pm Jul-Sep, core hours 10am-noon & 2-5pm daily Jun, Oct & Nov, Sat & Sun Dec-May), providing a fascinating insight into the culture and technology of the salt marshes.

Batz-sur-Mer is on the bus and rail route from St-Nazaire and La Baule to Le Croisic.

Normandy

SEINE-MARITIME

Seine-Maritime

CONTENTS

Rouen	202
Around Rouen	215
Pays de Bray	**218**
Neufchâtel-en-Bray	218
Forges-les-Eaux	219
Côte d'Albâtre	**220**
Le Havre	220
Around Le Havre	224
Dieppe	224
Varengeville-sur-Mer	230
Le Tréport	230
Fécamp	231
Around Fécamp	233
Étretat	234

To visit the Seine-Maritime *département* is to taste a little of everything that Normandy has to offer. From the fascinating city of Rouen, the River Seine winds sinuously along a valley dotted with ancient abbeys. The modern, almost futuristic, port of Le Havre stands sentinel over the Seine estuary on the Channel. As the coast curves north from Le Havre, fishing villages and rocky beaches cower under the white cliffs of the Côte d'Albâtre (Alabaster Coast). The coastal centres of Étretat, Fécamp and Dieppe supply Paris with seafood, while the national capital supplies them with a stream of seasonal and weekend visitors. A web of rivers laces the interior, watering the pastures that rise into forested hills and dip into lush valleys.

There's hours of good walking and cycling along the coast and through the interior, especially in the Forêt d'Eawy. From Gothic churches to the fine arts museums of Rouen and Le Havre, there are ample reminders of the region's rich cultural heritage that so inspired Normandy's luminaries and artists. Here you'll find the towering Romanesque abbeys that made Normandy a medieval religious centre and the milk, cream, butter, cheese and fish that define Norman cuisine. Except for the deep interior, transportation connections allow you to see a good part of the department by public transport, whether you enter it by boat from the UK or by train from Paris.

HIGHLIGHTS

- See the **cathedral** (p204) Monet loved in Rouen and his paintings in the **Musée des Beaux-Arts** (p209)

- Follow the Seine west of Rouen taking in **La Bouille** (p216) and the **abbeys** (p216) of St-Georges de Boscherville, Jumièges and St-Wandrille

- Tackle a plate of **fresh seafood** in Dieppe (p223); dig in to a **duck dish** in Rouen (p211)

- Stroll in the Bois des Moutiers park in **Varengeville-sur-Mer** (p230)

- Watch the sunset from the cliffs of **Étretat** (p234)

- POPULATION: 1,2400,000
- AREA: 6728 SQ KM

SEINE-MARITIME

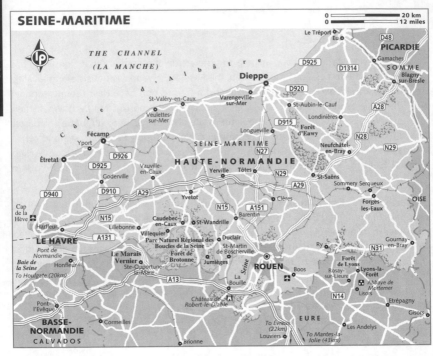

SEINE-MARITIME

ROUEN

pop 108,750

Half-timbered houses, craggy churches and lofty spires make the medieval centre of Rouen one of the most delightful in France. As the capital of Upper Normandy and the Seine-Maritime *département*, Rouen also has the political and economic muscle to support a thriving cultural scene, excellent restaurants, quirky bars and fashionable shops. Sprawled along the banks of the Seine 113km northwest of Paris, Rouen was badly damaged during the D-Day bombing campaigns but, with characteristic resilience, moved decisively to restore its most famous monuments and rebuild the ancient centre. The old city has around 2000 half-timbered houses, many with rough-hewn beams, posts and diagonals leaning this way and that. Some scars have not healed however. The rebuilt river banks are dreary and the part of the city that lies south of the Seine is a wasteland of tangled roads and haphazard development.

Fortunately, it's easy for a visitor to stay in the compact medieval centre. A wealth of sights recalls the history of a city that swung from Gothic glories to Joan of Arc's tragic martyrdom, and that produced Gustav Flaubert, Robert La Salle and nourished the genius of Claude Monet. With transportation links that stretch through all of Upper Normandy, Rouen is an excellent base for exploring the region.

History

Rouen is one of the oldest towns in Normandy, originating around the time of the Roman conquest in 50 BC. St Mellon Christianised the town in the 3rd century but little is known about Rouen until the 9th century, when the Vikings arrived in a looting frenzy and pillaged the town repeatedly for 50 years. The great Viking leader Rollo was baptised here. He made Rouen his capital and it became an important religious, political and administrative centre. The city expanded in importance and gained a substantial degree of autonomy under King Henry II of England until the French king, Philippe-Auguste, seized it in 1204 as the culmination of his conquest of Normandy. Once again, the city flourished, erecting its great cathedral with money earned from its flourishing textile business and its bustling port.

The 14th century saw a trio of troubles: famine, plague and the Hundred Years' War. Rouen fell into the hands of the English in 1419 and was, infamously, the place where Joan of Arc was tried, convicted and burned at the stake in 1431. The end of the Hundred Years' War in 1453 allowed the city to rebuild and resume its commercial activities. The 16th-century Renaissance brought a flurry of magnificent new construction, much of which still survives. The city reached a plateau in the latter half of the 17th century, but expanded again in the 19th century when the southern bank of the Seine was developed for manufacturing.

German troops set fire to the city in 1940 as part of their advance into France and the Allies bombed it ferociously in 1944, but as the city was rebuilt its infrastructure was improved and modernised.

Orientation

Rouen is a city with a dual character. Bisected by the Seine, the city is divided into the Rive Droite (right bank) on the northern bank and the Rive Gauche (left bank) south of the river. The Rive Droite is the oldest part of the city and contains almost all the churches, museums, hotels and restaurants. The main thoroughfare is rue Jeanne d'Arc, which runs from the main Right Bank train station (Gare Rouen-Rive Droite) south to the bank of the Seine. The old city is centred around rue du Gros Horloge between place du Vieux Marché and the cathedral. A long promenade filled with skaters, strollers and cyclists runs along much of the Seine's right bank. Rive Gauche is primarily commercial, residential and industrial but has a shopping centre at St-Sever and a giant conference centre further south. All buses depart from the bus station along quai du Havre and quai de la Bourse. The train station on the left bank (Gare St-Sever) mainly serves regional trains.

Information

BOOKSHOPS

ABC Bookshop (☎ 02 35 71 08 67; 11 rue des Faulx; ⊗ 10am-6pm Tue-Sat) English-language books.
L'Armitiere (☎ 02 35 70 57 42; 5 rue des Basnage) The local literary hang-out.

Arts Diffusion Loisirs (☎ 02 32 08 67 29; 31 rue du Bac) Has a good selection of books and magazines on Normandy.

INTERNET ACCESS

PlaceNet (☎ 02 32 76 02 22, 37 rue de la République; €1/15min; ⊗ 10am-midnight)

INTERNET RESOURCES

www.mairie-rouen.fr The town's website (French only).

LAUNDRY

Laundrette (47 rue d'Amiens)
Laundrette (55 rue d'Amiens)
Laundrette (75 rue Beauvoisine)

MEDICAL SERVICES

SOS Médicins (☎ 08 10 63 59 10) Will send a doctor to your hotel if necessary.
Hôpital Charles Nicolle (☎ 02 35 88 89 90; 1 rue de Germont) For emergency medical treatment.

MONEY

Banks line rue Jeanne d'Arc between the Théâtre des Arts and place Maréchal Foch, in front of the Palais de Justice. There are numerous ATMs, including one in the Right Bank train station.
Bureau de Change (7-9 rue des Bonnetiers; ⊗ 7am-10pm) Has decent exchange rates, long opening hours and no commission.
American Express (☎ 02 35 89 48 60; 25 place de la Cathédrale; ⊗ 9am-1pm & 2-6pm Mon-Sat) In the tourist office.

POST

Main Post Office (45 rue Jeanne d'Arc) It has a Cyberposte terminal.

TOURIST INFORMATION

Tourist Office (☎ 02 32 08 32 40; www.rouen tourisme.com; 25 place de la Cathédrale; ⊗ 9am-7pm Mon-Sat, 9.30am-12.30pm & 2-6pm Sun May-Sep, 9am-6pm Mon-Sat, 10am-1pm Sun Oct-Apr) In a lovely, early-16th-century building opposite the western façade of the cathedral. Staff make hotel reservations in the area for €2.30.
Centre Régional d'Information Jeunesse (CRIJ; ☎ 02 32 10 49 49; www.crij-haute-normandie.org; 84 rue Beauvoisine) Has information on hostels and student accommodation throughout Normandy as well as information on student discounts, courses and jobs.

TRAVEL AGENCIES

Voyages Wasteels (☎ 0825 88 70 57; 111 bis rue Jeanne d'Arc) Sells discount air tickets.

SEINE-MARITIME

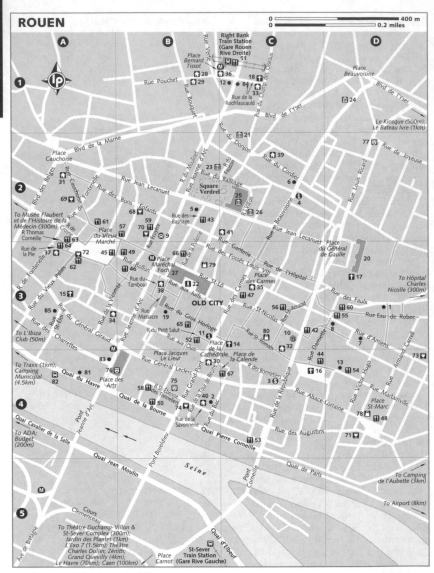

Cathédrale Notre Dame

As a part of his exploration of light, the Impressionist artist Claude Monet chose Rouen's **cathedral** (🕙 8am-6pm) as a subject, devoting some 30 canvases to immortalising its glory. Begun in 1201 and completed in 1514, this masterful cathedral spans the entire period of French Gothic architecture.

Like so many French churches, the Cathédrale Notre Dame was erected on the site of earlier churches. An early Christian sanctuary built by St Victrice was first on the spot at the end of the 4th century. A Romanesque cathedral followed, consecrated by William the Conqueror in 1063. In the middle of the 12th century, Archbishop Hugues d'Amiens

INFORMATION
ABC Bookshop...................................1 D3
American Express.........................(see 11)
Arts Diffusion Loisirs.......................2 B4
Bureau de Change............................3 C4
Centre Régional d'Information Jeunesse..4 C2
L'Armitiere...5 B2
Laundrette..6 C2
Laundrette..7 D3
Laundrette..8 D3
Main Post Office...............................9 B2
PlaceNet...10 C3
Tourist Office..................................11 B3
Voyages Wasteels...........................12 C1

SIGHTS & ACTIVITIES   (pp204–10)
Aître St-Maclou..............................13 D4
Cathédrale Notre Dame..................14 C3
Église St-Éloi..................................15 A3
Église St-Maclou............................16 C4
Église St-Ouen...............................17 D3
Église St-Romain............................18 C1
Gros Horloge..................................19 B3
Hôtel de Ville (Town Hall)...............20 D3
La Tour Jeanne d'Arc......................21 C2
Monument Juif................................22 B3
Musée de la Céramique...................23 B2
Musée des Antiquités......................24 D1
Musée des Beaux-Arts.....................25 C2
Musée Le Secq des Tournelles.........26 C2
Palais de Justice.............................27 B3

SLEEPING   (pp210–11)
Hôtel Anderson...............................28 B1
Hôtel Beauséjour............................29 B1

Hôtel Cardinal................................30 B4
Hôtel Dandy....................................31 A2
Hôtel de la Cathédrale....................32 C3
Hôtel de la Rochefaucauld..............33 C1
Hôtel de l'Europe............................34 A3
Hôtel des Carmes............................35 C3
Hôtel Dieppe..................................36 C1
Hôtel du Vieux Marché....................37 A3
Hôtel Le Palais................................38 B3
Hôtel Normandya............................39 C2
Hôtel Notre Dame...........................40 B4
Le Vieux Carré................................41 C2

EATING   (pp211–13)
Alimentation Générale....................42 C3
Au Temps Des Cerises.....................43 B2
Auberge St-Maclou.........................44 C4
Brasserie Paul............................(see 30)
Covered Food Market......................45 A3
Crêperie Tarte Tatin.......................46 B3
Flunch..47 C3
Food Market...................................48 D4
Fromagerie du Vieux Marché...........49 B3
Gill...50 B4
Gill, Le Bistrot du Chef… en gare....51 C1
Gourmand'grain.............................52 B3
Highlands Café...............................53 C4
La Petite Auberge...........................54 C4
La Petite Bouffe..............................55 D3
La Taverne St-Amand......................56 C3
La Toque d'Or.................................57 B2
Le 37..58 B4
Le Bistrot de Panurge......................59 B2
Le P'tit Bec.....................................60 D3
Le P'tit Zinc....................................61 A2

Les Maraîchers...............................62 A3
Les Nymphéas.................................63 A2
L'Orangerie....................................64 A3
Monoprix..65 B3
Pascaline..66 B3
Pub Station................................(see 51)
Thé Majuscule................................67 C4

DRINKING   (pp213–14)
El Guevara Café..............................68 B2
La Boîte à Bières............................69 A2
Le Buro...70 B2
Le Saxo..71 D4
L'Euro...72 A3
L'Insolite..73 D4
XXL...74 B4

ENTERTAINMENT   (p214)
Cinéma Le Melville..........................75 B4
Théâtre des Arts.............................76 A4
Théâtre des Deux Rives...................77 D2

SHOPPING   (p214)
Antiques &
  Bric-a-Brac Market........................78 D4
Centre Commercial..........................79 B3
Fayencerie Augy.............................80 C3

TRANSPORT   (p215)
Air France.......................................81 A4
Avis...(see 36)
Bus Station......................................82 A4
Espace Métrobus............................83 A4
Hertz..84 C1
Rouen Cycles..................................85 A3

undertook the expansion of the church, deciding to build the **Tour St-Romain** in what was considered an innovative Gothic style. A fire in 1200 destroyed the entire church, leaving only the Tour St-Romain, the two doors – Portes St-Jean and St-Etienne – and the **crypt**. Reconstruction was begun almost immediately and much of the basic structure was finished by 1250. A period of expansion and embellishment followed that lasted for three centuries. Huguenots pillaged the cathedral in 1562 and 18th-century revolutionaries turned it into a Temple of Reason, after destroying the tomb of Charles V. Bombs rained down on the cathedral the night of 19 April 1944 causing severe damage. The repairs are still being made, mostly to damaged statuary and some of the less obvious work. The major priority was work on the façade, which has been completed. The rest of the work is proceeding in bits and pieces, with no scheduled completion date.

EXTERIOR
Notice the contrast between the austere and early-Gothic Tour St-Romain on the left side and the Flamboyant Gothic **Tour de Beurre** on the right. Built between 1485 and 1506, the tower was paid for out of the alms donated by members of the congregation who wanted to eat butter during Lent. (Given the liberal use of butter in Norman cuisine, its absence must have been an intolerable hardship.) Within the tower is a carillon of 55 bells weighing 25 tonnes. The **central doorway** is surrounded by statues of patriarchs and prophets and topped by a sculpted Tree of Jesse. The central spire dates from 1822, replacing an earlier one that was destroyed by lightning.

INTERIOR
The overall impression of the 135m-long interior is of grace and harmony. Over the entrance is a 16th-century **rose window** that depicts God surrounded by angels. The transept is dominated by a majestic **lantern tower** and the aisles contain stained glass ranging from the 13th to 16th centuries. Notice the **Chapelle de Ste-Jeanne**, dedicated to Joan of Arc, in the south transept with a statue of the saint. The statue of her at the stake was placed there after WWII. The earliest part of the church is the **choir**. It dates from the 13th century and is notable for the simplicity and purity of its design. The recently restored **stalls** date from the 15th century and are decorated with ornate sculptures representing various professions.

On each side of the **altar**, which supports a lead sculpture of Christ, are angels that were rescued from the former Église St-Vincent on place du Vieux Marché. The **ambulatory** behind the choir has effigies of Rollo, his son and Richard the Lion-Heart, whose heart is in the cathedral treasury (the rest of him is in Fontevraud Abbey in the Loire Valley). Notice the size of the Rollo effigy. The nearby **Chapelle de la Vierge** is lit by original 14th-century windows representing the 24 archbishops of Rouen. Funerary art reached its apogee in the elaborate 16th-century **Tomb of the Cardinals of Amboise**. The kneeling cardinals are surrounded by a beautifully sculpted array of saints, apostles and allegorical figures. There are guided visits in French of the crypt, Tomb of the Cardinals and Chapelle de la Vierge at 3 pm daily in July and August, but weekends only from September to June.

Walking Tour

Begin your walk at **place de la Cathédrale (1)** (for details on the cathedral see p204) and notice the **Bureau des Finances (2)** – a striking Renaissance structure built in 1509 that now houses the tourist office. Turn onto rue St-Romain, the narrow street running along the northern side of the cathedral. Notice the house at **No 9–11 (3)**, a typical medieval structure of overhanging storeys, that dates from 1466. Across the street is **No 74 (4)**, which is a particularly handsome Gothic house from the 16th century, with niches

showing St Nicolas reviving three children and St Romain crushing a gargoyle. Further ahead on the right is **La Cour des Libraires (5**; the Booksellers Court) with a massive 15th-century gate carved with scenes from the Resurrection and Last Judgement above (unfinished), and scenes from Genesis below. Other figures include the Vices and Virtues, various professions and crafts, and a dragon with a human head.

Stretching from rue St-Romain to rue des Bonnetiers, the massive **archbishop's palace (6)** is still where the archbishop resides. On the rue St-Romain side, plaques remind you that Joan of Arc was tried here in 1431. Built in the 15th century it's possible to appreciate the majesty of the palace from the gate on rue des Bonnetiers. Before going up rue des Bonnetiers, cross rue de la République and visit **Église St-Maclou** and **Aître St-Maclou (7**; see p208).

Return to the cathedral and walk up rue du Gros Horloge – you'll see a plaque on the right, commemorating the **birthplace of Robert La Salle (8)**; he claimed Louisiana for France. Notice the harmonious façade of the **former Hôtel de Ville (9**; city hall) on your right at Nos 60–66. Built by the prestigious architect Jacques Gabriel in 1607, the building was never finished and now houses a clothing store.

The **Gros Horloge (10)** medieval clock – just up the street on the left – is something of a mascot to the Rouennais (people of Rouen). The clock's mechanism dates from the 14th

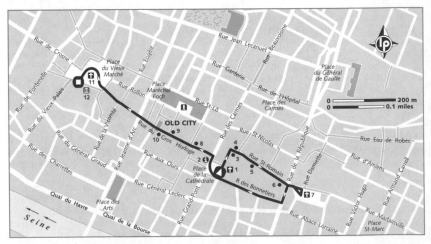

century when it was lodged in the adjacent belfry, but the citizens demanded a more conspicuous location. In 1529 the clock was given a flamboyant new façade in a Renaissance style and placed over its current arch. Its single hand points to the hour and, under the numeral VI, the day of the week appears in the form of the divinity associated with each day. On Monday, the moon is in a chariot drawn by deer; on Tuesday, Mars is drawn by wolves; and so on. Over the clock, a globe indicates the phases of the moon. The result was considered so admirable that the gender of the clock was 'elevated' from feminine to masculine. (In French, *horloge* is a feminine noun; the proper formulation should be 'grosse horloge'.) Restoration of the 14th-century belfry has been under way for some time; once it has reopened (expected for the 2004 tourist season) a visit to the tower will provide a magnificent view over the city. Its bell still rings 'curfew' each night at 9 o'clock.

At the end of rue du Gros Horloge is **place du Vieux Marché**, bounded on the south by a striking ensemble of half-timbered buildings. It was here that Joan of Arc was burned alive in 1431; a towering cross and a plaque marks the spot where she was executed. At the time of her death, place du Vieux Marché was considerably smaller and contained several churches, a marketplace, a pillory and a stake. Scattered stones are all that remain of the old structures.

The centrepiece of the square is the remarkable **Église Jeanne d'Arc, (11**; 10am-12.15pm & 2-6pm Mon-Sat), constructed in 1979 after the designs of architect Louis Arretche. The church is meant to resemble an upturned boat and its roofs sprawl over most of the square. An older church, Église St-Vincent, once stood here but it was destroyed in the bombing of 1944. Fortunately, its 16th-century stained-glass windows were removed for safekeeping in 1939 and now they grace the surprisingly lofty interior of the new church.

Also on the square is the **Musée Jeanne d'Arc, (12**; www.jeanne-darc.com; 33 place du Vieux Marché; admission €4; 9.30am-7pm May-Sep, 10am-noon & 2-6.30pm Oct-Apr), which recounts the life of La Pucelle (The Maid) in waxworks, documents and drawings. Kids like it, but the treatment is too superficial to interest most adults.

Palais de Justice

The ornate Palais de Justice (law courts) is a triumph of early 16th-century Gothic style. Typical of the period, the architects move your eye upwards from a relatively sober ground floor to increasingly elaborate upper levels, topped by spires, gargoyles and statuary. The oldest part of the structure is the west wing, the Palais du Neuf Marché, begun in 1499. The section that faces rue Jeanne d'Arc dates from the 19th century. Seriously damaged at the end of WWII, the building has been painstakingly restored, although the 19th-century western façade still shows extensive bullet and shell damage. It was during construction of the city's underground (subway) system that archaeologists discovered a 3rd-century Gallo-Roman settlement at this site.

Monument Juif

Under the courtyard of the Palais de Justice is Rouen's only reminder of its ancient Jewish community. Until their expulsion from Rouen by Philippe Le Bel in 1306, Rouen's Jews lived between rue du Gros Horloge, rue des Carmes, rue St-Lô and rue Massacre. This impressive two-storey stone building was discovered by accident in 1976 as the courtyard was being repaved. Although the building is in the heart of the Jewish ghetto and the presence of Hebrew graffiti confirms that it belonged to the Jewish community, its exact function is unknown. It may have been used either as a synagogue or a yeshiva, or it may have belonged to a rich merchant. Dating from around 1100, it is the oldest Jewish monument in France. As of the time of writing, the monument has been closed for security reasons but the situation may change.

Église St-Ouen

In any other town, **Église St-Ouen** (10am-noon & 2-6pm Wed-Mon mid-Mar–Oct, 10am-12.30pm & 2-4.30pm Wed, Sat & Sun Nov–mid-Mar) would be a star attraction but, in Rouen, it's often overlooked by visitors rushing to the cathedral. However, this 14th-century church is a jewel of Rayonnant Gothic style. Its imposing size (137m long, 26m wide) and relative lack of decoration focuses the eye on its sweeping vertical lines and balanced proportions. Vast windows of 14th- to 16th-century glass create an ethereal light that filters through a

SEINE-MARITIME

forest of slim columns. The wrought-iron grill around the choir and the organ with its 3914 pipes are exceptional.

The church was part of a powerful Benedictine abbey established in the mid-8th century on the site of St Ouen's grave. It was an active abbey until 1790 when it was sacked by revolutionaries. The entrance is through a lovely garden along rue des Faulx.

Église St-Maclou

This Flamboyant Gothic church (☺ 10am-noon & 2-6pm Mon-Sat, 3-5.30pm Sun) was built between 1437 and 1521, and it displays a remarkable unity of architectural style. The façade is an unusual arrangement of five pinnacled arches over a porch and three doors, richly decorated in Renaissance style. The left door recounts the parable of the Good Shepherd and the central door shows the circumcision and baptism of Christ. The tympanum over the central door represents the Last Judgment. The interior of the church is as sober as the exterior is ornate, with a Flamboyant Gothic staircase, 16th-century organ loft by Jean Goujon, 18th-century confessional, and oak doors from the mid-16th century. The 1944 bombing did a particularly nasty job on this church; most of the stained glass was destroyed and the church only reopened in 1980.

Aître St-Maclou

In 1348 Rouen was devastated by the plague; it took thousands of victims and provoked an urgent need for a new cemetery. Bodies were first buried near to the church in communal ditches. This curious ensemble of **half-timbered buildings** (186 rue Martainville; admission free; ☺ 8am-8pm), behind Église St-Maclou, was built between 1526 and 1533 around the graveyard and is one of the few remaining examples of a medieval charnel house. The carvings of skulls, crossbones, grave-diggers' tools and hourglasses adorning the walls would seem macabre in any other location.

THE WARRIOR SAINT

Nowhere in France is Joan of Arc (Jeanne d'Arc) more honoured than in Rouen, the place of her death. Here there is a church, a museum, a major avenue and numerous plaques testifying to the reverence in which the 'maiden warrior' is held. Imprisoned, tried, convicted and executed in Rouen, Joan of Arc achieved an enduring martyrdom here that rivals the enduring mystery of her life. Who was this illiterate teenage peasant girl? How did she persuade a king to give her an army? How did she inspire an army to follow her? Was she a visionary, a madwoman, or a girl-genius blessed with a laser-like will and an incendiary charisma?

Joan of Arc was born in Domrémy in 1412. The Hundred Years' War had been raging for over 70 years and a demoralised France was being governed by an English king.

When Joan was 12 years old, she began receiving visions of three saints. Their simple admonishments soon evolved into a more specific message: she was to save France and put the French Dauphin Charles on the throne. When she was 17, she rode off to Chinon, Charles' court, to inform him of her plans. After a private conversation, Charles fell under her spell and gave her command of the French army.

With a retinue of 4000 men Joan headed to Orléans, which the English had held under siege for six months. She chose the time if not the manner of the attack and fought alongside her men with strength and courage. Her example inspired others and led to a great victory. The English lifted the siege and, after several smaller defeats, left the Loire Valley.

The victory at Orléans was followed by the coronation of Charles at Reims. Joan was at the height of her power after the coronation. Her victory inspired young French men to volunteer for a rapidly growing army, but she mistakenly decided to attack Compiègne, where she was captured.

Threatened by her enormous popularity, the English brought her to their stronghold of Rouen for trial. The indictment contained a menu of charges, but the most serious was heresy, based on her insistence on communicating with God directly rather than through the church. Joan defended herself with panache, displaying tremendous stamina and mental agility, but unless she recanted her visions the result was a foregone conclusion.

She was convicted and, on 30 May 1431, she was led to place du Vieux Marché, tied to a stake and burned alive. She was 19 years old.

The cat's carcass displayed in a case to the right of the entrance was discovered in a wall. It was probably an unlucky black cat, believed to embody the devil, that was entombed in order to keep evil spirits at bay. The courtyard was used as a burial ground for victims of the plague as late as 1781 and is now the municipal École des Beaux-Arts (School of Fine Arts).

Musée des Beaux-Arts

Well-lit and well-organised, the **Musée des Beaux-Arts** (Fine Arts Museum; ☎ 02 35 71 28 40; 26 bis rue Jean Lecanuet; admission €3; ☺ 10am-6pm Wed-Mon) is one of the finest regional museums in France. With paintings from the 15th to 20th centuries, all the major movements in European art are represented.

The museum is organised chronologically, beginning in room one a major highlight *La Vierge entre les Vierges* (The Virgin amid the Virgins), by the 16th-century Flemish painter Gérard David. Of the Italian school in rooms three and four, notice *St-Barnabé Guéris-sant les Malades* (St Barnabas Healing the Sick) by Veronese. The painter Delacroix maintained that this alone justified a visit to Rouen. The Flemish school is represented by Marten De Vos, Van de Velde and a fine *Adoration des Bergers* (Adoration of the Shepherds) by Pierre-Paul Rubens in room five. The superb *Flagellation du Christ à la Colonne* (Flagellation of Christ on the Pillar) by Caravaggio in room six is another standout in the museum's collection.

The Fontainebleau school of painting that arose in 16th-century France is represented by Clouet's *Diane au Bain* (Bath of Diana) in room 12, which also contains the 17th-century *Vénus armant Énée* (Venus Arming Aeneas) by Poussin. Highlights of 18th-century French art include Fragonard's *Les Blanchisseuses* (The Washerwomen) room 15) and Jacques-Louis David's *Portrait de son Geôlier* (room 20), an affectionate look at his jailer painted while he was imprisoned for counter-revolutionary activity in 1794.

Naturally, painters who lived and worked in Rouen are strongly represented. Room 21 is entirely devoted to the works of Théodore Géricault, born in 1791 in Rouen and educated in Paris. Other French painters include the landscape painter Corot (room 22), Delacroix (room 25) and Monet (rooms 26, 27 and 28) although there is only one painting

of the cathedral. Of the 20th-century painters in rooms 31 to 34, notable are the works of Duchamp, Modigliani and the vast mural of the Seine painted by Raoul Dufy in 1937 for the Palais de Chaillot in Paris.

Other Museums

The fascinating **Musée Le Secq des Tournelles** (☎ 02 35 71 28 40; 2 rue Jacques Villon; admission €3; ☺ 10am-1pm & 2-6pm Wed-Mon) is in a desanctified 16th-century church. The collection is devoted to the blacksmith's craft, displaying some 12,000 locks, keys, scissors, tongs and other wrought-iron utensils made between the 3rd and 19th centuries. Larger works, such as balconies, staircase ramps and grills, are found in the nave and transept of the church; the upstairs floor is devoted to fashion accessories such as jewellery, belt buckles and combs. There are also instruments from various professions like gardening, dentistry, carpentry and surgery.

The **Musée de la Céramique** (☎ 02 35 07 31 74; 1 rue du Faucon; admission €3; ☺ 10am-noon & 1.30-5.30pm Wed-Sat, 2-6pm Sun) specialises in 16th- to 19th-century faïence (decorated crockery). Rouen is known for its fine ceramics, dating back to the 16th century when Italian artisans were imported into the court of François I. In 1645 a studio opened in the suburb of St Sever and the craft flourished until the end of the 18th century. Competition from English Wedgwood and a growing taste for porcelain sent Rouen's chinaware industry into decline. This museum has a fine collection from the height of the city's artistry in the 17th and 18th centuries, earlier pieces from the Italian Renaissance, and samples of Delft and Oriental works. The museum is in a 17th-century mansion with a fine courtyard.

History and archaeology buffs will want to stop at the **Musée des Antiquités** (☎ 02 35 71 78 78; 198 rue Beauvoisine; admission €3; ☺ 9.30am-noon & 1.30-6.30pm Wed-Mon) to review Rouen's past life. A beautiful 3rd-century mosaic is the highlight of the Gallo-Roman exhibit; there are glasses and jewels from the Merovingien era, religious gold and silverwork from the 12th century, medieval and Renaissance wood sculpture and splendid tapestries. The building was a 17th-century convent.

Musée Flaubert et de l'Histoire de la Médicine (☎ 02 35 15 59 95; 51 rue de Lecat; adult/concession €2.20/1.50; ☺ 10am-noon & 2-6pm Tue-Sat) is in the former hospital where Flaubert's father worked as a surgeon. The tiny museum is organised around the apartment where the Flaubert family lived and displays numerous family mementos as well as surgical instruments, hospital furniture and ceramic pharmacy containers. Just one of the more interesting exhibits is a contraption designed to teach midwives how to better assist the delivery process, in the hope that a better understanding of the process would help reduce the era's appalling infant-mortality rate.

La Tour Jeanne d'Arc (☎ 02 35 98 16 21; rue du Donjon; admission €1.50; 🕑 10am-12.30pm & 2-6pm Wed-Mon, 2-6.30pm Sun Apr-Sep, 10am-12.30pm & 2-5pm Wed-Mon, 2-5.30pm Sun Oct-Mar) is the sole survivor of eight towers that once ringed a huge chateau built by Philippe-Auguste in the 13th century. Joan of Arc was imprisoned and tortured here before her execution. A copy of her trial transcript is on the ground floor, while upstairs there are exhibits about the chateau and Joan of Arc's life.

Jardin des Plantes

Rouen is a busy, modern city and the **Jardin des Plantes** (☎ 02 32 18 21 30; admission free; 🕑 8am-sunset), between ave de la Résistance and rue Lethuillier in the St-Sever neighbourhood, is a good place to take a breather, especially if you have kids. This 9.5-hectare park is attractively landscaped with exotic plants and trees, including a giant Amazonian *Victoria regia* whose leaves can reach 1m in diameter. The park also has a shallow basin for kids to splash about or sail model boats. By public transport, take bus line 12 to the Dufay or Jardin des Plantes stop.

Tours

The tourist office conducts **guided tours** (French only; adult/concession €6/4; 2hr) of the city at least twice a week from March to November and daily in July and August.

Festivals & Events

First organised in 1989, the **Rouen Armada** (www.armada.org) was such a spectacular success that it has become a regular feature every four years. The next Armada is in July 2007 and is expected to draw at least 10 million visitors for the week-long festival that includes concerts, fireworks, boat rides and a parade of some 50 sailing boats and warships. Accommodation is booked up about a year in advance.

Other yearly events include the **Festival of African Cinema** in January, the antiques market in February, the **Festival of Nordic Cinema** in March, and the **Joan of Arc Festival** on the Sunday closest to 30 May. Joan of Arc's martyrdom is commemorated with parades and street events. The tourist office has exact dates and venues.

Sleeping

If you're staying over a weekend, ask the tourist office about its 'Bon Weekend' offer of two nights for the price of one in some hotels. You'll have to reserve at least 24 hours in advance (more in the high season) to qualify.

BUDGET

Camping Municipal (☎ 02 35 74 07 59; rue Jules Ferry, Déville-lès-Rouen; adult/site €3.50/4) Modern facilities, but five kilometres northwest of the city. From the Théâtre des Arts or the bus station on quai du Havre, take bus No 2 (last bus at 11pm) and get off at the *mairie* (town hall) of Déville-lès-Rouen.

Camping de l'Aubette (☎ 02 35 08 47 69; St-Léger -du-Bourg-Denis; adult/site €2.30/2.45) A more spartan site that's three kilometres east of Rouen.

Hôtel de la Rochefaucauld (☎ 02 35 71 86 58, 1 rue de la Rochefaucauld; s/d from €20/23) Close to Right Bank train station, this welcoming place has simple rooms with TV and phone. More expensive rooms have private facilities.

Hôtel Normandya (☎ 02 35 71 46 15; 32 rue du Cordier; r from €19) This is a pleasant, family-run place with no luxuries but all the necessities in spotless condition. More expensive rooms have showers and toilets.

Hôtel Le Palais (☎ 02 35 71 41 40; 12 rue du Tambour; r from €32) The main advantage of this hotel is its location, well-situated near the Palais de Justice and the Gros Horloge, but the rooms provide good value for money as well. All rooms have showers and for an extra €2 you can have an en suite toilet.

MID-RANGE

Hôtel de la Cathédrale (☎ 02 35 71 57 95; www.hotel-de -la-cathedrale.fr; 12 rue St-Romain; s/d €49/59) A wonderfully atmospheric hotel in a 17th-century house, right next to the cathedral. Rooms are well fitted out but not large, which encourages you to spend time in the leafy courtyard or the eye-catching lounge. Ask for a room looking onto the inner courtyard.

Hôtel Beauséjour (☎ 02 35 71 93 47; fax 02 35 98 0124; 9 rue Pouchet; s/d €35/55) It may be from the carpeted-wall school of decorating, but the rooms are comfortable and equipped with telephone, cable TV and modern bathrooms that include hairdryers.

Hôtel Cardinal (☎ 02 35 70 2442; fax 02 35 89 75 14; 1 place de la Cathédrale; s/d €57/64.50; P X) Businesslike but warm, this friendly hotel has many rooms with views of the nearby cathedral. The rooms are thoroughly modern, equipped with satellite TV and on nice days you can have breakfast on the terrace at the foot of the cathedral.

Hôtel de l'Europe (☎ 02 35 70 83 30; www.h-europe .fr; 87-89 rue aux Ours; s/d €65/75; P X X) Discreet and professional, this hotel is on a quiet street and offers elegant pastel rooms with a degree of comfort for the price.

Hôtel Notre Dame (☎ 02 35 71 87 73; www.hotelnotre dame.com; 4 rue de la Savonnerie; s/d €57/65; P) The new owners slapped this old place into a spanking new establishment with glistening, contemporary rooms in a 15th-century building.

Hôtel des Carmes (☎ 02 35 71 92 31, www.hoteldes carmes.fr.st - French only; 33 place des Carmes; r €39-55; P) If you're not on your honeymoon when you come here, you'll wish you were because this is the most romantic hotel in Rouen. Rooms are different sizes and bathrooms come with and without tubs, but all are decorated with flair.

Le Vieux Carré (☎ 02 35 71 67 70; www.vieux-carre.fr - French only; 34 rue Ganterie; r €51-55; P) Brimming with charm and good cheer, this little gem has 13 utterly fetching rooms and a cosy tea salon to hide from Normandy's all-too-frequent showers.

Hôtel Andersen (☎ 02 35 71 88 51; www.hotel andersen.com - French only; 4 rue Pouchet; s/d from €35/40) In this 19th-century mansion, you'll find bright, white rooms imaginatively decorated in the Directory style of post-Revolutionary France. You won't find a reception area, but you will find a warm welcome from the proprietor.

TOP END

Hôtel Dieppe (☎ 02 35 71 96 00; hotel.dieppe@ wanadoo.fr; place Bernard Tissot; s/d from €77.50/90; P X ▢) Well worth its three stars, this attractive place is across the street from the Right Bank train station. The century-old hotel has been lovingly restored and offers

smallish but plush rooms with all conveniences and a high level of service. Special weekend rates are available.

Hotel Dandy (☎ 02 35 07 32 00; www.hotels-rouen .net; 93 rue Cauchoise; r €72-95; P) Comfortable digs on a quiet street with the convenience of a coffee-maker in each room makes the Dandy a delightful option. The décor is an updated version of Old Normandy.

Hôtel du Vieux Marché (☎ 02 35 71 00 88; www.hotel duvieuxMarche.com; 15 rue de la Pie; s/d €89/99; P X) With a no-nonsense style, sleek, brightly decorated rooms and central location, this hotel is a favourite with businesspeople. Breakfast is an extra €7 and parking an extra €8 per night.

Eating
BUDGET
Crêperie Tarte Tatin (☎ 02 35 89 35 73; 99 rue de la Vicomté; menu €9; ⌚ 11.30am-10.30pm) This place does a good job with crepes and offers an excellent selection of salads. Come at lunch for the *menu* that includes a crepe or salad with dessert and a drink.

Pub Station (☎ 02 35 71 48 66; Right Bank train station; menus €9 & €16) Train stations are rarely dining destinations, but the all-you-can-eat salad bar and tempting array of bruschettas and pastas make this a worthwhile stop even if you're not waiting for a train.

Auberge St-Maclou (☎ 02 35 71 06 67, 224-226 rue Martainville; lunch menus €11 & €13; ⌚ closed Mon & dinner Sun) Planted on one of Rouen's more fetching streets, this rustic eatery is immensely popular for its simple, authentic dishes such as lamb in a garlic cream sauce and *saumon aux lardons* (salmon with bacon). The lunch menu even includes wine and coffee.

Le P'tit Bec (☎ 02 35 07 63 33; 182 rue Eau de Robec; menus €11 & €13.50; ⌚ closed Sun) Weight-conscious diners (especially women) love this dining room where Normandy's heavy cream sauces are banished. Instead, you'll find *tartes*, terrines, poached fish and tiny steamed vegetables. Dinner is only served Friday and Saturday nights. The restaurant becomes a tearoom in the afternoon.

La Petite Bouffe (☎ 02 35 98 13 14; 16 place du Lieutenant Aubert; menu €13.50; ⌚ closed Sun & Mon) When the going gets tough, the stressed-out set comes here to recharge the batteries with the kind of comfort food (*blanquette de veau, fricassée de volaille*) that *maman* used to make.

MID-RANGE

Les Maraîchers (☎ 02 35 71 57 73; 37 place du Vieux Marché; lunch menus €16) At least come and have a look at the dining room, gleaming with copper, mirrors, polished wood, pewter and tiles. Recently classified as *café historique d'Europe*, the cuisine is not on quite the same exalted level as the décor but, still, completely honourable.

La Petite Auberge (☎ 02 35 70 80 18; 164 rue Martainville; menus €14, €18, €26 & €35; ☺ closed Mon) Good home-cooked food is on the menu here and there are plenty of choices. The ambience is cosy and convivial and if you've ever yearned to try *tête de veau* (veal's head), this is the place to do it. The €14 *menu* is only available for lunch on weekdays.

Gill, Le Bistrot du Chef…en gare (☎ 02 35 71 41 15; Right Bank train station; menus €14.50; ☺ closed Sun, lunch Sat, dinner Mon & all of Aug) This lower-priced annexe of top-end Gill (right) offers fine cooking with less-expensive ingredients than its sister establishment. The *menu* is small and specialises in the greatest hits of traditional *cuisine bourgeoise* such as *suprême de poulet fermier* (free-range chicken breasts) or *riz au lait de ma grand-mére* (my grandmother's rice pudding).

Brasserie Paul (☎ 02 35 15 14 43; 1 place de la Cathédrale; menus €10.50 & €17.10) Next to Hôtel Cardinal, this sober brasserie was once a favourite of Rouen's artistic/literary scene, attracting such notables as Simone de Beauvoir, Marcel Duchamp and Guillaume Apollinaire. It's still popular, at least as much for its unbeatable view of the cathedral and cosy interior as for its well-produced bistro staples at reasonable prices.

La Toque d'Or (☎ 02 35 71 46 29; 11 place du Vieux Marché; menus from €9) It's on the square where poor Joan met her fiery fate, but you won't find any burned flesh here (unless you order it that way). The grilled meat is excellent here, drawing locals and, yes, quite a lot of tourists. There's no better *tarte normande* in all of Normandy!

Pascaline (☎ 02 35 89 67 44; 5 rue de la Poterne; menus €10.90, €12.95, €15.20 & €21.30) This old-time bistro with a player piano has some wonderful duck dishes. The chef is a master *canardier* who prepares the famous *Caneton Rouennais* (p53). The €10.90 *menu* is only available for weekday lunches.

L'Orangerie (☎ 02 35 98 16 03; 2 rue Thomas Corneille; menus €15.50 & €19.50-35) Occupying an 18th-century stone building, this restaurant makes a stunning impression. The cuisine is imaginative. Try the lamb braised in an orange caramel sauce. The €15.50 *menu* is only available for lunch on weekdays.

Au Temps Des Cerises (☎ 02 35 89 98 00; 4-6 rue des Basnage; menus €10 & €14-17; ☺ closed Sun, Mon & lunch Sat) Cheese, cheese and more cheese is served at this recently enlarged place. Turkey breast with Camembert, *oeufs cocotte* (eggs cooked in ramekins and topped with a cheese sauce) and, of course, fondue are well-prepared at reasonable prices. Vegetarians will be happy with the €14 *menu*. The €10 *menu* is only available for lunch.

Le Bistrot de Panurge (☎ 02 35 15 97 02; 91 rue Ecuyère; menus €11-25; ☺ closed Sun & Mon & lunch Sat) Everyone who's anyone makes a stop here for the most exquisitely prepared lamb you will ever taste. The wine list is also excellent, with a variety of reasonable choices from France's lesser-known vineyards.

Le 37 (☎ 02 35 70 56 65; 37 rue St-Étienne des Tonneliers; lunch menus from €16.50, dinner menus from €22.90; ☺ closed Sun & Mon) The busy Gilles Tournadre, who began Gill (below), moved on to Le Bistrot du Chef (left) and has found new success in this trendy place. The influence is modern Italian; you'll find parmesan, polenta and cannelloni all prepared with French panache.

TOP END

Gill (☎ 02 35 71 16 14; 8 quai de la Bourse; weekday menus €38, weekend menus €54 & €74; ☺ closed Sun & Mon) The mother ship is still captained by Gilles and Sylvie Tournadre and is still the finest restaurant in Rouen, if not all Upper Normandy. Although expensive, the quality of the food makes it excellent value. Let the chef seduce you with perfectly cooked scallops served with finely sliced truffles or the ravioli with fennel and crayfish in a sauce that must be divinely inspired.

Le P'tit Zinc (☎ 02 35 89 39 69; 20 place du Vieux Marché; meals from €23; ☺ closed Sun & dinner Sat) The casual style is deceptive for the excellent fish and meat are treated with the seriousness and respect they deserve. You won't find any odd spices here, but tradition has served this restaurant well and it remains one of Rouen's most popular addresses. The wine list is also first rate.

Les Nymphéas (☎ 02 35 89 26 69; 7 rue de la Pie; menus €27 & €33.50-61; ☺ closed Mon, lunch Tue &

dinner Sun) Patrice Kukrudz, the chef of this superb establishment, is one of the stars of Norman cuisine. Others may try, but he succeeds in using Norman cider, apples and Calvados to amplify rather than submerge the flavours of fine foie gras and soufflés. You won't regret sporting your best rags for this venture into fine dining. The €27 *menu* is not available on Wednesday.

VEGETARIAN
Gourmand'grain (☎ 02 35 98 15 74; 3 rue du Petit Salut; menus from €8; ⓨ lunch only, closed Mon) This would be the restaurant of choice for vegan vixens except that there isn't a choice – this is the only brown 'rice & veggie' place in town. It's still a cheery spot for a healthy lunch.

CAFÉS & TEAROOMS
Thé Majuscule (☎ 02 35 71 15 66; 8 place de la Calende; light meals €10-12; ⓨ lunch until 2pm, snacks until 6.30pm, closed Sun) A unique combination of a used bookshop and a tearoom, the literary ambience is supplemented by a selection of simple dishes including good salads and vegetable *gratins* served at lunchtime only.

Highlands Cafe (☎ 02 35 70 38 78; 2 quai Pierre Corneille; weekday menus €9 & €11; ⓨ closed Sun) This trendy bar, café and brasserie is known for its wide selection of beer and anything-can-happen musical evenings.

La Taverne St-Amand (☎ 02 35 88 51 34; 11 rue St-Amand; lunch menu €12; ⓨ closed Sun, Mon & lunch Sat) A favourite watering hole and feeding trough of the artistic set, this Old Rouen haunt is the place to come to drink and dine, just dine or just drink.

QUICK EATS
Flunch (☎ 02 35 71 81 81; 60 rue des Carmes; meals from €7) A good self-service place, Flunch offers a range of salads, cheese and desserts, as well as main courses.

SELF-CATERING
Rue Rollon has a number of good fruit stalls, cake shops and bakeries for buying prepared snacks and salads. There is a **covered market** (place du Vieux Marché; ⓨ 6.30am-1.30pm Tue-Sun) with dairy products, fish and fresh produce. There's also a daily **food and clothing market** (place St-Marc).

Fromagerie du Vieux Marché (☎ 02 35 71 11 00; 18 rue Rollon; ⓨ closed Sun) This place has an excellent selection of cheeses (try the Camembert

soaked in Calvados) as well as cider, *pommeau* and Calvados.

Alimentation Générale (78 rue de la République) has a good selection of groceries and long hours, while **Monoprix supermarket** (65 rue du Gros Horloge) has food and the utensils to eat it, plus a nice tablecloth.

Drinking
The tourist office has information about concerts and shows but serious nightcrawlers should check out *Le P'tit Normand* (€8), a yearly handbook with all the current venues. *Le Cyber Noctambule* is distributed free in most clubs and bars and is a good source of information about the late-night circuit.

PUBS & BARS
L'Euro (☎ 02 35 07 55 66; 41 place du Vieux Marché; ⓨ 10.30am-2am, from 3pm Sun) You can nibble and sip the day away on the terrace sampling tapas, tropical cocktails, bistro dishes and pasta. When the sun goes down there are theme nights and DJs to keep you dancing upstairs until the wee hours.

Le Bateau Ivre (☎ 02 35 70 09 05; 17 rue des Sapins) This is an easy-going place to enjoy varied music that might include rock, rhythm and blues or French songs in the style of Jacques Brel. To get there take bus T53 to the rue des Sapins stop.

La Boîte à Bières (☎ 02 65 07 67 47; 35 rue Cauchoise) Choose from an impressive selection of domestic or imported beers and then kick back to enjoy the mellow soundtrack in this half-timbered house of brew.

Highlands, Taverne St-Armand and the El Guevara Café are also good choices for tossing back a brewski.

DISCOS & NIGHTCLUBS
El Guevara Café (☎ 02 35 15 97 67; 31 rue des Bons Enfants) The succession of hot and humid cellars would have made Che feel like he was in his Bolivian jungle, but with lots of tropical cocktails and a torrid salsa scene. There are even free salsa lessons at 8.30pm when the music starts up in the downstairs bar.

Le Kiosque (☎ 02 35 88 54 50; 43 blvd de Verdun) Late-night 30-somethings like this place for dancing to a variety of nondeafening music, not just techno.

L'Exo 7 (☎ 02 35 03 32 30; 13 place des Chartreux) It's only rock 'n roll but they like it, like it, yes they do! And they've been coming here since 1983 to dance to the hottest rock acts, sometimes live. Take bus No 7 or 14 to the Chartreux stop.

Le Saxo (☎ 02 35 98 24 92; 11 place St-Marc) Jazz and blues have made this a must on the nightcrawler's itinerary, especially weekends when there are often live concerts.

L'Ibiza Club (☎ 02 35 07 76 20; 29 blvd des Belges) Singing, dancing, dining – they do it all here. Upstairs is the dining room with karaoke and downstairs is the dance floor.

GAY & LESBIAN VENUES

Le Buro (☎ 02 35 70 62 59; 81 rue Ecuyère; ✆ 7pm-2am, 7-10pm Sun) Rouen's oldest gay bar is the place to sip a cocktail on one of the plush sofas under subdued lighting.

XXL (☎ 02 35 88 84 00; 25 rue de la Savonnerie; ✆ noon-2am) It's a relaxed café during the day, but the action heats up at night.

L'Insolite (☎ 02 35 88 62 53; 58 rue d'Amiens) This is the newest bar on the gay and lesbian scene in Rouen but heteros are also welcome. Check out the 'vivarium' that includes reptiles and a parrot.

Traxx (☎ 02 32 70 72 02; 4 bis blvd Ferdinand de Lesseps) Techno-phobes, beware. This is the city's foremost venue for the genre. It's young, hot and attracts a mixed gay and straight crowd.

Entertainment

Rouen boasts a lively night scene with concerts, clubs, cinemas and theatres pulling in crowds from about October to May. The action quietens down during the summer and comes to a complete halt in August when the locals go on holiday before swinging into gear again in September. The tourist office has information about concerts and *L'Agenda Rouennais*, also free, covers a wide range of cultural events. Keep an eye on the daily *Paris-Normandie* as well, especially for the cinema schedule.

CINEMA

Cinéma Le Melville (☎ 02 35 98 79 79; 12 rue St-Étienne des Tonneliers) occasionally shows undubbed English-language films.

THEATRE

The **Théâtre des Deux Rives** (☎ 02 35 89 63 41; 48 rue Louis Ricard) offers a mixed bag of plays from classical and contemporary French theatre to more international works.

CLASSICAL MUSIC, OPERA & BALLET

Théâtre des Arts (☎ 02 35 71 41 36; place des Arts; tickets from €20) Rouen's premier music venue and home to the Opéra de Normandie, the theatre also presents concerts and ballets.

Théâtre Duchamp-Villon (☎ 02 32 18 28 10) In the St-Sever complex, this space offers an adventurous programme of contemporary music and dance from around the world.

Théâtre Charles Dullin (☎ 02 35 68 48 91; www .theatre-charles-dullin.com - French only, allée des Arcades; tickets from €20) Further to the south in Grand-Quevilly this theatre presents plays, variety acts, song-fests and dance.

Zénith (☎ 02 32 91 92 92; www.zenith-de-rouen.com - French only; ave des Canadiens, Grand Quevilly) As the name suggests, it's a big hall for big shows. Blockbuster rock, pop and classical stars do their acts here.

There are also music concerts in Rouen's churches. From mid-July to mid-August, **Église St-Maclou** (p208) hosts a regular series of classical music concerts and there are organ concerts held each Sunday in September in **Église St-Ouen** (p207). The tourist office will have details.

Shopping

Rouen is an important centre for the antiques business in Upper Normandy. Whether you are in the market for a piece of furniture or not, it's interesting to stroll around the stores on place St-Marc. There's an **antiques and bric-a-brac market** (✆ 8am-6.30pm Tue & Sat, 8am-1.30pm Sun) on the square. There are also some shops selling antiques and decorative objects on rue Damiette and rue Eau de Robec. The latter street is particularly scenic with an artificial brook and cunningly restored houses.

Centre Commercial (rue St-Lô) This is a shopping centre with various boutiques and a FNAC, which sells CDs and books as well as audiovisual equipment. Rue du Gros Horloge and the surrounding streets are also filled with shops.

St-Sever shopping centre (Rive Gauche) Just south of the city centre. This is where most Rouen residents come to do their shopping. Prices are cheaper than in the city centre and there is also a **bric-a-brac market** (place des Emmurées; ✆ 8am-6.30pm Tue, Thu & Sat).

Fayencerie Augy (☎ 02 35 88 77 47; 26 rue St-Romain) A good place to buy Rouen ceramics. It sells reproductions of traditional designs as well as original creations.

Getting There & Away

AIR
The **Aéroport Rouen Vallée du Seine** (☎ 02 35 79 41 00) is 8km southeast of town at Boos. **Air France** (☎ 08 02 80 28 02, 15 quai du Havre) has weekday direct flights to Lyons that connect with other cities in France as well as to international destinations.

BUS
Espace Métrobus (☎ 0825 07 60 27; 9 rue Jeanne d'Arc) dispenses information on all regional buses including Dieppe (€10.65, two hours, three daily) and towns along the coast west of Dieppe, like Fécamp (€14.45, 3¼ hours, one daily) and Le Havre (€12.65, three hours, five daily). Buses to Dieppe and Le Havre are much slower than the train and are more expensive.

Buses provide efficient connections to Évreux (€8.90, one hour, nine daily), Louviers (€5.60, 35 minutes, 11 daily), Clères (€3.65, one hour, nine daily), Lyon-la-Forêt (€6.70, one hour, one daily), Les Andelys (€7.49, 1¼ hours, twice daily), Gisors and Forges-les-Eaux (€7.60, 1¼ hours, one daily) and Neufchâtel-en-Bray (€8.35, 1¼ hours, three daily). The frequency given here is for Monday to Friday; there are far fewer connections on weekends. Buses leave from quai du Havre and quai de la Bourse.

TRAIN
Trains to Paris and other far-flung destinations depart from the main **Right Bank train station** (Gare Rouen-Rive Droite; ☎ 02 35 52 13 13).

From Right Bank station, there's a frequent express train to/from Paris' Gare St-Lazare (€17.40, 70 minutes). Others include Amiens (€15.50, 1¼ hours), Bernay (€11.30, one hour, six daily), Caen (€19.40, two hours, four daily), Dieppe (€9, 45 minutes, seven daily), Fécamp (€11, one hour, seven daily), Le Havre (€11.80, one hour, hourly), Lisieux (€14.80, 1½ hours, five daily) and Lyons via Paris (€78.20, four hours).

Getting Around

TO/FROM THE AIRPORT
There is no public transport into town; a taxi will cost about €20.

BUS & METRO
TCAR (also known as Espace Métrobus) operates Rouen's extensive local bus network as well as its metro line and high-tech buses. The metro runs between 5am (6am on Sunday) and 11.30pm. Tickets, valid for an hour of unlimited travel, cost €1.30, or €10.40 for a magnetic card for 10 rides. A **Carte Découverte** (1/2/3 days €3.50/5/6.50) public transport pass is available at the tourist office.

Rouen's public transport system has been designed to encourage residents of the suburbs to leave their car at home. Since the town centre is compact enough to explore on foot, it's unlikely you'll be taking too many buses or metros. For a visitor, the most convenient metro line runs from the train station under rue Jeanne d'Arc to Palais de Justice in the town centre and then on to the Théâtre des Arts, before continuing on to the St-Sever neighbourhood. Depending upon the line, the buses stop running between 6.30pm and 9.30pm. The last metro train leaves the station at 23.12pm.

CAR & MOTORCYCLE RENTAL
You can try **ADA** (☎ 02 35 72 25 88; 34 ave Jean Rondeaux) south of the town centre, **Avis** (☎ 02 35 88 60 94; place Bernard Tissot), **Budget** (☎ 02 32 81 95 00; 14 ave Jean Rondeaux) or **Hertz** (☎ 02 35 70 70 71; 130 rue Jeanne d'Arc) .

TAXI
Radio Taxis (☎ 02 35 88 50 50) operates 24 hours a day.

BICYCLE
Rouen Cycles (☎ 02 35 71 34 30; 45 rue St-Éloi) rents mountain bikes.

AROUND ROUEN

For a splendid taste of Normandy's open-air pleasures, head to the **Parc Naturel Régional des Boucles de la Seine Normande**. Straddling the Eure and Seine-Maritime *départements*, the protected area includes the beech and oak trees of the **Forêt de Brotonne** and the **Marais Vernier** wetlands. Within the Forêt de Brotonne are a number of bewitching villages, including Aizier, Bourneville, La Haye-de-Routot, Hauville, Heurteauville and Routot.

The Marais Vernier is a vast 4500-hectare plain, watered by 35km of canals. Don't miss the panoramic view from Ste-Opportune-la-Mare, near the intersection of the D95 and the N182. Bird-watchers flock to the lowlands of the Grande-Mare where herons, winter swallows and buzzards congregate.

SEINE-MARITIME

La Bouille

pop 800

This pretty riverside village 15km south of Rouen is a relaxing escape from the bustling city. Beneath the high coastal cliffs, flower-bedecked houses form a tiny medieval centre and a promenade runs along the Seine. In the 15th century it was an important port and later painters and poets fell in love with the enchanting vistas along the river. If you bring a bike, you can pedal up the river about 6km to Beaulieu. Otherwise, there's not much to do except eat, stroll and eat again, which is not a hardship since there are some excellent restaurants. With frequent buses into Rouen, La Bouille makes a good alternative place to stay if you're not on a tight budget.

In an elegant white building on the main road along the river, **Hôtel Restaurant Bellevue** (☎ 02 35 18 05 05; fax 02 35 18 00 92; 13 quai Hector Malot; s/d €47/63; P) has cheerful rooms with satellite TV and telephone. Some rooms have a river view. **Hôtel de la Poste** (☎ 02 35 18 03 90; fax 02 35 18 18 91; 6 place du Bateau; menus €17, €25.20 & €29.80; closed Tue) does have a couple of rooms (always full), but is mainly known for its fine **restaurant**. You can count on the *coquilles Saint-Jacques* (St-Jacques scallops), topped with plenty of sauce and a *tarte aux pommes* for dessert. There's also the **Restaurant de la Maison-Blanche** (☎ 02 35 18 01 90; 1 quai Hector Malot; menus €17 & €26-43). Classic cuisine plus classic furnishings equal a classic dining experience. The €17 menu is available weekdays only.

Bus No 31 connects Rouen with La Bouille (€1.30, 20 minutes, every 30 minutes).

Château de Robert-le-Diable

With a panoramic view over the Seine, this fortified **castle** (☎ 02 35 18 02 36; adult/concession €3.35/1.50; 9am-7pm Mar-Aug, closed Mon & Dec-Feb) is worth the dreary trip past Rouen's port installations. Robert the Devil was a mythical figure who reportedly had the ability to communicate with demons and ghosts. The character was probably inspired by William the Conqueror's father, Robert, and over the centuries his name became attached to the chateau.

Gallo-Roman wells in the courtyard indicate a long presence on the site, which clearly has a commanding and militarily useful view of Seine river traffic. The 11th-century chateau dates back to the earliest Norman dukes

but it was destroyed by Robert Lackland in 1204. Rebuilt by King Philippe-Auguste, the Rouennais again destroyed it in the 15th century in order to prevent the English from taking it over during the Hundred Years' War. The reconstructed castle now has a moderately interesting **museum** that traces the history of the Viking conquerors with waxworks and a reconstruction of a *drakkar* (Viking ship).

Bus No 31 connects Rouen with Château de Robert-le-Diable (€1.30, 20 minutes, every half-hour).

The Abbey Route

Following the Seine Valley west of Rouen, the D982 road winds through little towns, occasionally following the banks of the Seine as it climbs and descends. The minor resort towns such as Duclair, Caudebec-en-Caux and Villequier are scenic places to have a snack or stroll along the river, but the real highlights of the route are the three extraordinary abbeys.

Only 8km west of Rouen, the first abbey downstream is **L'Abbaye St-Georges de Boscherville** (☎ 02 35 32 10 82; www.abbaye-saint-geoges.com; admission low/high season €4/4.50; 9am-6.30pm Apr-Oct, 2-5pm Nov-Mar), in the village of St-Martin de Boscherville. Founded in 1114 on a pagan sanctuary, this sober but elegant abbey displays Norman Romanesque architecture at its finest. Unlike other abbeys, St-Georges was never destroyed, substantially remodelled or allowed to fall into decay, leaving a remarkable unity of style throughout. The geometric motifs that adorn the church façade seem curiously modern, although it was built from 1080 to 1125. The light, bright nave is supported by massive pillars forming majestic arcades.

The restored chapterhouse is adorned with statue columns illustrating themes from monastic life. The abbey is in continual restoration but you should be able to admire the arched ceilings of the monastery building, the 13th-century chamberlain chapel and some scattered vestiges of Gallo-Roman temples. A promontory over the garden planted with medicinal herbs affords a splendid view of the abbey.

With its ghostly white stone set off by a backdrop of trees, **Jumièges** (☎ 02 35 37 24 02; adult/concession €4/2.50, admission free first Sun every month; 9.30am-7pm mid-Apr–mid-Sep, 9.30am-1pm &

2.30-5.30pm mid-Sep–mid-Apr) is one of the most evocative ruins in the region. Little remains of the church – its nave is now open to the sky – but its imposing façade is flanked by 46m-high towers. It's easy to imagine the majesty of the structure from the sheer size of the remaining fragments – a tribune here, a chapel there, a noble arch sustaining a damaged bell tower. The church was begun in 1020 on the site of a 7th-century abbey destroyed by the Viking invasion. William the Conqueror attended its consecration in 1067 and the abbey soon took its place at the forefront of the spiritual and intellectual development of the age. It declined during the Hundred Years' War and then enjoyed a renaissance under Charles VII who stayed there with his mistress Agnes Sorel. The abbey continued to flourish until revolutionaries systematically destroyed it in the 18th century.

To get to the abbey take the D65 south from the D982.

Returning to the D982, the next abbey you come to is **L'Abbaye St-Wandrille** (☎ 02 35 96 23 11; www.st-wandrille.com; ☼ site 5.15am-1pm & 2-9.15pm), 19.5km west of Rouen, which harbours a community of 50 Benedictine monks. Founded in 649 by St Wandrille, the original structure was destroyed by the Vikings in the 9th century. A new abbey church was consecrated in 1031 and donations from William the Conqueror enlarged the abbey's property. The abbey flourished along with other Norman abbeys in the 11th century until the church was destroyed by fire in the mid-13th century. By the time a new church was completed, the Hundred Years' War ended the monastic life of St-Wandrille. The abbey reopened in the 16th century but, with little revenue, it wasn't until the 17th century that buildings were improved and expanded. Most of the structure dates from the 17th and 18th centuries, when the Revolution caused another suspension of monastic life. A Benedictine community moved in again in 1931 and began restoring the structure.

Guided visits (€3) are available daily at 3.30pm Tuesday to Saturday, and 11.30am and 3.30pm Sunday and holidays from April to mid-November. Visits are conducted by a monk and include the refectory, cloister, the new chapel of Notre Dame de Caillouville, and the ruins of the ancient abbey church. The monks sing Gregorian chants at 9.45am Monday to Saturday and 10am Sunday. In accordance with the Benedictine tradition of hospitality, it's possible to stay at the monastery for a maximum of 10 days. Write well in advance to Père Hôtelier, Abbaye St-Wandrille, 76490 St-Wandrille. If your image of monks is limited to prayers and chants, check out the superb abbey website, which leaves no stone unturned.

GETTING THERE & AWAY
CNA (☎ 0825 07 60 27) in Rouen has bus connections to the abbeys. There are up to 15 buses daily to St-Georges de Boscherville (€2.50, 20 minutes) and St-Wandrille (€5.20, one hour). Two buses go to Jumièges daily (€4.20, one hour).

Ry
pop 620
Flaubert's *Madame Bovary* was based on a real-life drama that occurred in Ry in the mid-19th century. Emma Bovary's adulterous prototype was Delphine Couturier Delamare, wife of Eugène Delamare, who was a student of Flaubert's father when he was teaching at the medical school in Rouen. As in the novel, Madame Delamare committed suicide after running up enormous and unpayable debts. Her husband died shortly after.

The pleasant but unremarkable town of Ry offers incessant reminders of its connection with Flaubert's groundbreaking novel. The small **Galerie Bovary Musée d'Automates** (☎ 02 35 23 61 44; admission €5; ☼ 11am-noon & 2-7pm Sat-Mon Easter-Oct, plus 3-6pm Tue-Fri Jul & Aug) presents scenes from the novel, animated by mannequins. An English translation of the scenes provides a good summary of the novel for those who haven't read it, can't remember it or haven't seen any of the Bovary movies. It also has a reconstruction of the pharmacy where Madame Delamare bought her lethal poison. You can also visit the Delamare graves behind **Église St-Sulpice**, built between the 12th and 16th centuries. The elaborately carved Renaissance wooden porch is unique in the region.

The **tourist office** (☎ 02 35 23 19 90; ☼ 10am-noon & 2.30-6pm Mon-Fri Apr-Oct, Sat & Sun Nov-Mar) is across the street from the museum and can provide free maps of suggested scenic walking, cycling and driving routes through the region.

Ry is 20km northwest of Rouen and an easy day trip by car, but there's only one bus daily from Rouen (one hour) and nowhere to stay in Ry if you must depend on public transport.

Clères

pop 1250

The main attraction of Clères is its fascinating **zoo** (☎ 02 35 33 23 08; adult/concession €4.60/3; ⏰ 10am-7pm Mar-Sep, 10am-5.30pm Oct, 1.30-5pm Nov) just steps away from the village marketplace. Established in 1920 around a Renaissance chateau, it has expanded to become a 13-hectare park containing 200 mammals and 2000 birds of 250 different species. Antelopes, wallabies, deer, peacocks, flamingos, cranes and gibbons live together amid a wide variety of exotic trees and plants. There's also a 19th-century chateau on the premises.

There are six trains daily between Clères and Rouen. The zoo is about 500m to the right when you leave the train station.

PAYS DE BRAY

To the northeast of Rouen, the Pays de Bray includes the Béthune, Andelle and Epte Valleys in a formation known as the 'buttonhole'. When the Alps were formed in the Tertiary period (65 million to 1½ million years ago) a large dome of land arose that eroded to form a valley 70km long and 15km wide. This fertile 'buttonhole' of land is marked by rolling hills, lush vegetation, meandering rivers and many pastures. No big cities mar the tranquillity. Never overpopulated, dairy farming has always been the region's mainstay. Neufchâtel cheese is on sale everywhere from local markets to family farms, while creamy Gervais-Danone dairy desserts, invented near Gournay-en-Bray, have pleased generations of French kids. The 6475-hectare Forêt d'Eawy, west of Neufchâtel-en-Bray, offers marvellous trails through giant beech trees.

NEUFCHÂTEL-EN-BRAY

pop 5350

For a town that suffered badly in the German bombardments of 1940, Neufchâtel has regained its balance nicely. The 15th- to 17th-century houses have been well reconstructed and the cheese industry has kept the town thriving. The cows-milk Neufchâtel cheese is the only heart-shaped French cheese (although it's sold in other shapes as well). The young cheese is chalk-white; the colour darkens as the cheese ages and develops a stronger flavour. Gervais-Danone 'petit suisse' dessert cheese is produced in a factory outside town. In addition to providing a good base for trips into the Forêt d'Eawy, Neufchâtel has a restored Renaissance church and an interesting town museum.

Orientation & Information

The main road through town is Grande Rue St-Pierre, which becomes Grande Rue Fausse Porte, Grande Rue Notre-Dame and Grande Rue St-Jacques. The town's **tourist office** (☎ 02 35 93 22 96; www.neufchatel-en-bray.com - French only; 6 place Notre Dame; ⏰ 9am-12.30pm & 2-6.30pm Tue-Sat year-round, plus 10.30am-12.30pm Sun mid-Jun–mid-Sep), across from the church on Grande Rue Notre Dame, has maps and brochures of the Forêt d'Eawy as well as a list of dairy farms open for visits and cheese tasting. The post office is on the corner of Grande Rue St-Pierre and Rue du Général de Gaulle.

Sights & Activities

The **Église Notre Dame** is notable for its Flamboyant Gothic porch and 16th-century nave topped with Renaissance capitals. Notice also the wooden statue of the Virgin at the entrance to the choir. The **Musée Municipal Mathon-Durand** (☎ 02 35 93 06 55; Grand Rue Saint-Pierre; admission €2.30; ⏰ 3-6pm Tue-Sat mid-Jun–mid-Sept, 3-6pm Sat & Sun rest of year) is down the street from the church near the post office. Five of the rooms in this medieval half-timbered house are devoted to illustrating traditional rural life in Normandy. Tools for roasting coffee, making butter, washing, making pottery as well as blacksmithing, iron-working and cheese-making are on display.

Market day is Saturday morning at place Notre-Dame; there's a *marché aux bestiaux* (livestock market) Wednesday morning in the Parc des Expositions, southwest of the town centre.

Sleeping & Eating

Camping de Ste-Claire (☎ 02 35 93 03 93; adult/site €3.05/3.05; ⏰ Apr-Oct) Less than 1km south of the town centre, this small camping ground is signed from the Parc des Expositions.

Hôtel Les Airelles (☎ 02 35 93 14 60; fax 02 35 93 89 13, 2 passage Michu; s/d €38/58; P) This central, two-star hotel in a pleasant ivy-covered stone building has discreetly furnished rooms with telephone and satellite TV.

Hôtel du Grand Cerf (☎ 02 35 39 91 14; fax 02 35 38 47 08; grand-cerf.hotel@wanadoo.fr; s/d €40/59; P) Also in the centre, this place is another good deal and also has an excellent Normandy **restaurant** (☺ closed Fri & lunch Sat).

Getting There & Away

All trains stop at Serqueux, 15km south, and are met by buses to Neufchâtel. There are three daily connections from Rouen to Neufchâtel (€9, 1½ hours); three from Dieppe (€5.50, one hour) and four from Paris (two hours). There are also four buses daily from Rouen to Neufchâtel (€8.30, 1¾ hours).

FORGES-LES-EAUX
pop 3750

Forges-les-Eaux, 40km northeast of Rouen, owes its existence to two precious commodities – iron and water. Iron has been mined from the region since antiquity, giving rise to forges powered by the River Andelle. The mineral-rich water spouting from La Chevrette spring developed a reputation for its curative powers in the 16th century, attracting such noble figures as Louis XIII, Anne of Austria and Cardinal Richelieu. It remained popular throughout the 19th century, even meriting a mention in Alexandre Dumas' *Les Trois Mousquetaires* (The Three Musketeers). Forges-les-Eaux is still very much a resort town, staid but relaxing. The wooded park around Andelle Lake is good for a healthy 5km stroll and its chic casino enlivens the nightlife.

Orientation & Information

The main road through town is ave des Sources, which becomes rue de la République, lined with stores and bakeries. The **tourist office** (☎ 02 35 90 52 10; www.ville-forges-les -eaux.fr - French only; rue du Maréchal Leclerc; ☺ 8.30am-12.30pm & 2-6pm Mon-Fri, 9am-noon & 2-6pm Sat, plus 10am-noon Sun mid-Jun–mid-Sep) is at the bottom of rue de la République, behind the town hall. The **post office** (rue de la République) is across from place Charles de Gaulle.

Sights & Activities

The unusual **Musée des Maquettes Hippomobiles et Outils Anciens** (admission €2; ☺ 2-5pm Tue-Sat, 2.30-6pm Sun Apr-Oct) was put together by a retired couple and displays models of horse-drawn vehicles from the 19th century. The museum is in the park behind the town hall.

The **Musée de la Faïence de Forges** (admission €2; ☺ by appointment only Mon-Fri) displays examples of pottery forged in the region. Located in the town hall, visits can be arranged through the tourist office.

Market days are Thursday and Sunday mornings on place Charles de Gaulle.

Sleeping & Eating

La Minière (☎ 02 35 90 53 91; blvd Nicolas Thiéssé; adult/site €3/5.50; ☺ open Apr-Sep) Less than 1km south of the town centre, this camping ground is a calm retreat beside a lake.

La Ferme de Bray (☎ 02 35 90 57 27; http: //fermedubray.fr.st; r €24-42) If you have your own transport you can hardly do better than staying on this working farm 6km north-west of Forges-les-Eaux, outside Sommery on the road to Dieppe. The Perriers are the 18th generation to run this dairy farm, turning it into a combination museum-inn. The farm buildings now house exhibits devoted to such traditional Norman activities such as pressing cider, baking bread and churning. There's a pond for trout fishing and equipment rental for those without tackle. The comfortable rooms of the inn are furnished in French country style with wooden furniture and Laura Ashley wallpaper.

DETOUR: AVENUE VERTE

The recently installed **Avenue Verte** is a 40km route open only to bicyclists, roller-bladers and walkers that runs from near **Forges** to **Aubin-le-Cauf**, near Dieppe. To find it, take the D1314 from Forges-les-Eaux about 3km north to **Beaubec-la Rosière**. The 'Green Road' starts in the centre of the village and follows a former train line through the heart of the pastoral **Pays de Bray**. The route is like an extensive park, with plenty of opportunities to veer away and explore villages along the way. Motorists can follow the D1314 until it becomes the D1 and take it nearly to Dieppe for similar country scenery.

La Paix (☎ 02 35 90 51 22; www.hotellapaix.fr - French only; 17 rue de Neufchâtel; r from €52.50; P) It's in the town centre and rooms are adequate if somewhat charm-impaired. The restaurant is good, however, specialising in fish and serving a decent house wine. Breakfast is an extra €6.10.

Hôtel Continental (☎ 02 35 89 50 50; fax 02 35 90 26 14; 110 ave des Sources; r from €60; P) In a restored half-timbered building across from the casino, this hotel offers all the comforts and some rooms have balconies.

Getting There & Around

All trains stop at Serqueux and are met by buses to Forges-les-Eaux. There are three connections daily from Rouen (€8.50, one hour) and three from Dieppe (€8.50, one hour). There is also a daily bus from Rouen (1½ hours).

Cycles Vauquet (☎ 02 32 89 02 64; 23 rue de la Libération) rents bicycles.

CÔTE D'ALBÂTRE

Stretching 120km from Le Tréport south to Cap de la Hève at Le Havre, the lofty white cliffs of the Côte d'Albâtre (Alabaster Coast) create the most dramatic coastal scenery in Normandy. Reminiscent of the southern coast of England, these chalky towers can reach 120m as they curve around stony beaches and crack open into dry valleys. The largest towns are built where rivers have been able to push their way to the sea: Le Havre at the mouth of the Seine, Dieppe on the River Arques, Fécamp on the Valmont and Le Tréport on the Bresle. Fishing ports and resorts complete the coastal picture while grain fields and pastures cap off the cliffs.

It's impossible to appreciate the Côte d'Albâtre by using the available public transport, but hikers, bikers and motorists will be treated to a series of ever-changing panoramas. Walkers can follow the coastal GR21 from Dieppe to Le Havre. If you are driving, take the more scenic coastal road (which starts as the D75 west of Dieppe) and not the inland D925. Good biking routes include the D211 from Étretat, the D79 from Fécamp northeast to St-Valéry-en-Caux and the D68 and D75 from St-Valéry-en-Caux to Dieppe.

LE HAVRE

pop 193,250

Le Havre, France's second-most-important port, is also a bustling gateway for ferries to Britain and Ireland. Like most gateways, people tend to pass through it on the way to someplace else but there's enough in the city to keep you busy for a day.

All but obliterated by WWII bombing raids, Le Havre was rebuilt around its historical remains by Auguste Perret. With a pressing need to shelter 80,000 suddenly homeless residents and little money to work with, it's not surprising that efficiency triumphed over design. The short three-storey buildings are out of proportion to the wide boulevards, which results in a cold, uninviting urban landscape. Yet, the very newness of the city can be intriguing. There's plenty of modern architecture to either admire or laugh at, and the sophisticated André Malraux fine-arts museum is one of the best in Normandy. You can also enjoy the wide, rocky beach with cold but clean water, good seafood restaurants, lots of parking and a number of good-value hotels, in case you want to use Le Havre as a base for exploring the Côte d'Albâtre.

History

Le Havre was created in 1517 by François I to replace the ports of Harfleur and Honfleur, which were silting up. The two-hour high tides made Le Havre attractive for maritime activities and the city quickly took its place as an important commercial centre. In the 17th century Cardinal Richelieu built a citadel and enlarged the ports just in time for the city to capitalise on emerging trade connections with the Americas. Ships loaded with cotton and coffee sailed into the port and, in the 18th century, sailed out with guns and supplies for American revolutionaries. The North American connection continued into the 20th century with the advent of luxury ocean liners that connected New York with Le Havre in 15 days.

Prewar Le Havre was a teeming port city, although probably lacking graciousness. After all, the city inspired Jean-Paul Sartre to write *La Nausée* (Nausea) during the 1930s, while teaching philosophy at a local high school. The Germans occupied Le Havre in 1940, turning it into an important garrison. The Allied offensive was fierce.

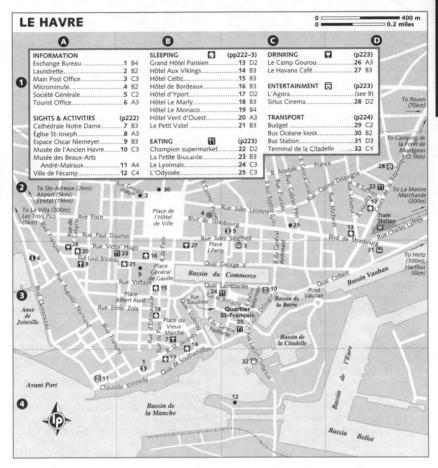

LE HAVRE

0 — 400 m
0 — 0.2 miles

INFORMATION		SLEEPING	(pp222–3)	DRINKING	(p223)
Exchange Bureau	1 B4	Grand Hôtel Parisien	13 D2	Le Camp Gourou	26 A3
Laundrette	2 B2	Hôtel Aux Vikings	14 B3	Le Havana Café	27 B3
Main Post Office	3 C3	Hôtel Celtic	15 B3		
Microminute	4 B2	Hôtel de Bordeaux	16 B3	ENTERTAINMENT	(p223)
Société Générale	5 C2	Hôtel d'Yport	17 D2	L'Agora	(see 9)
Tourist Office	6 A3	Hôtel Le Marly	18 B3	Sirius Cinema	28 D2
		Hôtel Le Monaco	19 B4		
SIGHTS & ACTIVITIES	(p222)	Hôtel Vent d'Ouest	20 A3	TRANSPORT	(p224)
Cathédrale Notre Dame	7 B3	Le Petit Vatel	21 B3	Budget	29 C2
Église St-Joseph	8 A3			Bus Océane kiosk	30 B2
Espace Oscar Niemeyer	9 B3	EATING	(p223)	Bus Station	31 D3
Musée de l'Ancien Havre	10 C3	Champion supermarket	22 D2	Terminal de la Citadelle	32 C4
Musée des Beaux-Arts		La Petite Brocante	23 B3		
André-Malraux	11 A4	Le Lyonnais	24 C3		
Ville de Fécamp	12 C4	L'Odyssée	25 C3		

From 2–12 September 1944, the city was subjected to a furious bombing campaign while the Germans, in a desperate last stand, blew up the port installations. The city was 85% destroyed.

Orientation

The main square is the enormous place de l'Hôtel de Ville. Avenue Foch runs west to the sea and the Port de Plaisance recreational area; blvd de Strasbourg goes east to the train and bus stations. rue de Paris cuts south past Espace Oscar Niemeyer, a square named after the Brazilian who designed two peculiar cultural centre buildings (which have been compared to a truncated cooling tower and a toilet bowl).

Rue de Paris ends at quai de Southampton and Bassin de la Manche, from where ferries to Britain dock at the Terminal de la Citadelle, southeast of the central square. Not far from the terminal is Quartier St-François, Le Havre's restaurant-filled 'old city'.

Information

INTERNET ACCESS
Microminute (☎ 02 35 22 10 15; 7 rue Casimir Periér; per hr €3.60; ☽ 2-7pm Mon, 10am-7pm Tue-Sat)

INTERNET RESOURCES
www.ville-lehavre.fr The city's website.

LAUNDRY
Laundrette (5 rue Georges Braque)

SEINE-MARITIME

MONEY

There are plenty of banks along blvd de Strasbourg.

Société Générale (2 place Léon Meyer)

Exchange Bureau (41 Chaussée Kennedy) Opposite the old Irish Ferries terminal.

POST

Main Post Office (62 rue Jules Siegfried) It has Cyberposte.

TOURIST INFORMATION

Tourist office (☎ 02 32 74 04 04; 186 blvd Clemenceau; www.lehavretourisme.com; ☺ 9am-7pm Mon-Sat, 10am-12.30pm & 2.30-6pm Sun Jun-Sep, 9am-6.30pm Mon-Fri, 9am-12.30pm & 2-6.30pm Sat, 10am-1pm Sun Oct-May) On the waterfront about 650m southwest of city hall. Staff reserve local accommodation for free.

Sights & Activities

The main highlight of Le Havre is the hypermodern **Musée des Beaux-Arts André-Malraux** (☎ 02 35 19 62 62; 2 blvd Clemenceau; adults/concession €3.80/2.20; ☺ 11am-6pm Mon & Wed-Fri, 11am-7pm Sat & Sun) Inaugurated in 1961 by former Minister of Culture André Malraux, this museum is marked by steel, glass and a cascade of light bathing a spacious interior. Le Havre native and long-term resident Eugène Boudin is represented by his many paintings of local beach scenes. Another sizeable section is devoted to Fauvist Raoul Dufy who was also born in Le Havre. The city has more than a passing connection with Impressionism since Monet's *Impression, Soleil Levant* (Impression, Sunrise) portrayed the sunrise over Le Havre's port, lending a name to the new movement. Several works by Monet including a *Les Nymphéas* (Water Lilies) series are displayed, as well as paintings by Sisley, Renoir and Manet.

The **Musée de l'Ancien Havre** (☎ 02 35 42 27 90; 1 rue Jérôme Bellarmato; admission €1.50; ☺ 10am-noon & 2-6pm Wed-Sun) gives historical depth to a city that can seem as though it was built yesterday. The museum is in a 17th-century building that emerged unscathed from the WWII bombing and now has a moderately interesting collection of photos, models, posters, drawings and documents focusing on the maritime traditions of Le Havre.

Cathédrale Notre Dame (place du Vieux-Marché) is Le Havre's oldest sight. Although it was severely damaged during 1944, clever restoration has revealed the church's unusual mixture of Gothic and Renaissance styles.

The magnificent 17th-century organ was a gift from Cardinal Richelieu.

The tallest building in Le Havre is **Église St-Joseph** (cnr rue de Caligny & rue Louis Brindeau), designed by Auguste Perret. Visible all over the city, the 107m-high bell tower was intended to be the first thing ship passengers from the USA saw as they neared Le Havre. Its angular lines wouldn't be out of place in New York, but the interior is suffused with a soft light created by the stained-glass windows.

Tours

From June to September the tourist office operates **walking tours** (adult/child €5/3; 1-1½hr) of various monuments and neighbourhoods in Le Havre. From late July to August, there are daily **boat rides** (☎ 02 35 28 99 53; adult/child 3-14 €12.50/8.50; 1½hr) around the port of Le Havre aboard *Ville de Fécamp*.

Sleeping

BUDGET

Camping de la Forêt de Montgeon (☎ 02 35 46 52 39; chlorophile1@wanadoo.fr; camping €12.20; ☺ Apr-Sep) Nearly 3km north of town in a 250-hectare forest this is a lovely shaded site. From the station, take bus No 11 and alight after the 700m-long Jenner Tunnel. Then walk north through the park another 1.5km.

Hôtel d'Yport (☎ 02 35 25 21 08; fax 02 35 24 06 34; 27 cours de la République; r from €34; Ⓟ) Hidden down an alley opposite the train station is this friendly place with a range of rooms, the more expensive ones include en suite facilities.

Hôtel Le Monaco (☎ 02 35 42 21 01; fax 02 35 42 01 01; 16 rue de Paris; r from €28 with shower only) Near the old Irish Ferries terminal, this hotel has shipshape but simple rooms. More expensive rooms are available with bath and toilet.

MID-RANGE

Grand Hôtel Parisien (☎ 02 35 25 23 83; fax 02 35 25 05 06; 1 cours de la République; r €40-8; Ⓟ) Also close to the station is this clean and pleasant place.

Hôtel Aux Vikings (☎ 02 35 42 51 67; www.peltierj .fr - French only; quai de Southampton; r €45; Ⓟ) Bland but acceptable rooms have telephones and TVs.

Hôtel Celtic (☎ 02 35 42 39 77; www.hotel-celtic .com; 106 rue Voltaire; r €31-47) Rooms in a variety of sizes are brightly painted and neatly furnished in a traditional style. The most expensive enjoy views over the Bassin du

Commerce but all are equipped with private facilities and satellite TV.

Le Petit Vatel (☎ 02 35 41 72 07; www.multimania .com/lepetitvatel - French only; 86 rue Louis Brindeau; s/d €35/43) This option with small bright rooms offers good value for money. All the rooms have satellite TV and windows are double glazed to assure a sound night's sleep. More expensive rooms are available with bathtubs and views.

TOP END

Hôtel Vent d'Ouest (☎ 02 35 42 50 69; www.vent douest.fr; 4 rue de Caligny; r €75-100; **P**) Carpeted and genteelly comfortable, each of the 33 rooms has its own artful decoration based upon the themes of mountain, countryside or sea.

Hôtel de Bordeaux (☎ 02 35 22 69 44; www.best western.com/fr/debordeaux; 147 rue Louis Brindeau; s/d €62 /78; **P** ⊠ 🖳) There are few surprises here, which can be a relief if you're simply looking for a comfortable place to relax. All rooms have modem plugs.

Hôtel Le Marly (☎ 02 35 41 72 48; www.hotel lemarly.com; 121 rue de Paris; r €66-82; **P** 🖳) With large, functional rooms that are equipped with modem plugs, it's no surprise that this place is often filled with business travellers. A copious buffet breakfast is an extra €10.

Eating

La Marine Marchande (☎ 02 35 25 11 77; 27 blvd amiral Mouchez; menu €10; ☒ closed Sun) All-you-can-eat buffets are a rarity in France, but here you can chow down with the hungry sailors at a full table of hors d'oeuvres, plus a main course, cheese, dessert and wine or cider (not all you can drink though). To get there take rue Charles Laffitte from the train station, then follow it to the right as it becomes rue Marceau, and onto blvd Amiral Mouchez.

L'Odyssée (☎ 02 35 21 32 42; 41 rue du Général Faidherbe; menus €19-32; ☒ closed Mon, lunch Sat & dinner Sun) One of Le Havre's best addresses for dipping into some superb fish dishes, this place offers a refined dining experience at prices that are fairly reasonable for the high quality.

La Petite Brocante (☎ 02 35 21 42 20; 75 rue Louis Brindeau; menu €22; ☒ closed Sun) The style is bistro-chic but the ambience is warm and the cooking brings bistro classics up a notch. Plus, the wine list is excellent.

Le Lyonnais (☎ 02 35 22 07 31; 7 rue de Bretagne; menus €12, €14, €17 & €22; ☒ closed Sun & lunch Sat) There's no place for romance in this crowded and noisy little neighbourhood bistro but you'll understand the brouhaha when you taste the delicious *marmite de poissons* (fish soup) or the seafood *feuilleté* (fish stew). If you still don't get it, try the chocolate cake.

La Villa (☎ 02 35 54 70 80; 66 blvd Albert 1er; weekday lunch menus €29.50, dinner menus €46, €69 & €125; ☒ closed Mon & dinner Sun & Wed) Gourmets from all over France make a pilgrimage here for the astonishing cuisine of master chef Jean-Luc Tartarin. It's useless to mention any specific dishes as the cuisine on offer changes according to the market and the chef's inspiration.

Les Trois Pics (☎ 02 35 48 20 60; Promenade des Régates, Sente Alphonse Karr, Ste-Adresse; lunch menus €17, dinner menus €23 & €35; ☒ closed Mon & dinner Sun) When the locals of Le Havre are looking for the very best in seafood, they head out to this address in Ste-Adresse for a whiff of salt air, excellent service and piles of shells.

The restaurant at the **Hôtel Le Monaco** (☎ 02 35 42 21 01; 16 rue de Paris) has excellent seafood *menus* from €10 and Quartier St-François is a good place to dine if you're in the mood for crepes or couscous.

Champion supermarket is on the corner of rue de la République and rue Turenne.

Drinking

Le Camp Gourou (☎ 02 35 22 00 92; 163 rue Victor Hugo) This raucous and highly popular student bar attracts lots of Australians.

Le Havana Café (☎ 02 35 42 35 77; 173 rue Victor Hugo) Despite the name, the musical programme is varied, although there is a Latin night once a month. The décor is cheerfully tropical and even Fidel would approve of the drink prices.

Entertainment

L'Agora (☎ 02 32 74 09 70; Espace Oscar Niemeyer) Not only do you get to see the inside of Le Havre's most striking building but there's a bar and concert hall that hosts an eclectic selection of musical acts from hip-hop to something called celtic-rock-latino.

Sirius Cinema (5 rue Duguesclin), just off cours de la République, often has movies in English with French subtitles.

Getting There & Away

AIR
The **airport** (☎ 02 35 54 65 00) is 6km north of town in Octeville-sur-Mer. There's no public transport to town; a taxi will cost about €12.

BUS
Caen-based **Bus Verts du Calvados** (☎ 08 01 21 42 14) and Rouen's **CNA** (☎ 0825 07 60 27) run frequent services from the bus station to Honfleur (€6.80, 30 minutes), Rouen (€12.65), Deauville-Trouville (1¼ hrs, €9.35) and Caen (€20, 1½ to three hours). **Autocars Gris** (☎ 02 35 22 34 00) has 10 buses daily to Fécamp (€7.25, 1½ hours) via Étretat (one hour) and five on Sunday.

TRAIN
Le Havre's **train station** (☎ 08 36 35 35 35; cours de la République) is east of the city centre. Chief destinations are Rouen (€11.80, one hour, 15 daily) and Paris' Gare St-Lazare (€25.20, 2¼ hours, 10 daily). A secondary line goes north to Fécamp (€6.70, 1¼ hours, five daily) with a change at Bréauté-Beuzeville.

BOAT
P&O European Ferries (☎ 08 02 01 30 13), which links Le Havre with Portsmouth, uses the new Terminal de la Citadelle on ave Lucien Corbeaux, just over 1km southwest of the train station. The information desk is open 9am to 7pm. A bus takes passengers from the terminal to the tourist office and the train station 15 minutes after ferry arrivals.

Getting Around

BUS
Bus Océane (☎ 02 35 43 46 00; place de l'Hôtel de Ville) runs 14 lines in Le Havre. Single tickets cost €1.40, a carnet of 10 is €9.20; a Ticket Ville is €3.20 for unlimited bus travel on that day.

CAR & MOTORCYCLE
For rentals try **Avis** (☎ 02 32 90 94 23) in the train station, **Hertz** (☎ 02 35 25 51 50; 70 rue Briquetiers) or **Budget** (☎ 02 35 22 53 52; 161 blvd de Strasbourg).

TAXI
For a **taxi** call ☎ 02 35 25 81 81 or ☎ 02 35 25 81 00). A **taxi tour** (in English; reservations ☎ 02 35 25 81 81; €50; 2hr) of Le Havre for up to four people is available. You can also reserve for Honfleur, Mont St Michel, Giverny, Étretat, and other destinations.

AROUND LE HAVRE
Boulevard Albert leads along the sea 2km to the Ste-Adresse village) which survived WWII intact. Built in the 14th century, the village became a fashionable watering spot for writers and artists at the end of the 19th century. Sarah Bernhardt, Alexandre Dumas, Monet and Raoul Dufy all came here to take the waters and enjoy the sea vistas. During WWI the Belgian government relocated to Ste-Adresse. It's still a popular spot for residents of Le Havre and makes a welcome change from the modern city. Bus No 1 runs to Ste-Adresse.

Harfleur is a quiet little village 6km east of Le Havre with cobblestone streets surrounding the 15th-century Église St-Martin. Harfleur's original claim to fame was as a port before the creation of Le Havre in 1517 rendered it useless. In 1415 the English army under the command of Henry V landed at Harfleur and laid siege to the town before proceeding to Agincourt for their famous victory. The **tourist office** (☎ 02 35 13 37 40, 1 rue du Grand Quai) in the town centre is trying to capture some overflow business from Le Havre by playing up Harfleur's history and pretty village appeal. The only hotel in town is the adequately comfortable **Les Calètes** (☎ 02 35 45 42 25, fax 02 35 49 12 42, 31-33 rue de la République; rooms €40). Bus Nos 9 and 13 from central Le Havre stop at the church.

DIEPPE
pop 35,700
Dieppe is an ancient seaside town and long a favourite among British weekend visitors. It's not the prettiest place in Normandy, but its location – set between two limestone cliffs – and its medieval castle are dramatic. Dieppe also has the attractive, gritty appeal of an old-fashioned port; it's the closest Channel port to Paris (175km). Like most Norman port cities, Dieppe was a coveted prize for invading armies throughout the centuries.

History
The Vikings came in the 7th and 8th centuries, followed by Philippe-Auguste of France who seized it from Richard the Lion-Heart in the 12th century. It changed hands several times in the Hundred Years' War, and was invaded by Prussians in the war of 1870. The most recent incursion into Dieppe took place in 1942 when an Anglo-Canadian

force of 6100 men landed in Dieppe in a show of force against the Germans. Though intended to demonstrate the British will and ability to launch a cross-Channel operation, the tragic loss of nearly two-thirds of the men in one day only demonstrated Allied military unpreparedness.

The port and wide sweep of beach has always defined Dieppe's culture and economy. Privateers made Dieppe their lair of choice as early as 1338 when they pillaged Southampton. Explorers launched expeditions from Dieppe, most notably Giovanni da Verrazano who sailed from here in 1524 to found New York. He was financed by the rich and powerful privateer, Jehan Ango, who became governor of Dieppe. In the 16th and 17th centuries, Dieppe flourished as the ivory and spice trade brought new wealth to its coffers. Protestants fleeing persecution left Dieppe's port in the 17th century when the Edict of Nantes was revoked, often on their way to Canada. A bout of plague and the bombardment of the city by the English and Dutch put an end to Dieppe's prosperity in the late 17th century.

It rebounded in the 19th century when aristocrats discovered the health benefits of sea bathing. With the construction of a railway link to Paris in 1848, fashionable Parisians began to spend Saturday and Sunday in Dieppe whereas the English came for longer periods. Parisians deserted Dieppe following WWII in favour of glamorous Deauville but Dieppe still keeps Paris well supplied with fish and seafood.

Orientation

The town centre is largely surrounded by water. Boulevard de Verdun runs along the lawns – a favourite spot for kite-flyers – that border the beach. Most of the Grande Rue and rue de la Barre has been turned into a pedestrian mall. Quai Duquesne and its continuation, quai Henri IV, follow the western and northern sides of the port area. The picturesque fishermen's quarter is on the eastern side of the canal. Roads lead up to the chapel Notre Dame du Bon-Secours from which there are stunning views.

Ferries dock at the terminal on the northeastern side of the port, just under 1km from the tourist office. The train station is south of the town centre, off blvd Georges Clemenceau – the bus station is in the same

building. The police station is west of the train station on the same road.

Information

INTERNET ACCESS
La Au Bar (☎ 02 35 40 48 35; 19 rue de Sygogne; ☽ 10am-2am Mon-Sat, 2-7pm Sun; per 15min/hr €1/4)

INTERNET RESOURCES
www.mairie-dieppe.fr The city website.

LAUNDRY
Laundrette (44 rue de l'Épée; ☽ 7am-9pm)

MONEY
Crédit Maritime Mutuel (3 rue Guillaume Terrien) One of the few banks open Monday.
Banque Populaire (15 place Nationale) One of several on place Nationale.

POST
Main Post Office (2 blvd Maréchal Joffre) It has Cyberposte.

TOURIST INFORMATION
Tourist Office (☎ 02 32 14 40 60; www.dieppetourisme .com; Pont Jehan Ango; ☽ 9am-1pm & 2-8pm Mon-Sat, 10am-1pm & 3-6pm Sun Jul & Aug, 9am-1pm & 2-7pm Mon-Sat, 10am-1pm & 3-6pm Sun May-Sep, 9am-noon & 2-6pm Mon-Sat Oct-Apr). On the western side of the port area. Hotel reservations in the Dieppe area cost €3.50.

Château Musée
High over the city on a western cliff, **Château Musée** (☎ 02 35 84 19 76; adult/concession €2.40/1.10; ☽ 10am-noon 2-6pm daily Jun-Sep, 10am-noon & 2-5pm Wed-Mon Oct-May) is Dieppe's most impressive landmark. The castle dates from the 15th century and served as a residence for the governors of Dieppe until the Revolution, receiving François I, Henri IV and Louis XIV as visitors. It was a prison and an army barracks before the city purchased it in 1906 and turned it into a museum. Damaged by the retreating German army in 1944, the structure has been restored and now offers sweeping views over the sea. The museum is devoted to Dieppe's maritime and artistic history, a large portion of which involved the dubious practice of separating African elephants from their tusks and shipping the ivory back to Dieppe.

The craft of ivory-carving reached extraordinary heights in Dieppe during the 17th century and the results are on display in a series of rooms. At one time, some 350

SEINE-MARITIM

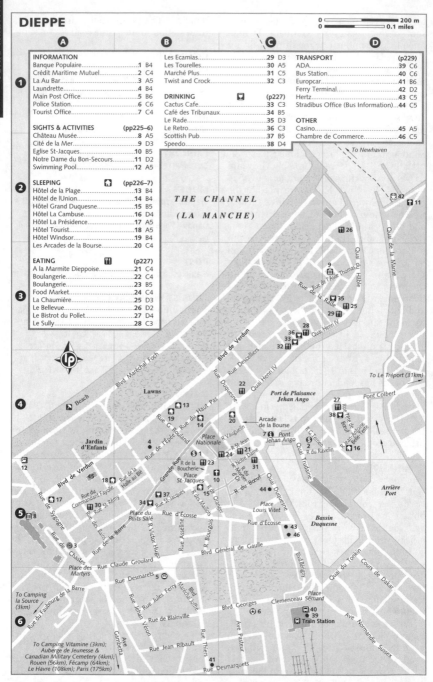

DIEPPE

0 — 200 m
0 — 0.1 miles

Ⓐ **Ⓑ** **Ⓒ** **Ⓓ**

INFORMATION
Banque Populaire.....................1 B4
Crédit Maritime Mutuel............2 C4
La Au Bar.................................3 A5
Laundrette...............................4 B4
Main Post Office.......................5 B6
Police Station...........................6 C6
Tourist Office...........................7 C4

SIGHTS & ACTIVITIES (pp225–6)
Château Musée.........................8 A5
Cité de la Mer...........................9 D3
Eglise St-Jacques....................10 B5
Notre Dame du Bon-Secours....11 D2
Swimming Pool.......................12 A5

SLEEPING (pp226–7)
Hôtel de la Plage....................13 B4
Hôtel de lUnion.....................14 B4
Hôtel Grand Duquesne............15 B5
Hôtel La Cambuse...................16 D4
Hôtel La Présidence................17 A5
Hôtel Tourist..........................18 A5
Hôtel Windsor........................19 B4
Les Arcades de la Bourse.........20 C4

EATING (p227)
A la Marmite Dieppoise...........21 C4
Boulangerie............................22 C4
Boulangerie............................23 B5
Food Market...........................24 C4
La Chaumière.........................25 D3
Le Bellevue............................26 D2
Le Bistrot du Pollet.................27 D4
Le Sully.................................28 C3

Les Ecamias............................29 D3
Les Tourelles..........................30 A5
Marché Plus............................31 C5
Twist and Crock......................32 C5

DRINKING (p227)
Cactus Cafe............................33 C3
Café des Tribunaux.................34 B5
Le Rade.................................35 D3
Le Retro................................36 C3
Scottish Pub...........................37 B5
Speedo..................................38 D4

TRANSPORT (p229)
ADA.......................................39 C6
Bus Station.............................40 C6
Europcar................................41 B6
Ferry Terminal........................42 D2
Hertz.....................................43 C5
Stradibus Office (Bus Information)..44 C5

OTHER
Casino...................................45 A5
Chambre de Commerce...........46 C5

To Newhaven

THE CHANNEL
(LA MANCHE)

Quai de la Marne

Quai du Hâble

Rue de l'Asile Thomas

Rue de la Rade

Quai Henri IV

Blvd de Verdun

Rue Descoliers

Rue Duquesne

To Le Tréport (31km)

Port de Plaisance
Jehan Ango

Pont Colbert

Blvd Maréchal Foch

Lawns

Rue C Ribault

Rue du Haut Pas

Rue de l'Épée

Arcade
de la Bourse

Pont
Jehan Ango

Quai Trudaine

Arrière
Port

Beach

Jardin
d'Enfants

Place
Nationale

R Vauquelin

R St-Jean

R de la
Boucherie

R Notre Dame

Bassin
Duquesne

Blvd de Verdun

Grande Rue

Rue St-Jacques

Place
St-Jacques

Rue du
Mortier d'Or

Rue du Bœuf

Quai Duquesne

Place
Louis Vitet

Quai du Tonkin Cours de Dakar

Rue de Sygogne

Rue du
Commandant Fayolle

Rue St-Rémy

Rue de la
Halle au Blé

Rue du
Four à Chaux

Place du
Puits Salé

Rue d'Écosse

Rue des
Maillots

R Boulganis

Rue d'Écosse

Rue de

Rue de la Barre

R Victor Hugo

Rue Asseline

Blvd Général de Gaulle

Blvd Bérigny

Place des
Martyrs

Rue Claude Groulard

Rue Desmarets

Rue Jules Ferry

Blvd Maréchal Joffre

Place
Sémard

Clemenceau Blvd

To Camping
la Source
(3km)

Rue du Faubourg de la Barre

Ave Cambeta

Rue Jehan Véron

Rue de Blainville

Blvd Georges

Ave Pasteur

Place
Sémard

Train Station

Ave Normandie Sussex

To Camping Vitamine (3km);
Auberge de Jeunesse &
Canadian Military Cemetery (4km);
Rouen (56km); Fécamp (64km);
Le Havre (108km); Paris (175km)

Rue Jean Ribault

Rue Desmarquets

artisans were working ivory in the town, with skills so finely honed it was rumoured that they had found a way to soften the ivory before carving it.

Other highlights of the museum include prints by Georges Braque, who periodically resided in Dieppe, and memorabilia of composer Camille St-Saëns, whose family was from Dieppe. To get to the museum on foot, take rue de la Barre and follow the signs up rue de Chastes.

Cité de la Mer

If you want to learn more about what Dieppe takes from – and gives back to – the sea around it, visit the **Cité de la Mer** (☎ 02 35 06 93 20; 37 rue de l'Asile Thomas; adult/concession €4.50/2.50; ❧ 10am-noon & 2-6pm). Those with an interest in boating will enjoy the 1st floor, which traces the history and evolution of boat building and navigation. Fishing techniques are the subject of the upper-floor exhibits, with a glance at the processes of freezing and distribution. Curious about cliffs? The formation, erosion and utility of Dieppe's cliffs are explained in detail. The visit ends with five large aquariums filled with happy living examples of fish and shellfish that are usually found on French plates: octopus, sole, lobsters, turbot and cod.

Other Sights & Activities

Although the white cliffs on either side of Dieppe have been compared to those at Dover, the **beach** is gravelly and at times very windy. The vast **lawns** between blvd de Verdun and the beach were laid out in the 1860s by that seashore-loving imperial duo, Napoleon III and his wife, Eugénie. **Église St-Jacques**, a Norman Gothic church at place St-Jacques, has been reconstructed several times since the early 13th century.

The **Canadian Military Cemetery** is 4km along the road to Rouen. To get there, take ave des Canadiens (the continuation of ave Gambetta) south and follow the signs.

The **GR21 hiking trail** follows the Côte d'Albâtre southwest from Dieppe all the way to Le Havre. Pick up a map from the tourist office. For some easy walks in the surrounding areas ranging from one to three hours, get a copy of *Topo-Guide Côte d'Albâtre*.

The sea may be cold but water in the Olympic-sized **swimming pool** is heated to 25°C and there are diving boards.

Special Events

Dieppe is kite-capital of the world for one week during September in even-numbered years. From all over the world kite-makers and kite-flyers come to show off their skills. One of the featured events is *l'Arche des Enfants* when 2500 kites fly over the beach, each one individually decorated by a child from Dieppe.

Sleeping

BUDGET

Camping La Source (☎ /fax 02 35 84 27 04; adult/site €4/6; ❧ mid-Mar–mid-Oct) This camping area is 3km southwest of Dieppe in a lovely creekside location, just off the D925 (well-signposted). Take bus No 4 to the Petit-Appeville train station (10 minutes), walk beneath the railway bridge and up the marked gravel drive.

Camping Vitamine (☎ 02 35 82 11 11; adult/site €4/5.50; ❧ mid-Apr–mid-Oct) is about 3km west of the train station. Take bus No 2 to the Vazarely stop.

Auberge de Jeunesse (☎ 02 35 84 85 73; dieppe@ fuaj.org; 48 rue Louis Fromager; dm €8.90, sheets €2.80; ❧ mid-Sept–mid-May; **P**) About 4km southwest of the train station, this hostel has a kitchen and laundry but breakfast is an extra €3.30. From the station, walk straight up blvd Bérigny to the Chambre de Commerce from where you take bus No 2 (direction: Val Druel) to the Château Michel stop.

MID-RANGE & TOP END

There are a number of popular small hotels along rue du Haut Pas and its continuation, rue de l'Épée.

Hôtel de l'Union (☎ 02 35 84 35 52; 47-49 rue du Haut Pas; r from €22.90) This family-run establishment has somewhat faded rooms of varying sizes. It also hosts a good little restaurant.

Hôtel La Cambuse (☎ 02 35 84 19 46; fax 02 35 84 13 27; 42 rue Jean-Antoine Belle-Teste; r from €30; **P**) Simple but correct, you'll find no-nonsense, clean rooms and a friendly welcome here.

Hôtel Tourist (☎ 02 35 06 10 10; touristhotel@ wanadoo.fr; 16 rue de la Halle au Blé; s/d from €21.50/26) Everything is as it should be here but there are few flourishes. There are more expensive rooms available with all facilities including telephone and TV.

Hôtel Grand Duquesne (☎ 02 32 14 61 10; www .augrandduquesne.fr - French only; 15 place St-Jacques; r from €37) In an older building, rooms have

SEINE-MARITIME

recently been polished up and now offer a good level of comfort complete with telephone and TV.

Les Arcades de la Bourse (☎ 02 35 84 14 12; fax 02 35 40 22 29; 1-3 Arcade de la Bourse; r from €49; P) This is an elegant, old-style hotel in the town centre with views over the port. All have private bath, TV and telephone. More expensive rooms have views over the port.

Hôtel Windsor (☎ 02 35 84 15 23; windsor@ hotelwindsor.fr; 18 blvd de Verdun; r from €51; P) This two-star hotel on the seafront (though a long way from the water across those lawns) has small, garishly decorated doubles with private facilities. More expensive rooms with sea views and balconies are available.

Hôtel de la Plage (☎ 02 35 84 18 28; 20 blvd de Verdun; r €48-73; P ▣) The more expensive rooms are larger and have sea views but all are modern, attractively decorated and equipped with satellite TV.

Hôtel La Présidence (☎ 02 35 84 31 31; www.hotel-la -presidence.com; blvd de Verdun; s/d €59/78; P ✕ ▣) Luxury on the sea is the hallmark of this sleek, modern hotel. It has all the comforts you would expect for the price, including a restaurant with a view of the sea.

Eating
RESTAURANTS

Twist and Crock (☎ 02 35 84 86 31; 67 quai Henri IV; dishes from €6) An inexpensive sandwich place that also serves brochettes, vegetarian salads and mussels. A good stop if you're in a hurry.

Les Écamias (☎ 02 35 84 67 67; 129 quai Henri IV; menus €12-23; ☽ closed Mon, dinner Sun & Tue) This simple, family-style place serves fresh, tasty seafood at reasonable prices. Be sure to try the mussels or *raie* (ray) with butter sauce.

Le Sully (☎ 02 35 84 23 13; 97 quai Henri IV; menus €11-28; ☽ closed Wed & dinner Tue) Also facing the port is this classic, offering a large selection of fish and shellfish simply or elaborately prepared. Vegetarians will enjoy the vegetarian *menu*. The *choucroute de la mer* (sauerkraut with seafood rather than ham and sausage) won't leave you hungry.

Les Tourelles (☎ 02 35 84 15 88; 43 rue du Commandant Fayolle; menus €9.50-19; ☽ closed Mon & dinner Sun) Tourists, families and local office workers on their lunch break come here for the fresh seafood and the convivial atmosphere.

La Chaumiére (☎ 02 35 40 18 54; 1 quai du Hâble; menus €10.50-13; ☽ closed Tue) Right on the water with delicious seafood and friendly service.

Le Bellevue (☎ 02 35 84 39 37; 70 blvd de Verdun; menus €13, €15, €20 & €26; ☽ closed Mon & dinner Sun) The undistinguished setting isn't the point here. The point is the fresh and well-prepared seafood served to a loyal clientele of penny-pinching gourmets. The €13 *menu* is for weekday lunches only.

Le Bistrot du Pollet (☎ 02 35 84 68 57; 23 rue Tête de Boeuf; weekday lunch menu €11.50; ☽ closed Sun & Mon) Away from the tourist crowds in the old fishermen's quarter is this gem for fish-lovers. The à la carte offerings might include *lotte* (monkfish) marinated in wine and *daurade* (sea bream) with herbs. The dining room is small so it's best to reserve.

À la Marmite Dieppoise (☎ 02 35 84 24 26; 8 rue St-Jean; menus €8-38; ☽ closed Mon & dinner Sun) If you really want to taste Dieppe's *fruits de la mer* at their best, head for this intimate establishment in the old city. Their speciality is *marmite Dieppoise*, a delicious fish stew.

SELF-CATERING

There's a **food market** (☽ 6am-1pm Tue & Thu, 7am-5pm Sat) between place St-Jacques and place Nationale and two wonderful **boulangeries** (15 quai Henri IV; ☽ Tue-Sun; 14 rue de la Boucherie; ☽ Thu-Tue). The **Marché Plus supermarket** (22 quai Duquesne) is open long hours.

Drinking

Dieppe has loads of pubs and bars full of interesting characters, but don't be surprised if you have to buzz to be let in.

Scottish Pub (☎ 02 35 84 13 16; 12 rue St-Jacques) This is a good place to start a crawl, and the friendly bar staff will point you in the right direction.

Café des Tribunaux (☎ 02 32 14 44 65; place du Puits Salé) This sprawling 18th-century building harboured the crowd of Impressionist painters in the late 19th century and still makes an excellent impression.

Cactus Cafe (☎ 02 35 82 59 38; 71 quai Henri IV; ☽ closed Sun) This lively spot offers a wide selection of beer and cocktails, as well as some Mexican-like dishes. Vegetarians have a good selection here.

Le Rade (☎ 02 35 82 34 15; 12 rue de la Rade; ☽ closed Mon) Where fishermen come to throw back a brew or two and discuss the day's catch.

Speedo (☎ 02 32 14 08 75; 9 rue de la Charpenterie; ☽ closed Tue) Right on Le Pollet Island is this laid-back new place with an atmospheric cellar.

MARMITE DIEPPOISE

This fish soup is the proud speciality of Dieppe although it can be found in many variations along the Côte d'Albâtre. Serve it with a sparkling dry cider.

4 servings

700g mussels
2 onions
5 tablespoons butter
1L cider
assorted fish heads and bones
2 leeks, washed and chopped
2 celery stalks, cut into rounds

1 bay leaf
3 stalks of fresh thyme or 1 teaspoon dried
900g firm-fleshed white fish (sole, turbot, monkfish) in fillets
250ml *crème fraîche*
2 tablespoons chopped fresh parsley
salt and pepper to taste

Scrub the mussels under cold running water to remove all sand, discarding any that do not close when firmly tapped. Peel and chop the onions. Put half of them in a large pot, add half the butter, 200ml of the cider and then the mussels. Cover and cook on high heat for a few minutes until the mussels open.

Shell the mussels, discarding any that have not opened, and set aside. Strain the cooking liquid and reserve.

Put the fish heads and bones in a pot. Add leeks, remaining chopped onions, celery, bay leaf and thyme. Add the remaining cider, 250mL of water and the cooking liquid from the mussels. Cook uncovered over medium heat for 30 minutes.

Season the white fish and put it into another pot. Pour the strained vegetable broth over it. Add the remaining butter, cut into pieces, and add the *crème fraîche*. Bring back to a simmer and cook over low heat for 15 minutes. Adjust seasoning to taste.

Add the mussels and reheat for two minutes. Pour into a large serving bowl, garnish with the parsley and tuck in!

Getting There & Away

BUS

The bus station is in the same huge building as the train station. Buses go to Fécamp (€11.40, 2¼ hours, at least two daily), Le Tréport (€6.40, 1¼ hours, four daily) and Rouen (€10.65, two hours, three daily). There are no buses Saturday or Sunday afternoon.

TRAIN

From Dieppe's **train station** (☎ 02 35 06 69 33), the paucity of direct trains to Paris' Gare St-Lazare (€22.80, 2¼ hours, four daily) is offset by frequent services to Rouen (€9, 45 to 60 minutes, 10 daily), where there is a connecting service to Le Havre (€16, two hours from Dieppe). The last train from Dieppe to Paris (via Rouen) leaves just before 7pm daily.

BOAT

The first ferry service from Dieppe to the UK (Brighton, to be exact) began in 1790. These days **Hoverspeed** (☎ 08 20 00 35 55) runs car and pedestrian ferries between Dieppe and Newhaven. Boats depart from the ferry terminal on the northeastern side of the port area at the end of quai de la Marne. For details on prices and times, see p339.

Getting Around

BUS

The local bus network **Stradibus** (☎ 02 32 14 03 03) runs 13 lines that run until either 6pm or 8pm, depending on the routes. All buses stop at either the train station or the nearby Chambre de Commerce, on quai Duquesne. It has an information office on this road. A single ticket costs €1, a 10-ticket carnet €6.80.

Buses meet incoming and outgoing ferries and shuttle foot passengers between the terminal and the tourist office (€2).

CAR & MOTORCYCLE

For rentals, there's **ADA** (☎ 02 35 84 32 28), which has an office in the train station, **Hertz** (☎ 02 32 14 01 70; 5 rue d'Écosse) and **Europcar** (☎ 02 35 04 97 10; 33 rue Thiers).

TAXI

Taxis can be called on ☎ 02 35 84 20 05. The fare from the ferry pier to the city centre is about €7.50.

VARENGEVILLE-SUR-MER

pop 1200

A country village just 8km west of Dieppe, **Varengeville-sur-Mer** is so small that you don't know you've been there until you leave it. Little more than a cluster of houses along the side of the road, Varengeville charmed painters such as Monet, Dufy, Miró and Braque. Miró included two paintings of Varengeville in his cycle *Constellations*, and Braque had a studio here towards the end of his life. Braque is buried in Varengeville outside a clifftop church for which he designed several vividly coloured stained-glass windows. His tomb is beneath a mosaic of a white dove on a blue background and there are bracing coastal views from the **cemetery** (8am-9pm summer, 9am-6pm winter).

Next door is the splendid garden-park **Bois des Moutiers** (☎ 02 35 85 10 02; adult/concession €6/2.50, adult €7 May & Jun; 10am-noon & 2-6pm mid-Mar–mid-Nov), a wonderland of flowers and trees from as far as China, North America, Chile and Japan as well as France. The gardens are an extension of a country house built for Guillaume Mallet at the turn of the century. The British architect Sir Edwin Lutyens designed the house in the popular Arts and Crafts style and the English landscape gardener Gertrude Jekyll collaborated with him on the gardens, which are some of the finest in France. Designed as a series of walled spaces, the gardens lead you to a 12-hectare park that winds down to the sea. Come in March and April for the flowering magnolias, in May and June for the azaleas and rhododendrons (some of which are 10m high), in the summer for roses and hydrangeas and in October and November for the Japanese maples. The house is also highly original but can only be visited by appointment. You can stay through lunch and until 8pm May to September. Bus No 60/61 from Dieppe stops at the park (25 minutes, twice daily except Sunday).

Since the cemetery and park are on a cliff high above town, it makes sense to visit them first if you're coming by bus and then walk down the hill to the town centre to visit **Le Manoir d'Ango** (☎ 02 35 85 80; admission €5; 10am-12.30pm & 2-6.30pm mid-Mar–mid-Nov). Built by the shipbuilder and privateer Jehan Ango in the 16th century, this manor has a stunning *colombier* (dovecote) with an unusual domed top and an Italian loggia decorated with frescos from the school of Leonardo da Vinci. The manor is fit for a king and, in fact, Ango received François I here in 1523. Despite his successful expeditions on behalf of the crown, Ango died in his manor almost penniless, still waiting for repayment of money he had lent to the Treasury years earlier.

LE TRÉPORT

pop 6000

Lying 30km north of Dieppe, Le Tréport is the northernmost point of the Côte d'Albâtre. Like many towns along the coast, Le Tréport was once a fishing port that became fashionable in the 19th century. It's not particularly fashionable now, very crowded only in the summer season. The beachfront has been developed to death but the wide, pebbly beach has its charms and the towering cliffs rising above the southwestern end provide a dramatic setting. If the summertime craziness gets too much, the quieter Mers-les-Bains resort lies just northeast of the port.

Orientation & Information

Le Tréport is separated from Mers-les-Bains by the canalised River Bresle, which opens into a port at the Channel. The restaurant-packed quai François 1er runs along the port to the seafront. The most interesting part of town is the old rope-makers quarter, wedged between the port and the beach. From rue de l'Hôtel de Ville on quai François 1er, 350 steps lead to the top of the cliff.

The train and bus station are shared with Mers-les-Bains, northeast of the town centre on the other side of the port. The **tourist office** (☎ 02 35 86 05 69; www.ville-le-treport.fr - French only; quai Sadi Carnot; 10-7pm Jul & Aug, 9am-noon & 2-6.30pm Apr-Jun & Sep, 10am-noon & 3-5pm Mon-Sat Oct-Mar) is east of quai François 1er.

Sights & Activities

On your way to the top of the cliffs, stop at **Église St-Jacques**. Built in the 15th century to replace a much earlier church that collapsed in a storm, the church has several Renaissance highlights including its main door and a polychrome Madonna from the 16th century. Notice the scallop decoration in the interior. Pilgrims on the way to Santiago de Compostela in Spain adopted the scallop as their emblem and it eventually took on a religious connotation.

The view from the top of the cliff is well worth the climb up and you can recuperate with a drink on the terrace of the Hôtel Le Trianon. On a rainy day, head to the **Musée du Vieux Tréport** (☎ 02 35 86 13 36; adult/concession €2/1; ◷ 10am-noon & 3-6pm Sat & Sun Apr-Sep), which has some moderately interesting exhibits devoted to Le Tréport's maritime history. More worthwhile is the **tourist train** (adult/concession €5.50/3) that runs weekends and holidays from April to September. It's a good way to take in the *belle époque* mansions in **Mers-les-Bains** and the vast chateau at **Eu**.

The tourist office has a map and suggestions for walking and cycling around the region.

Sleeping & Eating

Camping Les Boucaniers (☎ 02 35 86 35 47; fax 02 35 86 55 82; camping €14.80; ◷ Apr-Sep) This camping ground is in a quiet location on the road to Mers-les-Bains.

Le Saint-Yves (☎ 02 35 86 34 66; fax 02 35 86 53 73; 7 quai Albert Cauët; r €40-65) Only 300m from the sea, the Saint-Yves offers comfortably old-fashioned rooms equipped with TVs and telephones. A buffet breakfast will cost an extra €7.

Le Tréport is known for its giant plates of fresh seafood and you'll find a dozen equally good places on quai François 1er.

La Matelote (☎ 02 35 86 01 13; 34 quai François 1er) One of our favourites. Count on spending about €25 for a stack of shellfish but about half that for a fish-centred meal.

Pizzeria de la Tour (☎ 02 35 50 12 17; 1 rue de la Tour; menus €10.50-14; ◷ closed Mon) A simple pizza or decent plate of pasta can go a long way after a busy day on the beach.

La Crêperie du Musoir (☎ 02 35 86 69 41; 2 rue de Paris; menus €15) The crepes are delightful and you can get them every day.

Mon P'tit Bar (☎ 02 35 86 28 78; 3-5 rue de la Rade; ◷ 9am-midnight) It's not a big deal, just a friendly, local watering hole where you can also grab a bite to eat any time of the day.

Getting There & Away

The best way to reach Le Tréport is by bus from Dieppe. CNA has at least four buses daily (€6.40, 1¼ hours). There are also trains from Rouen (€15.50, 2¼ hours, three daily) and Paris (€21.50, three hours, five daily). You can also rent **bikes** (☎ 02 35 86 23 44) at the train station

FÉCAMP
pop 21,500

At the foot of the highest cliffs in Normandy (126m), Fécamp is a sturdy fishing town 41km north of Le Havre. Fishing boats and pleasure boats crowd its port and a promenade runs along an exhilarating stretch of rocky beach. Until the mid-1970s, Fécamp was the fourth largest fishing port in France with fishermen setting sail for the cod-filled waters of Newfoundland. In recent decades, fishing boats stay closer to home, bringing the daily catch to nearby freezing, drying and salting factories. Ship-repair and net-making are also important industries in Fécamp. The town's dramatic setting and neat rows of brick houses has made it a popular summer resort and there are fascinating reminders of its history scattered through the town.

History

Fécamp was little more than a fishing village until the 6th century, when a few drops of Christ's blood miraculously found their way here and it became a pilgrimage centre. The first dukes of Normandy built a fortified chateau in Fécamp in the 10th century that remained a ducal residence for over 100 years. The dukes also encouraged the formation of a Bénédictine abbey, which remained influential until the Revolution. In the early 16th century a Bénédictine monk concocted a 'medicinal elixir' from a variety of plants. Although the recipe was lost during the Revolution, it was rediscovered in the 19th century and the after-dinner liqueur was produced commercially. Today, Bénédictine is one of the most widely-marketed *digestifs* in the world. Visits to the abbey, the Bénédictine distillery and cod-fishing museum cover the main axes of Fécamp's development and the narrow streets remain much as they were in the 19th century when they served as a backdrop for the evocative tales of Guy de Maupassant.

Orientation

The town centre lies southwest of a series of ports and basins. Quai de la Vicomté and quai Bérigny along the Port de Plaisance and Bassin Bérigny form a busy commercial road packed with shops and restaurants. The pedestrianised streets between the St-Étienne church and place Charles de Gaulle are also good for shopping. The oldest part of town lies east of rue du Président René Coty, which is where you'll find most places of interest.

Information

The **tourist office** (☎ 02 35 28 51 01; www.fecamp.com - French only; 113 rue Alexandre Le Grand; ⏲ 9am-12.30pm & 2.30-6pm Apr-Sept, 9am-noon & 2.30-6pm Oct-Mar) in the town centre is the main source of information. There's another, smaller **tourist office** (☎ 02 35 29 16 94; quai de la Vicomté; ⏲ 11am-2pm & 3-7.30pm Jul & Aug) at the port that opens over the summer months.

Crédit Fécampois (23 rue Alexandre Legros) changes money. The **main post office** (place Bellet) has Cyberposte.

Palais Bénédictine

In an ornate 1900 building, mixing Flamboyant Gothic and eclectic styles, is the **Palais Bénédictine** (☎ 02 35 10 26 10; 110 rue Alexandre Le Grand; adult/concession €5/2.50; ⏲ 10am-6pm Jul & Aug, 10am-noon & 2-5pm Apr-Jun & Sep, 10.30-11.45am & 2-5pm Feb, Mar & Oct-Dec, closed Jan). It was inspired by the 15th-century Hôtel de Cluny in Paris. It's geared up to tell you everything about the history and making of its aromatic liqueur – except the exact recipe. We do know that it involves the prettily named melissa, angelica and hyssop plants – and 24 other herbs and spices.

Tours start in the art museum, which houses the private collection of founder Alexandre Le Grand. This rich merchant loved medieval art and the display includes carved ivory and wood, 15th- and 16th-century statues, manuscripts, wrought iron and a stained-glass window of Alexandre Le Grand commissioned by his son. The visit continues through a hall where hundreds of bottles of bootlegged Bénédictine are proudly displayed. In the fragrant Plant & Spice Room, you can smell a handful of some of the ingredients used to make the potent drink and then see the oak vats where it is fermented. Admission includes a free shot of Benedictine.

Abbatiale de la Ste-Trinité

Fortified by the Bénédictine, proceed to the **Abbatiale de la Ste-Trinité** (☎ 02 35 28 84 39; place des Ducs Richard; ⏲ 9am-6pm). Built from 1175 to 1220 under the instigation of Richard the Lion-Heart, this Benedictine abbey was the most important pilgrimage site in Normandy until the construction of Mont St-Michel. Its

primary draw for pilgrims has been the drop of holy blood that miraculously floated to Fécamp in the trunk of a fig tree. A fountain sprouted from the spot where the trunk landed and eventually the holy blood was placed in the custody of the abbey monks.

The exterior is a combination of primitive Gothic and a classical style dating from an 18th-century reconstruction. The spacious interior is 127m long and 23m high, which compares favourably with many of France's finest cathedrals. Among the many treasures inside is the late-15th-century *Dormition de la Vierge* (Assumption of the Virgin) – a polychrome bas relief of very lifelike faces crowding around a weeping Virgin. Nearby is the *Le Pas de l'Ange* (The Footprint of the Angel) sculpture, which represents the footprint of the angel that allegedly descended upon the church during its consecration, demanding that it be named after the Holy Trinity.

Across from the abbey are the remains of the **fortified chateau** built by the earliest dukes of Normandy in the 10th and 11th centuries.

Musée des Terres-Neuvas et de la Pêche

The typical life of a cod fisherman is evoked with extraordinary verve at the **Musée des Terres-Neuvas et de la Pêche** (☎ 02 35 29 76 22; 27 blvd Albert 1er; adult/concession €3/1.50; ⏲ 10am-7pm daily Jul & Aug, 10am-noon & 2-5.30pm Wed-Mon Sep-Jun). For centuries the men of Fécamp boarded sailing ships to Newfoundland, where they caught, cleaned and salted cod to be brought back to Spain and Portugal. The practice began in the 16th century and the last boat to make the crossing was in 1987. While some displays show fishing techniques, the emphasis is on men's relationship with the sea and their capacity for brutal, dangerous work.

Festivals & Events

On Ascension Thursday, the Fécampois pay homage to their sailing tradition with a mass in the ancient St-Trinity abbey, a procession and a blessing of the sea.

Tours

The boat **Ville de Fécamp** runs daily 1½-hour trips to Étretat (adult/concession €12/8) and 45-minute trips to Yport (adult/concession €8.50/6). Four-hour fishing trips (€29, with equipment included in the tour price) are also available between April and October, depending on the weather. Boats leave from the Grand Quai. Call ☎ 02 35 28 99 53 for further information.

Sleeping

Camping Renéville (☎ 02 35 28 20 97; fax 02 35 29 57 68; Côte de Renéville; camping €6.20) Dramatically situated on the western cliffs overlooking the beach, camping here makes a great holiday.

Hotels across from the beach are an appealing choice but since they are on a busy boulevard, the front rooms can be noisy.

Hôtel de la Mer (☎ 02 35 28 24 64; fax 02 35 28 27 67; 89 blvd Albert 1er; r with sink from €31, with bathroom €46) The best of the beachfront hotels is this coolly modern establishment, where many of the comfortably outfitted rooms have balconies with sea views.

Hôtel Les Embruns (☎ 02 35 28 31 31; fax 02 35 28 45 17; 73 blvd Albert 1er; r €45) Nearby is this smaller establishment that also has balconies facing the sea.

Hôtel de la Plage (☎ 02 35 29 76 51; hoteldelaplagefecamp@wanadoo.fr; 87 rue de la Plage; r from €50; ✗) Set back a block from the sea, this accommodating establishment offers stylish, well-furnished rooms kept in excellent condition. There are larger and more expensive rooms available that offer a view of the sea.

Hôtel d'Angleterre (☎ 02 35 28 01 60; fax 02 35 28 62 95; 93 rue de la Plage; r €40-57) The recent renovation has worked wonders for this young, friendly hotel. The rooms are cheery and colourful.

Hôtel le Grand Pavois (☎ 02 35 10 01 01; www.hotel -grand-pavois.com; r €80; P ✗ ⊠ ▣) Professional through and through, this well-run hotel offers large, sleek rooms with safes, minibars and balconies. More expensive rooms have panoramic sea views.

Eating

Hôtel Martin Restaurant (☎ 02 35 28 23 82; 18 place St-Etienne; menus from €11.40; ✕ closed Mon & dinner Sun) The hotel may not be any great shakes but the restaurant is one of the better-value eateries in town. In a cosy dining room, waiters bring out Norman dishes cooked with flair. Mussels with cider and fresh cod are standouts.

Le Vicomté (☎ 02 35 28 47 63; 4 rue du Président Coty; menu €14.60; ✕ closed Sun & dinner Wed) With its daily *menu* on a blackboard, moustachioed owner and cosy dining room, this could be a movie set for a typical French bistro. Now that you're in a good mood, try the *raie à la vinaigrette de noix* (skate with walnut sauce) or mackerel in mustard sauce.

Marée (☎ 02 35 29 39 15; 75 quai Bérigny; menus €17.60-33.50; ✕ closed Sun, Mon & dinner Thu) An extension of a fish shop, this place offers the freshest, tastiest fish in town. The *choucroute de la mer* (seafood with sauerkraut) has just the right touch of tang but all the fish and seafood is prepared with a minimum of fuss. Finish off with *crème brûlée à la Bénédictine*.

Le Maritime (☎ 02 35 28 21 71; 2 place Nicolas Selles; menus €17-29.50) There's a lot to choose from here, most of it from the sea, as the name would imply. The seafood platters are copious and can be ordered to take away.

SELF CATERING

Boulangerie Les Carolines (☎ 02 35 27 33 45; 44 rue Théagène Boufart; ✕ closed all day Wed & Sun afternoon) Bread lovers will revel in the chewy loaves here, named as one of the best *boulangeries* in France. Look for an old brick house with murals on bread-making themes.

There's a **Marché Plus** (83 quai Bérigny) supermarket and a **market** (place Charles de Gaulle) all day Saturday.

Getting There & Away

Fécamp is accessible by bus from Dieppe (p229), Le Havre (p224) and Rouen (p215), and by train from Le Havre. The **train station** (☎ 02 35 28 24 82) is conveniently located. The bus between Fécamp (30 minutes, seven daily) and Le Havre also connects Fécamp with Étretat.

Getting Around

Fécamp has a city bus line mainly to serve students. For a visitor, bus No 6 that runs from place St-Étienne to the beach, via the Palais Bénédictine would be the most useful, but there are only five buses daily.

Mountain bikes and 10-speeds are available for rent from **Rosalie Boutique** (☎ 02 35 10 73 39; 42 rue du Casino) .

For a **taxi** call ☎ 02 35 28 17 50.

AROUND FÉCAMP

Quiet **Yport** makes Fécamp, 6km to the west, look like a major metropolis. Also squeezed between giant cliffs, Yport has a rocky beach

SEINE-MARITIME

sadly marred by wooden bathhouses and an ugly casino. Yet, there's an endearing simplicity to Yport, which seems as though it's been left behind in the rush towards tourism along the coast.

The **tourist office** (☎ 02 35 29 77 31; place JP Laurens; ☺ 10am-noon & 3-7pm mid-May–mid-Sep). The post office is across the street. Places to stay are sparse but the tourist office has a list of *chambres d'hôtes* (B&Bs).

Hôtel Normand (☎ 02 35 27 30 76; fax 02 35 28 70 37; place JP Laurens) This two-star establishment has a traditional Norman look and appealing rooms with all the basic comforts.

Les Embruns (☎ 02 35 27 31 32; 2 rue Emmanuel Foy; menus €14.50-18.50; ☺ closed Wed) It's nothing fancy, but Normandy staples like cod in cider sauce, fisherman's platter and *moules marinière* (mussels with shallots in white-wine sauce) are very carefully and correctly prepared.

Yport is accessible by bus from Fécamp (15 minutes, eight daily).

ÉTRETAT

pop 1650

Étretat, a small village 20km southwest of Fécamp, is renowned for its two cliffs: the Falaise d'Amont and Falaise d'Aval. Featuring the most unusual rock formations in the area, you'll see them long before you arrive, appearing somewhat deceivingly to be one rock. Unlike other coastal towns, Étretat has no port and never amounted to much until painters and writers discovered its beauty in the 19th century. Guy de Maupassant spent part of his youth here and the stunning scenery made it a favourite of painters Camille Corot, Eugène Boudin, Gustav Courbet and Claude Monet. With the vogue for sea air at the end of the 19th century, fashionable Parisians came and built villas. Étretat has never gone out of style and swells to bursting point with visitors in summer and on long weekends. Count on huge traffic jams and overbooked hotels if you come during peak periods.

Orientation

The main road into town is ave de Verdun, which takes you down to the tourist office. Follow rue Monge east and you'll come to busy blvd du Président René Coty and the seaside promenade. Most hotels, shops and restaurants are in the compact town centre.

Information

Crédit Agricole (20 rue Prospero) Across from the tourist office.

Laundrette (78 ave de Verdun)

Main Post Office (25 rue George V) There's no Cyberposte.

Tourist Office (☎ 02 35 27 05 21; www.etretat.net; place Maurice Guillard; ☺ 10am-7pm mid-Jun–mid-Sep, 10am-noon & 2-6pm mid-Mar–mid-Jun & mid-Sep–mid-Nov, 10am-noon & 2-6pm Fri & Sat mid-Nov–mid-Mar) Accommodation lists for the area are posted on the door outside opening hours. It also has a map of the cliff trails and rents bicycles.

Sights & Activities

The big attraction of Étretat are the stony white cliffs that press in the town, the **Falaise d'Amont** to the northeast and **Falaise d'Aval** to the southwest. The latter is accessible via signposted stairs from place du Général de Gaulle. The cliff descends to the water in a delicate arch, the **Porte d'Aval**, that reminded writer Guy de Maupassant of an elephant dipping its trunk into the water. Behind the arch is the 70m-high **L'Aiguille** (Needle), which arises from the water like an obelisk. **Le Trou à l'Homme** grotto lies on the other side of the arch and can be reached on foot at low tide. Beyond the grotto is the stunning **La Manneporte** rock arch. The Falaise d'Amont is accessible by car, taking rue Jules Gerbeau, or on foot from the signposted path at the northeastern end of the promenade. At the top is a monument and little **museum** (☎ 02 35 27 07 47; admission €0.95; ☺ 10.30am-noon & 2.30-5.30pm Wed-Mon Jul & Aug, 10.30am-noon & 2.30-5.30pm Sat & Sun Sep-Jun) commemorating the spot where two aviators, Charles Nungesser and François Coli, were last seen before their attempt to cross the Atlantic in 1927. Count on about 1½ hours for each walk.

Serious walkers might enjoy continuing north on the GR21 from Falaise d'Amont to the **Aiguille de Belval** and Benouville for the splendid coastal views. Do *not* try to explore the base of the cliffs outside low tide. Ask the tourist office for the tide tables.

You can't miss the **old covered market** in the centre of town. This handsome wooden structure looks more like a church but was built in 1926 as a covered marketplace. It now houses various arts and crafts shops.

Special Events

The **Bénédiction de la Mer** (Blessing of the Sea) on Ascension Thursday commemorates the legend whereby fishermen were caught in a terrible storm. A monk prayed on bended knee for the winds to stop and they did, sparing the lives of all. The ceremony dates from the Middle Ages and includes music, a fair, a mass and, of course, a blessing of the sea in which flowers are spread on the water in homage to sailors who lost their lives in Great Blue.

Sleeping

Camping Municipal (☎ 02 35 27 07 67; adult/site €2.20/2.20; mid-Mar–mid-Oct) This camping ground is next to the road about 1km east of the town centre, taking rue Guy de Maupassant.

Camping Les Tilleuls (☎ 02 35 27 11 67; adult/site €2.50/4; Apr-Sep) This is a prettier site about 4km southwest of Étretat in the village of Tilleuls.

The cheaper hotels are in from the sea along ave George V or place Foch.

Hôtel de la Poste (☎ 02 35 27 01 34; fax 02 35 27 76 28; 6 ave George V; s/d €29/40) All fussiness has been banished from the attractively decorated rooms here but the ambience and the welcome remain warm.

Hôtel des Falaises (☎ 02 35 27 02 77; 1 blvd du Président René Coty; r from €29; P) There's a lot of polish for the price here. More expensive rooms with private facilities are available.

Hôtel La Résidence (☎ 02 35 27 02 87; fax 02 35 27 17 07; 4 blvd du Président René Coty; r €29-65) This may well be the most interesting hotel in Normandy. The 14th-century building with an appealingly dilapidated façade once belonged to an alchemist who adorned the windows with alchemy signs. Renovation of the interior has added modern bathrooms (some with a Jacuzzi) but left intact the creaky stairway, wooden floors and doors and overhanging beams. Rooms vary considerably in size and comfort but all are well-maintained.

Hôtel Le Corsaire (☎ 02 35 10 38 90; fax 02 35 28 89 74; rue Général Leclerc; r €55) For a room with a sea view, head here. The outside is pretty as a picture and if you find the rooms somewhat austere you can stroll out to your balcony for memorable views of the cliffs.

Hôtel Le Donjon (☎ 02 35 27 08 23, www.ledonjon -etretat.fr; chemin de St-Clair; r from €145-250; P   ) And to really wallow in luxury, there's this turreted wonder about 1km northeast of the town centre. The rooms are decorated with striking originality. Canopies over the beds, satellite TV, background music and hairdryers are in every room, but the more expensive rooms all have Jacuzzis, sea views, lounges and dressing rooms. There's an excellent restaurant.

Eating

The dining scene in Étretat has few standouts, but there are some good seafood places where you can feast well if you want to pay the price. The hotels **Le Corsaire** and **Le Donjon** turn out good food and there are a number of inexpensive **creperies**, **pizzerias** and **brasseries** on rue Alphonse Karr, blvd du Président René Coty and place Foch.

Le Galion (☎ 02 35 29 48 74; blvd du Président René Coty; menus €22-36; closed Tue & Wed) The 17th-century décor, filled with beams and style, creates a serious atmosphere to partake of such specialities as salmon with Muscadet sauce.

L'Huitrière (☎ 02 35 27 02 82; rue de Traz Perier; menus €17-32) There's a lot of scenery for the price here considering that the round dining room has a panoramic view of the Falaise d'Aval and the beaches. You won't be disappointed in the food either, especially the delicious mussels or the fish soup.

Pick up supplies at the **Point Coop** (40 rue Notre Dame; closed Sun afternoon) supermarket. The **market** (9am-1pm Thu) is held around the old covered market.

Drinking

La Salamandre (☎ 02 35 27 17 07; 4 blvd René Cody) This magnificent café is a congenial place to drink and snack, cloistered within its ancient wood walls.

Getting There & Away

The only way to reach Étretat is on the bus that runs from Fécamp to Le Havre, stopping at Yport. For information, see p224.

Eure

CONTENTS

Pays d'Ouche	**238**
Évreux	238
Around Évreux	241
Northeastern Eure	**243**
Vernon	243
Giverny	244
Les Andelys	246
Gisors	248
Forêt de Lyons	249
Côte des Deux Amants	251
Western Eure	**251**
Bernay	251
Around Bernay	252

Since it doesn't have a beach, the landlocked Eure *département* is untrampled by throngs of sun-worshippers. Tourists flock by the busload to Monet's luxuriant garden at Giverny, but fewer make it to the plains, valleys and forests of the interior. Yet the rewards are many. The magnificent Forêt de Lyons in the northeast offers a wide choice of walks and drives through beech trees that reveal forgotten chateaux and obscure old villages. The mighty fortresses of Gisors and Château Gaillard recall the turbulent time when the kings of England and France battled furiously to gain control of this *département*. In the 18th century, the region was settled by Belgian textile merchants who began the cultivation of flax and left the population awash with Flemish surnames.

Riversides are a large part of the Eure's appeal. Vernon and Les Andelys on the Seine, Évreux on the Iton and Bernay on the Charentonne have carefully groomed riverbanks that make the town centres gentle and relaxing. Forests cover about a fifth of the land area in this *département,* creating a pleasant contrast with the grain plains around Évreux and four gentle valleys created by the Rivers Eure, Risle, Iton and Charentonne. You'll need a car to do full justice to the *département*, since public transport is infrequent to nonexistent, especially to the circle of attractions – Le Bec-Hellouin and the chateaux of Beaumesnil and Champ de Bataille – around Bernay.

HIGHLIGHTS

- Cruise the Seine from **Vernon** (p243) to **Les Andelys** (p246)
- Stroll through Monet's luxuriant garden at **Giverny** (p244)
- Admire the views of the Seine from the **Château Gaillard** (p247)
- Peruse the Saturday morning market in **Bernay** (p251)
- Glimpse how the rich lived in the chateaux of **Beaumesnil** (p252) and **Champ de Bataille** (p253)
- Listen to the Gregorian chants in **Le Bec-Hellouin** (p253)

- POPULATION: 541,000
- AREA: 6040 SQ KM

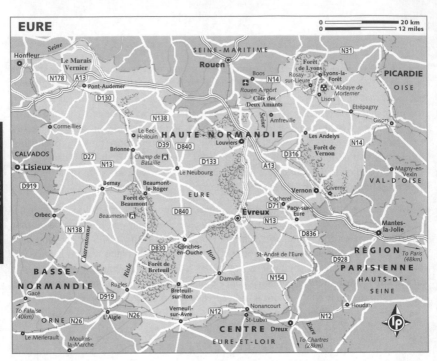

PAYS D'OUCHE

Picturesque Évreux, the capital of the Eure *département,* gives way to forested vales in the northwest and the humid hills of the Ouche country in the southwest. The Pays d'Ouche is a sparsely populated, forested plateau, well watered by rivers. With harsh winters and chalky soil, neither industry nor agriculture has taken root, but mysteries and tales of sorcerers have flourished in the evocative mists wafting through the valleys.

ÉVREUX
pop 51,000

Around 50km south of Rouen, Évreux is a tranquil provincial city on the River Iton. An archaeological museum and a fine cathedral recall its turbulent history, which began around the 1st century AD when the city was known as Mediolanum. Throughout the Middle Ages, Évreux was a battleground for every conquering army in Normandy. The Vandals destroyed the ancient city in the 5th century, the Normans destroyed it again in the 9th century and Henry I burned it in the 12th century. It was burned again by King Philippe-Auguste later in the 12th century after John Lackland (brother of Richard the Lion-Heart) invited 300 French soldiers garrisoned in Évreux for a nice dinner and then massacred them. During the 14th century Évreux was caught in the struggle between the French and English, and burned again, this time losing its Episcopal palace and priceless archives. It became part of France in 1441 but suffered again in 1791 when Revolutionaries razed six churches, two convents and two abbeys.

German bombs devastated the town in 1940 and Allied bombs rained down on it in 1944. Phoenix-like, Évreux has risen again. Careful reconstruction has created a warm, liveable centre with plenty of green spaces. The banks of the Iton are graced with tree-lined promenades, and old half-timbered houses are being restored. Although there's not enough in Évreux to keep most people engrossed for more than an afternoon, it makes a relaxing overnight stop or base for exploring other towns in the Eure.

Orientation

The train and bus stations are about 1km south of the town centre and adjacent to each other. The Tour de l'Horloge is the most conspicuous landmark in the centre of town. Shops, restaurants and cafés are clustered on and around rue Joséphine and rue du Docteur Oursel.

The river bank, promenade des Remparts and promenade Robert de Floques, run from the tourist office to the cathedral and museum. Rue Chartraine and rue de la Harpe are also lively streets, full of shops, banks and cafés.

Information

Cybernetics (☎ 02 32 38 06 03; 27 rue Edouard Feray; per 5min €0.50; ⏱ 10am-12.30pm & 2-7pm Mon-Sat)

Laundrette (27 rue St-Thomas; ⏱ 7am-9pm daily)

Main Post Office (25 rue du Docteur Oursel) Changes money and has Cyberposte facilities for Internet connection.

Tourist Office (☎ 02 32 24 04 43; www.ot-pays-evreux.fr; 3 place du Général de Gaulle; ⏱ 9.30am-12.30pm & 1.30-6.15pm Mon-Sat year-round, 10am-12.30pm Sun Jun-Sep) In the centre of town.

Sights & Activities

The **Cathédrale Notre-Dame** (rue Charles Corbeau; ⏱ 8am-noon & 2-7pm) has been destroyed and rebuilt so many times it has become a temple to changing architectural styles. The Romanesque arcades in the nave date from the late 12th century, and survived when the church went up in flames in 1194 as part of Philippe-Auguste's attack on the city. Reconstruction of the cathedral was slow, but by the end of the 13th century the choir was completed in an elegant Rayonnant Gothic style. Notice the fine 14th-century windows around the choir. The cathedral burned again in 1356 and 1378 in assaults by the Count of Évreux and Charles V, respectively. Under Louis XI in the 15th century, the transept, the lantern tower and a wonderful north door were built in a Flamboyant Gothic style. The Mère de Dieu (Mother of Christ) chapel, ornamented by a splendid series of stained-glass windows, reflects the end of the Gothic era. The church wasn't finished until the western façade was remodelled by a Parisian architect, and it was to suffer yet more indignities. All its statues were destroyed in the Revolution and a 1940

EURE

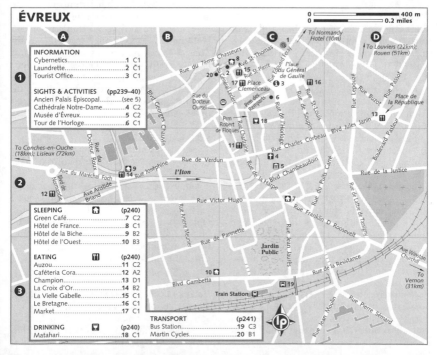

ÉVREUX

0 |——————| 400 m
0 |——————| 0.2 miles

INFORMATION
Cybernetics..................................1 C1
Laundrette....................................2 C1
Tourist Office..............................3 C1

SIGHTS & ACTIVITIES (pp239–40)
Ancien Palais Épiscopal............(see 5)
Cathédrale Notre-Dame..............4 C2
Musée d'Évreux............................5 C2
Tour de l'Horloge.........................6 C1

SLEEPING (p240)
Green Café.....................................7 C2
Hôtel de France............................8 C1
Hôtel de la Biche..........................9 B2
Hôtel de l'Ouest.........................10 B3

EATING (p240)
Auzou..11 C2
Caféteria Cora.............................12 A2
Champion.....................................13 D1
La Croix d'Or..............................14 B2
La Vieille Gabelle.......................15 C1
Le Bretagne.................................16 C1
Market..17 C1

DRINKING (p240)
Matahari.......................................18 C1

TRANSPORT (p241)
Bus Station..................................19 C3
Martin Cycles.............................20 B1

EURE

bombing caused terrible damage to its towers and the *clocher d'argent* (bell tower). As if it hadn't suffered enough, a hurricane in 1983 tore through the venerable old structure. Restorations are continuing.

Next to the church is the **Ancien Palais Épiscopal**, built on the vestiges of a Gallo-Roman rampart that surrounded the city in the 3rd century AD.

The **Musée d'Évreux** (☎ 02 32 31 52 29; 6 rue Charles Corbeau; admission €4; ☼ 10am-noon & 2-6pm Tue-Sun) presents an excellent overview of the town's history. As well as costumes, paintings and tapestries, there is an impressive segment of the 1700-year-old Gallo-Roman ramparts in the basement. Amid a display of prehistoric and Merovingian antiquities is a remarkable 1st-century bronze-and-silver statue of Jupiter and a later statue of Apollo. The exhibits are well presented but captioned only in French.

The noble **Tour de l'Horloge** is 44m high and was built between 1490 and 1497 on the site of the former city gates. The two-tonne bell, cast in 1406, strikes on the hour, with two chimes on the half-hour.

Sleeping

Green Café (☎ 02 32 39 05 46; 1 rue Franklin D Roosevelt; r without/with bathroom €25/31) The cheapest lodging in town is this small place, which is little more than 10 rooms over a brasserie. Make sure to call in advance as it is often closed.

Hôtel de l'Ouest (☎ 02 32 39 20 39; fax 02 32 62 37 19; 47-49 blvd Gambetta; r €38; (P)) Across the street from the train station, you'll find plain but adequate rooms equipped with TVs.

Hôtel de France (☎ 02 32 39 09 25; fax 02 32 38 38 56; 29 rue St-Thomas; r €42.50-70) This two-star place has pretty, old-fashioned rooms of different sizes on a quiet street.

Hôtel de la Biche (☎ 02 32 38 66 00; fax 02 32 33 54 05; 9 rue Joséphine; r €39-43; (P)) The most interesting hotel in town is this splashy place, which was a hunting lodge under François I and then a chic bordello. The theatrical interior of the lobby is topped by a *belle époque* skylight and ornamented in beige and cherry-toned wood. The rooms are somewhat faded but some overlook the river.

Normandy Hôtel (☎ 02 32 33 14 40; norman.hotel@ wanadoo.fr; 37 rue Edouard Feray; r €57-78; (P)) Known for its excellent restaurant, this three-star hotel also offers 20 lovely and comfortable rooms.

Eating

Several of the hotels listed above have good restaurants. Try the restaurants at **Hôtel de la Biche** (☼ closed Sun), **Hôtel de France** (☼ closed Mon, lunch Sat & dinner Sun) or the **Normandy Hotel** for *menus* starting at about €26.

Caféteria Cora (☎ 02 32 29 50 00; blvd de Normandie; menu €5; ☼ closed Sun) For a three-course meal, you can't beat the deal here.

La Croix d'Or (☎ 02 32 33 06 07; 3 rue Joséphine; menus €10.50 & €13.50-30.50) Everyone comes here for the fabulous bouillabaisse, but all the fish and seafood is fresh and expertly prepared. The €10.50 *menu* is available at weekday lunchtimes.

Le Bretagne (☎ 02 32 39 27 38; 3 rue St-Louis; menus €11.50 & €14-27.50; ☼ closed Mon & dinner Wed) The speciality of the house is chicken with Camembert sauce, but a loyal crowd of regulars comes for the other meaty wonders such as the beef *bourguignon* or *salade périgourdine* (green salad with bacon and chicken liver). The €11.50 *menu* is available at weekday lunch times.

La Vielle Gabelle (☎ 02 32 39 77 13; 3 rue de la Vielle Gabelle; menus €14 & €24; ☼ closed Mon, lunch Sat & dinner Sun; ☒) Picture a half-timbered house and a beamed dining room filled with Norman furniture and you'll think tradition. Nothing could be further from the truth. The cuisine is wonderfully imaginative and is permeated with influences from every region in France. And what could be more modern (in France, that is) than a separate room for nonsmokers? There's a €14 *menu* on weekdays.

SELF-CATERING

There's a Champion supermarket on place de la République, and a market on Saturday morning on place Clemenceau.

Auzou (rue Chartraine; ☼ closed Mon & Sun afternoon) sells boxes of scrumptious, almond-based pastries called *les caprices des Ursulines*, which were supposedly first developed by bored conscripts at the Ursuline convent. Congratulate yourself if you manage not to finish the entire box of 16 in one sitting.

Drinking

Matahari (☎ 02 32 38 49 88; 15 rue de la Petite Cité) The terrace on the river is a peaceful, trendy spot for a drink and a snack, and the interior often has exhibitions of local artists within its African-inspired décor.

AN UNLIKELY SAINT?

'Will no-one rid me of this turbulent priest?' cried Henry II about the rebellious Thomas Becket. The phrase may also have echoed around the Vatican in the early 1990s. Jacques Gaillot was named Bishop of Évreux in 1982 and ran into immediate difficulty with the Church. The Vatican's stand on homosexuality, the use of condoms to prevent the spread of HIV, birth control and the ordination of married men are unpopular in France and particularly with Bishop Gaillot. His espousal of a more open and inclusive church resonated beyond his see and attracted the attention of media outlets around the country. After Gaillot's declaration to a gay magazine that 'homosexuals will go to heaven before us', the Vatican began to ponder his more immediate earthly future within the Catholic Church. In a 1992 ceremony the Pope murmured to him, 'you have to sing inside the choir as well as outside it'.

When his song didn't change, the Vatican dismissed him from his see in 1995 and appointed him head of the obsolete diocese of Partenia in Mauritania. If they thought they were going to silence the outspoken priest, they were wrong. Thousands of people turned out for his last mass and Bishop Gaillot became an even bigger celebrity. Rather than disappear, he turned to cyberspace and set up the world's first virtual bishopric. He is now on line at www.partenia.org, where he ministers to the faithful in seven languages.

Although long an icon of the homosexual rights movement in France, Bishop Gaillot is active in a wide range of causes. He has travelled to the Middle East in support of the Palestinian people, and to Tunisia in support of political prisoners, and has recently allied himself with French activist Jose Bové against the spread of genetically modified food. Even as his media profile is deliberately kept low-key, his commitment to the rights of the downtrodden (les exclus) remains ardent and unwavering.

Getting There & Away

BUS

Cars Jacquemard (☎ 02 32 33 09 66) runs buses from L'Aigle (€9.30, one hour, three daily), Conches (€3.90, 40 minutes, three daily) and Le Bec-Hellouin (€8.10, one hour, twice daily). It also connects Évreux with Les Andelys (€5.80, one hour, twice daily), Pacy-sur-Eure (€3.70, 25 minutes, nine daily), Gisors (€9.30, one hour 40 minutes, twice daily) and Vernon (€5.30, 45 minutes, seven daily). **CNA** (☎ 08 25 07 60 27) connects Évreux with Rouen (€8.90, one hour, 10 daily). Call the **bus station** (☎ 02 32 39 40 60) for further information on schedules.

TRAIN

The **train station** (☎ 02 32 78 32 12) is open from 8am to 10pm. Trains from Évreux connect with Paris (€13.70, one hour, up to 16 daily), Caen (€16.50, 1½ hours, up to 15 daily), Lisieux (€11.50, one hour, up to five daily), Conches (€3.10, 10 minutes, up to five daily) and Bernay (€7.70, 45 minutes, up to 10 daily).

Getting Around

Trans Urbain (☎ 02 32 31 34 36) runs the local bus system. All buses from the train station go to the centre; tickets cost €1. **Martin Cycles** (☎ 02 32 39 17 08; 13 rue du Général Leclerc) rents mountain bikes. For a **taxi** call ☎ 02 32 33 43 33.

AROUND ÉVREUX
Conches-en Ouche

pop 4000

Conches-en-Ouche, 18km southwest of Évreux, is the capital of the Pays d'Ouche. Perched on a spur above the River Rouloir, it was once a prestigious stop on the road to Santiago de Compostela in Spain. The town was tossed back and forth during the Hundred Years' War, with fighting centred around its 12th-century chateau. These days the only fighting is likely to be for rooms in Conches' only hotel. With fresh air, half-timbered houses and valley views, the little town is a popular destination for weekending Parisians, many of whom have second residences in the region. An interesting feature of Conches' terrain is the network of passages and caves carved out of the subterranean rock.

ORIENTATION & INFORMATION

The main road through town is rue Ste-Foy, which contains almost all the local businesses, as well as the church, museum and

EURE

hotels. The **tourist office** (☎ 02 32 30 76 42; tourisme -cc.conches@wanadoo.fr; place Aristide-Briand; ⏰ 10am-12.30pm & 2-6pm Tue-Sat) is in the centre at the top of the hill; it rents bikes and organises cycling and walking trips. The **post office** and banks are downhill from place Aristide-Briand on rue Ste-Foy. The bus from Évreux stops at place Aristide-Briand and the train station is at the bottom of the hill.

SIGHTS & ACTIVITIES

The **Église Ste-Foy** (rue Ste-Foy; admission free; ⏰ 9am-7pm) is the town's proudest monument. Built at the end of the 15th century, the church is notable for its stunning ensemble of 22 Renaissance stained-glass windows and some well-carved interior and exterior statues.

Across the street is the **Maison du Fer Forgé** (☎ 02 32 30 20 50; 12 rue Ste-Foy; admission free; ⏰ 10am-12.30pm & 3-7pm Tue-Sun), which displays metalwork in a room that was once the local jail. Torture beams, cells and prison graffiti make a chilling visit.

Not much is left of the **12th-century chateau** that was a stronghold of Bertrand du Guesclin, except for the keep and the wells that provided water during the castle's many sieges. The interior can't be visited, but the surrounding park is agreeable and a woodsy path circles down around it.

SLEEPING & EATING

Camping Municipal (☎ 02 32 30 22 49; camping €7) This lovely spot is about 2km south of the town centre, next to a swimming pool.

Hôtel-Restaurant Le Cygne (☎ 02 32 30 20 60; 2 rue Paul Guilbaud; r €43-50) In a rustic old manor you'll find old-fashioned but pretty rooms. The **restaurant** (menus from €15; ⏰ closed Mon & dinner Sun) is excellent. Try the rabbit in cider aspic.

There are a few *boulangeries* (bakeries) and cafés around place Aristide-Briand; hours are from about 7am to 7pm, but they close about 2pm on Sunday.

Restaurant la Grand'Mare/Le Bistrot (☎ 02 32 30 23 30; 13 ave Croix-de-Fer; bistro menus €10 & €12, restaurant menus €20 & €30) The restaurant and its lower-priced annexe, the bistro, present remarkably sophisticated and imaginative cooking. The chef is the same but the *menu* is more varied and the setting glossier in the restaurant.

GETTING THERE & AWAY

Conches is an easy day trip from Évreux by bus or train. See p241 for details.

Louviers

pop 19,400

Halfway between Rouen and Évreux, Louviers has retained much of its original grace, despite ruinous bombardment in 1940. Several branches of the Eure cut through the town centre, softening the landscape and allowing quiet riverside walks. Some carefully restored half-timbered houses survive from the days when Louviers was renowned for the manufacture of woollen cloth. The wool industry that developed in the 13th century has been replaced by the manufacture of batteries and TV antennae, but the factories are mercifully far from town. Even if there's an unavoidably artificial quality to much of the reconstruction, the gaily decorated façades make for an eye-pleasing stroll.

ORIENTATION & INFORMATION

The main street in town is rue Maréchal Foch, leading from the south to the church, L'Église Notre-Dame, and most businesses. North of the church it becomes rue Pierre Mendès-France; the oldest part of town is northeast of the church. The Eure runs parallel to the main street.

Tourist Office (☎ 02 32 40 04 41; 10 rue du Maréchal Foch; ⏰ 10am-noon & 2-5.30pm Mon-Sat)

Post Office (2 rue de la Poste) Has Cyberposte.

www.ville-louviers.fr The town's website, in French only, with information about local organisations as well as tourist attractions and services.

SIGHTS & ACTIVITIES

The **Musée Municipal** (☎ 02 32 09 58 55; place Ernest Thorel; admission free; ⏰ 10am-noon & 2-6pm Wed-Mon) focuses on Louviers' cloth-making history, with displays of various tools involved in the process. The collection of ceramics, paintings and furniture from the 16th to 19th centuries is also interesting, and there are regular temporary exhibits of contemporary art.

L'Église Notre-Dame (⏰ 9am-5pm) dominates with its Flamboyant Gothic façade, a 16th-century overlay on the 13th-century structure. The best part is the exterior, especially the extravagantly decorated south door.

La Maison en Vaisselle Cassée (☎ 02 32 40 22 71; 80 rue du Bal-Champêtre) is one of the most eccentric residences in Normandy. For over 40 years the owner has amassed pieces of broken crockery and arranged them in whimsical, swirling designs on his house, garage and wall, in his garden – and even on his dog's kennel. All the flowers, plants and sea shells composed of coloured and mirrored ceramics create an almost hallucinatory effect that alone is worth the trip to Louviers. Although it's a private house, you can peek over the gate for a look at the garden. Take blvd Maréchal Joffre from place Ernest Thorel, turn left at the end and continue on rue de la Citadelle to rue du Bal-Champêtre.

SLEEPING & EATING
There's a limited choice of accommodation in Louviers.

Hôtel de Rouen (☎ 02 32 40 40 02; juhel.didier@ wanadoo.fr; 11 place Ernest Thorel; r €33.50-49) You wouldn't want to spend a lifetime here but the hotel is fine for a brief stop. Cheaper rooms have a sink only.

Hôtel le Pré Saint-Germain (☎ 02 32 40 48 48; www .le-pre-saint-germain.com; s/d €66/78; P 🖳) The finest hotel in town offers rooms that are both modern and warmly welcoming. The rooms have all modern conveniences, including modem plugs for Internet access. The **restaurant** (menus €15 & €26; ☽ closed Sun & lunch Sat) is also wonderful, offering an ambitious and finely executed selection of classics.

There are several brasseries and inexpensive cafés around the church. **Le Jardin de Bigard** (☎ 02 32 40 02 45; 39 rue du Quai; menus €9.50 & €12.50-25; ☽ closed Wed & dinner Sun), behind the church, offers typical Norman dishes such as trout with Camembert. The €9.50 *menu* is available at weekday lunch times.

GETTING THERE & AWAY
CNA (08 25 07 60 27) runs up to six buses daily from Rouen and Évreux to Louviers; the trips take about an hour.

DETOUR: THE EURE VALLEY

Leave Louviers by the D71. At **Acquigny**, at the confluence of the Rivers Eure and Iton, is a shady and romantic park. After a verdant drive from **Cailly-sur-Eure**, cross the Eure at Crève-Coeur and continue on through La Croix-St-Leufroy, picking up the D836 on to **Cocherel**, where the tree-lined river banks give way to a peaceful hamlet. Continue on the D836 to **Pacy-sur-Eure**, a charming village which stretches along the Eure. To return to Louviers, take the D181 to the A13. To go on to Évreux, pick up the N13 just south of town.

NORTHEASTERN EURE

VERNON
pop 23,000
Vernon's main draw is as a jumping-off point to visit Monet's house and gardens at Giverny. There's little reason to make a special journey to see Vernon itself, but the transport connections are good, making it a convenient stop on your way into or out of Normandy.

Although Vernon is an ancient city, with roots stretching back to the earliest Viking settlements, WWII bombs destroyed most of its medieval centre. The city has lavished attention on the few crooked streets and half-timbered houses that remain, creating an agreeably cosy feeling. With the Seine only steps away from the town centre, Vernon is also the easiest place in Normandy to board a boat for a river cruise.

Orientation
The town centre lies on the southwestern bank of the Seine. Both the train station on rue Emile Loubert and the bus station on place de la République are only a few hundred metres from the town centre, which is marked by the Notre Dame church.

The main street is rue Albuféra, which runs from place d'Évreux to the Seine. Most shops, restaurants and services lie between ave Pierre Mendès and rue Albuféra; the oldest part of town is around the tourist office.

Information
Crédit Mutual (37 rue Albuféra) There are a number of banks on this street.
Laundrette (5 rue Pontonniers)
Post Office (2 place d'Évreux) Cyberposte is available here.
Tourist Office (☎ 02 32 51 39 60; www.ville-vernon27.fr; 36 rue Carnot; ☽ 9am-12.15pm & 2.15-6.30pm Tue-Sat, 10.15am-12.15pm Sun) In a 15th-century house (Le Temps Jadis), the office has maps of suggested hikes in the region, walks in the town and cycle routes that take in Giverny.

Sights & Activities
The **Église Collégiale Notre Dame** is a stately Gothic structure dating from the 12th century but incessantly restored throughout the centuries. The 15th-century façade contains an exceptional rose window and the central tower dates from the 13th century. Highlights of the interior include a 15th-century

sculpted organ loft, a main altar in the style of Louis XVI and a number of 16th-century stained-glass windows.

The **Musée AG Poulain** (☎ 02 32 21 28 09; 12 rue du Pont; adult/concession €2.30/free; ☒ 10.30am-12.30pm & 2-6pm Tue-Sun Apr-Sep, 2-5.30pm Tue-Sat Oct-Mar) is a grab bag of antiquities, sculpture and paintings amassed by the collector AG Poulain and displayed in a 16th-century mansion. The highlights are two works by Monet, *Falaises à Pourville* (Cliffs at Pourville) and *Nymphéas* (Water Lilies), and there are also works by painters Pierre Bonnard, Rosa Bonheur and Alfred Sisley.

Tours
Fleuves et Réceptions (☎ 01 30 74 43 39; 6 ave Fernand Lefebvre, Poissy) runs a number of river cruises from Vernon. Every Sunday from mid-May to mid-September there's a 1¼-hour cruise down the Seine to Pressagny l'Orgueilleux and back. In July and August there are also departures on Wednesday, Thursday, Saturday and Sunday. The cruise leaves at 3.30pm and costs €8.50. Occasionally there are special cruises that include lunch and guided visits. All boats leave from Mail Anatole France, between the bridge and the swimming pool.

Sleeping & Eating
There are only two hotels in Vernon, although the tourist office can provide a list of *chambres d'hôtes* (B&Bs) in the region.

Hôtel d'Évreux-Le Relais Normand (☎ 02 32 21 16 12; fax 02 32 21 32 73; 11 place d'Évreux; r €33-54) Restful and well organised, there are only a few rooms in this traditional 17th-century hotel, so it's wise to reserve in advance. The cheaper rooms have shower only.

Hôtel Normandy (☎ 02 32 51 97 97; www.giverny-hotel-normandy.com; 1 ave Pierre Mendès; s/d €61/104; P) The rooms in this classic building are attractive without being especially distinctive, but the comfort level is definitely three-star, which is why it's often filled with a better class of weekending Parisians.

La Halle aux Grains (☎ 02 32 21 31 99; 31 rue de Gamilly; mains €7.50-15; ☒ closed Mon & dinner Sun) Whether you bite into a pizza, munch on a salad or go for a full meal, the offerings here won't disappoint. Everything is made on site and the wine list is entirely reasonable.

Restaurant and Le Bistro des Fleurs (☎ 02 32 21 29 19; 73 rue Carnot; restaurant menus from €26, bistro menus from €14; ☒ closed Sun & Mon) The restaurant is far and away the best dining experience in town, with a *menu* of tried and true classics. The bistro is also very good, using somewhat less expensive ingredients and a simpler presentation.

Pizzeria del Teatro (☎ 02 32 21 35 49; 34 rue d'Albuféra; pizzas from €7.50) Pizza makes a nice change, and this is one of the few establishments open on Sunday.

There's a market on Wednesday morning and all day on Saturday, and a Monoprix supermarket on place de la République.

Getting There & Away
The **train station** (☎ 02 32 51 01 72) opens from 5.30am to 8.30pm.

From Paris' Gare St Lazare there are two early-morning trains to Vernon (€10.80, 50 minutes). For the return trip there's roughly one train an hour between 5pm and 9pm. From Rouen (€8.80, 40 minutes), four trains leave before noon; the other way, there's about one train an hour between 5pm and 10pm.

There's a bus twice daily to Gisors (€4.80, one hour) and Évreux (€8.90, two hours), and three to Les Andelys (€3.90, one hour).

Getting Around
You can rent bikes at **Cyclo News** (☎ 02 32 51 10 59; 7 cours Manché aux Chevaux).

GIVERNY
pop 550
An ideal day trip from Rouen, this small village contains the Musée Claude Monet. The garden-museum attracts almost 500,000 visitors a year, many of whom also come to view the fine Impressionist collection of the Musée d'Art Américain.

Musée Claude Monet
From 1883 to 1926, this **museum** (☎ 02 32 51 28 21; adult/child/student €5.50/3/4; ☒ 10am-6pm Tue-Sun Apr-Oct) was the home and the flower-filled garden of one of France's leading Impressionist painters. Here Monet painted some of his most famous series of works, including *Nymphéas*. The property was bequeathed to the Académie des Beaux-Arts in 1966. In 1980 it was opened to the public, with Monet's house, studio, garden, water-lily pond and Japanese footbridge all gloriously restored. The only missing elements

CLAUDE MONET

One of the most important figures in modern art, Claude Monet, born in Paris in 1840, was the undisputed leader of the Impressionists. He grew up near Le Havre, where in his late teens he started painting nature in the open air, a practice that was to affect his work throughout the rest of his career.

By the time he was 17, Monet was studying in Paris at the Académie Suisse with such artists as Pissarro. His studies were interrupted by two years of military service in Algiers, where the intense light and colours planted the seeds of his future painting style. Returning to Le Havre, Monet painted Étretat, Fécamp and Trouville, aiming to capture on canvas the immediate impression of the scene before him, rather than precise detail.

During the Franco-Prussian War of 1870–71, Monet travelled to London, where he discovered the works of Turner and Constable. Consequently, painting from his houseboat on the Seine at Argenteuil, he focused on the effects of air and light, and in particular on the latter's effect on the water's surface. He also began using the undisguised, broken brush strokes that best characterise the Impressionist style.

It was in the late 1870s that Monet first began painting pictures in series, in order to study the effects of the changing conditions of light and the atmosphere. The best known of these include the Rouen Cathedral series, which were painted in the 1890s. In 1883, four years after the death of his first wife Camille, he moved to Giverny with Alice Hoschedé, his two sons and her five children from a previous marriage. Using his wealth to turn Giverny into the exact setting he required for his art, Monet planted his property with a variety of flowers to ensure he would have something to paint nearly all year. He dammed a branch of the Epte to create an artificial pond, planted it with water lilies and installed the Japanese footbridge. With the first morning light, Monet was before his lily pond with an easel capturing the reflection of sun and sky in the water. He worked on a dozen canvases at a time, attempting to portraying the fleeting light by day and pondering them in his studio at night.

Alice died in 1911, followed three years later by Monet's eldest son, Jean. Soon after, the portly, bearded artist built a new studio and started painting the *Nymphéas* (Water Lilies) series. The huge dimensions of some of these works, together with the fact that the pond's surface takes up the entire canvas, meant the abandonment of composition in the traditional sense and the virtual disintegration of form. Monet completed the series just before his death in 1926.

are Monet's paintings, although reproductions can be viewed in his studio.

The land that Claude Monet owned has become two distinct areas, cut by the Chemin du Roy, a small train line that, unfortunately, was converted into what is now the busy D5 road. The **studio** where Monet painted his *Nymphéas* murals is now the entrance hall, adorned with precise reproductions of his works and ringing with cash-register bells. Books about Monet are on sale for the same price you would pay anywhere else.

A few steps from the studio is Monet's pretty pink **house**. The painter's love of colour is evident in the sunny yellow kitchen and sky-blue upstairs rooms furnished in their original, cosy, warm style. Monet's collection of Japanese prints is on display, as well as photos and paintings by some of the many house guests who came to pay homage to the master.

In front of the house is the **Clos Normand garden** that Monet planted soon after he moved into the house in 1883. He constructed an arbour of climbing roses to replace the tree-lined path that once led to an orchard. A lawn is on the site of the former orchard, planted with Japanese cherry and flowering crab-apple trees, with irises and poppies scattered about. Surrounding the arbour are French-style symmetrical gardens with beds of gladioli, larkspur, daisies, asters and a lush profusion of other flowers.

From the Clos Normand's far corner, a tunnel leads under the D5 to the **Jardin d'Eau** (Water Garden). Having bought this piece of land in 1895 after his reputation had been established, Monet dug a pool (fed by the Epte, a tributary of the nearby Seine), planted water lilies and constructed the Japanese bridge, which has since been rebuilt. In contrast to the orderly Clos Normand, the Jardin d'Eau has a dreamy, mysterious ambience. Draped with purple wisteria, the bridge blends into the asymmetrical foreground and background, creating the intimate atmosphere for which the 'painter of light' is famous.

The seasons have enormous effects on the gardens at Giverny. From early to late spring, daffodils, tulips, rhododendrons, wisteria and irises appear, followed by poppies and lilies. By June, nasturtiums, roses and sweet peas are in flower. Around September, there are dahlias, sunflowers and hollyhocks.

Avoiding the camera-clicking crowds isn't easy, but here are some tips: be at the ticket window when it opens at 10am; visit between noon and 2pm when others are at lunch; or hold off until 4.30pm and visit until closing time at 6pm.

Musée d'Art Américain

The **American Impressionist Museum** (☎ 02 32 51 94 65; www.maag.org; 99 rue Claude Monet; adult/concession €5/3; ☼ 10am-6pm Tue-Sun Mar-Nov, closed last week in Aug) contains works of American Impressionist painters who flocked to France in the late 19th and early 20th centuries. Opened in 1992, the museum is intended to provide a link between Giverny and the Americans who briefly turned the village into an artists' colony and were involved in the Impressionist movement.

Highlights of the collection include *La Tasse de Chocolat* (A Cup of Chocolate) by Mary Cassatt, *Une Averse, Rue Bonaparte* (A Shower, Rue Bonaparte) by Frederick Childe Hassam and *Automne à Giverny, la Nouvelle Lune* (Autumn in Giverny, the New Moon) by John Leslie Breck. It is housed in a garish building 100m down the road from Musée Claude Monet.

Getting There & Away

Giverny is 66km southeast of Rouen. The nearest town is Vernon, nearly 7km to the northwest on the Paris–Rouen train line. See p244 for information on getting to and from Vernon.

Once you reach Vernon it is still quite a hike to Giverny. Shuttle buses (☎ 02 35 71 32 99) meet most trains and cost €2 each way. It is usually possible to get a taxi from the train station; alternatively call one on ☎ 06 09 31 08 99. The fare between Vernon and Giverny is around €10.

LES ANDELYS
pop 8500

Some 39km southeast of Rouen, Les Andelys is set like a jewel at the confluence of the mighty River Seine and modest River Gambon. From the 12th-century Château Gaillard, a breathtaking panorama takes in the bend of the grassy riverbanks that rise to forested hills and high, white bluffs.

As the name indicates, there are in fact two Andelys: modern Grand Andely, the commercial heart of the duo, and the older, more scenic Petit Andely, on the banks of the Seine. Most visitors gravitate to the riverside Andely for the winding streets of half-timbered houses or to scramble up the hill to the chateau.

Les Andelys developed as an extension of the Château Gaillard. By 1196, Richard the Lion-Heart's Norman territory was coming under increasing pressure from the French king Philippe-Auguste, who was pushing west from Paris along the Seine. Sensing that Rouen, his prize possession, was under threat, Richard looked for a position that would definitively close the door on Upper Normandy. On the promontory rising more than 100m above the Seine, Richard built the magnificent Château Gaillard, intending it to be an impenetrable bulwark against French expansion. The fortress lasted only seven years before falling to Philippe-Auguste, but the little village of Petit Andely took root and expanded northeast to Grand Andely. It was the birthplace of the neoclassical painter Nicolas Poussin, who was born in 1594, and it became the residence of French dramatists Thomas and Pierre Corneille in the 17th century. The bombs that fell on Grand Andely in 1940 destroyed a large chunk of the town, but it is still worth visiting for 13th-century Église Notre Dame.

Orientation & Information

Les Andelys are connected by ave de la République in Petit Andely, which becomes ave du Général de Gaulle in Grand Andely. The centre of Grand Andely is place Nicolas Poussin, which is around 1km northeast of Petit Andely. The bus station is across from the town hall and near place Nicolas Poussin.

The tiny **tourist office** (☎ 02 32 54 41 93; www .ville-andelys.fr; 24 rue Philippe-Auguste, Petit Andely;

🕑 9.30am-noon & 2-6pm Mon-Sat, to 5.30pm Sun Jun-Sep, 2-5.30pm daily Oct-May) is at the foot of the cliffs which form the base of the chateau. There is a **post office** (9 ave de la République) as well as numerous banks on place Nicolas Poussin.

Château Gaillard

The **chateau** (☎ 02 32 54 04 16; adult/concession €3/2; 🕑 10am-1pm & 2-6pm Wed-Mon) was built with extraordinary speed between 1196 and 1197 and according to the latest ideas in military architecture and engineering of the time. Workers rerouted tributaries of the Seine, leaving the mammoth cliff-top structure tenuously connected to the plateau by a narrow and easily defensible ridge, which was divided into two parts separated by a deep moat. The northern structure was the *châtelet* (the heart of the castle), protected by five towers, while the *fort principal* opposite featured a three-storey keep at its heart protected by a series of concentric circular 4m walls. Richard the Lion-Heart's defensive system included iron chains that reached from the chateau across the Seine, literally blocking all river traffic. Richard merrily pronounced it *gaillard*, a word that translates as saucy or gallant, reflecting its impregnability to mock French pretensions on the region. It's said that Philippe-Auguste defiantly shouted, 'If its walls were made of solid iron, yet would I take them!', to which Richard cried back, 'By the throat of God, if its walls were made of butter, yet would I hold them!'

After Richard's death in 1199, Philippe-Auguste laid siege to the chateau. A population of about 400 terrified civilians joined the English garrison, but when supplies dwindled they were abruptly ejected into the winter snow, resorting to cannibalism in a desperate attempt to survive. The siege dragged on for eight months, until a cavalryman noticed that the mighty fortress had one unprotected opening: the latrine. The French soldiers squirmed in and the battle for Château Gaillard – and Normandy – was over in hours.

Unfortunately, the chateau is now mostly in ruins thanks to Henry IV, who ordered its destruction in 1603, but the ghostly white walls still cut a dramatic silhouette against the sky and enough remains to give a reasonably good idea of its former majesty. More impressive than the ruins

is the fantastic view over the Seine, whose white cliffs are best seen from the viewing platform just north of the castle.

The chateau is a stiff 20-minute climb via a signposted path, Chemin de Château Gaillard, which begins about 100m north of the tourist office. By car, take the turn-off opposite the Église Notre Dame in Grand Andelys and follow the signs.

Musée Nicolas Poussin

Dedicated to the French classical painter Nicolas Poussin, who was born in the hamlet of Villers, this **museum** (☎ 02 32 54 31 78; rue Ste-Clotilde, Grand Andely; admission €2.50; 🕑 2-6pm Wed-Mon) exhibits one Poussin masterpiece, *Le Coriolan* (Coriolanus), and a number of works by other painters in the region, including René Sautin.

Sleeping & Eating

Hotels are fairly expensive in Les Andelys, but the tourist office has a list of *chambres d'hôtes* with doubles from about €25.

Camping Municipal (☎ 02 32 54 23 79; camping €11; 🕑 Apr-Oct) is conveniently located on the river in Petit Andely, but there's not much shade.

Camping Château Gaillard (☎ 02 32 54 18 20; fax 02 32 54 32 66; route de la Mare; adult/site €5/5; 🕑 closed mid-Dec–mid-Mar) This camping area is a much better bet, 800m southeast of the chateau and 200m from the Seine.

Hôtel Normandie (☎ 02 32 54 10 52; www.hotel normandie-andelys.com; 1 rue Grande; s/d €45/58; P) Rooms in the Normandie are comfortable and nicely outfitted, and from the flowery terrace along the Seine you can watch the boats come and go.

Hôtel and Restaurant de la Chaine d'Or (☎ 02 32 54 00 31; chaineor@wanadoo.fr; 27 rue Grande; r €72-122; P 💻) This romantic hideaway in Petit Andely has peaceful rooms and a renowned **restaurant** (menus €26, €42 & €55.50; 🕑 closed Mon & dinner Sun). The more expensive rooms in this 18th-century building have views over the Seine. A buffet breakfast is an extra €12 but is well worth it.

Villa du Vieux Château (☎ 02 32 54 30 10; 78 rue G Nicolle; menus €15; 🕑 closed Mon & Tue) In Petit Andelys, this restaurant has good fish.

There are numerous restaurants around place Nicolas Poussin in Grand Andely and, for self-caterers, a market on Saturday morning.

EURE

Getting There & Away

There's no train station in Les Andelys. **TCAR** (☎ 02 35 52 52 52) buses run between Grand Andely and Rouen at least twice a day (€7.77, 1¼ hours). **Cars Jacquemard** (☎ 02 32 33 09 66) connects Grand Andely with Évreux (€6.20, one hour, two daily) and Vernon (€3.80, one hour, three daily).

Getting Around

Local buses link Grand and Petit Andelys. From the bus station, take line C to reach the waterfront in Petit Andely. Tickets cost €0.80 (€7.40 for a booklet of 10). Bikes can be rented at the **Hôtel Modern** (☎ 02 32 54 10 41; 10 rue Clemenceau), behind the town hall, for €17 a day.

GISORS

pop 9000

Gisors, situated 64km northeast of Évreux, is a lively town at the confluence of the Rivers Epte, Troësne and Révillon. It is the capital of the Vexin Normand region, a vast plateau bordered by the Epte and Andelle Valleys. Although badly damaged in WWII, Gisors has restored its town centre to highlight the manicured banks of the Epte and its two most famous monuments: the chateau, built by the son of William the Conqueror, and the Église St-Gervais-St-Protais. The views from the chateau's tower are without match.

Orientation & Information

The train station is at the end of ave de la Gare, about 1km northeast of the town centre. The **tourist office** (☎ 02 32 27 60 63; www.ville-gisors.fr - French only; 4 rue Général de Gaulle; ☒ 10am-noon & 2-6pm Mon-Fri Apr-Sep, 9am-noon & 2-5pm Mon-Fri Oct-Mar) is closed weekdays, but on weekends you can get information at the chateau. The **post office** (rue Général de Gaulle) is at the other end of place des Carmélites. You can change money at **Crédit Agricole** (18 rue Général de Gaulle).

The main commercial street of Gisors is rue Vienne, running from the chateau to place des Carmélites. There are a number of shops, *boulangeries* and banks along it.

Chateau

Because of its strategic position at the eastern limit of the Norman duchy, the **chateau** (☎ 02 32 55 59 36; adult/concession €5/3; ☒ 9am-noon & 2-6pm Wed-Mon Apr-Sep, 10am-noon & 2-5pm Sat-Sun Feb-Mar & Oct-Nov) was at the centre of five centuries of Anglo-Norman conflict. To the east lay Paris and the perpetually ambitious French kings. The castle was begun by Guillaume le Roux (William the Redhead), son of William the Conqueror, in 1097. He began his fortress with a mound topped by a two-storey timbered keep. His successor, Henry I of England, added a large masonry keep, enlarged the interior and then added towers.

Henry II of England took over in 1181, raising the keep and reinforcing the exterior fortifications. After his death, the castle passed to Richard the Lion-Heart, who left it unchanged, but when Philippe-Auguste seized the castle in 1193 he immediately enlarged and expanded it. Up went the round Prisoner's Tower that is the current castle's most outstanding feature, as well as other towers and expanded residential quarters. Despite its strength, the castle was taken by the English during the Hundred Years' War, returned to the French when hostilities ceased, and seized by Henri IV during the Religious Wars. It was finally abandoned in the 16th century and slowly fell into disrepair.

The most impressive parts of the chateau are the Prisoner's Tower, so called because of the ancient graffiti on the walls scribbled by the prisoners incarcerated there, and Henry II's keep. Notice also the remains of the chapel Henry II built in commemoration of Thomas Becket, whom he had murdered.

There are tours (in French with English translations) at 10am, 11am, 2.30pm, 3.45pm and 5pm Wednesday to Monday, April to September. The park around the castle is open from 8am to 7.30pm daily.

L'Église St-Gervais-St-Protais

This **church** (rue Vienne; ☒ 9am-7pm Wed-Mon) is a remarkable combination of Gothic and Renaissance styles. Begun in 1119 and rebuilt from 1240 to 1249, the serious work on it took place at the height of the Renaissance in the 16th century. The pure Renaissance façade has a noble arch and a rich profusion of carvings flanked by classic Gothic towers. Inside, the purity of the Gothic structure sets off a series of fine Renaissance chapels. Notice the Chapelle du Rosaire, with a lavishly sculpted bas-relief of the Tree of Jesse, created between 1585 and 1593, and the

Chapelle de l'Assumption north of the choir, with a bas-relief of the Assumption.

Sleeping & Eating

Camping Municipal (☎ 02 32 55 43 42; Dangu; adult/ site €3.20/5.50; ⓨ Apr-Oct) In a pretty location on a lake near the River Epte is this attractive site, 5km southwest of Gisors in the tiny village of Dangu.

Hôtel Moderne (☎ 02 32 55 23 51; fax 02 32 55 08 75; place de la Gare; s/d €72/92; **P**) The rooms here are comfortable and in excellent condition, with attractive furnishings, but are somewhat overpriced.

Le Cochon Gaulois (☎ 02 32 27 30 33; 8 place Blanmont; menus €10.70 & €14.90; ⓨ closed Sun) Every part of the pig (cochon) is served here, from charcuterie to roast pork, and the weekday lunches are exceptionally fast. The €10.70 menu is available at weekday lunch times.

Le Cappeville (☎ 02 32 55 11 08; 17 rue Cappeville; menus €18, €23, €39; ⓨ closed Thu & dinner Wed) Under the same management as Le Cochon Gaulois, this distinguished establishment is the finest restaurant in the region. Try the artichokes and shrimp in a flaky pastry or the dramatic rognon de veau (calf kidneys) flambéed in Calvados. The €18 menu is available on weekdays.

Should you develop a bizarre yearning for a meal on Sunday night or Monday, there's Chinese, Vietnamese and Thai food at **Le Mirama** (☎ 02 32 27 27 17; 72 rue de Vienne; menus €10; ⓨ closed Wed).

There's a market all day Monday and on Friday morning on place des Carmélites.

Getting There & Away

The **train station** (☎ 02 32 55 01 30) opens from 6.30am to 10pm. There are 11 trains daily running between Paris and Gisors (€10.70, 1¼ hours), up to four from Forges-les-Eaux (€7.30, 45 minutes), and three from Rouen (€11.30, two hours, with a change at Serqueux).

There are two buses daily from Évreux (€9.30, two hours), one daily evening bus from Rouen (€10.31, 1½ hours), two from Les Andelys (€9.90, one hour and 10 minutes) and up to three daily from Dieppe (€12.20, 1½ to two hours).

Getting Around

Vexin Bus (☎ 02 32 27 41 00) runs three buses in the morning and three in the early evening

between place Blanmont, next to the chateau, and the train station.

FORÊT DE LYONS

Between Gisors and Rouen lies the Lyons-Andelle region, whose most outstanding feature is the Forêt de Lyons. This splendid old beech forest spreads over some 26,000 acres and offers excellent opportunities for walks, as well as a number of interesting chateaux. The forest has been a regional centre ever since it became favourite hunting turf for the Merovingian kings.

In the Middle Ages, monks from the Abbaye de Mortemer began clearing the terrain, creating hamlets that were quickly occupied by the kind of artisans that badly needed a supply of wood for their craft. The wood-gobbling glass industry took off and lasted until the 18th century. Even though the forest was exploited for firewood until the last century, careful planting and management has left it an extraordinary place in which to wander. A lack of undergrowth makes it a comparatively bright forest where the sun filters down through 20m-tall beech and oak trees.

The main centre for information is the tourist office at Lyons-la-Forêt (below), which has maps of the region and suggestions for walks to do on your own. It also provides a schedule of guided walks that take place on Friday, Saturday and Sunday, from July to September.

The only public transport within the Forêt de Lyons is the daily bus No 28 that runs from Rouen to Lyons-la-Forêt. You'll need wheels (four or two) and the nearest place to rent them is Rouen.

Lyons-la-Forêt

pop 795

In the middle of Forêt de Lyons and along the left bank of the River Lieure, Lyons-la-Forêt is the most postcard-perfect village in Upper Normandy. The brick and half-timbered houses clustered around the central square have survived nearly intact since the 17th century, giving the impression of a film set. In fact, it was a film set, for Jean Renoir's and Claude Chabrol's film versions of Madame Bovary. It's easy enough to imagine women in long dresses sweeping down the streets to meet their illicit lovers, even though you're more likely to

EURE

meet Parisians on their way to their weekend mansions in the woods. The composer Maurice Ravel found the village a peaceful spot, coming here in the prewar period to reflect and compose.

Once the location of a Gallo-Roman settlement 31km southeast of Rouen, Lyons-la-Forêt coalesced around the castle built by Henry I of England in the 12th century. The king died in his fortified castle in 1135 (supposedly from eating eels fished from the Lieure), but the village thrived until it was destroyed by a fire in 1590. It was rebuilt in the 17th century and reached its commercial heyday in the 18th century when Les Halles marketplace was built. Fortunately, the WWII bombing campaigns spared the town, making it a scenic base to launch excursions into the surrounding Forêt de Lyons and nearby Abbaye de Mortemer. The town is classified as a national historic monument.

ORIENTATION & INFORMATION

The centre of the town is place Benserade, marked by the 18th-century thatch-roofed Halles, which also presents the occasional art exhibition. The **tourist office** (☎ 02 32 49 31 65; otsi-pays-lyons-andelle@wanadoo.fr; 20 rue de l'Hôtel de Ville; 10am-noon & 2.30-5.30pm Mon-Sat, 10am-noon & 2-4pm Sun Jun-Sep, 10am-noon & 2-5pm Tue-Sat Oct-May) is near the main square and can supply you with information about walks into the forest.

SIGHTS & ACTIVITIES

On the right bank of the River Lieure, just west of the town centre, the 12th-century **Église St-Denis** is constucted of silex (flint) and

contains a 16th-century wooden statue of St Christopher. Opening hours are irregular; check with the tourist office.

From the Halles take the rue d'Enfer to the house called **Le Fresne** on the left, which is where Ravel stayed to orchestrate Moussorgski's *Pictures at an Exhibition* and to compose the *Tombeau de Couperin* (Tomb of Couperin). The **town hall** near the main square is a handsome 18th-century brick building.

Although the region is great for **cycling**, you'll have to bring your own bike as there are no rental shops in town.

SLEEPING & EATING

Lyons-la-Forêt is not a cheap town in which to stay or eat.

Camping St-Paul (☎ 02 32 49 42 02; camping €10.60; Apr-Sep) Roughly 2km northeast of the town centre, this is a lovely spot.

Le Grand Cerf (☎ 02 32 49 60 44; fax 02 32 49 72 96; place Benserade; r €45.75-53.40) This is the cheapest hotel in town and isn't bad value, especially if you get a room overlooking the gardens at the back.

Hôtel de La Licorne (☎ 02 32 49 62 02, www .licorne-hotel-restaurant.com; place Benserade; r €65-92; P) This three-star pad is located in a 400-year-old building with a lush garden terrace in the back. The style is traditional, both in the décor and in the offerings of the hotel's high-quality restaurant.

Café de Commerce (☎ 02 32 49 60 39; place Benserade; menus €10.50 & €16; closed Wed) This café has a pleasant pavement terrace from which you can contemplate the town square. It specialises in cuisine from Les Landes. The €10.50 *menu* is available at lunch time.

OF PEASANTS AND PIGEONS

The unique cylindrical *colombiers* (pigeon lofts or dovecotes) dotting the Normandy countryside were once a major status symbol for Norman nobility. In pre-Revolutionary France the right to erect a *colombier* was a rare privilege that the law awarded to the most important landholders. With only one *colombier* permitted for each fiefdom, the lords of the land tried to outdo each other in building elaborate pigeon houses. Brick and stone were often arranged in geometrical patterns, and halfway up the cylinder a stone band prevented rodents from reaching the top cone. The cone was usually topped with a small ornament in shiny metal or ceramic that pigeons on the wing could easily spot. Inside, a ladder led to the pigeon loft where the birds lived in thousands of niches.

The *colombiers* were a bitter source of grievance for the local peasantry, who watched in fury as pigeons ate their freshly sowed grain. For decades they agitated to close the *colombiers*, at least during the sowing season. It's significant that one of the Revolutionaries' first acts was to abolish the right to *colombiers* in a law dated 4 August 1789.

Around Lyons-la-Forêt

In addition to Lyons-la-Forêt, other highlights of the forest include the traditional villages of **Rosay-sur-Lieure**, **Ménesqueville** and **Lisors**.

L'ABBAYE DE MORTEMER

About 6km south of Lyons-la-Forêt and near Lisors, **L'Abbaye de Mortemer** (☎ 02 32 49 54 34; adult/concession €7/6; ☼ 11am-6pm Easter-Oct) is a Cistercian abbey convent founded in 1134 by Henry I Beauclerc, son of William the Conqueror. After the Revolution, stones from the abbey were removed and used to construct the village of Lisors. In the midst of a vast park, the abbey is falling to pieces but a remarkable *colombier* (pigeon loft or dovecote) is still standing. It has 934 niches which once sheltered the birds until they were caught and eaten. There is also an 18th-century chateau in the grounds, which has been transformed into a museum. Audiovisual equipment and wax figures are used to vividly re-create scenes from monastic life, and there's also a small doll museum.

It's said that the abbey is haunted. Mathilde, wife of the German emperor Henry V, was imprisoned here and cries out her anguish whenever there's a full moon. Other ghosts include the last four monks of the abbey, whose throats were cut by Revolutionaries. You might catch them floating around the *colombier*.

In addition to visitations from beyond, the abbey hosts a medieval fair on 15 August, which includes costumes, re-enactments and a son et lumière.

Guided visits (adult/concession €8/7, including admission) of the museum take place from 2pm to 6pm daily between May and August, and from 2pm to 5.30pm Saturday, Sunday and holidays during the rest of the year.

CHÂTEAU DE VASCOEUIL

On the northwestern edge of the forest, about 12km from Lyons-la-Forêt, is the **Château de Vascoeuil** (☎ 02 35 23 62 35; adult/concession €7/4.50; ☼ 11am-7pm daily Jul & Aug, 2.30-6.30pm daily mid-Apr–Jun & Sep–mid-Oct, 11am-7pm Sun rest of year), a stately manor built between the 14th and 16th centuries. In addition to the impressive courtyard and extremely well-preserved *colombier*, the chateau contains a museum dedicated to the historian of the French Revolution, Jules Michelet. It's worthwhile checking with the tourist office about any temporary art exhibitions held in the chateau, as they are of a high quality.

CÔTE DES DEUX AMANTS

On a limestone spur 150m above the Seine and Andelle Valleys is **Côte des Deux Amants**, 2km north of Amfreville-sous-les-Monts. The view is simply breathtaking and an indicator table lets you know what you're looking at. According to legend, the 'Two Lovers' hill got its name from the tragic tale of Edmond and Calliste. They fell in love when Edmond rescued her from a wild boar, but her father wouldn't consent to the marriage until Edmond proved his strength by running to the top of the hill with Calliste in his arms. He tried but collapsed and died at the summit, and Calliste immediately expired from a broken heart.

WESTERN EURE

BERNAY

pop 11,000

With so many towns in Normandy bombed to rubble in WWII, it seems almost miraculous that Bernay was spared. The town is a thriving regional centre, 42km northwest of Évreux, at the confluence of the Rivers Charentonne and Cosnier. The branches of the rivers meander through a town centre composed of ancient half-timbered houses and cobblestone streets, creating an extraordinarily attractive landscape of stone, water and wood, just as the tourist brochures boast. Bernay coalesced around an 11th-century abbey and owed its early prosperity to a now-defunct textile industry. As capital of the rustic Risle-Charentonne region, Bernay keeps the local economy humming by manufacturing small planes as well as marketing the region's cattle. If you have your own transport, Bernay makes an excellent base from which to explore several fine chateaux or the nearby village of Le Bec-Hellouin.

Orientation & Information

Rue Thiers is the main street in town, with the major shops and businesses. The most colourful part of town is around rue Folloppe, which leads to the river. The **tourist office** (☎ 02 32 43 32 08; www.bernay27.fr - French only;

29 rue Thiers; ⊗ 9.30am-12.30pm & 2-6pm Mon-Sat mid-Sep–mid-May, 9.30am-12.30pm & 2-7pm Mon-Sat, 10am-noon & 2-6pm Sun mid-May–mid-Sep) is in the centre of town. The **main post office** is at place Paul Derou and has Cyberposte. You can change money at **Crédit Lyonnais** (2 rue Gambetta).

Sights & Activities

Strolling the streets of the **old town**, especially for the extensive Saturday morning market, is one of the most agreeable activities in Bernay. The tourist office has a helpful map pointing out various historic buildings.

The **Église Abbatiale Notre-Dame** (☎ 02 32 43 32 08; ⊗ 8am-noon & 2-6pm Wed-Mon Jul & Aug, 2-6pm Wed-Mon Apr-Jun & Sep) is the oldest Romanesque church in Normandy, constructed sometime between 1017 and 1075 as part of an abbey. The abbey has been ravaged over the years, and has even been used as a warehouse and a granary. Part of it now houses the mayor's office and the courthouse. The church is under continuous restoration, but the great columned arcades of the nave and the high windows recall its ancient majesty. Part of the abbey is devoted to the **Musée Municipal**, which displays private collections that were bequeathed to the city. There's a collection of ceramics from Rouen, objects from Egypt and Mesopotamia gathered by a local archaeologist, 18th-century furniture, and French, Dutch, English and Italian paintings from the 17th to the 20th centuries. Entrance to the abbey is through the museum on place de la République.

Sleeping & Eating

Camping Municipal (☎ 02 32 43 30 47; rue des Canadiens; adult/site €2/2.50; ⊗ mid-May–mid-Sep) About 2km southwest of the town centre is this place with lots of shade.

Le Lion d'Or (☎ 02 32 43 12 06; hotelliondor@wanadoo.fr; 48 rue du Général de Gaulle; s/d €38/41; ✗ P 🖳) In the centre of town, this simple, friendly hotel is in an 18th-century building that has been well maintained. You'll find few luxuries but few problems either.

Restaurant Le Lion d'Or (☎ 02 32 44 23 85; 48 rue du Général de Gaulle; menus €13, €17, €26; ⊗ closed Mon, lunch Tue & dinner Sun) Terrines, foie gras, simmered sauces and home-made pastries are the hallmarks of this solid establishment. Try the *truite au Camembert* (trout with Camembert) if it's on the menu. The €13 *menu* is available on weekdays.

Rue Folloppe has several modestly priced eateries. Between **Au Lapin Gourmand** (☎ 02 32 43 42 32; 10 rue Folloppe; ⊗ closed Sun & Wed) and **Crêperie du Roy** (☎ 02 32 46 05 32; 9 rue Folloppe; ⊗ closed Sun & Mon) you'll find a good selection of pizza, salad, crepes, grilled meat or brasserie food. Crêperie du Roy is slightly more expensive but still manageable at less than €10 for a copious salad.

Entertainment

Le Piano (☎ 02 32 43 68 00; 32 rue Folloppe; ⊗ closed Mon) Nightlife is thin in Bernay but it does exist, as proven by this large bar with a vast choice of beers and the occasional live concert.

Getting There & Away

The **train station** (☎ 02 32 43 01 25) opens from 6am to 9pm and the connections from Bernay are good. There are trains to Évreux (€7.70, 45 minutes, up to 10 daily), Rouen (€11.30, one hour, four daily), Caen (€10.80, 45 minutes, 15 daily), Lisieux (€5.20, 20 minutes, 12 daily) and Conches-en-Ouche (€5.60, 20 minutes, one daily).

Getting Around

There are buses every half-hour between the train station and place Paul Derou, as well as several other points in the town centre. Tickets cost €0.50.

AROUND BERNAY
Château de Beaumesnil

Dubbed the 'Normandy Versailles', the exterior of the **Château de Beaumesnil** (☎ 02 32 44 40 09; adult/child €6/free; ⊗ 10am-noon & 2-6pm Wed-Mon Jul & Aug, 2-6pm Fri-Mon Apr-Jun & Sep) is almost as marvellous as that other chateau outside Paris. The baroque castle seems to float in the middle of an artificial pond that opens onto a magnificent 80-hectare landscaped park. Built by an obscure architect between 1633 and 1640, the ornate brick-and-stone façade is decorated with a profusion of sculpted heads, making it one of the finest examples of baroque style in Normandy. Don't miss the maze of privet bushes alongside the castle and take time to appreciate the park designed by a student of Le Nôtre, the landscaper of Versailles. The interior contains a museum of bookbinding, displaying hundreds of intricately decorated leather-bound books, and an unusual staircase suspended between two floors, but is not as interesting as the castle's exterior.

The chateau is 13km southeast of Bernay in a little village on the D140; there is no public transport.

Le Bec-Hellouin
pop 420

This peaceful little village buried in the lush Becquet Valley, 21km northeast of Bernay town centre, seems predestined to rest the eyes of weary tourists. The ivy-covered half-timbered houses cluster around an ancient abbey and a little river bubbles between tree-shaded banks. Except for paved roads, cars and a few art galleries, everything looks about the same as it must have around 900 years ago when the abbey was built.

After soaking up the scenery, a visit to **L'Abbaye** (☎ 02 32 43 72 60; admission €4; ✆ 8am-9pm, guided tours 10.30am, 3, 4 & 5pm Wed-Fri, Sun & Mon, 10.30am, 3 & 4pm Sat, noon, 3 & 4pm Sun Jun-Sep) is most worthwhile. It was founded in 1035 and soon became a highly influential intellectual centre. Its first abbot, Lanfranc, was one of the most learned men of the age and was summoned by William the Conqueror to straighten out the Pope's opposition to his marriage to Mathilde. Lanfranc and his successor, Anselm, became archbishops of Canterbury. The monastery, which remained a powerful force until the Revolution, when the monks were chased out and the invaluable library was vandalised.

The monastery stayed empty until 1948, when a new community of monks moved in and began restoring the church, cloister, chapter room and convent buildings. Try to time a visit for daily Mass (11.45am Monday to Friday, 10.30am Sunday), when the monks sing Gregorian chants.

If mechanical pianos and barrel organs are your passion, there's the **Musée de la Musique Mécanique** (☎ 02 32 46 16 19).

SLEEPING & EATING

There is no tourist office in Le Bec-Hellouin, but the **tourist office** (☎ 02 32 45 70 51; fax 02 32 45 70 51; 1 rue du Général de Gaulle) in neighbouring Brionne can give you some information about accommodation in and around the village.

Camping Municipal (☎ 02 32 44 83 55; camping €7) This is 1km north of the town centre.

Auberge de L'Abbaye (☎ 02 32 44 86 02; fax 02 32 46 32 23; r per person half-board €70) One of the most delightful little inns in the region, this has rustic but extremely comfortable rooms. The **restaurant** (✆ closed Mon) is a gourmet delight.

There are a few creperies around the abbey and a little grocery store across from the church on rue Lanfranc, but nothing is cheap in Le Bec-Hellouin.

GETTING THERE & AWAY

The only public transport available to Le Bec-Hellouin is the bus from Évreux. See p241 for details. Another option is to take the train to Brionne from Bernay, Rouen or Évreux, then take a **taxi** (☎ 02 32 45 50 00) 5km north to Le Bec-Hellouin; the taxi fare will cost about €10.

Château du Champ de Bataille

This sumptuous **chateau** (☎ 02 32 34 84 34; adult/concession €6/3 kitchens and gardens only; ✆ 2-6pm daily May-Sep, 2-6pm Sat-Sun Mar-Apr & Oct-Nov), at Ste-Opportune du Bosc, about 20km northeast of Bernay, contains an exquisite collection of 17th- and 18th-century furniture and *objets d'art*. Built in the 17th century, the chateau was purchased by French designer Jacques Garcia, who decorated the interior in opulent 18th-century style. Some of the items on display belonged to the royal family of Louis XVI before the Revolutionaries looted the palaces at Versailles and Tuileries. Panelled walls, chandeliers, Flemish tapestries, Chinese porcelain, portraits, busts and vases have been arranged with impeccable taste in order to evoke the royal lifestyle in pre-Revolutionary France. The gardens are also in a French classical style, with Italian statuary, lawns and a maze. The overall effect of the visit is eye-popping, but it's a shame that admission to the entire chateau is a whopping €46 (by appointment only)!

There's no direct public transport to the chateau, but it's possible to take a morning bus from Évreux to Le Neubourg and then a **taxi** (☎ 02 32 35 09 34) from the train station 2km to the chateau. The taxi fare is around €9.

Calvados

CONTENTS

Caen	256
Bayeux & the D-Day Beaches	**266**
Bayeux	266
Balleroy	271
Arromanches	272
Longues-sur-Mer	272
D-Day Beaches	272
Côte Fleurie	**274**
Honfleur	274
Deauville-Trouville	279
Around Deauville-Trouville	283
Pays d'Auge	**283**
Lisieux	283
Pont l'Évêque	285
St-pierre-sur-Dives	286
Château de Vendeuvre	287
Central Calvados	**287**
Falaise	287
La Suisse Normande	289

CALVADOS

The *département* of Calvados stretches from Honfleur in the east to Isigny-sur-Mer in the west, and is famed for its rich pastures and farm products: butter, cheese, cider and Calvados. The capital and largest town is Caen, but many people come for Bayeux and its renowned tapestry. The D-Day beaches and museums also draw millions of visitors a year, making Calvados one of the most touristed regions in France.

Calvados boast the region's most developed coastline, which includes the Côte Fleurie and Côte de Nacre. For stretching out along the sand, there's the classy Deauville-Trouville and the quieter Houlgate and Cabourg. The D-Day beaches extend along almost the entire coast, with sobering museums and cemeteries illustrating the human cost of the Normandy liberation. Of all the *départements* in Normandy, Calvados suffered the worst destruction during the Battle of Normandy. Only a handful of towns and villages survived unscathed, poignant reminders of a lost heritage.

Much of the interior is given over to the vast cereal plains extending from Caen to Falaise. Pastures are another feature of the Calvados landscape, as are many kilometres of apple orchards. When the apple trees blossom in spring, the region takes on a light and festive tone, particularly if you've been imbibing the three main apple drinks: cider, Calvados and *pommeau* (an aperitif of Calvados and apple juice).

CALVADOS

HIGHLIGHTS

- Honour the fallen of WWII at **Le Mémorial de Caen** (p257), the **American Military Cemetery** (p273) at **Omaha Beach** (p272) and **Pointe du Hoc** (p273)

- Witness William's conquest of England on the **Bayeux Tapestry** (p266)

- Enter the surreal mind of Erik Satie at quirky **Les Maisons Satie** (p277), Honfleur

- Walk across the **Pont de Normandie** (p278)

- Sip **Calvados** (p279) at a portside café in Honfleur

- Spend a day at the **races** (p281) in Deauville

▪ POPULATION: 648,400	▪ AREA: 5548 SQ KM

CALVADOS

THE CHANNEL (LA MANCHE)

To Portsmouth (UK)

HAUTE-NORMANDIE
SEINE-MARITIME

LE HAVRE

D - D A Y   L A N D I N G   Côte de Nacre
BEACHES

Utah Beach
Grandcamp-Maisy
Pointe du Hoc
Omaha Beach
Colleville-sur-Mer
Longues-sur-Mer
Carentan
Arromanches
Plateau du Calvados
Gold Beach
Juno Beach
Courseulles-sur-Mer
Bayeux
Côte Fleurie
Pont de Normandie
Baie de la Seine
Honfleur
Trouville
Deauville
Rade de Caen
Sword Beach
Houlgate
Cabourg
Ouistreham
Dives-sur-Mer
Pont-l'Évêque
Cormeilles

EURE

St-Lô
To Countances (18km)
Balleroy
CAEN
Lisieux
To Bernay (15km)
Caumont-l'Eventé
Villers-Bocage
Dampierre
Orne
CALVADOS
BASSE-NORMANDIE
St Pierre-sur-Dives
Livarot
Orbec
Thury-Harcourt
Suisse Normande
Clécy
Pont d'Ouilly
Villedieu-les-Poêles
Vire
Falaise
Vimoutiers
To Flers (1km)
La Roche d'Oëtre (120m)
Orne
ORNE
To Argentan (3km)
Gacé

0 ——— 20 km
0 ——— 12 miles

CALVADOS

CAEN

pop 117,000

Caen, the capital of Basse Normandie, is a bustling university city with several fine museums, two historic abbeys and a massive 11th-century chateau. Unfortunately, there's little else in Caen to hold a visitor's attention. The city burned for over a week in the Battle of Normandy and has been rebuilt in a utilitarian, although not entirely unpleasing, style. Only a nugget of medieval streets remains as a sad reminder of all that was lost. At least the wide boulevards have been able to accommodate the traffic that accompanied the city's rapid postwar expansion.

Caen makes a good base from which to explore Normandy's D-Day beaches and has good transport connections to other towns in the region. It is also the gateway for Ouistreham, a minor passenger port for ferries to England.

History

Until the 11th century Caen was little more than a ragtag collection of villages scattered around the confluence of the Rivers Orne and Odon. Its fortunes changed upon the marriage of William the Conqueror and his cousin, Matilda of Flanders, in 1050. A marriage between cousins displeased the pope and in order to receive a dispensation each spouse promised to build an abbey in Caen. William built the Abbaye aux Hommes, or Men's Abbey, and Matilda the Abbaye aux Dames, or Ladies' Abbey. The town apparently pleased William and, after becoming king of England in 1066, he made Caen his secondary residence, building a massive fortified castle on a rocky spur.

Caen flourished under William's rule. The city's intellectual tradition was born in its abbeys and creamy Caen limestone was used to build Westminster Abbey and Canterbury Cathedral in England. Caen's prosperity attracted the attention of England's King Edward III, who sacked the city in 1346 during the Hundred Years' War.

The city had hardly recovered when the English returned under Henry V in 1417 for another bout of looting and pillage. This time the English stayed for a 33-year occupation that turned out rather well for Caen.

The monarchy established a university in 1432 that long outlasted the occupation, currently attracting some 30,000 students. In 1850 Caen was linked to the sea by a canal running parallel to the River Orne, which aided the growth of the steel industry that is now at the heart of its economy.

Orientation

Caen's modern heart is made up of a few pedestrianised shopping streets and some busy boulevards. The largest, ave du 6 Juin, links the centre, which is based around the southern end of the chateau, with the canal and train station to the southeast. Bassin St-Pierre is the city's pleasure port, its quays serving as favourite promenades in mild weather.

Information

BOOKSHOPS
Hemisphères (☎ 02 31 86 67 26; 15 rue des Croisières) Guidebooks in English, including Lonely Planet titles.

INTERNET ACCESS
M.I.G. (☎ 02 31 93 09 09; 74-76 ave de la Libération; per hr €3; ☟ 2.30-7pm Mon, 10am-noon & 2.30-7pm Tue-Sat)

LAUNDRY
Laundrette (127 rue St-Jean)

MONEY
Crédit Agricole (1 blvd Maréchal Leclerc) There's an exchange bureau here. The tourist office also offers exchange services from May to September.

POST
Main Post Office (place Gambetta) It has Cyberposte.

TOURIST OFFICES
Tourist Office (☎ 02 31 27 14 14; fax 02 31 27 14 18; www.caen.fr/tourisme; place St-Pierre; ☟ 9am-7pm Mon-Sat, 10am-1pm & 2-5pm Sun Jul & Aug, 9.30am-6.30pm Mon-Sat & 10am-1pm Sun Jun & Sep) Information on Caen life, including extensive entertainment listings.
Centre Regional d'Information Jeunesse (CRIJ; ☎ 02 31 27 80 80; fax 02 31 27 80 89; crij.bn@wanadoo.fr; 6 rue Neuve St-Jean) Has a wealth of information for students, including available discounts, lodging referrals and courses.

TRAVEL AGENCIES
OTU (☎ 02 31 56 60 93; www.otu.fr - French only; Maison de l'Étudiant, ave de Lausanne) This student travel agency can help book cheap flights and is a good source of information on transportation discounts.
SNCF Boutique (8 rue St-Pierre) For train information and reservations.

Le Mémorial de Caen

Le Mémorial de Caen (☎ 02 31 06 06 44; www.memorial-caen.fr; esplanade Dwight Eisenhower; adult/child €18/12, WWII veterans free; ☟ 9am-6pm daily Oct-May, 9am-7pm daily Jun-Sep, closed 1st 3 weeks of Jan) is the most vivid and comprehensive treatment of the Battle of Normandy in the region – possibly in the world. The exhibits use lights, sound, video, film footage, documents, photos and animated maps to trace the rise of Nazi Germany, the world's descent into war, the occupation of France,

---

THE BATTLE OF CAEN

Caen was a thriving industrial, commercial and intellectual centre when on 6 June 1944 the first Allied bombs began raining down on the city. Although brutal, the bombing was intended to block German Panzers from reinforcing their divisions on the Cotentin beaches. Caen went up in flames and burned for 11 days, reducing the medieval quarters of St-Pierre and St-Jean to ruins. Having been told to evacuate the city, many residents had fled south to the quarries of Fleury-sur-Orne, while others took refuge in the ancient Abbaye aux Hommes, but thousands more were entombed in the rubble. Although planning had called for a rapid occupation of the city, the Germans quickly launched a counter-offensive that blocked Allied troops just outside the city. The stalemate continued for three weeks, but Caen had to be wrested from the Germans in order to allow a clear advance south along the vast plains. On 7 July the northern part of the city was targeted, but the actual bombing pushed further into the centre, which received 2500 tons of explosives. More than 80% of the city was destroyed and some observers felt that the operation achieved dubious results. The heaps of rubble impeded the Allied advance through the city and it did not delay the transfer of German divisions from the British to the American sectors as was originally intended. Caen's role in the Battle of Normandy is evoked in the outstanding museum Le Mémorial de Caen (above).

CALVADOS

CAEN

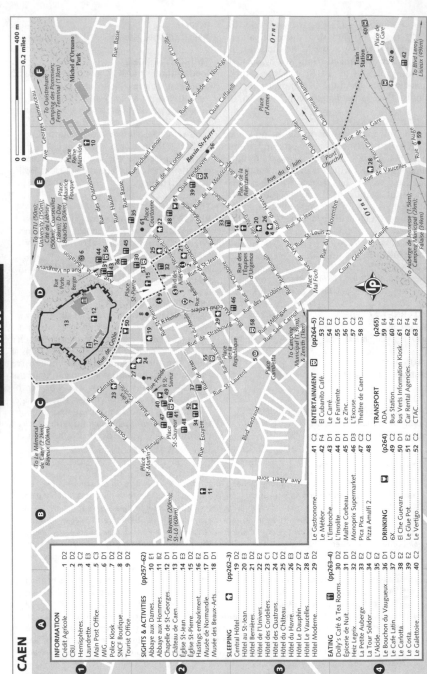

INFORMATION	
Crédit Agricole	1 D2
CRIJ	2 D2
Hemisphères	3 C3
Laundrette	4 E3
Main Post Office	5 C3
MIG	6 D1
Police Kiosk	7 D2
SNCF Boutique	8 D2
Tourist Office	9 D2

SIGHTS & ACTIVITIES	(pp257–62)
Abbaye aux Dames	10 E1
Abbaye aux Hommes	11 B2
Chapelle de St-Georges	12 D2
Château de Caen	13 D1
Église St-Jean	14 E3
Église St-Pierre	15 D2
Hastings embarkment	16 E2
Musée de Normandie	17 D1
Musée des Beaux-Arts	18 D1

SLEEPING	(pp262–3)
Central Hôtel	19 D2
Hôtel au St-Jean	20 E3
Hôtel Bernières	21 D2
Hôtel de l'Univers	22 E2
Hôtel des Cordeliers	23 C1
Hôtel des Quatrans	24 C2
Hôtel du Château	25 D2
Hôtel du Havre	26 E3
Hôtel Le Dauphin	27 C2
Hôtel Le Vaucelles	28 E4
Hôtel Moderne	29 D2

EATING	(pp263–4)
Dolly's Café & Tea Rooms	30 D2
Épicerie de Nuit	31 D1
Heiz Legrix	32 E2
La Petite Auberge	33 E2
La Tour Solidor	34 C2
L'Alcide	35 E2
Le Bouchon du Vaugueux	36 D1
Le Cafe Latin	37 C2
Le Carlotta	38 E2
Le Costa	39 E2
Le Galetoire	40 C2

Le Gastronome	41 C2
Le Météor	42 F4
L'Embroche	43 D1
L'Insolite	44 D1
Maître Corbeau	45 D1
Monoprix Supermarket	46 D3
Pica Pica	47 C2
Pizza Amalfi 2	48 C2

DRINKING	(p264)
6X	49 C2
El Che Guevara	50 D1
Le Glue Pot	51 E2
Le Vertigo	52 C2

ENTERTAINMENT	
El Cubanito Café	53 D2
Le Carré	54 E2
Le Famiente	55 C2
Le Zinc	56 D1
L'Excuse	57 C2
Théâtre de Caen	58 D3

TRANSPORT	(p265)
ADA	59 F4
Bus Station	60 F4
Bus Verts Information Kiosk	61 E2
Car Rental Agencies	62 F4
CTAC	63 C2

and the preparations, execution and aftermath of D-Day.

The museum is intended not merely to commemorate the liberation of Europe but to promote peace. A concluding section dealing with the establishment of the UN and global conflicts since WWII ends on a note of cautious optimism without glossing over some of the major obstacles to world peace. The museum packs a powerful punch, although the emotional effect can be diluted by the hordes of noisy French school children swarming through the rooms. Try to visit on weekends or during school holidays.

Built over the command post of the German General Richter and inaugurated on 6 June 1988, the museum was financed by various governmental committees as well as American, Canadian, British and other Allied organisations. Visitors enter through a jagged crack in the stark white façade, meant to symbolise the broken city of Caen and the Allied breach of the German juggernaut. The French inscription across the wall reads: 'I was crushed by grief, but fraternity revived me, and from my wound there sprang a river of freedom.'

In the middle of the vast entrance hall is a replica of an RAF Hawker Typhoon that looks poised to strike. The museum's exhibits, captioned in English, French and German, are divided into distinct parts.

A tunnel spiralling downwards shows Europe's descent into total war. Documents, posters and photos trace the failure of the Versailles agreement that ended WWI, leading to the rise of fascism in Germany and the fear of Bolshevism in France. Vichy France is recalled as well as the Resistance. Photos of German concentration camps and Hitler's voice booming over the loudspeakers convey the sense of urgency facing Allied leaders.

Three segments of un-narrated film footage (50 minutes in total) are taken from the archives of both the German and Allied sides. Most startling is the split-screen film footage of D-Day from both viewpoints. The documentary material is further enlivened by scenes from the fictional film *The Longest Day*. The second segment deals with the Battle of Normandy and the third with struggles against oppression since WWII.

An exhibit on Nobel Peace Prize laureates is housed in a former German command post underneath the main building and reached via a futuristic tunnel.

The most recently installed section in the museum focuses on the Cold War, the colonisation of the Third World and the emergence of the European Union.

There's a cafeteria in the museum and a park around it, good for a contemplative stroll. The little-used Centre de Documentation above the main hall has an extensive library of books (some in English) covering WWII. There's also a collection of videos in French and English that include documentaries and films about WWII. They can be watched for free.

Le Mémorial de Caen is around 3km northwest of the tourist office. To reach the museum, take bus No 17 from opposite the tourist office at place St-Pierre; the last bus back departs at 8.45pm (earlier on Sunday). By car head towards Bayeux, following the multitude of signs with the word 'Mémorial'. Allow about 2½ hours for a visit.

Château de Caen

This huge **fortress** (www.chateau.caen.fr; ☺ 6am-7.30pm, 6am-10pm May-Sep) was begun by William the Conqueror in 1060 and extended by his son Henry I. It was a royal residence until the reign of Richard the Lion-Heart and then turned into a garrison when Normandy became part of France in 1204. Eventually it became a town within a town, containing residences, workshops, a church, a prison and a cemetery. From the Revolution until WWII it served various military functions. Until 1944 a nest of houses pressed up against the fortress, but the bombardment had the salutary effect of revealing the entire structure.

A walk around the **ramparts** is an excellent way to appreciate the harmonious layout of reconstructed Caen and its many church steeples. You can visit the 12th-century **Chapelle de St-Georges**, built for the people who were living within the walls of the castle, and the **Échiquier** (Exchequer), which dates from about AD 1100 and is one of the oldest civic buildings in Normandy. Of particular interest is the **Jardin des Simples**, a garden of medicinal and aromatic herbs that were cultivated during the Middle Ages – some of which are poisonous. A book (in French) on the garden is on sale inside the **Musée de Normandie** (☎ 02 31 30 47 50; adult/child/student

€1.50/free/0.70, admission free Sun, combined ticket with Musée des Beaux Arts €3.90; 9.30am-6pm Wed-Mon), which contains historical artefacts illustrating life in Normandy. Utensils, tools, coins, jewellery, farm implements and pottery from the Neolithic era to the 20th century are on display. There are explanatory signs in English.

The **Musée des Beaux-Arts** (☎ 02 31 30 47 70; www .ville-caen.fr/mba; adult/child €3.80/free, combined ticket with Musée de Normandie €3.90; 9.30am-6pm Wed-Mon), in an extravagant modern building nearby, houses an extensive collection of paintings dating from the 15th to 20th centuries, including the wonderful *Le mariage de la Vierge ou Sposalizio* (Marriage of the Virgin) painted by Perugino in 1504. The Venetian school is represented by Veronese's *La tentation de Saint Antoine* (Temptation of St Anthony). From Flanders, the collection highlights Rubens' *Abraham et Melchisédech* (Abraham and Melchizedek), while the French rooms include Poussin's *Vénus pleurant Adonis* (Venus Mourning Adonis), Courbet's *La mer* (The Sea), Boudin's *La plage de Deauville* (The Beach at Deauville) and *Nymphéas* (Water Lilies) by Monet. The collection of engravings is particularly noteworthy, including works by artists ranging from Dürer and Rembrandt to Tiepolo and Van de Weyden. For reasons of conservation, not all the engravings are on display at any given time.

Abbaye aux Hommes

With its multi-turreted Église St-Étienne, **Abbaye aux Hommes** (☎ 02 31 30 42 81; adult/child under 12 €2/free, admission free Sun; 8.50am-noon & 2-7.30pm, guided visits 9.30am, 11am, 2.30pm & 4pm) is a triumphant mixture of Romanesque, Gothic and classical architecture. 'When St-Étienne comes tumbling down, the kingdom of England will perish,' wrote 12th-century Norman poet Robert Wace, and it seems nothing short of miraculous that the church and convent buildings remained standing after the fearsome 1944 bombardments.

Built by William the Conqueror, it was his chosen resting place, but now only his thighbone remains here. His tomb was desecrated during the 16th-century Wars of Religion, but his corpse was badly treated even before he was buried. His thieving servants stripped him almost naked and the funeral procession caught fire. Finding him too large for the funeral bier, the pallbearers tried to fold him in half, causing his stomach to burst open. As a final indignity, a peasant launched the ancient cry of 'Haro' at his tomb (see the boxed text, p261), claiming that he owned the land upon which the grave had been constructed and had not been compensated for its seizure. The peasant was hastily paid off and William was finally laid to rest.

The **Église St-Étienne** (admission free; 8.15am-noon & 2-7.30pm) was built relatively quickly – from 1066 to 1077 – which explains the unity of its style. The austere, undecorated façade creates an impression of sobriety and grandeur, accentuated by the church's perfect proportions. The 11th-century towers topped by Gothic steeples became a model for churches around the region. The interior has the same minimalist decorative scheme and the Gothic choir is one of the oldest in Normandy. A modern plaque in front of the altar marks the burial place of William.

Alongside the church are the convent buildings, which now house the majestic town hall. Very little remains of the original abbey, which was rebuilt by the 18th-century monk-architect Guillaume de la Tremblaye in a classical style. The monks were ejected from the abbey during the French Revolution and Napoleon subsequently turned it into a school. The guided visit takes you through the sumptuous interior, outfitted in sculpted oak panelling, classical paintings and such wonders as an exquisitely designed staircase that seems to be suspended in midair.

Also within the convent buildings is the interesting **Musée d'Initiation à la Nature** (☎ 02 31 30 43 27; admission free; 2-6pm Mon-Fri), which has a child-friendly series of exhibits on the fauna and flora of the Normandy countryside. There are dioramas, games, a botanical garden and stuffed animals.

Abbaye aux Dames

At the eastern end of rue des Chanoines, **Abbaye aux Dames** (☎ 02 31 06 98 98; admission free; guided tours 2.30pm & 4pm) incorporates the **Église de la Trinité**, an even starker church than the Église St-Étienne. The highlights of the church are the stained-glass windows behind the altar and the 11th-century crypt with its finely sculpted capitals. Look for Matilda's tomb behind the main altar. William and

Matilda's daughter Cécile was one of the first nuns at the convent, but its most famous boarder was Charlotte Corday. In July 1793, she got a pass from the abbess, headed to Paris and stabbed revolutionary extremist Marat in his bath. She was guillotined within a week. Access to the abbey, which houses regional government offices, is by guided tour only.

The abbey opens onto the 5¼-hectare **Michel d'Ornano Park** (admission free; ☼ 8am-nightfall), which was once part of the abbey grounds. With paths as wide as boulevards, manicured flowerbeds and a maze, the park is a restful breather from the city.

Other Sights

The most popular old neighbourhood in Caen is **rue du Vaugueux** and its offshoots. The tiny neighbourhood can be overrun with tourists and nightcrawlers, but the cobblestone streets and creaky houses convey the charm of working-class Caen. Most of the stone houses date from the 18th century, although a couple of half-timbered houses were built in the 16th century. Edith Piaf's grandparents had a bistro here.

Less touristy **rue Froide** also escaped bombing and has fine examples of 17th- and 18th-century bourgeois architecture. Behind the elegant façades there are often courtyards

---

WILLIAM CONQUERS ENGLAND

Edward the Confessor, king of England and William's cousin, promised William that upon his death the throne would pass to the young Norman ruler. And when the most powerful Saxon lord in England, Harold Godwinson of Wessex, was shipwrecked on the Norman coast, he was obliged to swear to William that the English crown would pass to Normandy.

In January 1066 Edward died without an heir. The great nobles of England (and very likely the majority of the Saxon people) supported Harold's claim to the throne, and he was crowned on 5 January. He immediately faced several pretenders to his throne, William being the most obvious. But while William was preparing to send an invasion fleet across the Channel, a rival army consisting of an alliance between Harold's estranged brother Tostig and Harold Hardrada of Norway landed in the north of England. Harold marched north and engaged them in battle at Stamford Bridge, near York, on 25 September. He was victorious, and both Harold Hardrada and Tostig were killed.

Meanwhile, William had crossed the Channel unopposed with an army of about 6000 men, including a large cavalry force. They landed at Pevensey before marching to Hastings. Making remarkably quick time southwards from York, Harold faced William with about 7000 men from a strong defensive position on 13 October. William put his army into an offensive position, and the battle began the next day.

Although William's archers scored many hits among the densely packed and ill-trained Saxon peasants, the latter's ferocious defence terminated a charge by the Norman cavalry and drove them back in disarray. For a while, William faced the real possibility of losing the battle. However, summoning all the knowledge and tactical ability he had gained in numerous campaigns against his rivals in Normandy, he used the cavalry's rout to draw the Saxon infantry out from their defensive positions, whereupon the Norman infantry turned and caused heavy casualties on the undisciplined Saxon troops. The battle started to turn against Harold – his two other brothers were slain, and he was killed late in the afternoon. The embattled Saxons fought on until sunset and then fled, leaving the Normans effectively in charge of England. William immediately marched to London, ruthlessly quelled the opposition and was crowned king of England on Christmas Day.

William thus became king of two realms and entrenched England's feudal system of government under the control of Norman nobles. Ongoing unrest among the Saxon peasantry soured his opinion of the country, however, and he spent most of the rest of his life after 1072 in Normandy, only going to England when compelled to do so. He left most of the governance of the country to the bishops.

In Normandy William continued to expand his influence by military campaigns or by strategic marriages. In 1077 he took control of the Maine region, but then fought Philip I of France over several towns on their mutual border. In 1087 he was injured during an attack on Mantes. He died at Rouen a few weeks later and was buried at Caen.

CALVADOS

with dormer windows and stone staircases. Although these apartments are private residences there's usually not a problem opening the outside door for a look around. Try Nos 10, 22 bis and 49.

Rue Écuyère is a little more run down but also contains some interesting old buildings. Notice the façade of No 9, the string of interior courtyards at No 32 and the 15th-century courtyard of No 42.

Festivals & Events

On the first Saturday of September Caen remembers its prewar incarnation as an important port by presenting its boat collection and boat entertainments in the **Festival du Port**. The tourist office is the place for more information.

Tours

Boat trips on board the **Hastings** (☎ 02 31 34 00 00; adult/child return €12/6) leave from quai Vendeuvre four times daily in July and August, and on Sunday only the rest of the year. The 1¼-hour cruise travels along the Caen canal to Ouistreham, passing by the Pegasus bridge and other sites.

The tourist office runs **guided tours** (adult/concession €4.50/4; ☼ 10.30am Mon-Sat Jul & Aug) of the historic old centre of Caen that take in the backstreets of the old town and finish at the St-Etienne cloister in the Abbaye des Hommes.

Le Mémorial de Caen organises guided minibus tours of the D-Day beaches, including Arromanches, Pointe du Hoc, Omaha Beach, the American Military Cemetery and Longues-sur-Mer. The tour leaves at 1pm daily, April to September (with additional departures at 9am and 2pm from June to August), and at 1pm on weekends and holidays the rest of the year. The tour costs €61.60 (students and WWII veterans €55.20). The ticket includes a visit to the museum and this can be used on a different day. Reservations are essential.

Sleeping

BUDGET

Auberge de Jeunesse (☎ 02 31 52 19 96; fax 02 31 84 29 49; 68 rue Eustache Restout; dm €10, breakfast €2.50; ☼ Jun-Sep) This hostel is 2km southwest of the train station – take bus No 5 or 17 (the last one leaves at 9pm) to the Cimetière de Vaucelles stop.

Cité de Lébisey (☎ 02 31 46 74 74; fax 02 31 46 74 76; rue de Lébisey; student/nonstudent per day €7.50/11, per 2 weeks €60.25/78.85, per month €120.45/153; 🖳) These university dormitories offer a good deal for clean doubles with shower in the hall. Reservations must be made by mail or fax to Cité de Lébisey, 114-116 rue de Lébisey, BP 5153, 14070 Caen Cedex 5. The dormitories are just north of the chateau.

Hôtel Le Vaucelles (☎ 02 31 82 23 14; levaucelles@wanadoo.fr; 13 rue de Vaucelles; r from €22.50) If you don't mind the lack of private facilities, this place offers basic but clean rooms and hall showers are free.

Hôtel Bernières (☎ 02 31 86 01 26; www.hotel bernieres.com; 50 rue de Bernières; s/d €35/40) Cosy and friendly, this establishment offers excellent value for the price. In some of the rooms there's only a curtain separating the shower from the sleeping area though, which could be just a little too much intimacy for some people.

Hôtel au St-Jean (☎ 02 31 86 23 35; fax 02 31 86 74 15; 20 rue des Martyrs; r with bathroom/shower €38/35; Ⓟ) The rooms here are nicely decorated without being cutesy or eccentric, and parking is free.

Hôtel du Havre (☎ 02 31 86 19 80; www.hoteldu havre.com; 11 rue du Havre; s/d €39/43; Ⓟ) With efficient, professional service and relatively good-sized and recently brushed-up rooms, this place offers good value. Cheaper rooms with shower only are available, but all have double-glazed windows.

Central Hôtel (☎ 02 31 86 18 52; fax 02 31 86 88 11; 23 place J Letellier; s €36, d €39-43) The building is drab but the interior is cheerfully coloured in yellow and peach. Rooms are fine and offer good value for money.

Hôtel de l'Univers (☎ 02 31 85 46 14; fax 02 31 38 21 33; 12 quai Vendeuvre; s/d €33/44) The location is good as the hotel overlooks the port. Windows are double glazed to block out noise and each room has a telephone and TV, although the decorative scheme is uninspiring.

MID-RANGE

Hôtel du Château (☎ 02 31 86 15 37; www.hotel -chateau-caen.com; 5 ave du 6 Juin; s/d €45/55; Ⓟ) It's a stone's throw from the chateau and has good-sized rooms decorated in a rainbow of colour schemes. Front windows are double glazed and there's an elevator.

Hôtel des Cordeliers (☎ 02 31 86 37 15; fax 02 31 39 56 51; 4 rue des Cordeliers; r from €38) As one of the rare Caen hotels in an 18th-century building, this hotel has more character than most. The interior garden is a relaxing haven and some of the rooms open directly onto it. With white walls and plain pine furniture, the rooms are easy on the eye. The hotel is located on a quiet old street.

Hôtel des Quatrans (☎ 02 31 86 25 57; www.hotel -des-quatrans.com; 17 rue Gémare; s/d €47/54; **P**) In the centre of town, this sleek, modern establishment has an elevator and sound-proofed rooms that area equipped with TV and telephone.

TOP END
Hôtel Moderne (☎ /fax 02 31 86 04 23; www.hotel -caen.com; 116 blvd Maréchal Leclerc; s/d €76/109; **P** **✕**) Although it has a plain exterior, the modern rooms are large and brightly decorated and the rooftop breakfast room offers a superb view of the city.

Hôtel Le Dauphin (☎ 02 31 86 22 26; dauphin.caen @wanadoo.fr; 29 rue Gémare; s/d €70/130; **P** **✕**) For a touch of class, it's hard to beat this priory turned hotel. Features such as antiques, polished wood doors and beamed ceilings create an atmosphere of refinement and luxury, and the restaurant is one of the best in town. Room 310 is a particularly romantic selection.

Eating
CAFÉS
Pedestrianised rue St-Pierre and rue Écuyère have a number of cafés to take a break from shopping during the day or meet friends at night. Both of the following cafés serve food only between noon and 2pm.

Le Cafe Latin (☎ 02 31 85 26 36; 135 rue St-Pierre; ☾ closed Sun) This casual student hang-out has caught the salsa wave and ridden it to shore. Some people start their day here; others start a night of revelry.

La Tour Solidor (☎ 02 31 86 10 35; 24 rue Écuyère; ☾ closed Sun) Larger and warmly decorated in mustard tones, this place is slightly more staid than the Latin.

RESTAURANTS
Caen's restaurants serve a variety of cuisine, from local specialities to those from further afield. There's something to suit all tastes in food and budget. The pedestrianised quarter around rue du Vaugueux is a popular dining area with a wide range of prices and cuisines in one of Caen's few remaining old quarters.

Le Galettoire (☎ 02 31 85 45 28; 33 rue St-Sauveur; dishes from €6; ☾ open daily) A young and casual crowd comes here to sample of wide variety of crepes and *galettes*.

Le Météor (☎ 02 31 82 31 35; 55 rue d'Auge; menus €10; ☾ lunch only Mon-Sat) The joy of this tiny haunt is that the perfectly acceptable three-course *menu* includes a glass of wine.

Pica Pica (☎ 02 31 86 37 41; 1 place St-Sauveur; dishes €8-10; ☾ closed Mon & lunch Sun) Spanish tapas culture has caught fire in Caen and this friendly, young spot is the place to nibble away at a selection of spicy Iberian specialities.

La Petite Auberge (☎ 02 31 86 43 30; 17 rue des Équipes d'Urgence; menus €11 & €17; ☾ closed Sun & Mon) This homely little place turns out simple but scrumptious dishes, including, of course, tripe. The €11 *menu* is available on weekdays only.

Le Bouchon du Vaugueux (☎ 02 31 44 26 26; 12 rue de Graindorge; menus €11.50-16; ☾ closed Sun & Mon) A crowd of regulars who come for the home-spun cooking and hearty, imaginative salads keeps this place humming.

L'Insolite (☎ 02 31 43 83 87; rue du Vaugueux; menus €15-27.50; ☾ closed Sun & Mon) Fish and seafood are prepared to a high standard here. You can enjoy the copious platters from a pleasant heated terrace or the welcoming interior.

Maître Corbeau (☎ 02 31 93 93 00; 8 rue Buquet; menus €9.45-19; ☾ closed Sun & lunch Mon & Sat) Cheese is the star here, as an appetiser, main course and dessert, just as at Au Temps des Cerises in Rouen (it's the same management). It's a young, fun place and the cooking is tasty and uncomplicated. The €9.45 *menu* is available at weekday lunch times.

Dolly's Café & Tea Rooms (☎ 02 31 94 03 29, 16-18 ave de la Libération; breakfast €6-12, dishes around €8.50; ☾ 10am-7.30pm Tue-Sat, 9.30am-6pm Sun) A hearty, full English breakfast can be a welcome antidote to the French bread and coffee routine. This inviting store/restaurant serves up bacon, eggs, beans, toast, coffee and juice all day. The daily specials might include fish and chips, and English products such as tea, jam and newspapers are available next door at The English Shop.

Pizza Amalfi 2 (☎ 02 31 86 08 09; 23 rue Vauquelin; pastas & pizzas €8-12; ☾ closed Sun & dinner Mon) The atmosphere here is convivial and familial; it's extremely kid-friendly. Portions are large and the pizza is of good quality.

CALVADOS

L'Alcide (☎ 02 31 44 18 06; 1 place Courtonne; menus €13.20-21.50; ⊙ closed Sat) This is an excellent address for sampling some traditional Caen cuisine, especially the infamous *tripes à la mode de Caen*, served here in a sauce so savoury you can almost forget you're eating intestines.

Le Gastronome (☎ 02 31 86 57 75; 43 rue St-Sauveur; weekday only menu €12.50, other menus €16-32; ⊙ closed Sun & dinner Tue) Now that you've acquired a taste for tripe, try some more sophisticated versions here. The chef puts his own spin on local classics, much to the delight of local gastronomes.

L'Embroche (☎ 02 31 93 71 31; 17 rue Porte au Berger; menus €16 & €20; ⊙ closed Sun & lunch Mon & Sat) This is one of the more appealing restaurants in the restaurant-ridden Vaugueux quarter, with a nifty dining room and a good list of daily specials prepared with flair. The €16 *menu* is only available at weekday lunchtime.

Le Carlotta (☎ 02 31 86 68 99; 16 quai Vendeuvre; menus €20-30; ⊙ closed Sun) Decked out in a very Parisian *belle époque* style, this is an elegant spot to tuck into a heaping platter of fresh shellfish or one of the Calvados-based local specialities.

Le Costa (☎ 02 31 86 28 28; 13 rue Guilbert; menus from €18; ⊙ closed Sun) A revolving door takes trendoids into the sleek, Art Deco interior to feast on modern updates of French classics. Try the wild salmon for a real treat.

Restaurant Le Dauphin (☎ 02 31 86 22 26; 29 rue Gémare; menus €28-50; ⊙ closed Sat, lunch Sun in summer & dinner Sun in winter) At the hotel of the same name (see Sleeping, p263), this temple to fine cuisine has accumulated a loyal clientele from locals as well as from regular visitors to the hotel. The cuisine is thoroughly Norman, well-executed and reasonably priced considering the quality.

SELF-CATERING

There's a supermarket downstairs at **Monoprix** (45 blvd Maréchal Leclerc; ⊙ 8.30am-8.30pm Mon-Sat). Late-night purchases can be made at **Épicerie de Nuit** (23 rue Porte au Berger; ⊙ 8pm-2am Tue-Sun). Exquisite gateaux and dozens of types of bread are available at **Heiz Legrix** (8 blvd des Alliés).

For **food markets** head to place St-Sauveur on Friday, blvd Leroy (behind the train station) on Saturday and place Courtonne on Sunday.

Drinking

El Che Guevara (☎ 02 31 85 10 75; 53 rue de Geôle) A young crowd of beer drinkers fills this colourful space early in the evening, only to be replaced later on by smart 30-somethings who sip on the excellent tall cocktails. The music is Cuban, naturally, and you can puff on your Cuban cigars in the downstairs cellar.

Le Glue Pot (☎ 02 31 86 29 15; 18 quai Vendeuvre) This pub brings a touch of England to the bar scene along the *quai*. There's usually a live band on Saturday night.

6X (☎ 02 31 86 36 98; 7 rue St-Sauveur; ⊙ noon-1am Mon-Sat, 4pm-1am Sun) Drinks are cheap at this funky student joint where the crowds spill out onto the street.

Le Vertigo (☎ 02 31 85 43 12; 14 rue Écuyère) The university set also flocks here, especially for the nightly happy hours that run from 7pm to 9pm.

Entertainment

DISCOS & CLUBS

Le Farniente (☎ 02 31 86 30 00; 13 rue Paul Doumer) Cementing the Caen-Havana connection, a cool crowd dances to hot Latin sounds.

El Cubanito Café (☎ 02 31 94 34 16; 12 ave de la Libération) Yes, it's another one. If there wasn't a Cuba, would there even be a bar scene in Caen? We report, you decide – while sloshing down more rum-laced cocktails.

Le Carré (☎ 02 31 28 90 90; 32 quai Vendeuvre) This is the slickest disco you'll find in the region, with theme nights, a strict door policy and the latest DJs. You must be over 27 to be allowed in.

L'Excuse (☎ 02 31 38 80 89; rue Vauquelin; ⊙ 10pm -4am Thu-Sat) Tiny and hot in all senses of the word, this is the place to dance until you drop into the arms of a stranger.

GAY & LESBIAN VENUES

Le Zinc (☎ 02 31 94 05 06; 12 rue du Vaugueux) Although you'll sometimes find a mixed crowd, this remains the trendiest gay bar in town. The DJ spins house and techno and it can get pretty crowded.

CLASSICAL MUSIC, OPERA & BALLET

Théâtre de Caen (☎ 02 31 30 48 00; 135 blvd Maréchal Leclerc) Located in the centre of town, this hall offers a season of opera, dance, jazz and classical concerts that run from October to May.

DETOUR: ROUTE DES TRADITIONS

From the A84 south of Caen, take exit 43 into the green, rolling land of **Pre-Bocage**. Look for the signs (white with a navy-blue rim) marked **Route des Traditions**, which take you through the back roads where local family businesses ply their unique products. Follow the D6 to Villers Bocage, and then the D67, which turns into the D71. About 6km further on, watch for **Le Clos D'Orval** (☎ 02 31 77 02 87), producers of Calvados, *pommeau* (an aperitif of Calvados and apple juice) and cider in Amaye-sur-Seulles. After a little – burp – refreshment, forge on past Caumont-l'Éventé, perched precariously on a cliff, to bees and honey at **Le Miel et les Abeilles** (☎ 02 31 77 40 79) in Le Haut Hamel, which has a picnic area. Follow the D9 to Dampierre and the pigeon lofts, pigeon terrine and roast pigeons at **Le Pigeonnier des Pelletiers** (☎ 02 31 68 70 32). Follow the D185 to the D53, which takes you back to the A84.

Zenith (☎ 08 36 68 17 57; www.zenith-caen.fr - French only; rue Joseph Philippon) This is the place where big events with big stars are held. To get here take bus No 12 or 16 to the Parc des Expositions stop.

Getting There & Away

AIR

Caen's **airport** (☎ 02 31 71 20 10) is 5km west of town in Carpiquet. Bus No 1 runs from Carpiquet to Caen's train station. A taxi costs about €15.

BUS

Bus Verts (☎ 08 10 21 42 14) serves the entire Calvados *département*, including Bayeux (€5.80, 50 minutes), Courseulles-sur-Mer (€4.80, 30 minutes), Deauville-Trouville (€8.50, 1¼ hours), Honfleur (€10.20 via Cabourg and Deauville, or €13.70 by express bus) and the ferry port at Ouistreham (€3.40, 25 minutes). It also runs two buses a day to Le Havre (€20, 1½ hours). Go to the relevant sections for information on buses to Falaise (p288), Lisieux (p285) and Pont l'Évêque (p287).

During the summer the school holidays (July to August, more or less), the Ligne Côte de Nacre goes to Bayeux (one hour and 20 minutes) twice a day via Ouistreham and the eastern D-Day beaches. Bus No 44 to Bayeux takes in Le Mémorial de Caen, Arromanches, Pointe du Hoc and the American Military Cemetery at Omaha Beach.

Most buses stop both at the bus station and in the centre of town at place Courtonne, where there's a Bus Verts information kiosk. If you arrive in Caen by bus, your ticket is valid on CTAC city buses for one hour. If you purchase your intercity ticket in advance, your ride to the bus station to catch your bus is free.

TRAIN

Caen is on the Paris–Cherbourg line. There are connections to Paris' Gare St-Lazare (€26.20, 2½ hours, 13 daily), Pontorson (€20.40, 2½ hours, daily), Bayeux (€5.10, 20 minutes, 15 per day), Rennes (€27.30, three hours, two daily), Rouen (€19.40, two hours, 10 daily), and Tours (€28.40, 3¾ hours, five daily) via Le Mans.

CAR

There are the usual car-rental places.
ADA (☎ 02 31 34 88 89; 26 rue d'Auge).
Avis (☎ 02 31 84 73 80; 44 place de la Gare)
Europcar (☎ 02 31 84 61 61; 36 place de la Gare)
Hertz (☎ 02 31 84 64 50; 34 place de la Gare)

BOAT

Brittany Ferries (☎ 02 31 36 36 36) operates vessels from Ouistreham, 14km northeast of Caen, to Portsmouth in England. For more information, see p389.

Getting Around

BUS & TRAM

CTAC (☎ 02 31 15 55 55) operates the city bus No 7 and the more direct No 15 between the train station and the tourist office near the chateau (stop: St-Pierre). There's also a tram line connecting the train station with the University, stopping at quai de Juillet, rue de Bernières, place St-Pierre and the chateau, as well as running out to the suburbs. A single ride on either the buses or trams costs €1.02, and a carnet of 10 tickets costs €8.70. Services end between 6pm and 8pm, depending on the route.

TAXI

To order a **taxi**, ring ☎ 02 31 26 62 00 or ☎ 02 31 52 17 89.

CALVADOS

BAYEUX & THE D-DAY BEACHES

This quiet little corner of France records two of history's great cataclysms. William the Conqueror's 1066 invasion of England is celebrated in the marvellous Bayeux Tapestry and the evocative D-Day beaches recall events that occurred in the 20th century's defining war. The D-Day landings, code-named Operation Overlord, were part of the largest military operation in history. Early on the morning of 6 June 1944, swarms of landing craft – part of a flotilla of almost 7000 boats – hit the beaches, and tens of thousands of soldiers from the USA, UK, Canada and other nations began pouring onto French soil.

The majority of the 135,000 Allied troops stormed ashore along 80km of beach north of Bayeux code-named (from west to east) Utah and Omaha (in the US sector), and Gold, Juno and Sword (in the British and Canadian ones). The Allied landings on D-Day – known as Jour J in French – were followed by the Battle of Normandy, which would lead to the liberation of Europe from Nazi occupation (see p25). In the 76 days of fighting, the Allies suffered 210,000 casualties, including 37,000 deaths. German casualties are believed to be around 200,000, and another 200,000 German soldiers were taken prisoner.

Le Mémorial de Caen (see p257) provides the best introduction to the history of what took place here and also attempts to explain the rationale behind each event. Once on the coast, travellers can take a well-marked circuit that links the battle sites, close to where holiday-makers sunbathe.

Fat Norman cows with udders the size of beach balls use the bombed-out bunkers to shield themselves from the wind. Many of the villages near the D-Day beaches have small museums with war memorabilia on display, collected by local people after the fighting.

Maps of the D-Day beaches are available at *tabacs* (tobacconists), newsagents and book-shops in Bayeux and elsewhere. The best one is called *D-Day 6.6.44 Jour J*. The area is also known as the Côte de Nacre (Mother of Pearl Coast).

BAYEUX
pop 15,400

Stately Bayeux is the proud possessor of the only pictorial record of William the Conqueror's trans-Channel invasion in 1066 – the Bayeux Tapestry. This invaluable stretch of embroidered cloth is the magnet for several million tourists each year and, with a majestic cathedral, the British War Cemetery and museums of art, lace and WWII, a visitor can easily pass an absorbing day or two here. The River Aure cuts through the town centre composed of austere stone buildings, some dating as far back as the 16th century. Bayeux was the first town liberated after the D-Day landings and is one of the few in Calvados to have survived WWII unscathed.

Orientation
Cathédrale Notre Dame, the major landmark in the centre of Bayeux and visible throughout the town, is 1km northwest of the train station. The River Aure, with several attractive little mills along its banks, flows northwards on the eastern side of the centre.

Information
LAUNDRY
Laundrette (13 rue du Maréchal Foch)

MONEY
Caisse d'Épargne (59 rue St-Malo)
Société Générale (26 rue St-Malo)

POST
Main Post Office (14 rue Larcher) Has Cyberposte and changes money.

TOURIST OFFICE
Tourist Office (☎ 02 31 51 28 28; www.bayeux-tourism .com; pont St-Jean; ⏰ 9am-noon & 2-6pm Mon-Sat, 9.30am-noon & 2.30-6pm Sun Jul & Aug; 🖳) Just off the northern end of rue Larcher. Will change money when the banks are closed (Monday and public holidays), and staff can book accommodation for a €2 fee. You can use the Internet here with a Cyberis card (€10 for 1½ hours' access) bought from the counter.

Bayeux Tapestry
The world-famous Bayeux Tapestry recounts the story of the Norman invasion and the events that led up to it – from the Norman perspective. From Harold's perfidy to his grisly death, the whole tale springs to life in a remarkable series of embroidered scenes. It

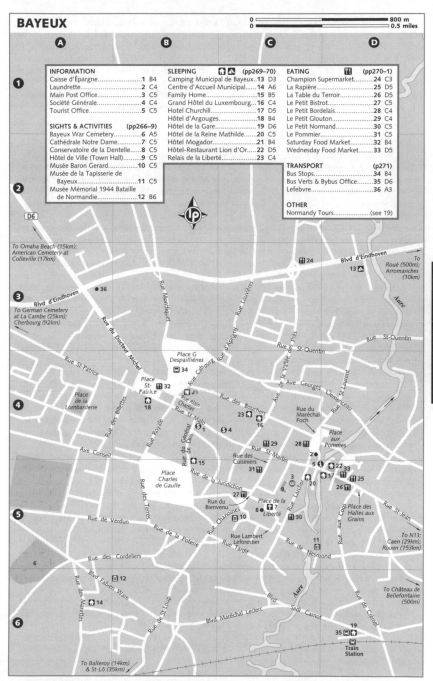

BAYEUX

CALVADOS

INFORMATION
Caisse d'Épargne.....................1 B4
Laundrette..............................2 C4
Main Post Office......................3 C5
Société Générale......................4 C5
Tourist Office..........................5 C5

SIGHTS & ACTIVITIES (pp266–9)
Bayeux War Cemetery................6 A5
Cathédrale Notre Dame.............7 C5
Conservatoire de la Dentelle......8 C5
Hôtel de Ville (Town Hall).........9 C5
Musée Baron Gerard...............10 C5
Musée de la Tapisserie de
   Bayeux..............................11 C5
Musée Mémorial 1944 Bataille
   de Normandie......................12 B6

SLEEPING (pp269–70)
Camping Municipal de Bayeux..13 D3
Centre d'Accueil Municipal......14 A6
Family Home.........................15 B5
Grand Hôtel du Luxembourg....16 C4
Hotel Churchill......................17 D5
Hôtel d'Argouges...................18 B4
Hôtel de la Gare....................19 D6
Hôtel de la Reine Mathilde.......20 C5
Hôtel Mogador......................21 B4
Hôtel-Restaurant Lion d'Or......22 D5
Relais de la Liberté.................23 C4

EATING (pp270–1)
Champion Supermarket............24 C3
La Rapière............................25 D5
La Table du Terroir.................26 D5
Le Petit Bistrot......................27 C5
Le Petit Bordelais...................28 C4
Le Petit Glouton....................29 C4
Le Petit Normand..................30 C5
Le Pommier.........................31 C5
Saturday Food Market.............32 B4
Wednesday Food Market.........33 D5

TRANSPORT (p271)
Bus Stops.............................34 B4
Bus Verts & Bybus Office.........35 D6
Lefebvre..............................36 A3

OTHER
Normandy Tours...................(see 19)

0 ———————— 800 m
0 ———————— 0.5 miles

To Omaha Beach (15km);
American Cemetery at
Colleville (17km)

To German Cemetery
at La Cambe (25km);
Cherbourg (92km)

To Roué (500m);
Arromanches
(10km)

Blvd d'Eindhoven

Rue Montilaquet

Rue St-Patrice

Rue du Docteur Michel

Place
de la
Lombarderie

Place G
Despaillières

Rue Cabourg

Rue d'Aprigny

Rue de la Vallée des Prés

Rue St-Quentin

Ave Georges Clemenceau

Rue des Bouchers

Rue du
Maréchal
Foch

Place
St-
Patrice

Rue Alain
Chartier

Rue St-Malo

Rue des Billettes

Rue Royale

Rue du Général de Dais

Rue St-Martin

Place
aux
Pommes

Ave Conseil

Place
Charles
de Gaulle

Rue de la Juridiction

Rue des
Cuisiniers

Rue du
Bienvenu

Rue de Verdun

Rue des Terres

Rue de la Poterie

Rue Chânoines

Place de la
Liberté

Rue Larcher

Place des
Halles aux
Grains

Rue St-Jean

Rue Lambert
Leforestier

Rue Tardif

Rue de Nesmond

To N13;
Caen (29km);
Rouen (153km)

Rue des Cordeliers

Blvd Fabien Ware

Rue des Marettes

Rue aux Coqs

To Château de
Bellefontaine
(500m)

Rue de Crémel

Blvd Marechal Leclerc

Blvd Sadi Carnot

Aure

Train
Station

To Ballerey (14km)
& St-Lô (35km)

was the epic that defined the 11th century in much the same way as the D-Day landings defined the 20th century, and the tapestry itself has had a turbulent history. In 1792 it was narrowly saved from use as a wagon cover, and in 1794 it was almost cut up into decorative little pieces. Napoleon displayed it in Paris for a few years to drum up support for an invasion of England, but the tapestry was eventually returned to Bayeux, where the priceless work underwent a careful restoration. In 1939 it was placed in an air-raid shelter, then in 1944 it was sent to Paris and hidden in a cellar of the Louvre.

The tapestry is housed in the **Musée de la Tapisserie de Bayeux** (☎ 02 31 51 25 50; rue de

THE BAYEUX TAPESTRY

The Norman conquest of England changed the course of history and the Normans had no doubt that they were right to vanquish the duplicitous Harold at the Battle of Hastings. Soon after, Bayeux's Bishop Odo, along with an unknown artist and a team of highly skilled embroiderers, set out to tell this tale of ambition, betrayal, war and conquest. The result was the splendid Bayeux Tapestry, a vivid pictorial record of the Norman conquest of England and a window upon 11th-century life.

Although once called 'Queen Matilda's tapestry' in the erroneous belief that William the Conqueror's wife was responsible for it, it is unlikely that the busy queen could have accomplished it herself. Because the earliest reference to the tapestry indicates that it hung in Bayeux's cathedral, scholars believe that Bishop Odo of Bayeux, William's half-brother, commissioned it for the opening of the cathedral in 1077.

The story of the Norman conquest is presented cartoon style, with 58 scenes, briefly captioned in Latin, and a cast of hundreds. The main narrative fills up the centre of the canvas, while the daily life of Norman France unfolds in the top and bottom edges. In addition to the lead roles, William (the Good) and Harold (the Very Bad), and supporting players King Edward and Bishop Odo, there are 619 extras, from knights and nobles to peasants ploughing the fields. Like modern blockbusters, it's a man's story – there are only five female figures – with men's labours, animals, weapons, feasts and battles rendered in startling detail.

From the tapestry we have learned that 11th-century Saxons wore moustaches and had long hair, while the Normans were clean-shaven. We see that weapons decorated with dragon motifs were popular on both sides, that the Saxons preferred to fight with battle axes and that they had few archers during the Battle of Hastings. We see men hunting birds with a sling, felling trees and sharpening axes. Animals were an important part of 11th-century life – there are more than 200 horses galloping and prancing across the tapestry; 55 dogs hunting, playing or dashing into battle; and hundreds of birds, including eagles, falcons and peacocks.

Norman spiritual life included myths, fables, superstitions and astrology, all of which are alluded to in the tapestry. The Normans considered Halley's Comet to be an important omen, and its appearance in 1066 is depicted in the tapestry along with a cluster of clearly astonished onlookers. Mythical creatures decorate the upper and lower borders of the tapestry. There are griffins with the head and wings of an eagle but the body of a lion, fish that represent the Pisces constellation, dragons and half-man, half-beast figures. Aesop's fable of an ape asking a lion to become king of the animals is depicted in the tapestry, with the implication that Harold is the ape and William is the lion.

The epic moves to a thrilling climax at the Battle of Hastings. A woman flees a burning house; cavaliers hurl javelins; archers unleash their arrows; and men tumble to the ground, their bodies broken and their heads severed. The artist's conception of battle seems curiously modern: there is more death than glory on this battlefield. Finally Harold falls, either by an arrow in the eye or under the hooves of a Norman horse. Some scholars identify Harold as the man under the final inscription, while others place him in the middle of the picture. With the death of Harold the battle is over and the tapestry ends with the fleeing English soldiers.

The furthest border of the tapestry is unfinished, indicating that there may have been another scene. Having vanquished the faithless Harold, William became the King of England – an image that might have furnished the tapestry's final scene.

Nesmond; adult/concession €7.40/3, incl admission to Musée Baron Gérard; 9am-6.30pm mid-Mar–Apr & Sep-Nov, 9.30am-12.30pm & 2-6pm Nov–mid-Mar, 9am-7pm May–Aug). The excellent taped commentary (€1) makes viewing the upstairs exhibits a bit unnecessary. A 14-minute film on the 2nd floor is screened eight to 13 times a day in English (last screening 5.15pm, or 5.45pm May to August).

Cathédrale Notre Dame

Most of Bayeux's spectacular **cathedral** (place de la Liberté; 8.30am-6pm Oct-Jun, 8.30am-7pm Jul-Sep) is a fine example of Norman Gothic architecture, dating from the 13th century. However, the crypt, the arches of the nave and the lower portions of the towers on either side of the main entrance are 11th-century Romanesque. The central tower was added in the 15th century; the copper dome dates from the 1860s.

Musée Baron Gérard

This pleasant **museum** (02 31 92 14 21; 6 rue Lambert Leforestier; adult/concession €2.60/1.60; 10am-12.30pm & 2-6pm), near the cathedral at place de la Liberté, specialises in local porcelain, lace and 15th- to 19th-century paintings (Italian, Flemish, Impressionist). Admission is free if you buy a ticket to the tapestry museum. The museum is housed in the mansion, Hôtel du Doyen.

Conservatoire de la Dentelle

The fascinating **Lace Conservatory** (02 31 92 73 80; 6 rue du Bienvenu; admission free; 10am-12.30pm & 2-6pm Mon-Sat) is dedicated to the preservation of traditional Norman lace-making. It is claimed that this is the only place where you can watch some of France's most celebrated lace-makers, who create the intricate designs using dozens of bobbins and hundreds of pins.

The Conservatory also gives lace-making classes and sells materials (pins, bobbins, thread and so on). Small lace objects, the product of something like 50 hours' work, are on sale for around €150.

Musée Mémorial 1944 Bataille de Normandie

Bayeux's huge **war museum** (02 31 92 93 41; blvd Fabien Ware; adult/concession €5.50/2.60; 9.30am-6.30pm May–mid-Sep, 10am-12.30pm & 2-6pm mid-Sep–Apr) rather haphazardly displays thousands of photos, uniforms, weapons, newspaper clippings and lifelike scenes associated with D-Day and the Battle of Normandy. A 30-minute film in English is screened two to five times a day (always at 10.45am and 5pm).

Bayeux War Cemetery

This peaceful cemetery, situated on blvd Fabien Ware a few hundred metres west of the war museum, is the largest of the 18 Commonwealth military cemeteries in Normandy. It contains 4868 graves of soldiers from the UK and 10 other countries. Many of the 466 Germans buried here were never identified, and the headstones are simply marked 'Ein Deutscher Soldat' (A German Soldier). There is an explanatory plaque in the small chapel to the right as you enter the grounds. The large structure across blvd Fabien Ware commemorates the 1807 Commonwealth soldiers missing in action.

Festivals & Events

The **Fêtes Médiévales de Bayeux** takes place on the first weekend in July to commemorate the anniversary of the Battle of Formigny, which put an end to the Hundred Years' War. Expect medieval songs, dances, parades and street theatre. In July and August the city sponsors a series of concerts around town for the **Été Musical** (Musical Summer). Rock fans won't want to miss the **Calvados Rock Festival**, which takes place over two days at the beginning of August. The tourist office has the schedule.

Sleeping

BUDGET

Camping Municipal de Bayeux (02 31 92 08 43; blvd d'Eindhoven; adult/site €2.90/3.60; mid-Mar–mid-Nov) This camping ground is about 2km north of the town centre. Bus No 3 stops three times daily at nearby Les Cerisiers.

Family Home (02 31 92 15 22; fax 02 31 92 55 72; 39 rue du Général de Dais; dm incl breakfast €16, d €28) This is an excellent, friendly old hostel and a great place to meet other travellers. The hostel opens all day, but curfew is (theoretically) at 11pm; just ask for a key to the main door. Multicourse French dinners, including wine, cost €11. Vegetarian dishes are available on request or you can cook for yourself. You can also pitch a tent out back for €6.10.

Centre d'Accueil Municipal (02 31 92 08 19; fax 02 31 92 12 40; 21 rue des Marettes; s €11.90) This large, modern building 1km southwest of the cathedral has antiseptic but comfy singles that offer a great deal. You can even have breakfast for an extra €2.45. Telephone reservations are usually accepted.

Hôtel de la Gare (☎ 02 31 92 10 70; fax 02 31 51 95 99; 26 place de la Gare; r €22-37; P) Old but well-maintained, here you'll find slightly cramped rooms but full facilities. There are no late trains so it's usually pretty quiet at night. Normandy Tours (see p273) operates from the hotel.

Relais de la Liberté (☎ /fax 02 31 92 67 72; 22 rue des Bouchers; r €30-38) This warm and friendly B&B offers nice rooms right in the centre of town. Breakfast is an extra €4.50.

Hôtel Mogador (☎ 02 31 92 24 58; hotel.mogador@ wanadoo.fr; 20 rue Alain Chartier; r €42-47; P) This two-star establishment has restful, comfortable rooms, some of which face a pleasant interior courtyard. The beamed ceilings and old-fashioned décor add a touch of warmth to the ambience.

Hôtel de la Reine Mathilde (☎ 02 31 92 08 13; fax 02 31 92 09 93; 23 rue Larcher; r €45; P ✕) Rooms in this cosy hotel are named after Anglo-Saxon kings and queens, who probably would have been happy with the *en suite* bathrooms and good value for money. All rooms are non-smoking.

MID-RANGE

Hôtel d'Argouges (☎ 02 31 92 88 86; dargouges@ aol.com; 21 rue St-Patrice; r €67-93; P) Staying in an 18th-century mansion with a peaceful inner garden and elegant rooms gets you into the spirit of Bayeux. It's within walking distance of the town centre.

Hotel Churchill (☎ 02 31 21 31 80; www.hotel -churchill.com; 14-16 rue St-Jean; s/d €68.50/100; P) This sober structure is decorated with elegance and good taste. Service is first-rate and there's a patio.

Grand Hôtel du Luxembourg (☎ 02 31 92 00 04; hotel.luxembourg@wanadoo.fr; 25 rue des Bouchers; r €74-100; P ✕) This hotel combines businesslike comfort with a warm and friendly welcome. It manages to connect with tradition without appearing old-fashioned, and contains an excellent restaurant.

TOP END

Hôtel-Restaurant Lion d'Or (☎ 02 31 92 06 90, lion.d-or.bayeux@wanadoo.fr; 71 rue St-Jean; r €79-114 P) This sprawling three-star hotel is in an old coaching inn, part of which dates from the 17th century. The cheerful rooms are quiet because they face a courtyard but the hotel is often booked out.

Château de Bellefontaine (☎ 02 31 22 00 10; hotel .bellefontaine@wanadoo.fr; 49 rue de Bellefontaine; s/d €103/105; P ✕) You can live like the duke of Normandy in this superb hotel surrounded by a groomed five-acre park. A canal runs through the property and the hotel is in a luxuriously renovated 18th-century building. The best rooms are Nos 4, 5 and 6, which have chimneys and views over the park. Best of all, the hotel is not too far from the centre of Bayeux.

Eating
RESTAURANTS

Le Petit Normand (☎ 02 31 22 88 66; 35 rue Larcher; menus €9.50-23; ☼ closed Thu Oct-Apr) Serving traditional Norman food prepared with apple cider, this is popular with English tourists as much for the reasonable prices as for the view of the cathedral. The €9.50 *menu* is available on weekdays.

La Rapière (☎ 02 31 21 05 45; 53 rue St-Jean; menus €15, €24, €30; ☼ closed Wed & Thu) The entire family pitches in here to make this restaurant a success. Not to be missed is the wonderful salad Rapière with foie gras, *gesiers* (gizzards – it sounds better in French!) and langoustines. Finish with a Camembert in Calvados. The €15 *menu* is available at lunchtime on weekdays.

Le Petit Bistrot (☎ 02 31 51 85 40; 2 rue du Bienvenu; menus €16 & €28; ☼ closed Sun & Mon Sep-Jun) This is a charming little eatery with excellent fish and duck *menus*. Its secret is the intelligent use of fresh local ingredients.

Le Pommier (☎ 02 31 21 52 10; 40 rue des Cuisiniers; menus €9.50-23; ☼ closed Tue & Wed mid-Sep–mid-Jun) The Norman dishes are impeccably executed and there's a little terrace. Try out the special D-Day *menu* inspired by the Norman meals served to soldiers after the landings. The €9.50 *menu* is available at weekday lunch times.

Le Petit Bordelais (☎ 02 31 92 06 44; 15 rue du Maréchal Foch; dishes €7.20-16; ☼ lunch Tue-Sat) For lunch, pop into this tiny wine bar, an extension of a wine cellar. The vintages are inexpensive and good for washing down the plat du jour or an assortment of cheeses. The wine bar is open until 7pm, even if no meals are served after 2.30pm.

La Table du Terroir (☎ 02 31 92 05 53; 42 rue St-Jean; menus €11, €14 & €26; ✆ closed Sun & Mon) Vegetarians abstain. The big wooden tables fill up with a carnivorous crowd who come to chow down on the meat-only *menus*. The restaurant is an extension of a butcher shop so the cuts are of high quality. The €11 *menu* is available at weekday lunch times.

SELF-CATERING
There are plenty of takeaway shops along or close to rue St-Martin and rue St-Jean, including **Le Petit Glouton** (☎ 02 31 92 86 43; 42 rue St-Martin).

Rue St-Jean has an open-air **food market** on Wednesday morning, as does place St-Patrice on Saturday morning. Don't miss *tergoule*, a sweet, cinnamon-flavoured rice pudding typical of the Bayeux region.

The **Champion supermarket** (blvd d'Eindhoven; ✆ 9am-8pm Mon-Sat) is across the road from Camping Municipal.

Entertainment
Bayeux is not known for its hot nightlife, but there are frequent concerts and theatrical events staged in venues around town. The free booklet *Sorties Plurielles* highlights the various concerts, exhibitions and festivals in Bayeux and is available at the tourist office.

Getting There & Away
BUS
Bus Verts (in Bayeux ☎ 02 31 92 02 92, in Caen ☎ 02 31 44 77 44) offers rather infrequent services from the train station and place St-Patrice to Caen, the D-Day beaches (see p273 for details), Vire and elsewhere in the Calvados *département*. The schedules are arranged for the convenience of school children coming into Bayeux for school in the morning and going home in the afternoon. The Bus Verts office, across the car park from the train station, opens from 10am to noon and from 3pm to 6pm Monday to Friday, year-round except most of July.

TRAIN
Services from Bayeux include Paris' Gare St-Lazare (€28.80) via Caen (€5.10, 20 minutes, 15 per day), as well as Cherbourg (€13.30, one hour, 10 per day). There's a service to Quimper (€45.80, 5¾ hours, three per day) via Rennes.

Getting Around
BUS
The local bus line, **Bybus** (☎ 02 31 92 02 92), which shares an office with Bus Verts, has two routes traversing Bayeux, all of which end up at place St-Patrice. From the train station, take bus No 3 (direction J Cocteau). The bus service is geared to students and is thus infrequent. There's no bus service on Sunday.

BICYCLE
Family Home (☎ 02 31 92 15 22; 39 rue du Général de Dais) and **Roué** (☎ 02 31 92 27 75; 14 blvd Winston Churchill) rent bikes for about €12 per day.

TAXI
You can order a **taxi** 24 hours a day on ☎ 02 31 92 92 40 or ☎ 02 31 92 04 10.

BALLEROY
pop 850
Fourteen kilometres southwest of Bayeux, Balleroy is a humble village with a grand avenue leading to a grandiose **chateau** (☎ 02 31 21 60 61; adult/child €3.30/2.50; ✆ 9am-noon & 2.30-6pm).

In 1631 one of Louis XIII's top advisors commissioned François Mansart, the most prestigious architect of the day, to construct a magnificent residence. For the next several centuries, the counts of Balleroy presided over the grounds, but in 1970 leather-clad press prince Malcolm Forbes bought the property and restored it. He also created a museum devoted to ballooning, a hobby he pursued avidly in his time away from running *Forbes* magazine. Balloon history and examples of elephant, sphinx, Beethoven and minaret balloons are amusing, even if you're not allowed to forget Forbes, his exploits, his friends or his magazine for an instant. Every two years, in the third week of June, there's a balloon festival (the next one is in June 2005) on the grounds of the chateau.

In case you're not a balloon buff, there's always the sumptuously outfitted residential area to explore. Staid royal portraits, oak panelling and floors alternate with more whimsical features such as a ceiling painted with, you've guessed it, balloons.

There's no public transport to the chateau. Take the D572 to Le Tronquay and then turn onto the D73.

CALVADOS

ARROMANCHES

pop 560

To make it possible to unload the quantities of cargo necessary for the Normandy invasion, the Allies established two prefabricated ports code-named Mulberry Harbours. The harbour established at Omaha Beach was completely destroyed by a ferocious gale just two weeks after D-Day, but the other, at Port Winston, can still be viewed at Arromanches, a seaside town 10km northeast of Bayeux.

The harbour consists of 146 massive cement caissons towed from England and sunk to form a semicircular breakwater in which floating bridge spans were moored. In the three months after D-Day, 2.5 million men, four million tonnes of equipment and 500,000 vehicles were unloaded here. At low tide you can walk out to many of the caissons. The best view of Port Winston is from the hill, east of town, topped with a statue of the Virgin Mary.

In addition to its historical interest, Arromanches is a low-key resort with a wide, sandy beach. The **tourist office** (☎ 02 31 22 36 45; www.arromanches.com; 2 rue Maréchal Joffre; ⏰ 10am-12.30pm & 2-5pm) is one block in from the sea. You can change money there and it has a list of *chambres d'hôtes*.

Sights & Activities

The well-regarded **Musée du Débarquement** (Invasion Museum; ☎ 02 31 22 34 31; place de 6 Juin; adult/child €6/4; ⏰ 9am-7pm Jul & Aug, 9.30am-12.30pm & 1.30-5.30pm Sep-Jun), right in the centre of town, explains the logistics and importance of Port Winston and makes a good first stop before visiting the beaches. The last guided tour (in French, with text in English) leaves 45 minutes before closing time. An unimpressive seven-minute slide show in English is held throughout the day.

Sleeping & Eating

Camping Municipal (☎ 02 31 22 36 78; ave de Verdun; adult/site €3.50/3) It's only a block away from the tourist office.

Hôtel de la Marine (☎ 02 31 22 34 19; www.hotel -de-la-marine.com, 2 quai du Canada; r with half-board per person €68; P) The hotel is right on the sea and has nicely renovated rooms, some of which overlook the beach. Half-board is obligatory from June to September but negotiable in the off season. The **restaurant** (menus €18-35) is

a good place to sample Norman specialities, with an €18 *menu* on weekdays.

Hôtel d'Arromanches (☎ 02 31 22 36 26; www.hotel darromanches.fr; 2 rue du Colonel René Michel; r €48-55; P ⌧) A block inland, this familial hotel has a comfortably old-fashioned look both inside and outside, but the rooms have some modern amenities such as satellite TVs and hairdryers. The **restaurant** (menus €14.50-24.50; ⏰ closed Tue & Wed) specialises in seafood and offers excellent value.

LONGUES-SUR-MER

The massive 152mm German guns on the coast near Longues-sur-Mer, 6km west of Arromanches, were designed to hit targets 20km away, which in June 1944 included both Gold Beach (to the east) and Omaha Beach (to the west). Half a century later, the mammoth artillery pieces are still sitting in their colossal concrete emplacements. (In wartime they were covered with camouflage nets and tufts of grass.)

Parts of an American film about D-Day, *The Longest Day* (1962), were filmed both here and at Pointe du Hoc. On clear days, Bayeux's cathedral, 8km away, is visible to the south.

D-DAY BEACHES
Omaha & Juno Beaches

The most brutal fighting on D-Day took place 15km northwest of Bayeux along 7km of coastline known as Omaha Beach, which had to be abandoned in storms two weeks later. As you stand on the gently sloping sand, try to imagine how the US soldiers must have felt running inland towards the German positions on the nearby ridge. A memorial marks the site of the first US military cemetery on French soil, where the soldiers killed on the beach were buried. Their remains were later re-interred at the American Military Cemetery at Colleville-sur-Mer or in the USA.

These days Omaha Beach is lined with holiday cottages and is popular with swimmers and sunbathers. Little evidence of the war remains apart from a single concrete boat used to carry tanks ashore and, 1km further west, the bunkers and munitions sites of a German fortified point (look for the tall obelisk on the hill).

Dune-lined Juno Beach, 12km east of Arromanches, was stormed by Canadian troops on D-Day. A Cross of Lorraine marks the spot where General Charles de Gaulle came ashore shortly after the landings.

American Military Cemetery

The **American Military Cemetery** (☎ 02 31 51 62 00; ☿ 9am-5pm) at the town of Colleville-sur-Mer, 17km northwest of Bayeux, contains the graves of 9386 American soldiers. The remains of an additional 14,000 soldiers were repatriated to the USA.

The huge, immaculately tended expanse of lawn, with its white crosses and Stars of David, set on a hill overlooking Omaha Beach, testifies to the extent of the killings that took place in this area in 1944. At the overlook is an orientation table marked with the landing sites of all the invasion forces, making it easy to visualise the D-Day actions. Steps and a path to the beach lead down from the orientation table.

There's a large colonnaded memorial with a map carved into the north loggia showing the progress of the invasion forces across Europe. Behind the memorial is a wall inscribed with the names of 1557 soldiers missing in action whose remains were never found. Opposite the visitors centre and embedded in the lawn is a time capsule containing news reports of the invasion. It is dedicated to the journalists who covered the war and is due to be opened on 6 June 2044. A reflecting pond and a chapel encourage silent meditation.

Veterans are invited to sign a special register at the visitors centre. The visitors centre will also help you locate a specific grave. It can be reached from Bayeux by Bus Verts' bus No 70, but the service is infrequent. Bus No 44 from Caen also stops here.

Pointe du Hoc Ranger Memorial

At 7.10am on 6 June 1944, 225 US Army Rangers scaled the 30m cliffs at Pointe du Hoc, where the Germans had emplaced a battery of huge artillery guns. The guns, as it turned out, had been transferred elsewhere, but the Americans captured the gun emplacements (the two huge circular cement structures) and the German command post (next to the two flagpoles), and then fought off German counterattacks for two days. By the time they were relieved on 8 June, 81 of the rangers had been killed and 58 more had been wounded.

Today the site, which France turned over in perpetuity to the US government in 1979, looks much as it did half a century ago. The ground is still pockmarked with 3m bomb craters. Visitors can walk among and inside the German fortifications, but they are warned not to dig; there may still be mines and explosive materials below the surface. In the German command post, you can see where the wooden ceilings were charred by American flame-throwers. As you face the sea, Utah Beach, running roughly perpendicular to the cliffs here, is 14km to the left.

Pointe du Hoc, which is 12km west of the American Military Cemetery, is always open. The command post is open the same hours as the cemetery.

Tours

A bus tour is an excellent way to see the D-Day beaches. **Normandy Tours** (☎ 02 31 92 10 70, Hôtel de la Gare, Bayeux) has four-hour tours stopping at Arromanches, Longues-sur-Mer, Omaha Beach, the American Military Cemetery and Pointe du Hoc for €35, not including museum admission fees.

D-Day Tours (☎ 02 31 22 00 08; fax 02 31 51 74 74; www.d-daybeaches.com; BP 48525, 14400 Bayeux) are best booked through the Family Home hostel (see p269). An afternoon tour to major D-Day sites costs €45 (students €35), including museum admission fees. They'll collect you from your hotel or the tourist office in Bayeux. See p262 for details of tours of the beaches from Caen.

Getting There & Away

BUS

Bus No 70, run by **Bus Verts** (☎ 08 25 07 60 27), goes west to the American Military Cemetery at Colleville-sur-Mer and Omaha Beach, and on to Pointe du Hoc and the town of Grandcamp-Maisy. Bus No 74 (No 75 during summer) serves Arromanches, Gold and Juno Beaches, and Courseulles. During July and August, the Côte de Nacre line goes to Caen via Arromanches, Gold, Juno and Sword Beaches, and Ouistreham; Circuit 44 links Bayeux and Caen via Pointe du Hoc, the American Military Cemetery, Le Mémorial de Caen and Arromanches. You can commence the journey in Caen (€17 return), Courseulles (€15 return), Arromanches (€12 return) or Bayeux (€13 return). Prices are for all bus lines.

CALVADOS

CAR

For three or more people, renting a car can be cheaper than a tour. **Lefebvre Car Rental** (☎ 02 31 92 05 96; blvd d'Eindhoven), at the Esso petrol station in Bayeux, charges €78 per day with 200km free (more than enough for a circuit to the beaches along coastal route D514), or €135 for two days with 400km free.

CÔTE FLEURIE

Côte Fleurie, lying between Honfleur and Cabourg, is a lovely but highly developed string of beach resorts along a sandy coast. Glamorous Deauville-Trouville attracts the chic set from Paris, Cabourg is more sedate, whereas Honfleur and Houlgate retain traces of their medieval past amid the summer hoopla. The landscape is gentle, with low cliffs and dunes rising behind wide swaths of sand.

HONFLEUR

pop 8350

In its strategic coastal position at the mouth of the River Seine some 200km northwest of Paris, Honfleur is a step back in time to an era when fishermen, pirates and explorers set sail from its harbour to seek their fortunes. The stone dwellings constructed at the height of Honfleur's glory in the 17th and 18th centuries survive largely intact in a warren of streets around its old harbour. Even though Parisian weekenders sometimes outnumber residents, and cruise ships can be more plentiful than fishing boats in the summer, it's still an active maritime centre dispatching shrimp, scallops and mackerel to the interior.

Honfleur may still be gatekeeper to the sea, but the sea is further away now. The Seine has been dumping silt on the seafront for centuries, leaving the houses along blvd Charles V staring across parkland. Further west are two wide sandy beaches, but the main attraction of Honfleur is the amazingly picturesque old harbour. The changing play of light over slate-fronted buildings proved irresistible to a procession of 19th-century artists. Eugène Boudin was born in Honfleur and was an early mentor of Claude Monet. Painters such as Paul Huet, Corot, Seurat and Dufy came to try their hand at capturing Honfleur's particular charm. The poet

Baudelaire spent time in Honfleur and the composer Erik Satie was born and worked in the town. There are still a number of artists' studios in Honfleur, especially along rue du Puits, rue de l'Homme de Bois and rue des Lingots.

History

Honfleur's seafaring tradition dates back over a millennium. After the Norman invasion of England in 1066, goods bound for the conquered territory were shipped across the Channel from Honfleur. During the Hundred Years' War Charles V fortified the town, but it was conquered by the English and remained in English hands until 1450. With the return of peace, the town rebuilt and re-established its commercial links. Even the creation of Le Havre as a rival port in 1517 only served to spur the town on to developing trade relations with the New World.

In 1608 Samuel de Champlain set sail from here with a crew of local sailors on his way to found Quebec City. More than 4000 Normans migrated to Canada in the 17th century, working as fishermen, merchants and fur traders. In 1681 Cavelier de la Salle started out from Honfleur to explore the New World. He reached the mouth of the Mississippi and named the area Louisiana in honour of King Louis XIV, the ruler of France at the time. During the 17th and 18th centuries, Honfleur achieved a certain degree of prosperity through trade with the West Indies, the Azores and the colonies on the western coast of Africa. In order to accommodate the growing maritime traffic, Louis XIV's minister Colbert ordered the construction of a sheltered port, now the Vieux Bassin (old harbour), completed in 1684. It was followed by the construction of the Bassin de l'Est in the 18th century, but the age of maritime adventure was passing as England assumed control of the seas. Honfleur's diminishing importance made it unnecessary to undertake any grand renovation projects, leaving the town much as it was when its moment in the spotlight had passed.

Orientation

Honfleur is centred around the Vieux Bassin. To the east is the heart of the old city, known as the Enclos because it was once enclosed by fortifications. To the north is the Avant

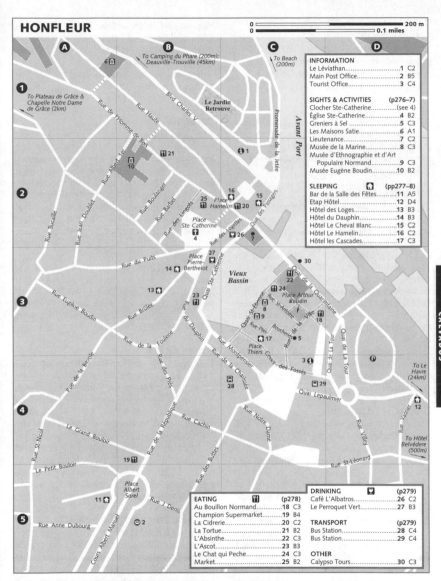

HONFLEUR

INFORMATION	
Le Léviathan	1 C2
Main Post Office	2 B5
Tourist Office	3 C4

SIGHTS & ACTIVITIES	(p276–7)
Clocher Ste-Catherine	(see 4)
Église Ste-Catherine	4 B2
Greniers à Sel	5 C3
Les Maisons Satie	6 A1
Lieutenance	7 C2
Musée de la Marine	8 C3
Musée d'Ethnographie et d'Art Populaire Normand	9 C3
Musée Eugène Boudin	10 B2

SLEEPING	(pp277–8)
Bar de la Salle des Fêtes	11 A5
Etap Hôtel	12 D4
Hôtel des Loges	13 B3
Hôtel du Dauphin	14 B3
Hôtel Le Cheval Blanc	15 C2
Hôtel Le Hamelin	16 C2
Hôtel les Cascades	17 C3

EATING	(p278)
Au Bouillon Normand	18 C3
Champion Supermarket	19 B4
La Cidrerie	20 C2
La Tortue	21 B2
L'Absinthe	22 C3
L'Ascot	23 B3
Le Chat qui Peche	24 C3
Market	25 B2

DRINKING	(p279)
Café L'Albatros	26 C2
Le Perroquet Vert	27 B3

TRANSPORT	(p279)
Bus Station	28 C4
Bus Station	29 C4

OTHER	
Calypso Tours	30 C3

CALVADOS

Port (outer harbour), where the fishing fleet is based. Quai Ste-Catherine fronts the Vieux Bassin to the west, while rue de la République runs southwards from it. The Plateau de Grâce, with the Chapelle Notre Dame de Grâce on top, is west of town. To reach the beach walk up promenade de la Jetée and head west along the coast.

Information

Le Léviathan (☎ 02 31 87 92 95; 11 blvd Charles V; per 30min €1.50; ☷ 2.30pm-1am Mon-Sat) Internet access.
Main Post Office (rue de la République) Southwest of the centre, just past place Albert Sorel. It has a Cyberposte terminal.
Tourist Office (☎ 02 31 89 23 30; www.ot-honfleur.fr; quai Lepaulmier; ☷ 9.30am-7pm daily Jul-Aug, 9.30am-12.30pm

---

PASSE MUSÉE

The **Passe Musée** (adult/concession €8.50/5.50) is on sale in museums and includes visits to all town museums, except the Clocher. It is good for one year.

& 2-6.30pm Mon-Sat Apr-Jul & Sep, 9.30am-noon & 2-6pm Mon-Sat Oct-Mar) Will help visitors find accommodation, with an added cost of €0.30 for a telephone booking, and runs two-hour guided tours of Honfleur (3pm Mon; adult/concession €8.50/5.50) in English.

Église Ste-Catherine

This wooden **church** (place Ste-Catherine; 10am-noon & 2-6pm, except during services), whose stone predecessor was destroyed during the Hundred Years' War, was built by the people of Honfleur during the second half of the 15th and the early 16th centuries. It is thought that they chose wood, which could be worked by local shipwrights, in an effort to save stone in order to strengthen the fortifications of the Enclos. The structure that the town's carpenters created, which was intended to be temporary, has a vaulted roof that looks like an overturned ship's hull. The church is also remarkable for its twin naves, each topped by vaulted arches supported by oak pillars.

Clocher Ste-Catherine

The church's free-standing wooden bell tower, **Clocher Ste-Catherine** (02 31 89 54 00; adult/concession €4.30/2.60, incl admission to Musée Eugène Boudin; 10am-noon & 2-6pm Wed-Mon mid-Mar–Sep, 2.30-5pm Mon-Fri, 10am-noon & 2.30-5pm Sat & Sun Oct–mid-Mar), dates from the second half of the 15th century. It was built apart from the church for both structural reasons (so the church roof would not be subject to the bells' weight and vibrations) and for safety (a high tower was more likely to be hit by lightning). The former bell-ringer's residence at the base of the tower houses a small museum of liturgical objects, but the huge, rough-hewn beams are of more interest.

Musée Eugène Boudin

Named in honour of the early Impressionist painter born here in 1824, this **museum** (02 31 89 54 00; rue de l'Homme de Bois; adult/concession €4.30/2.60, incl admission to Clocher Ste-Catherine; 10am-noon & 2-6pm Wed-Mon mid-Mar–Sep, 2.30-5pm Mon-Fri,

10am-noon & 2.30-5pm Sat & Sun Oct–mid-Mar) has a good collection of Impressionist paintings from Normandy, including works by Dubourg, Dufy and Monet. An entire room is devoted to the works of Eugène Boudin, whom Baudelaire called the 'king of skies' for his luscious skyscapes.

Harbours

The **Vieux Bassin**, from where ships bound for the New World once set sail, now shelters mainly pleasure boats. The nearby streets, especially **quai Ste-Catherine**, are lined with tall, narrow houses dating from the 16th to the 18th centuries. The **Lieutenance**, which was once the residence of the town's royal governor, is at the mouth of the old harbour. It is the sole remaining vestige of the fortifications that once completely circled the town.

The **Avant Port**, on the other side of the Lieutenance, is home to Honfleur's 50 or so fishing vessels. Further north, dykes line both sides of the entrance to the port.

Either harbour makes a pleasant route for a walk to the seashore.

Musée de la Marine

Honfleur's small **maritime museum** (02 31 89 14 12; adult/concession €3/1.70, incl admission to Musée d'Ethnographie et d'Art Populaire Normand; 10am-noon & 2-6pm Tue-Sun Apr-Sep, 2-6pm Mon-Fri, 10am-noon & 2-6pm Sat & Sun Oct–mid-Nov & mid-Feb–Mar, closed mid-Nov–mid-Feb) is on the eastern side of the Vieux Bassin in the deconsecrated Église St-Étienne, which was begun in 1369 and enlarged during the English occupation of Honfleur (1415–50). Displays include numerous assorted model ships, ships' carpenters' tools and engravings.

Musée d'Ethnographie et d'Art Populaire Normand

Next to the Musée de la Marine on rue de la Prison (an alley off quai St-Étienne), this **museum** (02 31 89 14 12; adult/concession €3/1.70, incl admission to the Musée de la Marine; 10am-noon & 2-6pm Tue-Sun Apr-Sep, 2-6pm Mon-Fri, 10am-noon & 2-6pm Sat & Sun Oct–mid-Nov & mid-Feb-Mar, closed mid-Nov–mid-Feb) occupies a couple of houses and a former prison dating from the 16th and 17th centuries. It contains 12 furnished rooms of the sort you would have found in the shops and wealthy homes of Honfleur between the 16th and 19th centuries.

Les Maisons Satie

This delightful **museum** (☎ 02 31 89 11 11; 67 blvd Charles V; adult/concession €5/3.50; ☺ 10am-7pm Wed-Mon Jun-Sep, 11am-6pm Wed-Mon Oct-May) captures the spirit of composer Erik Satie in an unusual way. 'Esoteric' Satie was known for his surrealistic wit ('Like money, piano is only agreeable to those that touch it') as much as for his starkly beautiful compositions. Visitors wander through the museum (located in Satie's birthplace) with a headset playing Satie's music and excerpts from his writings (in French or English). Each room is a surprise. One features a winged pear, another has a light display around a basin, and a room called the Laboratory of Emotions has a whimsical contraption that you pedal.

Greniers à Sel

The two huge **salt stores** (☎ 02 31 89 02 30; rue de la Ville), along from the tourist office, were built in the late 17th century to store the salt needed by the fishing fleet to cure its catch of herring and cod. There were originally three warehouses but one burned down in 1892. All three could store up to 10,000 tonnes of salt. For most of the year the only way to see the Greniers à Sel is to take a guided tour, which is part of the town tour available from the tourist office. During July and August the stores host art exhibitions and concerts.

Chapelle Notre Dame de Grâce

This chapel, built between 1600 and 1613, is at the top of the Plateau de Grâce, a wooded, 100m-high hill about 2km west of the Vieux Bassin. There's a great view of the town and port.

Tours

Honfleur is a good launching pad for boat tours of the region. There are 40-minute boat tours of the Vieux Bassin for €3. These tours leave from the quai de la Quarantaine.

There is a 50-minute Promenade en Mer operated by Vedettes Stéphanie, Alphée and Evasion for €6.50 and the Vedette la Jolie France has a tour that goes to the Pont de Normandie (€8). These tours run from April to mid-October, and boarding is either from the quai des Passagers or the quai de la Quarantaine. The schedule depends on the tides.

Festivals & Events

Every year on Whit Sunday (the seventh Sunday after Easter) Honfleur's sailors organise a blessing of the sea in front of the old harbour. On Whit Monday (the next day) there's a procession up to Chapelle Notre Dame de Grâce, where a ceremony is held. During the two-day festival there's an exposition of model ships at the Greniers à Sel. The third week of September is the time to celebrate prawn fishing. Expect sailing songs and water jousting.

Sleeping

BUDGET

Camping du Phare (☎ 02 31 89 10 26; blvd Charles V; per person/site €4.75/5.35; ☺ Apr-Sep) This camping ground is the closest to town. From the town centre, follow rue Haute about 500m northwest of the Vieux Bassin.

Bar de la Salle des Fêtes (☎ 02 31 89 19 69; 8 place Albert Sorel; r €30-50) There are only four simple, unadorned rooms in this tiny place over a bar about 400m southwest of the Vieux Bassin. Breakfast costs an extra €6.

Etap Hôtel (☎ 02 31 89 71 70; fax 02 31 89 77 88; rue des Vases; r €31.50; P) It has the charm you would expect from a chain hotel, but then the price is right and so is its central location. Rooms have private bathroom and satellite TV, and can sleep up to three people.

Hôtel les Cascades (☎ 02 31 89 05 83; fax 02 31 89 32 13; 17 place Thiers; r from €31) This hotel has sparse but attractive rooms with TV and telephone, and a decent restaurant downstairs.

MID-RANGE

Hôtel Belvédere (☎ 02 31 89 08 13; fax 02 31 89 51 40; 36 rue Emile Renouf; s/d €51/62; P) Less than 1km east of the town centre is this tranquil retreat. The garden and terrace are relaxing. Room 11 has a view of the Pont de Normandie.

Hôtel des Loges (☎ 02 31 89 38 26; www.hoteldes loges.com - French only; 18 rue Brûlée; r from €90; P) The soft lighting, candy-like colours and lack of fussiness are both kid-friendly and romantic. Rooms are simple but comfortable and the ambience is friendly and relaxed. Families will like the baby-sitting service available at €8 per hour.

TOP END

Hôtel du Dauphin (☎ 02 31 89 15 53; www.hotel-du -dauphin.com; 10 place Pierre-Berthelot; r €61-137; P ▢ ▢) Behind a 17th-century, half-timbered

CALVADOS

façade lies this delightfully modern and charming hotel. The colourful rooms are bound to cheer you up on a grey Norman day, and the more expensive rooms even have spa baths.

Hôtel Le Cheval Blanc (☎ 02 31 81 65 00; www.hotel -honfleur.com; 2 quai des Passagers; r €70-200; P ⊠) This luxurious establishment is in a 15th-century mansion overlooking the port. The rooms are stunningly furnished in a style you could call updated traditional and have views over the Vieux Bassin. Suites and studios with spa baths are available, and prices include breakfast.

Eating
RESTAURANTS
Places to dine are abundant (especially along quai Ste-Catherine) but the food here doesn't come cheap. Menus usually centre on fish and seafood.

La Cidrerie (☎ 02 31 89 59 85; 26 place Hamelin; week-day lunch menu €9; ⊠ closed Tue-Wed Oct-Jun) Crêpes and *galettes* with every kind of topping are wonderful, but the main attraction here is the wide selection of drinks that are almost exclusively based on apples and pears. *Cidre* (cider), *pommeau*, *poiré* (pear cider) and Calvados are served in surprising forms and combinations.

Au Bouillon Normand (☎ 02 31 89 02 41, 7 rue de la Ville; menus €16 & €23; ⊠ closed Wed & dinner Sun) In the bright, modern dining room, the blackboard specials might include a *brandade de poisson* (fish and potato puree) with shrimp, crusty Camembert and *tarte tatin* (upside-down apple tart). If your kids get bored they can improve their French by perusing the comic books and games set aside for them.

La Tortue (☎ 02 31 89 04 93; 36 rue de l'Homme de Bois; menus €15.50 & €23; ⊠ closed Tue & dinner Mon) The cute dining room and informal service set a relaxed tone for fine dining. Vegetarians put off by the fried foie gras in truffle juice can choose the excellent vegetarian *menu*.

Le Chat qui Peche (☎ 02 31 89 35 35; 5 place Arthur Boudin; menus €13.50, €19 & €25; ⊠ closed dinner Sun Oct-May) The outdoor umbrella-covered terrace is inviting, and the fish dishes could tempt even the most avid fish-o-phobe. Try the superb fish soup as a starter.

L'Ascot (☎ 02 31 90 88 791; 76 quai Ste- Catherine; menus €20.50 & €27; ⊠ closed Thu & dinner Wed) The cuisine is exquisite in this romantic spot on the Vieux Bassin. On the terrace or in the candlelit dining room, your tastebuds will be titillated by the delicately prepared seafood.

L'Absinthe (☎ 02 31 89 39 00; 10 quai de la Quaran-taine; menus €29, €48, €63) Located in a ravishing 18th-century mansion, this is one of the finest restaurants in Normandy. The cuisine is sophisticated, even on its cheapest *menu*, which might include crispy veggies, fish and a crepe with fresh fruit, flavoured with tantalising spices. Do reserve in advance.

SELF-CATERING
The **market** (place Ste-Catherine; ⊠ 9am-1pm Sat) has an excellent selection of local products and an organic food market. There's a **Champion supermarket** just west of rue de la République, near place Albert Sorel.

THE PONT DE NORMANDIE

The Pont de Normandie between Le Havre and Honfleur is a remarkable feat of engineering and a majestic work of architecture. Opened in January 1995, the original idea had been to build the world's longest cable-stayed bridge to connect Upper and Lower Normandy. With a total length of 2141m, the Pont de Normandie was surpassed in 1998 by the Tatara bridge in Hiroshima, Japan, but its elegant structure is unequalled. A delicate web of cables connects the arched span of the bridge with two soaring 215m towers, etching a bold silhouette against the sky. At night the theatrically placed lights create an even more dramatic effect.

The decision to construct a cable-stayed bridge was based in part upon the softness of the riverbed, which probably would not have supported a suspension bridge. The two towers descend to a depth of 50m to rest upon a sufficiently solid bedrock. Also, one malfunctioning stay doesn't affect the entire bridge. Its aerodynamic design keeps the bridge stable even in tornado-level winds and a battery of computers monitor its stress level.

The bridge is 88km from Caen, 16km from Le Havre and 2km from Honfleur. A **visitors centre** (☎ 02 35 24 64 90; ⊠ 8am-noon & 2-5pm) on the Le Havre side has photos and explanations of the construction. There's no charge for walking across the bridge but drivers pay €5 each way.

Drinking

Café L'Albatros (☎ 02 31 89 25 30; 32 quai Ste-Catherine)
Sailors, students, philosophers and layabouts are all at home at this café-bar, from breakfast through beer and sandwiches and on to nightcaps.

Le Perroquet Vert (☎ 02 31 89 14 19; 52 quai Ste-Catherine) This is more of a 'bar' bar, with an excellent selection of beer and a good terrace for people-watching.

Getting There & Away

The **bus station** (☎ 02 31 89 28 41) is southeast of the Vieux Bassin on rue des Vases. **Bus Verts** (in Caen ☎ 02 31 44 77 44) Line No 20 runs via Deauville-Trouville (€3.40, 30 minutes, five per day) to Caen (€10.20, €13.70 by express bus, one hour). The same line goes northwards to Le Havre (€6.80, 30 minutes, five per day) via the Pont de Normandie. Line No 50 goes to Lisieux (€10.80, one hour). Bus Verts offers a 12% discount for people aged under 26 on Wednesday, Sunday and Saturday afternoon.

DEAUVILLE-TROUVILLE

Some 15km southwest of Honfleur lie the two seaside resorts of Deauville (population 4500) and Trouville (population 5600), which share many of the same amenities but maintain distinctly different personalities. Chic Deauville couldn't be more impressed with itself. With designer boutiques, an exclusive casino, a racetrack and the yearly Festival of American Film, the town is clearly more comfortable with world-class shoppers, gamblers and film stars. Trouville is more down-to-earth. Hotels and restaurants are less expensive and the town is proud of the 19th-century artists and writers that once flocked to its picturesque port. Both towns boast a wide, sandy beach, marred by lines of bathhouses.

The town of Trouville developed before Deauville. When the painter Paul Huet and the writer Alexandre Dumas first came here in 1826, Trouville was merely a small fishing village. Its proximity to Paris (200km) attracted a series of painters and writers at a time when the concept of therapeutic baths was gaining popularity. Flaubert came in 1836 when he was still a teenager and the landscape painter Charles Mozin produced several Trouville paintings. In the 20th century, writer-director Marguerite Duras wrote fondly of her long visits to Trouville and was inspired to make several films in the town.

Deauville became fashionable in the early 20th century after construction of a racetrack and casino. Designer Coco Chanel opened a boutique in 1913 that was soon patronised by the fashionable set fleeing WWI for their secondary residences. Throughout the 1920s and 1930s, Deauville glittered with international royalty, industrialists and such political heavyweights as Winston Churchill. The Festival of American Film arrived in 1975, bringing a parade of stars and new glamour to Deauville. Events revolving around horses, polo and film attract the highest rungs of Parisian society, who sometimes refer to the town as Paris' 21st arrondissement.

Orientation

The two towns are separated by the River Touques, with Trouville on the eastern bank and Deauville on the western bank, linked by the Pont des Belges. The combined train and bus station is just west of the bridge. Beaches line the coast to the north of both towns on either side of the port. Note that there are no beach showers; you must rent a swimming hut (monthly) and they are reserved at least a year in advance for the July/August season.

Information

INTERNET ACCESS

Gestimedia (☎ 02 31 14 04 61; 6 rue Thiers, Deauville; per 10 min/1hr €1/6; ☺ 9am-1pm & 2-6pm Mon-Fri)

LAUNDRY

Laundrette (41 ave de la République)

MONEY

Crédit du Nord (84 rue Eugène Colas, Deauville) Has an ATM.
Société Générale (9 place Morny, Trouville) Has an ATM.

POST

Post Office (rue Robert Fossorier, Deauville) Has Cyberposte and exchanges currency.
Post Office (16 rue Amiral de Maigret, Trouville)

TOURIST OFFICE

Deauville Tourist Office (☎ 02 31 14 40 00; www.deauville.org; place de la Mairie; ☺ 9am-7pm daily Jul-Sep, 9am-6.30pm daily May & Jun, 9am-12.30pm & 2-6.30pm Mon-Sat, 10am-1pm & 2-5pm Sun mid-Sep–Apr) You can pick up a copy of the free, outlandishly glossy magazine *Deauville Passions* for an overview of annual events.

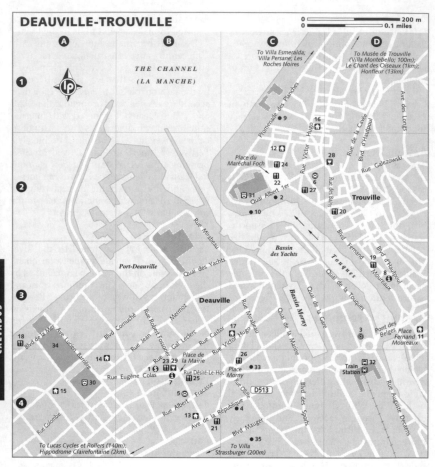

DEAUVILLE-TROUVILLE

Trouville Tourist Office (☎ 02 31 14 60 70;
www.trouvillesurmer.org; 32 blvd Fernand Moureaux;
⏰ 9am-7pm daily May-Aug, 9.30-noon & 2-6.30pm
Mon-Sat Apr-Jun & Sep-Oct, 9.30am-noon & 1.30-6pm
Mon-Sat Nov-Mar)

TRAVEL AGENCIES
Fournier (☎ 02 31 88 16 73; place du Maréchal Foch,
Trouville) Handles air tickets.

Sights & Activities
In Deauville the rich, famous and various
assorted wannabes strut their stuff along
the elegant beachside **promenade des Planches**,
a 500m-long boardwalk lined with private
swimming huts, before losing a wad at the
casino.

About 1km northeast of Trouville's tour-
ist office stands the **Musée de Trouville** (☎ 02 31
88 16 26; 64 rue du Général Leclerc; adult/concession €2/1.50;
⏰ 2-6.30pm Wed-Mon Apr-Sep), which is located
in the magnificent Villa Montebello. This
former summer residence of Napoleon III
was built at the height of Trouville's popularity in 1865 for the marquise of Montebello. The villa has a panoramic view over
the beaches, and the museum recounts the
history of Trouville in posters, drawings and
paintings. Featured artists include Trouville
painters Eugène Isabey, Charles Mozin and
Eugène Boudin, and there are temporary
exhibitions by local artists.

On the beach at Trouville, La Plage, is
the remarkably varied **Aquarium Vivarium de**

INFORMATION			Hôtel Le Chantilly	13	B4	DRINKING		(p282)
Crédit du Nord	1	B4	Hôtel Normandy	14	A4	La Maison	28	D2
Fournier	2	C2	Hôtel Royal	15	A4	Zoo Bar	29	B4
Gestimedia	3	D3	La Maison Normande	16	C1			
Laundrette	4	C4	L'Espérance	17	C3	ENTERTAINMENT		(p282)
Main Post Office Deauville	5	B4				Casino de Deauville	30	A4
Main Post Office Trouville	6	C2	EATING		(p282)	Louisiane Follies	31	C2
Tourist Office	7	B4	Bar du Soleil	18	A3			
Tourist Office	8	D3	Bistro Sur Le Quai	19	D3	TRANSPORT		(p283)
			Brasserie Le Central	20	C2	Bus Station	32	D4
SIGHTS & ACTIVITIES		(pp280-1)	Champion Supermarket	21	B4	Rent a Car	33	C4
Aquarium Vivarium de Trouville	9	C1	Food Market	22	C2			
Gulfstream	10	C2	Glacerie Lambert	23	B4	OTHER		
			La Petite Auberge	24	C2	Centre International de Deauville (CID)	34	A3
SLEEPING		(pp281-2)	Mamy Crêpe	25	B4	Hippodrome La Touques	35	C4
Hôtel de la Paix	11	D3	Market	26	C4			
Hôtel La Reynita	12	C2	Monoprix	27	C2			

Trouville (☎ 02 31 88 46 04; adult/concession €6.50/4.50; 10am-noon & 2-6.30pm Easter-Jun & Sep-Oct, 10am-7pm Jul & Aug, 2-6pm Nov-Easter), which aside from wild and wonderfully colourful fish also houses some fearsome reptiles (snakes, crocodiles and iguanas among them) and weird insects.

Walking up Trouville's beachside promenade, you'll come to several illustrious **19th-century villas**. Notice the half-timbered Villa Esmeralda, the oriental style Villa Persanc, and Les Roches Noires, where Marguerite Duras lived and worked. Following rue Général Leclerc past the Villa Montebello takes you to La Corniche, a hilly road with spectacular views along the coast.

In Deauville the **Villa Strassburger** (admission €2.30), on ave de Strassburger near the Hippodrome, was built by the Rothschild family and then given to the town. The exterior is an eye-pleasing mixture of towers and gables coalescing within a unique Alsatian-Norman style, and the interior is furnished in its original American style. The tourist office conducts visits three times daily on Tuesday and Wednesday in July and August.

Tours
Fournier (see p280) offers a programme of excursions to the D-Day beaches, Mont St-Michel and other Normandy highlights for about €45 a day. From quai Albert 1er the *Gulfstream* goes on a half-hour coastal tour (€6.50), as well as longer trips that take in the Pont de Normandie and Honfleur.

Festivals & Events
Deauville's answer to Cannes' famous film festival is the **Festival of American Film**, open to all and attracting a procession of Hollywood stars during the first week of Sep-

tember. Tickets cost €40/130 per day/week and are available during the festival at the **Centre International de Deauville** (CID; ☎ 02 31 14 14 14; www.festival-deauville.com; ave Lucien Barrière) or through the website. One ticket includes the entire daily or weekly programme.

Deauville is renowned for its equestrian tradition. The horse-racing season, which runs from early July to the middle of October, is held at two local racetracks: Hippodrome La Touques (300m southwest of the train station) for gallop races, and Hippodrome Clairfontaine (2km further west) for galloping, trotting and steeplechase. Horse-lovers will also enjoy the **Equi'days** (☎ 02 31 84 61 18; www.equidays.com), which take place for a week in mid-October with seminars, horse shows, jumping and sales.

The new **Asian Film Festival** takes place in March. Tickets are free and available at the tourist office. Trouville hosts a **Festival Folkorique**, which fills the streets with colourfully clad musicians and dancers in the third week of June, and celebrates mackerel and the fisherman that bring them in during the **Fête de la Mer et du Maquereau** at the end of July and beginning of August.

Sleeping
Le Chant des Oiseaux (☎ 02 31 88 06 42; fax 02 31 98 16 09; 11 route d'Honfleur; adult/site €2.50/5; Apr-Oct) About 1km east of Trouville, this place has a sweeping view of the coast.

The best-value hotels are all in Trouville, and the town participates in the 'Bon Weekend en Villes' two-nights-for-the-price-of-one programme from November to March. Check at the tourist office for details.

Hôtel de la Paix (☎ 02 31 88 35 15; hoteldelapaix@hotmail.com; 4 place Fernand Moureaux, Trouville; r €36.50-66) The recent renovation has been tasteful

CALVADOS

here, and leaving in place the hotel's many traditional features while brushing up the amenities. The more expensive rooms overlook the port.

Hôtel La Reynita (☎ 02 31 88 15 13; fax 02 31 87 86 85; 29 rue Carnot, Trouville; r €40-80; ☐) The spacious and quiet rooms are kept in tiptop shape and the new modem plugs are a welcome addition.

La Maison Normande (☎ 0231881225; www.maison normande.com - French only; 4 place de Lattre de Tassigny, Trouville; r with shower €44, with bathroom €52-64) As its name indicates, you'll enjoy ultra-Norman style, with crisscrossing beams outside and an interior that resembles a local family home where the furnishings are meant to have a lived-in look.

Hôtel Le Chantilly (☎ 02 31 88 79 75; www.123france .com; 120 ave de la République, Deauville; r from €79) In Deauville, this is a good, moderately priced hotel with renovated, relatively large rooms.

L'Espérance (☎ 02 31 88 26 88; fax 02 31 88 33 29; 32 rue Victor Hugo, Deauville; r €34-67) This peaceful, agreeable hotel has stuck with tradition and it works. The restaurant is also worth a stop.

The most luxurious establishments in Deauville are the **Hôtel Normandy** (☎ 02 31 98 66 22; www.lucienbarriere.com; 38 rue Jean Mermoz; r from €238; P ✕) and the **Hôtel Royal Barrière** (☎ 02 31 98 66 33; www.lucienbarriere.com; 14 blvd Cornuché; r €229-1165; P ✕ ▨ ☐), which are under the same management and are as much tourist attractions as hotels. Both are outstanding hotels; the Hôtel Normandy is slightly more Norman in style and offers more facilities for kids (nursery, games room, children's restaurant). Whether or not you decide to indulge with a lavishly outfitted room, do stroll in for a look at the lobbies and bars or feast in one of the fine restaurants.

Eating

Deauville has a somewhat overpriced dining scene. For better value, try the options in Trouville.

Mamy Crêpe (☎ 02 31 14 96 44; 16 rue Désiré-Le-Hoc, Deauville; light meals from €2.50) This hugely popular takeaway stand sends out excellent crepes, quiches and sandwiches.

Bar du Soleil (☎ 02 31 88 04 74; blvd de la Mer; Deauville; weekday menu €18.50; ☽ noon-4pm Easter-Oct) Its wide terrace right on the boardwalk is always filled even though the seafood is not especially cheap. At least come for a drink and watch the sunset.

Bistrot Sur Le Quai (☎ 02 31 81 28 85; 68 blvd Fernand Moureaux, Trouville; menus €10-25; ☽ closed Wed) Among the waterfront eateries in Trouville, this one serves the best seafood at the best prices and has a pleasant front terrace.

Brasserie Le Central (☎ 02 31 88 13 68; 158 blvd Fernand Moureaux, Trouville; menus €16.20 & €23.90) Parisians will feel right at home in the large dining room reminiscent of some of the capital's most celebrated brasseries. Portions are large; one main course is usually sufficient.

La Petite Auberge (☎ 02 31 88 11 07; 7 rue Carnot, Trouville; menus €24-40; ☽ closed Tue & Wed) It's Norman all the way, from the décor to the well-chosen menu. Prices are reasonable considering the quality of the cuisine.

SELF CATERING

Look for fine regional products at the market, place Morny, every morning in July and August, and on Tuesday, Friday and Saturday off season. **Champion supermarket** is on ave de la République and opens from Tuesday to Sunday. Try the **Glacerie Lambert** (76 bis rue Eugène Colas), which serves delicious home-made ice cream. There's also **Monoprix** (blvd Fernand Moureaux; ☽ closed Sun) and a **food market** (place du Maréchal Foch; ☽ Wed & Sat mornings).

Drinking

Zoo Bar (☎ 02 31 81 02 61; 53 rue Désiré-Le-Hoc, Deauville) This is not a jeans-and-trainers kind of place. Designer clothes wouldn't be out of place in the postmodern décor, even if the dim lighting makes it hard to show off.

La Maison (☎ 02 31 81 43 10; 66 rue des Bains, Trouville) The primary purpose of this wine bar is to sample wines from all over France, but the accompanying snacks are also delightful. The ambience is casual and there are occasional exhibitions and events.

Entertainment

Casino de Deauville (☎ 02 31 14 31 14; ave Lucien Barrière; ☽ 11am-2am Mon-Thu, 11am-3am Fri, 10am-4am Sat, 10am-3am Sun) Dress is formal but men can borrow a jacket and tie from reception. There is an admission charge to some rooms but slot machines start at only €0.20.

Louisiane Follies (☎ 02 31 87 75 00; place du Maréchal Foch; ☽ 10am-2am Sun-Thu, 10am-3am Fri, 10am-4am Sat) On the beachfront, this is a more relaxed affair with an adjoining cinema and nightclub.

Getting There & Away

BUS

The bus is generally faster and cheaper than the train. **Bus Verts** (☎ 08 01 21 42 14) has very frequent services to Caen (€8.50, 1¼ hours), Honfleur (€3.40, 30 minutes) and Le Havre (via Honfleur; €9.35, one hour).

TRAIN

Most trains from Deauville-Trouville require changes at Lisieux (€5.10, 20 minutes, 10 daily). There are trains to Caen (€12.40, one to 1½ hours, 13 daily), Rouen (€19.90, 3¼ hours, four daily) and Dieppe (via Rouen; €28.90, three to 3½ hours, four daily).

Getting Around

For car rental try **Rent a Car** (☎ 02 31 88 08 40; 38 bis rue Désiré-Le-Hoc), or **Avis** through the Fournier agency in Trouville. Bike rentals are available at **Lucas Cycles et Rollers** (☎ 02 31 88 53 55; 92 ave de la République).

AROUND DEAUVILLE-TROUVILLE

About 22km to the southwest of Deauville-Trouville, **Cabourg** is a staid resort. Its main claim to fame is as the inspiration for Balbec, a town appearing in Proust's *Du Côté de Chez Swann* (The Way by Swann's). Sprawling along a wide beach promenade, the opulent **Grand Hôtel** (☎ 02 31 91 01 79; fax 02 31 24 03 20; promenade Marcel Proust; r €146-249; **P** ☒) is where Proust stayed during his Normandy sojourns – you can even stay in his room. Built at the height of Cabourg's early-20th-century popularity, its over-the-top décor has to be seen to be believed. The **tourist office** (☎ 02 31 91 20 00; www.cabourg.net; Jardins du Casino; ☼ 9.30am-7pm Jul & Aug, 9.30am-12.30pm & 2-6pm Mon-Sat, 10am-noon & 2-4pm Sun Sep-Jun) can direct you to cheaper accommodation and provides a useful brochure and town map.

The quiet family resort of **Houlgate**, 14km southwest of Deauville-Trouville, is also composed of Victorian-era mansions but, unlike Cabourg, there has been little disfiguring new construction. The town's 19th-century elegance has remained intact and prices are more reasonable than at other coastal resorts. The **tourist office** (☎ 02 31 24 34 79; www.ville-houlgate.fr - French only; blvd des Belges; ☼ 10am-12.30pm & 2-6.30pm daily Jun-Sep, closed Sun Oct-May) can provide information.

Cabourg shares a train station with Dives-sur-Mer. There are daily trains from Paris to Houlgate and Cabourg in summer, changing at Deauville-Trouville (€32, 2¼ hours), but the service drops to Saturday and Sunday only the rest of the year. There are five trains daily from Deauville-Trouville to Cabourg (30 minutes) and Houlgate (20 minutes) in summer, and on weekends only in winter. Bus Verts bus No 20 runs year-round from Houlgate and Cabourg to Caen (one hour), Deauville-Trouville (30 minutes) and Honfleur (45 minutes).

PAYS D'AUGE

Inland from the Côte Fleurie, the Pays d'Auge is a luscious green landscape of hills, pastures and apple trees. The Risle, Dives and Touques water the lowlands, sprouting streams and brooks that add to the visual allure. Apart from Lisieux, the largest city, Pays d'Auge is composed of the kinds of small towns and villages that make French people sentimental about rural life. The landscape is dotted with half-timbered family farms that usually contain a dairy, an apple barn and a cider press. Parisians have been steadily acquiring the farms as secondary residences, preserving their traditional architecture. Cheese rules the region, with three of the finest French cheeses (Camembert, Pont L'Évêque and Livarot) produced here, as well as the lesser-known Pavé d'Auge. Apple products from the Pays d'Auge are also highly prized; Normandy's best cider and Calvados are made here. Thoroughbred horses from more than 200 stables in the region fetch high prices at Deauville's international horse markets.

LISIEUX

pop 24,200

Forty-seven kilometres east of Caen, Lisieux is the largest city in the Pays d'Auge. After 13 bombardments between 6 June and 31 July 1944, very little remains of its medieval centre. Postwar reconstruction was graceless in Lisieux, replacing the sinuous streets with straight wide roads and squat buildings. Yet there is a stunning Gothic cathedral and the city makes a good base to explore the surrounding countryside. Lisieux is of particular interest to devotees of Ste Thérèse, as she grew up here at the end of the 19th century.

CALVADOS

The city was inhabited by an ancient Gallic tribe that succumbed to the Romans in the 1st century BC. Traces of the Roman occupation are visible in excavations on the place de la République. Lisieux became the seat of a bishopric in the 6th century and controlled most of the Pays d'Auge by the 12th century. Henry II and Eleanor of Aquitaine were married in Lisieux in 1152 (or so it's thought), and the town remained important until the triple troubles of the 14th century – war, famine and plague – reduced its influence. The town's association with Ste Thérèse, which has been assiduously promoted, has made it one of the more important pilgrimage destinations in Europe, attracting about 1½ million pilgrims each year.

Orientation & Information

The town centre is dominated by the imposing Cathédrale St-Pierre. The train station is about 1km south of the town centre. The **tourist office** (☎ 02 31 48 18 10; www.ville-lisieux.fr - French only; 11 rue Alençon; ☺ 8.30am-6.30pm Mon-Sat, 10am-12.30pm & 2-5pm Sun mid-Jun–Sep, 8.30am-noon & 1.30-6pm Mon-Sat Oct–mid-Jun) is 400m north of the train station (follow rue de la Gare). There's a **temporary tourist office** across from Cathédrale St-Pierre, open in July and August only. The **post office** (rue Condorcet) is across from the cathedral. For information on fly-fishing in La Touques river (see the boxed text opposite), contact **Parages** (☎ 02 31 31 37 42; www.touques -parages.com - French only; 14 rue de Verdun).

Sights & Activities

The town's main attraction is **Cathédrale St-Pierre** (rue Condorcet; 9am-noon & 2-7pm Jun-Sep, 9.30am-noon & 2-6pm Oct-May), begun in 1170 and largely completed by the mid-13th century. The interior is marked by an elegant sobriety, characteristic of early Gothic architecture. A statue of Ste Thérèse stands in the choir where she came to pray, and the main altar was a gift from her father. The chapel was built to the order of Pierre Cauchon, who became bishop of Lisieux after presiding over the trial and sentence of Joan of Arc. His tomb is to the left of the altar. The stained-glass windows date from the 13th century and the side chapels contain fine examples of painting and sculpture from the 14th to 18th centuries. Behind the church, the **Jardin de l'Evêché** was designed by Le Nôtre, who also designed the gardens of Versailles.

Basilique Ste-Thérèse (☺ 8.30am-8pm Jun-Sep, 9am-6pm Oct-May), which is just behind the train station, is hard to miss. Grand and grandiose, it combines Romanesque and Byzantine styles in one of the largest churches built this century. Construction of this stone-and-concrete behemoth was begun in 1924 and it was consecrated in 1954. The interior, which can accommodate 4000 people, is covered with mosaics; take a look, especially, at the multicoloured mosaics that cover the crypt. It's possible to climb to the top of the 100m dome.

Sleeping & Eating

Camping Municipal de la Vallée (☎ 02 31 62 00 40; fax 02 31 48 18 11; route de la Vallée; adult/site €2.05/2.50; ☺ closed mid-Sep–mid-Apr) This site is 2km east of the town; take bus No 1.

Les Capucines (☎ 02 31 62 28 34; 6 place Fournet; r €20-32.50) About 200m north of the train station on the way into town, this simple place has adequate but hardly luxurious rooms with showers in the hall.

Hôtel de Lourdes (☎ 02 31 31 19 48; fax 02 31 31 08 67; 4 rue au Char; r with bathroom €44, without bathroom €30-40; P) Closer to the centre of town, this place has simple, bright rooms. The rooms without full bathroom facilities have a shower and sink.

Azur Hôtel (☎ 02 31 62 09 14; www.azur-hotel.com; 15 rue au Char; r from €65; P ⌨) This colourful and fully renovated three-star establishment near the cathedral is the town's best hotel. A small breakfast buffet costs an extra €8.40.

Le France (☎ 02 31 62 03 37; 4 rue au Char; menus €14.50-25; ☺ closed Mon & dinner Sun) For a special meal try the meals at this place, a favourite haunt of actors from the nearby theatre. It was founded by two burnt-out Parisians, and many of the dishes use such local products as cider, *pommeau* and Livarot cheese.

Rue Henry Chéron along the side of the cathedral is awash in cheap eateries.

Self-caterers can stock up on supplies at the **Champion supermarket** in the Nouvelle Galleries shopping centre, located on place de la République.

The Saturday morning **market** on place de la République is replete with local food products, and there's a Wednesday **market** from 4pm in July and August that offers more elaborate gastronomic adventures accompanied by music.

THE TROUT OF LA TOUQUES

More than their first Calvados, even more than Maman's *tarte tatin*, any man born in the Pays-d'Auge will remember the first *truite de mer* (sea trout) they reeled in from La Touques river. The elusive and hard-fighting sea trout has acquired an almost mystical aura in the region; catching one is a rite of passage for local boys. The season begins in May just after the fish swim up the river from Deauville, but locals know that the good fishing probably won't start until July, when the water level has risen. The timing is perfect for summer vacation. As the sunlight fades, the banks of La Touques fill up with fly-fishing anglers. After passing their days in the cool, relatively deep reaches of the river, the trout head to the shallows to spend the nights, occasionally darting out of the water with a soft splash.

Catering to anglers is a thriving business in the region. The fame of the river has now spread far beyond Normandy, but old-timers remember (maybe with rose-coloured glasses) the nights of their boyhood when the river was still peaceful. All have a preferred spot, but the confluence of the Calonne and La Touques rivers seems to be a particularly desirable spot for the 2kg fish and the anglers who pursue them.

Until the season ends in October, everyone has trout mania. The pinkish flesh has a distinctive and delectable flavour that makes all other fish taste insipid. The trout eat little during their sojourn in the river, but fatten up all winter on tasty little sea shrimp that impart their aroma. If you want to sample this delicacy, though, you'll have to catch a trout yourself or become very good friends with a very skilled angler. The sale of sea trout in restaurants or markets is strictly forbidden.

After a summer spent cleverly dodging hooks, the trout set about the business of reproducing, leaving behind legions of frustrated anglers and a few happy diners. While the new trout families enjoy the frigid open water of the North Atlantic, local fly-fishing aficionados plan their attack for the following summer. Maybe it's time to thread a new set of flies?

Getting There & Away

There are no buses from Caen but trains run at least hourly from there to Lisieux (€7.30, 30 minutes), and there are five direct trains from Rouen daily (€14.80, 1½ hours). There are also up to 10 trains daily from Deauville-Trouville (€5.10, 20 minutes).

One bus connects Lisieux and Le Havre daily (1½ hours); there's one bus Monday to Friday from Deauville-Trouville (one or two hours, depending on the route) and up to seven from Honfleur (one hour).

PONT L'ÉVÊQUE
pop 4200

Located about 18km north of Lisieux, Pont l'Évêque is an unpretentious little town that has been known for its cheese since the 13th century. Pont l'Évêque is a strongly flavoured soft cheese with a rind that, as an *appellation contrôlée* (official standard, see p55), must be produced in the region. Although 65% of the town was destroyed in the 1944 bombings, a careful reconstruction has preserved much of its layout. The rivers meandering through the town centre give a sense of connection to the surrounding countryside and the banks contain pleasant footpaths.

Orientation & Information

The church, tourist office, bank and post office are grouped together along rue St-Michel in the town centre, about 200m north of the train station. The **tourist office** (☎ 02 31 64 12 77; www.pontleveque.com; 16 bis rue St-Michel; ☺ 10am-1pm & 2.30-6.30pm daily Jul & Aug, 10am-12.30pm & 2.30-5.30pm Mon-Sat Sep-Jun) makes hotel reservations.

Sights & Activities

Église St-Michel, in the centre of the town, was built between 1483 and 1519, although the stained-glass windows date from 1963. **Place du Tribunal** has a number of 16th-century residences and the nearby **Couvent des Dames Dominicaines** is marked by a Renaissance building with a lovely balustrade and stone stairway. The most intact part of the town is along **rue de Vaucelles**, an extension of rue St-Michel. Notice the old houses leaning into the River l'Yvie just after ave de la Libération.

The tourist office has information about chateaux to visit in the region, notably **Château du Breuil** (☎ 02 31 65 60 00; ☺ 9am-noon & 2-6pm). It can also direct you to cheese-making farms that offer visits and tastings. The lake southwest of the train station has a **leisure** centre (☎ 02 31 65 29 21) with sailing, jet-skiing, canoeing and horse riding.

Two **Calvados distilleries** outside town offer visits. The closest is **Père Magloire** (☎ 02 31 64 30 31; admission €2.30 incl tastings; ✹ 10am-12.30pm & 2-6.30pm Apr-Nov), about 1km northeast of the town centre on the road to Deauville. Tours are given hourly in July and August and twice daily the rest of the year.

Cheese-lovers won't want to miss the **Fête du Fromage** (cheese festival) held on place Foch in the second weekend in May, where there are prizes for the best cheese and displays of regional products. If you miss the cheese festival try for the **Marché Campagnard à l'Ancienne**, regularly held on Sunday from 10am to 1pm on place des Dominicaines, where you can enjoy folk dances, craft demonstrations and local costumes while downing your fill of cider and cheese.

Sleeping & Eating

La Cour de France (☎ 02 31 65 29 21; fax 02 31 65 03 46; adult/site €2.75/7; ✹ Mar-Oct) This is an excellent camping area, near the leisure centre on the lake.

La Stade (☎ 02 31 64 15 03; rue de Beaumont; adult/site €4/3.50) This is another good camping ground, 1km northwest of the town centre on the route to Beaumont.

Hôtel de France (☎ 02 31 64 30 44; fax 02 31 64 98 90; 1 rue de Geôle; r €27-42) In the town centre, this place is kept in beautiful shape and has rooms decorated in the style of a country house. From some of them you can even see cows grazing.

Restaurant Le Rollon (☎ 02 31 64 28 13; 44 rue Hamelin; menus €12 & €19.60; ✹ closed Sun & dinner Wed) Hands down, this place offers the best value in town. It's firmly anchored in the Normandy basics – you'll find plenty of duck, Calvados and excellent cheese.

Auberge de l'Aigle d'Or (☎ 02 31 65 05 25; 68 rue de Vaucelles; menus €25-46; ✹ open daily Jul & Aug, closed dinner Tue, Wed & Sun Sep-Jun) It's expensive but definitely worth it if only for the atmosphere. The building dates from 1520 and is an architectural marvel. The classic Normandy cuisine won't disappoint either. Free-range chicken from the region is its best feature but you'll find plenty of other delights.

Getting There & Away

Pont l'Évêque is on the train line that runs from the coast to Lisieux. There are up to 15 trains a day between Deauville-Trouville and Pont l'Évêque (€2.40, 10 minutes) and an equal number to Lisieux (€3.10, 12 minutes). Less practical are the late-afternoon buses from Deauville (€5.80, one hour) or the early-morning bus from Lisieux (€3.20, 35 minutes). There are also three daily buses from Caen (€9.35, one hour).

ST-PIERRE-SUR-DIVES

pop 4000

St-Pierre-sur-Dives, midway between Falaise and Lisieux, is a marketplace for regional produce and is also Normandy's box-maker. The town doesn't produce cheese but manufactures the light wooden boxes that protect Norman cheeses. There's also a substantial tannery trade.

The town formed around a powerful 11th-century Benedictine abbey that endured until the French Revolution. The abbey is the official highlight of St-Pierre-sur-Dives but the Monday markets afford an indelible glimpse of small-town Norman life.

Orientation & Information

The **tourist office** (☎ 02 31 20 97 90; www.mairie -saint-pierre-sur-dives.fr; rue St-Benoit; ✹ 9.30am-12.30pm & 1.30-6pm Mon-Fri, 9.30am-12.30pm Sat mid-Apr–mid-Oct, 9.30am-12.30pm & 1.30-5.30pm Mon-Fri mid-Oct–mid-Apr) is in the town centre, west of rue de Lisieux (the main road running through town). The post office is on the other side of rue de Lisieux next to place du Marché.

Sights & Activities

Established in the 11th century, reconstructed in the 12th and 13th centuries and modified in the 16th and 17th centuries, the **abbey** (admission free; ✹ 9.30am-12.30pm & 2.30-6pm) is the most extensive monastic structure in Normandy. The church towers have the tapered elegance that characterises Norman Gothic architecture, and the bright, harmonious interior has carved Renaissance choir stalls and a gold-leaf altar that dates from the 17th century. The chapter room has been restored to its former glory and now displays works by the painter André Lemaître.

One of the convent buildings houses the **Musée des Techniques Fromagères** (adult/child €2.29/1.83; ✹ 9.30am-12.30pm & 1.30-6pm Mon-Fri, 10am-noon & 2-5pm Sat mid-Apr–mid-Oct; 9.30am-12.30pm & 1.30-5.30pm Mon-Fri mid-Oct–mid-Apr) and the tourist office. The museum is well conceived and covers every aspect of cheese-making from the production of milk to the latest techniques. The visit also includes a tasting. Guided tours take place every 30 minutes.

The market building in the town centre, **Les Halles**, is almost as impressive as the abbey. Although it was burned in 1944, the 13th-century building was faithfully reconstructed using the 290,000 original, handmade, wooden pegs. The regular markets in Les Halles are local events. The weekly market is on Monday morning and offers local produce and regional dishes, as well as being the supplier of pigs, calves, sheep and goats to local breeders. The first Sunday of the month is given over to the **Marché aux Antiquaires** (8am-6pm), where everything from crafted furniture to postcards is for sale. Not enough markets? Try the Monday **cattle auction** (from 10am) in the Zone Industrial Sud and pick up a Normandy heifer.

Sleeping & Eating
Camping Municipal (02 31 20 73 28; adult/site €2.30/1.85; May Sep) This well-kept site is 1km south of town on the D102 and is next to a sports complex.

Les Agriculteurs (02 31 20 72 78; les.agriculteurs @wanadoo.fr; 118 rue de Falaise; r from €28) This hotel-restaurant in the centre of town has a rustic flavour and serves inexpensive meals.

Getting There & Away
Getting to St-Pierre-sur-Dives on public transport is highly problematic since it is only connected by school bus with Falaise and Lisieux, which means that there's no bus service during school holidays. There's a midday bus on Wednesday, and two late-afternoon buses from Lisieux and Falaise (50 minutes) as well as early buses in either direction Monday to Friday, so it's possible to stop in St-Pierre-sur-Dives overnight on your way to either Lisieux or Falaise.

CHÂTEAU DE VENDEUVRE
The **château** (02 31 40 93 83; adult/child €7.80/6.20 gardens, chateau & museum, €6.30/4.80 chateau & gardens; 11am-6pm daily May-Sep, 2-6pm Sun Apr & Oct–mid-Nov), 6km south of St-Pierre-sur-Dives along the road to Falaise, is an 18th-century manor that testifies to the enviably luxurious life of pre-Revolutionary aristocrats. The manor presides over a vast estate with several manicured gardens enlivened by

a marvellous water park with a shellfish grotto. The interior re-creates the 18th-century lifestyle with period furniture and *objets d'art*.

The chateau's main feature is the unique **Musée des Meubles Miniatures**, which presents one hundred or so miniature pieces of furniture created bewteen the 16th and 19th centuries. Made with the same materials as standard furniture, these exquisite pieces served as models for larger items and were sometimes created simply as a hobby by furniture artisans. Among other wonders, notice the bed made for the cat of Louis XV's daughter.

You'll need your own transport in order to get here.

CENTRAL CALVADOS

Falaise lies on the River Ante in the southern part of Calvados *département*, 38km south of Caen. Due west of Falaise, spanning the Calvados and Orne *départements*, the Suisse Normande in the Orne Valley is a paradise for active travellers.

FALAISE
pop 8800
The rocky promontory in the western part of town overlooks the Ante Valley, giving it a strategic importance that was obvious to the earliest Norman dukes. The 12th-century fortified castle on the hill was the birthplace of William the Conqueror and is now the town's main attraction. Falaise later emerged as a prosperous trade and crafts centre in the early Middle Ages, known throughout France for its trade fairs. Although disrupted during the Hundred Years' War, the fairs returned in full force in the 16th century and were the basis of the Falaise economy until the 19th century.

Falaise was devastated during WWII. Canadian forces liberated the city on 16 August 1944 and then joined other Allied forces intending to encircle remnants of the German army south of the city in the 'Falaise Pocket'. The Allied failure to close off the German retreat has been one of the more controversial subjects of WWII military history. Eighty-five percent of Falaise was destroyed in the fighting but it has been tidily rebuilt.

Orientation & Information

The town centre of Falaise is compact. The **tourist office** (☎ 02 31 90 17 26; www.otsifalaise.com; Le Forum, blvd de la Libération; ☼ 9.30am-12.30pm & 1.30-6.30pm Mon-Sat, 10am-noon & 2.30-5.30pm Sun May-Sep, 9.30am-12.30pm & 1.30-5.30pm Mon-Sat Oct-Apr) is in the centre of town, as is the **post office** (rue St-Michel), which has Cyberposte. There's a **laundrette** (3 rue Trinité).

Sights & Activities

With its thick, square walls and circular tower, **Château Guillaume-le-Conquerant** (☎ 02 31 41 61 44; adult/child €5.50/3.50; ☼ 10am-7pm Jul & Aug, 10am-6pm mid-Feb–Jun & Sep-Dec) cuts a striking figure. Although the promontory upon which it rests was the site of a 9th-century chateau, it wasn't until the 11th century that Robert, duke of Normandy, built the chateau that served as the birthplace of his son, William, in 1027. Little remains of the 11th-century structure, which was probably the oldest chateau in Normandy. In 1123 Henry Beauclerc, the son of William the Conqueror, built a square keep and chapel and, later in the century, Henry II Plantagenet built a small keep on the western side. When Normandy fell to the forces of Philippe-Auguste in 1204, the new king built the round tower, known as the Talbot Tower. After suffering a siege by Henri IV in 1590 during the Wars of Religion, the castle fell into disuse and was left to moulder for several centuries.

In 1986 architect Bruno Decaris was hired to restore the castle and completed his work in 1997 to a storm of criticism. Rather than attempting to re-create the original forecourt, the architect decided to 'suggest' its military function by erecting unattractive walls of grey concrete. Angry petitions and lawsuits ensued but the walls remain. His other architectural ideas were better received. Replacing the stone floors with translucent glass allows visitors to gaze down at the remains of the 11th-century castle. The rooms have an austere beauty and plans are afoot to present a 'scenography' with multimedia effects tracing the castle's history within its walls. The top of the tower gives a splendid view of the surrounding landscape.

Across the River Ante behind the castle is **La Fontaine d'Arlette**, which commemorates the meeting between Robert and Arlette (William's father and mother). Legend has it that Robert, son of the duke of Normandy, spotted Arlette, daughter of a successful tanner, washing clothes by the river. Struck by her beauty, Robert invited her to spend the night in his chateau. Arlette agreed but, rather than slink in secretly, she entered through the front gate on horseback, dressed magnificently. Nine months later, little William entered the world. A bas-relief tells the story of their encounter next to an old wash house.

The **Musée Août 1944** (☎ 02 31 90 37 19; chemin des Roches; adult/child €5.35/2.30; ☼ 10am-noon & 2-6pm daily, closed Tue Apr-May & Sep-Nov) illustrates the battle of the Falaise Pocket with an impressive collection of tanks, jeeps, war memorabilia and figurines, explained by a series of multilingual panels.

Sleeping & Eating

Camping Municipal (☎ 02 31 90 16 55; mairie@ville -falaise.fr; route du Val d'Ante; adult/site €3/2.50; ☼ May-Sep) This is a lovely location at the foot of the chateau, near tennis courts and a pool.

Le Gars de Falaise (☎ 02 31 90 16 79; fax 02 31 90 72 09; 1-3 place Belle-Croix; r €24-32) Located over a popular pub, this is the cheapest hotel in town. Only the more expensive rooms have private facilities.

Hôtel de la Place (☎ 02 31 40 19 00; fax 02 31 90 08 90; 1 place St-Gervais; r €30) Rooms are simple but have private facilities, and the hotel is well located in the town centre. The attached restaurant is also good.

Hotel-Restaurant La Poste (☎ 02 31 90 13 14; hotel.delaposte@wanadoo.fr; 38 rue Georges Clemenceau; r €49-65; P) Comfortable and friendly, this hotel offers freshly redecorated rooms and a restaurant good enough to consider taking half-board.

La Fine Fourchette (☎ 02 31 90 08 59; 52 rue Georges Clemenceau; menus €13.50-28) The owner-chef has an impressive pedigree, honing his skills in some of the best Parisian restaurants. Even the cheapest *menu* offers some fine Normandy dishes and the cheese selection is excellent. The cuisine and décor are sophisticated without being pretentious.

The **Aux Delices du Midi** (21 rue St-Gervais) sells groceries.

Getting There & Away

Bus 35 links Caen and Falaise (€7.90, one hour) up to six times a day from Monday to Friday, and less often on Saturday; there's no service on Sunday.

LA SUISSE NORMANDE

Lying 25km south of Caen and 14km west of Falaise, the Suisse Normande is defined by jagged cliffs and forested slopes along the path of the River Orne and its tributaries. In summer kayakers and canoeists paddle up and down the rivers, hang-gliders drift overhead, cyclists pedal the back roads and walkers make their way through the meadows and forests. For further information on what you can do in the area, contact the tourist offices in Clécy or Thury-Harcourt or check out the region's website www.suisse -normande.com (French only).

Bus No 34 from Caen runs frequently to the main centres of Clécy (50 minutes, four daily) and Thury-Harcourt (40 minutes, nine daily), but your own transport is handy for appreciating the beauty of this unique region.

Thury-Harcourt

pop 1840

On the northernmost edge of the Suisse Normande, Thury-Harcourt is built along a hill rising from the Orne. Most shops and services are clustered around place St-Sauveur. A scattering of houses and a hotel lie on the other side of the river. The **tourist office** (☎ 02 31 79 70 45; otsi.thury@libertysurf.fr; 2 place St-Sauveur; ❥ 10am-12.30pm & 2.30-6.30pm daily Jul & Aug, Tue-Sun rest of year) is on the main square.

The **Kayak Club** (☎ 02 31 79 40 59; impasse des Lavandières) rents out canoes/kayaks/mountain bikes for €14/10/10.70 for two hours.

SLEEPING & EATING

Camping du Traspy (☎ 02 31 79 61 80; camping €11.70) This is beautifully situated along the river bank, next to an aquatic centre with a toboggan and waterfalls.

Hôtel Stop (☎ 02 31 39 23 50; 5 rue St-Sauveur; r €23) Rooms are basic with facilities in the hall.

Hôtel du Val d'Orne (☎ 02 31 79 70 81; fax 02 31 79 16 12; 9 route d'Aunay-sur-Odon; s/d €21/30; ❥ closed Sat afternoon) This rustic establishment with a façade half-buried under ivy has modest but pleasant rooms, a small terrace and a decent restaurant. The cheapest rooms have a sink only.

Le Relais de la Poste (☎ 02 31 79 72 12; fax 02 31 39 53 55; ave du 30 Juin; r from €53) Although this is the more expensive option, the rooms are exquisitely decorated and the restaurant is excellent.

Clécy

pop 1270

Self-proclaimed 'capital' of the Suisse Normande, Clécy is an engaging town of narrow streets, granite houses and white shutters. The town is on top of a hill which affords marvellous views of the Orne Valley. At the bottom of the hill, the leafy banks of the Orne are lined with *guinguettes* – cafés with riverside terraces. With its natural charms and array of outdoor activities, it's not surprising that Clécy is packed with tourists on sunny weekends and during summer holidays.

The **tourist office** (☎ /fax 02 31 69 79 95; otsi.clecy@ libertysurf.fr; place Tripot; ❥ 10am-12.30pm & 2.30-6.30pm Tue-Sun) is on a pretty square behind the town hall and has a list of *chambres d'hôtes*. It'll also point you in the right direction for walks, hikes and other activities.

ACTIVITIES

Canoeing and kayaking are major attractions in Clécy. Rental places are along the river around the Pont de Vey. Try **Le Beau Rivage** (☎ 02 31 69 79 73) or **La Potinière** (☎ 02 31 69 76 75). **A Le Relais du Grand Camp** (☎ 02 31 69 69 06) rents out mountain bikes as well as canoes and kayaks.

The **Centre de Pleine Nature Lionel Terray** (☎ 02 31 69 72 82), also along the banks of the Orne, will equip you with a canoe, kayak, mountain bike or archery equipment, or take you rock climbing. The activities are priced according to session and each session costs €9.60

Four kilometres northeast of Clécy at St-Omer, there's a **parachuting centre** (☎ 02 31 26 89 13) where hang-gliding costs €35.

Across the River Orne the 205m Pain de Sucre (Sugar Loaf) massif looms over the valley. Several paths lead up to the top.

SLEEPING

Camping Municipal (☎ /fax 02 31 69 70 36; adult/site €4/3.50) This is along the Orne in Vey, 1km from Clécy and just across the river.

Au Site Normand (☎ 02 31 69 71 05; fax 02 31 69 48 51; 1 rue des Châtelets; r €44-55; P) In the centre of Clécy, this place has a shady, plant-covered terrace and attractive rooms. The more expensive rooms have a terrace or balcony.

Hostellerie du Moulin du Vey (☎ 02 31 69 71 08; reservations@moulinduvey.com; Vey; r €69.50-97; P) This unusual hotel is in a converted flour mill on the river at Vey. The lush and flowery setting is enchanting, and the romantic rooms have every comfort.

Pont d'Ouilly

At the confluence of the Rivers Orne and Noireau, Pont d'Ouilly is an inconspicuous little village known for its water sports. The centre is an unremarkable postwar reconstruction but the serene river banks overhung with trees and rising to gentle slopes on either side create a lovely setting for a stroll or drive. The **tourist office** (☎ 02 31 69 29 86 or 02 31 69 39 54; blvd de la Noë; ☒ 10am-1pm & 2.30-6.30pm Wed-Sun Jul & Aug, 10am-1pm Wed-Sun May, Jun & Sep, closed Oct-Apr) is just over the river.

ACTIVITIES

Base de Plein Air (☎ 02 31 69 86 02), on the river, rents out canoes and kayaks and organises trips down the River Orne. It also organises competitions in kayak polo, a unique sport played only in Pont d'Ouilly.

You can hire mountain bikes from the **service station** (☎ 02 31 69 80 35) across from the tourist office. Fishing enthusiasts can try their luck at Les Sources de la Here pond, north of Pont d'Ouilly at St-Christophe.

SLEEPING

Camping Municipal (☎ 02 31 69 46 12; rue du Stade; adult/site €3.50/4) This is well located along the river.

There are two hotels in town.

Hôtel de la Place (☎ /fax 02 31 69 40 96; place des Halles; r €22-27) Near the post office and marketplace, on a hill overlooking the river, this place has simple but comfortable rooms.

Hôtel du Commerce (☎ 02 31 69 80 16; fax 02 31 69 78 08; rue de Falaise; r €33-40) Near the Hôtel de la Place, this friendly hotel has slightly more elaborate rooms.

La Roche d'Oëtre

About 7km south of Pont d'Ouilly, this is the most dramatic sight in the Suisse Normande. From this immense cliff rising almost 120m over the gorge of the River Rouvre, waves of forested slopes and steep valleys unfold in a breathtaking panorama. A number of paths lead down and across the cliff, but be careful after rainfall as the rocks can get slippery. Notice the profile of a human face that the wind has carved into the rock face supporting the upper plateau. The site is isolated but easily reachable and signposted from the D167 in Pont d'Ouilly.

Manche

CONTENTS

Cotentin Peninsula   **293**
Cherbourg   294
Barfleur   298
Valognes   298
Ste-Mère-Église   299
Parc Naturel Régional des
    Marais du Cotentin et
    du Bessin   300
The Hague Peninsula   300
Central Manche   **301**
St-Lô   301
Coutances   301
Granville   303
Villedieu-les-Poêles   306

The *département* of Manche, surrounded on three sides by the Channel (La Manche), includes the entire Cotentin Peninsula. Its 320km coastline stretches from Utah Beach northwest to the port city of Cherbourg and then south to the magnificent Mont St-Michel. Much of the coast is wild and undeveloped, perfect for solitary wind-blown walks above a pounding sea.

The fertile inland areas, crisscrossed with hedgerows, produce an abundance of cattle, dairy products and apples. The mild climate has encouraged the production of fruits and vegetables and the gentle landscape is perfect for horses – the *département* is a major breeding ground for some of France's finest.

Sadly, over the past 20 years, part of the Manche region has become known as 'Europe's nuclear dump'. On the peninsula's western tip at Cap de la Hague is France's first nuclear-waste treatment plant, which is well hidden until you reach its heavily fortified perimeter. Further south at Flamanville is a sprawling nuclear power plant, and at the Cherbourg shipyards the latest nuclear submarines are built.

Trains run to and from Cherbourg, but local buses are few and far between in the Manche region.

HIGHLIGHTS

- Set out from **Ste-Mère-Église** (p299) to follow La Voie de la Liberté (Liberty Way), which follows the route of the 1944 march by General Patton's Third Army across Normandy
- **Hike the coast** (p300) between the Nez de Jobourg and the Baie d'Ecalgrain
- Experience the splendour of Coutances' **cathedral** (p302)
- Party at the **Granville Carnival** (p305)
- Shop for copper pots in **Villedieu-les-Poêles** (p306)

Baie d'Ecalgrain ★
Nez de Jobourg ★
Ste-Mère-Église ★
★ Coutances
Granville ★   Villedieu-les-Poêles ★
★ Avranches
Mont St-Michel ★

■ POPULATION: 481,500	■ AREA: 5938 SQ KM

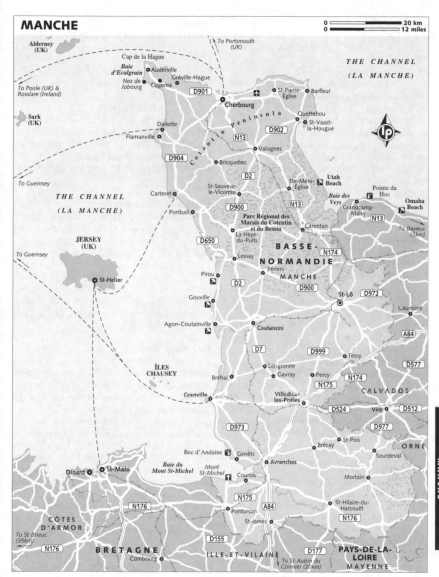

COTENTIN PENINSULA

The Cotentin Peninsula's northwestern corner is especially captivating, with unspoiled stretches of rocky coastline which shelters some delightful tranquil bays and quaint villages. Due west of the peninsula lie the Channel Islands of Jersey (25km from the coast) and Guernsey (45km), which are both accessible by ferry from St-Malo in Brittany and, in the high tourist season, from the Norman towns of Carteret, Granville and Dielette. The peninsula's rugged tip is Cap de la Hague, marking the western- and northernmost point of Normandy.

CHERBOURG

pop 26,750

At the tip of the Cotentin Peninsula sits Cherbourg, one of the largest artificial ports in the world. Transatlantic cargo ships, passenger ferries from Britain, yachts, warships and nearly everything else that floats on water pass in and out of Cherbourg's monumental port. It was Napoleon's idea to build a port here in preparation for the invasion of England he never got around to launching. Napoleon III completed the project around the same time that the Paris to Cherbourg train line opened in 1831. The port welcomed transatlantic passenger ships at the turn of the century and took on an enormous strategic importance during the D-Day landings. As the region's only deepwater port, Cherbourg was indispensable in resupplying the invasion forces.

Cherbourg has a small old town huddled behind the sprawl of maritime installations, but the city is not nearly as romantic as that portrayed in Jacques Demy's 1964 classic film *Les Parapluies de Cherbourg* (The Umbrellas of Cherbourg). There is an umbrella factory, although the city is no rainier than any other in Normandy. Residents even recall that the downpours and drizzles in the film were artificially produced. There are enough shops and cafés, an excellent aquarium and a couple of museums to keep you occupied but the main reason to come to Cherbourg is the excellent sailing opportunities.

Orientation

The Bassin du Commerce, a wide central waterway, separates the 'living' half of Cherbourg to the west from the deserted streets to the east. The attractive Avant Port (outer harbour) lies to the north.

Information

INTERNET ACCESS

Forum Espace Culture (☎ 02 33 78 19 30; place Centrale; per 10/30min €1.50/2.35; ✆ 2-7pm Mon, 10am-7pm Tue-Sat) The Internet café is on the upper floor of this cultural centre.

INTERNET RESOURCES

www.ville-cherbourg.fr The city's website.

LAUNDRY

Laundrette (62 rue au Blé)

MONEY

Crédit Lyonnais (16 rue Maréchal Foch)

POST

Main Post Office (1 rue de l'Ancien Quai) It has a Cyberposte and exchanges currency.

TOURIST INFORMATION

Tourist Office (☎ 02 33 93 52 02; www.ot-cherbourg -cotentin.fr - French only; 2 quai Alexandre III; ✆ 9am-6.30pm Mon-Sat, 10am-12.30pm Sun Jul & Aug, 9am-12.30pm & 2-6.30pm Mon-Sat Sep-Jun)
Annexe (☎ 02 33 44 39 92; at the ferry terminal) Open for ferry arrivals.

Musée Thomas Henry

This **museum** (☎ 02 33 23 02 23; 4 rue Vastel; adult/child €2.3/1.10; ✆ 10am-noon & 2-6pm Tue-Sat, 2-6pm Sun & Mon May-Sep, 2-6pm Wed-Sun Oct-Apr), upstairs in a cultural centre, has 200 works by French, Flemish, Italian and other artists. Highlights include *Atalante et Maleagre* by Van Dyck, *Conversion de St-Augustin* by Fra Angelico and 30 paintings by Jean-François Millet, born in nearby Gréville-Hague, which alone make it worth the visit.

Cité de la Mer

This new **museum** (☎ 08 25 33 50 50; www.cite delamer.com adult/child €13/9.50, children under 6 not admitted; ✆ 9.30am-7pm Jun–mid-Sep, 10am-6pm mid-Sep–May) is a celebration of the sea and the submarines that penetrated its secrets. You can visit an actual submarine and marvel at the sea life contained within the largest aquarium in Europe. The visit begins at the top of a 350,000-litre 12m-high aquarium where 3000 flashy fish from Tahiti circulate near the top, and continues down and around to other smaller tanks containing various forms of sea life. The submarine on display is the first French nuclear submarine, now decommissioned and disarmed. Visiting the room of ballistic missiles is liable to send a chill down your spine. Photos and documents on submarine exploration are available in the Médiathèque. Count on about 3½ hours for the visit.

Musée de la Libération

Devoted to the role played by Cherbourg's port in the Battle of Normandy, this interesting **Musée de la Libération** (☎ 02 33 20 14 12; adult/child €3/1.50; ✆ 9.30am-7.30pm Jul & Aug, 9.30am-7pm Jun & Sep, 10am-6pm mid-Mar–May & Oct–mid-Nov)

CHERBOURG

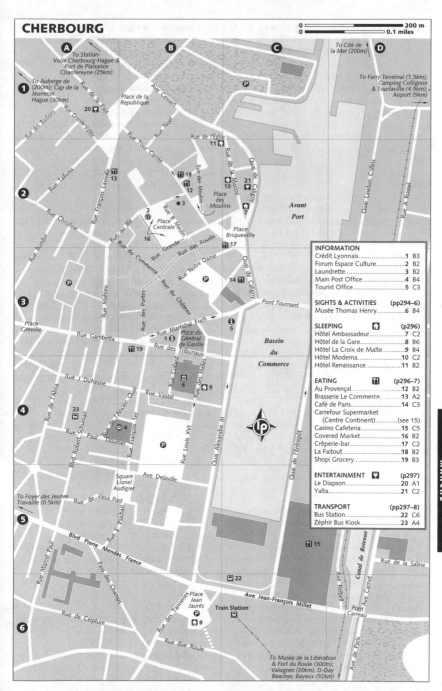

To Station-
Voile Cherbourg-Hague &
Port de Plaisance
Chantereyne (25km)

To Auberge de
(200m); Cap de la
Jeunesse
Hague (30km)

To Cité de
la Mer (200m)

To Ferry Terminal (1.5km);
Camping Collignon
& Tourlaville (4.5km);
Airport (9km)

Place de la
Republique

Avant
Port

Place
des
Moulins

Place
Briqueville

Place
Centrale

Place
Greville

Pont Tournant

Bassin
du
Commerce

Place du
Général
de Gaulle

Square
Lionel
Audigier

To Foyer des Jeunes
Travaille (0.5km)

Bassin
du
Commerce

Quai de l'Entrepot

Canal de Retenue

Rue de la Saline

Train Station

Place
Jean
Jaurès

To Musée de la Libération
& Fort du Roule (300m);
Valognes (20km); D-Day
Beaches; Bayeux (92km)

Pont
Carreau

MANCHE

INFORMATION
Crédit Lyonnais	1 B3
Forum Espace Culture	2 B2
Laundrette	3 B2
Main Post Office	4 B4
Tourist Office	5 C3

SIGHTS & ACTIVITIES (pp294–6)
Musée Thomas Henry	6 B4

SLEEPING (p296)
Hôtel Ambassadeur	7 C2
Hôtel de la Gare	8 B6
Hôtel La Croix de Malte	9 B4
Hôtel Moderna	10 C2
Hôtel Renaissance	11 B2

EATING (p296–7)
Au Provençal	12 B2
Brasserie Le Commerce	13 A2
Café de Paris	14 C3
Carrefour Supermarket (Centre Continent)	(see 15)
Casino Cafeteria	15 C5
Covered Market	16 B2
Crêperie-bar	17 C2
La Faitout	18 B2
Shopi Grocery	19 B3

ENTERTAINMENT (p297)
Le Diapson	20 A1
Yalta	21 C2

TRANSPORT (pp297–8)
Bus Station	22 C6
Zéphir Bus Kiosk	23 A4

0 — 200 m
0 — 0.1 miles

is housed in the strategically located Fort du Roule. Built under Napoleon III, the fort was intended to defend against an English attack. After falling into disuse, it was again occupied by French soldiers in the 1930s. On 19 June 1940 it finally fell to Field Marshal Rommel. The German troops stationed there put up a fierce resistance to Allied liberators In 1944, but the fort fell on 26 June. Photos, posters, and audiovisual aids document the period of the occupation and the fall of Cherbourg.

Walking
The tourist office organises walks of 12km or more in the surrounding countryside some Saturdays from April to October, and every Saturday in July and August.

Sailing
Cherbourg is a major sailing centre and an excellent place to learn the basics or polish your skills. **Station-Voile Cherbourg-Hague** (☎ 02 33 78 19 29; www.cherbourg-hague-nautisme.com - French only), at the entrance to the Port de Plaisance Chantereyne, offers introduction-to-sailing courses for €92 for a morning or afternoon session, and a range of other watery activities such as kayaking, rowing and paragliding.

Sleeping
BUDGET
Camping Collignon (☎ 02 33 20 16 88; camping €17.50; ☺ May-Sep) This is the nearest camping ground. It is on the coast in Tourlaville, about 5km northeast of Cherbourg. Bus No 5 makes two runs a day Monday to Saturday

LA CLAMEUR DE HARO

Norman tradition allows someone who has been wronged to invoke their rights by raising *la clameur*. In front of two witnesses, the injured party sinks to their knees, recites the Lord's Prayer in French and cries 'Haro! Haro! À l'aide mon Prince, on me fait tort!' (Haro! Help me my Prince, someone is wronging me). The accused must then stop the offending acts and wait for the legal system to run its course. 'Haro' is thought to derive from the cry of 'Ha' and 'Roi' or 'Rollo', the first duke of Normandy. Although the custom has fallen out of use in Normandy, it survives in parts of the Channel Islands.

from the train station and there are frequent shuttles *(navettes)* in summer. There's a large indoor swimming pool nearby.

Auberge de Jeunesse (☎ 02 33 78 15 15; cherbourg@fuaj.org; 55 rue de l'Abbaye; dm €12.70) This comfortable, ultramodern hostel opened in 1998 and is still going strong. Take bus No 3 or 5 to the Hôtel de Ville stop.

Foyer des Jeunes Travailleurs (☎ 02 33 78 19 78; fax 02 33 78 19 79; 33 rue Maréchal Leclerc; dm incl breakfast €14) It is 1km from the centre of town and offers clean, efficient rooms with a shared bathroom. Rooms are doubles, triples, quads and quins. Take bus No 8 to the cemetery.

MID-RANGE
Quai de Caligny has plenty of mid-range options. There are cheaper places in the backstreets north of the tourist office.

Hôtel Moderna (☎ 02 33 43 05 30; www.moderna-hotel.com; 28 rue de la Marine; r €26-48; P ✗) The comfortable, well-equipped rooms (ask for a port view) are decorated in soft pastels and are equipped with satellite TVs and telephones. The most expensive rooms have bathrooms with tubs.

Hôtel Renaissance (☎ 02 33 43 23 90; fax 02 33 43 96 10; 4 rue de l'Église; r €49-58) Recently renovated rooms with views of the port make this hotel a highly desirable option in the centre of town.

Hôtel La Croix de Malte (☎ 02 33 43 19 16; hotel.croix.malte@wanadoo.fr; 5 rue des Halles; r €30-39) Close to the sumptuous Théâtre de Cherbourg (built in 1882), this hotel has well-equipped doubles.

Hôtel de la Gare (☎ 02 33 43 06 81; fax 02 33 43 12 20; 10 place Jean Jaurès; r €38) Rooms are decent here, if unexceptional.

Hôtel Ambassadeur (☎ 02 33 43 10 00; www.ambassadeurhotel.com; 22 quai de Caligny; s/d from €29/37; P 💻) This classic is in the centre of the action, overlooking Avant Port, but the comfortable rooms have double glazed windows to ensure quiet. Larger and more-expensive rooms are available.

Eating
RESTAURANTS
Rue de la Paix and the area around place Centrale offer a wide choice of both cuisine styles and price.

Café de Paris (☎ 02 33 43 12 36; 40 quai de Caligny menus €17-21; ☺ closed Mon & dinner Sun Oct-May) It's not the place for a romantic tête-à-tête with the constant crowds and bustle, but the seafood is the freshest in town.

La Faitout (☎ 02 33 04 25 04; 25 rue Tour Carrée; menu €18; ☻ closed Sun & Mon) This atmospheric place has wonderful lunch dishes and a show-stopping crusty duck. It's best to book weekends.

Brasserie Le Commerce (☎ 02 33 53 18 20; 42 rue François Lavieille; menus from €12; ☻ closed Sun) There are no culinary surprises here but this bustling brasserie serves copious, tasty food nonstop from 11am to midnight.

Au Provençal (☎ 02 33 53 38 24; 29 rue Tour Carrée; dishes €6-11) This cute little spot serves pizzas topped with vegetables, cheese and seafood as well as pasta and salad.

If you can forgo the need for atmosphere, the **Casino Cafeteria** (1st fl, Centre Continent, quai de l'Entrepôt) has cheap two-course *menus* .

SELF-CATERING
There are markets on Tuesday and Thursday until about 5pm at place de Gaulle and place Centrale. The latter, which is covered, also operates on Saturday morning. Other options are the huge **Carrefour supermarket** (Centre Continent quai de l'Entrepôt) and the little **Shopi grocery store** (57 rue Gambetta).

Entertainment
Yalta (☎ 02 33 43 02 81; 46 quai de Caligny) This is the sizzling centre of Cherbourg nightlife, attracting sailors, students and sophisticates alike. There are usually two or three jazz, rock or blues concerts a month and occasionally French singers.

Le Diapson (☎ 02 33 01 21 43; 21 rue de la Paix) This place has a little bit of everything – a philosophy night, art exhibits, an occasional concert. There's a good selection of beer to wash down a varied musical programme.

Getting There & Away
AIR
Cherbourg's airport is 9km east of town at Maupertus-sur-Mer.

BUS
The main regional bus line (which stops at the station on ave Jean-François Millet) is **STN** (☎ 02 33 44 32 22), which has services to the camping ground in Tourlaville (€2.60). There are also buses to Valognes (€3.90, 30 minutes, six daily) and Barfleur (€4.10, 40 minutes, two daily).

TRAIN
Services from the **train station** (☎ 02 33 57 50 50; ☻ 6am-10pm) include one to Paris' Gare St-Lazare (€36.60, 3½ hours, seven daily) via Caen (€60, 1½ hours, eight daily). Most destinations involve a change at either Caen or Lisons.

There are connections to:

destination	cost	duration	frequency
Avranches	€15.40	2¼hr	4
Bayeux	€13.30	1hr	8
Bernay	€23.70	2-3½hr	11
Évreux	€28.20	2½-3½hr	11
Lisieux	€21	2-3hr	9
Pontorson	€22	2½hr	2
Rennes	€28.80	3½hr	2
St-Lô	€28.80	1½hr	10

BOAT
The three companies with services to either England or Ireland have bureaus in the ferry terminal *(gare maritime)*. Their desks are open two hours before departure and for 30 minutes after the arrival of each ferry.

Brittany Ferries (☎ 02 33 88 44 44) covers the route to Poole in England; **Irish Ferries** (☎ 02 33 23 44 44) sails to Rosslare, Ireland; and **P&O** (☎ 02 33 88 65 70) handles the link to Portsmouth. For further details and schedules see p339. Local buses run between the ferry terminal and the tourist office between three and 10 times daily, depending on the season. The fare is €1.

Getting Around
TO/FROM THE AIRPORT
There's no public transportation into town and a taxi will cost about €20.

BUS
City buses are run by **Zéphir** (☎ 08 10 81 00 50; 40 blvd Robert Schuman). Buses leave from either outside the kiosk or at various points around place Jean Jaurès, in front of the train station. Single tickets cost €1 and a carnet of 10 is €8. There's a shuttle-bus service linking the ferry terminal, the town centre and the train station.

TAXI
Taxis can be called on ☎ 02 33 53 36. The trip between the train station and ferry terminal costs about €8.

MANCHE

BICYCLE

Station-Voile (see p296) rents out mountain bikes for €10 per half-day.

BARFLEUR

pop 650

Little more than a cluster of granite houses on a finger of land, Barfleur is the smallest village in the Manche. The sea has been creeping up on the town for centuries turning the most important commercial harbour on the Cotentin Peninsula into a scenic but relatively minor fishing port. At one time Barfleur had a population of 9000 installed on much more than the sliver of land that now constitutes the town centre. Dikes have been erected on the northern shore, but the town still seems on the verge of disappearing under the waves, which lends it a fragile beauty. There's a small beach but Barfleur is mainly attractive for its laid-back, village-on-the-sea ambience.

In its heyday under the Norman dukes, Barfleur was involved in two pivotal events. It was a local, Étienne, who built and piloted the ship – the *Mora* – that carried William the Conqueror to England in 1066. A stele across from the tourist office commemorates the fact.

Less happily, it was from Barfleur that the infamous *Blanche Nef* was launched in 1120. William the Conqueror's son, Henry I of England, was returning home to England and entrusted a local seaman with the boat carrying his son and heir to the throne, William, William's wife and 300 courtiers. King Henry's vessel set out and began to outpace the *Blanche Nef*. Considerably intoxicated, the sailors of the *Blanche Nef* tried to out-manoeuvre the king's boat, but were swept away by currents and crashed onto the offshore rocks. All the nobles were drowned, ending the line of William the Conqueror and giving rise to the Plantagenet dynasty. The site is marked by a lighthouse, visible from the town centre.

Orientation & Information

The two main streets of Barfleur are quai Henri Chardon, which runs along the western side of the port, and the intersecting rue St-Thomas à Becket, where you'll find most hotels and restaurants. The main square is place Général de Gaulle near the post office, which will change money.

The **tourist office** (☎ 02 33 54 02 48; www.ville -barfleur.fr; quai Henri Chardon; ☼ 10am-12.30pm & 2.30-6.30pm Mon-Sat Apr-Oct, 10am-12.30pm & 2.30-5.30pm Tue-Sat Nov-Mar) is at the tip of the port near the church and the monument to William the Conqueror.

Sights & Activities

Barfleur is museum-free but there is a simple 17th-century church, **Église St-Nicolas**, clearly built to withstand maritime gusts.

Admiring the granite houses that line the straight, narrow streets, strolling along the coast and waiting for the fishing boats to return are typical Barfleur activities. For livelier pursuits, there's the **sailing school** at the camping ground.

The best time to be in Barfleur is on the second Sunday in August for the **Regattas**, which have been taking place for one hundred years.

Sleeping & Eating

Camping de la Blanche Nef (☎ 02 33 23 15 40; fax 02 33 23 95 15; camping €10.70) Next to the seaside promenade. This camping ground offers plenty of seaside activities.

Hôtel Le Conquérant (☎ 02 33 54 00 82; fax 02 33 54 65 25; 16 rue St-Thomas à Becket; r €56-80; P) In a handsome 17th-century house with a flourishing rear garden, this hotel promises a quiet, contemplative holiday in prettily furnished rooms.

Le Moderne (☎ 02 33 23 12 44; fax 02 33 23 91 58; 1 place Général de Gaulle; r €40-54) There are only three rooms in this rustic house but they do have an indelible charm. The **restaurant** (menus from €16.80; ☼ closed Wed & dinner Tue) is particularly good. Try the *choucroute de poisson* (fish with sauerkraut) for a real treat.

Getting There & Away

There are two buses from Cherbourg daily (€4.10, 40 minutes).

VALOGNES

pop 7800

The architectural unity of Valognes creates a startling effect. From the banks of the narrow river to mansions, townhouses and bridges, everything is constructed from the same beige-grey granite. At first glance the town centre seems to be all angles, corners and walls, but closer examination reveals elaborate decoration on the sober façades.

In the late 17th and early 18th centuries many noble families with chateaux in the countryside constructed opulent winter quarters in Valognes. With its new burst of money and prestige, Valognes became known as the 'little Versailles of Normandy'. Its moment of glory ended abruptly with the Revolution of 1789, but the town continued to prosper, turning out porcelain for a while, then butter and now material for the nearby nuclear industry. Proud of its heritage, Valognes was rebuilt with style after WWII, recovering a large part of its aristocratic allure.

Orientation & Information

The centre of town is place du Château and the main thoroughfare is blvd Division-Leclerc, which becomes blvd Félix Buhot in the northwest and blvd de Verdun in the southeast. The **tourist office** (☎ 02 33 40 11 55; www.mairie-valognes.fr; place du Château; ⏰ 10am-noon & 2-6.30pm Jul & Aug, 10am-noon & 3-6pm Mon-Sat Sep-Jun) distributes a helpful leaflet of walking tours of the city. The **post office** (place du Château) is across from the tourist office and it has Cyberposte terminal. You can change money at **Crédit Mutuel** (25 blvd Division-Leclerc).

Sights & Activities

The 18th-century **Hôtel de Beaumont** (☎ 02 33 40 12 30; cnr rue Barbey d'Aurevilly & rue Petit Versailles; adult/child €4.60/2.60; ⏰ 2.30-6.30pm daily Jul & Aug, 2.30-6.30pm Sat & Sun Jun, closed rest of year except Easter weekend) is an elegant mansion, south of the tourist office, featuring a fine columned façade and wrought iron balcony. It is still inhabited but in the part open to visitors you'll find a monumental stairway leading to rooms furnished in 17th-, 18th- and 19th-century styles. The visit is completed by a stroll of the manicured gardens.

Off blvd de Verdun the **Abbaye de Valognes** (☎ 02 33 21 62 82; 8 rue des Capucins; admission free) makes an interesting visit. The abbey was built for Bénédictine monks in the 17th century and was reconstructed after damage caused during WWII. It now houses a community of nuns. Seventeenth-century sculptures and windows in the church contrast with more recent acquisitions. Expect heavy sales pressure to buy the sweets that are made in the abbey.

A two-part museum (one admission price, same hours) is devoted to Normandy's most famous thirst-quenchers – cider and Calvados. **Le Musée Regional du Cidre** (☎ 02 33 40 22 73; rue du Petit Versailles; adult/child €4/2; ⏰ 10am-noon & 2-6pm Mon & Wed-Sat, 2-6pm Sun Apr-Sep) has three floors of cider tools and equipment, plus a video explaining the process in one building. Up the street, **Le Musée du Calvados et des Vieux Métiers** (☎ 02 33 40 26 25; rue Pelouze) is in a 17th-century mansion that functioned as a lace factory, barracks and firehouse before it became a museum displaying the barrels, pipes and casks used to make Calvados. The stone, iron and leather trades are also described.

Sleeping & Eating

Hôtel des Rivieres (☎ 02 33 40 07 82; www.hoteldes rivieres.fr.st - French only; 5 place Camille Blaisot; s/d from €22.50/24.50; P) Everything is clean and proper but the decorating theme is simple to say the least. More expensive rooms have showers, toilets or both.

Hôtel du Louvre (☎ 02 33 40 00 07; fax 02 33 40 13 73; 28 rue des Religieuses; r €34-54; P) As a former post office dating from the 19th-century, the building has a lot of character. Even with modern bathrooms and TVs, the rooms still have a classical appeal; they don't make them like this anymore.

Hôtel de l'Agriculture (☎ 02 33 95 02 02; www.hotel-agriculture.com; r €35-45; P) It's rustic but in the good sense of the word, with ivy climbing over the rough stone walls and large comfortable rooms. The **restaurant** (menus €12-30; ⏰ closed Mon & dinner Sun) is equally rustic with good home cooking.

Getting There & Away

For transportation options from Cherbourg see p297.

STE-MÈRE-ÉGLISE

pop 1610

In perhaps the most celebrated image of D-Day, an American parachutist John Steele drifted down from the skies on the night of 6 June 1944 and entangled himself on the church clock in Ste-Mère-Église. The episode was featured in the film *The Longest Day*, and Mr Steele became something of a local celebrity, returning every so often to re-enact the drama. Since his death, a mannequin has taken his place on the church roof. Ste-Mère-Église was the first village to be invaded on D-Day. (For more about the

D-Day landings and beaches, see p26 and p272). It is now point zero for La Voie de la Liberté (Liberty Way) the route marked out by white milestones that follows the 1944 march of General Patton's Third Army across Normandy.

The 12th-century **church** is probably the only one in existence that has a stained-glass window depicting the Virgin and Child surrounded by parachutists. Another recent window shows St Michel, the patron saint of parachutists.

The only other venue of interest in Ste-Mère-Église is **Musée des Troupes Aéroportées** (☎ 02 33 41 41 35; adult/child €5/2; ⏲ 9am-6.45pm Apr-Sep, 9.30am-noon & 2-6pm Feb, Mar, Oct & Nov), which tells the story of the landings through films, documents and photos. Jeeps, tanks and even a C47 transport plane help convey the intensity of the experience.

Getting There & Away

STN bus No 5 travels between Cherbourg and Ste-Mère-Église on Monday to Friday (about 50 minutes, five times daily).

PARC NATUREL RÉGIONAL DES MARAIS DU COTENTIN ET DU BESSIN

Straddling Manche and Calvados *départements*, the **Parc Naturel Régional des Marais du Cotentin et du Bessin** (www.parc-cotentin-bessin.fr) comprises 250 sq km of lowlands. Crisscrossed with rivers, canals and hedgerows, the park area teems with flora and fauna but the highlight is undoubtedly the Baie des Veys in the east. Seagulls, woodcocks, cormorants and grebes make the bay one of France's most important habitats for migratory birds.

THE HAGUE PENINSULA

The wild landscape on the northwestern tip of Normandy has often been compared to Ireland.

Pastures roll up to the edge of cliffs while below an ice-blue sea pounds the lonely coves. The sound of wind and waves is not broken by any whirring motors since the area has few residents and only a smattering of visitors. It feels like the end of the world – or at least the end of Europe – although it is clearly neither.

Perhaps it was the remoteness of the site that inspired the French government to turn a hunk of the peninsular territory over to the nuclear-power industry. The eerie constellation of white tanks, tubes, towers and offices at the sprawling **COGEMA plant** (☎ 02 33 02 61 04; ⏲ 10am-6pm daily Apr-Sep, Sat & Sun rest of year) at La Hague are devoted to the reprocessing and disposal of spent nuclear fuel. Because of the controversy surrounding the site, the COGEMA people are happy to offer free guided tours in which they will explain that the disposal of radioactive material is as sanitary as their lustrous facilities suggest. By the time they're done, you'll be ready to take a bath in the stuff. There are several visits per week for which you must reserve one week in advance. The minimum age for visits is 13.

For further enlightenment on the wonders of nuclear power you can tour the **Flamanville nuclear power plant** (☎ 02 33 04 12 99; admission free; ⏲ 8.30am-12.30pm & 1.30-5.30pm Mon-Fri). Each tour lasts about three hours, and you must present your passport or national ID card. There is one afternoon tour per day in July and August, for which you must book no later than the morning of the visit. Tours are scarcer the rest of the year and reservations must be made one month in advance. No wandering about nuclear power plants on your own!

At 126m, the cliff at **Nez de Jobourg** is the highest in continental Europe. The GR223 trail (Sentier des Douaniers) winds along the steep cliffs offering breathtaking sea views. You can follow it north to the **Baie d'Ecalgrain**, a majestic coastal curve that qualifies as the most romantic spot in Normandy. Windswept skies, tossing waves and low cliffs capped with meadows create an unforgettable sight.

From Ecalgrain, the trail takes you to **Auderville**, 22km northwest of Cherbourg and with the only places to stay in the area. The tiny village is an artful arrangement of stone houses built to withstand the gusty winds that rip over the peninsula.

Sleeping & Eating

Hôtel de la Hague (☎ /fax 02 33 52 71 00; r €35.50) This sturdy stone house in town has rooms with views of the sea.

Hôtel du Cap (☎ 02 33 52 73 46; fax 02 33 01 56 30; r €41-50; ℗) A little further down is this place complete with a garden, sea view and private baths in all rooms.

Auberge d'Auderville (☎ 02 33 52 77 44; menus €9.50-15; ⏲ closed Tue) Next to the church, you

---

DETOUR: AUDERVILLE TO LA ROCHE

From **Auderville**, follow on foot the D901, lined by low stone walls to **Goury** and its lighthouse. One of the world's most powerful and dangerous currents, the **Raz Blanchard**, runs just offshore. On a clear day, there are views of the Jersey Islands. Leave town by the southern coastal foot trail, enjoy the dramatic scenery until the rustic little hamlet of **La Roche**. Notice the covered well and *lavoir* (washhouse) outside the hamlet. Follow the D401 through the rugged countryside back to Auderville.

---

can enjoy home-smoked fish crepes and other local treats in a rustic, beamed dining room.

Getting There & Away

There's no public transport out here so you'll need your own wheels.

CENTRAL MANCHE

World War II veterans remember with a shudder the 'bocage' country that stretches from the bottom of the Cotentin Peninsula southeast to Vire (in Calvados) and the Suisse Normande. The zigzagging hedgerows that lend the region its distinctive character were used to devastating effect by the defending Germans, who were able to launch surprise attacks from their leafy hideouts. From low bushes to higher trees, the bocage was designed to delineate small or irregular parcels of land and has existed for centuries. Its green patchwork carpets the low hills and gentle valleys formed by the Rivers Soulles and Sienne. Small towns and hamlets dot this region, which is predominantly agricultural, producing milk by the tanker.

ST-LÔ

pop 21,600

Totally razed during the Allied bombing of 1944, St-Lô rose from the ashes to reclaim its place as the principal administrative and transportation hub of the Manche. Possibly qualifying as the most charmless city in Normandy, St-Lô nevertheless can be an interesting stop for lovers of art or horses.

The **Musée des Beaux-Arts** (☎ 02 33 72 52 55; Centre Culturel Jean-Lurç,at, place du champ-de-Mars; admission €1.50; ☉ 10am-noon & 2-6pm Wed-Mon) is a fine regional museum where Millet, Boudin, Rousseau, Corot and Moreau are well represented. **Le Haras National** (National Stud Farm; ☎ 02 33 55 29 09; rue du Maréchal-Juin; admission €4.50, guided

tours 2.30pm, 3.30pm & 4.30pm Jun-Sep plus 11.30am Jul & Aug) houses over 60 stallions and specialises in the Norman Cob horse and the French Saddle horse. The **Jeudis du Haras** presents horses and carriages in a colourful parade every Thursday at 3pm from late July to early September.

The St-Lô **tourist office** (☎ 02 33 77 60 35; place du Général de Gaulle; www.saint-lo.fr; ☉ 9am-6pm Mon-Sat Jul & Aug, 10am-noon & 2-6pm Tue-Fri, 2-6pm Mon, 10am-noon & 2-5pm Sat Sep-Jun) can advise you on various accommodation options and events around town.

St-Lo is connected by train to nearly every significant town in Normandy as well as to Paris (€32.40, three hours, five daily). The closest town is Coutances (€5.10, 20 minutes, hourly), about 26km to the west.

COUTANCES

pop 9700

The medieval hilltop town of Coutances, 77km south of Cherbourg, is the administrative and commercial centre of bocage country but its remarkable old cathedral recalls the days when it was an influential episcopal centre. The contours of the cathedral are visible from afar and its lofty towers and steeples dwarf the modest structures surrounding them. Religious life in Coutances reached its apogee in the 16th century, attracting wealthy and powerful people to set up residences in the town. For a while, it was the capital of the Manche *département* but since it lost that role in 1796, Coutances has resigned itself to serving as a market for local agricultural products. In addition to the cathedral, Coutances boasts splendid botanical gardens.

Orientation & Information

The town centre is compact and confined by blvd Alsace-Lorraine in the northwest and blvd Jeanne Paynel to the east. At the centre of town is the cathedral and town hall.

MANCHE

The **tourist office** (☎ 02 33 19 08 10; tourisme-coutances@wanadoo.fr; place Georges Leclerc; ☺ 10am-12.30pm & 2-5.30pm Mon, 10am-12.30pm & 2-6pm Tue, Wed & Fri, 10am-6pm Thu, 10am-12.30pm & 2-5pm Sat).

The train and bus stations are about 1km southeast of the town centre.

There's a **Société Générale** (8 rue Daniel) opposite the tourist office. The **post office** (10 rue St-Dominique) exchanges money and it has a Cyberposte terminal.

Cathédrale de Coutances

The soaring, 13th-century Gothic **cathedral** (admission free; ☺ 9am-7pm) is one of France's finest, prompting Victor Hugo to call it the prettiest he'd seen after the one at Chartres. Constructed in creamy limestone, the cathedral combines Gothic and Romanesque styles to stunning effect. Initially erected in the 11th century, the cathedral was transformed by the wave of Gothic architecture that accompanied Philippe-Auguste's takeover of Normandy in the 1200s. A new layer of stone created soaring Gothic towers over the original Romanesque structures.

A rare octagonal lantern tower is the focal point of the light, bright interior and a series of parallel arches makes the cathedral look higher than it is. The dizzying sense of verticality was meant to create the impression that the church was rising to the floors of heaven. Look for the 13th-century stained-glass window in the north transept, which shows scenes from the lives of Thomas à Becket, St George and St Blaise. In the Chapel of St-Lô is one of the cathedral's oldest windows, dating from the early 13th century. In the south transept, notice the 14th-century window showing a frightening *Last Judgment*. There are **tours** (adult/concession €5/3; 3.30pm Mon-Fri summer) in English available, which also afford sweeping views from the galleries in the lantern tower.

Jardin des Plantes

Opposite place Georges Leclerc is this grand 19th-century landscape garden. Conceived by a civil engineer and painter, the garden tastefully blends symmetrical French lines with Italianesque terraces, English-style copses, a maze and fountains. Its varied stock of ornamental trees includes giant redwood, cedar of Lebanon, New Zealand beech and Canadian nut. Look out for the hedges trimmed into the shape of human figures and flower beds arranged to suggest a boat. Kids will like the labyrinth in the southwestern corner. Like the cathedral, the gardens are illuminated on summer nights.

Other Sights & Activities

The **beaches** of Agon-Coutainville, Gouville and Pirou lie a short distance from the town. The beach at Agon-Coutainville is the oldest and also the most popular; Pirou has the longest beach and a remarkable **chateau** surrounded by an artificial lake.

Festivals & Events

The jazz festival during Ascension week in May, **Jazz Sous les Pommiers** (☎ 02 33 76 78 65; www.jazzsouslespommiers.com) is the most important annual music event in Normandy. In cafés, churches and on the streets, local and international musicians strut their stuff to an appreciative public.

Sleeping & Eating

Camping Municipal Les Vignettes (☎ 02 33 45 43 13 route de Coutainville; adult/site €2.60/2.60; ☒) About 1.2km northwest of town on the D44, this place has about 100 places.

The **Hôtel des Trois Piliers** (☎ 02 33 45 01 31; 11 rue des Halles; r with sink/shower €21/23) Rooms are smallish but well equipped. The **bar** downstairs draws a young, noisy crowd and the hotel is often booked out by students during vacation periods.

Hôtel de Normandie (☎ 02 33 45 01 40; fax 02 33 46 74 54; 2 place Général de Gaulle; r €30.50-45) It may be old-fashioned but this place is well run and has comparatively spacious rooms for the price, some with a cathedral view. The restaurant does great fish meals.

Hôtel le Parvis (☎ 02 33 45 13 55; fax 02 33 45 68 00; place de la Cathédrale; r €42-67) The most comfortable digs in town are here even though they are nothing particularly special.

Le Râtelier (☎ 02 33 45 56 52; 3 bis rue Georges Clémenceau; menus €7.50-15.20; ☺ closed Sun & Mon Oct-May) If you can't find a crepe here to suit your taste, you probably won't find one anywhere as there are some 50 varieties of these sweet or salty treats.

Restaurant le Vieux Coutances (☎ 02 33 47 94 78; 55 rue Geoffroy de Montbray; menus €10.70-32; ☺ closed Mon) This former post office is a small and intimate Norman eatery offering excellent fish or meat *menus*. It is, by a long way, the best address in town.

HAVE STILL, WILL TRAVEL

It was a sad day in Lower Normandy when the government decided to phase out home-brewed spirits. Until 1960 most households had the inherited right to distil about 20L of alcohol per year for their personal consumption without paying taxes. In the Manche, Calvados and the Orne, that liquor was likely to be Calvados and it was strong – up to 70 proof. Rather than abruptly terminating production of the firewater (and possibly risking mass DTs), it was decided that the 'privilege' could only be passed on to a surviving spouse. No longer could it be passed down from generation to generation.

The immediate effect of the law was an explosion in the black-market trade of soon-to-be-scarce, home-made Calvados. For a few years, it was Chicago-on-the-Orne as the *gendarmeries*, often tipped off by spiteful neighbours, battled a new network of gangsters. Local newspapers had a field day recounting tales of clandestine meetings, car chases and midnight busts.

The criminality gradually simmered down, but one centuries-old profession went into long-term decline. Very few families could afford their own still, so most used the services of a *distillateur ambulant* (travelling moonshine-maker). From October to December, the *distillateur ambulant* took his still from town to town to distil the local apple stock into precious liquor. His arrival was a festive occasion, celebrated with – *bien sur!* – lots of Calvados.

There are still a few old folk out there brewing up their spirits legally – and certainly some illegal brewing going on – but artisanal Calvados is extremely difficult to find. Old Norman families are bound to have a few bottles stashed away but you'll probably have to marry into the family (and stay married for a while) in order to taste it.

The market is Thursday morning. Look for the delicious local Coutances cheese with its creamy centre.

Getting There & Away

The SNCF runs buses to Granville (€7.40, 30 minutes, up to five daily). In July and August there are buses to the beaches (20 minutes, three daily). Regular train services include Cherbourg (€15.30, two hours, six daily), Caen (€13.50, 1½ hours, six daily) and Paris' Gare du Nord (€34.70, four hours, twice daily).

GRANVILLE

pop 13,500

At the foot of the Cotentin Peninsula, the coastal port of Granville likes to call itself the 'Monaco of the North'. Like the tiny principality to the south, Granville has an old town crowded onto a rocky promontory overlooking the sea and a lower town built on land reclaimed from the sea. The straight rows of granite houses and white shutters in the walled upper town, however, have a uniquely Norman austerity. Despite the no-nonsense buildings, Granville is a popular destination for pleasure-seekers. In summer, the narrow beach is crowded with visitors and the coastal views from the upper town are extraordinary.

Much of the upper town is 18th century, when shipbuilders and privateers built residences. The 19th-century vogue for sea bathing brought the first beach lovers, speeded by a new train line. Liberated on 31 July 1944, Granville was surprised to find itself under assault by German commandos everyone had forgotten were still garrisoned at Jersey. The Germans left 20 dead before making off with a cargo of coal and GI prisoners.

Orientation

Granville is divided into two parts – a modern lower town that contains most shops and services, and a walled upper town overlooking the sea. The beach runs northeast of the casino and the southern part of town is given over to several ports. There are promenades along the beach, around the upper town and along rue du Port. The train station is on ave de la Gare, 1km east of the town centre.

Information

INTERNET RESOURCES
www.ville-granville.fr The town's website (French only).

LAUNDRY
Laundrette (10 rue St-Sauveur)

MONEY
Caisse d'Epargne (18 cours Jonville; ☺ closed Sun & Mon)

POST
Post Office (cours Jonville) A block east of the tourist office, and there's Cyberposte.

TOURIST INFORMATION
Tourist Office (☎ 02 33 91 30 03; 4 cours Jonville; ⏰ 9am-1pm & 2-7.30pm Mon-Sat, 11am-12.30pm Sun Jul & Aug, 9am-12.30pm & 2-6.30pm Mon-Sat Sep-Jun)
STN Office (☎ 02 33 50 77 89) Across the street from the tourist office, it's a good source of information for local and regional buses.

TRAVEL AGENCIES
Luce Voyages (☎ 02 33 90 62 24; 1 rue Lecampion) Sells train, air and sea tickets.

Sights & Activities
All of Granville's sights are found within the walled upper city. **Musée du Vieux Granville** (☎ 02 33 50 44 10; 2 rue Le Carpentier; adult/concession €1.60/1; ⏰ 10am-noon & 2-6pm Wed-Mon Apr-Sep, 2-6pm Wed, Sat & Sun Oct-Mar) concentrates on the maritime history of the town, displaying painted and ceramic seascapes, model boats, posters, postcards and photographs. There are also rooms of local furniture,

traditional Norman costumes and *coiffes* (headdresses worn by women).

Musée d'Art Moderne Richard Anacréon (☎ 02 33 51 02 94; place de l'Isthme; adult/concession €2.50/1.30; ⏰ 11am-6pm Wed-Mon Jul-Sep, 2-6pm Wed-Sun Oct-Jun) houses an eclectic collection of modern art that includes such well-known names as Picasso, Derain, Vlaminck, Utrillo, Laurencin and Signac. The collection was a donation from Granville resident Richard Anacréon, who owned a bookshop for many years in Paris' Latin Quarter. The shop window of his bookshop has been re-created and the museum contains mementos from Colette, Cocteau, Apollinaire, Genet and other Parisian literary figures.

Musée et Jardin Christian Dior (☎ 02 33 61 48 21; villa Les Rhumbs; admission €5; ⏰ 10am-12.30pm & 2.30-6.30pm) It's the childhood home of the great French fashion designer – a must-see for *fashionistas*. The collection of outfits is wonderful enough and the designs and watercolours help trace Dior's evolution as a designer. Temporary exhibits each summer illuminate other aspects of the revolutionary changes he brought to women's fashion.

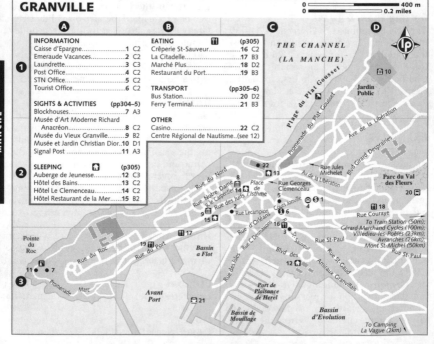

La Pointe du Roc at the southwestern tip of the upper town has a **lighthouse** built in 1869, a **signal post** and several **blockhouses** built by the Germans between 1942 and 1944.

Tours

Boat trips (☎ 02 33 50 31 81; return €16.80) aboard the ferry *Jolie France II* or the catamaran *Jeune France* take in the rugged Îles Chausey, 17km offshore. Departures are between 9am and 10am Wednesday, Saturday and Sunday, depending on the tides. Boats leave from the ferry terminal *(gare maritime)*.

Festivals & Events

The unmissable event in Granville is the **Grand Pardon**, which takes place each year at the end of July and beginning of August. The port is filled with decorated boats, there's a Blessing of the Sea and lots of seafood to sample.

Sleeping

Camping La Vague (☎ 02 33 50 29 97; camping €17; ☿ May Sep) Two kilometres south of the town centre and 200m from the beach, this camping ground has 145 places.

    Auberge de Jeunesse (☎ 02 33 91 22 62; www .crng.asso.fr; r with/without bathroom per person €18.50/ 14.50; P) It's well-situated in the Centre Régional Nautisme (Regional Nautical Centre) at Port de Plaisance de Herel.

    Hôtel Le Clemenceau (☎ 02 33 50 19 87; clemenceau .hotel@wanadoo.fr; 1 rue Georges Clemenceau; r with sink/ bathroom €25.50/37) Centrally located with small but well-kept rooms, this hotel has friendly, professional service.

    Hôtel Restaurant de la Mer (☎ 02 33 50 67 56; 74 rue du Port; r €34-39) This hotel right on the port has recently been redecorated on a marine theme; that is, in several different shades of blue. It's all very pretty and prices are reasonable.

    Hôtel des Bains (☎ 02 33 50 17 31, 02 33 50 89 22; 19 rue Georges Clemenceau; s/d from €37/48; P ✗) Modern three-star establishment across from the casino and near the beach has cheerful, bright rooms. More-expensive rooms with sea views are available. Breakfast costs an extra €8, but the restaurant is excellent.

Eating

There are a number of inexpensive creperies in the upper town especially on rue Cambernon and rue Notre Dame.

Crêperie St-Sauveur (☎ 02 33 90 20 77; 4 rue St-Sauveur; crepes from €5.50; ☿ closed Tue) In the lower town, this attractive place is on a colourful street and turns out tasty crepes and *galettes* in a friendly atmosphere.

    Restaurant du Port (☎ 02 33 50 00 55; 19 rue du Port; menus from €11.50; ☿ closed Mon & dinner Sun) In addition to being a delightful waterfront spot on the port with a cosy dining room and an outdoor terrace you can graze on an assortment of fabulous seafood or the delicious seafood paella.

    La Citadelle (☎ 02 33 50 34 10; 34 rue du Port; menus €15-30; ☿ closed Tue & Wed Oct-Mar) The talented young chef concocts such treats as oysters with camembert sauce and a special grilled lobster in an appetite-inspiring setting right on the port.

    The supermarket **Marché Plus** (107 rue Couraye) is open long hours.

Getting There & Around

There is a daily evening bus that goes to Coutances, Valognes and Cherbourg, four weekday buses to Coutances (€6 20, one hour and 10 minutes), and seven weekday buses to Avranches (€7.10, one hour). There are regular train services to Paris (€33.50, three hours, six daily), Coutances (€6.60, 30 minutes, four daily) and Villedieu-les-Poêles (€5.10, 20 minutes, four daily).

STN runs local buses in Granville. There are infrequent services between the train station and the post office. Tickets cost €1.10. You can hire a bicycle at **Gérard March-and Cycles** (☎ 02 33 61 53 62; 35 ave Maréchal Leclerc).

VILLEDIEU-LES-POÊLES
pop 4300

Twenty-three kilometres east of Granville is a 'city of God' *(villedieu)* and 'pans' *(poêles)*. Villedieu-les-Poêles was founded in 1130 by the Hospitallers of St John of Jerusalem, who eventually became the Knights of Malta. This ancient stone town is known for its copper pans. The origins of the copper industry remain obscure, but it seems that the religious character of the town in the 12th century gave rise to various tax breaks that favoured artisans. Workshops began to produce church ornaments and eventually developed an expertise in kitchen implements, church bells and in pewter.

After a decline in the 19th century, the industry has once again flowered to feed a demand for luxury kitchenware. A number of workshops in town are open for visits, from which you can also buy copper pans. **Atelier du Cuivre** (☎ 02 33 51 31 85; 54 rue Général Huard; admission €3.50; ☺ 9am-noon & 1.30-6pm Mon-Sat) presents a short film and a tour of the facilities.

The **tourist office** (☎ 02 33 61 05 69; www.ot-ville dieu.fr; place des Costils; ☺ 9am-12.30pm & 2-6.30pm daily Apr-Sep, 9am-noon & 2-6pm Mon-Sat Oct-Mar) has information on other workshop tours, accommodation and excursions.

Villedieu-les-Poêles is linked by train to Granville (see left for details) and Paris (€31.30, three hours, four daily).

Orne

CONTENTS

Alençon 309
Around Alençon 312
Bagnoles de l'Orne 313
Mortagne-au-Perche 315

Two major autoroutes circle around the Orne *département*, forming a kind of shell that has protected it from urbanisation. Normandy's most rural *département* has been left to its forests, hillsides, horses and rivers. Cities are few and far between and the region is among the least polluted in France. To appreciate the Orne, take the back roads – there's hardly anything but back roads anyway – and stop off in the rural villages and hamlets that have sprouted up along the region's many rivers. The blight of modern housing has not infected the Orne, which sparkles with pre-industrial charm. Even the capital of Alençon is remarkably stress-free for a city. This isn't the region for uplifting museums and flashy shopping. Come to enjoy the outdoors and the culinary delights, which are often cheaper here than other, more touristed, regions.

The River Orne in the northwest stretches into the Suisse Normande while the Sarthe Valley in the south offers ravishing vistas. Take a walk or bike ride through the Forêt d'Écouves north of Alençon or the Perche forests – Forêt de Bellême, Forêt de Saussay and the Parc Naturel Régional de Normandie-Maine. If you want to unwind, there's always the curative waters of Bagnoles de l'Orne. The Orne is not a good *département* to explore by public transport – buses throughout the region are either rare or nonexistent.

HIGHLIGHTS

- Stroll through Alençon's **town centre** (p309)
- Walk along the **River Sarthe** from St-Céneri-le-Gérei to St-Léonard-des-Bois (p312)
- Take the waters at **Bagnoles de l'Orne** (p313)
- Attend the annual *boudin* (blood sausage) fair in **Mortagne-au-Perche** (p315)

- POPULATION: 292,200
- AREA: 6103 SQ KM

ORNE

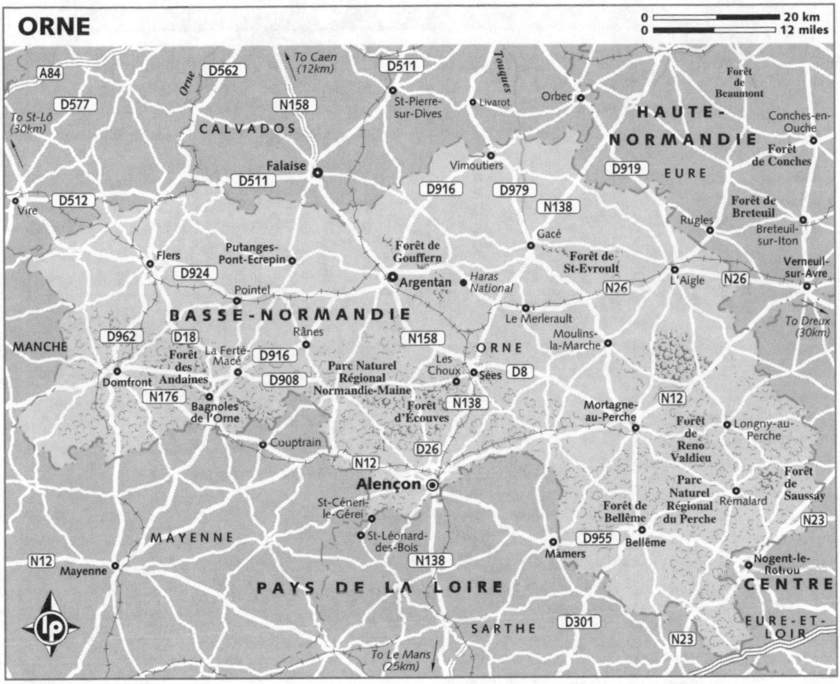

ALENÇON

pop 30,400

In the far south of Normandy, on the edge of the Parc Naturel Régional de Normandie-Maine, lies the vibrant town of Alençon. The elegant buildings that make up the town centre recall the days when Alençon was the lace-making hub of Europe. From the 17th to 19th centuries, Alençon supplied fashionable women everywhere with astonishingly intricate lace, and grew prosperous in the process. The lace industry has withered away but, thanks to the opening of Moulinex appliance factories, Alençon is still thriving. With the Rivers Sarthe and Briante meandering through a town centre largely composed of pedestrianised shopping streets, Alençon makes a perfect base from which to explore the Orne.

Orientation & Information

The old town and its sights are about 1.5km southwest of the train station, via ave du Président Wilson and rue St-Blaise. The bus station is 800m southwest of the train station on square des Déportés.

INTERNET ACCESS
Espace Internet (☎ 02 33 32 40 33; 6-8 rue des Filles Notre Dame; ☼ 8.30am-7pm Mon-Sat) Internet access is free but it's often packed.

INTERNET RESOURCES
www.ville-alencon.fr The city website.

LAUNDRY
Laundrette (5 rue du Collège)

MONEY
Crédit Mutuel (89 bis rue aux Sieurs)

POST
Post Office (16 rue du Jeudi) It has Cyberposte and exchanges currency.

TOURIST INFORMATION
Tourist Office (☎ 02 33 80 66 33; alencon.tourisme@ wanadoo.fr; place La Magdelaine; ☼ 9.30am-6pm Mon-Sat, 10am-12.30pm & 3-5.30pm Sun Jul & Aug, 9.30am-noon & 2-6.30pm Mon-Sat Sep-Jun) In the turreted Maison d'Ozé. Its accommodation-booking service is free and it provides an English-language brochure, *Alençon on Foot*, showing a walking tour of the town.

ORNE

ORNE

ALENÇON

INFORMATION	
Bureau Information Jeunesse	1 C2
Crédit Mutuel	2 B3
Espace Internet	3 B2
Laundrette	4 B2
Main Post Office	5 B2
Tourist Office	6 C3

SIGHTS & ACTIVITIES	(p311)
Château des Ducs	7 A3
Eglise Notre Dame	8 C3
Musée de la Dentelle Au Point	
d'Alençon	9 C3
Musée des Beaux-Arts et de la	
Dentelle	10 B2
Musée Leclerc	(see 9)
St-Theresa's Birthplace	11 D2

SLEEPING	(p311)
Hôtel de L'Industrie	12 D1
Hôtel de Paris	13 E1
Hôtel Le Grand St-Michel	14 B2
Hôtel-Restaurant Le Grand Cerf	15 C2

EATING	(p311)
Restaurant Au Petit Vatel	16 B2
Restaurant au Point d'Alençon	17 D3

DRINKING	(p311)
Le Shetland	18 C2

ENTERTAINMENT	(p312)
L'Arc-en-Ciel	19 C2

TRANSPORT	(p312)
Bayi Cycles	20 C4
Bus Station	21 D2

Bureau Information Jeunesse (☎ 02 33 80 48 90; www.bijbus.com - French only; 4-6 place Poulet Malassis) It provides information about local transport and accommodation options.

Sights & Activities
The old town, especially along **Grand Rue**, is full of atmospheric Second Empire houses with forged iron balconies dating from the 18th century. To the southwest looms the crowned turret of the **Château des Ducs**, which was used by the Nazis as a prison during WWII. It is closed to the public.

The **Musée des Beaux-Arts et de la Dentelle** (☎ 02 33 32 40 07; 12 rue Charles Aveline; adult/child €2.90/2.40; ⏰ 10am-noon & 2-6pm daily Jul & Aug, Tue-Sun Sep-Jun) is in a restored Jesuit school building. It houses a so-so collection of Flemish, Dutch and French artworks from the 17th to 19th centuries, and an exhaustive exhibit on the history of lace-making and its techniques. The intricacy of the works is remarkable. There's also an unexpected section of Cambodian artefacts – including Buddhas, spears and tiger skulls – donated by a former (French) governor of Cambodia.

Serious lace-lovers can try the **Musée de la Dentelle 'Au Point d'Alençon'** (☎ 02 33 26 27 26; 33 rue du Pont Neuf; adult/child €3.05/1.80; ⏰ 10am-noon & 2-6pm Apr-Sep, 10.30am-noon & 2-5.30pm Oct-Mar), which offers guided visits that include a short film on lace-making and about 60 pieces of lace. There's also a shop where you can buy it.

Église Notre Dame (Grande Rue; 8.30am-noon & 2-5.30pm) has a stunning Flamboyant Gothic portal from the 16th century, and some superb stained glass in the chapel where St Theresa was baptised.

St Theresa's birthplace (☎ 02 33 26 09 87; 58 rue St-Blaise; admission free; ⏰ 9am-noon & 2-6pm Jun-Sep, 9.30am-noon & 2.30-5pm Wed-Mon Oct-Dec & Feb-May) is remarkable for its extreme simplicity. The entrance is through an adjacent chapel dedicated to the saint.

The **Musée Leclerc** (☎ 02 33 26 27 26; 33 rue du Pont Neuf; adult/child €2.25/1.20; ⏰ 10am-noon & 2-6pm Apr-Sep, 10.30am-noon & 2-5.30pm Oct-Mar) details the history of Alençon during WWII and has some fascinating wartime photos. The town was liberated in August 1944 by General Leclerc, whose statue stands proudly out front.

Sleeping
Camping Municipal (☎ 02 33 26 34 95; 69 rue de Guéramé; adult/site €2.10/2.45) Southwest of town

on the Sarthe, this well-outfitted location has 87 places.

Hôtel de Paris (☎ 02 33 29 01 64; fax 02 33 29 44 87; 26 rue Denis Papin; r with washbasin/bathroom from €25/30; ℗) One of a number of small hotels around the train station, this one is just east and has modest, quiet rooms.

Hôtel de L'Industrie (☎ 02 33 27 19 30; hotel .industrie@wanadoo.fr; 20 place du Général de Gaulle; r €40-50; ℗) Close to the town centre, this is a friendly place with 1950s-style rooms and a good restaurant. Oddly enough, the hotel is closed Friday night and all day Saturday, but it makes a good weekday choice.

Hôtel Le Grand St-Michel (☎ 02 33 26 04 77; fax 02 33 26 71 82; 7 rue du Temple; r with washbasin/bathroom €28/54; ℗) On a quiet street in the centre of old Alençon, this place has the air of a traditional country house. The rooms are comfortable in a casual, thrown-together way.

Hôtel-Restaurant Le Grand Cerf (☎ 02 33 26 00 51; 21 rue St-Blaise; s/d €49/57; ℗ ✕ 🖳) This stately old building on the edge of the old town offers more luxury, with plush rooms and a delightfully traditional décor. It also has a good **restaurant** (menus €15.50 & €19-27; ⏰ closed Sat & Sun). The €15.50 menu is only available for weekday lunches.

Hotel-Restaurant Le Chapeau Rouge (☎ 02 33 26 20 33; fax 02 33 26 54 05; 3 blvd Duchamp; r with washbasin/shower €29/40; ℗) This little hotel possesses an ineffable charm probably due to the garden and the furniture, which looks as though it had belonged to a princess fallen upon bad times. The **restaurant** (weekday lunch menus €12, other menus to €25; ⏰ closed Sat-Mon) also offers good value with a selection of dishes from all of France's regions.

Eating & Drinking
Restaurant Au Petit Vatel (☎ 02 33 26 23 78; 72 place du Commandant-Desmeulles; menus €18-37; ⏰ closed Wed & dinner Sun) This is one of the town's older dining addresses, under new management. The cuisine is as refined and elegant as the dining room, presenting such tasty titbits as *beignet de Camembert* (Camembert fritters) and chicken liver in aspic.

Restaurant au Point d'Alençon (☎ 02 33 26 01 68; 116 rue Cazault; menus €10.10-22.10; ⏰ closed Sun & Mon) This family-style restaurant attracts crowds of students who come for its cheap and tasty meals.

Le Shetland (☎ 02 33 26 05 39; 4 rue de la Halle aux Toiles) It's open all day, but the action really

ORNE

heats up after the sun goes down when a relaxed crowd of regulars waters its thirst with a great selection of beer in preparation for a night at the disco across the street.

Entertainment

L'Arc-en-Ciel (☎ 02 33 26 32 15; 11 rue de la Halle aux Toiles; ⊗ from 10pm Wed-Sun) Finally, a disco right in the centre of town. The danceable beats range from techno and house to disco and funk.

La Luciole (☎ 02 33 32 83 33; www.laluciole.org - French only; 171 route de Bretagne) With an excellent concert programme in its main hall that covers everything happening in jazz, rock, pop and electro and regular concerts by local artists in its Musical Cafe, this is the region's premier cultural centre. Plus there's a little Tex Mex restaurant and a bar.

Getting There & Away

STAO (☎ 02 33 26 06 35) runs buses between Alençon and Le Mans (€7.95, 1¾ hours, three to four daily), 49 km to the south, and connects Alençon with Sées (€4.60, 20 minutes, once daily) and Mortagne-au-Perche (€6.10, one hour, four daily).

Alençon has frequent train services to the Gare Montparnasse in Paris (€47.20, 1¾ hours), Caen (€14.50, 1¾ hours), Granville (€20.50, three hours), Pontorson (€30.40, four hours) and Le Mans (€8.10, 45 minutes), among other destinations.

Getting Around

Altobus (☎ 08 00 50 02 29) has three routes that serve the city including one, Line A, that runs from the train station to the town centre.

Bikes can be rented at **Bayi Cycles** (☎ 02 33 29 65 13; 104 blvd de la République).

AROUND ALENÇON
Sarthe Valley

Following the Sarthe southwest of Alençon takes you through an enchanting landscape of steep forested hills and fairy-tale villages. The most delightful is **St-Céneri-le-Gérei**, 13km from Alençon. Classified as one of France's most beautiful villages, its allure has the government seal of approval. The stone village is on a tiny peninsula in the midst of the Sarthe and gives the impression of just holding its own against the encroaching greenery. A map posted at the entrance

---

> ### DETOUR: FORÊT D'ÉCOUVES
>
> From **Sées**, follow the D908, which takes you to the lovely **Forêt d'Écouves** in the Parc Naturel Régional de Normandie-Maine, beginning at les Choux. Pass Carrefour de la Rangée, head up a hill and turn left onto the D226, which runs through a forest of tall spindly pines. At the **Carrefour de la Croix de Médavy**, notice the block of granite commemorating the visit of the brother of Louis XVI. You can leave your car here and follow the signposted trails through the forest or take the D26 up to the **Signal d'Écouves** (417m), one of the highest points in the region. Follow the D26 past the **old glass factory** (Verrerie de Gast) to rejoin the D908.

---

to the village is a helpful aid in finding the main highlight – the Romanesque church built in the 11th century. Campers can stay at **Camping de St-Céneri** (☎ 02 33 26 60 00; adult/site €3/3.50), an idyllic spot along the river only 100m from the village.

St-Léonard-des-Bois, 6km south of St-Céneri, is a sleepy town along the Sarthe at the foot of high cliffs. There's a tourist office at the **Camping Municipal** (☎ 02 43 33 81 79) that can provide you with a list of *chambres d'hôtes* (B&Bs).

There's no public transport to either town, but the back roads make a pretty bike ride and there's a path from St-Céneri that takes you along the river to St-Léonard.

Sées

It's no surprise that French director Luc Besson chose Sées, 17km north of Alençon, as the setting for several scenes in his movie *Jeanne d'Arc*. The town centre is crammed with medieval buildings, mostly religious structures dating from the days when Sées was the seat of the archbishop. Of the churches, chapels, basilicas, convents and abbeys, the most outstanding building is the **cathedral**. Built from the 13th to 14th centuries, but badly damaged in the Hundred Years' War, the 70m towers dwarf the town centre. Passing through the elaborate central doorway, you're faced with a cavernous interior marked by splendid 13th-century rose windows in the north and south transepts.

The **tourist office** (☎ 02 33 28 74 79; sees.tourisme@ wanadoo.fr; place Charles de Gaulle; ☽ 9.30am-12.30pm & 2-6pm Mon-Fri) is a few metres north of the cathedral.

There's only just one impractically scheduled bus from Alençon each day (€4.60, 20 minutes), so it's best to have your own transport.

Le Pin au Haras

Horse-whisperers and horse lovers will be pleased to discover that this noble animal finally is housed within a palatial residence worthy of its status. Called the Versailles of the Horse, the **Haras National** (National Stud; ☎ 02 33 36 68 68; adult/concession €4/2.50; ☽ 2-5pm Jan-Mar, 9.30am-6pm Apr-mid–Oct, guided visits every 30 minutes) was founded in the 18th century by Louis XIV's minister Colbert to preserve France's great pedigreed horses. Designed in the same sumptuous style as Versailles, the chateau and gardens provide a magnificent setting for the 60 or so stallions kept there to breed. In addition to a stroll in the grounds and the stables, the tour includes a peek at the collection of buggies and the saddlery. From June to September, there are **horse-riding displays** (admission €3; 3pm Thu), and races the first Sunday in September and a few Sundays in October. If you want to see the stallions, bear in mind that their reproductive duties make them unavailable from mid-February to mid-July.

You'll need your own wheels to visit the stud farm as the public transport options are impractical. Take the N26 and head 15km east of Argentan.

BAGNOLES DE L'ORNE

pop 900

Hugging the banks of the River Vée and its lake, Bagnoles is the most attractive spa town in Normandy. The vast Forêt des Andaines presses around the town, leaving the air fresh and fragrant. The town is also architecturally interesting. Avenues of opulent buildings date from the turn of the century when the rich and titled found various ailments to send them down to Bagnoles for a relaxing 'cure'. It may no longer be royalty's spa of

FROM A TROT TO A GALLOP

Thoroughbreds, trotters and workhorses alike find Lower Normandy to be a horse's paradise. The climate is mild, the landscape is softly contoured and the grass is particularly rich. The Orne, Calvados and Manche *départements* raise some 70% of French thoroughbreds and trotters, bred in the national stables of St-Lô and Le Pin as well as scattered private stud farms. Horses that don't make the cut for a racing career are pressed into service for weekend riders and horse lovers at hundreds of local stables.

Normandy's tradition of breeding racehorses dates back to the early 18th century and is concentrated in the Orne and Calvados *départements*. The elite thoroughbreds are descended from Arabian stallions and English mares, carefully chosen for speed and endurance. With an average career of only three years, these elegant horses are evaluated early. Deauville (see p279) hosts a yearling sale each August while brood mares and foals go to market in November.

Norman trotters date from the 19th century and originated in the Orne. They have a somewhat longer career, working first at the racetrack and then as hire horses. Descended from Norman mares and English stallions, the trotter is also a pure breed, with a carefully charted heritage.

Cobs are sturdy horses with short legs and a comfortable riding gait, good for a long day in the saddle touring the farm. Although not strong enough for heavy loads, they are often used for pulling small carriages of tourists on sightseeing jaunts.

Normandy's most famous horse breed is the Percheron, named after the Perche region where they originated. These grey or black horses are immensely powerful and were once indispensable on the farm. Although the breed may extend back to the Middle Ages, all of today's Percherons are descended from one (busy) 19th-century stallion, Jean Le Blanc. Their docility and strength made them the workhorse of choice a century ago, but modern farming had less need of their powerful fore- and hindquarters. For a while, it looked as though the Percherons were going from harvesting dinner to being dinner, but Percheron appreciation associations emerged around the world to save the breed from the butcher's knife. Their strong backs, easy stride and adaptability, whether pulling carriages, sleighs or prancing in a parade, have ensured the breed's survival.

choice, but Bagnoles has no trouble attracting clients to its luxurious thermal baths. The median age of its visitors stretches into the higher double-digits but there's plenty to do apart from relaxing in warm baths or getting pummelled by water jets. Paths lead along the river and around the lake; there's tennis, golf, horse-riding, rock-climbing, a casino, buggy rides and a packed schedule of concerts and shows during the summer season.

Orientation & Information

The lake provides an orientation point in the town. The casino is on its northwestern shore and the commercial centre of town stretches down from the southeastern shore. The thermal baths are in the midst of the Parc Thermal, a spacious wooded park, along the southern course of the Vée.

The **tourist office** (☎ 02 33 37 85 66; www.bagnoles -de-lorne.com; place du Marché; 🕙 9.30am-1pm & 2-6.30pm Mon-Sat, 10am-12.30pm & 2-6pm Sun Apr-Oct, 9.30am-1pm & 2-6.30pm Mon-Sat Nov-Mar) has ample documentation on the sporting and cultural activities in and around Bagnoles as well as accommodation and information about special hotel packages including a cure at the thermal baths.

Sights & Activities

L'Établissement Thermal (☎ 02 33 30 38 00; 2hr bath & massage €40.70; 🕙 6.15am-1pm, free visits 5pm Tue & Fri) is worth a visit if only for its eye-catching *belle époque* architecture. According to a local legend, the underground spring that furnishes its famous water was discovered by a local landholder who noticed that his tired old horse gained new vitality after daily baths in the fountain. The elderly gentleman began bathing in the spring and found himself blessed with a youthful new vigour. The water comes from a granite pocket about 5m deep and is lightly radioactive. Doctors prescribe it for circulatory troubles, skin disorders and, naturally enough, stress. While the French healthcare system pays for extended, prescribed treatments, it's possible to enjoy a two-hour curative bath with water-jet massages.

The **old town** is an exuberant mixture of over-the-top architectural flourishes on villas built during Bagnoles' golden age. The tourist office publishes a small free brochure containing a map and explanations.

Sleeping & Eating

It's gratifying that a town as well-heeled as Bagnoles still provides plenty of affordable accommodation, but book well in advance. Bagnoles has a long season that runs from April to October. During those months it's crammed, and outside them it's deserted.

Camping de la Vée (☎ 02 33 37 87 45; camping-de -la-vee@wanadoo.fr; camping €8.20; 🕙 Apr-Oct) Two kilometres south of town along ave Président Coty, this is a nice spot, although it lacks shade.

All of the hotels below have good restaurants, making it worthwhile to consider taking half-board.

Hôtel Les Capucines (☎ 02 33 37 82 59; hotel.les capucines@wanadoo.fr; 36 blvd Lemeunier-de-la-Raillère; r with washbasin/bathroom €23/39; **P**) One of the most agreeable of the budget hotels, this stately old place is in the old town. The high-ceilinged rooms are well maintained and some have balconies. The **restaurant** (menus €12-24) turns out nicely prepared fish dishes, among other choices.

La Potinière du Lac (☎ 02 33 30 65 00; www.hotel delapotiniere.com - French only; rue des Casinos; r with washbasin/bathroom €20/42; 🕙 closed 4pm Sun-Tue Nov-Mar; **P**) You can't miss this stunning establishment close to the lake. Look for the conical tower and the cross-hatched half-timbered façade that just screams out 'Normandy'!

Nouvel Hôtel (☎ 02 33 30 75 00; perso.wanadoo.fr /nouvelhotel; 8 ave du Docteur-Noël; r €40-62; **P**) Just walking up the impressive stairway to the lobby puts you in the mood to be pampered. The rooms are comfortable without being especially eye-catching but the service is good and you will enjoy the **restaurant** (menus €14-26).

Le Cetlos (☎ 02 33 38 44 44; fax 02 33 38 46 23; rue des Casinos; www.le-cetlos.com; r per person incl breakfast from €39; **P** ✗ 🖳 🖳) This peachy place overlooks the lake and offers amazing luxury for the price. Rooms are large and comfortable and there's an indoor swimming pool, sauna, steam room and gym.

Getting There & Around

There are three buses daily from Alençon during the week. They are scheduled to make a day trip possible (€7.40, 70 minutes).

You can rent mountain bikes from **Librairie du Lac** (☎ 02 33 30 80 27; 4 rue des Casinos) for €11 per day.

MORTAGNE-AU-PERCHE
pop 4900

Located about 34km northeast of Alençon, Mortagne-au-Perche sits on a hill overlooking the Perche region, an underpopulated land marked by the massive Parc Naturel Régional du Perche in its southern reaches. The park was created in 1998 and covers 2035 sq km (nearly half a million acres). Known for its particular breed of horse, the Percheron (see the boxed text, p313), much of the region is given over to fields and forests. There are no cities, no autoroutes and just a few large towns. In addition to exporting its popular horses, the Perche exported many of its people to Canada centuries ago, furnishing much of the population for French Canada.

Mortagne-au-Perche makes an excellent base for exploring the area. Its 18th-century buildings have been immaculately restored, recalling the days when the town was the capital of the Perche region. Although Mortagne-au-Perche is no longer the key commercial centre it once was, the town remains a vital marketplace for the agricultural products of the region. If blood sausage *(boudin)* is to your taste, this is the place to sample it. The annual Lent **boudin fair** draws many locals and even more Parisians, many of whom have second homes in and around town.

Orientation & Information
The centre of the town is the busy place du Général de Gaulle, dominated by the 19th-century Halle aux Grains (grain market). The **tourist office** (☎ 02 33 85 11 18; office-mortagne@wanadoo.fr; Halle aux Grains; ☼ 9.30am-12.30pm & 2.30-6pm Mon-Sat mid-May–mid-Sep) has a wealth of information about walks and cycle routes in the region. The **Caisse d'Épargne** (10

place du Général de Gaulle) changes money. The **post office** (16 rue des 15 Fusillés) is on the main street leading from place du Général de Gaulle.

Sights & Activities
The tourist office publishes a helpful pamphlet mapping out the aristocratic residences that were constructed during the town's heyday. Along the route is the **Porte St-Denis** on rue du Portail St-Denis, which is the last remnant of the walls that once surrounded the town.

Also of note is **Église Notre Dame**, reconstructed at the end of the 16th century in Flamboyant Gothic style. Notice the 18th-century wood panelling around the choir.

There are over 1000km of signposted trails in the **Parc Naturel Régional du Perche** (www.le-perche.org) that are ideal for walkers, cyclists and horse riders. The Forêt de Bellême, 15km south of Mortagne, and Forêt de Saussay, about 20km southeast, are two popular havens.

Sleeping & Eating
Hôtel de la Poste (☎ 02 33 25 08 01; 15 place de la République; r with washbasin/bathroom €21/35) In the centre of town, this place has only 10 simple rooms. The **restaurant** (☼ closed Sun) below the hotel is a lunch favourite serving up tasty €10 *menus*.

Hôtel du Tribunal (☎ 02 33 25 04 77; hotel.du.tribunal@wanadoo.fr; 4 place du Palais; r €46-95) It's the best place in town, housed in a beautifully renovated 16th-century building. The old features have been preserved while modern comforts have been added.

Getting There & Away
STAO (☎ 02 33 26 06 35) in Alençon runs four buses daily between Mortagne-au-Perche and Alençon (€6.10, one hour).

DIRECTORY

Directory

CONTENTS

Accommodation	316
Activities	319
Business Hours	320
Children	320
Climate Charts	320
Courses	321
Customs	321
Dangers & Annoyances	322
Disabled Travellers	322
Discount Cards	322
Embassies & Consulates	323
Festivals & Events	324
Food	324
Gay & Lesbian Travellers	324
Government	324
Holidays	325
Insurance	325
Internet Access	326
Legal Matters	326
Maps	326
Money	327
Photography & Video	328
Post	328
Solo Travellers	329
Telephone	329
Tourist Information	330
Visas	330
Women	331
Work	331

PRACTICALITIES

■ To call France, dial 33 (the country code) and the local number without the initial zero

■ To call overseas from France, dial 00 (for international access), the country code and the number

■ Buy stamps for the EU (€0.50) at a *tabac* and international stamps (€0.90) at the post office

■ France is one hour ahead of GMT/UTC except during daylight-saving (or summer) time when it is two hours ahead.

ACCOMMODATION

Normandy and Brittany have accommodation of every sort and for every budget. The listings in the accommodation sections of this guidebook are ordered from budget to mid-range to top-end options. We generally treat any place that charges up to €50 as budget accommodation. Mid-range facilities are usually in the range of €50 to €100 per double, while the top-end tag is applied to places charging more than €100 per night. In heavily touristed areas, accommodation is somewhat more expensive and the categories are adjusted upwards. Remember that local authorities impose a *taxe de séjour* (tourist tax) on each visitor in their jurisdiction. The prices charged at camping grounds, hotels and so on might therefore be as much as €0.20 to €1.25 per person higher than the posted rates.

Advance reservations save the hassle of looking for a place to stay each time you pull into a new town. At times of heavy domestic or foreign tourism (for example, around Easter and Christmas, during the February–March school holiday and in July and August), having a reservation can mean the difference between finding a room in your price range and moving on.

Some tourist offices will help travellers make local hotel reservations, usually for a small fee. In some cases, you pay a deposit that is later deducted from the first night's bill. The staff might also have information on vacancies but they will usually refuse to make specific recommendations. You cannot take advantage of reservation services by phone – you have to stop by the office.

Most places will hold a room only until a set hour, rarely later than 6pm or 7pm (and sometimes earlier). If you're running late, let them know or they're liable to let the room to someone else.

Gîtes & Chambres d'Hôtes

Several types of accommodation – often in charming, traditional-style houses with gardens – are available for people who would like a more informal atmosphere and have a vehicle. All are represented by **Gîtes de France** (☎ 01 49 70 75 75; www.gites-de-france.fr; 59 rue St-Lazare;

DIRECTORY

75439 Paris Cedex) an organisation that acts as a liaison between owners and renters.

A **gîte d'étape** is a comfortable form of accommodation geared for walkers and cyclists passing through the region. A night's accommodation costs around €10 or €12 per person and places are listed in *Gîtes d'Étape et de Séjour*, published annually by Gîtes de France. Another good resource is www.gite-etape.com (French only).

A **gîte rural** is a holiday cottage (or part of a house) in a village or on a farm. Amenities always include a kitchenette and bathroom facilities and you usually must rent weekly, beginning on Saturday. Sometimes you will need to supply your own linen. Rates start at about €300 per week.

A **chambre d'hôte**, basically a guesthouse or B&B (bed and breakfast), is a room in a private house rented to travellers by the night. Breakfast is included and you can also sometimes arrange for lunch and/or dinner. It's a much more intimate experience than staying in a hotel, but usually more expensive. Prices run from €35 to €45 per night for a double room and most homes are out of town, making a car essential.

Details on how to contact the nearest Gîtes de France office are available at any local or *département* tourist office, which can usually supply a brochure listing *gîtes* and *chambres d'hôtes* in the area.

Camping

Camping, either in tents or in motor caravans, is immensely popular in Normandy and Brittany. Most camping grounds close from October or November to March or April. Hostels sometimes let travellers pitch tents in the back garden.

Rates are generally the same for tents and motor caravans, except that the latter are charged an extra fee for electricity. Some places have *forfaits* (fixed-price deals) for two or three people that includes a space for a car and tent or caravan. Children up to about age 12 enjoy significant discounts. Few camping grounds are near major sights, so campers without their own wheels might spend a fair bit of money (and time) commuting.

For details on camping grounds not mentioned in the text, ask at a local tourist office or consult www.campingfrance.com.

In July and especially August, when most camping grounds are completely packed, campers who arrive late in the day have a much better chance of getting a spot if they arrive on foot (ie without a vehicle). Camping offices are often closed for most of the day – the best times to call for reservations are in the morning (before 10am or 11am) and in the late afternoon or early evening.

Remember that camping is generally permitted only at designated camp sites. Pitching your tent anywhere else is usually illegal, although sometimes tolerated if you're not on private land and at least 1500m from a camping facility.

Homestays

Under an arrangement known as *hôtes payants* (literally 'paying guests') or *hébergement chez l'habitant* (lodging with the owners or occupants of private homes), young people, students and tourists can stay with French families. In general you rent a room and have access (sometimes limited) to the family's kitchen and telephone. Many language schools (p321) arrange homestays for their students.

Students and tourists alike should count on paying around €25 to €55 per day, €200 to €265 per week or €550 to €900 per month for a single room, including breakfast.

Hotels

Most French hotels have between one and four stars; the fanciest places have four stars plus an L (for 'luxury'). A hotel that has no stars (ie that has not been rated) is known as *non-homologué*, sometimes abbreviated as NH. The letters 'NN' after the rating mean that the establishment conforms to the *nouvelle norme* (new standards), introduced in 1992. Hotel ratings are based on certain objective criteria (such as the size of the entry hall), not the quality of the service, the decor or cleanliness, so a one-star establishment may be more pleasant than some two- or three-star places. Prices often reflect these intangibles far more than they do the number of stars.

Most hotels offer a continental breakfast consisting of a croissant, French rolls, butter, jam and either coffee or hot chocolate. The charge for this is usually €5 to €7 per person, a bit more than you would pay at a café. Some places in tourist-heavy areas require guests to take breakfast, especially during the summer.

Very few hotels have single rooms. In the budget category the smallest room with a double bed is usually sold to singles even though it's adequate for (intimate) couples. Unless otherwise stated, all prices are for rooms with one double bed. If you require two twin beds, there will be a supplement.

BUDGET HOTELS

The days of the cheap, bathless rooms are numbered as hotels upgrade and improve their facilities. Most budget rooms are small but equipped with private facilities, although there are usually a few rooms with a *lavabo* (wash basin) only and bathrooms in the hall. Taking a shower in the hall bathroom is usually free but sometimes *payant*, which means there's a charge of €1.50 to €3.80 per shower.

If you're travelling by car, you'll be able to take advantage of the remarkably cheap hotel chains on the outskirts of the region's cities and larger towns, usually on a main access route. The best known, **Formule 1** (☎ 08 36 68 56 85; www.hotelformule1.com), charges from €23 to €27 for a clean but bland room for up to three people; toilets and showers are in the hall but there's a wash basin in the room. Breakfast is €3.40 extra. **Etap Hôtel** (☎ 08 36 68 89 00; www.etaphotel.com) is one step up, offering rooms with private facilities for €30 to €45 with a breakfast that includes orange juice for €4.

MID-RANGE HOTELS

Many places that are listed as 'budget' also have rooms that, from the point of view of amenities and price, fall into the mid-range category.

Some hotels – many of them family-run places in the countryside or by the sea – belong to Logis de France, an organisation whose members meet strict standards of service and amenities. They generally offer very good value. The **Fédération Nationale des Logis de France** (☎ 01 45 84 83 84; www.logis-de-france.fr; 83 ave d'Italie; 75013 Paris) has a convenient, searchable website and issues an annual guide with prices and maps of how to find each hotel.

TOP-END HOTELS

Big international chains have largely steered clear of Normandy and Brittany, leaving the top-end option open to creative local own-ers. Staying in an 18th-century manor house surrounded by gardens or a 19th-century villa overlooking the sea can be a delightful accommodation option. Many fascinating old houses, crammed with antiques and family memorabilia, have been renovated and converted into hotels.

Hostels & Foyers

Official hostels that belong to one of the three hostel associations in France are known as *auberges de jeunesse*. FUAJ and LFAJ affiliates require a Hostelling International (HI) card. Otherwise, you can get a 'Guest Card' at your hostel and buy a Welcome Stamp (for €2.90) for your first 6 nights (€17.40), at which point you have full membership and can stay at any hostel around the world. They also require that you either bring a sleeping sheet or rent one for €2.80 per stay.

HOSTEL ORGANISATIONS

Most of France's hostels belong to one of three major hostel associations:

Fédération Unie des Auberges de Jeunesse (FUAJ; ☎ 01 44 89 87 27; www.fuaj.org; 27 rue Pajol, 75018 Paris)

Ligue Française pour les Auberges de la Jeunesse (LFAJ; ☎ 01 44 16 78 78; www.auberges-de-jeunesse.com; 67 rue Vergniaud, 75013 Paris)

Union des Centres de Rencontres Internationales de France (Ucrif; ☎ 01 40 26 57 64; if www.ucrif.asso.fr; 27 rue de Turbigo, 75002 Paris)

Rental Accommodation

If you don't speak French or have a local person helping you, it may be very difficult to find a flat for long-term rental. Since it is costly and time-consuming to evict people in France, landlords usually require substantial proof of financial responsibility for three-year leases. One-year or summer leases of furnished apartments entail less of a commitment from the landlord, making them more likely to take a chance on a foreigner. After you've exhausted your personal connections, the places to look include the *petites annonces* (classified ads) in local newspapers. Each Wednesday free newspapers are dropped off in bundles at many bars, tobacconists and residences. Named after the number of their *départe-ment* (17 in Seine Maritime, 27 in the Eure, 14 in Calvados, 50 in the Manche, 61 in the Orne, 22 in Côtes d'Armor, 29 in Finistère,

35 in Ille-et-Vilaine, 56 in Morbihan and 44 in Loire-Atlantique), they contain hundreds of classifieds. Students may wish to try the Crous office of the nearest university. Estate agents require lots of paperwork and can charge commissions of up to one month's rent.

ACTIVITIES

The varied geography of Brittany and Normandy makes the region ideal for a range of outdoor pursuits. The regional tourism organisations (see p330) publish several free brochures on popular activities.

See the Brittany & Normandy Outdoors chapter (p46) for details about walking, sailing and canal cruising, cycling and diving.

Fishing

With abundant waterways and long coastlines, fishing is an important activity in the region. Fishing requires a licence and may be limited to certain dates. There are also rules about the size of a catch and the type of lures and hooks you can use. Each *département* has a fishing organisation that publishes brochures (in French) and tourist offices (see p330) have information about casting a line.

Hang-Gliding, Paragliding & Parachuting

The thrill of *deltaplane* (hang-gliding) and *parapente* (paragliding) can be experienced throughout Normandy and at a couple of sites in Brittany. The main centres for getting off the ground in Normandy are **Optivol** (☎ 02 35 42 67 90; http://optivol.free.fr/ - French only; 9 rue du Perrey, 76600 Le Havre) for paragliding and the **Aéro-Club de Dieppe** (☎ 02 35 84 86 55; http://acdieppe.free.fr/ - French only). In Brittany the **Club Celtic de Vol Libre** (☎ 02 98 81 50 27; www.ifrance.com /vol-libre-bretagne/Celtic-Vol-Libre.html - French only; Ménez-Hom) is the place to go.

Horse-Riding

Équitation is a popular pastime, especially in Lower Normandy. There are many places throughout the region to take lessons, hire a mount or even stay on a horse farm. Some of the loveliest rides are through the forests of the Parc Naturel Régional du Perche (p315) and Baie du Mont St-Michel (p71). *Département* tourist offices (see p330) have information about horse-riding centres.

Kayaking & Canoeing

Canoeing and kayaking are practised on the rivers and canals across the region. There is little white water in Brittany, but the rivers of the Suisse Normande are particularly fast-moving. Sea-kayaking is especially suited to Brittany's creek-riddled coast and numerous islands – but the strong tides and exposed coastline make it for experienced paddlers only. The **Fédération Française de Canoë-Kayak** (☎ 01 45 11 08 50; www.ffck.org - French only; 87 quai de la Marne, BP 58, 94344 Joinville le Pont Cedex) is a good source of general information.

Sailing

The indented coastline of Brittany and Normandy offers a host of opportunities for sailing. The stunning scenery has made it a popular cruising ground for British yachties on summer holidays who join the thousands of French boat-owners. You can rent boats and sailboards at coastal resorts, and overall advice is available from **Fédération Française de Voile** (☎ 01 40 60 37 00; www.ffvoile.org - French only; 17 rue Henri Bocquillon, 75 015 Paris).

Spas & Thalassotherapy

For over a century, the French have been keen fans of *thalassothérapie* (sea-water therapy) and *thermalisme* (water cures). Visitors with ailments ranging from rheumatism to serious internal disorders flock to hot-springs and thalassotherapy resorts.

France's first thalassotherapy centre was founded in Roscoff in 1899 by Dr Louis Bagot. There are thalassotherapy centres in St-Malo (p75), Perros-Guirec (p113), Roscoff (p123), Belle-Île-en-Mer (p168), La Baule (p196) and Deauville-Trouville (p279). The most popular thermalist (spa) centres are Bagnoles de l'Orne (p313) and Forges-les-Eaux (p219).

For further information, contact the **Fédération Internationale de Thalassothérapie** (☎ 01 44 70 07 57; www.thalassofederation.com; 8 rue Isly, 75008 Paris).

Surfing & Windsurfing

The big swells rolling in from the Atlantic Ocean create ideal surfing conditions at a few places in Brittany. The main surfing beach is found at Pointe de la Torche (p150), in the southwestern corner of Finistère. Stiff breezes and big waves provide a challenge for expert windsurfers all around the Brittany coast, while the more sheltered bays are ideal for beginners. The relatively new sport of kite-surfing (*flysurf* in French) is also popular in Brittany. The vast expanses of firm sand exposed at low tide in many of the bays of Brittany and Normandy provide a perfect arena for sand-yachting (*char à voile*). The **Fédération Française de Char à Voile** (☎ 03 21 89 99 10, www.ffcv.org - French only; 19 rue des Sables, 62600 Berck-sur-Mer) lists a handful of approved sand-yachting schools.

More detail about these activities are given in the individual destination sections.

Swimming

Swimming is popular during summer on the beaches of Brittany – from the crowded strands of Dinard and La Baule to the remote coves of the Île d'Ouessant – and Normandy – from the pebbly shores of the Côte d'Albâtre to the sandy Côte Fleurie. The water is cold most of the year but temperate in July and August when the beaches are at their most crowded. The public is free to use any beach not marked as private. Most popular beaches have a lifeguard, and swimming conditions are rated by coloured flags: green for safe; orange for cautious; red when swimming is forbidden; violet for polluted waters.

Topless bathing for women is pretty much the norm in France – if other people are doing it, you can assume it's OK.

BUSINESS HOURS

Most museums are closed on either Sunday or Monday and almost always shut for a midday break – except in July and August. Many close or operate with greatly reduced hours from November through to March.

Small businesses open daily, except Saturday afternoon, Sunday and often Monday. Hours are usually 9am or 10am to 6.30pm or 7pm, with a break from noon or 1pm to 2pm or 3pm. Laundrettes are usually open 7am or 8am to 7pm or 8pm daily.

Banks usually open from 8am or 9am to sometime between 11.30am and 1pm, and 1.30pm or 2pm to 4.30pm or 5pm, Monday to Friday or Tuesday to Saturday. Exchange services may end half an hour before closing time. Post offices generally open 8.30am or 9am to 5pm or 6pm on weekdays, usually with a two-hour break at midday, and Saturday mornings. Moral: at lunchtime, sit down and eat; there's nothing else to do.

Supermarkets and hypermarkets are open from around 8am to 7pm Monday to Saturday and on Sunday morning. Small food shops mostly close on Saturday afternoon, Sunday and Monday, so Saturday morning may be your last chance to stock up on provisions until Tuesday, unless you come across a supermarket. Restaurants serve between noon and 2pm and from 7pm or 7.30pm to 9.30pm (later on weekends). Many restaurants are closed on Sunday and/or Monday but their closing days are so idiosyncratic that we've specified them in the text.

In July and August, loads of city businesses tend to shut down as the owners and employees take their annual vacation. Small family-run hotels may also close for a week or two in July and August and some close one or two nights a week – or close down completely for a month or three – in winter.

CHILDREN

Successful travelling with young children requires planning and effort. Don't try to overdo things; packing too much into the time available can cause problems even for adults. Include the kids in the trip planning; if they've helped to work out where you will be going, they will be much more interested when they get there. Lonely Planet's *Travel with Children* is a good source of general information.

Most car-rental firms in France have children's safety seats for hire at a nominal cost, but it is essential that you book them in advance. The same goes for highchairs and cots (cribs); they're standard in most restaurants and hotels, but numbers are limited. The choice of baby food, infant formula, soy and cow's milk, disposable nappies (diapers) and the like is as great in French supermarkets as it is back home, but the opening hours may be quite different. Run out of nappies on Saturday afternoon and you could be facing a very long and messy weekend.

CLIMATE CHARTS

Normandy and Brittany have maritime climates, strongly influenced by the temperate winds from the Atlantic. Summers are comfortable, and winters rarely become cold along the coast but are colder in the interior. However, there are regional variations and some marked 'microclimates' within the region. Certain parts of Brittany, notably the

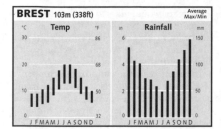

BREST 103m (338ft)

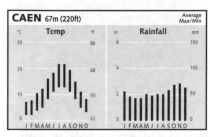

CAEN 67m (220ft)

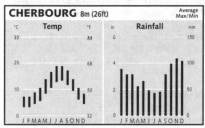

CHERBOURG 8m (26ft)

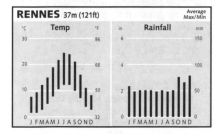

RENNES 37m (121ft)

Île de Bréhat and Île de Batz, enjoy a very mild microclimate (warmed by the currents of the Gulf Stream), while Normandy is rainy. With its exposed situation, strong winds are a regular feature of Brittany's weather.

COURSES

Learning the language is a great way to experience Normandy and Brittany. French courses are not abundant but you can contact the following centres:

Centre d'Études des Langues de St-Malo (☎ 02 99 19 15 46; www.cel-saint-malo.com; Centre Christian Morvan, BP 6, 35430 St-Jouan-des-Guérêts) Two-, three- and four-week courses (20 or 25 hours a week) are available in July and August. Fees range from €491 for two 20-hour weeks to €939 for four 25-hour weeks (excluding accommodation). A two-week course, including board with a local family, costs from €790.

Centre International d'Étude des Langues (CIEL; ☎ 02 98 30 57 57; www.ciel.fr; rue du Gué Fleuri, BP 35, 29480 Le-Relecq-Kerhuon, Brest) Courses are available beginning in January, April, June, July, August and September, and take up 20 or 25 hours a week. Fees range from €520 for two 20-hour weeks and €221 for each additional week (excluding accommodation).

Alliance Française (☎ 02 35 98 55 99; www.alliance-francaise-rouen.asso.fr; 29 rue de Buffon, 76000 Rouen) Courses are available all year for 15 or 20 hours a week. Beginners start in January, July and October and accommodation is possible with private residences or rental of studios or rooms. The fees are €96 for a 15-hour week, €128 for 20 hours a week and €380/€505 a month. Less than 15 hours a week, the cost is €10 per hour and there's a registration fee of €60.

Centre d'Enseignement Universitaire International pour Étrangers, Université de Caen (☎ 02 31 56 55 38; www.unicaen.fr/ceuie; BP 5186, 14032 Caen) There are sessions for three weeks in September (€300) and two 14-week sessions (€725) beginning in October and May that include all levels. Accommodation can be arranged in the university dormitory, in private residences or in hotels.

Centre d'Études de Lisieux (☎ 02 31 31 22 01; centre.normandie@wanadoo.fr; 14 blvd Carnot BP 176, 14404 Lisieux) Courses are available spring to autumn, and accommodation can be in private residences or a dormitory. Prices start at €638 per week, including room and board.

Inlingua (☎ 02 35 69 81 61; www.inlingua.fr/rouen; 75144 Le Petit Quevilly) Courses from March to October are either individual or in small groups and can focus on a cultural theme such as cooking. Accommodation can be arranged within private residences or in a hotel.

CUSTOMS

The usual allowances apply to duty-free goods purchased at airports or on ferries outside the EU: 200 cigarettes, 50 cigars or 250g of loose tobacco; 1L of strong liquor or 2L of less than 22% alcohol by volume *and* 2L of wine; 500g of coffee or 200g of coffee extracts; 100g of tea or 40g of tea extracts; 50g of perfume and 0.25L of eau de toilette.

Do not confuse these with duty-paid items (including alcohol and tobacco) bought at normal shops and supermarkets in another EU country and brought into France. Then the allowances are more than generous: 800 cigarettes, 200 cigars or 1kg of loose tobacco;

DIRECTORY

10L of spirits (more than 22% alcohol by volume), 20L of fortified wine or aperitif, 90L of wine or 110L of beer.

DANGERS & ANNOYANCES

In general, Brittany and Normandy are safe places. The problems you're most likely to encounter are thefts from (and of) cars, pickpocketing and the snatching of daypacks or handbags, particularly in dense crowds, at the airport, train or bus station. A common ploy is for one person to distract you while another zips through your pockets. Be especially careful in the big cities in port areas. Either carry your money, credit cards and documents in a money belt or leave them in the hotel, preferably in the safe. A photocopy of your passport will usually suffice for identification; keep the original locked up.

Parked cars and motorbikes, as well as the contents of vehicles (especially those cars with a rental-company sticker or out-of-town, red-coloured purchase-repurchase or foreign plates) are favourite targets. Never, ever leave anything inside your car. Even a few old clothes, a handkerchief or an umbrella left lying in the backseat might attract the attention of a passing thief, who won't think twice about breaking a window or smashing a lock to see if there's a camera hidden underneath.

Tides along the Brittany and Normandy coastline are among the biggest and most powerful in the world. If you plan to explore any low-tide area, or an island accessible only at low tide, make sure you know the tide times. Always check with the local tourist office. Don't go swimming from a beach unless you are sure it is safe – again, ask locally. Undertows and tidal currents can easily sweep you out to sea.

Although the rocky coasts look appealing, huge swells can roll in from the Atlantic – even when the weather is fine – and sweep unsuspecting hikers and anglers from rocks a few metres above the water level. Take care.

DISABLED TRAVELLERS

France is not particularly well equipped for *handicapés* (disabled people); kerb ramps are few and far between, older public facilities and budget hotels often lack lifts, and cobblestone streets are a nightmare to navigate in a wheelchair. But people with mobility problems who would like to visit France can overcome these problems. Most hotels with two or more stars are equipped with lifts and Michelin's *Guide Rouge* indicates hotels with facilities for disabled people.

In recent years the national rail company, SNCF, has made efforts to make its trains more accessible to people with physical disabilities. A traveller in a *fauteuil roulant* (wheelchair) can journey in the wheelchair on both TGV and regular trains provided they make a reservation by phone or at a train station at least a few hours before departure. Details are in SNCF's booklet *Guide du Voyageur à Mobilité Réduite*. You can also contact **SNCF Accessibilité** (☎ 0800 15 47 53 toll free).

General publications are useful:

Gîtes Accessibles aux Personnes Handicapés A guide in French to holiday cottages and B&Bs with disabled access. It is published by Gîtes de France (see p316).

Holidays and Travel Abroad: A Guide for Disabled People An annual publication that gives a good overview of facilities available to disabled travellers in Europe. Published in even-numbered years by the **Royal Association for Disability & Rehabilitation** (Radar; ☎ 020-7250 3222; www.radar.org.uk; 12 City Forum, 250 City Rd, London EC1V 8AF)

DISCOUNT CARDS
Senior Cards

Reduced admission prices are charged for people aged over 60 at most cultural centres, including museums, galleries and public theatres. SNCF issues the **Carte Senior** to those aged over 60, which gives reductions of 20% to 50% on train tickets. See the boxed text (p337) for further information.

Student & Youth Cards

An **International Student Identity Card** (ISIC; €12) can pay for itself through half-price admissions, discounted air and ferry tickets, and cheap meals in student cafeterias. Many places stipulate a maximum age, usually 24 or 25. In Nantes and Rouen ISIC cards are issued by the Centre Régional d'Information Jeunesse (CRIJ). For more details, check the **International Student Travel Confederation** (ISTC; www.istc.org) website.

If you're under 26 but not a student, you can apply for an **International Youth Travel Card** (ITYC), also issued by ISTC, giving much the same discounts as an ISIC. You can buy one (€12) from student unions or student travel agencies. The **European Youth Card** (Euro<26 card) offers similar discounts across 35 European countries for nonstudents under 26 (see www.euro26.org).

Teachers, professional artists, museum conservators and certain categories of students are admitted to some museums free. Bring along proof of affiliation, for example, an **International Teacher Identity Card** (ITIC).

EMBASSIES & CONSULATES
French Embassies & Consulates
Don't expect France's diplomatic and consular representatives abroad to be helpful or even civil at times, though you do come across the odd exception. Visa and other travel information is posted on the website www.france.diplomatie.fr. Contact details for some embassies follow.

Australia Embassy (☎ 02-6216 0100; www.ambafrance -au.org; 6 Perth Ave; Yarralumla, ACT 2600) Consulates in Adelaide, Brisbane, Canberra, Darwin, Hobart, Melbourne, Perth and Sydney.

Belgium Embassy (☎ 02-548 8711; www.ambafrance -be.org 65 rue Ducale, 1000 Brussels)

Canada Embassy (☎ 613-789 1795; www.ambafrance-ca .org; 42 Sussex Dr, Ottawa, Ont K1M 2C9) Consulates in Montreal, Québec, Toronto, Moncton, Halifax, Calgary, Chicoutimi, Edmonton, North-Sydney, Regina, Rouyn-Noranda, Jean du Nouveau Brunswick, Vancouver and Winnipeg.

Germany Embassy (☎ 030-590 039 000; www.botschaft -frankreich.de; Pariser Platz 5, D-10117 Berlin) Consulates in Breme, Dusseldorf, Frankfurt, Freiburg, Hannover, Hamburg, Mannheim, Munich, Sarrebruck and Stuttgart.

Ireland Embassy (☎ 01-277 5000; www.ambafrance-ie .org; 36 Ailesbury Rd, Ballsbridge, Dublin 4) Consulates in Cork, Dunway, Galway and Limerick.

Italy Embassy (☎ 06-686 011; www.france-italia.it; Piazza Farnese 67, 00186 Rome) Consulates in Florence, Genoa, Milan, Naples, Turin and Venice.

Netherlands Embassy (☎ 070-312 5800; www.amba france-nl.org; Smidsplein 1, 2514 BT, The Hague) Consulates in Amsterdam and Utrecht.

New Zealand Embassy (☎ 04-384 2555; www.amba france-nz.org; Rural Bank Bldg, 34-42 Manners St, Wellington) Consulates in Auckland and Christchurch.

South Africa Embassy (☎ 012-425 1600; www.amba france-rsa.org; 250 Melk St, New Muckleneuk 0181, Pretoria) Consulates in Durban, Johannesburg and Port Elizabeth.

Spain Embassy (☎ 91-423 8900; www.ambafrance-es .org; Calle de Salustiano, Olozaga 9, 28001 Madrid) Consulate in Barcelona.

Switzerland Embassy (☎ 031-359 2111; www.amba france-ch.org; Schosshaldenstrasse 46, 3006 Berne) Consulates in Geneva and Zurich.

UK (www.ambafrance.org.uk) Embassy (☎ 020-7073 1000; 58 Knightsbridge, London SW1X 7JT); Consulate (☎ 020-7073 1250; 21 Cromwell Rd, London SW7 2EN); Visa Section (☎ 020-7838 2051; 6A Cromwell Pl, London SW7 2EW). Other consulates in Aberdeen, Belfast, Brighton, Cardiff, Chester, Dover, Dundee, Edinburgh, Gibraltar, Guernsey, Glasgow, Jersey, Leeds, Liverpool, Manchester, Newcastle, Norwich, Nottingham, Plymouth and Portsmouth.

USA Embassy (☎ 202-944 6000; www.ambafrance-usa .org; 4101 Reservoir Rd NW, Washington DC 20007) Consulates in Anchorage, Atlanta, Austin, Birmingham, Boise, Boston, Chicago, Houston, Los Angeles, Miami, New York New Orleans and San Francisco.

Embassies & Consulates in France
All foreign embassies can be found in Paris. Canada, the UK and the USA also have consulates in other major cities.

To find an embassy or consulate not listed here, consult the *Yellow Pages* (Pages Jaunes; look under 'Ambassades et Consulats') in Paris.

Countries with representation in Paris include the following:

Australia Embassy (☎ 01 40 59 33 00; www.austgov.fr; 4 rue Jean Rey, 15e; metro Bir Hakeim)

Belgium Embassy (☎ 01 44 09 39 39; www.diplobel.org /france/; 9 rue de Tilsitt, 17e; metro Charles de Gaulle-Étoile)

Canada Embassy (☎ 01 44 43 29 00; www.amb-canada.fr; 35 ave Montaigne, 8e; metro Franklin D Roosevelt)

Germany Embassy (☎ 01 53 83 45 00; www.amb-alle magne.fr; 13-15 ave Franklin D Roosevelt, 8e; metro Franklin D Roosevelt)

Ireland Embassy (☎ 01 44 17 67 00; 4 rue Rude, 16e; metro Argentine)

Italy Embassy (☎ 01 49 54 03 00; 51 rue de Varenne, 7e; metro rue du Bac)

Netherlands Embassy (☎ 01 40 62 33 00; www.amb -pays-bas.fr; 7 rue Eblé, 7e; metro St-François Xavier)

New Zealand Embassy (☎ 01 45 01 43 43; www.nzembas sy.com; 7 ter rue Léonard de Vinci, 16e; metro Victor Hugo)

Spain Embassy (☎ 01 44 43 18 00; www.amb-espagne.fr; 22 ave Marceau, 8e; metro Alma Marceau)

Switzerland Embassy (☎ 01 49 55 67 00; www.eda .admin.ch/paris/embassy/; 142 rue de Grenelle, 7e; metro Varenne)

UK (www.amb-grandebretagne.fr) Embassy (☎ 01 44 51 31 00; 35 rue du Faubourg St-Honoré, 8e; metro Concorde); Consulate (☎ 01 44 51 31 00; 16 bis rue d'Anjou, 8e; metro Madeleine) Consular representation in Cherbourg, Le Havre, Lorient, Nantes and St-Malo.

USA (www.amb-usa.fr) Embassy (☎ 01 43 12 22 22; 2 ave Gabriel, 8e; metro Concorde); Consulate (☎ 01 43 12 47 08; 2 rue St-Florentin, 8e; metro Concorde) Consular represent ation in Rennes.

FESTIVALS & EVENTS

Most cities in Normandy and Brittany have at least one major music, dance, theatre, cinema or art festival each year and many are held in summer. Brittany's special culture is manifested in a kaleidoscope of colourful festivals. Some villages hold *foires* (fairs) and *fêtes* (festivals) to honour anything from a local saint to the *coquille St-Jacques* (scallop). Many of the festivities have their roots in religion – notably the many religious *pardons* (p31) for which Brittany is famous – but others are resolutely secular and celebrate Celtic music and culture (see p32). Others focus on a pillar of the local economy, often fishing. Normandy celebrates its maritime tradition, its luscious seafood and also throws a glance at culture with a few important film festivals.

In this book, important annual events are listed under Festivals & Events in many city and town listings; for precise details about dates, which may change from year to year, contact the local tourist office. Remember that the largest festivals can make it very difficult to find accommodation, so make reservations as far in advance as possible.

D-DAY COMMEMORATIONS

On 6 June many towns in Normandy and some in Brittany have small ceremonies in which veterans' groups lay wreaths at the local war memorial. Along the D-Day beaches, the commemorations can be more elaborate and often involve visiting veterans' groups. To find out about specific locales and activities, check on the website at www .normandiememoire.com.

EQUI-DAYS IN CALVADOS

The essential horsiness of Calvados is on display for two weeks on October. Look for horse shows, races, sales and events in Cabourg, Caen, Deauville, Falaise, Lisieux and Vire. For more information, consult www .equidays.com.

FOOD

In this book we've used the term budget to describe places where you can grab a meal for less than €15; mid-range places cost between €15 and €30, while a top-end place will cost over €30 a head.

For more on what to eat in Brittany and Normandy, see Food & Drink (p50).

GAY & LESBIAN TRAVELLERS

France is one of Europe's most liberal countries when it comes to homosexuality, in part because of the long French tradition of public tolerance towards groups of people who choose not to live by conventional social codes. Predictably, attitudes towards homosexuality tend to be more conservative in the countryside than in the large cities. France's lesbian scene is much less public than its gay counterpart and is centred mainly around women's cafés and bars.

Têtu is a monthly national magazine that is available at newsstands everywhere. Be on the lookout for *e.m@le*, which has interviews, gossip and articles (in French) and among the best listings of gay clubs, bars and associations and personal classifieds. It is available free at gay venues. Also check out the website http://cybergay.nfrance.com (French only).

Guidebooks listing pubs, discos, restaurants, beaches, saunas, sex shops and cruising areas include *Spartacus International Gay Guide* – a male-only guide to travelling the world.

The monthly national magazine *Lesbia* provides a run-down of what's happening around France. *Les Nanas*, a freebie appearing every other month, is for women only. Both are in French only.

Écoute Gaie (☎ 01 44 93 01 02; ☉ 6-10pm Mon-Fri & 6-8pm Sat) is a national hotline for gays and lesbians. **SOS Homophobie** (☎ 01 48 06 42 41; ☉ 8-10pm Mon-Fri) accepts anonymous calls concerning discriminatory acts against gay people.

GOVERNMENT

Brittany, Upper Normandy and Lower Normandy are three of the 22 *régions* created by the French government for administrative purposes in 1972. Each is governed by a Conseil Régional with members elected to office every five years. Each *région* is divided into *départements*. In Brittany the four *départements* are Ille-et-Vilaine, Côtes d'Armor, Finistère and Morbihan – much to the annoyance of Breton nationalists, who still mourn the loss of Loire-Atlantique, which was transferred to the Pays de la Loire in 1941. Upper Normandy consists of the Seine-Maritime and Eure, whereas Lower Normandy consists of the Manche, Calvados and the Orne. Within the *départements*

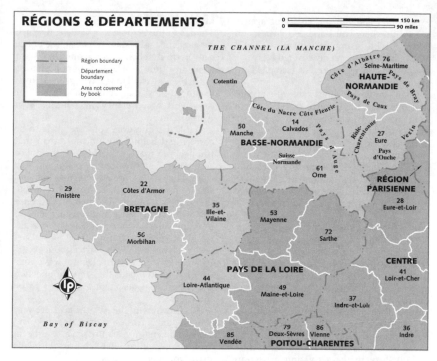

RÉGIONS & DÉPARTEMENTS

of Normandy, there are a number of areas *(pays)* that serve no administrative purpose but reflect various geographical and geological features. The Pays d'Auge, le Perche, Pays de Bray, Pays de Risle-Charentonne, Pays d'Ouche, Suisse Normande, Cotentin, Côte d'Albâtre, Côte Fleuri and Pays de Caux are some of the regions-within-regions mentioned in this book.

HOLIDAYS
Public Holidays
The following *jours fériés* (public holidays) are observed in France:
New Year's Day (Jour de l'An) 1 January – parties in larger cities, fireworks tend to be subdued by international standards
Easter Sunday & Monday (Pâques & lundi de Pâques) Late March/April
May Day (Fête du Travail) 1 May – traditional parades
Victoire 1945 8 May – celebrates the Allied victory in Europe that ended WWII
Ascension Thursday (L'Ascension) May – celebrated on the 40th day after Easter
Pentecost/Whit Sunday & Whit Monday (Pentecôte & lundi de Pentecôte) Mid-May to mid-June – celebrated on the 7th Sunday after Easter

Bastille Day/National Day (Fête Nationale) 14 July – the national holiday
Assumption Day (L'Assomption) 15 August
All Saints' Day (La Toussaint) 1 November
Remembrance Day (Le Onze Novembre) 11 November – celebrates the WWI armistice
Christmas (Noël) 25 December

Most French museums and shops are closed on public holidays. Cinemas, restaurants or most bakeries are not. When a holiday falls on a Tuesday or a Thursday, the French have a custom of making a *pont* (bridge) to the nearest weekend by taking off Monday or Friday as well. The doors of banks are a good place to look for announcements of upcoming long weekends.

INSURANCE
You should seriously consider taking out travel insurance. This covers you for medical expenses and luggage theft or loss, as well as for cancellation or delays in your travel arrangements (including ticket loss). The level of cover depends on your insurance and type of airline ticket, so ask both

your insurer and your ticket-issuing agency to explain where you stand. EU citizens on public health-insurance schemes should note that they're generally covered by reciprocal arrangements in France (see p344 for more details).

Paying for your airline ticket with a credit card often provides limited travel accident insurance and you might be able to reclaim the payment if the operator doesn't deliver. In the UK, for instance, institutions issuing credit cards are required by law to reimburse consumers if a company goes into liquidation and the amount in contention is more than UK£100. Ask your credit-card company what it's prepared to cover.

INTERNET ACCESS

Around 1000 post offices across France are equipped with a Cyberposte, a modern, card-operated Internet terminal for public use – mostly stylish Apple iMacs, *naturellement*. This is about the cheapest reliable way to check your emails in France. To use the Cyberposte – restricted to post-office opening hours (see p320) – buy a chip card at the counter for €7.60, which includes an hour's connection time, and go through the activation procedure (you'll need a post office staff member for this part). When the card's exhausted you can recharge it for €4.50, good for another hour. There's a list of post offices with a Cyberposte at www.laposte.net (in French). Post offices with Cyberposte are noted in the text.

Otherwise you can seek out one of the growing ranks of Internet cafés in French towns. They aren't cheap: expect to pay €3 to €4.50 for 30 minutes of Web surfing (note that some places charge by the minute). The more reliable outlets are listed in the destinations sections of the text.

Another solution for keeping in touch by email is to seek out one of the increasingly numerous Bornes Netanoo, managed by France Telecom. These Internet posts are scattered around the region (usually in the larger cities) in supermarkets, tourist offices, hotels, bars and other public places. They work with a *télécarte* (see p329) at the same cost (ie €2.40/3 for a 120-/50-unit card) and are broken down into three-minute units. For a list of outlets, see www.neta noo.com (in French).

LEGAL MATTERS

Thanks to the Napoleonic Code (on which the French legal system is based), the police can pretty much search anyone they want to at any time – whether or not there is probable cause. They have been known to stop and search chartered coaches for drugs just because they are coming from Amsterdam.

If asked a question, cops are likely to be correct and helpful but no more than that (though you may get a salute). If the police stop you for any reason, be polite and stay calm. They have wide powers of search and seizure and, if they take a dislike to you, they may choose to use them. The police can, without any particular reason, decide to examine your passport, visa, *carte de séjour* (residence permit) and so on.

French police are very strict about security, especially at airports. Do not leave your baggage unattended: they're serious when they warn that suspicious objects will be blown up.

As elsewhere in the EU, the laws are very tough when it comes to drinking and driving and for many years the slogan has been: 'Boire ou conduire, il faut choisir' (Drink or drive, you have to choose). The legal blood-alcohol limit is 0.05% and drivers exceeding this amount face fines of up to €4500 plus up to two years in jail. Licences can be suspended immediately.

MAPS

Road maps and city maps are available at Maisons de la Presse (large newsagents found all over the region), bookshops and even some newsstands. Check with the local tourist offices, which often have easy-to-read and helpful town maps, as well as maps that detai interesting itineraries. Where relevant, advice on maps and where to buy them is given the city or town listings throughout this guide.

Road Maps

A variety of *cartes routiéres* (road maps) are available, but if you're driving a lot the best road atlas is Michelin's yellow-jacketed 1:200,000-scale fold-out map No 230. IGN's *Carte Touristique Locale* series covers all of Brittany at a scale of 1:100,000 in five maps (Nos 13, 14, 15, 16 and 24; green covers) and the No 231 map of Normandy.

DIRECTORY

City Maps

Rare is the town or village in France whose tourist office doesn't provide a free map for travellers. They can be of surprisingly good quality as well as quite detailed. Blay-Foldex issues a range of orange-jacketed town maps with helpful street indexes; its main competitor is Grafocarte's blue *Plans Bleu & Or*. With a scale of at least 1:10,000, the maps are easy to read and also cover the towns' outskirts.

Walking & Cycling Maps

The IGN *Bleu* series covers all of Brittany's walking trails at a 1:25,000 scale. The *Top 25* series covers the coast and islands, and includes information about tourist offices, camping and horse trails. There's also an IGN *Plein Air* series map that covers the Golfe du Morbihan and Belle-Île-en-Mer with information on various outdoor activities. IGN map No 906, *France – VTT & Randonnées Cyclos*, indicates dozens of suggested bicycle tours of rural France and includes Brittany.

The Fédération Française de la Randonnée Pédestre (FFRP) publishes 13 topoguides covering many of the major walks throughout the region.

Didier et Richard publishes a series of 1:50,000-scale trail maps, which are perfect for hoofing it or cycling.

MONEY
Currency

On 18 February 2002 France ditched the franc and embraced the euro. Francs can be changed at branches of the Banque de France until 17 February 2005 for coins and 17 February 2012 for banknotes.

There are seven euro notes in different colours and sizes; they come in denominations of €5, €10, €20, €50, €100, €200 and €500. Try to keep them in denominations below €50 as large bills can be difficult to change. There are eight euro coins, in denominations of one, two, five, 10, 20 and 50 cents, then €1 and €2. Although France and the other euro zone countries have decorated the coins with their own designs, all euro coins can be used anywhere that accepts euros.

See the inside back cover for a handy table to help you calculate the exchange rate. See p9 for information on costs.

Exchanging Money

Wherever you change money, you can tell how good the rate is by checking the spread between the rates for *achat* (buying – what they'll give you for foreign cash or travellers cheques) and *vente* (selling – the rate at which they sell foreign currency to people going abroad). The greater the difference, the further each is from the interbank rate (printed daily in newspapers, including the *International Herald Tribune*).

Banks, post offices and exchange bureaux often give a better rate for travellers cheques than for cash. Major train stations and fancy hotels have exchange facilities, which usually operate in the evening, at the weekend and during holidays, but the rates are often poor. Rates are generally good in post offices.

Bring along the equivalent of about US$100 in low-denomination notes (which makes it easier to change small sums of money if necessary). Because of the risk of counterfeiting it may be difficult to change US$100 notes.

Commercial banks usually charge a stiff €3 to €5.50 per foreign currency transaction. The rates offered vary so it pays to compare.

TRAVELLERS CHEQUES & EUROCHEQUES

Note that you will not be able to pay merchants directly in travellers cheques, even if they are in euros. The most flexible travellers cheques are issued by American Express and Visa – they can be changed at many post offices. American Express offices don't charge commission on their own travellers cheques (but 3% or at least €6 on other brands). If your American Express travellers cheques are lost or stolen in France, call ☎ 0800 90 86 00 (24-hour toll free).

If you lose your Thomas Cook cheques, contact any Thomas Cook bureau or its customer-service bureau on ☎ 0800 90 83 30 (toll free).

ATMs

Known in French as DABs (*distributeurs automatiques de billets*) or *points d'argent*, ATMs can draw on your home account at a superior exchange rate. Most ATMs will also give you a cash advance through your Visa or MasterCard (see the Credit Cards & Debit Cards section following). You must have a four-digit PIN code. There are plenty of ATMs linked to the international Cirrus, Plus and Maestro networks. If you normally remember your PIN code as a string of letters, translate it back into numbers, as keyboards may not have letters indicated. When you get a cash advance, many banks charge a commission of €4.50 or more.

CREDIT CARDS & DEBIT CARDS

Overall, the cheapest way to pay during your stay in Brittany and Normandy is by credit or debit card. Visa (Carte Bleue) is the most widely accepted, followed by MasterCard (Access or Eurocard). American Express cards are only useful at more upmarket establishments.

It might be impossible to get a lost Visa or MasterCard reissued until you get home, so two different credit cards are safer than one. If your Visa card is lost or stolen, call **Carte Bleue** (☎ 0836 69 08 80, 0800 90 20 33, both 24hr). To get a replacement card you'll have to deal with the issuer.

Report a lost MasterCard, Eurocard or Access to **Eurocard France** (☎ 0800 90 13 87) and, if you can, to your credit-card issuer back home (for cards from the USA, call ☎ 314-275 6690 in the USA).

If your American Express card is lost or stolen, call ☎ 0800 900 888 (24 hours). American Express card holders from the USA can call collect (reverse charges) on ☎ 202-783 7474 or ☎ 202-677 2442. On-the-spot replacements can be arranged at any American Express office.

Report lost Diners Club cards on ☎ 0820 000 764.

PHOTOGRAPHY & VIDEO

Unlike the rest of Western Europe and Australia, which use PAL, and the USA, which uses NTSC, French TV broadcasts are in SECAM format. French videotapes can't be played on non-SECAM video recorders and TVs. In case you are tempted to buy DVDs of French movies, remember that they are coded to prevent disks bought in one region from playing on machines bought in another country. France and Europe are coded for region two, the USA and Canada are region one and Australasia is region four. Some (few) DVDs have not been coded and will play on any system. Check the back of the package for details. Some DVD players are multisystem and others can be modified .

Film & Equipment

Colour-print film produced by Kodak and Fuji is widely available in supermarkets, photo shops and FNAC stores. It's fairly expensive in France compared to a lot of other countries so it does pay to stock up before you leave home. One-hour developing is widely available. Getting a roll of film developed (24 exposures) costs anywhere between €8 and €13. Photographic services are often cheaper in the main towns and cities. For slides *(diapositives)*, stay away from Kodachrome; it's difficult to process quickly in France and can give you lots of headaches if not handled properly.

You can obtain video cartridges for your video camera easily in large towns but it's usually worth buying a few from home.

Airports are all fully equipped with modern inspection systems that do not damage most film or other photographic material that is carried in hand luggage.

For tips on how to make the most of your camera during your travels try Lonely Planet's *Travel Photography*.

POST

Postal services in France are fast, reliable, bureaucratic and expensive. About three-quarters of domestic letters arrive the day after they've been mailed. Each of France's 17,000 post offices is marked with a yellow or brown 'La Poste' sign; older branches may also be marked with the letters PTT. The notation 'Cedex' after a town name simply means that mail sent to that address is collected at the post office, rather than delivered to the door.

Worldwide express-mail delivery, called **Chronopost** (☎ 08 25 80 18 01), costs a fortune – around €50 for a 1kg parcel to EU countries!

To have mail sent to you via poste restante (general delivery), which is available at all French post offices, have it addressed as follows:

SMITH, Jane
Poste Restante
Recette Principale
76000 Rouen
France

There's a €0.50 charge for every piece of poste restante mail you pick up weighing less than 20g; for anything between 20g and

100g, the fee is €0.90. You'll need to present your passport or national ID card when you pick up your mail.

SOLO TRAVELLERS

The joy of travelling solo is that it is a compromise-free trip. You do what you want when you want to do it but you will pay for the privilege. Very few hotels have special rates for singles, although you may be able to knock a few euros off the double-room price. If you find that dining out alone is a forlorn experience, make lunch the main meal of your day when the dining room is more likely to contain solo business diners. Solo diners can often get short shrift but if you take out a notebook and start writing you might be mistaken for restaurant critic. Your treatment will improve dramatically.

TELEPHONE

If you do not know the required country code *(indicatif pays)* and it's not posted in the telephone cabin, consult a telephone book or dial ☎ 12 (directory inquiries). International Direct Dial (IDD) calls to almost anywhere in the world can be made from public telephones. Faxes can be sent from most post offices.

To make a reverse-charge (collect) call or a person-to-person call dial ☎ 3123 or ☎ 0800 990 011 (for the USA and Canada) and ☎ 0800 990 061 for Australia. Expect to pay about €12 for a three-minute call.

For France Telecom's directory inquiries *(services des renseignements)*, dial ☎ 12. Not all operators speak English. The call is free from public phones but costs a breathtaking €1.70 from private lines (for one or two numbers). You can not make domestic reverse-charge calls.

For directory inquiries for numbers outside France, dial ☎ 3212. The cost is about €2.50. If you make telephone calls from your hotel room none of the above rates applies. Hotels, *gîtes*, hostels, and *pensions* are free to meter their calls as they like. The surcharge is usually around €0.30 per minute but can be higher.

Telephone Cards

Nearly all the public telephones in France require a phonecard *(télécarte)*, which can be purchased at post offices, *tabacs* (tobacconists) and anywhere you see a blue sticker

reading 'télécarte en vente ici'. Cards worth 50/120 calling units cost €7.50/15.

You can purchase prepaid phonecards in France that make calling abroad cheaper than with a standard *télécarte*. France Telecom's Le Ticket de Téléphone, the Carte Intercall Monde and Carte Astuce are among the more popular cards, and offer up to 60% off standard French international call rates. You should be able to make a one-minute call to Europe and North America for €0.15, and to Australasia for €0.29. Because they work with numbers and codes rather than magnetic chips, they can be used from your hotel room as well as public phones.

Phone Codes

France is divided into five telephone-dialling areas. You dial the same 10-digit number no matter where you are but calls from one dialling area to another are more expensive. There are five regional area codes:
- ☎ 01 the Paris region
- ☎ 02 the northwest
- ☎ 03 the northeast
- ☎ 04 the southeast (including Corsica)
- ☎ 05 the southwest

Domestic Rates

Domestic rates are billed at about €0.15 for three minutes with a *télécarte* but there are many numbers beginning with 08 that are billed at special rates. Emergency numbers and 0800 numbers can be dial from public telephones without inserting a *télécarte*.

Mobile Phones

France uses GSM 900/1800, which is compatible with the rest of Europe and Australia but not with the North American GSM 1900 nor the entirely different system used in Japan (but some North Americans have GSM 1900/900 phones that do work here). If you have a GSM phone, check with your service provider about using it in France, and beware of calls being routed internationally (very expensive for a 'local' call).

A prepaid *mobicarte* is cheaper. Sold by France Telecom, this deal costs from €79 for the cellular phone and €10 worth of included time. For more time you buy a recharge card for €15, €25 or €35 from tobacconists and places you'd buy a phonecard. Check out the website at www.orange.fr (French only) and click on the 'Découvrez la mobicarte' link.

Mobile phone numbers begin with 06 and France has a caller pays system which means that you do not pay to receive a call on your mobile phone unless it's an international call but you pay as a caller.

Minitel
Minitel is a screen-based information service peculiar to France, set up in the 1980s. Many post offices have minitels which are either free or paid through a phonecard. For a traveller, the most useful service is 3511 which allows you to find addresses and phone numbers throughout France.

TOURIST INFORMATION
Local Tourist Offices
Every city, town, village and hamlet seems to have either an *office de tourisme* (a tourist office run by some unit of local government) or a *syndicat d'initiative* (a tourist office run by an organisation of local merchants). Both are excellent resources and can almost always provide a local map at the very least. Some will also change foreign currency (especially when banks are closed), although the rate is rarely good, and will make local hotel reservations, sometimes for a small fee.

Details on local tourist offices appear under Information at the beginning of each city, town or area listing in this guide.

There are also *département* tourist offices that are invaluable sources of information when planning your trip. Tourist offices have compiled lists of companies and individuals offering outdoor activities, off-the-beaten-track accommodation and special tours. Most of the more general brochures are in English, but the brochures in French are also helpful in locating addresses. If you have a special interest, it pays to contact the relevant tourist office before your visit since whatever information you're looking for undoubtedly appears in one of the region's countless brochures. Address your request to the Comité Départemental de Tourisme:

BRITTANY
Côtes d'Armor (☎ 02 96 62 72 00; www.cotesdarmor .com; 7 rue St-Benoît, BP 4620, 22046 St-Brieuc Cedex 2)
Finistère (☎ 02 98 76 20 70; www.finisteretourisme.com; 11 rue Théodore Le Hars, BP 1419, 29104 Quimper Cedex)
Ille-et-Vilaine (☎ 02 99 78 47 47; www.bretagne35 .com; 4 rue Jean Jaurès, BP 6046, 35060 Rennes Cedex 3)

Morbihan (☎ 02 97 54 06 56; www.morbihan.com; Hôtel du Département, BP 400, 56009 Vannes Cedex)
Loire-Atlantique (☎ 02 51 72 95 30; www.cdt44.com; 2 allée Baco, 45005 Nantes, BP 20502)

For information on the region as a whole, contact **Comité Régional de Tourisme de Bretagne** (☎ 02 99 28 44 30; www.brittanytourism.com; 1 rue Raoul Ponchon, 35069 Rennes Cedex).

NORMANDY
Seine-Maritime (☎ 02 35 12 10 10; www.seine -maritime-tourisme.com - French only; 6 rue Couronné, BP 60, 76420 Bihorel-les-Rouen)
Eure (☎ 02 32 62 04 27; www.cdt-eure.fr; rue du Commandant Letellier BP 367, 27003 Évreux)
Calvados (☎ 02 31 27 90 30; www.calvados-tourisme .com - French only; 8 rue Renoir 1404 Caen Cedex)
Manche (☎ 02 33 05 98 70; www.manchetourisme.com; Maison du Département, 50008 St-Lô Cedex)
Orne (☎ 02 33 28 88 71; www.ornetourisme.com; 88 rue St-Blaise, BP 50, 61002 Alençon Cedex)

For information on the entire Normandy region, contact **Comité Régional de Tourisme** (☎ 02 32 33 79 00; www.normandy-tourism.org; Le Doyenné, 14 rue Charles Corbeau, 27000 Évreux).

VISAS
Tourist Visas
There are no entry requirements for EU nationals. Citizens of Australia, the USA, Canada, New Zealand and Israel do not need visas to visit France as tourists for up to three months. Except for people from a handful of other European countries (including Switzerland and Poland), everyone else needs a Schengen Visa, named after the Schengen Agreement that abolished passport controls among Belgium, France, Germany, Luxembourg, the Netherlands, Austria, Denmark, Finland, Greece, Iceland, Italy, Norway, Portugal, Spain and Sweden. A visa for any of these countries should, in theory, be valid throughout the area, but it pays to double-check with the embassy or consulate of the countries you intend to visit.

If you do need a visa, fees depend on the current exchange rate, but a transit visa, a visa valid for up to 30 days, and a single or multiple-entry visa of up to three months costs €35. You will need your passport (valid for a period of three months beyond the date of your departure from France), a return ticket, proof of sufficient funds to support yourself, some proof of prearranged accommodation (possibly), two passport-sized photos and the visa fee in cash.

If all the forms are in order, your visa will be issued on the spot. South African visas take two days to process. You can also apply for a French visa after arriving in Europe – the fee is the same but you may not have to produce a return ticket. If you enter France overland, your visa may not be checked at the border, but major problems can arise if you don't have one later on (for example, at the airport as you leave the country).

Long-Stay & Student Visas

If you'd like to work or study in France or stay for over three months, apply to the French embassy or consulate nearest where you live for the appropriate sort of *long séjour* (long-stay) visa. Unless you live in the EU, it's extremely difficult to get a visa that will allow you to work in France. For any sort of long-stay visa, begin the paperwork in your home country several months before you plan to leave. Applications cannot usually be made in a third country nor can tourist visas be turned into student visas after you arrive in France. People with student visas can apply for permission to work part-time (inquire at your place of study).

If you are issued a long-stay visa valid for six or more months, you'll probably have to apply for a *carte de séjour* within eight days of arrival in France. For details, ask at your place of study or the local *préfecture*.

Tourist visas *cannot* be extended except in emergencies (such as medical problems). If you have an urgent problem, you should get in touch with the local *préfecture*. If you need a visa to enter France, you'll need to leave, re-apply and re-enter when it expires. Make sure to get your passport stamped when you leave the country (or any other EU/Schengen country) so you can't be suspected of overstaying your visa, which would preclude you from getting another one.

As a practical matter, if you don't need a visa to visit France you can stay as long as you like. The days of travelling to Geneva or Brussels to get a stamp on your passport are past. Just don't try to work, get social services or commit a crime. Without the *carte de séjour*, however, you can face real problems renting an apartment, opening a bank account or getting car insurance.

People entering France by rail or road often don't have their passports checked, much less stamped, and even at airports don't be surprised if the official just glances at your passport and hands it back without stamping the date of entry. If you prefer to have your passport stamped (for example, because you expect to have to prove when you last entered the country), it may take a bit of running around to find the right official.

If you are serious about living and working in France on a long-term basis, it pays to consult a qualified immigration attorney in France who can advise you on surmounting some of the hurdles. Your consulate may be able to provide a list of names.

WOMEN TRAVELLERS

Women tend to attract more unwanted attention than men, but female travellers need not walk around in fear: people are rarely assaulted on the street. If you're going to be harassed anywhere, it would probably be on the train, particularly on an overnight journey. Don't hesitate to ask the conductor to change your couchette compartment if you feel uncomfortable. A two- or three-person sleeping compartment affords greater privacy and security than a *couchette*.

As a general rule, the more you pay for your hotel room, the less likely you are to be harassed. Cheap hotels staffed by apparently unattached men might pay far more attention to your comings and goings than you would like. Be alert to the vibes when you check in. If it's not feasible to find another arrangement, make it clear that you are married (even if you're not) preferably to someone involved in law enforcement who may be arriving soon. Be careful about inviting unknown men to your hotel room as date rape is unlikely to be taken seriously.

WORK

With an unemployment rate of over 9% and laws that forbid non-EU nationals from working in France, working 'in the black' (that is, without any documents) is difficult. People without documents probably have their best chance of finding work as an au pair, which can be done by non-EU citizens. For practical information, pick up *The Au Pair and Nanny's Guide to Working Abroad* by Susan Griffith and Sharon Legg. Another option is to look for work as a courier for one of the package-tour companies bringing Brits to Brittany or Normandy for short holidays. Look in the classified ads of major newspapers starting in early February.

Non-EU nationals cannot work legally unless they obtain a work permit *(autorisation de travail)* before landing in France. Obtaining a work permit is not easy, because a prospective employer has to convince the authorities that there is no French – and, increasingly these days, no EU – citizen who can do the job being offered to you.

For practical information on employment in France, you might want to pick up a copy of *Living and Working in France* by David Hampshire.

Nationals of EU and EEA countries have the right to work in France without special authorization.

Employment Agencies

The Centre Régional d'Information Jeunesse (CRIJ), which provides all sorts of information for young people on housing, professional training and educational options, have notice boards with work possibilities and works with the Agence National pour l'Emploi (ANPE), France's national employment service (whose services are available to all EU citizens). For details on CRIJ offices see the Information sections of Caen (p257) and Rouen(p203).

Transport

CONTENTS

Getting There & Away	**333**
Land	335
Sea	337
Getting Around	**339**
Bicycle	339
Bus	340
Car & Motorcycle	340
Local Transport	342
Train	342

GETTING THERE & AWAY

AIR

Although there several airports in Brittany and Normandy, there are few international flights. Most international visitors enter through Paris via either Charles de Gaulle or Orly airport. France is a heavily touristed destination, making it wise to book ahead, especially if you are travelling around Christmas, Easter or any time during the summer holiday period. If you are travelling from one of France's far-flung *départements* (Guadeloupe, Martinique, Mauritius,

WARNING

The information in this chapter is particularly vulnerable to change: prices for international travel are volatile, routes are introduced and cancelled, schedules change, special deals come and go, and rules and visa requirements are amended. You should check directly with the airline or a travel agent to make sure you understand how a fare (and ticket you may buy) works and be aware of the security requirements for international travel.

The upshot of this is that you should get opinions, quotes and advice from as many airlines and travel agents as possible before you part with your hard-earned cash. Details given in this chapter should be regarded as pointers and are not a substitute for your own careful, up-to-date research.

Réunion, French Guiana) or territories in the South Pacific (Tahiti, New Caledonia), be aware that flights may be booked solid many months in advance.

Airports & Airlines

France's main international gateway is Paris, with three airports: Charles de Gaulle, Orly and Beauvais. Airports in Rouen, Caen, Cherbourg and Le Havre serve the local market in Normandy, and there are local airports at Brest, Lannion, Lorient, Quimper and St-Brieuc in Brittany.

Beauvais (code BVA; ☎ 08 92 68 20 66, 03 44 11 46 66; www.aeroportbeauvais.com)

Brest (code BES; ☎ 02 98 32 01 00; www.airport.cci-brest.fr)

Caen (code CFR; ☎ 02 31 71 20 10; www.caen.aeroport.fr - French only)

Charles de Gaulle (code CDG; ☎ 01 48 62 22 80; www.paris-cdg.com)

Cherbourg (code CER; ☎ 02 33 23 32 00; www.aeroport-cherbourg.com)

Dinard (code DNR; ☎ 08 25 08 35 09)

La Rochelle (code LRH; ☎ 05 46 42 30 26; www.larochelle.aeroport.fr - French only)

Le Havre (code LEH; ☎ 02 35 54 65 00; www.havre.aeroport.fr - French only)

Nantes-Atlantique (code NTA; ☎ 02 40 84 80 00; www.nantes.aeroport.fr)

Orly (code ORY; ☎ 01 49 75 15 15; www. adp.fr)

Rennes (code RNS; ☎ 02 99 29 60 00; www.rennes.aeroport.fr - French only)

Rouen (code URO; ☎ 02 35 79 41 00)

Following are airlines that regularly have flights to and from selected destinations in Normandy and Brittany.

Air Atlantique (airline code ES; ☎ 02 35 19 71 90)

Air Canada (airline code AC; ☎ 08 25 88 08 81; www.aircanada.com)

Air France (airline code AF; ☎ 0820 820 820; www.airfrance.com)

Aer Lingus (airline code EI; ☎ 01 70 20 00 72; www.aerlingus.ie)

American Airlines (airline code AA; ☎ 08 10 87 28 72; www.aa.com)

Aurigny (airline code AUR; ☎ 02 99 46 70 28; www.aurigny.com)

British Airways (airline code BA; ☎ 08 25 82 50 40; www.britishairways.com)

TRANSPORT

British Midland (airline code BD; ☎ 01 48 62 55 65; www.flybmi.com)

Continental Airlines (airline code CO; ☎ 01 42 99 09 09; www.continental.com)

Delta Air Lines (airline code DL; ☎ 08 00 30 13 01; www.delta.com)

EasyJet (airline code U2; ☎ 08 25 08 25 08; www .easyjet.com)

FlyBE (airline code BE; ☎ 0871 700 0535; www3 .flybe.com)

Ryanair (airline code FR; ☎ 08 92 55 56 66; www .ryanair.com)

Qantas (airline code QF; ☎ 08 20 82 05 00; www .qantas.com.au)

Twin Jet (airline code T7; ☎ 08 92 70 77 37)

United Airlines (airline code UA; ☎ 08 10 72 72 72; www.united.com)

US Airways (airline code US; ☎ 08 20 30 49 23; www.usairways.com)

Tickets

World aviation has never been so competitive, making air travel better value than ever. But you have to research the options carefully to make sure you get the best deal. The Internet is an increasingly useful resource for checking air fares. Online ticket sales work well if you are doing a simple one-way or return trip on specified dates. However, online superfast fare generators are no substitute for a travel agent who knows all about special deals, has strategies for avoiding layovers and can offer advice on everything from which airline has the best vegetarian food to the best travel insurance to bundle with your ticket. Note that departure tax is included in your ticket price. Some of the better international online ticket sites:

Expedia (www.expedia.msn.com) Microsoft's travel site caters to the US market.

Flight Centre (www.flightcentre.com) A respected operator for direct flights with sites for Australia, New Zealand, the UK, the USA and Canada.

Flights.com (www.tiss.com) A truly international site for flight-only tickets; cheap fares and an easy-to-search database.

STA (www.statravel.com) The leader in world student travel, but you don't necessarily have to be a student. Also has links to worldwide STA sites.

Travel.com.au (www.travel.com.au) A good Australian site. You can look up fares and flights into and out of the country.

Travelocity (www.travelocity.com) This US site allows you to search fares (in US dollars) to or from practically anywhere.

From Australia & New Zealand

From Melbourne or Sydney, return tickets to Paris on Qantas cost from A$1830 (low season) to A$3000 (high season, ie June to August and around Christmas). Fares from Perth are about A$200 cheaper. A return flight from Auckland in low season is about NZ$1900 and is often routed through Asia. Small agencies often advertise in the Saturday travel sections of the *New Zealand Herald*, *Sydney Morning Herald* and the Melbourne *Age*. Other major dealers in cheap air fares, with many branches:

Flight Centre (in Australia ☎ 133 133, in New Zealand ☎ 0800 24 35 44; www.flightcentre.com)

STA (in Australia ☎ 1300 733 035, in New Zealand ☎ 0508 782 872 in; www.statravel.com)

From Canada

From Toronto or Montreal, return flights on Air Canada to Paris are available from about C$820 in the low season; it costs C$200 or C$300 more from Vancouver. To find lower fares, you might scan the travel agencies' ads in the *Globe & Mail*, *Toronto Star* and *Vancouver Province*.

The main travel agency, with numerous outlets throughout Canada is **Travel CUTS** (☎ 1 888 359 2887; www.travelcuts.com).

From Continental Europe

Most European airlines fly to Paris, but Air France offers competitive fares on most routes and good youth rates for those aged between 12 and 24. Seniors and those travelling as couples (married or legally cohabiting) also get special rates.

Check with local travel agencies and at online ticket sites:

DENMARK

Kilroy Travels (☎ 70 80 80 15; wwww.kilroytravels.com; Skindergade 28, Copenhagen)

STA Travel (☎ 33 14 15 01; www.statravel.dk; Fiolstraede 18, Copenhagen)

GERMANY

STA Travel (☎ 030-310 00 40; www.statravel.de; Hardenbergstrasse 9, Berlin)

ITALY

CTS Viaggi (☎ 06 462 043 116; www.cts.it; Via Genova, Rome) One of many branches throughout Italy.

Viaggi Wasteels (☎ 091 34 96 86; Viale Piemonte, Palermo)

THE NETHERLANDS
ISSTA (☎ 020-618 80 31; 226 Overtoom Straat; Amsterdam)
Kilroy Travels (☎ 020-524 51 00; wwww.kilroytravels .com; Singel 413, Amsterdam)

NORWAY
Kilroy Travels (☎ 81 55 96 33; Nedre Slottsgate 23, Oslo)
STA Travel (☎ 81 55 99 05; www.statravel.no; Karl Johansgate 8, Oslo)

SWEDEN
Kilroy Travels (☎ 0771-545769; wwww.kilroytravels .com; Kungsgatan 4, Stockholm)
STA Travel (☎ 0771-611010; www.statravel.se; Kungs-gatan 30, Stockholm)

SWITZERLAND
STA Travel (☎ 022-818 02 00; www.statravel.ch; rue de Rive 10, Geneva)

From the UK & Ireland
You can get incredible deals from London Stansted to Dinard, Brest and La Rochelle (just south of Brittany) via low-cost Ryanair. Prices vary wildly from a ridiculously low UK£17, depending on the flight and the day. Alternatively, you can take a British Airways flight from Gatwick to Nantes for between UK£50 and UK£71. FlyBE also offers good rates if you purchase in advance. There are no flights from the British mainland to Normandy, but Twin Jet makes a regular run from Jersey to Cherbourg, with prices as low as UK£49, and Aurigny links Dinard with the Channel Islands.

Otherwise you have to go through Paris. Ryanair runs from Glasgow-Prestwick to Paris' Beauvais airport for prices that begin at UK£24 on selected flights, and from Dublin or Shannon airports to Beauvais for €42. Aer Lingus flies from Dublin or Shannon to Paris' Charles de Gaulle for €115 return. Another low-cost carrier, EasyJet, has regular daily flights from London's Luton airport to Charles de Gaulle at prices that start at UK£33, while British Airways flies from London's Heathrow airport to Charles de Gaulle for UK£54 on some flights. Air France and British Midland link London and a variety of other British cities (such as Birmingham, Belfast, Edinburgh, Glasgow and Manchester) with Paris.

There are a number of local travel agencies and online ticket sites:

Cheap Flights (www.cheapflights.co.uk)
Cheapest Flights (www.cheapestflights.co.uk)
Online Travel (www.onlinetravel.com) Good deals on flights from more than a dozen British cities.
STA Travel (☎ 0870 1 600 599; www.statravel.co.uk) Caters especially to students or travellers under 26 years.

From the USA
The flight options across the North Atlantic, the world's busiest long-haul air corridor, are bewildering. The *New York Times*, *LA Times*, *Chicago Tribune* and *San Francisco Chronicle* all have weekly travel sections in which you'll find any number of travel agencies' ads. Independent periodicals such as the *San Francisco Guardian* and New York's *Village Voice* are other good places to check.

You should be able to fly from New York to Paris and back for about US$350 in the low season and US$800 in the high season; even lower promotional fares are sometimes on offer. Tickets from the west coast are US$150 to US$250 higher.

Local travel agencies and online ticket sites:

Expedia (www.expedia.msn.com) Microsoft 's travel site.
Flight Centre (www.flightcentre.com)
STA Travel (☎ 800 781 40 40; www.statravel.com)
Travelocity (www.travelocity.com)

From Within France
Air France links a dozen or so French cities, including Avignon, Biarritz, Bordeaux, Clermont-Ferrand, Marseilles, Metz, Nice and Perpignan, with Rennes and Nantes through Lyon (€147 return) and Paris (€155 return). Air France also connects a dozen or so cities with Caen through Lyon (€148 return). Good ticket agencies with online sales:

Degriftour (☎ 08 92 70 50 00; www.degriftour.fr)
Nouvelles Frontières (☎ 08 25 00 07 47; www.nouvelles-frontieres.fr)

LAND
From Continental Europe
BUS
Eurolines (www.eurolines.com, with links to each national company's website) is a consortium of European coach companies that links points all over Europe and Morocco. Buses are slower and less comfortable than trains, but they are cheaper, especially if you qualify for the 10% discount available to those aged under 26 or over 60, or take advantage of the discount

fares on offer from time to time. The main hub is Paris, but there are connections to Brittany and Normandy. There are two to three buses a week to Nantes from Amsterdam (€67, 16 hours) and Brussels (€58, 11½ hours) and to Rennes from Amsterdam (€67, 15¼ hours) and Brussels (€58, 10¼ hours). There are also buses several times a week to Caen from Madrid (€78, 18 hours). Otherwise, you'll have to go through Paris, which is linked with all major cities in Europe, including Amsterdam (€46, eight hours), Berlin (€73, 14 hours), Madrid (€87, 17 hours) and Prague (€75, 16 hours).

Intercars (in Paris ☎ 01 42 19 99 35; www.intercars.fr - French only; 139 bis rue de Vaugirard) links Paris with Berlin (€77, 13 hours), Moscow (€234, 50 hours) and other Eastern European cities.

TRAIN
Rail services link France with every country in Europe; schedules are available from major train stations in France and abroad. The closest hub to Normandy and Brittany is Paris. Following are the national rail companies linking to Paris.

Austria (☎ 01-93 00 00; www.oebb.at)
Belgium (☎ 02-528 28 .28; www.b-rail.be)
Germany (☎ 0800 1 50 70 90; www.bahn.de)
Italy (☎ 89 20 21; www.trenitalia.it)
Netherlands (☎ 06 92 96; www.ns.nl)
Spain (☎ 902 24 02 02; www.renfe.es)
Switzerland (☎ 0900 300 300; www.sbb.ch)

The Thalys (www.thalys.com) service links Paris' Gare du Nord to Brussels-Midi (from €65, one hour and 25 minutes, 20 per day), Amsterdam CS (from €87, 4¼ hours, five per day) and Cologne's Hauptbahnhof (€78, four hours, seven per day). Youth fares cost half (or less) of the regular adult fare; seniors also get discounts.

For details on discount rail passes and tickets, see the boxed text (opposite).

From the UK
BUS
The Channel Tunnel, inaugurated in 1994, is the first dry-land link between the UK and France since the last Ice Age and, given the cost overruns, there isn't likely to be another one before the next Ice Age. In addition to regular services to Paris (UK£30, 7½ hours), Eurolines has coach services from London's Victoria Coach Station direct to Caen (UK£40, 11½ hours, at least twice weekly), and Rennes (UK£50, 12 hours, at least twice weekly).

Eurolines (in the UK ☎ 0870 580 8080, in Paris ☎ 01 49 72 51 51; www.nationalexpress.com)
Intercars (in Paris ☎ 01 42 19 99 35; www.intercars.fr - French only) Has a Manchester–London–Paris bus service.

TRAIN
The highly civilised Eurostar (in the UK ☎ 08705 186 186, in France ☎ 08 36 35 35 39; www.eurostar.com) takes only three hours (not including the one hour time change) to get from London to Paris. There are direct services from London and Ashford to Paris and the three other stations in France: Calais-Fréthun, Lille and Disneyland Paris. A full-fare, 2nd-class ticket from London to Paris can be as low as UK£50. You'll get the best deals if you stay over a Saturday night, if you book 14 or seven days ahead, if you're under 25 or if you're a student. Student travel agencies often have youth fares not available directly from Eurostar.

CAR & MOTORCYCLE
High-speed Eurotunnel shuttle trains (in the UK ☎ 0870 535 3535, in France ☎ 03 21 00 61 00; www.eurotunnel.com) whisk cars, motorbikes and coaches from Folkestone through the Channel Tunnel to Coquelles, 5km southwest of Calais, in air-conditioned and soundproofed comfort. Shuttles run 24 hours a day, every day of the year, with up to five departures an hour during peak periods (one an hour from 1am to 5am). LPG and CNG tanks are excluded, which eliminates many campers and caravans.

Prices vary with market demand, but the regular one-way fare for a passenger car, including all its passengers, costs from UK£150 (in February or March) to UK£250 (in July or August); return passage costs twice as much. Return fares valid for less than five days are much cheaper. The fee for a bicycle, including its rider, is UK£32 return; advance reservations are mandatory. To take advantage of promotional fares you must book at least one day ahead. From Coquelles, count on a 2½-hour drive to Le Tréport, the first town in Normandy.

From Within France
Long-distance bus travel in France is almost unknown. To get to Brittany and Normandy

TRAIN PASSES & DISCOUNT FARES

The following passes are sold at student travel agencies, major train stations within Europe, and the SNCF subsidiary **Rail Europe** (in the UK ☎ 08705 848 848, in the US ☎ 1 877 257 2887, in Canada ☎ 800 361 7245; www.raileurope.com).

SNCF Discount Fares & Passes

Children aged under four travel free of charge; those aged four to 11 travel for half-price. Discounted fares (25% reduction) automatically apply to travellers aged 12 to 25, seniors aged over 60, one to four adults travelling with a child aged four to 11, two people taking a return journey together or anyone taking a return journey of at least 200km and spending a Saturday night away. Purchasing tickets well in advance will also usually get you a discounted fare. The Découverte J30, which must be purchased 30 to 60 days before the date of travel, offers savings of 45% to 55%. The Découverte J8, which you must buy eight days ahead, gets you 20% to 30% off.

Purchasing a one-year travel pass can yield a 50% discount (25% if the cheapest seats are sold out): a **Carte 12-25** aimed at travellers aged 12 to 25 costs €48, the **Carte Enfant Plus** for one to four adults travelling with a child aged four to 11 costs €63, and a **Carte Sénior** for those aged over 60 costs €49.

The **France Railpass** entitles nonresidents of France to unlimited travel on SNCF trains for four days over a one-month period. In 2nd class, it costs US$218; each additional day of travel costs US$28. The **France Youthpass** entitles holders to four days of travel over a one-month period. In 2nd class it costs US$164, plus US$21 for each extra day.

European Train Passes

Eurail (www.eurail.com) passes are available to non-European residents, while **InterRail** (www.raileurope.co.uk/inter-rail) and **Euro-Domino** passes are available to European residents. All are valid on the national train network and allow unlimited travel for varying periods of time. The passes are useful only if you plan to travel extensively around France by train.

from other parts of France, you'll need to take a train.

TRAIN

Services are handled by France's national company, **SNCF** (☎ 08 92 35 35 35; www.sncf.fr). Most lines out of Normandy or Brittany pass through Paris (for information about train connections to Paris, see the Getting There & Away sections under individual destinations), but if you take the **TGV** (Train à Grande Vitesse; www.tgv.com) from Brittany you can get in and out of the region speedily. Cities in Brittany have frequent and fast rail connections to the French capital on the TGV Atlantique network. There are several TGVs daily from Paris' Gare Montparnasse to Nantes (€61.40, 2¼ hours), Rennes (€57.50, 2¼ hours), Lorient (€59.10 to €69.70, four hours), Quimper (€64, five hours) and Brest (€63.80, 4½ hours). There are two TGV lines that operate into Brittany. The northern line serves Rennes, Lamballe, Guingamp, Morlaix and Brest. The southern line serves

Rennes, Vannes, Auray, Lorient, Quimperlé and Quimper. A third line links Paris to the Loire Valley. TGV services to Brittany from other parts of France go via Paris, eg Lyon to Nantes (€67, 4½ hours) and Lyon to Rennes (€67 to €99, 4½ hours). There is also a direct service on ordinary trains from Bordeaux to Nantes (€37, four hours).

SEA

Tickets for ferry travel to/from the UK, Channel Islands and Ireland are available from most travel agencies in France and the countries served. Except where noted, the prices given below are for standard one-way tickets; in some cases, return fares cost less than two one-way tickets. Children aged four to somewhere between 12 and 15 (depending on the company) travel for half to two-thirds of the cost of an adult fare.

Note that if you're travelling with a vehicle you are usually denied access to it during the voyage.

From the Channel Islands

Passenger-only catamarans operated by **Hugo Express** (☎ 02 33 61 08 88), based in Granville, link the Channel Islands with two small ports on the western coast of Normandy: Granville (daily April to September, weekends only in March) and Carteret (daily April to September). The one-way pedestrian fare is UK£35.

Émeraude Lines (☎ 01534 766 566; www.emeraude .co.uk) runs express car ferries between Jersey and St-Malo (foot passenger/car and two adults from UK£35/129, 1¼ hours).

From Ireland

Eurail pass holders pay 50% of the adult pedestrian fare for crossings between Ireland and France on Irish Ferries (make sure you book ahead).

Irish Ferries (☎ 01-638 3333; www.irishferries.ie) has overnight runs from Rosslare to either Cherbourg (18 hours) or Roscoff (16 hours) every other day (three times a week from mid-September to October, with a possible break in service from November to February). Pedestrians pay around €50 (€40 for

students). There are special prices for five- and nine-day returns.

From April to September, Brittany Ferries runs a car ferry every Saturday from Cork (Ringaskiddy) to Roscoff (14 hours), and every Friday in the other direction. Foot passengers pay around €53 one way.

Freight ferries run by **P&O Irish Sea** (www.po irishsea.com) link Rosslare with Cherbourg (18 hours, three per week); cars with two passengers cost from €154. From April to September there is also a weekly Dublin–Cherbourg route (18 hours); cars with two adults cost €174. Foot passengers are not accepted on either service.

From the UK

Fares vary widely according to demand, which in turn depends on the season (July and August are especially popular) and the time of day (a Friday night ferry can cost much more than a Sunday morning one); the most-expensive tickets can cost almost three times as much as the cheapest ones. Three- or five-day excursion (return) fares generally cost about the same as the regular

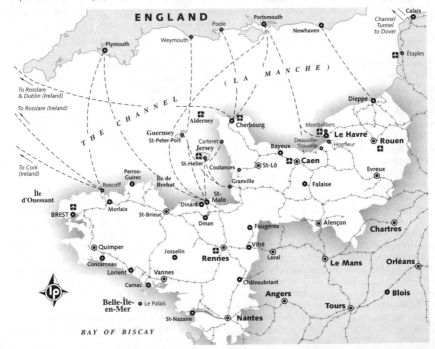

one-way ticket; special promotional return fares, often requiring advance booking, are sometimes cheaper than a standard one-way fare. On some overnight sailings you have to pay extra for a mandatory reclining seat (UK£5) or sleeping berth (UK£16 to UK£38). Check on **Ferry Savers** (☎ 0870 990 8492; www.ferrysavers.com), which guarantees the lowest prices on Channel crossings. Ferry companies may try to make it hard for people who use supercheap, one-day return tickets for one-way passage – a huge backpack is a dead giveaway that you're not out for an afternoon outing.

Eurail passes are *not* valid for ferry travel between the UK and France. Transporting bicycles is often (but not always) free.

TO NORMANDY

The Newhaven–Dieppe route is handled by **Hoverspeed** (☎ 0870 240 8070; www.hoverspeed.co .uk) and **Transmanche Ferries** (☎ 0800 917 1201; www.transmancheferries.com). The hovercraft trip (one to three daily) takes 2¼ hours, while the ferry trip (two daily) takes four hours. Pedestrians pay from UK£27 one way, with special deals available.

It's a 4¼-hour crossing (one or two per day) from Poole to Cherbourg using **Condor Ferries** (☎ 0845 345 2000; www.condorferries.co.uk) or **Brittany Ferries** (☎ 0870 366 5333; www.brittany -ferries.com). Foot passengers pay from UK£22 to UK£35 one way.

On the Portsmouth–Cherbourg route, Brittany Ferries, Condor Ferries and **P&O Portsmouth** (☎ 0870 598 0555, 0870 520 2020; www.po ferries.com) have two or three car ferries a day (five hours by day, eight hours overnight) and, from April to September, two faster catamarans a day. Foot passengers pay from UK£29 one way.

The Portsmouth–Le Havre crossing is handled by P&O Portsmouth (5½ hours by day, 7¾ hours overnight, three car ferries a day, fewer in winter). Passage costs somewhat more than Portsmouth–Cherbourg.

Brittany Ferries also has car ferries from Portsmouth to Caen (Ouistreham; six hours, three per day). Tickets cost the same as for Poole–Cherbourg.

VIA FAR NORTHERN FRANCE

The fastest way to cross the English Channel is between Dover and Calais, served by Hoverspeed's SeaCats (catamarans), which take 50 minutes. For foot passengers, a one-way trip (or a return completed within five days) costs UK£27. From Calais, there are five daily trains to Le Tréport, the northernmost town in Normandy (€19, five hours).

The Dover–Calais crossing is also handled by car ferries, run by SeaFrance (www.sea france.com; 1½ hours, 15 daily) and P&O Stena (one to 1¼ hours, 29 daily) for about the same price.

TO BRITTANY

From mid-March to mid-November, Plymouth is linked to Roscoff (six hours for day crossings, one to three per day) by Brittany Ferries. The one-way fare for foot passengers is around UK£35.

Brittany Ferries also links Portsmouth and Plymouth with St-Malo (8¾ hours for day crossing, one per day). Pedestrians pay from UK£27 one way.

From April to September, Condor Ferries has at least one daily ferry linking Weymouth with St-Malo (UK£35) that can take anywhere from seven to 10 hours, including a stopover in Guernsey. From late May to September, Condor runs one catamaran a day linking Poole with St-Malo. The 4¼-hour crossing costs UK£32 one way for pedestrians.

GETTING AROUND

France's domestic transport network, much of it owned or subsidised by the government, tends to be monopolistic: the state-owned SNCF takes care of virtually all interdepartmental land transport, and short-haul bus companies are either run by the *département* or grouped so each local company handles a different set of destinations.

BICYCLE

French law dictates that bicycles must have two functioning brakes, a bell, a red reflector on the back and yellow reflectors on the pedals. After sunset and when visibility is poor, cyclists must turn on a white light in front and a red one in the rear. When being overtaken by a car or lorry, cyclists must ride in single file.

Bicycles are not allowed on most local or intercity buses or on trams. On some of the regional trains you can take a bicycle free of charge. On train timetables, a bicycle symbol indicates that bicycles are allowed on particular trains. On some regional trains, bikes have to be stored in the luggage van.

BUS

Normandy and Brittany have an extensive network of buses linking the major cities and many small towns, but schedules are mostly designed to accommodate the needs of students and workers. Some smaller villages in the interior are not served at all by bus links. The coast has a more reliable service than the interior, but services through the region are cut dramatically on Saturday and are often nonexistent on Sunday. School holidays also involve a rearrangement of bus schedules. In addition, SNCF has replaced some uneconomic train services with buses. Travellers can often (but not always) take advantage of any train pass they have when travelling on SNCF bus services.

CAR & MOTORCYCLE
Bringing Your Own Vehicle

A right-hand drive vehicle brought to France from the UK or Ireland must have deflectors affixed to the headlights to avoid dazzling oncoming traffic. A motor vehicle entering a foreign country must display a sticker identifying its country of registration. In the UK, information on driving in France is available from the **RAC** (☎ 0870 010 6382; www.rac.co.uk) and the **AA** (☎ 0870 600 0371; www.theaa.com). *Motoring in Europe*, published in the UK by the RAC, gives an excellent summary of road regulations in each European country, including parking rules.

If your car is *en panne* (breaks down), you'll have to find a garage that handles your *marque* (make of car). There are Peugeot, Renault and Citroën garages all over the place, but if you have a non-French car you may have trouble finding someone to service it in more remote areas. Michelin's *Guide Rouge* lists garages at the end of each entry.

Note that service stations in many towns and villages are closed on Sunday. The local tourist office should be able to direct you to a service station that's open after hours, but you'll have to pay by credit card.

Try not to be on the roads when the French are involved in their massive seasonal shift from home to holiday spot. On

the first and last weekends of August roads can be completely clogged, and the weekend around 15 August is also a time of heavy traffic. Tune in to 107.7MHz FM, which gives traffic reports in English every 30 minutes during the summer.

Tolls are charged for travel on almost all autoroutes (except around major cities) and many bridges. Watch out for the A14, which is substantially more expensive than the A13. Rouen–Caen costs €6.90 on the A13 but nearly twice as much on the A14. Nantes–Le Havre costs €8.70 and Rennes–Caen costs €15.40. The website www.autoroutes.fr is a useful source of information on budgeting for car travel, as it includes tolls and petrol estimates.

Driving Licence

You are not required to have an international driving licence in order to drive in France, and there is no particular reason to get one if you have a valid driving licence in your home country.

Insurance

Unlimited third-party liability insurance is mandatory for all automobiles entering France, whether the owner accompanies the vehicle or not. As proof of insurance, the owner must present an international motor insurance card showing that the vehicle is insured in France. A temporary insurance policy is available from the vehicle insurance department of the French Customs Office with a validity of eight to 30 days. Third-party liability insurance is provided by car-rental companies, but things such as collision-damage waivers (CDW) vary greatly from company to company. When comparing rates, the most important thing to check is the *franchise* (excess/deductible), which is usually €350 for a small car. Some US credit-card companies (such as Amex) have built-in CDW, but you may have to cover all expenses in the event of an accident and claim the damage back from the credit-card company later.

Purchase-Repurchase Plans

If you'll be needing a car in Europe for 17 days to six months (one year if you're studying or teaching in France), by far your cheapest option is to 'purchase' a brand-new one from

ROAD DISTANCES (KM)

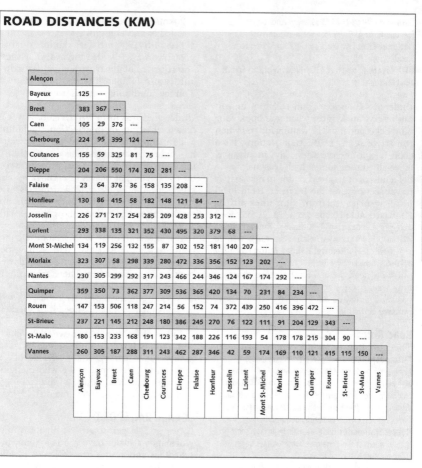

	Alençon	Bayeux	Brest	Caen	Cherbourg	Courances	Dieppe	Falaise	Honfleur	Josselin	Lorient	Mont St-Michel	Morlaix	Nantes	Quimper	Rouen	St-Brieuc	St-Malo	Vannes
Alençon	---																		
Bayeux	125	---																	
Brest	383	367	---																
Caen	105	29	376	---															
Cherbourg	224	95	399	124	---														
Coutances	155	59	325	81	75	---													
Dieppe	204	206	550	174	302	281	---												
Falaise	23	64	376	36	158	135	208	---											
Honfleur	130	86	415	58	182	148	121	84	---										
Josselin	226	271	217	254	285	209	428	253	312	---									
Lorient	293	338	135	321	352	430	495	320	379	68	---								
Mont St-Michel	134	119	256	132	155	87	302	152	181	140	207	---							
Morlaix	323	307	58	298	339	280	472	336	356	152	123	202	---						
Nantes	230	305	299	292	317	243	466	244	346	124	167	174	292	---					
Quimper	359	350	73	362	377	309	536	365	420	134	70	231	84	234	---				
Rouen	147	153	506	118	247	214	56	152	74	372	439	250	416	396	472	---			
St-Brieuc	237	221	145	212	248	180	386	245	270	76	122	111	91	204	129	343	---		
St-Malo	180	153	233	168	191	123	342	188	226	116	193	54	178	178	215	304	90	---	
Vannes	260	305	187	288	311	243	462	287	346	42	59	174	169	110	121	415	115	150	---

Peugeot (www.peugeot-openeurope.com) or Renault (www.eurodrive.renault.com) and then, at the end of your trip, 'sell' it back to them. In reality, you pay only for the number of days you use the vehicle. Eligibility is restricted to people who are not residents of the EU (citizens of EU countries are eligible if they live outside the EU).

Prices include unlimited kilometres, 24-hour towing and breakdown service, and comprehensive insurance with – incredibly – no excess (deductible), so returning a damaged car is totally hassle-free. Extending your contract is possible (using a credit card), but you'll end up paying about double the prepaid per-day rate, in part because of the added paperwork.

Cars can be picked up in many cities all over France and returned to any other purchase-repurchase centre, including other European capitals.

Rental

Prebooked and prepaid rates, which are arranged before you leave home, are often a much better deal than on-the-spot rentals.
ADA (☎ 08 25 16 91 69; www.ada-sa.fr - French only) Somewhat cheaper than the international outfits.
Avis (☎ 08 20 05 05 05; www.avis.com)
Budget (☎ 08 25 00 35 64 www.budget.com)
Easycar (☎ 0906 33 33 33 3; www.easycar.com) The cheapest deal for renting subcompacts from Paris. The super-low prices for a day's rental makes the annoying Easycar logo on the side of the car bearable.

TRANSPORT

Europcar (☎ 08 25 35 93 59; www.europcar.com)
Hertz (☎ 01 41 91 95 25; www.hertz.com)
National-Citer (☎ 08 25 16 12 12. www.citer.com - French only)
OTU Voyages (☎ 08 20 81 78 17; www.otu.fr - French only) For students.

Under SNCF's pricey Train + Auto plan, you can reserve an Avis car when you book your train ticket and it will be waiting for you when you arrive at any of 195 train stations. It's a good idea to reserve a few days in advance, especially during tourist high seasons.

Details of deals are available in newspaper travel sections, on the Internet, from local travel agencies and from companies such as US-based **Auto Europe** (☎ 1 888 223 5555; www .autoeurope.com), and UK-based **Holiday Autos** (☎ 0870 530 0400; www.holidayautos.co.uk), whose US affiliate is **Kemwel Holiday Autos** (☎ 1 877 820 0668; www.kemwel.com).

If you need a car for more than three or four weeks, see Purchase-Repurchase Plans (p340) for details on some incredibly inexpensive options.

Road Rules
There are four types of intercity roads:
Autoroutes These multilane, divided motorways/highways, usually requiring the payment of tolls, have alphanumeric designations that begin with A. Marked by blue signs depicting a divided highway receding into the distance, they often have lovely *aires de repos* (rest areas), some with restaurants and pricey petrol stations.
Routes Nationales These are main highways, some of them divided for short stretches, whose names begin with N (or, on older maps and signs, RN).
Routes Départmentales These are local roads whose names begin with D.
Routes Communales These are minor rural roads whose names sometimes begin with C or V.

French law requires that all passengers, including those in the back seat, wear seat belts, and children who weigh less than 18kg must travel in backward-facing child seats. A passenger car is permitted to carry a maximum of five people. North American drivers should remember that turning right on a red light is illegal in France.

Unless otherwise posted, a speed limit of 50km/h applies in *all* areas designated as built-up, no matter how rural they may appear. Outside built-up areas, speed limits vary according to the type of road:

■ 90km/h (80km/h if it's raining) on undivided N and D highways
■ 110km/h (100km/h if it's raining) on dual carriageways (divided highways) or short sections of highway with a divider strip
■ 130km/h (110km/h in the rain, 60km/h in icy conditions) on autoroutes

Under the *priorité à droite* rule, any car that is entering an intersection (including a T-junction) from a road on your right has right-of-way, unless the intersection is marked 'vous n'avez pas la priorité' (you do not have right of way) or 'cédez le passage' (give way). *Priorité à droite* is also suspended on priority roads, which are marked by an up-ended yellow square with a black square in the middle.

It is illegal to drive with a blood-alcohol concentration (BAC) over 0.05% (0.5g per litre of blood) – the equivalent of two glasses of wine for a 75kg adult. There are periodic random breathalyser tests.

Mobile phones may only be used when accompanied by a hands-free kit or speakerphone.

Riders of any type of two-wheeled vehicle with a motor (except motor-assisted bicycles) must wear a helmet. No special licence is required to ride a motorbike whose engine is smaller than 50cc, which is why you often find places renting scooters rated at 49.9cc.

LOCAL TRANSPORT
Cities and larger towns in Brittany and Normandy usually have a bus system, but schedules and routes are designed to take people back and forth to school or a market. Details of routes, fares, tourist passes etc are available at tourist offices and from local bus-company information offices; see Getting Around at the end of each destination listing.

TRAIN
Details on the countrywide rail passes available for Europeans and non-Europeans are outlined in the boxed text (p337), but if you'll be confining your travel to Normandy and Brittany, it's unlikely that you'll rack up enough kilometres to make most passes worthwhile. In Lower Normandy there's a weekend pass, the Carte Sillage Loisirs, that offers a 50% reduction for the passholder and a second person and only a €0.15 charge

for additional people. The journey must be completed on either Saturday or Sunday; the pass costs €7and is valid for a year. Children under four travel free; those aged four to 11 pay 50% of the adult fare.

Tickets & Reservations

You can buy your ticket with a credit card via the SNCF's website (www.sncf.com) and have it sent to you by post or pick it up at any SNCF ticket office using your reference number and the credit card used to purchase the ticket. Almost every SNCF station in the region has at least one *billeterie automatique* (automatic ticket machine) that accepts credit cards for purchases of at least €2. Tickets *can* be purchased on board the train, but unless the ticket window where you boarded was closed, prohibitive surcharges apply. If you search out the *contrôleur* (conductor), rather than letting yourself be discovered ticketless, the surcharge is much less.

Reserving in advance is optional unless you're travelling by Eurostar or during holiday periods (for example, around Easter and 14 July) when trains may be full.

Validating Your Train Ticket

Before boarding the train you must validate your ticket by time-stamping it in a *composteur*, one of those orange posts situated somewhere between the ticket windows and the tracks. If you forget, find a conductor so they can punch it for you (if you wait for your crime to be discovered, you're likely to be fined).

TRANSPORT

Health

CONTENTS

Before you go	**344**
Insurance	344
Recommended Vaccinations	344
Internet Resources	344
In Transit	**344**
Deep Vein Thrombosis (DVT)	344
In Brittany & Normandy	**345**
Availability & Cost of Health Care	345
Traveller's Diarrhoea	345
Environmental Hazards	345
Travelling with Children	345
Women's Health	345

Travel health depends on your predeparture preparations, your daily health care while travelling and how you handle any medical problems that do develop. Brittany and Normandy are healthy places to travel. Hygiene standards are high and there are no unusual diseases to worry about.

BEFORE YOU GO

Prevention is the key to staying healthy while abroad. A little planning before departure, particularly relating to pre-existing illnesses, will save trouble later: see a dentist before a long trip; carry a spare pair of contact lenses and glasses, and take your optical prescription with you. Bring medications in their original, clearly labelled, containers. A signed and dated letter from your physician describing your medical conditions and medications, including generic names, is also a good idea. If carrying syringes or needles, be sure to have a physician's letter documenting their medical necessity.

INSURANCE

If you're an EU citizen, an E111 form, available from health centres or, in the UK, from post offices, covers you for most medical care. E111, however, will not cover any non-emergencies or emergency repatriation to a home country. Non-EU citizens should find out if there is a reciprocal arrangement for free medical care between their country and the country visited. If you do need health insurance, be sure you get a policy that covers you for the worst possible scenario, such as an accident needing an emergency flight home. Find out in advance if your insurance will make payments directly to providers or reimburse you later for health expenditures. Some policies require the holder to carry an E111 form if they are an EU citizen.

RECOMMENDED VACCINATIONS

The WHO recommends all travellers are covered for diphtheria, tetanus, measles, mumps, rubella and polio, as well as Hepatitis B, regardless of destination. Since most vaccines don't produce immunity until at least two weeks after they're given, visit a doctor at least six weeks before departure.

INTERNET RESOURCES

The WHO's publication *International Travel and Health* is revised annually and is available online at www.who.int/ith/. Other useful websites:

www.mdtravelhealth.com Travel health recommendations for every country; updated daily.

www.fitfortravel.scot.nhs.uk General travel advice for the layman.

www.ageconcern.org.uk Advice on travel for the elderly.

www.mariestopes.org.uk Information on women's health and contraception.

IN TRANSIT

DEEP VEIN THROMBOSIS (DVT)

Blood clots might form in the legs during plane flights, chiefly because of prolonged immobility. The longer the flight, the greater the risk. The chief symptom of DVT is swelling or pain of the foot, ankle, or calf, usually but not always on just one side. When a blood clot travels to the lungs, it may cause chest pain and breathing difficulties. Travellers with any of these symptoms should immediately seek medical attention.

To prevent the development of DVT on long flights, walk about the cabin, contract the leg muscles while sitting, drink plenty of fluids and avoid alcohol and tobacco.

IN BRITTANY & NORMANDY

AVAILABILITY & COST OF HEALTH CARE

Good health care is readily available in both Brittany and Normandy, and for minor self-limiting illnesses pharmacists (pharmaciens) can give valuable advice and sell over-the-counter medication. They can also advise when more specialised help is required and point you in the right direction. In major towns you are likely to find English-speaking doctors or a translator service available. The standard of dental care is usually good, however, it is sensible to have a dental check-up before a long trip.

TRAVELLER'S DIARRHOEA

If you develop diarrhoea, be sure to drink plenty of fluids, preferably an oral rehydration solution, eg dioralyte. A few loose stools don't require treatment but, if you start having more than four or five stools a day, you should start taking an antibiotic (usually a quinolone drug) and an antidiarrhoeal agent (such as loperamide). If diarrhoea is bloody, persists for more than 72 hours or is accompanied by fever, shaking, chills or severe abdominal pain you should seek medical attention.

ENVIRONMENTAL HAZARDS
Heat Exhaustion & Heatstroke

Heat exhaustion occurs following excessive fluid loss with inadequate replacement of fluids and salt. Symptoms include headache, dizziness and tiredness. Dehydration is already happening by the time you feel thirsty – aim to drink sufficient water to produce pale, diluted urine. To treat heat exhaustion, replace fluids with water and/or fruit juice, and cool the body with cold water and fans. Treat salt loss with salty fluids such as soup or Bovril, or add a little more table salt to foods than usual.

Heat stroke is much more serious, resulting in irrational and hyperactive behaviour and eventually loss of consciousness and death. Rapid cooling by spraying the body with water and fanning is ideal. Emergency fluid and electrolyte replacement by an intravenous drip is recommended.

Hypothermia

Proper preparation will reduce the risks of getting hypothermia. Even on a hot day, the weather can change rapidly. Acute hypothermia follows a sudden drop of temperature over a short time. Chronic hypothermia is caused by a gradual loss of temperature over hours.

Hypothermia symptons start with shivering, loss of judgment and clumsiness. Unless rewarming occurs, the sufferer deteriorates into apathy, confusion and coma. Prevent further heat loss by seeking shelter, warm dry clothing, hot sweet drinks and shared bodily warmth.

Water

Tap water in Brittany and Normandy is safe to drink. However, Bretons are distrustful of it and tend to stick to bottled water. In Normandy people are much more comfortable with good old tap water.

TRAVELLING WITH CHILDREN

All travellers with children should know how to treat minor ailments and when to seek medical treatment. Make sure the children are up to date with routine vaccinations, and discuss possible travel vaccines with your doctor well before departure, as some vaccines are not suitable for children under 12 months old. Lonely Planet's Travel with Children includes advice on travel health for younger children.

WOMEN'S HEALTH

Emotional stress, exhaustion and travelling through different time zones can all contribute to an upset in the menstrual pattern. If using oral contraceptives, remember some antibiotics, diarrhoea and vomiting can stop the pill from working and lead to the risk of pregnancy – remember to take condoms with you just in case. Time zones, gastrointestinal upsets and antibiotics do not affect injectable contraception.

Travelling during pregnancy is usually possible but always consult your doctor before planning your trip. The most risky times for travel are during the first 12 weeks of pregnancy and after 30 weeks.

HEALTH

Language

CONTENTS

French	**346**
Pronunciation	346
Be Polite!	346
Gender	347
Accommodation	347
Conversation & Essentials	347
Directions	348
Health	348
Emergencies	349
Language Difficulties	349
Numbers	349
Paperwork	349
Question Words	349
Shopping & Services	349
Time & Dates	350
Transport	350
Travel With Children	351
Breton	**351**
Greetings & Useful Words	351

French is the principal language of communication in both Brittany and Normandy. Some English is spoken, especially by young people.

The indigenous language of Brittany is Breton *(breiz)*, a Celtic language related to Cornish and Welsh and, more distantly, to Irish and Scottish Gaelic. See the Breton section on p351 for some basic words and greetings in Breton.

The Norman dialect died out several centuries ago and remains in only a few words that you may hear older people using. They may refer to a *cheval* (horse) as a *qu'va*, or a *coq* (rooster) as a *cô*. Unlike regions such as Brittany or Provence, there is no movement to revive the dialect.

FRENCH

Modern French developed from the *langue d'oïl*, a group of dialects spoken north of the River Loire that grew out of the vernacular Latin used during the late Gallo-Roman period. The *langue d'oïl* – particularly the Francien dialect spoken in the Île de France –

eventually displaced the *langue d'oc*, the dialects spoken in the south of the country and from which the Mediterranean region of Languedoc got its name.

Around 122 million people worldwide speak French as their first language. The French, rightly or wrongly, have a reputation for assuming that all human beings should speak French – until WWI it was *the* international language of culture and diplomacy – and you'll find that any attempt to communicate in French will be much appreciated. Probably your best bet is always to approach people politely in French, even if the only sentence you know is *'Pardon, madame/monsieur/mademoiselle, parlez-vous anglais?'* (Excuse me, madam/sir/miss, do you speak English?).

For a more comprehensive guide to the language, pick up a copy of Lonely Planet's *French phrasebook*.

PRONUNCIATION

Most letters in French are pronounced more or less the same as their English counterparts. Here are a few that may cause confusion:

j	as the 's' in 'leisure', eg *jour* (day)
c	before **e** and **i**, as the 's' in 'sit'; before **a**, **o** and **u**, it's pronounced as English 'k'. When undescored with a 'cedilla' (**ç**), it's always pronounced as the 's' in 'sit'.
r	pronounced from the back of the throat while constricting the muscles to restrict the flow of air
n, m	where a syllable ends in a single **n** or **m**, these letters are not pronounced, but the preceding vowel is given a nasal pronunciation

BE POLITE!

An important distinction is made in French between *tu* and *vous*, which both mean 'you'; *tu* is only used when addressing people you know well, children or animals. If you're addressing an adult who isn't a personal friend, *vous* should be used unless the person invites you to use *tu*. In general, younger people insist less on this distinction between polite and informal, and you will find that in many cases they use *tu* from the beginning of an acquaintance.

GENDER

All nouns in French are either masculine or feminine and adjectives reflect the gender of the noun they modify. The feminine form of many nouns and adjectives is indicated by a silent **e** added to the masculine form, as in *ami* and *amie* (the masculine and feminine for 'friend').

In the following phrases both masculine and feminine forms have been indicated where necessary. The masculine form comes first and is separated from the feminine by a slash. The gender of a noun is often indicated by a preceding article: 'the/a/some', *le/un/du* (m), *la/une/de la* (f); or one of the possessive adjectives, 'my/your/his/her', *mon/ton/son* (m), *ma/ta/sa* (f). With French, unlike English, the possessive adjective agrees in number and gender with the thing in question: 'his/her mother', *sa mère*.

ACCOMMODATION

I'm looking for a ...	*Je cherche ...*	zher shersh ...
camping ground	*un camping*	un kom·peeng
guesthouse	*une pension (de famille)*	ewn pon·syon (der fa·mee·ler)
hotel	*un hôtel*	un o·tel
youth hostel	*une auberge de jeunesse*	ewn o·berzh der zher·nes

Where is a cheap hotel?
Où est-ce qu'on peut trouver un hôtel pas cher?
oo es·kon per troo·vay un o·tel pa shair
What is the address?
Quelle est l'adresse?
kel e la·dres
Could you write it down, please?
Est-ce que vous pourriez l'écrire, s'il vous plaît?
e·sker voo poo·ryay lay·kreer seel voo play
Do you have any rooms available?
Est-ce que vous avez des chambres libres?
e·sker voo·za·vay day shom·brer lee·brer

I'd like (a) ...	*Je voudrais ...*	zher voo·dray ...
single room	*une chambre à un lit*	ewn shom·brer a un lee
double-bed room	*une chambre avec un grand lit*	ewn shom·brer a·vek un gron lee
twin room	*une chambre*	ewn shom·brer

MAKING A RESERVATION
(for phone or written requests)

To ...	*A l'attention de ...*
From ...	*De la part de ...*
Date	*Date*
I'd like to book ...	*Je voudrais réserver ...* (see the list under 'Accommodation' for bed and room options)
in the name of ...	*au nom de ...*
from ... (date) **to ...**	*du ... au ...*
credit card number	*carte de crédit numéro*
expiry date	*date d'expiration*
Please confirm availability and price.	*Veuillez confirmer la disponibilité et le prix.*

---

with two beds	*avec des lits jumeaux*	a·vek day lee zhew·mo
room with a bathroom	*une chambre avec une salle de bains*	ewn shom·brer a·vek ewn sal der bun
to share a dorm	*coucher dans un dortoir*	koo·sher don zun dor·twa

How much is it ...?	*Quel est le prix ...?*	kel e ler pree ...
per night	*par nuit*	par nwee
per person	*par personne*	par per·son

May I see the room?
Est-ce que je peux voir la chambre?
es·ker zher per vwa la shom·brer
Where is the bathroom?
Où est la salle de bains? oo e la sal der bun
Where is the toilet?
Où sont les toilettes? oo·son lay twa·let
I'm leaving today.
Je pars aujourd'hui. zher par o·zhoor·dwee
We're leaving today.
Nous partons aujourd'hui. noo par·ton o·zhoor·dwee

CONVERSATION & ESSENTIALS

Hello.	*Bonjour.*	bon·zhoor
Goodbye.	*Au revoir.*	o·rer·vwa
Yes.	*Oui.*	wee
No.	*Non.*	no
Please.	*S'il vous plaît.*	seel voo play
Thank you.	*Merci.*	mair·see

LANGUAGE

You're welcome.	*Je vous en prie.*	zher voo·zon pree
	De rien. (inf)	der ree·en
Excuse me.	*Excuse-moi.*	ek·skew·zay·mwa
Sorry. (forgive me)	*Pardon.*	par·don

What's your name?
Comment vous		
appelez-vous? (pol)	ko·mon voo·za·pay·lay voo
Comment tu	ko·mon tew ta·pel
t'appelles? (inf)		

My name is ...
Je m'appelle ... zher ma·pel ...

Where are you from?
De quel pays êtes-vous?	der kel pay·ee et·voo
De quel pays es-tu? (inf)	der kel pay·ee e·tew

I'm from ...
Je viens de ... zher vyen der ...

I like ...
J'aime ... zhem ...

I don't like ...
Je n'aime pas ... zher nem pa ...

Just a minute.
Une minute. ewn mee·newt

DIRECTIONS
Where is ...?
Où est ...? oo e ...

Go straight ahead.
Continuez tout droit. kon·teen·way too drwa

Turn left.
Tournez à gauche. toor·nay a gosh

Turn right.
Tournez à droite. toor·nay a drwat

at the corner
au coin o kwun

at the traffic lights
aux feux o fer

behind	*derrière*	dair·ryair
in front of	*devant*	der·von
far (from)	*loin (de)*	lwun (der)
near (to)	*près (de)*	pray (der)
opposite	*en face de*	on fas der

beach	*la plage*	la plazh
bridge	*le pont*	ler pon
castle	*le château*	ler sha·to
cathedral	*la cathédrale*	la ka·tay·dral
church	*l'église*	lay·gleez
island	*l'île*	leel
lake	*le lac*	ler lak
main square	*la place centrale*	la plas son·tral
museum	*le musée*	ler mew·zay
old city (town)	*la vieille ville*	la vyay veel
palace	*le palais*	ler pa·lay

SIGNS

Entrée	Entrance
Sortie	Exit
Renseignements	Information
Ouvert	Open
Fermé	Closed
Interdit	Prohibited
Chambres Libres	Rooms Available
Complet	Full/No Vacancies
(Commissariat de)	Police Station
Police	
Toilettes/WC	Toilets
Hommes	Men
Femmes	Women

quay	*le quai*	ler kay
riverbank	*la rive*	la reev
ruins	*les ruines*	lay rween
sea	*la mer*	la mair
square	*la place*	la plas
tourist office	*l'office de*	lo·fees der
	tourisme	too·rees·mer
tower	*la tour*	la toor

HEALTH
I'm ill.	*Je suis malade.*	zher swee ma·lad
It hurts here.	*J'ai une douleur*	zhay ewn doo·ler
	ici.	ee·see

I'm ...	*Je suis ...*	zher swee ...
asthmatic	*asthmatique*	(z)as·ma·teek
diabetic	*diabétique*	dee·a·bay·teek
epileptic	*épileptique*	(z)ay·pee·lep·teek

I'm allergic	*Je suis*	zher swee
to ...	*allergique ...*	za·lair·zheek ...
antibiotics	*aux antibiotiques*	o zon·tee·byo·teek
aspirin	*à l'aspirine*	a las·pee·reen
bees	*aux abeilles*	o za·bay·yer
nuts	*aux noix*	o nwa
peanuts	*aux cacahuètes*	o ka·ka·wet
penicillin	*à la pénicilline*	a la pay·nee·see·leen

antiseptic	*l'antiseptique*	lon·tee·sep·teek
aspirin	*l'aspirine*	las·pee·reen
condoms	*des préservatifs*	day pray·zair·va·teef
contraceptive	*le contraceptif*	ler kon·tra·sep·teef
diarrhoea	*la diarrhée*	la dya·ray
medicine	*le médicament*	ler may·dee·ka·mon
nausea	*la nausée*	la no·zay
sunblock cream	*la crème solaire*	la krem so·lair
tampons	*des tampons*	day tom·pon
	hygiéniques	ee·zhen·eek

EMERGENCIES – FRENCH

Help!
Au secours!   o skoor
There's been an accident!
Il y a eu un accident!   eel ya ew un ak·see·don
I'm lost.
Je me suis égaré/e. (m/f)   zhe me swee·zay·ga·ray
Leave me alone!
Fichez-moi la paix!   fee·shay·mwa la pay

Call ...!	*Appelez ...!*	a·play ...
a doctor	*un médecin*	un mayd·sun
the police	*la police*	la po·lees

LANGUAGE DIFFICULTIES

Do you speak English?
Parlez-vous anglais?   par·lay·voo ong·lay
Does anyone here speak English?
Y a-t-il quelqu'un qui   ya·teel kel·kung kee
parle anglais?   par long·glay
How do you say ... in French?
Comment est-ce qu'on   ko·mon es·kon
dit ... en français?   dee ... on fron·say
What does ... mean?
Que veut dire ...?   ker ver deer ...
I understand.
Je comprends.   zher kom·pron
I don't understand.
Je ne comprends pas.   zher ner kom·pron pa
Could you write it down, please?
Est-ce que vous pouvez   es·ker voo poo·vay
l'écrire?   lay·kreer
Can you show me (on the map)?
Pouvez-vous m'indiquer   poo·vay·voo mun·dee·kay
(sur la carte)?   (sewr la kart)

NUMBERS

0	*zero*	zay·ro
1	*un*	un
2	*deux*	der
3	*trois*	trwa
4	*quatre*	ka·trer
5	*cinq*	sungk
6	*six*	sees
7	*sept*	set
8	*huit*	weet
9	*neuf*	nerf
10	*dix*	dees
11	*onze*	onz
12	*douze*	dooz
13	*treize*	trez
14	*quatorze*	ka·torz
15	*quinze*	kunz
16	*seize*	sez
17	*dix-sept*	dee·set
18	*dix-huit*	dee·zweet
19	*dix-neuf*	deez·nerf
20	*vingt*	vung
21	*vingt et un*	vung tay un
22	*vingt-deux*	vung·der
30	*trente*	tront
40	*quarante*	ka·ront
50	*cinquante*	sung·kont
60	*soixante*	swa·sont
70	*soixante-dix*	swa·son·dees
80	*quatre-vingts*	ka·trer·vung
90	*quatre-vingt-dix*	ka·trer·vung·dees
100	*cent*	son
1000	*mille*	meel

PAPERWORK

name	*nom*	nom
nationality	*nationalité*	na·syo·na·lee·tay
date/place	*date/place*	dat/plas
of birth	*de naissance*	der nay·sons
sex/gender	*sexe*	seks
passport	*passeport*	pas·por
visa	*visa*	vee·za

QUESTION WORDS

Who?	*Qui?*	kee
What?	*Quoi?*	kwa
What is it?	*Qu'est-ce que c'est?*	kes·ker say
When?	*Quand?*	kon
Where?	*Où?*	oo
Which?	*Quel/Quelle?*	kel
Why?	*Pourquoi?*	poor·kwa
How?	*Comment?*	ko·mon

SHOPPING & SERVICES

I'd like to buy ...
Je voudrais acheter ...   zher voo·dray ash·tay ...
How much is it?
C'est combien?   say kom·byun
I don't like it.
Cela ne me plaît pas.   ser·la ner mer play pa
May I look at it?
Est-ce que je peux le voir?   es·ker zher per ler vwar
I'm just looking.
Je regarde.   zher rer·gard
It's cheap.
Ce n'est pas cher.   ser nay pa shair
It's too expensive.
C'est trop cher.   say tro shair
I'll take it.
Je le prends.   zher ler pron

LANGUAGE

Can I pay by ...?	Est-ce que je peux payer avec ...?	es·ker zher per pay·yay a·vek ...
credit card	ma carte de crédit	ma kart der kray·dee
travellers cheques	des chèques de voyage	day shek der vwa·yazh

more	plus	plew
less	moins	mwa
smaller	plus petit	plew per·tee
bigger	plus grand	plew gron

I'm looking for ...	Je cherche ...	zhe shersh ...
a bank	une banque	ewn bonk
the ... embassy	l'ambassade de ...	lam·ba·sahd der ...
the hospital	l'hôpital	lo·pee·tal
the market	le marché	ler mar·shay
the police	la police	la po·lees
the post office	le bureau de poste	ler bew·ro der post
a public phone	une cabine téléphonique	ewn ka·been tay·lay·fo·neek
a public toilet	les toilettes	lay twa·let
the telephone centre	la centrale téléphonique	la san·tral tay·lay·fo·neek

TIME & DATES

What time is it?	Quelle heure est-il?	kel er e til
It's (8) o'clock.	Il est (huit) heures.	il e (weet) er
It's half past ...	Il est (...) heures et demie.	il e (...) er e day·mee
in the morning	du matin	dew ma·tun
in the afternoon	de l'après-midi	der la·pray·mee·dee
in the evening	du soir	dew swar
today	aujourd'hui	o·zhoor·dwee
tomorrow	demain	der·mun
yesterday	hier	yair

Monday	lundi	lun·dee
Tuesday	mardi	mar·dee
Wednesday	mercredi	mair·krer·dee
Thursday	jeudi	zher·dee
Friday	vendredi	von·drer·dee
Saturday	samedi	sam·dee
Sunday	dimanche	dee·monsh

January	janvier	zhon·vyay
February	février	fayv·ryay
March	mars	mars
April	avril	a·vreel
May	mai	may
June	juin	zhwun
July	juillet	zhwee·yay

August	août	oot
September	septembre	sep·tom·brer
October	octobre	ok·to·brer
November	novembre	no·vom·brer
December	décembre	day·som·brer

TRANSPORT
Public Transport

What time does ... leave/arrive?	À quelle heure part/arrive ...?	a kel er par/a·reev ...
boat	le bateau	ler ba·to
bus	le bus	ler bews
plane	l'avion	la·vyon
train	le train	ler trun

I'd like a ... ticket.	Je voudrais un billet ...	zher voo·dray un bee·yay ...
one-way	simple	sum·pler
return	aller et retour	a·lay ay rer·toor
1st class	de première classe	der prem·yair klas
2nd class	de deuxième classe	der der·zyem klas

I want to go to ...
Je voudrais aller à ...   zher voo·dray a·lay a ...
The train has been delayed.
Le train est en retard.   ler trun et on rer·tar
The train has been cancelled.
Le train a été annulé.   ler trun a ay·tay a·new·lay

the first	le premier (m)	ler prer·myay
	la première (f)	la prer·myair
the last	le dernier (m)	ler dair·nyay
	la dernière (f)	la dair·nyair
platform number	le numéro de quai	ler new·may·ro der kay
ticket office	le guichet	ler gee·shay
timetable	l'horaire	lo·rair
train station	la gare	la gar

Private Transport

I'd like to hire a/an...	Je voudrais louer ...	zher voo·dray loo·way ...
car	une voiture	ewn vwa·tewr
4WD	un quatre-quatre	un kat·kat
motorbike	une moto	ewn mo·to
bicycle	un vélo	un vay·lo

Is this the road to ...?
C'est la route pour ...?   say la root poor ...
Where's a service station?
Où est-ce qu'il y a   oo es·keel ya
une station-service?   ewn sta·syon·ser·vees
Please fill it up.
Le plein, s'il vous plaît.   ler plun seel voo play
I'd like ... litres.
Je voudrais ... litres.   zher voo·dray ... lee·trer

ROAD SIGNS

Cédez la Priorité	Give Way
Danger	Danger
Défense de Stationner	No Parking
Entrée	Entrance
Interdiction de Doubler	No Overtaking
Péage	Toll
Ralentissez	Slow Down
Sens Interdit	No Entry
Sens unique	One-way
Sortie	Exit

petrol/gas	essence	ay·sons
unleaded	sans plomb	son plom
leaded	au plomb	o plom
diesel	diesel	dyay·zel

(How long) Can I park here?
(Combien de temps) (kom·byun der tom)
Est-ce que je peux es·ker zher per
stationner ici? sta·syo·nay ee·see?
Where do I pay?
Où est-ce que je paie? oo es·ker zher pay?
I need a mechanic.
J'ai besoin d'un zhay ber·zwun dun
mécanicien. may·ka·nee·syun
The car/motorbike has broken down (at ...)
La voiture/moto est la vwa·tewr/mo·to ay
tombée en panne (à ...) tom·bay on pan (a ...)
The car/motorbike won't start.
La voiture/moto ne veut la vwa·tewr/mo·to ner ver
pas démarrer. pa day·ma·ray
I have a flat tyre.
Mon pneu est à plat. mom pner ay ta pla
I've run out of petrol.
Je suis en panne zher swee zon pan
d'essence. day·sons
I had an accident.
J'ai eu un accident. zhay ew un ak·see·don

TRAVEL WITH CHILDREN

Is there a/an ...?	Y a-t-il ...?	ya teel ...
I need a/an ...	J'ai besoin ...	zhay ber·zwun ...
baby change room	d'un endroit pour changer le bébé	dun on·drwa poor shon·zhay ler bay·bay
car baby seat	d'un siège-enfant	dun syezh·on·fon
child-minding service	d'une garderie	dewn gar·dree
children's menu	d'un menu pour enfant	dun mer·new poor on·fon

disposable nappies/diapers	de couches-culottes	der koosh·kew·lot
formula	de lait maternisé	de lay ma·ter·nee·zay
(English-speaking) babysitter	d'une baby-sitter (qui parle anglais)	dewn ba·bee·see·ter (kee parl ong·glay)
highchair	d'une chaise haute	dewn shay zot
potty	d'un pot de bébé	dun po der bay·bay
stroller	d'une poussette	dewn poo·set

Do you mind if I breastfeed here?
Cela vous dérange si ser·la voo day·ron·zhe see
j'allaite mon bébé ici? zha·lay·ter mon bay·bay ee·see
Are children allowed?
Les enfants sont permis? lay zon·fon son pair·mee

BRETON

GREETINGS & USEFUL WORDS

Hello.	Demad/Demat.
Welcome.	Degemermat.
Goodbye.	Kenavo.
See you again.	D'ur wech all.
Thank you.	Trugarez.
Cheers.	Yehed mad/Yec'hed mat.

The following are some Breton words you may come across, especially in place names. Note that the spelling may vary.

aber	river mouth
ar	the
aven	river
bae	bay
bed	world, land
bihan	little
braz	big
coz	old
deiz	day
dol	table
dour	water
du	black
enez	island
fao, faou	beech tree
fest-noz	night festival
gall	French
gwenn	white
hir	long, tall
-ig, -ic	diminutive suffix
iliz	church

LANGUAGE

kastell	castle	**poull**	pond
kember, kemper	confluence	**pred**	lunch
koad, goat	forest	**raz**	strait
koan	dinner	**roc'h**	rock, pointed hill
kromm, crom	curved	**roz, ros**	hillock, mound
lam, lan	monastery	**ster, stêr, steir**	river
loc	hermitage	**stif, stivell**	spring
men/mein	stone	**tann**	oak tree
menez	mountain	**telenn**	Celtic harp
mor	sea	**ti, ty**	house
nant	valley	**trev, tre, treo**	parish division
plou-, plo-, ple-	parish (used only as a prefix in place names)	**trez**	sand
		uhel	high

LANGUAGE

Also available from Lonely Planet:
French Phrasebook

Glossary

For a glossary of food and drink terms, see the Food & Drink chapter (p50).

(m) indicates masculine gender, (f) feminine gender and (pl) plural

accueil (m) – reception
alignements (m pl) – a series of standing stones, or menhirs, in straight lines
alimentation (f) – grocery store
allée – alley
allée-couverte (f) – covered corridor or gallery tomb
auberge de jeunesse (f) – youth hostel

baie (f) – bay
baptême en mer (m) – beginner's dive
billet (m) – ticket
billet jumelé (m) – combination ticket, good for more than one site, museum etc
billeterie (f) – ticket office or counter
billeterie automatique (f) – automatic ticket machine
biniou kozh – double-reed bagpipe, specific to Brittany
bisquine (f) – traditional ocean-going fishing boat
bois (m) – wood
boisson comprise (f) – drink included
boîte (f) – night-club, literally box
bombarde (f) – Breton version of the shawm, a precursor of the oboe
boucherie (f) – butcher
boucherie chevaline (f) – butcher selling horse meat
boulangerie (f) – bakery, bread shop
BP – *boîte postale* (post office box)
brasserie (f) – restaurant usually serving food all day
brocante (f) – second-hand goods
brut (m) – dry
bureau de change (m) – exchange bureau
bureau de poste (m) or *poste* (f) – post office

cairn (m) – a heap of dry stones, usually covering a burial chamber
calvaire (m) – calvary cross; representation of the Crucifixion
canard (m) – duck
carnet (m) – a book of five or 10 bus, tram or metro tickets sold at a reduced rate
carrefour (m) – crossroads
carte (f) – card; menu; map
carte de séjour (f) – residence permit

cave (f) – wine cellar
chambre (f) – room
chambre d'hôte (f) – B&B accommodation/guesthouse
char à voile (m) – sand-yachting
charcuterie (f) – pork butcher's shop and delicatessen
chasse-marée (f) – traditional sailing ship built for the coasting trade
château (m) – castle
cimetière (m) – cemetery
cloître (m) – cloister
coiffe (f) – woman's lace headdress
col (m) – pass; lowest point on a ridge between two peaks
colombier (m) – pigeon house, or dovecote
commissariat de police (m) – police station
confiserie (f) – chocolate/sweet shop
coquillier (f) – scallop-fishing boat
côte (m) – coast
couchette (f) – sleeping berth on a train or ferry
cour (f) – courtyard
crêmerie (f) – dairy, cheese shop
crêperie (f) – pancake restaurant
CRIJ – Centre Régional d'Information Jeunesse (regional youth association)
cromlech (m) – a circle of standing stones
Cyberposte (f) – the post office's Internet access service

déjeuner (m) – lunch
deltaplane (m) – hang-gliding
demi-pension (f) – half-board (B&B with either lunch or dinner)
demi-tarif (m) – half-price
dentelle (f) – lace
département (m) – department, administrative division of France
dîner (m) – dinner
dolmen (m) – from the Breton *dol men* (stone table); a horizontal stone slab supported by two vertical slabs set on edge to create a chamber
douane (f) – customs
dundée (m) – traditional cray-fishing boat

eau (f) – water
eau non potable (f) – non-drinking water
église (f) – church
embarcadère (m) – pier, jetty
enclos paroissiaux (m) – parish enclosures
épicerie (f) – small grocery store
équitation (f) – horse riding

faïence (f) – ceramics
fauteuil (m) – seat on trains, ferries or at the theatre
fest-noz (pl *festoù-noz*) – night festival
fête (f) – festival, party
FFRP – Fédération Française de la Randonnée Pédestre (French ramblers' association)
foire (f) – fair
fôret (f) – forest
forfait (m) – fixed-price deal at camping grounds
formule (f) or **formule rapide** – similar to a menu but allows choice of whichever two of three courses you want (eg starter and main course or main course and dessert)
foyer de jeunes travailleurs/travailleuses (m) – student dormitory converted for male/female travellers' use during the summer holidays
fromagerie (f) – cheese shop
FUAJ – Fédération Unie des Auberges de Jeunesse (united federation of youth hostels)

galerie (f) – covered shopping centre or arcade
gare (f) – railway station
gare interurbaine (f) – intercity bus station
gare maritime (f) – ferry terminal
gare routière (f) – bus station
gendarmerie (f) – police station; police force
gîte d'étape (m) – walkers' accommodation, usually in a village
gîte rural (m) – country cottage
golfe (m) – gulf
GR – *grande randonnée* (long-distance hiking trail)
granite rose (m) – pink granite

halles (f pl) – covered market, central food market
hébergement chez l'habitant (m) – homestays
horaire (m) – timetable or schedule
horaires des marées (m) – tide tables
hôtel de ville (m) – city or town hall
hôtes payants (m pl) or *hébergement chez l'habitant* (m) – homestays
hypermarché (m) – hypermarket

interdit – prohibited

jardin (m) – garden
jardin botanique (m) – botanical garden
jours fériés (m pl) – public holidays

lande (f) – moor, heath
lavabo (m) – wash basin

laverie (f) or **lavomatique** (m) – laundrette
LFAJ – Ligue Française pour les Auberges de la Jeunesse (French league of youth hostels)

mairie (f) – city or town hall
maison de la presse (f) – newsagent
maison du parc (f) – a national park's headquarters and/or visitors centre
marché (m) – market
marché aux puces (m) – flea market
marché couvert (m) – covered market
menhir – from the Breton *men hir* (standing stone); a single upright stone
menu (m) – fixed-price meal with two or more courses
météo (f) – weather forecast
musée (m) – museum

navette (f) – shuttle bus, train or boat
nettoyage à sec – dry cleaning

office du tourisme (m) – tourist office
ordonnance (f) – prescription

palais de justice (m) – law courts
parapente (m) – paragliding
parc (m) – park
parc naturel régional – regional natural park
parcs à huîtres (m) – oyster beds
parlement (m) – parliament
pâtisserie (f) – cake and pastry shop
petit déjeuner (m) – breakfast
phare (m) – lighthouse
pharmacie de garde (f) – pharmacy on weekend/night duty
piste cyclable (f) – cycle path
place (f) – square, plaza
plage (f) – beach
plan (m) – city map
plan du quartier (m) – map of nearby streets
plat du jour (m) – daily special in a restaurant
poissonnier (m) – fish monger
pont (m) – bridge
port (m) – harbour, port
port de plaisance (m) – marina or pleasure-boat harbour
porte (f) – door, gate in a city wall
poste (f) or **bureau de poste** (m) – post office
pourboire (m) – tip
préfecture (f) – prefecture, capital of a regional *département*
préservatif (m) – condom
presqu'île (f) – peninsula

quai (m) – quay, railway platform
quart (m) – quarter of a litre (25cL)
quartier (m) – quarter, district

refuge (m) – mountain hut, basic shelter for hikers
rive (f) – river bank
riverain (m) – local resident
rond point (m) – roundabout
rue (f) – street

salon de thé (m) – tearoom
SAMU – Service d'Aide Médicale d'Urgence (emergency medical aid service)
sentier (m) – trail
sentier de grande randonnée (m) – long-distance footpath
sentier des douaniers (m) – customs officers' trail
service des urgences (m) – hospital accident and emergency department
SNCF – Société Nationale des Chemins de Fer (state-owned railway company)
sortie (f) – exit
square (m) – public garden
supermarché (m) – supermarket
supplément (m) – supplement, additional cost
syndicat d'initiative (m) – tourist office

tabac (m) – tobacconist (also sells bus tickets, phonecards)
table d'orientation (f) – viewpoint indicator
taxe de séjour (f) – municipal tourist tax
télécarte (f) – phonecard
TGV – *train à grande vitesse* (high-speed train, bullet train)
thalassothérapie (f) – sea-water therapy
thermalisme (m) – water cures
toilettes (f pl) – public toilets
tour (f) – tower
tour d'horloge (f) – clock tower
TTC – *toutes taxes comprises* (all taxes included)
tumulus (m) – a mound of stone and/or earth covering a burial chamber
TVA – value added tax

vallée (f) – valley
vedette (f) – ferry
venelle (f) – alley
vente (f) – sale, or the selling rate when changing money
V.F. (f) – *version française*; a film dubbed in French
vieille ville (f) – old town or old city
ville neuve (f) – new town or city
vin (m) – wine
V.O. (f) – *version originale*; a nondubbed film with French subtitles
voie (f) – train platform
VTT (m) – *vélo tout terrain*; mountain bike

Behind the Scenes

THIS BOOK

The 1st edition of *Brittany* was researched and written by Neil Wilson and Jeanne Oliver was the author of the 1st edition of *Normandy*. Jeanne was also the coordinating author of this 1st edition of *Brittany & Normandy*, writing the front and back sections and the chapters on Normandy. Miles Roddis contributed the chapters on Brittany and wrote the Brittany & Normandy Outdoors section. Dr Caroline Evans reviewed and contributed to the Health chapter.

THANKS from the Authors

Jeanne Oliver A most heartfelt thanks and *gros bisous* are due to my favourite Norman, John Enée for his invaluable insight into the life and culture of Normandy. *Bon peche!* A big *merci* also to Yves Enée for filling me in on Norman traditions. As ever, Jean-Philippe Touzet provided me with a wealth of practical information and knowledge that made the writing of this book so much easier. The staff of all the tourist offices of Normandy should be commended for their friendly efficiency as well as their patience in answering thousands of questions.

Miles Roddis Special thanks to *les copains* of Lonely Planet, France, for the reliability of their research and some great leads from their *Bretagne et ses Îles* guide. Also to Lucy and James Arnold for taking me into their homestead.

Thanks too to tourist office staff who enthusiastically responded to my queries: Sébastien Monnier (Dinan), Fabienne Pinsard (St-Malo), Mme Fermin (Dinard), Nathalie (Erquy), Gaëlle le Men (St-Quay Portrieux), Anne le Roux (Paimpol), Alexia le Tirant (Île de Bréhat), Fabienne (Rennes), Isabelle Goossens (Pléneuf-Val-André), Karina (Mont St-Michel), Cécile Paillard (Avranches), Pascale (Morlaix), Philippe Leroy and Florence Seité (Roscoff), Valérie Brouard (Brest), Chrystelle le Bris (Crozon), Sabine Kerdommarec (Camaret), Christelle (Quimper), Jeanne (Douarnenez), Jean-Christophe (Audierne), Katell (Bénodet), Anne Soriano (Lorient), Martine (Pontivy), Alexandra (Mur-de-Bretagne), Patricia (Josselin), Cécile Gallard (Belle-Île), Sonia and Delphine (Carnac), Delphine Pepion (Vannes), Rodolphe Legendre (St-Nazaire) and Véronique (Nantes).

THANKS from Lonely Planet

Many thanks to the following travellers who used the last edition and wrote to us with helpful hints, useful advice and interesting anecdotes.

Annemarie Bekker, Kees Bouman, Chris Burin, Leif Costantini, Theadis & Doug Damewood, Jay Davidson, Debashis De, Michael Dewick, Amy Guttman, Pat Keehan, DC Langmead, Jim Laniok, Lucy Leroy, Mary Lisko, William Loneskie, Sheila Miller, Shawn Morris, Ed Mueller, Jeanne Nadal, Gladys O'Flynn, Graham Patten, Lauren Payne, Michael Stopp, Alison Stott, Angelique Su, Bob Taylor

---

THE LONELY PLANET STORY

The story begins with a classic travel adventure: Tony and Maureen Wheeler's 1972 journey across Europe and Asia to Australia. There was no useful information about the overland trail then, so Tony and Maureen published the first Lonely Planet guidebook to meet a growing need.

From a kitchen table, Lonely Planet has grown to become the largest independent travel publisher in the world, with offices in Melbourne (Australia), Oakland (USA), London (UK) and Paris (France).

Today Lonely Planet guidebooks cover the globe. There is an ever-growing list of books and information in a variety of media. Some things haven't changed. The main aim is still to make it possible for adventurous travellers to get out there – to explore and better understand the world.

At Lonely Planet we believe travellers can make a positive contribution to the countries they visit – if they respect their host communities and spend their money wisely.

CREDITS

Series Publishing Manager Susan Rimerman oversaw the redevelopment of the regional guides series with the help of Virginia Maxwell and Maria Donohoe, and Regional Publishing Managers Katrina Browning and Amanda Canning steered the development of this title. The series was designed by James Hardy, with mapping development by Paul Piaia. The series development team included Shahara Ahmed, Jenny Blake, Anna Bolger, Erin Corrigan, Nadine Fogale, Dave McClymont, Leonie Mugavin, Rachel Peart, Lynne Preston, Howard Ralley, Valerie Sinzdak and Bart Wright.

This title was commissioned and developed in Lonely Planet's London office by Judith Bamber. Sam Trafford took over the commissioning role from Judith and steered the project through to its conclusion.

This project was managed by Rachel Imeson. Editing was co-ordinated by Yvonne Byron with assistance from Katie Evans, Charlotte Harrison, Margedd Heliosz, Lucy Monie and Stephanie Pearson. Cartography was coordinated by Helen Rowley with assistance from Kim McDonald, Hunor Csutoros, Huw Fowles, Karen Fry, Jenny Jones, Chris LeeAck and Jacqui Saunders. Thanks also to Lachlan Ross, Chris LeeAck and Paul Piaia for their usual excellent assistance on the technical cartography side. The layout team consisted of Cris Gibcus and Kate McDonald. The cover was designed by Pepi Bluck with artwork by Annika Roojun.

SEND US YOUR FEEDBACK

We love to hear from travellers – your comments keep us on our toes and help make our books better. Our well-travelled team reads every word on what you loved or loathed about this book. Although we cannot reply individually to postal submissions, we always guarantee that your feedback goes straight to the appropriate authors, in time for the next edition. Each person who sends us information is thanked in the next edition – and the most useful submissions are rewarded with a free book.

To send us your updates – and find out about LP events, newsletters and travel news – visit our award-winning website: **www.lonelyplanet.com**.

Note: We may edit, reproduce and incorporate your comments in Lonely Planet products such as guidebooks, websites and digital products, so let us know if you don't want your comments reproduced or your name acknowledged. For a copy of our privacy policy visit www.lonelyplanet.com/privacy.

Thanks also to Quentin Frayne and Fabrice Rocher for their help with the Language chapter, and to Bruce Evans and Mark Griffiths.

Index

A

Abbey Route 216-17
abbeys
    Abbatiale de la Ste-Trinité,
      Fécamp 232
    Abbaye aux Dames, Caen 36, 260-1
    Abbaye aux Hommes, Caen 36,
      260
    Abbaye de Beauport 108
    Abbaye de Bon Repos, Lac de
      Guerlédan 176-7
    Abbaye de Mortemer, Forêt de
      Lyons 251
    Abbaye de Valognes 299
    Abbaye du Mont St-Michel 70
    Abbaye St-Guenolé,
      Landévennec 139
    Abbaye St-Mathieu, Le Conquet 129
    Jumièges 36, 216-17
    Le Bec-Hellouin 253
    Mont St-Michel 36
    St-Georges de Boscherville 216
    St-Pierre-sur-Dives 286
    St-Wandrille 36, 217
Abelard, Peter 33
Aber-Benoit 42, 128
Aber-Ildut 128, 8
Aber-Wrac'h 42, 126, 128
accommodation 316-19
    chambres d'hôtes 317
    gîtes 316-17
    homestays 317
    hostels 318
    hotels 317-18
    rental 318-19
Acquigny 243
activities 46-9, 319, *see also*
    individual entries
Aiguilles de Port-Coton 169
Aiguille de Belval 234
air travel
    fares 334-5
    to/from the region 333-5
    websites 334
Airbus factory, St-Nazaire 193
airlines 333
airports 333
Aître St-Maclou, Rouen 38, 208-9
Alençon 309-12, **310**
alignements 35

Alignements de Kerlescan 165
Alignements de Kermario 165
Alignements de Lagatjar 141
Alignements du Ménec 165
American Military Cemetery 273, 7
Ancienne Usine LU, Nantes 189
animals 43
Anne de Bretagne 21, 171, 187
Anse de Sordan 176, 177
Appellation d'Origine Contrôlée
    (AOC) 55
aquariums
    Aquarium Marin, Trégastel 116
    Aquarium Vivarium de Trouville 280
    Audierne 144
    Grand Aquarium, St-Malo 78
    Marinarium, Concarneau 152
    Océanopolis, Brest 134-5
    Océarium, Le Croisic 198
architecture 35-9
    École de Rouen 40
    Fauvists 40
    Flamboyant Gothic 38
    Gothic 36-8
    prehistoric 35-6
    Renaissance 38-9
    Romanesque 36
arctic auks 43
Armorican massif 42
arrefour de la Croix de Médavy 312
Arromanches 272
arts 32-41, *see also individual entries*
Arzon 176
Aubin-le-Cauf 219
Auderville 300
Audierne 144-5
Auray 171-2
Avenue Verte 219
Avranches 71-2

B

Bagnoles de l'Orne 313-14
Baie d'Ecalgrain 300
Baie des Trépassés 145
Baie des Veys 43
Baie du Mont St-Michel 69
Balleroy 271
ballooning 271
Barbe-Torte, Alain 19
Barfleur 298

Barrage de Guerlédan 176
Barrage de la Rance 81
basilicas, *see* churches & cathedrals
Battle of Caen 257
Battle of Hastings 19, 261, 268
Battle of Normandy 25-8, 71, 257-9,
    294
Batz-sur-Mer 198
Bayeux 266-71, **267**
Bayeux Tapestry 35, 266-9
beaches 320
    Bénodet 150
    Concarneau 152-3
    Coutances 302
    Dinard 82-3
    Douarnenez 142
    Île de Bréhat 110
    Île d'Houat 170
    Île d'Ouessant 130
    La Baule 196
    Le Conquet 129
    Le Croisic 198
    Perros-Guirec 113
    Pléneuf-Val-André 103-4
    Plouescat 127
    Presqu'île de Crozon 139
    Quiberon 167
    St-Cast-le-Guido 100
    St-Malo 78
Beaubec-la-Rosière 219
Beau Rivage 176
Bécherel 90
beer 54, 121
Belle-Île-en-Mer 42, 47, 168-70, **168**
Bénédiction de la Mer, Étretat 234-5
Bénodet 150-1
Bernay 251-2
bicycle travel, *see* cycling
Binic 106
birds 43
bird-watching
    Baie des Veys 43
    Cap Sizun 144
    Île d'Ouessant 43
    Île Grande 116
    Marais Vernier 43, 215
    Morbihan 175
    Réserve Naturelle de Séné 175
    Sept-Îles 115
Blessing of the Sea, Honfleur 277

boat travel
  to/from the region 337-9, **338**
boat trips
  Aber-Wrac'h 128
  Blavet river, Lorient 161
  Caen 262
  Camaret-sur-Mer 140-1
  Golfe du Morbihan 174
  Le Croisic 198
  Odet River 148, 150, 153
  Pont-Aven 155
  Rance River 78, 82, 98-9
  Vernon 244
Bois d'Amour 155
Bois des Moutiers, Varengeville-
  sur-Mer 230
books 10, 11, *see also* literature
  D-Day 10
  food 51, 56, 59, 60, 61
  history 17, 19, 20, 21, 22
boudin 53, 56, 315
Boudin, Eugène 39, 276
Braque 230
Brest 132-6, **133**
  accommodation 135
  attractions 134-5
  festivals 134, 135
  food 135-6
  information 133-4
  travel to/from 136
Brest Boat Festival 134, 135
Brignogan-Plages 127
British Film Festival, Dinard 41
Brittany 65-198
Breton language 29, 31, 351-2
Brouel-Kerbihan 175
Buguélès 113
Bureau des Finances, Rouen 38, 206
bus travel
  to/from the region 335-6
  within the region 340
business hours 320

C
Cabourg 283
Caen 256-65, **258**
  accommodation 262-3
  attractions 257-62
  entertainment 264-5
  food 263-4
  information 257

travel to/from 265
  travel within 265
Cailly-sur-Eure 243
Cairn de Gavrinis 176
Calvados *département* 254-90, **256**
Calvados (drink) 55, 265, 286, 299,
  303
Camaret-sur-Mer 140-1
canal cruising 48
  Nantes–Brest Canal 178, 180
Cancale 74-5
canoeing 319
  La Suisse Normande 289-90
Cap d'Erquy 102
Cap de la Chèvre 139
Cap Sizun 144
car travel 336, 340-2
  driving licence 340
  insurance 340
  purchase-repurchase plans 340-1
  rental 340-2
  road distance map 341
  road rules 342-3
  road signs 351
  security 322
Carnac 163-6, **164**
Cartier, Jacques 78
Castennec 178
castles, *see* chateaux & palaces
cathedrals, *see* churches & cathedrals
Celtic traditions 14, 32, 99, 324
Channel Tunnel 336
Chantiers de l'Atlantique,
  St-Nazaire 193
chapels, *see* churches & cathedrals
chateaux & palaces
  Balleroy 271
  Château de Beaumesnil 252-3
  Château de Bienassis, Pléneuf-
    Val-André 103
  Château de Brest 134
  Château de Caen 259-60
  Château de Josselin 39, 179
  Château de la Roche-Jagu 108-9
  Château de Robert-le-Diable 216
  Château de St-Malo 77
  Château de Suscinio 176
  Château de Vascoeuil, Forêt de
    Lyons 251
  Château de Vendeuvre,
    St-Pierre-sur-Dives 287
  Château des Ducs, Alençon 311
  Château des Ducs de Bretagne,
    Nantes 186
  Château des Rohan, Pontivy 178

Château du Breuil, Pont l'Évêque 285
Château du Champ de Bataille,
  Ste-Opportune du Bosc 253
Château Gaillard, Les Andelys 247
Château Guillaume-le-Conquerant,
  Falaise 288
Château Musée, Dieppe 225-7
citadel, Lorient 162
Coutances 302
Dinan 97-8
Fort La Latte 101
Fougères 91
Gisors 248
Palais Bénédictine, Fécamp 232
Villa Strassburger, Deauville 281
Vitré 92
cheese 52, 55, 58, 109, 285, 286-7, 6, 8
Cherbourg 294-8, **295**
children, travel with 59, 320, 345, 351
Chouan Rebellion 23, 90
churches & cathedrals
  Basilique de Notre Dame du
    Folgoët 127
  Basilique Notre Dame de Bon
    Secours, Guingamp 39, 111
  Basilique Notre Dame du Roncier,
    Josselin 179
  Basilique St-Gervais, Avranches 72
  Basilique St-Sauveur, Dinan 97
  Basilique Ste-Thérèse, Lisieux 284
  books 20
  Cathédrale de Coutances 36, 302
  Cathédrale Notre Dame, Bayeux 269
  Cathédrale Notre-Dame,
    Évreux 239-40
  Cathédrale Notre Dame,
    Le Havre 222
  Cathédrale Notre Dame, Rouen
    36, 204-6, 6
  Cathédrale St-Corentin, Quimper
    38, 146-7, 5
  Cathédrale St-Étienne, St-Brieuc 104
  Cathédrale St-Pierre, Lisieux 284
  Cathédrale St-Pierre, Rennes 87
  Cathédrale St-Pierre, Vannes 173
  Cathédrale St-Pierre et St-Paul,
    Nantes 186
  Cathédrale St-Pol de Léon 125
  Cathédrale St-Samson, Dol de
    Bretagne 73-4
  Cathédrale St-Tugdual,
    Tréguier 111-12
  Cathédrale St-Vincent, St-Malo 77
  Chapelle de Kermaria-an-Iskuit,
    Kermaria 106-7

Chapelle de Notre Dame Sous Terre, Mont St-Michel 70
Chapelle Notre Dame de Grâce, Honfleur 277
Chapelle Notre Dame de Rocamadour, Camaret-sur-Mer 38, 140
Chapelle Notre Dame du Kreisker, St-Pol de Léon 38, 125
Chapelle St-Gonéry, Plougrescant 38, 112
Chapelle St-Ninian, Roscoff 123
Collégiale St-Aubin, Guérande 196
Église Abbatiale, Mont St-Michel 70
Église Abbatiale Notre-Dame, Bernay 252
Église Collégiale Notre Dame, Vernon 243-4
Église de Brélévenez, Lannion 117
Église de la Trinité, Caen 260-1
Église de St-Armel, Ploërmel 180
Église Jeanne d'Arc, Rouen 207
Église Notre Dame, Alençon 311
Église Notre Dame, Louviers 242
Église Notre Dame, Mortagne-au-Perche 315
Église Notre Dame, Neufchâtel-en-Bray 218
Église Notre Dame, Vitré 92
Église Notre Dame de Kroaz-Batz, Roscoff 124
Église Notre Dame de Pontorson 73
Église St-Denis, Lyons-la-Forêt 250
Église St-Étienne, Caen 260
Église St-Gervais-St-Protais, Gisors 248-9
Église St-Jacques, Dieppe 227
Église St-Jacques, Le Tréport 230
Église St-Jacques, Perros-Guirec 113
Église St-Joseph, Le Havre 222
Église St-Maclou, Rouen 38, 208
Église St-Melaine, Morlaix 121
Église St-Michel, Pont l'Évêque 285
Église St-Nicolas, Barfleur 298
Église St-Ouen, Rouen 38, 207-8
Église St-Sulpice, Ry 217
Église Ste-Catherine, Honfleur 276
Église Ste-Croix, Quimperlé 36, 156
Église Ste-Foy, Conches-en-Ouche 242
Ermitage de Gueltas, Castennec 178
Ry 38
St-Pierre, Caen 38
Sées 312

cider 54, 55, 299
cinema 11, 25, see also films
    website 41
Clécy 289-90
Clères 218
climate 9, 10, 320-1
    website 10
Clocher Ste-Catherine, Honfleur 276
cloth-making 242
Cocherel 243
COGEMA 45, 300
Colleville-sur-Mer 273
Concarneau 151-4, **152**
Conches-en-Ouche 241-2
consulates 323
copperware 306
Cornouaille 142-56
Cosmopolis, Trébeurden 116
costs 9-10, 324, see also money
Cotentin Peninsula 42, 293-301
Côte d'Albâtre 42, 220-35
Côte de Granit Rose 111-17
Côte de Nacre 42
Côte de Penthièvre 101-6
Côte d'Émeraude 74-85
Côte des Ajoncs 113
Côte des Deux Amants 251
Côte du Goëlo 106-11
Côte Fleurie 42, 274-83
Côte Sauvage 167, 169
Côtes d'Armor département 94-117, **196-7**
courses
    cooking 61
    language 321
Coutances 301-3
cow-breeding 43, 52
credit cards 328
Croisic Peninsula 198
Crozon 139-40
cultural considerations 60
culture 30-41, 296
    website 30
customs regulations 321-2
cycling 31, 48-9, 339-40
    Avenue Verte 219
    Côte d'Albâtre 220
    Croisic Peninsula 198
    Dinard 83
    Forêt de Lyons 250
    Forêt de Paimpont 180
    La Suisse Normande 289-90
    maps 327
    Parc Naturel Régional du Perche 315

D
D-Day 24-7, 49, 257-9, 266-74, 299-300, see also individual landing beach entries
    books 10
    commemorations 324
    films 25
    tours 262, 273, 281
    website 24
D-Day memorials, see also military cemeteries
    Le Mémorial de Caen 257-9
    Mémorial 39–45 78
    Musée Août 1944, Falaise 288
    Musée de la Libération, Cherbourg 294-5
    Musée des Troupes Aéroportées, Valognes 300
    Musée du Débarquement, Arromanches 272
    Musée Mémorial 1944 Bataille de Normandie, Bayeux 269
    Pointe du Hoc Ranger Memorial 273
Deauville 279-83, **280-1**
deep vein thrombosis (DVT) 344
départements 324-5, **325**
Dieppe 224-9, **226**
    accommodation 227-8
    attractions 225-7
    food 228
    information 225
    travel to/from 229
    travel within 229
Dinan 96-100, **98**, 4
Dinard 81-5, **82**
Dior, Christian 304
disabled travellers 322
diving 49
    Aber-Benoit 128
Dolmen des Pierres Plates 165
Dol de Bretagne 73-4
Douarnenez 142-3
drinks 53-5, 121
    vocabulary 64
Dufy, Raoul 40

E
ecomuseums, see museums & galleries
economy 16
Edict of Nantes 22
electricity generation 83
email access 326
embassies 323
emergencies, see also inside back cover
    vocabulary 349

enclos paroissiaux 136-8
  Guimiliau 136-7
  Lampaul-Guimiliau 137
  La Martyre 137
  La Roche-Maurice 137
  Plougastel-Daoulas 137
  St-Thégonnec 136
  Sizun 137-8
endangered species 43
environmental issues 29, 44-5, 83, 128
  websites 43, 45
Equi'days 281, 324
Erquy 101-3
Étretat 40, 234-5, 7
Eu 231
Eure *département* 236-53, **238**
Eure River 42
Eure Valley 243
Eurotunnel 336
Évreux 238-41, **239**
exchange rates 10, *see also inside back cover*

F
faïence 147, 148, 219
Falaise 287-8
Falaise d'Amont 234, 7
Falaise d'Aval 234
Fécamp 231-3
festivals 9, 11, 30, 31, 33, 324, *see also individual entries and special events*
  films 11, 41, 187, 210, 281
  food 55-6, 315
  sailing 142, 210
Festival de Cornouaille, Quimper 148, 4
Festival Interceltique, Lorient 161
Festival of American Film, Deauville 41, 281
festoù-noz 33
Fêtes Médiévales de Bayeux 269
Fête de la Coquille St-Jacques 56, 102, 106
Fête de la Morue, Binic 56, 106
Fête des Remparts, Dinan 99
Fête Medievále, Guérande 195
films 11, *see also* cinema
  festivals 11, 187, 210, 281
  website 41
Finistère *département* 118-56, **120**

fishing 145, 150, 319
  Bénodet 150
  Camaret-sur-Mer 141
  Concarneau 153
  Le Croisic 198
  Touques River 285
Flamanville nuclear power plant 300
Flaubert, Gustave 35, 209-10, 217
Foire au Boudin 56
food 50-3, 55-63, 8
  books 51, 56, 59, 60, 61
  Brittany 50-1
  children 59
  cooking courses 61
  customs 59-61
  festivals 55-6, 315
  Normandy 51-3
  self-catering 57
  vegetarian 59
  vocabulary 61-3
  websites 50, 52
football (soccer) 31
Forêt de Bellême 315
Forêt de Brotonne 215
Forêt de Lyons 249-51
Forêt de Paimpont 46, 180
Forêt de Saussay 315
Forêt d'Écouves 312
Forges-les-Eaux 219-20
Fougères 91-2
  walking tour **91**

G
Gaillot, Jacques 241
galleries, *see* museums & galleries
gardens, *see* parks & gardens
Gauguin, Paul 39, 155
gay travellers 10, 324
Géant du Manio 165
Genêts 71
geography 16, 42
geology 42
Géricault, Théodore 39
Gisors 248-9
Giverny 244-6
Gold Beach 27
Golfe du Morbihan 42, 175-6
Goury 301
government 324-5
Grande Brière 194
Grand Menhir Brisé 165
Grand Pardon, Granville 305
Granville 303-6, **304**
Granville Carnival 305
Greniers à Sel, Honfleur 277

Gros Horloge, Rouen 38, 206-7, 7
Grotte de l'Apothicairerie, Belle-Île-en-Mer 169
Guéhenno 179
Guérande 195-6
Guesclin, Bertrand du 19-20, 242
Guimiliau 136-7
Guingamp 111

H
Hague Peninsula 300-1
hang-gliding 319
  La Suisse Normande 289-90
  Ménez-Hom 139
Harfleur 224
health 344-5
  vocabulary 348
  websites 344
Hédé 47, 90
hiking, *see* walking
history 17-29
  books 17, 19, 20, 21, 22
  websites 21, 23, 24
  WWII 24-8
holidays 325
Honfleur 40, 274-9, **275**, 6
horse-breeding 43, 301, 313
horse-racing 31, 279, 281
horse-riding 281, 319
  Mont St-Michel 71
  Parc Naturel Régional du Perche 315
Houlgate 283
Huelgoat 46, 138
Huguenots, the 21-2
Hundred Years' War 20-1

I
Île aux Moines (Côtes d'Armor) 115
Île aux Moines (Morbihan) 175
Île d'Arz 175
Île de Batz 126
Île de Beaufor 179
Île de Bréhat 109-11, **110**
Île de Fédrun 195
Île de Gavrinis 175-6
Île de Groix 162-3
Île de Sein 145-6
Île de St-Nicolas 154
Île d'Hoëdic 170-1
Île d'Houat 170-1
Île d'Ouessant 43, 47, 129-32, **130**
Île du Grand Bé 78
Île Feydeau 187
Île Grande 116
Île Molène 132

Îles Chausey 305
Îles de Glénan 153, 154
Ille-et-Rance Canal 47, 48, 89-90
Ille-et-Vilaine *département* 66-93, **68**
insurance
    health 344
    motor vehicle 340
    travel 325-6
Internet access 326
Internet resources 10
    air tickets 334
    cinema 41
    culture 30
    D-Day 24
    food 50, 52
    health 344
    history 21, 22, 23, 24
    society 32
    weather 10
itineraries 12-14, 15, *see also* gatefold
    map

J
Jazz Sous les Pommiers 302
Joan of Arc 21, 203, 207, 208
    festival 210
    website 21
Josselin 39, 179
Juno Beach 26, 272-3

K
kayaking 319
    Dinard 83
    La Suisse Normande 289-90
    Plage de Penthièvre 167
Keremma 127
Kerhinet 195
Kérity 150
Kermaria 106-7
kite-surfing
    Plage de Penthièvre 167
kite festival, Dieppe 227
kouign amann 51, 142

L
La Baule 196-7, 4
La Bouille 216
La Calebasse 198
La Grande Pêche 107
La Grande Troménie 144
La Hague 300
La Magdeleine 89
La Maison Entre Les Deux Rochers 113
La Maison en Vaisselle Cassée 242
La Martyre 137

La Merveille 38
La Pointe du Roc 305
La Roche 301
La Roche-Maurice 137
La Roche aux Fées 93
La Roche d'Oëtre 290
La Suisse Normande 90, 289
Lac de Guerlédan 176-7
lace making 269, 311
Lampaul-Guimiliau 137
Landévennec 139
Landrézac 176
language 346-52, 353-5, *see also
    inside back cover*
    Breton 29, 31, 351-2
    courses 321
    food 61-4
    French 346-51
Lannion 117
Le Bec-Hellouin 253
Le Conquet 129
Le Croisic 197-8
Le Folgoët 127
Le Gouffre 113
Le Guilvinec 150
Le Haras National 301
Le Havre 220-4, **221**
Le Letty 150
Le Mémorial de Caen 257-9
Le Palais 168
Le Pays Bigouden 149-50
Le Pin au Haras 313
Le Quadrilatère 165
Le Tréport 230-1
Les Andelys 246-8
Les Arts Dînent à l'Huile 143
Les Forges des Salles 177
Les Maisons Satie 277
Les Monts d'Arrée 138-9
lesbian travellers 10, 324
Liberty Way 300
lighthouses 101, *see also individual
    entries* at Phare
Lilia 126, 127
Lisieux 283-5
Lisors 251
literature 33-5, *see also* books
lobster fishing 146, 8
local transport 342
Locmariaquer 165
Locronan 143-4
Loire-Atlantique *département* 42,
    181-98, **183**
Lorient 159-62, **160**

Louviers 242-3
Lyons-la-Forêt 249-50

M
magazines 32
Malestroit 180
Manche *département* 291-306, **293**
maps 326-7
    cycling 48-9
marais salants 196
Marais Vernier 43, 215
marées noires (black tides) 128
marées vertes (green tides) 44
Marmite Dieppoise 229
Matisse, Henri 169
Maupassant, Guy de 35
measures, *see* weights & measures
medical services 345, *see also* health
Ménesqueville 251
Ménez-Hom 139
Merlin the Magician 180
Mers-les-Bains 231
military cemeteries
    American Military Cemetery,
        Colleville-sur-Mer 273, 7
    Bayeux War Cemetery 269
    Canadian Military Cemetery,
        Dieppe 227
Millet, Jean-François 39
mobile phones 329-30
Monet, Claude 39, 40, 169, 244-6
money 9-10, 327-32
    costs 9-10, 324
    credit cards 328
    discount cards 322-3
    exchange rates 327
Mont-Dol 74
Montagu's harrier 43
Monts d'Arrée 42
Mont Frugy 148
Mont St-Michel 36, 68-71
Morbihan *département* 157-80, **159**
Morgat 139-40
Morlaix 120-3, **122**
    walking tour **121**
Mortagne-au-Perche 315
motorcycle travel 336, 340-2, *see
    also* car travel
Moulins de Kerouat 139
museums & galleries
    Abbaye St-Guenolé,
        Landévennec 139
    Archéoscope, Mont St-Michel 70
    ballooning museum, Balleroy 271

Cathédraloscope, Dol de Bretagne 74
Château Musée, Dieppe 225-7
Cité de la Mer, Cherbourg 294
Cité de la Mer, Dieppe 227
Conservatoire de la Dentelle,
    Bayeux 269
Écomusée de St-Nazaire 193
Écomusée d'Ouessant 130
Écomusée – La Mémoire de l'Île, Île
    de Groix 162
Escal'Atlantic, St-Nazaire 193
Espace des Sciences, Rennes 87
Galerie Bovary Musée d'Automates,
    Ry 217
Grenier à Sel, Honfleur 227
Haliotika, Le Guilvinec 150
Hôtel de Beaumont, Valognes 299
La Maison de la Mariée, Parc
    Naturel Régional de Brière 195
La Maison des Paludiers,
    Guérande 196
La Tour Jeanne d'Arc, Rouen 210
Le Mémorial de Caen 257-9
Le Musée du Calvados et des Vieux
    Métiers, Valognes 299
Le Musée Regional du Cidre,
    Valognes 299
Le Radôme, Trébeurden 116
Les Maisons Satie, Honfleur 277
Les Forges des Salles 177
Maillé Brézé, Nantes 187
Maison de la Rance, Dinan 98
Maison de la Reine Anne,
    Morlaix 121
Maison de la Rivière, Sizun 138
Maison de l'Éclusier, Parc Naturel
    Régional de Brière 195
Maison des Johnnies, Roscoff 124
Maison du Fer Forgé,
    Conches-en-Ouche 242
Moulins de Kerouat 139
Musée AG Poulain, Vernon 244
Musée Août 1944, Falaise 288
Musée Baron Gérard, Bayeux 269
Musée Bigouden, Pont-l'Abbé 150
Musée Claude Monet, Giverny 244-6
Musée d'Art Américain, Giverny 246
Musée d'Art et d'Histoire,
    St-Brieuc 105
Musée d'Art Moderne Richard
    Anacréon, Granville 304

Musée de Bretagne, Rennes 87
Musée de Dinan 97-8
Musée de la Céramique, Rouen 209
Musée de la Cohue, Vannes 173
Musée de la Compagnie des Indes,
    Port-Louis 162
Musée de la Dentelle 'Au Point
    d'Alençon' 311
Musée de la Faïence, Quimper 147
Musée de la Faïence de Forges,
    Forges-les-Eaux 219
Musée de la Libération,
    Cherbourg 294-5
Musée de la Marine, Brest 134
Musée de la Marine, Honfleur 276
Musée de la Mer, Paimpol 107
Musée de la Mer et de l'Écologie,
    Mont St-Michel 70
Musée de la Musique Mécanique,
    Le Bec-Hellouin 253
Musée de la Pêche, Concarneau
    151
Musée de la Poupée, Guérande 196
Musée de Préhistoire, Carnac 163-4
Musée de la Résistance Bretonne,
    Malestroit 180
Musée de la Tapisserie de
    Bayeux 268
Musée de l'Ancien Havre,
    Le Havre 222
Musée de l'Horlogerie Ancienne,
    Fougères 91
Musée de Normandie, Caen 259-60
Musée de Pont-Aven 154
Musée de Trouville 280
Musée Départemental Breton,
    Quimper 147
Musée des Antiquités, Rouen 209
Musée des Beaux-Arts, Caen 260
Musée des Beaux Arts, Nantes 187
Musée des Beaux-Arts, Quimper 147
Musée des Beaux-Arts, Rennes 87
Musée des Beaux-Arts, Rouen 209
Musée des Beaux-Arts André-
    Malraux, Le Havre 222
Musée des Beaux-Arts et de la
    Dentelle, Alençon 311
Musée des Jacobins, Morlaix 121
Musée des Maquettes Hippo-
    mobiles et Outils Anciens,
    Forges-les-Eaux 219
Musée des Marais Salants,
    Batz-sur-Mer 198
Musée des Meubles Miniatures,
    St-Pierre-sur-Dives 287

Musée de Bretagne, Rennes 87
Musée des Phares et Balises, Île
    d'Ouessant 130
Musée des Poupées, Josselin 179
Musée des Techniques Fromagères,
    St-Pierre-sur-Dives 286-7
Musée des Terres-Neuvas et de la
    Pêche, Fécamp 232
Musée des Troupes Aéroportées,
    Valognes 300
Musée d'Ethnographie et d'Art Popu-
    laire Normand, Honfleur 276
Musée d'Évreux 240
Musée d'Histoire et d'Archéologie,
    Vannes 173
Musée du Bateau, Douarnenez 142
Musée du Bord de Mer, Bénodet 150
Musée du Château, St-Malo 77-8
Musée du Château, Vitré 92
Musée du Château de Guérande 195
Musée du Chaume, Parc Naturel
    Régional de Brière 195
Musée du Costume Breton,
    Paimpol 107
Musée du Débarquement,
    Arromanches 272
Musée du Drummond Castle, Île
    Molène 132
Musée du Vieux Granville 304
Musée du Vieux Tréport 231
Musée et Jardin Christian Dior,
    Granville 304
Musée Eugène Boudin, Honfleur 276
Musée Flaubert et de l'Histoire de
    la Médicine, Rouen 209-10
Musée Historique,
    Belle-Île-en-Mer 168
Musée International du Long Cours
    Cap-Hornier, St-Malo 78
Musée Jacques Cartier, St-Malo 78
Musée Jeanne d'Arc, Rouen 207
Musée Jules Verne, Nantes 187
Musée Le Secq des Tournelles,
    Rouen 209
Musée Leclerc, Alençon 311
Musée Mémorial 1944 Bataille de
    Normandie, Bayeux 269
Musée Municipal, Bernay 252
Musée Municipal d'Avranches 72
Musée Municipal, Louviers 242
Musée Municipal Mathon-Durand,
    Neufchâtel-en-Bray 218
Musée National de la Marine,
    Lorient 162
Musée Nicolas Poussin,
    Les Andelys 247

000 Map pages
000 Location of colour photographs

Musée Thomas Dobrée, Nantes 187
Musée Thomas Henry,
    Cherbourg 294
Muséum d'Histoire Naturelle,
    Nantes 187
Palais Bénédictine, Fécamp 232
Port-Musée, Douarnenez 142
Poul Fétan 178-9
Sous-Marin Espadon, St-Nazaire 193
Terre de Sel, Guérande 196
Thalassa, Lorient 160-1
Tour Tanguy, Brest 134
Village Gaulois, Trébeurden 116
music 32-3
mussels 51

N

Nantes 183-91, **184-5**
    accommodation 188
    activities 187
    attractions 186-7
    entertainment 190
    food 188-90
    information 183-6
    travel to/from 190-1
    travel within 191
Nantes–Brest Canal 47, 48, 178, 180
Napoléonville 178
national parks, see regional parks &
    reserves
Neufchâtel-en-Bray 218-19
newspapers 32
Nez de Jobourg 300
night festivals, see festoù-noz
Normandy 199-315
Notre Dame de Tronoën, Le Pays
    Bigouden 150
Notre Dame des Naufragés statue 145
nuclear power 16, 300
nuclear waste 45

O

Omaha Beach 27, 49, 272, 7
Onion Johnnies 123-4
Orne *département* 307-15, **309**
Orne Valley 289-90
otters 43
oysters 74

P

Pacy-sur-Eure 243
Paimpol 107-8
Paimpont 180
painting 14, 39-41
palaces, see chateaux & palaces

parachuting 319
paragliding 319
    Ménez-Hom 139
Parc Naturel Régional d'Armorique
    44, 138-9
Parc Naturel Régional de Brière 44,
    194-5
Parc Naturel Régional de Brotonne 44
Parc Naturel Régional de Normandie-
    Maine 44, 312
Parc Naturel Régional des Boucles de la
    Seine Normande 215
Parc Naturel Régional des Marais du
    Cotentin et du Bessin 44, 300
Parc Naturel Régional du Perche 44, 315
pardons 31, 324
    Grand Pardon, Granville 305
    Grand Pardon de Notre Dame du
        Folgoët 127
    Kermaria 106
    Pardon de St-Christophe 127
    Pardon de St-Yves, Tréguier 112
parish enclosures, see enclos paroissiaux
parks & gardens
    Bois des Moutiers,
        Varengeville-sur-Mer 230
    Clos Normand garden, Giverny
        245
    Jardin d'Eau 245-6
    Jardin des Plantes, Coutances 302
    Jardin des Plantes, Nantes 186-7
    Jardin des Plantes, Rouen 210
    Jardin des Simples, Caen 259
    Michel d'Ornano Park 261
passports, see visas
Patton, General George S 71, 300
Pays d'Auge 42, 283-7
Pays de Bray 218-20, 219
Pays de Caux 42
Pays de Fréhel 101
Pays des Abers 127-8
Pays d'Iroise 128-36
Pays d'Ouche 238-43
Perros-Guirec 113-15, **114**
petit beurre 189
Phare de Kermorvan 129
Phare de la Vieille 145
Phare d'Eckmühl 150
Phare d'Île Vierge 101, 126, 127
Phare du Créac'h 101, 130
Phare du Paon 109
Phare du Stiff 101
Phare St-Mathieu 101
Phare Vauban 101
photography 328

pick-pocketing 322
pigeons 250, 265
pilgrimages 144
Pissarro, Camille 40
Plage de Penthièvre 167
planning 9-11, 322-3, see also
    itineraries
    health 344
    holidays 325
plants 43
Pléneuf-Val-André 103-4
Pleumeur-Bodou 116
Ploërmel 180
Plouescat 126, 127
Plougastel-Daoulas 137
Plougrescant 112
Plouguerneau 127
Ploumanac'h 113
Pointe de Corsen 128
Pointe de Dinan 139
Pointe de la Torche 150
Pointe de Pen-Hir 141
Pointe de Penmarc'h 150
Pointe des Espagnols 141
Pointe des Poulains 169
Pointe du Château 113
Pointe du Croisic 198
Pointe du Décollé 85
Pointe du Grouin 75
Pointe du Hoc Ranger Memorial 273
Pointe du Raz 145, 5
Pointe St-Mathieu 129
politics 16, 28-9
pollution 29, 44, 128
pommeau 54, 265
Pommelin 108
Pont-Aven 154-5
Pont d'Ouilly 290
Pont de Normandie 278
Pont de St-Nazaire 193
Pont-l'Abbé 149-50
Pont l'Évêque 285-6
Pontivy 177-8
Pontorson 72-3
population 16, 30-1
Port-Blanc 113
Port-Louis 162
Port-Manech 155
Port-Navalo 176
Port-Solidor 78
Portsall 128
Port Winston 272
postal services 316, 328-9
Poulain, AG 244
Poul Fétan 178-9

Poussin, Nicolas 39, 247
pre-bocage 265
prehistoric sites 35-6, *see also*
    individual entries
    books 17
    Camaret-sur-Mer 141
    Carnac 17, 35, 163-5
    Grand Menhir Brisé 35
    Île de Gavrinis 176
    La Roche aux Fées 35, 93
    Locmariaquer 165
    Tumulus de Barnenez 36, 123
    Vallée du Blavet 178
Presqu'île de Crozon 139-41
Presqu'île de Guérande 195-8
Presqu'île de Rhuys 176
Presqu'île Renote 116
Presqu'île Ste-Marguerite 128
Proust, Marcel 35, 283

Q
Quiberon 166-8
Quimper 146-9, **147**, 5
Quimperlé 156
Quistinic 178

R
radio 32
Rance River 81
Raz Blanchard 301
Regattas, Barfleur 298
regional parks & reserves 46
    Forêt de Bellême 315
    Forêt de Brotonne 215
    Forêt de Paimpont 46, 180
    Forêt de Saussay 315
    Forêt d'Écouves 312
    Parc Naturel Régional d'Armorique 44, 138-9
    Parc Naturel Régional de Brière 44, 194-5
    Parc Naturel Régional de Brotonne 44
    Parc Naturel Régional de Normandie-Maine 44, 312
    Parc Naturel Régional des Boucles de la Seine Normande 215
    Parc Naturel Régional des Marais du Cotentin et du Bessin 44, 300
    Parc Naturel Régional du Perche 44, 315

Réserve du Cap Sizun 144
Réserve Naturelle de Séné 175
    wesbites 44, 46
régions 324-5, **325**
Rendez-Vous des Marins 142
Rennes 85-9, **86**
Réserve du Cap Sizun 144
Réserve Naturelle de Séné 175
Ria d'Étel 42
Roc'h de Trévézel 138-9
Rosay-sur-Lieure 251
Roscoff 123-5, **124**
Rouen 202-15, **204-5**, 7
    accommodation 210-11
    attractions 204-10
    drinking 213-14
    entertainment 214
    food 211-13
    information 203
    shopping 214
    travel to/from 215
    travel within 215
    walking tour **206**
Rouen Armada 210
Route des Traditions 265
Rozé 195
Ry 217-18

S
safe travel 322
sailing 31, 47-8, 142, 319
    Barfleur 298
    Cherbourg 296
    Erquy 102-3
    festivals 134, 210, 298
St Bartholomew's Day Massacre 22
St-Briac-sur-Mer 85
St-Brieuc 104-6, **104**
St-Cast-le-Guido 100-1
St-Guénolé 150
St-Joachim 195
St-Lô 301
St-Lunaire 85
St-Malo 75-81, **76**, **77**, 5
    accommodation 79
    attractions 77-8
    food 79-80
    information 76
    travel to/from 80-1
    travel within 81
St-Nazaire 191-4, **192**
St-Nicolas des Eaux 178
St-Pierre-sur-Dives 286-7
St-Pol de Léon 125-6
St-Quay-Portrieux 106

St Ronan 144
St Samson 128
St-Thégonnec 136
St Theresa 311
Ste-Mère-Église 299-300
Ste-Opportune-la-Mare 215
salons de thé 57
salt-harvesting 196, 277
sand-yachting 167, 320
sardine fisheries 142, 143, 166
Sarthe Valley 312
Sartre, Jean-Paul 35
Satie, Erik 277
Sauzon 169
scallops 51, 56, 102
sea bass 145
sea trout 285
seafood 50, 52, 56
seaweed harvesters 124, 108, 109
Sées 312-13
Seine-Maritime *département* 200-35, **202**
Seine River 42
Sentier des Douaniers 113, 116, 300
separatism 16, 24, 28-9
Sept-Îles 115
Sillon de Talbert 108, 109
Signal d'Écouves 312
Site de Castennec 178
Sizun 137-8
soccer 31
society 16, 28-9, 30
    website 32
spas, *see also* thalassotherapy
    Bagnoles de l'Orne 313-4
    Forges -les-Eaux 219-20
special events 9, 11, 31, 324, *see also* festivals
sport 31
submarine base, St-Nazaire 193
surfing 319-20, *see also* windsurfing
    Pointe de la Torche 150
swimming 320, *see also* beaches
Sword Beach 26

T
Table des Marchands 165
Tas de Pois 141
telephone services 316, 329-30, *see also inside back cover*
    area codes 329
    mobile phones 329-30
thalassotherapy 319, *see also* spas
    Grand Hôtel des Thermes, St-Malo 79

000 Map pages
000 Location of colour photographs

Grand Hôtel de Trestraou,
  Perros-Guirec 114
Thalasso Roscoff 124
theft 322
thermal baths, *see* thalassotherapy
  and spas
Thury-Harcourt 289
tides 69, 70, 83, 145, 322
time 316
Tombeau de Merlin, Paimpont 180
tourist information 330
tours
  cycling 49
  D-Day beaches 262, 273, 281
Tour de Beurre, Rouen 38, 205
Tour de France 31
Tour de la Brière, Parc Naturel
  Régional de Brière 195
Tour Tanguy, Brest 134
train travel **338**
  discount fares 337
  passes 337
  to/from the region 336-7
  within the region 342-3
Tréac'h Er Gouréd, Île d'Houat 170
Treaty of Union 21, 171
Trébeurden 116-17
Trégastel 115-16
Tréguier 111-12
Trouville 40, 279-83, **280-1**
Trou de l'Enfer 162
Tumulus de Barnenez 123
Tumulus de Kercado 165
Tumulus St-Michel 165
Turner, Joseph 39
TV 32

U
Usine Marémotrice de la Rance 83
Utah Beach 27

V
Vallées des Traouïero 113
Vallée du Blavet 178-9
Valognes 298-9
Vannes 172-5, **171**
  walking tour **173**
Van Gogh, Vincent 169
Varengeville-sur-Mer 230
Vasarely, Victor 169
vegetarian travellers 59
Verne, Jules 34, 187
Vernon 243-4
video systems 328
Villedieu-les-Poêles 306
visas 330-1
  website 10
  work 331
Vitré 92-3
  walking tour **92**

W
walking 46-7
  Avenue Verte 219
  Belle-Île-en-Mer 47, 169
  Cherbourg 296
  Concarneau 153
  Côte d'Albâtre 220
  Dieppe 227
  Dinard 83
  Erquy 102
  Étretat 234
  Forêt de Paimpont 46, 180
  GR21 220, 227, 234
  GR3 194
  GR34 46, 74, 75, 176
  GR39 194
  GR223 300
  GR341 176
  Hédé 47
  Huelgoat 46

Île de Groix 162
Île d'Ouessant 47, 130-1
Ille-et-Rance Canal 47, 89
Josselin 179
Lac de Guerlédan 176
Le Conquet 129
maps 327
Mont St-Michel 71
Nantes–Brest Canal 180
Parc Naturel Régional
  d'Armorique 138
Parc Naturel Régional de Brière
  194-5
Parc Naturel Régional du Perche 315
Perros-Guirec 113
Plouescat 126
Pont-Aven 155
Quimper 147-8
Tour de la Brière 195
Trégastel 116
weather, *see* climate
weights & measures, *see inside back
  cover*
wildlife, *see* animals, birds and plants
William the Conqueror 19, 34, 261,
  268, 288
windsurfing 319-20, *see also* surfing
  Dinard 83
  Perros-Guirec 113
  Plage de Penthièvre 167
  Pointe de la Torche 150
  Roscoff 124
wine 54
women travellers 331, 345
work 331-2
WWI 24
WWII 24-8, 257-9

Y
Yport 233-4

INDEX

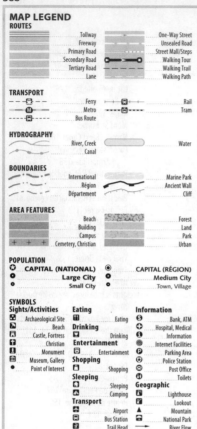

MAP LEGEND

ROUTES

Tollway
Freeway
Primary Road
Secondary Road
Tertiary Road
Lane
One-Way Street
Unsealed Road
Street Mall/Steps
Walking Tour
Walking Trail
Walking Path

TRANSPORT

Ferry
Metro
Bus Route
Rail
Tram

HYDROGRAPHY

River, Creek
Canal
Water

BOUNDARIES

International
Région
Département
Marine Park
Ancient Wall
Cliff

AREA FEATURES

Beach
Building
Campus
Cemetery, Christian
Forest
Land
Park
Urban

POPULATION

CAPITAL (NATIONAL)
Large City
Small City
CAPITAL (RÉGION)
Medium City
Town, Village

SYMBOLS

Sights/Activities
Archaeological Site
Beach
Castle, Fortress
Christian
Monument
Museum, Gallery
Point of Interest

Eating
Eating

Drinking
Drinking

Entertainment
Entertainment

Shopping
Shopping

Sleeping
Sleeping
Camping

Transport
Airport
Bus Station
Trail Head

Information
Bank, ATM
Hospital, Medical
Information
Internet Facilities
Parking Area
Police Station
Post Office
Toilets

Geographic
Lighthouse
Lookout
Mountain
National Park
River Flow

LONELY PLANET OFFICES

Australia
Head Office
Locked Bag 1, Footscray, Victoria 3011
☎ 03 8379 8000, fax 03 8379 8111
talk2us@lonelyplanet.com.au

USA
150 Linden St, Oakland, CA 94607
☎ 510 893 8555, toll free 800 275 8555
fax 510 893 8572, info@lonelyplanet.com

UK
72–82 Rosebery Ave,
Clerkenwell, London EC1R 4RW
☎ 020 7841 9000, fax 020 7841 9001
go@lonelyplanet.co.uk

France
1 rue du Dahomey, 75011 Paris
☎ 01 55 25 33 00, fax 01 55 25 33 01
bip@lonelyplanet.fr, www.lonelyplanet.fr

Published by Lonely Planet Publications Pty Ltd
ABN 36 005 607 983

1st Edition – July 2004

© Lonely Planet 2004

© photographers as indicated 2004

Cover photographs by Masterfile (front) and Lonely Planet Images (back): Lily pond in Monet's garden, Giverny, Scott Gilchrist (front); Colourful reels of rope used for fishing boats, Jean-Bernard Carillet (back). Many of the images in this guide are available for licensing from Lonely Planet Images: www.lonelyplanetimages.com.

Printed through SNP SPrint Singapore Pte Ltd at
KHL Printing Co Sdn Bhd Malaysia